# The Smile That Broke:

## How We Learned the Difference Between a Bully and a Manipulator

## Children's Edition

Garrick David Pattenden

To: _____

*Best Wishes,*

*Garrick David Pattenden*

Copyright © 2025 Garrick David Pattenden

All rights reserved.

ISBN: 978-1-83417-011-4

# DEDICATION

This book is dedicated to Myles Casey Benson Neuts — a boy whose life mattered, whose smile deserved to last, and whose story should never have had an ending like it did. We remember you not as a headline, not as a case file, but as a child who should have been safe.

Birth: 14 Aug 1987, Ontario, Canada
Death: 12 Feb 1998, London, Middlesex, Ontario, Canada

We remember your laughter, your light, and the life that was yours to live. To your family — Mike and Brenda Neuts — and to everyone who loved you, I offer this work as a testament that your fight, your grief, and your truth are not forgotten.

But this dedication does not end with one name alone. It extends to every child who has ever been cornered in a hallway, mocked in a classroom, shoved on a playground, or silenced by fear. It extends to the children who have survived bullying but carry its marks in hidden ways, and to those who were not given the chance to grow older because the harm was too great, too ignored, or too late to be stopped. Your lives matter. Your voices matter. Your absence is felt.

This dedication belongs also to the parents who have stood at kitchen tables late at night, trying to find words for a hurting child. To the guardians who have carried unanswered questions. To the teachers who have tried, sometimes against systems that failed them, to protect. And to the friends who stood up when others turned away. This book is for you, too.

What happened to Myles must never happen to another child. His story, and the stories of countless others, must be carried forward until silence no longer protects the aggressor and fear no longer binds the victim. This book exists to tell the truth, to protect those still here, and to stand against the silence that too often lets harm continue.

It contains a truthful account of the death of a ten-year-old boy named Myles, who died as a result of a bullying-related incident. His story is told without euphemisms and without apology. While no unnecessary graphic detail is included, the events are described honestly, because the truth matters more than comfort. This account is included so that Myles is not forgotten — and so that other children may be spared.

To every child who reads these pages: you are not alone. To every parent or teacher who reads beside them: do not turn away.

We dedicate this book to Myles, to his family, and to every child past, present, and future who deserves the right to live without fear.

"Make Children Better Now"
https://makechildrenbetternow.com

## CARRYING FORWARD

This is not the beginning. It is the continuation of a story already set into motion.

In The Lie That Sounded Nice: How I Learned the Difference Between Truth and Control, we faced the subtler enemy — the manipulator who worked not with fists, but with words. That first book uncovered the darkness of gaslighting, the kind of cruelty that bends memory and reshapes truth until a child begins to doubt their own eyes, their own voice, their own worth. It was about lies wrapped in kindness, words twisted into traps, control disguised as love. It was about the silence forced upon children when they were told that what they felt was wrong, what they saw was imagined, what they lived was somehow their fault. That silence was not passive — it was heavy, it pressed on the chest, it taught a child to accept shadows as truth.

But manipulation is not the only enemy a child must face. Where the first book traced the scars left by lies and deceit, this book places its hand on bruises left by fists, the sudden sting of a shove, the humiliation of laughter weaponized. The Smile That Broke: How We Learned the Difference Between a Bully and a Manipulator is not about the quiet kind of breaking — it is about the visible one. Here, the mask slips. The smile is still present, yes, but it is no longer a smile meant to deceive with charm. It is the grin of one who takes satisfaction in another's pain, the smirk of someone who believes power is proven by dominance, not dignity.

The bully is not more dangerous than the manipulator — nor less. They are two sides of the same coin, two faces of control. One tears at the mind, the other at the body. One whispers that you are wrong, the other shouts it with blows. Both break the child's smile, and both leave wounds that carry forward into adulthood. The child who was silenced learns distrust. The child who was beaten learns fear. And both learn, unless the cycle is broken, to carry those weapons themselves. Some become bullies because they were manipulated. Some manipulate because they once feared fists. The cycle is not simple, but it is real.

That is why this book must carry forward from the first. To stop at manipulation would be to name only half of the truth. To stop at bullying would be to ignore the foundation upon which bullying often grows. The lies and the fists are not separate worlds — they belong to the same house of cruelty, and both must be torn down.

This book belongs to the children who already know too much of fear. It belongs to the teachers who have watched a smile break but said nothing, perhaps because they themselves once lived through the same silence. It belongs to parents who must finally see what their children see, hear what their children hear, believe what their children say.

For those who read The Lie That Sounded Nice, this book is its echo and its extension. The first revealed the hidden chains, this one shows the open wounds. Together, they tell one story: how children are made small by those who take power from them, and how that power can be named, resisted, and defeated.

If you are reading this book first, you are entering through another door, but it leads to the same house. You will find the children here the same, the voices honest, the lessons unbroken. And if you choose to turn back and read the first, you will hear the foundation of the struggle. Together, they complete each other.

This carrying forward is not simply a continuation. It is a reminder: the fight against cruelty cannot pause. When one book ends, the work must carry on. When one voice falls silent, another must speak. And when one child's smile breaks, the world must stop and ask why.

Only then, together, can those smiles begin to heal.

## FOREWORD

This book was not written to comfort. It was written to confront.

For too long, stories of children harmed by bullying have been softened, trimmed, or hidden away in whispers. That silence has never protected a single child. The truth, however, can.

You hold in your hands not only a story but also a mirror. The children within these pages are fictional, but what they endure—and what they learn—is drawn from a reality we can no longer pretend does not exist. The beating heart of this book belongs to a boy named Myles Casey Benson Neuts, a ten–year–old whose life ended in 1998 in a way no child's life should. He is not forgotten here. His story forms the foundation of this work, because when the truth of a child's suffering is hidden, it leaves space for the same cruelty to repeat itself.

This is not a book about despair. It is a book about recognition and repair. The students in this story learn what bullying really is—not the cartoon version, not the simple push on a playground, but the manipulation, the silence, and the fear that grow when people look away. They learn the difference between strength and cruelty, between leadership and intimidation. Most importantly, they learn that courage does not always mean standing tall with fists raised. Sometimes it means standing firm with words, or simply standing beside someone who is alone.

The writing here does not use softened phrases for death. Myles did not "pass away." He died. His life was ended. That truth matters, because language shapes how we remember and how we act. Euphemisms protect the listener, not the victim. This book chooses honesty, because children deserve nothing less.

To the parents and educators who read alongside children: you may find moments here that are difficult to face. That is deliberate. Shielding young people from the reality of bullying does not keep them safe; it leaves them unprepared. But honesty, presented with clarity and respect, can equip them with the tools to see harm, to name it, and to stop it.

To the children who will read these pages: know that you are not alone. If you have ever been hurt, ignored, or silenced, this book is proof that your experience matters. And if you have ever been tempted to hurt another, or to look away when someone else is being harmed, let this be your moment to choose differently.

The story that follows belongs to all of us. It belongs to Myles Neuts, whose memory insists that truth must be told. It belongs to his family, who live with a loss no book can heal. It belongs to every student who has ever been bullied and every teacher who has ever wished they had acted sooner. And now, it belongs to you.

Read it with care. Carry it with courage. And let it remind you that one honest voice—one act of standing beside another—can break the silence that lets harm grow.

— Garrick David Pattenden

## PREFACE

This book was written because silence has never saved a child. Silence protects the bully, not the victim. When we soften words or look away, the harm grows until it claims what cannot be returned — a life. In February of 1998, a boy named Myles Casey Benson Neuts died as a direct result of bullying. He was ten years old. He was not a headline, not a symbol, not a statistic. He was a child who should have been safe in his school, a boy who loved and was loved, a boy who deserved to grow old. His story is here because stories like his cannot be erased if we hope to protect those who come after him.

I do not use softened phrases. Myles did not "pass away." He died. His parents buried their son because the cruelty of other children, and the failure of adults to act, cost him his life. That truth must be spoken plainly, even when it is painful. This book does not aim to shock for the sake of shock, nor to linger in darkness. Instead, it holds a mirror to what happens when cruelty is allowed to grow, and it offers a way to confront that reality before it becomes another funeral.

The narrative within these pages is told through students, teachers, and the unseen voices of those who refuse to look away. The characters may be fictional, but the pain they confront, and the truths they carry, are not. Bullying is not just about fists or shoves; it hides in whispers, manipulation, silence, and the refusal to intervene. The line between a bully and a manipulator is thin, but both leave scars that can outlast childhood.

To Myles's family — Mike and Brenda Neuts, and all those who loved him — this book is offered as one small piece of remembrance. To Myles himself — though your life was stolen too soon, your name remains. We write it, we say it, we carry it. You will not be forgotten.

This is not a gentle story. It was not meant to be. But it is a truthful one, and truth is what saves lives. If one child who reads this book finds the courage to speak, or if one teacher decides to intervene, then the work has mattered. That is the purpose of these words: to honour the boy who should still be here, and to make sure no one else is left in silence.

## AUTHOR'S NOTE

This book is dedicated to Myles Casey Benson Neuts, a ten-year-old boy from Chatham, Ontario, who in 1998 lost his life after being found hanging in a school washroom. He was a son, a brother, a student, and a child whose story should never have ended the way it did. Myles's death left a wound in his family, in his community, and in this country. His parents, Mike and Brenda Neuts, turned their grief into advocacy, speaking to thousands of children so that no life would be forgotten, and no silence would ever again become an accomplice to cruelty.

This story remembers Myles. It does not sensationalize him, nor does it bury him in silence. It memorializes a child who should have lived a long and full life. His name deserves to be spoken, his memory deserves to be held, and his story deserves to be told. Children deserve the truth—not sugar-coated, not hidden, not softened into polite words. The truth is that Myles died because bullying was ignored, and the response came too late. That is the truth we owe him, and it is the truth this book carries forward.

If you are a student reading this, remember that your voice matters. Speak when you see wrong. Stand for those who are afraid to stand for themselves. Do not be silenced by fear or by the threats of a bully. Your courage may be the difference between life and death for someone who believes they are alone. If you are a parent or a teacher, know that children can see through false comfort. They deserve honesty. They deserve action. They deserve more than empty words like "ignore them" or "walk away."

This book carries Myles's story so that he will never be forgotten. It is also for every child who has been bullied, every child who has felt unseen, every child who has fought silently in hallways, bathrooms, or playgrounds while the world turned its head. May you know that you are not alone. May you find strength in truth. And may you, like Tom, learn that a smile can belong again.

## CONTENT WARNING

This book contains the truthful account of the death of a ten–year–old boy, Myles Casey Benson Neuts, who died in 1998 as a direct result of bullying. His story is told with honesty, without euphemism, and without apology.

No unnecessary graphic detail is included, but the description of what happened is plain and unsoftened. Myles did not "pass away." He died. That truth matters, and it is told here so that his memory is not erased, and so other children may be protected.

Parents, guardians, and educators should be aware that children reading this story will encounter frank language about death, cruelty, and the failures of adults to act. Shielding children from this reality does not prepare them — but honesty, handled with clarity and respect, can.

This story is not written to shock for the sake of shock. It is written so that Myles's life, and the lives of children like him, are remembered with dignity, and so the silence that allows bullying to grow is broken.

Readers should expect difficult truths, told directly. If you choose to share this book with a child, read it with them. Speak openly about what you encounter together. The intent is not despair, but recognition, courage, and hope — that no other name will ever be added to the silence Myles was forced into.

## NOTE TO PARENTS AND TEACHERS

This book is written in the voice of children, for children, yet it does not shy away from hard truths. It is not designed to comfort with platitudes or to repeat the tired refrain of "just ignore them." Children know when they are being lied to, and they deserve more than softened words. To lie to a child, even with good intentions, is to teach them that adults cannot be trusted — and trust once lost is rarely regained.

Bullying, whether physical, verbal, or psychological, leaves marks that cannot be dismissed. The story told here is not fiction alone. It carries within it the real death of a child, Myles Casey Benson Neuts, and it carries the lived experiences of countless children who have stood in hallways and playgrounds with fear in their chests and no hand beside them. It carries the testimony of those who had to strike back, those who endured in silence, and those who were never given the chance to grow older. These stories matter. They are not exaggerations, and they are not for entertainment. They are warnings and reminders that the cost of inaction is always paid by the child.

Your role as a parent, guardian, or teacher is not to explain away the story, but to stand with your child as they face it. Read with them if possible. Ask them what they hear, what they feel, and most importantly, listen. Do not rush to correct, to dismiss, or to soften their perception. Children do not need polished answers; they need your honest presence. If the story makes them angry, let them be angry. If it makes them sad, sit with their sadness. If it sparks questions you cannot answer, admit it. Humility teaches more than false certainty.

This book offers lessons, not instructions. It tells the truth of what bullying can do, and it shows how children can stand together, speak up, and refuse silence. It shows the role of adults — not as distant authorities, but as people who must act, who must tell the truth, who must intervene without hesitation. When a child tells you their truth, your first responsibility is to believe them. Your second is to act.

If a child comes to you with their own story after reading, hear them. Believe them. Do not tell them to "walk away" unless you are willing to walk beside them. Do not tell them to "ignore it" when their pain is real. Do not ask them to be silent when their voice is the first step toward safety. Children will measure you by what you do, not by what you say.

The aim of this book is not fear. Its aim is recognition, strength, and hope — that children may learn they are not alone, and that adults may remember that their duty is not to dismiss, but to act. It is a reminder that silence is complicity, and that every broken smile is one too many.

If this book unsettles you, let it. That discomfort is a call to vigilance. If it stirs your conscience, follow it. Change is not born from ignoring the hard things but from facing them with courage. This is what children need from you most: truth without evasion, love without condition, and action without delay.

## PROLOGUE – THE WEIGHT OF A SMILE

There are stories we inherit whether we want them or not. They live in hallways, in classrooms, in the whispered warnings passed down from one generation of students to the next. Some stories are softened until they sound like rumours. Others are sharpened into weapons. And some — the rarest kind — stand as unmovable truths, carved into memory because the price of forgetting is too great. This is one of those truths. It begins with a boy whose life should never have been lost.

Myles Casey Benson Neuts was ten years old, in fifth grade, and by every measure he should have grown into the ordinary joys of life: birthday cakes, ball games, awkward first crushes, and the long march of seasons that carry a child into adulthood. But he was not allowed that chance. What happened to Myles was not an accident, nor an act of fate. It was the result of cruelty left unchecked, of laughter at another's expense allowed to grow too long, too loud, too often. His death was the end of a chain that could have been broken at any point had someone chosen to act sooner. And that is the truth this book carries.

Children deserve honesty, not fairy tales dressed up to hide pain. To say that Myles "passed away" would be a betrayal. He did not drift off into some soft dream. He died. He was killed by the weight of bullying that turned from words and shoves into something that stole the breath from his body. He was found where no child should ever be found, and the silence that followed nearly swallowed his name whole. That is why his story is here — to keep his name spoken, his smile remembered, and his truth alive.

This is not just a book about Myles, though he remains at its centre. This is a book about every child who has been pushed to the margins, about every voice smothered under laughter that was never kind. It is about the difference between a bully — loud, obvious, reckless — and a manipulator, who twists truth until it bends and convinces others to believe lies. Both destroy, but in different ways. Both must be stopped, and both are named here without apology.

The children in these pages are not perfect. They fight, they stumble, they sometimes fail each other. But they also learn. They listen. They change. And that is where hope lives — not in pretending cruelty doesn't exist, but in proving it can be confronted, dismantled, and replaced with something stronger.

If you are a child reading this, know that you are not alone. The words you will hear from Jeremy and the others are meant for you, not for strangers. They are told straight because you deserve straight answers. They are told with courage because you deserve protection. And they are told with love because you deserve nothing less.

If you are an adult reading this, remember that silence has never saved a child. Too often, silence has buried them. The lesson of Myles Neuts is not that tragedy strikes without warning — it is that tragedy gives every warning possible, if only we dare to listen.

This prologue stands as both a promise and a warning. A promise that Myles's story will not fade into dust, and a warning that ignoring the signs of cruelty means writing another child's name beside his. That is something we cannot and will not allow.

So let this book be more than a story. Let it be a shield for the children still walking into classrooms every morning. Let it be a reminder that truth, even when it hurts, is worth telling. And let it be the place where Myles's smile, though broken once, belongs again in the hearts of all who refuse to forget him.

## CONTENTS

| | | |
|---|---|---|
| | Acknowledgments | i |
| 1 | The Story That Stopped the Room | 1 |
| 2 | When Smiles Break | 26 |
| 3 | The Girl Harley Fears | 47 |
| 4 | Shadows in the Hall | 67 |
| 5 | The Old Wounds of Leo and Alex | 105 |
| 6 | The Unseen Fights | 144 |
| 7 | Lines Crossed | 174 |
| 8 | Jarod's Homelife | 212 |
| 9 | When Jeremy Decides | 241 |
| 10 | The First Sparks | 271 |
| 11 | Shadows of the Uncle | 304 |
| 12 | The Library Confrontation | 334 |
| 13 | The Toss Up | 360 |
| 14 | The Uncle Unmasked | 387 |
| 15 | Tom's Breaking Point | 417 |
| 16 | The Conversation | 447 |
| 17 | Small Steps Forward | 477 |
| 18 | The Smile That Came Back | 501 |

# CHAPTER 1: THE STORY THAT STOPPED THE ROOM

*Narrator: **Nico***

 I walked into the front hall and could already tell it was going to be one of those days. You know the kind — the air feels heavier, like even the light from the windows has decided it doesn't want to stick around. Harley was slouched against the lockers, not talking, just tapping the sole of his shoe against the tile in that restless way he does when he's looking for trouble but hasn't picked his target yet. I caught his eye for half a second. He didn't smile. That was the first clue. Harley always smirks at me in the mornings, even if it's the fake kind, just to see if I'll react. Not today. Something had already sunk its teeth into him before the bell even rang. I tightened my grip on my books and kept walking, but I kept him in my peripheral. That's what you do when you know a storm's brewing.

 At the far end of the hall, Lisa was leaning against the trophy case, pretending to be fascinated by the silver cup from the basketball championship five years ago. She wasn't even looking at it. I knew that trick. She was listening — always listening — catching bits of conversations so she could twist them into something useful later. Her hair was loose today, falling into her eyes in a way that looked casual but wasn't. She liked to watch people from behind it, so you never knew exactly where she was looking. When she noticed me noticing her, she gave the smallest raise of her eyebrow, like she'd already filed me under "to deal with later." I kept moving toward the library, not because I wanted to read before class, but because it was the one place neither of them usually followed this early.

 Even in the library, the tension seeped in. You could feel it through the walls, like a vibration in the floorboards. Mrs. Duncan, our math teacher, was at one of the tables talking quietly with Mr. Clarke, the librarian. It wasn't the kind of quiet you use for friendly conversation. It was the kind you use when you're trying to decide whether to say something at all. I caught a few words — "incidents," "recess," "complaints" — and knew they weren't talking about missing homework. Teachers don't use that tone for homework. Mr. Clarke saw me hover near the new arrivals shelf and gave me a nod, the kind that says, "I see you, but I'm busy, give me a minute." So, I sat at the far table, close enough to listen without looking like I was listening.

 The door opened again, and Harley walked in. That wasn't normal. Harley didn't come into the library unless he had to, and he definitely didn't come in without an audience to show off for. He moved past me without a glance and stopped at the counter. Mr. Clarke's eyes flicked up, and I saw him tense, just for a second, before schooling his face back into neutral. Harley muttered something too low for me to catch, but I saw Mr. Clarke shake his head. Then Harley turned and left, just like that, his sneakers squeaking against the polished floor. I thought I saw something in his face — not anger, not exactly, but something that looked like a crack in his usual armour. I made a mental note. Cracks always mean something's coming.

Lisa came in a few minutes later, and unlike Harley, she spotted me right away. She walked past with a smile so faint it was almost polite, which is exactly why I didn't trust it. Lisa only smiled like that when she wanted people to think she wasn't interested. That's how she got them to talk without realising they were telling her anything. She headed straight to the magazine rack, flipping through the pages without looking down, her eyes tracking the reflection of the teachers in the glass of the fire alarm case on the wall. I kept my head down and started sorting through the books in front of me, pretending to be busy.

When the first bell rang, I stayed seated for a moment, just watching the doorway. Harley hadn't come back, and Lisa slipped out without looking behind her. The library emptied out in a slow shuffle, but the air still felt thick, like there was something unfinished hanging in it. Mr. Clarke started gathering papers from the counter, stacking them neatly. I wondered if he knew how obvious it was that he was waiting for the right moment to tell someone something. I'd seen that look before — it meant a story was coming, and not the kind you find in the fiction section.

By the time I got up to leave, I knew this wasn't just any morning. The looks, the silences, the way Harley avoided eye contact and Lisa kept herself too still — it all added up to something I couldn't name yet. But I've learned that when the day starts this way, you don't ignore it. You listen harder. You notice more. And you keep your seat near the front, because when the story comes, you want to be where you can hear every word.

When the last student left for first period, the library door clicked shut and the sound changed. It wasn't silence — not really. It was the low, careful hum of voices meant to stay inside these walls. I'd only meant to return my book before the bell, but when I saw Mrs. Duncan leaning on the counter, arms folded, and Mr. Clarke lowering his voice instead of raising it, I knew this wasn't a conversation about overdue returns. They were talking about us. About the school. About the things we don't put on posters.

Mrs. Duncan glanced toward the door, then back at him. "Three complaints this week. Same names, same pattern." She didn't have to say which names. If you've been here longer than a month, you know. Mr. Clarke slid a thin stack of papers across the counter, his fingers resting on the top page like he was weighing down more than paper. "It's escalating," he said, and there was no mistaking the steel in his voice. "We can't keep treating these as isolated events."

I kept to the corner by the returns cart, one book in my hand, pretending to check for a ripped page. I've learned that teachers forget you're there if you make yourself small enough. Mrs. Duncan's voice softened, not in kindness but in the way people do when they're talking about something they don't want to wake up. "You've seen the younger ones," she said. "Some of them are already afraid to go outside at recess. That's not school — that's…" She didn't finish the sentence. She didn't have to.

Mr. Clarke leaned back, the chair groaning under him. "I'm going to tell them," he said finally. "All of them. It's overdue." His tone carried the kind of weight you don't argue with, but Mrs. Duncan did anyway. "You can't just drop that story on them without warning. You'll scare the—" He cut her off with a shake of his head. "Good. They should be scared. Not of each other — of what happens when this is ignored."

I felt my grip tighten on the book. I knew what story he meant. The one whispered about by the older grades when they thought we couldn't hear. The one no one ever told in full. Mrs. Duncan lowered her eyes, and for a moment, neither of them spoke. Then she sighed. "Alright. But you'd better tell it right." He nodded once, like he'd been waiting years to hear those words.

Footsteps sounded in the hallway — heavier than a student's. I ducked around the shelf as the door opened, but it was only Mr. Khan, the gym teacher, joining them. He didn't even sit down before saying, "Got another one. Grade six this time." Mr. Clarke pinched the bridge of his nose, and Mrs. Duncan closed her eyes. I didn't hear the name, but I didn't need to. This wasn't about one kid anymore. This was a list.

I slipped out before they noticed me, the bell ringing above my head. The halls were full again, but the sound of their voices followed me — low, sharp, and heavy with something I couldn't yet name. Whatever Mr. Clarke was about to tell us, it wasn't just a story. It was going to land like a stone in the middle of the room and change the way we all looked at each other.

When Mr. Clarke pushed his chair back from the table, the scrape echoed like a cue for everyone else to go still. He didn't have notes in front of him anymore — just his hands flat on the wood, steady, like he didn't need paper to remember what he was about to say. "This happened in Ontario," he began, looking at Mrs. Duncan, then at Mr. Khan, "to a boy in fifth grade. Ten years old. His name was Myles Neuts."

I had heard the name before, but not from a voice that low and certain. He told us Myles wasn't a troublemaker. He wasn't even the kind of kid who drew attention. He liked baseball, rode his bike everywhere, and could spend hours on a Lego set without looking up. He was the kind of kid who'd wave to a neighbour without thinking about it. And maybe that's why no one saw it coming.

Mr. Clarke's eyes didn't move from the table as he told us Myles was lured into the school gym one afternoon by two other students — boys older than him. They told him they wanted to "play a game." It wasn't a game. It was a setup. Once the doors were closed, there were no teachers, no classmates, no one to see. They grabbed him by the hood of his sweatshirt. They laughed. And then they hung him by it from the basketball net.

Someone at the table swore under their breath. Mr. Clarke didn't pause. He said Myles was still alive when they left him there. Struggling. Kicking. But by the time another student wandered in, thinking the gym was empty, it was too late. He was gone. Ten years old. Fifth grade.

He described the funeral — the school gym packed wall to wall with classmates, parents, strangers who had only heard the name a week before. The teachers who couldn't stop crying. The mother who stood so still, it was like her body had given up on moving altogether. And the father who kept asking why, as if someone in that crowd might have an answer.

Mr. Clarke's voice stayed calm, but the words didn't soften. He told us the boys who did it were charged, but no charge could bring Myles back. He said the hardest part was knowing this didn't start in the gym. It started months before, in hallways and lunch lines, with shoves and names and laughter that made Myles smaller every time. And no one stopped it. Not once. Not until it was too late.

That's when I noticed the shadow in the doorway. Harley. Leaning just far enough in to catch every word, like the air was holding him there. His usual smirk was gone. His eyes were locked on Mr. Clarke, and if he saw me, he didn't let on.

Mr. Clarke finished by saying this wasn't a warning for other schools. It was a warning for ours. "If you see it starting, you stop it," he said. "You don't wait for someone else to do it. Because there might not be someone else."

The room stayed quiet long after he stopped talking. No one shuffled papers or cleared throats. Even Harley didn't move. He just stood there, still as the boy in the story, until the sound of footsteps in the hall broke the air and sent him walking away — not fast, not slow, but with a weight in his step I hadn't seen before.

I knew Harley was still there because I could hear the faint scuff of his shoe against the tiled floor every now and then, like he wasn't even aware he was doing it. He had planted himself just beyond the library's open door, tucked against the edge of the wall so no one inside could see him. He wasn't leaning like he usually did, casual and careless; he was rigid, like his spine had locked him upright. I kept my eyes forward so the teachers wouldn't know I'd spotted him. If they knew he was there, the story might stop, and I didn't want that — not for my sake, and not for his.

From where I sat, I could see only the faint shadow his presence cast across the beige carpet, wavering whenever he shifted his weight. He stayed in that half-lit space, caught between walking away and stepping inside, as Mr. Clarke's voice spilled out in steady, unbroken lines. Harley's breathing was shallow, just enough to keep from being heard. It wasn't the kind of hiding you do when you're avoiding trouble — this was the kind of hiding you do when you can't face what you're hearing, but you can't bring yourself to miss it either.

I thought about the way Harley normally moved through the school — loud in the halls, shoulders squared, eyes sharp like he was always measuring the distance to his next strike. Now, he seemed smaller, like the words were pressing in on him, closing the space he usually took up. Every detail from Mr. Clarke's telling seemed to land heavier on him than anyone else. When the part came about the hood of Myles' sweatshirt, Harley's shadow shifted, a quick jerk like he'd stepped back an inch.

The teachers didn't know they had another audience, but I did. I watched the invisible dialogue unfold in the doorway: Mr. Clarke speaking to the room, Harley catching the words like they were meant for him alone. The air between them felt tight, charged, like one wrong sound would snap it. I wondered if Harley even understood why he hadn't left yet, or if something deep inside him had decided for him.

The hall outside the library was usually a stream of noise at this time of day — lockers clanging, sneakers squeaking, voices bouncing off walls — but now it was empty, the sound dampened by the weight of the story. Harley's stillness was so complete that if I didn't know better, I might have thought he was part of the building itself. Every pause in Mr. Clarke's voice seemed to hold him in place, like the next sentence might either keep him rooted there or finally send him walking.

I kept wondering how much of this he was matching to his own life. Harley wasn't the kind to flinch at stories. He liked to pretend nothing could touch him. But this one — this was different. He wasn't just hearing what happened to Myles; he was measuring himself against it, and maybe, for the first time, he didn't like the comparison. There's a kind of discomfort that shows in the way a person breathes, and from where I sat, I could tell his had changed.

His head must have been tilted just enough for his ear to catch every word, because he never shifted in a way that broke the line between him and the voice coming from the table. If he heard the shuffle of chairs or the scratch of a pen, he didn't react. He was tuned only to the rise and fall of Mr. Clarke's story. The mention of the older boys who'd cornered Myles made his shadow edge closer to the doorframe, but not enough to reveal him. It was as though he wanted to step in but didn't trust what it would do to him if he did.

I thought about standing up and walking past him, just to see the look on his face, but I didn't. Something told me this was a moment I shouldn't disturb. Some things you ruin just by making them aware they're being watched. If Harley needed to hear the rest without knowing anyone knew, then I would let him. Maybe this was the only way it would work — the truth reaching him without any eyes to challenge him.

Mr. Clarke's voice carried the final part of the story with a steadiness that made it even heavier. He spoke of the silence that followed Myles' death, the way the whole town seemed to move slower, like they were afraid any sudden sound might bring back the memory of it. He told us about the parents who never forgave themselves for not seeing the signs sooner. Through it all, Harley's shadow never left its place. I knew he was still listening, because when the story turned to what could have been done to stop it, his stance shifted again, just slightly, like something in him had moved without his permission.

The bell hadn't rung yet, but the hallway outside had begun to stir faintly with the noise of students returning from recess. Harley stayed until the very end, until Mr. Clarke's last words fell like a stone into the centre of the room: If you see it starting, you stop it. And then, finally, Harley's shadow pulled away from the light, melting into the movement of the hallway before anyone else knew he'd been there.

I watched the empty space where he had stood for a moment longer, wondering if he would ever admit to himself — or to anyone — that he had heard it all. I knew better than to ask him then. Sometimes, the hardest truths need to sit in the dark before they can survive the light.

Mr. Clarke's voice didn't rise or fall for drama. It didn't lean on the crutch of suspense or the comfort of softening the edges. He told the story of Myles Neuts like he was laying down bricks — each fact set in place with purpose, each detail a weight that couldn't be ignored. The dates, the ages, the places, the sequence — all of it was exact. There were no gaps where someone could slip away and pretend they didn't hear. His delivery made sure of that.

He spoke of the day Myles went to school, just like any other. He wore his hooded sweatshirt, his jeans, his sneakers. Nothing about him screamed for attention. He was just a kid in the fifth grade, ten years old, with no reason to think the day would be anything but ordinary. But the ordinary was the first thing stolen from him. Mr. Clarke made us feel the weight of that — that the cruelty didn't come as a warning. It came like a shadow creeping closer until it was too late to step away.

The facts about the gym were placed in front of us like cold photographs. The older boys, two of them, pulling Myles into a corner where no teacher could see. The hands grabbing the strings of his hood. The tightening. The sudden absence of air. The shock that stole the fight from him before he could even make a sound. Mr. Clarke's words didn't rush this part. They held us there, in that terrible stillness, until the picture was burned into the back of our minds.

He told us that Myles was left hanging from his own sweatshirt, suspended in a way no child should ever be. The older boys didn't stop because they felt remorse — they stopped because someone walked in. That detail, Mr. Clarke said, was the one most people tried to ignore when they read the headlines. The idea that cruelty often ends not from guilt, but from the fear of getting caught. And then, when the eyes turn away, it grows back again, ready to strike.

I noticed the teachers weren't moving in their seats anymore. No scribbling pens, no quiet sips from coffee mugs. Even the faint hum of the library lights seemed to dull. Mr. Clarke had built a space where nothing but the truth existed, and no one dared interrupt it. His words didn't feel like a story being told — they felt like a weight being passed from his hands into ours, demanding we feel every ounce of it.

He didn't stop with the moment Myles was found. He carried us into the chaos — the rush of footsteps, the panicked calls for help, the frantic hands trying to undo what had been done. He made us see the teachers who didn't yet understand the scope of what they were looking at, who thought maybe this was some terrible accident that could be fixed if they just moved fast enough. But Mr. Clarke's voice told us it was already too late, and that the truth would take longer to sink in than anyone wanted to admit.

When he spoke of Myles' family, the room seemed to grow smaller. His parents had sent him to school believing he would come home. They'd packed his bag, told him to be good, maybe kissed the top of his head without knowing it was the last time. Mr. Clarke didn't dress those moments in sentiment — he left them bare, because that's how they happened. The cruelty of it wasn't just in the act itself, but in how quietly the world moved on from it.

He told us about the trial — how the boys responsible were seen not as the architects of a tragedy, but as children themselves, deserving of leniency. And yet, the damage they had done could never be undone. "They didn't serve time the way you think of it," Mr. Clarke said, his eyes fixed on the far wall. "And they went back into the world, carrying the same tools they'd used before." That was the part that lodged in my throat, because it wasn't about punishment — it was about the risk of repetition.

The statistics came next, but they weren't numbers you could forget. Mr. Clarke spoke of how many children were lost each year to bullying, how many parents lived with the hollow space where a laugh used to be. He gave us the reality that this wasn't just one name, one town, one moment in 1998. It was a thread that stretched across years, across countries, tying together strangers in grief they never asked to share.

I watched as the teachers' eyes shifted, not to each other, but down into their laps, like the truth was too much to hold head-on. And still, Mr. Clarke didn't let up. He explained that the only way to break the cycle was to see it clearly — every corner, every shadow, every place it hides when no one's looking. That meant admitting that children, even the ones we think we know, can be capable of destroying someone else's life.

There was a part where he stopped speaking for a moment, not because he was searching for words, but because he was letting us feel the silence. It was the kind of pause that filled itself, heavy and slow, until it pressed down on your chest. He didn't need to tell us that Myles' absence had become permanent — we could feel it sitting there among us.

When he spoke again, it was to tell us exactly why he had chosen to share every detail. "If you tell it soft, they forget," he said. "If you tell it straight, maybe they'll carry it." And I knew then that this wasn't just a story. It was a warning set in stone, meant to outlast the people hearing it.

By the time he reached the end, his voice had not once cracked or wavered. But it had carried something else — the unspoken demand that now we knew, we could never unknow it. The teachers didn't clap. They didn't thank him. They sat there, holding the weight, maybe not sure what to do with it yet.

And in the quiet that followed, I thought about Harley still somewhere just outside that door. If Mr. Clarke had meant for this to lay the foundation for change, then maybe, just maybe, it had already started to settle in the place it was most needed.

When the bell rang to pull everyone back in from recess, most of the school poured toward the doors in a wave of coats and chatter. But Jeremy didn't follow the stream toward his classroom. He moved in the opposite direction, his steps measured, his eyes fixed ahead like he already knew exactly where he was going. I followed from the far end of the hallway, curious but careful not to interrupt. Jeremy had that air about him — the kind that told you if you spoke now, you'd only be intruding on something important.

The library was nearly empty when we stepped inside. The air carried that quiet, paper-dusted stillness that makes you feel like you're walking into a memory rather than a room. Mr. Clarke was still at his desk, but the small gathering of teachers from earlier had dispersed, leaving only the faint echo of their earlier conversation lingering in the corners. Jeremy didn't hesitate; he went straight to the tall cabinet tucked into the far wall — the one marked Archives.

I'd seen the drawers in that cabinet before, the way their heavy metal handles caught the light, the small labels typed in a neat, old-fashioned font. But I'd never had a reason to open them. Jeremy did. He pulled the bottom drawer with a slow scrape of metal on metal, revealing rows of manila folders that seemed to breathe dust with every shift. His hand hovered for a moment before settling on one with a single word typed in black ink: Neuts.

He slid the file free and placed it carefully on the nearest table, almost as if touching it too roughly would change what was inside. When he opened it, the paper's edges were yellowed, the print faint in some places, bold in others. The headline stretched across the top in block letters — Boy, 10, Dies After Playground Incident. Even before I read a word, the gravity of it hit me. The photograph of Myles sat just below, the kind of school portrait where the smile was small, almost uncertain.

Jeremy leaned over the article, his hands braced against the table, eyes scanning line after line. I stayed back, not out of disinterest, but because something about the way he was reading made it feel private, like a conversation between him and the boy in the picture. I could see his jaw tighten every time his eyes moved over certain sentences — the ones about the older boys, the lack of supervision, the way the school tried to word it as a "tragic accident."

Mr. Clarke noticed us and came over quietly, his steps barely making a sound on the carpet. He didn't ask why Jeremy was there at first. He just looked at the open file, then at Jeremy, and I saw something pass between them — a kind of mutual recognition that didn't need words. "You want to borrow that?" Mr. Clarke asked, his tone even, no hint of surprise. Jeremy nodded once, still looking down.

"What for?" Mr. Clarke pressed, though not unkindly. Jeremy's answer came without him looking up. "Because I need to understand something," he said. His voice was steady, but there was a current under it — not curiosity, not exactly anger, but something that carried the weight of both. It was the kind of tone you don't argue with if you've heard it before. And Mr. Clarke had.

I remembered then that he'd told me about Jeremy's part in helping Leo last year, how he'd been one of the few who didn't just see trouble and look away. Mr. Clarke respected that. You could hear it in the way he didn't push for more explanation. He simply gave a small nod, slid the file closed, and placed it gently into Jeremy's hands like passing on something sacred.

Jeremy held it as if the weight wasn't in the paper but in the truth it carried. "I won't damage it," he said, and I believed him without question. Mr. Clarke's eyes softened. "I know you won't," he replied. Then he stepped back, letting Jeremy decide the next move. There was trust in that gesture, and it seemed to settle over the room like another layer of quiet.

For a moment, Jeremy didn't leave. He reopened the file, just enough to glance again at the photo of Myles. His thumb traced the edge of the page, careful not to smudge or tear it. It was as though he wanted to memorize the boy's face before taking the story with him. He didn't smile. He didn't frown. He just looked — and kept looking until he finally closed the file for good.

As we walked out together, he didn't speak. The hallway was louder now, filled with footsteps and voices, but the silence between us wasn't awkward. It was the kind that comes when you're carrying something too heavy to set down yet. I didn't ask what he was going to do with the article. I didn't have to. I already knew it wouldn't stay locked away in that file for long.

And as we reached the doors to the classroom wing, I thought about the way Mr. Clarke had told the story earlier that morning. It had stopped a room full of adults. I wondered what it would do when Jeremy chose to place it in the hands of kids who had never heard the name Myles Neuts before.

The moment Jeremy's eyes locked on the headline, I saw the shift in his expression. It wasn't surprise — not exactly. It was recognition. That small tightening around the corners of his mouth, the way his brow drew in ever so slightly, told me this wasn't the first time he'd heard the name. Myles Neuts. It was as though the letters themselves carried weight, pulling him into some connection the rest of us couldn't see yet.

He didn't touch the paper right away. He stood there, leaning over it like he was trying to decide whether to step closer or turn away. But his hesitation didn't last. His fingertips brushed the edge of the page, light at first, then firmer as though accepting something inevitable. I stayed quiet, close enough to notice the way his lips moved silently — testing the name, saying it to himself like he needed to hear how it sounded in his own voice.

When his eyes reached the third paragraph, something settled in his posture. Not a relaxation, but a resolve. He read the words twice, then a third time, as if measuring their truth against something already stored in his mind. The room around us might as well have been empty; the faint hum of the library lights was the only sound between us. And then, without looking away from the page, Jeremy spoke. "This is the same story," he said, more to himself than to me.

I asked him what he meant, but he didn't answer right away. Instead, he lifted the article by its corners, careful not to crease it, and scanned it again from top to bottom. When he finally looked up, his eyes didn't dart or wander. They went straight to Mr. Clarke. "Can I borrow this?" he asked, his voice low but carrying the kind of weight that makes you listen.

Mr. Clarke glanced at the file in Jeremy's hands, then back at him. "Borrow it?" he repeated, not with suspicion, but as if giving Jeremy the chance to explain. Jeremy nodded once. "Yes. I need to take it with me." He didn't fidget. He didn't break eye contact. It wasn't a request made lightly, and Mr. Clarke could see that.

"What for?" The question came in the same measured tone, no pressure in it, but enough to give Jeremy space to answer truthfully. He took a breath before speaking. "Because I need to understand something," he said. "Not just from hearing it — I need to see it for myself. I need to read every word until it makes sense." His words were calm, but there was an urgency beneath them, like a door in his mind had been unlocked and he had no choice but to step through.

Mr. Clarke studied him for a long moment. I could tell he was weighing more than just whether to hand over a piece of paper. He was deciding if Jeremy could carry the weight of the story outside the safety of the library. And then, slowly, he nodded. "All right," he said. "But bring it back the way you found it." His voice was steady, but the approval in it was unmistakable.

Jeremy's fingers tightened slightly on the folder, not in possession, but in gratitude. "I will," he promised. And I knew from the way he said it that the promise wasn't just about the paper. It was about the boy whose name was printed in bold across that headline.

As we stepped toward the door, Jeremy paused. He looked back at the table where the file had been, as though picturing it still there. "He was only ten," he murmured, almost too quiet to hear. But I caught it. The words carried no question, no disbelief — just a fact that refused to fade.

The walk back to the hallway was slow, not because Jeremy was stalling, but because it felt wrong to rush when you were carrying something like that. The file wasn't heavy in his hands, but it seemed to press on the air around us, pulling our steps down into the quiet. I didn't ask what he was going to do next. Some things don't need to be asked when the answer is already written in the way someone holds on to a name.

When the library door closed behind us, the noise of the school returned — lockers slamming, voices calling down the hall, shoes squeaking on polished tile. But none of it seemed to touch him. Myles Neuts had taken root in his thoughts, and I knew it wouldn't be long before that name found its way into someone else's.

Mr. Clarke didn't move right away after Jeremy made his request. He leaned one arm on the edge of the table, the way he does when he's sifting through more than just the words he's hearing. His gaze wasn't on the paper anymore. It was on Jeremy, steady and weighing, like he was measuring what kind of truth sat behind those eyes.

I'd seen that look before, the year Leo almost burned himself completely out. Back then, Clarke had been the one to keep the boy in the building when every other adult had given up. And I remember Jeremy being the one who wouldn't stop showing up for Leo, even when Leo didn't want him there. Clarke knew that too. You don't forget a kid who holds the line for another kid like that.

It wasn't just the act of taking care — it was the way Jeremy had done it. Quietly. Without fuss. Without needing to be told twice. There had been nights after school when Clarke had found Jeremy in the corner of the library, waiting until Leo was done with whatever detentions or extra work the staff had piled on him. He'd wait, hand over a granola bar or just walk beside him in silence. Those aren't the kind of things you fake.

Now, looking at Jeremy with that file in his hands, Clarke was seeing the same thing I was — the same kid, only older, standing at another turning point. It wasn't about curiosity or gossip. Jeremy wasn't asking for the story so he could pass it around. He was asking because something in him needed to know exactly what had happened to Myles Neuts, and what it meant for the rest of us.

Clarke's fingers tapped once on the table, slow and deliberate. "You'll treat this with care?" It wasn't a challenge — it was an invitation to confirm what he already knew. Jeremy's answer was simple. "Yes." He didn't fill the space with explanations or promises he didn't need to make.

That was enough for Clarke. He pulled the folder a little closer, slipped the article back into its plastic sleeve, and handed it to Jeremy like someone passing along more than paper. I could see the exchange for what it was — not a loan, not even permission. It was trust, plain and unadorned, offered because Jeremy had earned it before.

"You bring it back exactly as it is now," Clarke said, his voice low but firm. "And if it changes you, that's between you and the boy in that story." There was a finality in the way he said it, as if he knew the change was inevitable and maybe even necessary.

Jeremy nodded once, and I caught that flicker in his eyes — the kind that says a person has just agreed to carry something heavier than they've ever held. Clarke didn't need to explain the details. He knew Jeremy would find them himself, line by line.

I thought about the first time I'd seen Clarke trust a student like that. It had been Leo, in the mess of his worst days, and even then it had been a risk. But it worked because Clarke doesn't hand trust to everyone. He waits for the moment when he knows it'll be used right, and then he commits without hesitation.

Jeremy slid the folder under his arm and stepped back from the table, careful not to bump the corners. It was a strange thing — seeing him walk away with something so small and knowing it carried the weight of a life lost. Clarke's eyes followed him to the door, not out of doubt, but like a man watching a torch being carried into the dark.

The library stayed quiet after that, though the sounds of the hallway beyond kept leaking in. Clarke busied himself with straightening a stack of returned books, but I noticed he didn't take his eyes off the door for a good while after Jeremy left.

It's a rare thing, watching two people exchange more than words without needing to say what it is. Clarke had just handed Jeremy the beginning of something — maybe the start of a fight, maybe the root of a lesson the whole school would feel. And Jeremy had accepted it without pretending it was light.

When Clarke finally sat down again, he exhaled in that way he does when a decision has settled into him. I think he knew Myles' story wasn't going to stay in that file much longer. Once Jeremy carried it, it would start moving through the halls in a different way. Not as gossip. Not as rumour. But as a warning carried by someone who believed in the power of telling it right.

And I knew, even before the next bell rang, that the boy who had once fought to keep Leo from falling was about to use every ounce of that same resolve for Myles Neuts — even if Myles had never had the chance to stand in this school's hallways himself.

Jeremy didn't open the folder right away. He waited until the halls thinned, the clatter of lockers faded, and the only sounds left were the hum of the vents and the scratch of pencils from a distant classroom. He settled into the far corner table in the library, the one under the window where the morning light cut across the grain of the wood. That's where he laid the folder down and unfastened the brass clasp with slow, measured care, as though noise might change the truth waiting inside.

I watched from the next table, pretending to skim a book I wasn't actually reading. The article wasn't just a page. It was a memory trapped in print — dated, but still breathing in the way a story never fully dies. The paper had yellowed at the edges, but the ink was still sharp, the headline bold enough to stop anyone mid-step. Jeremy's eyes landed on it first, and for a long moment, he didn't move past it.

His fingers traced the words without touching the ink, hovering just close enough to feel the groove where the letters had been pressed into the page. He read slowly, not skimming, not skipping. Each sentence seemed to land heavy in him, pulling him deeper into the account of a boy who had been alive one moment and gone the next — not from sickness, not from accident, but because other children had decided he shouldn't feel safe in his own skin.

The first few paragraphs painted Myles Neuts in the small details — his grade, his smile, the way his teachers described him. Jeremy lingered there, I could tell, because those pieces were easy to connect with. The kind of details that make you think, I've met that kid before, or worse, I could have been that kid. It was only when the story shifted into what had happened that his posture changed, shoulders curling slightly as though bracing for a blow.

The words didn't spare him. The account wasn't dressed up or softened. It described the events in plain, chronological order, each line a strike of truth that didn't ask permission to be felt. Jeremy read about the isolation, the quiet cruelties, the moments no adult had seen or had chosen not to notice. Every time his eyes paused, I knew he was picturing them in our own hallways, hearing the same silences between the shouts.

He turned the page only when he had finished everything on the first, right down to the caption beneath a grainy photo of Myles in a hockey jersey. I caught the way he blinked a little slower there, the kind of blink that holds back more than it lets go. Then he moved to the second page, the part that detailed the day everything came to a head — where Myles had been, who had been there, and how quickly the situation had turned from bullying to something fatal.

The description of that final day wasn't long, but it didn't need to be. It was exact, and that precision was what made it hurt. Jeremy didn't rush it. His eyes stayed on each paragraph until I thought he might memorize them. I knew then that this wasn't just about knowing the story. He was letting it rewrite something in him — the same way it had once done when he learned about Leo's breaking point.

When he reached the last section, the article shifted again. It spoke about the aftermath, the memorials, the debates that flared up about school safety and responsibility. But Jeremy read those parts with a different expression — not disbelief, not even anger, but something heavier. The understanding that all those debates hadn't saved Myles. That they were words spoken too late.

He folded the article back into its sleeve when he was done, but he didn't close the folder right away. His hands stayed resting on it, fingers spread like he was holding something fragile that couldn't be dropped, even though the paper was in no danger of tearing. It was more than just a story now — it was a weight he'd chosen to carry, even if no one else had asked him to.

I could see the moment he decided this wasn't staying with him alone. He didn't say it out loud, but it was in the set of his jaw, in the way he pushed the folder an inch forward on the table before pulling it back, like testing its readiness to be handed off.

Clarke didn't come over. He didn't need to. This was between Jeremy and the boy on those pages. And I knew that in the days ahead, it would become between Jeremy and every kid in this school. The kind of truth you can't unknow has a way of spreading without being shouted.

Jeremy finally closed the clasp and slid the folder into his bag, careful to keep it upright. He didn't rush out. He sat there for another few minutes, eyes on the window, as if he was trying to see the world the way Myles might have once seen it — before anyone decided to take it away from him.

When the bell rang, he stood and slung his bag over his shoulder, but I caught one last glance in his eyes that told me he wasn't walking into the next class as the same person who had sat down here twenty minutes ago. This was the start of something. And I had the uneasy feeling that everyone, even Harley, was going to feel the edge of it soon enough.

When the second bell rang, the chatter in our classroom was still thick enough to trip over. Desks scraped, chair legs dragged, and someone in the back was still telling a half-finished joke that died the moment Jeremy stepped in. He didn't drop his bag in the usual careless way. He placed it against the leg of his desk like the file inside was made of glass. There was something in the way he looked at us — not sharp, but steady — that made even Harley stop tapping his pencil against the edge of his desk.

I had seen Jeremy stand in front of this class before. He could talk about anything — history, sports, what happened on the playground — without making it a performance. But today there was no casual lean against the whiteboard, no sideways smile. He stood straight, hands braced lightly on the desk in front of him, and waited until every last shuffle quieted. Even the clock seemed louder in the stillness.

"You remember what I told you about Myles Neuts," he began. His voice didn't rise or drop dramatically. It carried the weight of someone who had already decided the words were more important than the way they sounded. "You remember the reason I told you." That was all he said at first, and in the pause that followed, you could feel people's minds pushing back to the earlier moment in the week when he had told us the story for the first time.

He didn't repeat the details. He didn't have to. The look in his eyes made the memory of it sharper than any retelling could. "If we can stop that from happening again, if we can keep even one person from reaching that point, then it's worth every bit of effort we put in. Every bit." He tapped the edge of his desk once, not in impatience but as though marking the thought.

I saw Sophie's eyes drop to her notebook. Ty leaned back slightly, his arms crossed but his focus locked on Jeremy. Even Leo and Alex, who usually looked anywhere but at the speaker, didn't move. It wasn't guilt in their faces — not anymore — but a recognition that they had once walked too close to the same edge that had pushed Myles over.

Jeremy didn't point fingers. He didn't name names. "Bullying doesn't just happen when someone throws a punch," he said. "It happens in whispers. In looks. In the way people choose not to see." There was a ripple through the room at that — small shifts in posture, eyes darting to the side before snapping back. He let the silence hang there, unhurried, until it settled deep enough to matter.

"You don't have to be best friends with everyone," he went on, "but you do have to be human. You do have to remember that the person sitting next to you is carrying something you can't see." The way he said it, you could tell he meant everyone, even the people who thought they were untouchable. Harley shifted in his seat. Not fidgeting — more like recalculating.

I watched him then, Jeremy, standing there with nothing in his hands, no paper to read from, no teacher to back him. It was just his voice and the weight behind it. He wasn't pleading. He wasn't lecturing. He was setting down a line that no one in the room could step over without knowing exactly what they were doing.

Harley tried to catch my eye, maybe to see if I was buying into this. But when I didn't give him anything, he looked back at Jeremy. And for the first time, I thought I saw something flicker in him — not fear exactly, but an awareness that this wasn't going away. That this story was going to follow him through the halls whether he wanted it to or not.

Jeremy's last words were the quietest, but they landed the hardest. "We stand together. Not just this class. All of us. And if you think it's not your problem, you've already made it worse." No one moved when he stopped. He didn't ask for a response, didn't demand agreement. He just stepped back to his desk and sat down, pulling his notebook out like we were starting any other lesson.

But it wasn't any other lesson. You could feel it in the way no one rushed to fill the silence. In the way even the sound of the next door classroom moving into group work felt distant. The air had shifted. Not permanently, not yet. But enough that people would think twice before letting their mouths run the way they had before.

Ty finally broke the stillness by clearing his throat, not to speak but to remind us that time hadn't stopped. The teacher moved to the board, starting the day's math problems, but no one was looking at the numbers. They were still looking, even from the corners of their eyes, at Jeremy.

That was the thing about him. He didn't need to keep talking to keep being heard. The story of Myles Neuts was sitting in every one of us now, and Jeremy knew it would do its own work long after he'd gone quiet. I knew it too. And so, I think, did Harley — though he'd never admit it, not yet.

When Jeremy sat down, the room didn't immediately snap back to normal. You'd expect someone to crack a joke, drop a pencil, or even just shuffle in their seat to shake off the heaviness, but nothing happened. It was like the air had settled too thick to stir. I watched Sophie turn her pen in slow circles between her fingers, her gaze fixed somewhere on the middle of her desk. She wasn't bored — she was far away, replaying every word.

Leo's chair creaked as he shifted, but he didn't say anything. That was unusual for him. Normally, he would have added his own edge to Jeremy's point, not because he wanted to upstage him, but because he understood what it was like to be on the wrong side of a story like Myles'. Alex glanced at him once, as if deciding whether to speak, but his eyes dropped before the thought could take shape.

Ty stayed motionless, his arms crossed, but I could see the measured breath in his shoulders. I've known Ty long enough to tell when he's running scenarios in his head — when he's thinking about what someone said and how it lines up with what he's seen before. He'd heard Jeremy's tone and filed it in that unspoken place where he keeps things that matter.

Even Harley wasn't his usual restless self. He sat back in his chair, eyes aimed at the whiteboard, but I noticed his fingers had stilled on his pencil. Not tapping, not spinning, not breaking it in half the way he sometimes did. He wasn't giving away much, but I knew enough to catch the subtle drop in his guard. It was quick, almost nothing, but it was there.

The teacher began writing on the board, her voice carrying over the stillness with the rhythm of someone who's used to filling gaps. She moved through the math lesson like she didn't notice the undercurrent in the room. But some of us weren't ready to fill that gap yet. The numbers landed on the page without meaning. The real weight was still sitting between us.

From where I sat, I could see Ella's mouth tighten, the way it does when she's holding back something sharp. She kept glancing toward the window, her reflection caught faintly in the glass. Whatever she was thinking, she wasn't going to say it in front of the whole class. Not now.

Jasmin chewed at the edge of her pencil, then set it down entirely. Her usual quick energy seemed to have drained, replaced by a careful kind of stillness. It wasn't fear — more like she was cataloguing her own choices, trying to measure where she stood in the shadow of that story.

Even the hum of the fluorescent lights seemed louder in the absence of chatter. The clock's tick felt like it was marking more than minutes — it was marking the space between what we'd been before and what we might be after this.

Nobody said it, but I could tell some people were feeling a strange mix of relief and discomfort. Relief that the truth had been spoken out loud, discomfort that it now lived in the same room with them, pressing against their own unspoken memories.

Jeremy didn't turn around. He didn't need to. The shift in posture, the way people's eyes didn't dart to the corners as much, the absence of those low side conversations — he'd feel it without looking. I did too.

Harley leaned forward once, probably to make it look like he was focused on the math problem on the board. But I caught the faint line in his forehead, the kind that appears when he's thinking about something he doesn't want to think about.

A couple of kids glanced at each other like they wanted to say something but couldn't figure out how to start without unravelling the whole moment. That's the thing about silences like this — break them too soon, and you waste the weight they carry.

By the time the lesson moved on, the quiet wasn't as sharp, but it hadn't gone entirely. It shifted into the kind of quiet that follows you, even after the noise comes back. People picked up their pens again, their voices started to return in fragments, but there was a difference.

And I knew, just by looking around, that whatever anyone said for the rest of the day, the story of Myles Neuts would be replaying somewhere in their minds. They might not talk about it, but they'd carry it. That kind of story doesn't just leave when the bell rings.

The teacher didn't let the moment fade into just another stretch of classroom quiet. She set her marker down on the ledge beneath the whiteboard and turned toward us, hands folded in front of her like she'd been waiting for the right time to speak. "Jeremy's right," she said, her tone even but carrying enough weight to cut through the low hum of thought in the room. No one shifted. It wasn't the kind of thing you answered. It was the kind of thing you absorbed.

I watched her eyes move across the rows, not darting, not skipping over anyone. She gave each of us a moment under that steady gaze, the kind that makes you feel seen whether you want to be or not. "Bullying doesn't just stop because someone tells you to stop," she said. "It stops when the people who see it decide they won't let it happen anymore." Her words hung there, not accusing, not pleading, just plain and solid.

She didn't raise her voice. She didn't need to. Every sentence landed like she was putting another brick in the wall behind Jeremy's point, building it taller so no one could knock it down without effort. Her pace was slow enough that each thought had space to settle before the next one came. It was the kind of speaking you couldn't hide from, even if you wanted to look busy with your notebook.

When she stepped closer to the middle of the room, it wasn't to intimidate anyone — it was to close the gap. "Some of you might think it's not your problem if it's not happening to you," she said. "But that's how it keeps happening. Silence is what bullies rely on most." I could feel that one hit certain people harder than others. Alex glanced at Leo. Harley's pencil rolled to the edge of his desk and stopped.

She paused just long enough for the sound of the clock to slip back in, like it was reminding us we were still in the middle of a school day. Then she added, "You don't have to fight with your fists to stop something wrong. Sometimes all it takes is telling the truth where someone can hear it." She looked toward Jeremy, and there was no mistaking it — that was a thank you.

From my seat, I could see Sophie sit a little straighter, like she'd been given permission to keep thinking about what she'd just heard. Jasmin set her pencil down again, no fidgeting this time. Ty stayed still, but his eyes had narrowed slightly, not in suspicion, but in calculation — the way he looks when he's deciding what to do next.

Harley didn't meet her eyes. Not once. He kept his attention fixed somewhere over her shoulder, like the safest place for him was outside the line of direct contact. Still, his shoulders had lost that usual forward hunch. It was a subtle shift, but I caught it.

The teacher let the quiet fill back in for a beat before picking up the marker again. She turned to the board, wrote a single line at the top — "You can be the reason it stops" — and then moved into the day's work as if that sentence could sit there above the math problems all period. She didn't erase it.

I don't think anyone missed the fact that the lesson for the day had just doubled in size. There was the one in the textbook, and then there was the one that had been spoken out loud — the kind that follows you out the door. Some of us would forget the math by next week. But the other lesson? That one would stay.

As I looked around, I noticed the smallest nods, the kind people give themselves when they've made up their mind about something. It wasn't loud agreement. It wasn't a rally cry. But it was enough to tell me that Jeremy hadn't been talking to an empty room.

Even after she turned back fully to the board, her voice stayed a little heavier, like she was still carrying the message with her as she wrote. She called on students, checked answers, kept the class moving, but that line at the top of the board never stopped being the loudest thing in the room.

And maybe that was the point. Not to hammer it into us with repetition, but to leave it sitting there, waiting for each of us to decide what to do with it. Some would take it seriously right away. Others might tuck it away and not touch it for months. But once you hear something like that, you can't unhear it.

It didn't take long for word to move beyond our classroom walls. I'd barely packed my notes back into the folder when I heard the low hum from the hallway — the kind of hum that meant teachers were talking, but not about lesson plans or lunch duty. The door had been open just enough for me to see Mrs. Dalton from the science wing standing outside, her hand cupped near her chin as she spoke to Mr. Carson. They weren't exchanging small talk. Their voices carried that measured tone people use when they're weighing something important.

By the time the next bell rang, I caught sight of two more teachers heading into the library. It was too early in the day for them to be off schedule, which meant they were either on a mission or already part of the conversation. I followed at a slow pace, not because I was trying to listen in — though I admit, curiosity was winning — but because it was obvious this wasn't going to stay quiet for long.

When I stepped just inside the library doorway, I caught Mr. Clarke speaking with a kind of deliberate care I'd heard only once before — last year, when he addressed the entire staff after Leo's turning point. He was explaining that Jeremy had taken the initiative to speak to our class about bullying, using the Myles Neuts case as the backbone of his point. There was no dramatizing, no stretching for effect. Just facts. And in that stillness, the weight of it seemed to land on every ear within reach.

Mrs. Patterson from the art department leaned against one of the bookshelves, arms folded, not in dismissal but in focus. She asked Mr. Clarke for specifics, and when he gave them, she nodded slowly, as if filing the details away for later use. I'd seen her take that same posture before she planned one of her mural projects — only this time, it wasn't paint she was thinking about.

A few feet over, Mr. Jennings was already suggesting that maybe this should be brought up at the next faculty meeting. He said it like someone testing the water, but you could hear in his tone that he already knew the answer. Mrs. Dalton agreed before he'd even finished the sentence. It wasn't enthusiasm in their voices — it was conviction.

From where I stood, I could see the quiet chain reaction building. One teacher passing the idea to another, each one adding their own layer to it. It was like dropping a pebble in the centre of a pond; the ripples were faint at first, then growing, touching every edge they could reach. You don't always get to watch momentum start, but when you do, it looks exactly like this.

I didn't step forward or announce myself. This wasn't my scene to take over. But I stayed close enough to catch the way their body language shifted — leaning in, hands no longer tucked away but moving as they spoke, eyes scanning for others to join in. That's how you know an idea's taking root.

At one point, Mr. Clarke glanced toward the door and spotted me. He didn't wave me in, but he didn't send me out either. Just that slight narrowing of his eyes, like he knew I was putting the pieces together. And I was. What had started as Jeremy standing at the front of our class was already turning into something bigger than he'd planned.

By the time the group broke apart, Mrs. Dalton had already moved toward the main office, no doubt to speak with the principal. Mrs. Patterson stayed behind to ask Mr. Clarke if he had any archived material she could use for her elective classes. He promised to look into it. I knew then this wasn't going to fade into one of those "good talks" that people forget by Monday.

Even in the hallway, you could hear snippets of the conversation trailing off — a mention of "student-led initiatives," another about "peer accountability." Those weren't throwaway phrases. They were the kind of terms teachers used when they were getting ready to shift the way things worked.

I made my way back toward our classroom, thinking about the pace of it all. The message had been spoken less than an hour ago, and already the people who shaped the school's tone were deciding it mattered enough to spread. That's not normal. Most things die in the classroom they start in. But not this.

Inside, Jeremy was back in his seat, flipping his pencil between his fingers like nothing had happened. But I knew he knew. There was a faint pull at the corner of his mouth — not a smile exactly, but something close. It was the look of someone who'd planted a seed and trusted the ground to do its work.

The hum of voices outside our door kept rising and falling, like the tide coming in. I could picture it travelling even further — to the lunchroom, to the gym, to places where students who hadn't been in our class would hear about it secondhand. And sometimes, secondhand stories have more power than the first.

Harley hadn't said a word since the talk ended, but his stillness was louder than usual. He didn't tap his pencil. He didn't slouch into the corner of his desk. Just sat there, staring at the faint writing still on the whiteboard: You can be the reason it stops. I wasn't sure if it unsettled him or anchored him.

The thing about ripples is you can't always tell which direction they'll move next. You can only watch, and wait, and notice who's listening. And right now, I could tell — the right people were listening.

You learn to read people's rhythms after enough time in the same building. Harley's was easy to spot — the lazy swagger to his walk, the half-smirk when teachers looked away, the way his eyes always scanned for something to poke at, someone to needle. That morning, though, something was off. It wasn't dramatic, not yet. But there was a fracture in the rhythm, a half-step that didn't quite land. He still slouched in his seat, but the smirk never came. And his eyes, usually quick to dart toward any hint of weakness, seemed to keep slipping back to the same point on the whiteboard where Jeremy's words had been written.

I caught it during our math block, when the teacher called on him for an answer. Normally he'd toss back a lazy, sarcastic remark to get a laugh. This time, he stared at the problem, cleared his throat, and muttered something about not being sure. The laugh didn't come, because he didn't want it. I could see the difference — his performance mode was switched off. That's when I knew whatever he'd overheard in the library had taken root somewhere under his skin.

At lunch, Harley sat with the same crew he always did, but he wasn't steering the conversation. Usually, his voice would be the loudest, tossing out jabs that kept him in control of the table's attention. Instead, he chewed his sandwich slowly, letting others talk over him. When a friend cracked a joke about someone in the next line, Harley glanced at them, didn't laugh, and went back to his food. It was the smallest gesture, but small gestures are sometimes the loudest signals.

I passed their table on the way to the vending machine, keeping my eyes ahead so it didn't look like I was watching. Still, I caught that sideways flicker in his gaze — the kind of look someone gives when they think they've been caught thinking about something they shouldn't be. That's when it clicked: Harley wasn't afraid of the teachers' talk about bullying. He was afraid of where it might lead if enough people decided to act on it.

Later, when the lunch bell sent us all spilling back into the hallway, I saw him slow down as we passed the library. He didn't go in, didn't stop to talk, but his eyes lingered just long enough to confirm that yes, he remembered exactly where he'd been standing when Mr. Clarke's story started. People say fear shows in your hands, your shoulders, your jaw. But in Harley, it showed in his pace — slower, more careful, as though the floor might give way if he stepped too hard.

The thing about unease is that it's rarely about what's happening in the moment. It's about what might come next. Harley wasn't panicking; he was bracing. He'd heard enough to know there were details in that story that didn't just describe someone else — they pressed too close to the shape of his own behaviour. And once you see yourself in the story of a victim or a villain, you can't unsee it.

In the afternoon, I watched him from across the room. Our teacher had us working in small groups, but Harley's group might as well have been silent. He did his part, answered when spoken to, but kept his head low. No joking, no nudging the kid next to him to whisper some insult. Just quiet. Even Lisa, who was in another group, glanced at him a few times like she'd noticed the shift too. If Lisa was curious, that meant something — she didn't pay attention unless there was an angle to play.

Once, during the last fifteen minutes of class, Harley's pen stopped moving entirely. He sat there, staring at the lined paper as if it might give him an answer he wasn't ready to write. His friends didn't notice; they were too busy trying to finish the assignment. But I did. That pause was longer than any I'd ever seen from him. It was the kind of stillness that comes when someone's trying to decide whether to double down or change course.

By the time the final bell rang, Harley was the first out the door. No backward glance, no calling out to anyone to walk home with him. Just straight down the hall, shoulders pulled in tighter than usual. The swagger was gone, and in its place was something heavier, something that didn't want to be seen but couldn't help showing through.

And here's the thing — I didn't know yet whether that flicker of unease would fade by tomorrow morning or grow into something bigger. People like Harley are experts at burying it, covering the cracks before anyone can pry them open. But sometimes, even the best cover doesn't hold forever. And if I was reading him right, this was the first sign that Harley's cover had been shaken.

I didn't mention it to anyone, not even Jeremy. Partly because I wanted to see if it was real, partly because I knew the wrong kind of attention could push Harley right back into his old posture. You can't force a shift. You can only notice it, let it breathe, and hope it grows.

Still, as I packed my bag and headed out, I thought about Mr. Clarke's words in the library, about how one story could ripple into places you never expected. Harley had heard it. He couldn't unhear it. And whether he wanted to admit it or not, a seed had been planted. It was small, fragile, and easy to stomp out — but it was there.

By the time the last bell echoed through the halls, it wasn't just Harley carrying that strange weight. The air in the corridors felt slower, like someone had turned the volume down on the usual end-of-day chatter. Kids still talked, still moved in clumps toward the doors, but there was less bouncing in their steps, fewer bursts of laughter ricocheting off the lockers. It was as if that story in the library had somehow seeped into the brickwork and started working its way through the rest of us without needing to be retold.

I could see it in the way friends walked together — side by side, but not pushing or shoving like they usually did. Even the loud group from the corner stairwell, the ones who thought every day was an audition for a comedy show, kept their jokes softer. Smiles weren't gone, but they weren't the careless kind anymore. They sat differently on faces, held back by thought. And I knew exactly when they'd start breaking, because it had already started.

Passing the trophy case, I caught sight of my own reflection and almost laughed at the serious look on my face. I hadn't planned on letting the day stick to me like this, but once you've heard something you can't unhear, you start to see how it fits into the cracks of other people's lives. That's what was happening here. Every kid walking past seemed to be carrying the thought: What if that happened to someone I knew? What if it happened to me?

At the lockers, groups that usually mixed without thinking were sticking to their own. It wasn't hostility — it was caution. Maybe everyone was taking stock, wondering if the way they treated each other would hold up under the weight of a real story. And maybe, for the first time in a long time, the answer wasn't so clear. That uncertainty showed on faces, stretched tight under those "harmless" smiles that now felt anything but.

I noticed it especially when Harley came down the hall. He wasn't looking at anyone, but people noticed him. Not in the usual way, with rolled eyes or whispered warnings, but with something sharper — the way you look at someone when you're weighing new information against what you already know. No one said anything, but the silence followed him. It wasn't the respect he was used to; it was the start of doubt.

In the gym doors' reflection, I caught Jeremy watching, too. He didn't need to say a word. His eyes tracked the same thing mine did — the slight tightening of Harley's jaw when he realized he wasn't invisible, but also wasn't being given his usual space out of fear. The balance had shifted. He was walking through a school that had started to think differently, and he could feel it.

Even Lisa looked different. She wasn't rattled like Harley — her stride was as confident as ever — but she glanced at people longer, her eyes searching for any sign of hesitation. She didn't like changes she hadn't caused, and this was one of them. Her smile stayed fixed, but it was the kind of smile that works too hard, stretched a little too thin, as if to say, Don't think I've changed just because the air feels different.

As I moved toward the exit, I felt the weight of a school at the edge of something. It wasn't fear exactly, but awareness — the kind that sits in your chest and makes every look, every word, every laugh feel like it could mean more than it used to. Even the simple "see you tomorrow" exchanges sounded softer, as if no one wanted to press too hard on the day we'd just had.

Outside, the usual rush for the buses was slower. Conversations clustered in smaller groups, hands stayed in pockets, and the laughter, when it came, was brief. I watched a few kids glance back at the building before climbing the bus steps, like they were leaving behind something unsettled. And maybe they were.

Harley stood off to the side, waiting for his ride. For the first time I could remember, no one approached him. He didn't approach anyone either. His head was down, hands shoved deep into his hoodie pocket, and his foot tapped against the curb without rhythm. He looked less like a king in his corner and more like someone who wasn't sure if his corner was still there.

Jeremy came out a few minutes later, giving Harley a passing nod without slowing down. It wasn't a challenge, but it wasn't submission either — just a simple acknowledgment that the ground had shifted and everyone knew it. Harley didn't return the nod. He just kept staring at the road, like he was waiting for something he couldn't name.

As the buses pulled away, the schoolyard emptied faster than usual. The stragglers walked with quieter steps, and even the last burst of chatter at the crosswalk felt muted. I stayed back a moment, taking in the way the building stood there against the fading light. It looked the same, but it didn't feel the same. And that's how I knew the smile had already cracked — not in one clean break, but in hairline fractures you only notice when you're close enough to see the surface give way.

Walking home, I thought about how cracks work. They don't announce themselves all at once; they spread, slow and quiet, until the whole shape changes. Today had been the first line drawn across the surface. What came next would depend on whether people tried to smooth it over — or let it widen until the truth showed through.

I caught up to Jeremy just as he stepped off the curb, the newspaper article folded with such precision you'd think it was a letter from someone he couldn't bear to lose. He didn't rush, didn't tuck it away like a kid hiding something forbidden — he carried it in plain sight, held neatly between his fingers, like he wanted the world to know he wasn't letting it go. There was a finality in the way he pressed his thumb against the crease, sealing it in more ways than one.

"Gonna read it again?" I asked, half knowing the answer already. Jeremy didn't look at me, just adjusted his grip so the folded square sat tighter in his palm. "Not just me," he said. "It's not ready for everyone else yet. But when it is, they'll hear it." The way he said when instead of if made it clear — this wasn't something to pass around casually. This was ammunition for the right moment.

We walked a few steps in silence. Every so often, his thumb would move over the paper's edge, as if checking it was still there. That article wasn't just newsprint anymore — it was a piece of Myles Neuts' voice, and Jeremy had claimed responsibility for it. He was treating it like you would a borrowed heirloom, something you protect not because it's yours, but because you've been trusted with it.

I thought about the way Mr. Clarke had looked at him when he handed it over. There had been no hesitation, no list of rules or warnings. Just trust. It takes a lot for a teacher to hand something like that to a student, especially knowing it's not coming back in the same day. But Clarke knew Jeremy — knew what he'd done for Leo, knew he wouldn't let it gather dust in the bottom of a backpack.

At the corner, we stopped for the light. Jeremy shifted the article into his jacket pocket, sliding it flat so it wouldn't bend. The movement was deliberate, almost ceremonial, like locking a door after the last guest leaves. He didn't pat the pocket afterward to check; he didn't have to. He already knew it was exactly where it needed to be.

"You think Harley heard all of it?" I asked. Jeremy nodded once. "Enough." He didn't explain what enough meant, but I understood. Some truths don't hit you all at once. They lodge somewhere, work their way in slow, until they're impossible to ignore. That article would be part of that process.

We crossed when the light changed. A gust of wind lifted the edge of Jeremy's jacket, and for a moment the corner of the folded paper showed, stark against the dark fabric. He caught it quickly, pressing it flat again. It struck me that the paper looked too small to carry the weight it held — but maybe that's how most important things are.

At the next block, he glanced sideways. "You know what the worst part is?" he said. "It's not that he died. It's that there were a hundred chances for someone to stop it, and no one did." His voice was steady, but the way he tightened his jaw told me that thought would be the one that stayed with him the longest.

When we reached his street, he paused before turning in. "This isn't for shock value," he said. "It's not for pity either. When the time's right, it's for clarity." He didn't explain further, but I didn't need him to. That article wasn't a warning; it was a mirror. And sooner or later, he was going to hold it up to the right faces.

I watched him walk up his driveway, the folded paper now completely hidden from sight. His shoulders didn't sag under it — they squared, as if the weight gave him something to stand against. For all the quiet around us, there was something in his stride that made the air feel charged.

From the sidewalk, I saw him disappear through his front door without looking back. I knew he wouldn't pull that article out again tonight, not yet. This wasn't about rushing the impact. This was about keeping the truth intact until it could land where it needed to.

Walking away, I couldn't help but think of it as a fuse. Not lit yet, but ready. The right words, the right moment, and the story inside that folded page would ignite. When it did, I had no doubt it would leave a mark deep enough that no one in this school would ever forget it.

# CHAPTER 2: WHEN SMILES BREAK

**Narrator: *Nico***

The first sound of the day is not the usual rush of sneakers across the tiled floor or the high notes of laughter ringing from the lockers. It is quieter — an in-between sort of quiet, the kind you hear before a storm breaks. I step through the main doors and feel the shift instantly, the kind that doesn't announce itself but hangs in the air all the same. The hallway smells faintly of wet coats and pencil shavings, but the energy is not what it was yesterday. Where there was once a hum of voices filling every corner, there's a hesitation, as if words are now measured before they're sent out into the open. It's not fear exactly, but it's not comfort either. Something about yesterday has travelled through the walls overnight, and it's waiting for the right moment to speak.

The clock above the office door reads 8:18, two minutes before the first bell, when Harley pushes through the side entrance. He's never been early in the time I've known him, but today he's cutting it close enough to draw glances from both ends of the hallway. His stride is the same — shoulders loose, chin tilted just enough to pretend he isn't aware of the attention — but the eyes that follow him are different now. They track him, yes, but they do not greet him. No waves, no shouts of his name, not even a hand lifted in passing. It's a pause too long to be mistaken for distraction.

I stand near the trophy case, pretending to check the dust on the lower shelf, and watch the scene unfold. Harley swings his backpack over one shoulder with the usual exaggerated arc, letting it thump against his back as if the sound alone should announce his arrival. The strap slips halfway down his arm, but he doesn't adjust it. He's playing his part as if nothing at all has shifted since yesterday. The trouble is, everyone else has stopped playing theirs. The group that used to gather near his locker has thinned to two — and even those two look like they're there out of habit, not choice.

The sound of his locker door opening echoes more sharply than it should in a hallway filled with people. He moves slowly, lining up his books as if the neatness will prove something. The first bell still hasn't rung, but the space between him and the nearest conversation is bigger than I've ever seen it. He glances up once, maybe twice, catching the eye of someone across the hall, but they turn to the side before he can read them. He smiles — or something like it — but it slides away when no one returns it.

I know enough about these shifts to understand they rarely happen without cause. Yesterday's story in the library planted something in this place, and it has already started to grow. You don't see it outright; it works under the surface, in the tilt of a head, in the half-second pause before answering a question. It moves through the school without permission, and even those who weren't in the room feel it. Harley may not admit it yet, but he feels it too.

Lisa is nowhere in sight, which is unusual for this time of morning. She likes to arrive before the second bell, giving herself the advantage of choosing where she'll be when everyone else walks in. Her absence now adds to the oddness of the moment. Without her, Harley looks less like a leader and more like someone walking into a play without his co-star. I'm not sure he knows how to carry the scene alone.

He shifts his weight from one foot to the other, eyes moving between the office door and the stairwell. I can tell he's deciding whether to head up early or wait for someone to fall into step beside him. No one does. Instead, students pass with a nod or a glance but keep moving. The conversations that do happen seem pitched lower than usual, as if no one wants to be overheard saying the wrong thing.

The air in the hallway grows heavier the longer I watch. It's not a weight you can measure, but it's there in the way people walk. The pace is slower, the footsteps more deliberate. Someone drops a pencil, and the sound rings out far longer than it should. Harley turns at the noise, expecting a greeting, but gets nothing more than a polite smile that doesn't reach the eyes. He closes his locker with more force than needed, the metallic clang snapping a few heads around before they go back to what they were doing.

The first bell finally cuts through the silence, its sharp tone bouncing off the walls like a reminder that the day must move forward whether anyone's ready or not. Harley starts toward the stairs, but the gap around him is still there — not obvious enough to call a separation, but wide enough that he walks alone. For someone who has always filled the centre of the hall, that space will not go unnoticed.

I fall in behind him as the crowd shifts toward their classrooms. There's no talking between us — he hasn't noticed me watching — but I'm already measuring the change. It's not enough to break him yet, but it's the first sign the ground under his feet isn't as solid as he thought. And once the ground shifts, you either learn to balance, or you fall. I think Harley has just felt the first tilt.

From the edge of the tarmac, I lean against the cold metal of the fence, the grid of it leaving faint marks on my palms as I watch the morning unfold. The air smells faintly of wet asphalt and the faint tang of last night's rain. Balls roll across the painted lines, skipping over puddles where the drains are slow. The games begin in their usual territories — soccer in the far corner, four-square along the wall, the loose clusters of jump ropes and hopscotch chalk near the middle — but the rhythm is different. The teasing that usually hangs in the air like harmless static is now edged with something sharper. Not louder, not even more frequent, but more calculated. It's like watching the same play acted out by new performers who have all decided to rewrite their lines.

From where I stand, I can map the subtleties — who is watching whom, who steps into a game without being asked, who takes a step back before the ball even comes their way. A few kids still toss out the same taunts they used yesterday, but there's less conviction in them now, as if they're testing how far they can go before someone steps in. Others have learned to lace their words with pauses, glancing toward teachers on duty before deciding whether to follow through. It's small enough that you could miss it if you weren't looking, but once you've seen that pull between instinct and caution, you can't unsee it.

Harley is in the middle of the soccer game, his long strides carrying him up the field with a kind of ease that used to command the attention of everyone watching. He yells for the ball, but the pass doesn't come. Not the first time, not the second. It's not defiance yet — more like they didn't hear him — but I can tell he's keeping count. The shift in their play is subtle, a fraction of a second's hesitation before they make their choice. To Harley, though, those fractions will add up fast.

I track the faces of the players nearest to him, the ones who usually take their cues from his smirk or nod. Today, they keep their eyes on the ball, not on him. One kid even passes in the opposite direction, sending the game veering toward the far corner. Harley recovers, masking his irritation with a grin, but it's the kind of grin you wear when you've bitten into something sour and won't admit it. He jogs back to position, calling out instructions in a voice a little louder than necessary, and I can see the weight of being ignored pressing against him.

Lisa has taken up her usual post near the hopscotch squares, one foot balanced on the chalked-out border, her arms folded like she's surveying a kingdom. She's not playing, but she's watching everything — who trips, who stumbles, who laughs a second too long. Her gaze sweeps across the yard with the precision of someone looking for leverage. When a younger boy drops his rope mid-turn, she leans down, picks it up for him, and says something that makes his smile falter. I can't hear the words from here, but I know the tone. She can layer it in such a way that you'll spend the rest of recess wondering if she was helping or mocking you.

The teacher on yard duty, Mr. Blake, walks a slow circuit along the far fence, his hands in his pockets and his eyes scanning without much urgency. He doesn't see the way Lisa's smile hooks at one corner when she turns away from the boy. He doesn't see the way Harley's calls for the ball are just a fraction more insistent than before. But I do. I see the invisible lines being redrawn, and I see who's testing their strength.

The playground has its own order, unspoken and rarely questioned, but today that order has been nudged. Not overturned, not replaced — just nudged. And that's enough to send ripples across the games. The four-square players take longer to serve the ball, the jump rope swings slow down when someone new approaches, and the soccer game pauses for the briefest of moments when Harley's path crosses another's. Each pause is like a bead of water rolling across glass — tiny, almost imperceptible, but impossible to reverse once it moves.

From my spot by the fence, I make myself part of the background. I know how to look like I'm only half paying attention, tracing the lines of the court with my eyes while my ears gather every piece of the conversations drifting my way. There's less laughter now, and when it does come, it's quieter, as if no one wants to give too much away. I wonder if the story from yesterday is still lingering in the back of their minds, reshaping their choices even when they don't realise it.

Harley scores a goal — or at least, he's the last to touch the ball before it rolls into the net — but even that doesn't draw the cheer it might have last week. A couple of claps, a muttered "nice one," and the game moves on. He looks toward Lisa, perhaps expecting a nod or smirk in approval, but she's busy fixing her hair, letting the elastic snap back around her wrist before she ties it up again. The dismissal isn't obvious, but it's there in the lack of acknowledgement.

The whistle blows from across the yard, signalling the end of recess. The players scatter, gathering coats and half-drunk juice boxes, and I push off the fence, falling into step with the crowd heading back toward the doors. As we pass the soccer net, Harley catches my eye for half a second, his grin still fixed in place but thinner now, stretched over something heavier. I don't stop walking, and neither does he. But I know we both felt the shift today. And shifts, once they start, have a way of gaining ground.

Harley comes back inside with the rest of us, still riding the momentum of recess like he's just won something worth bragging about. His voice cuts through the shuffle of boots on tile, tossing out quick remarks at anyone close enough to hear. The first is aimed at a boy balancing his lunch tray a little too carefully — "Don't trip, champ, it'd be a shame if your sandwich hit the floor before you did." It's the kind of line that usually earns him a few chuckles, but this time it floats in the air and drops flat, like a ball that didn't bounce. One kid smirks faintly, more out of habit than humour, while another keeps walking without so much as a glance. Harley notices, even if his grin stays put.

He gives a playful shoulder bump to a girl in a red sweater, the same one he's targeted with these so-called friendly hits all year. Normally she'd roll her eyes and say something like, "Watch it, Harley," half-laughing as she does. Today, though, she sidesteps before he can connect fully, leaving his arm swinging through empty space. It's subtle, not confrontational, but her eyes flick past him instead of meeting his. He masks the miss with a shrug, tossing his hands into his pockets as though he'd planned to walk that way all along.

The smirk is still there, but I've been around long enough to see the difference between confidence and maintenance. Right now, Harley's wearing it like armour, keeping it in place because letting it slip would mean admitting that something is off. He throws another line at a boy fiddling with his locker, "Careful with that thing, it might bite you back." It earns him half a grin, but the boy doesn't look up. The exchange dies before it has a chance to grow, and Harley turns away, pretending he's got somewhere else to be.

We file into the classroom, the usual chatter weaving through the air, but it's thinner somehow. Harley takes his seat with a kind of casual drop, leaning back like the room belongs to him, one ankle hooked over his knee. From that perch, he scans the crowd for someone willing to play along. His eyes land on a smaller boy near the window, and I can almost see the calculation — the quick assessment of who's safe to target, who won't push back. He makes a comment about the boy's hair sticking up in the back, loud enough for the row to hear. A couple of snickers bubble up, but they're shallow, uncertain. The boy just runs a hand over his head and keeps looking out the window.

It's not that Harley's words have lost all effect — it's that they're no longer unquestioned currency. The automatic laughter, the unspoken permission, it's all thinning out, like a rope fraying strand by strand. He adjusts, leaning into the back of his chair with that practiced ease, as if to signal that none of this matters. But the way his fingers tap the armrest tells me otherwise. He's measuring responses, clocking the drop in energy, and storing it away for later.

Lisa walks past his desk on her way to sharpen a pencil, her eyes sliding toward him in a silent, almost imperceptible check-in. She doesn't speak, doesn't smile, but her glance is enough to say she's watching. Harley tilts his head slightly, an unspoken "I've got this" in the motion, though I'm not sure who he's trying to convince — her or himself. She moves on without breaking stride, leaving him to sit with the space between who he thinks he is and how the room is starting to see him.

Mr. Clarke steps in a moment later, carrying a stack of papers that lands on the desk with a soft thud. The noise pulls everyone's attention forward, but Harley is still scanning the room, still looking for the reaction he's not getting. It's in the smallest things — the way people choose their seats without gravitating toward his, the way conversations lower slightly when he leans in. None of it is enough to confront outright, but it's there, a steady undercurrent that even he can't pretend not to feel.

From my desk near the middle row, I watch him settle into a quieter rhythm, his smirk softening into something less certain. He's not retreating, not yet, but the edges are starting to show. This is how it begins — not with a blowout, but with a slow shift in the weather, the kind you only notice when you've been standing in it long enough to feel the change in the air.

By the time we spill into the hallway, the shuffle of shoes and locker doors opening is loud enough to cover the quiet reshaping of the crowd. It's not dramatic, not the kind of shift you'd catch if you weren't looking for it, but it's there — like the way water starts to pull back before a wave breaks. The kids who used to flank Harley without thinking, orbiting him the second he showed up, now seem to pause just long enough to miss their cue. When he veers toward his usual spot near the trophy case, they're still at their lockers, still adjusting books, still talking to someone else. It's not rejection. It's a delay. But in Harley's world, even a delay is a crack.

He notices, of course. You can tell by the way his eyes sweep sideways, measuring the gap that wasn't there before. He tries to plug it with motion, shifting his backpack higher on his shoulder, spinning his combination lock even though he's already opened it. He calls over his shoulder to one of the taller boys, a comment about how slow he's moving, the kind of jab that used to pull a quick laugh. The boy glances up, offers a half-smile that dies before it reaches his eyes, then turns back to his books. That's all it takes for the silence to harden a little more.

The distance isn't just physical — it's in the way people choose where to look. They're not avoiding him outright, but their eyes keep finding somewhere else to land. A group by the bulletin board leans in together, shoulders tight, their laughter carrying in bursts that don't include him. Another pair shifts down the hallway when he starts moving their way, pretending to be headed somewhere they weren't a moment ago. No one says it's because of him. No one says anything at all. But that's the point — no explanation is needed.

Even Lisa, who usually threads herself into his path without fail, keeps a slight diagonal today. She's still watching him, still keeping her read on the room, but she doesn't close the space between them. Her gaze skims over him like a hand on a closed door, and for once she doesn't push it open. Harley catches it — I can see the flicker in his expression — but he doesn't call her on it. He just shifts his weight and keeps walking.

It's strange how quickly the air changes when unspoken rules start to rewrite themselves. A week ago, Harley could step into a group and the conversation would bend toward him like metal to a magnet. Now it's like the magnet's been flipped — the pull is weaker, and sometimes there's even a push. The jokes he tosses out hang too long before someone decides whether to catch them. A couple don't get caught at all.

I'm not sure if Harley understands yet that this is a warning. Not the loud, in-your-face kind, but the kind you only get once. When silence starts to replace laughter, it means people have begun thinking twice. And when people start thinking twice, the ground beneath you shifts whether you want it to or not. Harley keeps moving, wearing his smirk like a shield, but the gap between him and the others is no longer something he can pretend isn't there.

From where I'm standing, the whole hallway feels like it's holding its breath — not waiting for him to speak, but waiting to see if he notices he's speaking into a space that isn't listening the same way anymore.

She doesn't walk onto the playground — she claims it, the same way a cat steps into a room and makes you believe it's hers. Lisa's pace is unhurried, each step deliberate, as though she's giving everyone enough time to notice she's arrived. Her eyes, sharp and calculating, move in slow sweeps from one end of the tarmac to the other, weighing and sorting people without ever letting her expression give her away. She's done this so often it's practically a ritual: spot the weakest link, gauge who's watching, then strike at the right moment. But today there's something in the air she hasn't quite measured yet.

She stops short of Harley, tilting her head in that subtle way of hers, as if she's running the numbers on whether he's still worth her time. Normally, her greeting to him is long enough to draw attention — a smug remark, a private smirk, something that tells anyone within earshot that the two of them are a united front. This time it's nothing more than a quick nod and a clipped "Hey." The word lands flat, without the usual performance, before she pivots away and begins her slow march toward the far corner of the playground.

That corner is hers — not officially, of course, but in the unspoken geography of recess it might as well be fenced off and marked with her name. It's where she can see everything without having to be in the middle of it, where her chosen audience comes to her rather than the other way around. Today, though, fewer kids drift her way. A couple glance in her direction, start to move, then change their minds and join a different game. She notices — I can see it in the way her gaze lingers a fraction longer on their backs — but she doesn't call them out. She'll bide her time.

Harley's watching her too, though he tries to hide it. He knows Lisa's moods the way some people know the weather; one wrong read and you end up caught in a storm. But she doesn't give him much to work with today. There's no wink, no signal, no silent agreement to corner someone later. Just that clipped greeting and the distance she keeps. For someone like Harley, that absence is louder than a shout.

The rest of the playground seems to sense it too. The kids who usually tighten up when Lisa scans the field aren't shrinking quite as much. They still keep her in the corner of their eye — old habits die hard — but they're not bending under her gaze the way they used to. It's subtle, a shade lighter than defiance, but enough to make her readjust the tilt of her head, to scan again as if she's missed something.

Lisa leans against the fence, crossing her arms in that trademark stance of hers, chin slightly up, as though the air itself should respect her space. A soccer ball rolls too close, and instead of kicking it back, she traps it under her foot. The boy who comes to retrieve it hesitates, waiting for the verbal jab or the mocking laugh. None comes. She lets the silence hang a second longer than necessary before sending the ball back with a casual nudge. It's not kindness — it's calculation.

If Harley notices her shift, he doesn't show it outright, but there's a stiffness in the way he stands now, like he's bracing for a move she hasn't made yet. The two of them have always worked in an unspoken rhythm, feeding off each other's timing. Today, that rhythm is off. It's not broken — not yet — but it's faltering. And for bullies like Lisa and Harley, even a small misstep is enough to make the whole act wobble.

From where I'm standing, the playground feels different with her in it. Not safer — not by a long stretch — but quieter, like everyone's waiting to see if she's still playing the same game or if the rules are about to change.

## THE SMILE THAT BROKE

From where I stand, the space between Harley and Lisa is only a stretch of cracked tarmac, but it might as well be a wall. He keeps stealing glances her way, short and sharp, like someone checking a shadow that's grown too close. It's not admiration — there's no trace of that cocky grin he uses when he wants someone to think he's in control. This look is different, measured, and edged with something I've never caught on his face before: wariness. Even from a distance, I can read the stiffness in his jaw, the faint set of his mouth that says he's weighing every move before he makes it.

Lisa doesn't seem to notice him, or maybe she does and she's just too good at pretending otherwise. Her eyes skim the playground in slow, deliberate passes, never stopping long enough to suggest she's looking for anyone in particular. But I've seen her work before; she's not scanning for entertainment — she's gauging power. The way her weight shifts on one hip, the slow roll of her shoulders, it's all part of her control. And Harley, for all his bluster, is caught on the edge of her radius like a bird that's just realized it's flown into a hunter's line of sight.

He masks it quickly, straightening his posture, pulling that easy swagger back onto his frame. But it's too late — I've already seen it. The tightness in his shoulders doesn't fade, even when he turns away. His steps are more measured now, not the loose, overconfident strides he usually throws around like a badge of ownership. He's thinking, calculating, and I can almost hear the unspoken question rattling around in his head: did something change, or has he just been too blind to notice it until now?

A group of younger kids runs between them, breaking the visual thread for a moment. Harley uses it as cover, shifting his position so he's no longer directly in Lisa's line. He pretends to watch a basketball game starting up near the fence, but I can tell his attention's still tethered to her. Every so often, his eyes flick back, quick and unsteady, as if he's testing to see if she's watching him too.

Lisa, meanwhile, stands anchored in her corner, arms still crossed, one foot resting lightly on the ball she's claimed. She doesn't need to look his way — not directly — to know she's holding some part of his attention. That's the thing about Lisa: she doesn't have to chase her influence. It just hangs there, a quiet threat in the air, until the person on the receiving end either steps closer or steps back. Right now, Harley's doing both, and he doesn't even seem to realize it.

I've been watching these two for a long time, long enough to understand that bullies like Harley don't usually get rattled by other bullies. They compete, they challenge, but they don't flinch. And yet here it is — the first hairline crack in his armour, showing in something as simple as the way he stands, the way he keeps track of her without meaning to. It's small, maybe even invisible to anyone else on the playground, but I see it clear as day.

If this were any other morning, he'd already have made a move to prove himself — to her, to the crowd, to anyone watching. But he doesn't. Instead, he keeps that careful distance, eyes shifting between her corner and the games happening just out of reach. It's not fear, not exactly, but it's the closest I've seen Harley come to it. And once you spot that in someone, you can't unsee it.

The rest of the playground hums along, but there's a different current under it now. Two watchers, pretending not to watch each other, caught in some silent measurement neither of them is ready to name. For everyone else, it's just recess. For Harley, it's the beginning of something he's not going to be able to hide.

Harley steps into the four square court like it's his personal stage, tossing the ball once in his palm before serving it hard into the nearest square. Normally, he'd be fully locked in, using the game to assert himself — fast returns, quick smirks, and that fake-friendly taunt that dares someone to challenge him. But today, there's a looseness to his focus, a sliver of space between the moment and his attention. His eyes keep straying toward the far side of the playground, to clusters of kids who aren't even looking at him. It's not subtle, not to me. He's watching them in quick, sidelong glances, like someone checking whether a door is still locked.

The ball comes toward him, low and fast, but he misses it entirely, caught in mid-glance at a group by the tetherball poles. Someone else scoops up the point, and Harley lets out a laugh — too loud, too sharp — as if the noise alone will erase the fact that he didn't even try. There's a hollowness in that laugh, the kind that makes you think of an empty tin can rolling down a road. It rattles, but it's not full of anything real.

He steps back into the game, serves again, and this time he gets the point. The smirk returns for a heartbeat, but it fades almost as quickly, his eyes cutting sideways again toward another knot of kids. They're sitting cross-legged in the shade, passing around a snack, and they don't look up at him once. That absence of attention seems to pull at him more than if they'd been staring outright. He misses the next ball too, and again the laugh comes — bigger, brasher, but no one joins in.

The players in the court keep the game moving, but there's a slight shift in the air. The others don't make eye contact with him the way they used to. They don't jostle for his approval after each point. Instead, they're locked in on the rhythm of the game, letting Harley orbit around it without inviting him into the centre of its gravity. It's not exclusion in the obvious sense — no one's telling him to get out — but the subtlety of it stings more.

Harley bounces the ball in place, waiting for his serve, but his gaze is already sliding again, this time toward Lisa's corner. She's leaning against the fence, talking to a younger boy who looks equal parts nervous and curious. Harley's mouth tightens, but he forces it into a half-smile when he notices me watching. It's the same look someone gives when they've been caught reading over a stranger's shoulder — a silent admission they didn't want you to see.

The ball rolls past his feet while he's distracted again, and this time no one bothers to toss it back right away. A younger player steps out to retrieve it, and Harley makes another show of laughing it off. But the sound rings even thinner now, the edge of strain creeping in. His jokes fall into the air like flat stones, rippling only once before sinking.

From my spot near the court, I can feel it happening — the slow, quiet loosening of Harley's grip on the space around him. It's not a collapse, not yet, but it's the first hint that his hold isn't as tight as it used to be. Every sideways glance, every missed ball, every too-loud laugh is a thread fraying from the edge of a fabric he's spent years stitching together. And the thing about threads is that once they start to unravel, the rest follows faster than you think.

By the time the whistle blows to end recess, he's standing just outside the square, ball in hand, but not looking at anyone in particular. His eyes skim the playground one last time, checking those groups again, as if he's looking for something he can't quite name. Maybe it's control. Maybe it's certainty. Either way, it's not there anymore — and I don't think he knows what to do without it.

Lisa doesn't need a ball or a court to hold her ground. Her game is slower, quieter, and far more deliberate than anything Harley plays. She moves through the playground like she's mapping it, her eyes always landing a beat longer than they should on the faces she chooses. There's no raised voice, no obvious shove, no flash of temper — just a lean in close enough to make someone's shoulders stiffen, her lips shaping words that no one else can hear. Whatever she says, it works fast. I watch a boy's face drop mid-sentence, his laugh folding into a tight-lipped nod before he steps back, unsettled but not sure why.

This isn't the kind of trouble you can catch on a whistle blow or call out in front of a crowd. Lisa's skill is in planting something that grows in the other person's head long after she's gone. One look, one tilted eyebrow, one remark phrased like a fact — it's all she needs to seed doubt. She doesn't linger afterward; she moves on before her target can think of a reply. By the time they realize the weight of what she said, she's already speaking to someone else. It's not chaos she's after. It's control. And it's a control that feels colder than Harley's obvious swings.

Harley might bruise your arm and laugh when no one's looking, but Lisa makes you second-guess your own footing. She'll have you thinking you misheard, that the way she looked at you wasn't as sharp as you felt it. The best part — for her — is that no one else notices. If they do, they're not quick to admit it. On the surface, she's just another kid leaning on the fence, brushing hair out of her face. Underneath, she's measuring distance and adjusting her aim like someone setting traps.

I catch her watching Harley once, but not in the way friends watch each other. Her eyes narrow, assessing, the way a cat watches a dog from a high ledge. There's no trust there, no real alliance — only convenience. She'll use his noise to mask her moves when it suits her, and she'll step over him without hesitation when it doesn't. Harley senses it too, though he tries to keep it out of his posture. His laugh gets a shade louder when she's within earshot, but it's not the sound of someone enjoying themselves. It's a warning bell disguised as a joke.

The thing about Lisa's game is that it works best when the rest of the playground is distracted. She doesn't need everyone's attention; she just needs one person's focus at a time. And the quieter she plays, the longer her words last. I see it happen with a girl near the basketball court. Lisa leans in, says something I can't hear, and walks away. The girl stays frozen for a moment, like she's replaying the sentence over and over in her head, trying to decide whether it was an insult, a threat, or just nothing at all. That's how Lisa gets you — by leaving you unsure which it was, but certain you felt it.

There's a precision to her cruelty that makes it hard to counter. With Harley, you can see the hit coming; you can brace for it or block it. With Lisa, you only realize you've been struck when you feel the bruise later, and by then she's already moved on to the next target. Her pace is slow enough to look casual, but it's steady, and it covers more ground than you think. Every step, every pause, every glance is placed exactly where she wants it.

She's not reckless like Harley. She's patient. And patience in someone like her is dangerous, because it means she's willing to wait until her work takes hold. You don't get the satisfaction of catching her mid-act. You just notice the change in people days later — a quieter voice, a shift in where someone stands at recess, a sudden reluctance to look certain kids in the eye. That's when you know Lisa's been there.

From where I stand, I can see both of them — Harley making noise in the open, Lisa operating in the shadows. They're not a team, not really, but their presence overlaps enough to make the air feel tight. If Harley's the shove that knocks you off balance, Lisa's the hand that keeps you from finding your footing again. And right now, she's playing her part with the kind of calm that tells me she knows exactly how effective she is.

When the bell finally rings, Lisa doesn't rush. She walks in slow, eyes ahead, not looking at anyone directly. But I can see the faint curve at the corner of her mouth — not a smile, exactly, but close enough to one that I know she's satisfied. Whatever she planted out here today will grow on its own, and she'll be ready to water it when the time comes.

It begins like most shifts do — quiet enough that you could mistake it for coincidence if you weren't watching closely. A cluster of kids heading toward the basketball court breaks apart just before reaching Harley's path. One veers toward the swings, the others angle to the far end of the tarmac. No words are exchanged, no warnings spoken aloud, but the avoidance is deliberate. These aren't accidents of movement. They're small, tactical changes made by people who've started to weigh the cost of proximity. Harley notices. I can tell because his eyes flick toward each one, marking who chose the detour and how quickly they took it.

It's not in Harley's nature to let something like that pass without a response. Distance feels like a challenge to him, and challenges demand a show of strength. So he steps into the space they left, making sure his presence fills it. His stride gets longer, his shoulders square a little more, and his smirk hardens into something that doesn't bother pretending to be friendly. The air around him feels heavier now, and the noise of the playground dips for a moment before recovering. People laugh again, but the sound is thinner, stretched over something taut.

I watch him adjust his route so he's always where people might have to cross paths with him. If a group heads for the hopscotch squares, Harley drifts in that direction. If they slow near the sandbox, he quickens his pace to meet them there. It's a silent contest — him trying to close the space they're trying to widen. And the more they sidestep, the more obvious his efforts become. There's an edge to his movements, like he's daring someone to call out what's happening. No one does. Instead, they adapt again, creating new lines of movement that snake around him without ever touching.

He plays it off at first, tossing casual remarks to anyone within earshot, but the words are a shade sharper than usual. A compliment with a twist, a joke that sounds like it's missing a punchline, a "just kidding" that hangs in the air too long. It's as if he's testing whether people will still engage, still give him the reaction he's looking for. When they don't, he pushes harder. His voice rises, his laughter gets louder, and his gestures grow bigger — all of it an attempt to reclaim the space he feels slipping away.

Some of the avoidance is practical. Kids choose games on the far side of the field, or they linger near the doors where a teacher might step out. But some of it is instinctive, the kind of body language you adopt without thinking. Shoulders turning, eyes glancing down, steps shifting just enough to create a buffer. Harley reads these cues like a map, and every time he spots one, his jaw tightens. For someone who prides himself on being in control, the loss of even an inch of ground feels like an insult.

Lisa notices, too. She doesn't step in to help him, though. She watches from her usual post by the fence, her gaze sliding over the small changes in the playground's flow. If Harley's retreating in any way, she's not about to close the gap for him. In fact, I think she's measuring how much of this is his doing and how much is just the natural outcome of people finally taking a step back. Her detachment seems to bother him more than the avoidance itself.

By the time recess is halfway over, the pattern is set. Harley moves, others move away. He advances, they redirect. It's a dance no one rehearsed but everyone understands. The bell will end it soon enough, but the unspoken message will stick. You can't fake comfort, and right now, comfort around Harley is in short supply. He knows it, and it's making him restless. Restlessness in Harley has never ended quietly.

When the whistle blows, there's no rush to line up near him. Kids filter into place from different angles, leaving him just enough room to make it clear the space is intentional. He's not alone, not yet, but the distance is growing. And the more he pushes to prove otherwise, the more obvious that truth becomes.

The first thing I notice isn't the move he makes toward the hopscotch lines — it's the mark on his face. The bruise sits high on his cheekbone, an ugly bloom of purple and yellow that wasn't there yesterday. It draws the eye whether you mean to look or not, and Harley knows it. He wears it like an accessory, letting it speak for him before he says a word. When he drifts toward the smaller boy standing alone near the faded chalk squares, there's a rhythm to his steps — slow, deliberate, almost lazy. But I've seen Harley's kind of lazy before. It's the same calculated ease a cat uses before it pounces.

The boy's shoulders tense before Harley even says anything. That's the thing about fear: it remembers. Harley doesn't have to raise his voice or step too close; his reputation does the work for him. He leans just far enough forward to block the kid's view of the rest of the playground, his shadow falling long across the hopscotch grid. The boy looks down, but Harley tilts his head until their eyes meet. No words yet — just a stare that says, I still own this space.

When he finally speaks, it's in a low tone I can't quite catch from where I stand. It's not what he says that matters, though. It's the way he says it — measured, almost casual, but with that clipped edge that turns even the smallest remark into a warning. The boy nods once, quick and jerky, and Harley takes a half-step closer, closing the space between them until there's nowhere left to back up. There's no shove, no grab, nothing that a teacher could point to and call an infraction. Harley's smarter than that. This is about presence, not proof.

The moment breaks when Harley steps back, slow and deliberate. He lets his gaze linger on the boy a second too long, then glances sideways as if something in the distance has caught his interest. But before he walks away, he delivers the part that chills me more than anything else — the smile. It's wide, slow, and utterly hollow, stretching just enough to be seen from across the yard. There's no humour in it, no warmth. It's a performance for anyone watching, a reminder that he's still capable of making someone's day turn cold in seconds.

I feel my stomach twist because I know that smile. It's the same one I've seen on faces that enjoy the discomfort they cause. The kind that thrives on the quiet victories, the unspoken I win that doesn't need an audience. And from the way the boy's shoulders stay tight even after Harley's gone, the message landed exactly as intended.

Around us, games keep going. A ball bounces off a wall, laughter spikes from the swings, and somewhere a whistle blows, calling kids toward the water fountain. But near the hopscotch lines, the air still feels heavy. The boy glances over his shoulder twice before moving, his steps quick, as if putting distance between himself and the chalk squares might erase what just happened.

Harley doesn't follow. He doesn't have to. He's already planted what he came to plant — the seed that says the shift on this playground might be real, but he's not going quietly. The bruise on his face only deepens the message: someone might have gotten to him, but that doesn't mean he's out of the game. If anything, it makes him more dangerous, because now he has something to prove.

I catch Lisa watching from her corner, expression unreadable. She doesn't step in, doesn't even move, but I see the faint curve of her mouth, the kind of smirk that knows a piece of the board just shifted. Whether she's pleased or simply taking note, I can't tell. But I know this — Harley's pushback today isn't the last we'll see of it.

It's strange how one moment can hang in the air long after it's passed. Watching Harley turn away from the hopscotch lines, I find my mind slipping back to yesterday in the library, to Mr. Clarke's voice carrying over the hum of the heating vents as he told the story that silenced the room. He'd said there are moments — small, almost invisible at first — when you can stop something before it becomes irreversible. He said if you miss them, you don't always get another chance. That line has been replaying in my head since, and now it lands harder than ever. The way Harley moved, the way he smiled without smiling — it feels like the first chapter of something that could turn darker if no one interrupts the writing.

I scan the yard, wondering if anyone else sees it the same way. Most of the kids are back in their games, as if what happened was just another ripple in the morning. But the boy Harley cornered hasn't joined anyone. He stands at the far edge of the fence, his back pressed lightly against it, head lowered, hands stuffed deep in his pockets. His friends are scattered elsewhere, maybe not even aware he's alone. I think of Mr. Clarke's words again — how the early signs don't always look dramatic, how sometimes they're just in the shift of a shoulder or the way someone avoids the places they used to stand without thinking.

Harley walks toward the basketball court now, slipping back into a group as if nothing happened. They greet him, not warmly, but out of habit. There's a pause in their rhythm when he arrives, a small gap in the conversation, and then they keep going. He laughs too loudly at a joke that wasn't meant to be funny, his voice cutting across the court like a misplaced chord in a song. No one tells him to stop. They just keep playing, adjusting around him the way people adjust around a puddle they don't want to step in.

The sunlight catches the bruise on his face, and I see him touch it briefly, almost like a reminder. I can't tell if it hurts him or fuels him. That's the danger with someone like Harley — pain can turn either way. It can soften you, or it can sharpen you into something you don't want to see coming. Yesterday's story was about a boy who didn't get enough softening, who met too much sharpening from the people around him until there was nothing left to blunt the edge.

I can almost hear Mr. Clarke's voice again, steady and deliberate, when he said the saddest thing isn't when someone gets hurt — it's when everyone sees the signs and still does nothing. I glance at the teachers on yard duty. They're watching in that general way that covers a lot of space but doesn't settle on any one thing for too long. If they saw Harley's little performance, they don't show it.

The boy at the fence finally moves, slow steps toward the school door, cutting across the blacktop like someone who just remembered they forgot something inside. I don't know if he'll tell anyone. Most kids don't. You learn early that saying something can sometimes make it worse. That's what bothers me — knowing Harley is counting on that silence. He's banking on it, the same way a gambler counts on the cards no one else has seen yet.

I keep my eyes on him as he joins the game, but my thoughts keep drifting back to yesterday. It's not just the story of Myles Neuts that's sticking — it's the feeling in the room when we all heard it. That tightness in the chest, that sense that you can't go back once you know certain things. I think maybe this morning is one of those "certain things." The kind that will sit in the corner of your mind, waiting to see which way it turns.

The whistle blows for the end of recess, and the yard begins to funnel toward the doors. Harley jogs ahead, tossing a ball to someone with a grin that looks almost real. The boy from the fence slips in behind a different crowd, careful not to pass too close. I hang back for a moment, just to watch the space between them grow, and I wonder if anyone else can hear the echo of yesterday in the way today is already shaping up.

Lisa comes down the steps from the portable, her hands tucked into the pockets of her jacket, chin lifted just enough to look over the heads in front of her. She doesn't break stride when she sees Harley near the basketball court. No smile. No nod. Not even the smallest flicker of acknowledgment. It's the kind of pass-by that says, you're not worth my time. To anyone else, it might look like she's ignoring him completely, but I know better. Lisa doesn't waste opportunities. She stores them. She's the type who lets the air go still before she makes her move, so when she does, the change is sudden enough to knock you off balance.

Harley notices her — I see it in the way his eyes track her for half a second longer than they should. He masks it quickly, spinning the ball on his palm like it's just another ordinary moment. But the spin falters, the ball slipping from his fingertips to the ground. He recovers it, laughing in that offhand way he uses when he doesn't want people thinking he's rattled. His friends don't even seem to notice, but I catch the way his jaw tightens as he watches her walk away.

Lisa's silence is its own kind of presence. She doesn't need to fill the space with words to make herself heard. She just lets her absence speak. It's the absence of alliance, of loyalty, and in this kind of playground economy, that's worth more than anything she could have said out loud. Harley knows it. The unspoken rule here is simple — if Lisa decides you're not worth standing beside, the rest of the school will start wondering why they should.

She crosses to her usual spot near the far fence, leaning against it with her arms folded. A small group gathers there, the ones who always seem to orbit her without quite touching her centre. She says something low to the girl nearest her, who immediately glances over at Harley before looking away. I can't hear the words, but I can feel the temperature shift. Whatever Lisa just said, it wasn't random.

Harley keeps playing, but his movements are sharper now, like he's putting just a little too much into each pass. He scores a point and calls it louder than necessary, his voice carrying across the tarmac. Lisa doesn't even look up. That's her power — she doesn't give him the dignity of reacting. She makes him work for attention he's not going to get. And the harder he works for it, the more obvious it becomes to anyone watching that she's the one holding the strings, even if she hasn't pulled them yet.

I've seen Lisa operate before. She's not the type to push in the middle of a crowd. She prefers the edges — the in-between moments, the quiet conversations when no one else is listening. That's where she plants her seeds. You won't see them sprout until later, and by then, you've forgotten the moment they were sown. Harley may think he's safe because she's not confronting him, but if he knew her game, he'd know this is the most dangerous stage.

From where I stand, I can almost map out the invisible line she's drawing around herself. Everyone in her circle is inside it. Harley's outside. And once Lisa decides you're outside, you stay there until she says otherwise. He might not feel the full weight of that yet, but he will.

The bell rings, scattering everyone toward the doors. Lisa waits, letting her group go ahead before she follows. Harley lingers too, bouncing the ball against the wall, watching her retreat. He thinks she's not paying attention. He's wrong. She's paying attention to everything — she's just waiting for the right moment to make it count. And I've learned enough about her to know she always gets her moment.

The bell cuts through the playground noise with its sharp, hollow clang, but Harley doesn't move. Most kids drop what they're doing at the first ring, already halfway to the door before the sound fades. Not him. He lingers in the middle of the tarmac, one hand hooked through the strap of his backpack, the other shoving the basketball between his palm and the ground with slow, deliberate thumps. He's scanning, his gaze sliding from one group to another like he's testing the waters before stepping in. From where I'm standing, it looks less like confidence and more like searching.

Kids move past him in a steady stream, the usual flow toward the doors. He glances at a pair of boys from his class, the ones who used to slap his palm every morning like it was part of some unspoken ritual. Today, they keep walking. One looks at the ground. The other adjusts his hat like it suddenly matters more than acknowledging Harley. If he notices, he doesn't show it, but the basketball hits the pavement a little harder the next time.

The yard is almost empty now, only a few stragglers left. Harley's eyes keep sweeping, moving too quickly to settle on any one face. Maybe he's looking for a sign that someone's still in his corner. A nod. A grin. Something. But the kids who meet his gaze are the ones who only hold it for half a second before shifting away. It's subtle — you'd miss it if you weren't looking for it. But I'm looking, and it's there.

Lisa's already gone, her group swallowed by the tide heading inside. Without her in sight, Harley looks unanchored. He spins the ball once, catches it, and tucks it under his arm. The action feels less like a show and more like retreat — the way someone pockets a coin they're not sure is worth playing. He glances toward the entrance, and for a moment, I think he's finally going in. He doesn't.

Instead, he shifts his weight from one foot to the other, watching the last few kids disappear into the school. The yard feels bigger now, emptier. He's the only one left in the open, framed by the painted lines and faded hopscotch squares. I've seen him stand alone before, but this is different. This isn't a choice. This is what's left when no one chooses you.

A teacher pokes their head out the door to call the final warning, voice carrying just enough authority to pull him in. Harley turns, walking at an unhurried pace, the basketball bouncing once more before he catches it and holds it still. He doesn't look around this time. If there's anyone left willing to meet his eyes, I can't see them from here.

Inside, the noise of the hallway swallows him. I follow at a distance, and even from behind, I can tell — something in the way his shoulders sit lower, something in the way his steps drag half an inch longer — that he didn't find what he was looking for out there. Whatever it was, it's gone for now. And he knows it.

The hallway swallows the sound of the playground behind us, replacing it with the softer hum of lockers opening, shoes squeaking on polished floors, and the steady murmur of voices that don't carry the same sharp edges as they did outside. It's almost disorienting, the way the atmosphere changes between the door and the first row of hooks. Out there, every step felt like a performance; in here, it feels like the curtain's already down and no one's watching. Harley moves slower than usual, his strides measured, almost hesitant, like the hallway has suddenly grown longer. He keeps his eyes forward, but I notice how they flick, just briefly, toward certain groups.

# THE SMILE THAT BROKE

It's not the swagger I'm used to seeing from him. Normally, Harley owns these corridors — leaning on doorframes, tossing half-smiles at anyone who passes, finding a reason to stall near the water fountain just to claim the space. Today, his pace is steady, but not for the sake of confidence. It's like he's bracing himself for the reception. And the thing is, no one's going out of their way to greet him. No elbows jab in friendly familiarity. No hands shoot up for an incoming high five. If someone makes eye contact, it's fleeting, a glance that bounces away before it can land.

The air in here feels safer, like it's been cleared out by something unseen. Conversations are lighter — not because they're happier, but because the tension that's usually tethered to him isn't trailing behind as strongly. I think he feels it too. The gap between him and the next cluster of students is wider than it needs to be, but he doesn't close it. Instead, he carries the basketball low against his hip, a shield without a fight to defend against.

As we pass the grade five classrooms, a couple of kids step aside to let him through, but they don't speak. It's not fear that's keeping them quiet; it's something closer to uncertainty, like they're trying to figure out where the lines are now. He notices — of course he notices — and his jaw shifts just enough to tell me he's biting back a comment. That silence is louder than anything he could have said.

By the time we reach our own classroom, Harley has adjusted his grip on the ball three times, rolling it over his palms as if searching for something to hold onto that isn't slipping through. The door's open, voices spilling out, and for the first time in a long while, I see him hesitate. Just for half a second, his shoulders lift and fall, almost imperceptibly, before he steps inside.

The difference hits immediately. In here, the light falls softer, the walls are closer, and the distance between people is dictated by choice, not by the flow of recess. Harley's spot — the one near the back where he can see everyone — is still empty, but he doesn't head there right away. He takes the longer path around, weaving past desks, as if searching for some silent confirmation that nothing's changed.

But it has. He can see it in the way heads turn to track him, not in admiration or expectation, but in quiet observation. No one flinches. No one challenges him. They're just… watching. And for the first time, I think he knows that watching and waiting might be more dangerous to him than any open opposition.

When he finally sinks into his chair, he sets the ball on the floor beside him instead of spinning it on his knee like usual. His fingers tap once against the desk, then stop. Whatever game he thought he was playing this morning, the rules shifted somewhere between the blacktop and the hallway. And judging by the way his gaze stays fixed on the front of the room, Harley hasn't yet figured out how to play by them.

The hallway is nearly empty now, most of the class already at their desks, but Harley lingers by his locker. I slow down just enough to see his hand falter on the dial, spinning past the numbers once, then again. The clang of the metal lock snapping back into place is sharper than it needs to be, and when he mutters under his breath, it's low enough to be missed by anyone not paying attention. But I'm paying attention. His voice carries that edge — the kind that comes when someone's holding too much in, and the pressure's beginning to show. The smirk he wore this morning has softened, but not in kindness; it's sagging, slipping at the corners, as if keeping it in place takes more energy than he has left.

A teacher walks past, arms full of books, and I catch the quick glance they exchange with another staff member down the hall. It's not just casual notice — it's the kind of look that says news has already made its way through the staffroom. I don't have to wonder long, because the fragments reach me in pieces: a whisper by the water fountain, a hushed conversation at the library door. By the time I get to my own locker, the truth lands heavy — Harley's mother died last night. No illness drawn out over months, no slow goodbyes, just gone. And before the sun was even fully up, his father sent him here, to school, like it was any other day.

There's no funeral being planned, no chance for him to see her one last time. Straight cremation, just like that — the kind of decision that leaves no room for ritual or closure. I think about that as I watch him tug the locker door open with more force than necessary. The sound echoes, metallic and hollow, a noise that belongs more in a factory than in a school hallway. He doesn't look at anyone. He just shoves his books into the bag, slamming the door shut again before spinning the lock with an abrupt twist.

It's no wonder his anger's been burning hotter than usual, though this isn't the kind of blaze that lights up for show. This is a deep, searing fury, the kind that scorches from the inside and doesn't care what gets caught in the path. And yet, under it, I see something else — not weakness, exactly, but a rawness. Like a wire that's been stripped of its coating, left exposed, humming with a current no one should touch.

He catches me watching and holds my gaze for a fraction of a second too long. There's no threat in it this time. No dare, no smug defiance. Just an unspoken message I can't quite read, a warning and a plea knotted together. Then he swings the strap of his bag over his shoulder and heads for the classroom, leaving the faint scent of cold air and something sharper in his wake.

The teachers don't stop him, though I can see in their faces they want to. Maybe they know there's nothing to say that won't make it worse. Maybe they've already decided to let him burn through the day on his own terms. Either way, the space he leaves behind feels heavier than the one he occupied. It's like the hallway is holding its breath, waiting to see what comes next.

And I realize then that this — this fumbling at the locker, this slip in his armour — is the first real crack I've seen in him. Not the staged hesitations or the calculated smirks, but something honest, even if it's jagged. I don't know if that makes him more dangerous or more human. I just know that the smile he's worn like a shield is losing its shape, and once it's gone, we'll all see what's been hiding underneath.

By the time the first bell has faded and the scrape of chairs settles into a low hum, Harley is already in his seat. His arms are folded tight across his chest, not in the lazy sprawl he usually claims but in that rigid, locked-in way that says he's building walls. His eyes stay fixed on the desk, not moving even when the shuffle of books and whispers of conversation flow around him. There's no swagger, no casual glances thrown to make sure the room is orbiting him. He's anchored now, and it's not by choice. It's as if he's bracing for something, or maybe trying to keep himself from unravelling any further.

Two rows over, Lisa leans back in her chair, one leg stretched under the desk, already half turned toward a girl she's speaking to in a voice too soft for anyone else to catch. She doesn't so much as glance at Harley. If there's any history in their usual alliance, it's gone from her posture. She's operating on a different track, her gaze settling on a new target without hesitation. Watching her, I realise that whatever game she plays, she never stays in one place long enough to get tied to anyone else's downfall. She moves when the ground shifts. And right now, Harley is sinking ground.

The room feels… different. Not louder, not quieter, but lighter, like the air has been holding its weight back for a long time and finally let some of it go. The front row is focused on the teacher as she begins, but there's an unspoken current in the way heads turn and voices pause just before they speak. Harley doesn't hold the room anymore, not even in the way an unspoken threat can. That space has thinned, replaced by a strange kind of collective ease.

I watch it settle over the class, the way it works in small moments. A pencil passed without hesitation. A question asked without checking his reaction first. Even the clatter of a dropped ruler near the back doesn't draw his eyes. For once, the centre of gravity in here is somewhere else entirely, and everyone can feel it. It's not victory — not yet — but it's a shift, and shifts matter.

Harley's shoulders stay locked, his jaw tense. I wonder if he notices the change, if he can feel the way people aren't revolving around him anymore. It's subtle enough he could miss it if he's trying to, but I don't think he is. Not now. He's too still. Too closed in. And that stillness is new.

The teacher moves into the day's lesson, her voice steady, her eyes scanning the room in a way that lands on everyone equally. No extra weight on Harley. No signs of walking on eggshells. The whole scene plays out like a test, and the class passes without even realising they're being tested. Harley stays quiet. Lisa keeps her focus elsewhere. And for the first time in a long time, the room doesn't feel claimed by either of them.

That's new. And in the quiet of that realisation, I know this isn't an ending. It's only the beginning of something neither of them planned for — a slow turning of the tide that doesn't crash all at once, but pulls steady and sure until the shore looks different and they're standing in a place they don't recognise. Whatever happens next will come from here.

# CHAPTER 3: THE GIRL HARLEY FEARS

The bell had not yet rung, but the yard was already alive with the restless shuffle of students finding their places in the morning's unspoken order. From where I stood by the bike racks, the air felt different — still charged from yesterday's undercurrents, but now sharpened in a way that made people watch each other more carefully. Lisa arrived as if she owned the path beneath her shoes, the faint crunch of gravel announcing her before her face came into view. She was smaller than most of the kids clustered at the tarmac's edge, her frame slight enough to disappear into the crowd if she wanted. But she didn't vanish; she moved with the kind of deliberate pace that told you she knew exactly who was watching and exactly what they would see. Her hair was tied back in a way that showed her eyes clearly, sharp and still, cutting through the noise of the playground without ever breaking stride.

I saw Harley before he saw her. He was leaning against the wall by the basketball nets, backpack slung over one shoulder, wearing the same mask of false ease he'd been holding onto since yesterday. It slipped the instant his gaze found her. No one else seemed to notice the way his posture changed — the slow stiffening of his spine, the way his fingers twitched against the strap of his bag. But I did. His grief was still a raw, ticking presence in him, and Lisa's arrival seemed to pull that fuse shorter. He didn't step forward to greet her, didn't call her name, didn't so much as nod in acknowledgment. Instead, his weight shifted toward the doors, as if retreat was an option he might take if no one else was looking.

Lisa didn't rush to meet him either. She paused at the outer edge of the yard, letting her gaze sweep over the playground like she was checking the pieces on a board before deciding on her move. Her eyes passed over Harley once — just once — but in that brief contact, something unspoken passed between them. It wasn't the look of an enemy meeting another in open battle; it was the look of someone who knew exactly where to place the next blow, and that it didn't need to come right now. She kept walking, choosing a route that kept her in his sightline without ever approaching close enough to speak. The air between them tightened, invisible but solid, the kind of thing you could feel pressing against your skin.

Jeremy came up beside me, his hands shoved deep in his jacket pockets, following my gaze toward the two of them. "He's rattled," he murmured, not bothering to hide the observation. His tone wasn't mocking, but there was no sympathy in it either. "Didn't think I'd see him flinch for her." I didn't answer, because flinch wasn't quite the right word. It wasn't fear the way you might expect from someone facing a bigger opponent — it was something quieter, deeper, the kind of unease that digs in where you can't shake it off. Harley's grief was like a wound that hadn't scabbed over, and Lisa, whether she knew it or not, had just walked straight toward it.

Across the yard, Harley's friends tried to pull him into conversation, but he wasn't listening. His responses were delayed, the kind that made the others glance at each other like they were wondering if he'd heard the question at all.

His eyes kept shifting toward Lisa's path, even when she wasn't looking his way anymore. It was like watching someone track a stormcloud moving in slow motion — too far to drench you yet, but close enough to feel the air change. The more he tried to mask it with his usual smirk, the more obvious it became that the mask didn't fit today. It sagged in the corners, his grin not quite reaching his eyes, his shoulders too rigid to sell the performance.

Lisa reached the benches near the hopscotch squares and stopped there, leaning one hip against the seat. A couple of girls joined her, their voices low but their eyes flicking toward Harley with the kind of curiosity that made me think she'd said something worth hearing. She laughed once — short, sharp, deliberate — and though I couldn't hear the words, I didn't need to. Whatever she said, it had Harley pushing his weight off the wall, shifting his stance in that restless way people do when they want to walk away but can't without showing they've been pushed.

"Do you think she knows about his mom?" Jeremy asked quietly, his voice low enough that it wouldn't carry. I considered it for a moment before answering. "Maybe. Maybe not. Doesn't change much. If she does, she'll use it when she wants to. If she doesn't, she'll find something else." Jeremy frowned, eyes narrowing as he tracked Harley's movements. "She doesn't look like she'd bother with him. But she is." I didn't disagree. Some people don't need to look dangerous to be dangerous. Lisa was one of them.

The wind picked up just enough to stir the loose leaves near the fence, rattling them against the chain links. Harley finally tore his gaze away from Lisa long enough to toss his bag on the ground and join a game near the nets. But his movements were jerky, his voice too loud when he called for the ball. Lisa didn't move from her spot. She just watched, chin tilted slightly, that unreadable half-smile playing at the edge of her mouth. It wasn't the kind of smile you give someone you like — it was the kind you give when you know the game's already yours, and you're just waiting for the other player to figure it out.

From where I stood, it was already clear: whatever Harley's reputation had been before, whatever weight he thought his presence carried, Lisa wasn't impressed. And more than that — she wasn't afraid. If anything, she seemed to know something he didn't want the rest of us to see. I could almost feel the shift in balance happening, not in a crash, but in a slow, deliberate slide. Harley might not have realized it yet, but this morning was the first step toward a place where he wouldn't be the one people measured themselves against anymore.

Lisa leaned forward on the bench, speaking to a boy from our class whose name I couldn't catch over the wind. Her voice was low enough that I had to watch his reaction instead of her mouth. On the surface, it looked like a normal exchange — a friendly tilt of the head, a half-smile that suggested a shared joke. But then his eyes shifted down, his answer slow to come, and I saw the flicker of caution cross his face. Whatever she'd said, it carried more than the light tone implied. Words like that don't just pass through the air; they settle in the other person's head and keep echoing long after. Lisa didn't break her smile. She just leaned back, folding her arms like she'd done exactly what she meant to do.

Leo appeared at my side without warning, his gaze fixed on the same scene. "You ever seen two cats fight over one yard?" he asked, his voice pitched low so it stayed between us. I shook my head, still watching Lisa's small frame against the backdrop of the playground. "Well," he went on, "same thing happens here. Two people like that can't run the same ground. Sooner or later, one of 'em moves." His tone wasn't casual — it was the tone of someone who'd thought about it longer than he should have. Alex joined us then, dragging his feet in the gravel before stopping with his arms crossed. "Leo's right. You can't have two people trying to be the one everyone else watches. They'll keep circling each other until one makes the first real hit."

Jeremy stepped up a moment later, not asking what we were looking at because it was obvious. "She's not afraid of him," he said flatly. "And he knows it." His eyes narrowed on Harley, who was still forcing his way through the game near the nets, making louder calls for the ball than the play required. "He's used to being the one people step back for. She's not going to give him that." Jeremy's voice had that thoughtful edge I'd heard yesterday when he spoke about the Myles Neuts article — the kind that meant he was already connecting threads in his head, laying them out in a line only he could see.

Lisa glanced over then, just for a second, catching Harley mid-pass. She didn't hold the look long enough to start a staring match, but long enough to let him know she'd been watching. The boy she'd been talking to excused himself quickly after that, heading toward the far end of the yard without looking back. "See?" Leo murmured. "She doesn't have to raise her voice. She just plants something and lets it grow." He sounded almost impressed, though the edge in his tone said he knew it wasn't something to admire. Alex nodded slowly. "And Harley's the kind who reacts without thinking. That's going to make it worse for him."

Jeremy pulled a small notebook from his jacket pocket — the one he always carried, scribbling in during quiet moments like he was storing pieces of the day for later. Without looking up, he muttered, "Two predators, same territory. Won't last. One's going to get louder, the other's going to get smarter. My guess? She's the smarter one." He jotted something down quick before sliding the pencil back into the spine and closing it with a snap. His eyes didn't leave Lisa. "She's not testing him yet. She's just mapping the ground."

The wind carried a sudden burst of laughter from the four-square court, and Harley's head turned sharply toward it, as though making sure no one was laughing at him. The movement was too fast to be casual, the kind of reflex that told you he was already feeling the ground shift under him. Lisa caught it, I could tell by the faint lift of her eyebrow. She didn't smile this time. She just adjusted her stance, still leaning against the bench like she had all morning to watch how he played this out. There was something unnerving in how still she could be when everyone else was in motion.

Jeremy's pencil made a slow turn between his fingers. "That's the thing about people like her," he said, speaking more to himself than to us. "They don't rush. They wait until the other person does something they can use, and then they make it look like it was their plan all along." Leo glanced at him sideways. "You're talking like you've seen this before." Jeremy didn't answer directly. He just tucked the notebook away again and said, "I've seen what happens when you don't notice it soon enough."

Alex tilted his head toward Harley, who had just missed another play, drawing groans from his teammates. "He notices her," he said. "He just doesn't know what to do about it yet." His voice carried a note of certainty, the kind you get when you've seen the ending of a story but have to watch everyone else catch up. Jeremy's eyes narrowed again, and I knew he was filing away every small detail — Harley's missed passes, Lisa's stillness, the way the other kids moved around them both like currents avoiding rocks.

I kept my gaze on the two of them, thinking about what Leo had said — about how two bullies couldn't share the same ground. It wasn't just about size or strength. It was about space, about who people looked at, whose words got remembered. Harley had always been the loudest voice in the room, but Lisa's wasn't about volume. Hers was about precision, and precision can cut just as deep as brute force, if not deeper. I didn't say it aloud, but I knew in my gut: this wasn't going to stay a stalemate for long.

Harley planted himself at the edge of the basketball game like he had every right to be there, but even from where I stood, it was obvious his attention was anywhere but on the ball. His body was turned half away from the court, eyes scanning the yard but never quite landing on Lisa. It was the kind of not-looking that only made it clearer he knew exactly where she was. He laughed at something one of the boys said, the sound too quick, too high, and followed it with a shove to someone's shoulder that didn't seem connected to anything. His smirk didn't reach his eyes, and in that small gap between performance and reality, I saw the first real retreat.

Jeremy noticed it too. He had a way of tracking people without making it obvious, his gaze drifting just enough to catch patterns no one else thought to follow. He leaned slightly toward me, his voice low. "Watch his feet." I did, and sure enough, Harley was angling himself in tiny increments — not so much stepping back as shifting his weight so he could keep a barrier of moving bodies between himself and Lisa. It was calculated in the way a cornered animal calculates, choosing open space over confrontation. He wasn't about to give her a straight line to him.

Lisa, for her part, didn't seem to be pressing for one. She lingered by the bench, her hands tucked into the pockets of her jacket, eyes flicking toward Harley now and then without any urgency. That was what made it worse for him, I think — the fact that she wasn't chasing, wasn't pushing, just existing in the same space without bending to the unspoken rule that people moved for him. Her stillness was a quiet defiance, and I could see it scratching at him under the surface. He masked it well enough for most, but not for Jeremy.

The ball rolled toward Harley's side of the court, and he bent to scoop it up, dribbling twice before passing it off faster than necessary. His hands brushed the sides of his jeans afterward, a restless gesture that made it clear his focus wasn't on the game. Jeremy's eyes narrowed slightly, and I knew he was writing the moment down in his mind, another thread to add to whatever quiet map he was drawing of the tension between them. The air felt stretched thin, like we were all waiting for one of them to make the move that would push this from subtle to obvious.

When Harley finally did glance toward Lisa, it was quick, like a flash of light in a shuttered room. But even in that instant, I caught the flicker in his expression — not fear exactly, but the stiff awareness of someone watching their opponent in a match they never agreed to play. He looked away immediately, calling for the ball again even though it was nowhere near him. The sound of his voice was louder than it needed to be, another tell in the long list of tells that Jeremy was quietly collecting.

Leo wandered up beside us, chewing on the inside of his cheek as he followed our gaze. "He's keeping his distance," he said flatly. "That's not Harley." Jeremy didn't look away from the court when he replied, "No, it's Harley adjusting. He's not sure what she'll do yet, so he's staying where he can see her without looking like he's watching." His tone was almost clinical, but there was a current underneath — the same one I'd heard when he talked about Myles Neuts, like he'd seen this play out before and knew the steps too well.

The group Harley was with shifted toward the far side of the tarmac, and I saw him take the chance to widen the gap between himself and Lisa. It was subtle enough that most would miss it, but once Jeremy pointed out the way his steps angled instead of moving straight, I couldn't unsee it. Lisa's eyes followed, and though she didn't move, there was something in the way her lips pressed together that told me she'd clocked it too. Harley was playing defense, but in a game where she had more patience than he did, defense wouldn't hold forever.

I found myself wondering if Harley even understood how much of this she was controlling without a word. Jeremy's pencil made another slow turn between his fingers, and I suspected he was wondering the same thing. This wasn't about who could shove harder or shout louder. This was about who could hold their ground without showing strain — and right now, Harley was the only one showing it. The retreat was small, but in a place where everyone watched everyone else, small was all it took for the cracks to start showing.

Lisa didn't march over like someone picking a fight. She drifted, weaving through the edges of games until her path became impossible to mistake for anything but deliberate. The bench where she'd been leaning was now behind her, and each step shaved off the careful buffer Harley had been keeping. I watched the moment he noticed — a fractional pause in his dribble, a flick of his eyes toward the right as though looking for an exit. His voice called out something to his group, but the words were filler, just enough noise to mask the tightening in his jaw. The boys around him glanced between the two, sensing the line about to be crossed, yet none moved to intercept her.

"Morning, Harley," she said when she was close enough for it to be just between them. Her tone was light, almost friendly, but it carried that weight she could pack into anything — a weight that made the word sound like it had a hook hidden inside. Harley forced a smile, tossing the ball once before catching it again, holding it like a shield. "Morning, Lisa," he replied, matching her casualness in pitch but not in ease. The muscles in his neck gave him away, pulled tight like a rope bracing for strain.

"You missed a spot," she said, nodding toward his shoulder as though brushing invisible lint from the air. It was nothing, just a comment, but it landed in the space between them like a dare. Harley chuckled — a low, short sound — and said, "Yeah, I'll survive." He wanted to sound dismissive, but the way he gripped the ball, fingertips pressing hard against the rubber, told another story. Her eyes flicked to it, then back to him, the corner of her mouth curling like she'd just confirmed something.

"Survival's good," she murmured. "But some people get tired of just surviving." She didn't move closer, didn't need to. Harley's shoulders stiffened another notch, and the angle of his stance shifted so he was no longer half-facing her — he was full-on squared, ready but not sure what for. "You talking about someone in particular?" he asked, injecting a sharpness into his words that didn't quite mask the uncertainty underneath. Lisa shrugged, letting the silence do the work for her.

One of Harley's boys let out a low laugh, more nervous than amused, and quickly looked away when Harley shot him a glare. That glare was meant to rally them, to close ranks, but no one stepped forward. It was the smallest betrayal — not that they were siding with her, but that they wouldn't pick a side at all. In the schoolyard economy, that silence was worth more than a shouted challenge. Harley saw it. I saw him see it.

"Must be nice," Lisa said softly, "having a crowd when you want one." The words weren't a jab — they were bait. Harley tossed the ball to one of his group without looking, freeing his hands, but the motion read more like buying himself a moment than gearing up to strike. "What do you want, Lisa?" he asked finally, keeping his tone flat. She tilted her head, studying him, and for a moment I thought she might actually answer. Instead, she smiled — the kind that never reached her eyes — and said, "Just checking in."

It wasn't the words that made his jaw clench; it was the way she turned her back on him mid-reply, already walking away as though he'd been dismissed. Harley stood there, hands flexing once at his sides before shoving them into his pockets. The boys shifted awkwardly, their attention scattering back to the game like nothing had happened, but the energy was fractured now. Harley didn't call them back. He just stood, staring at the space she'd left behind, and for a heartbeat, he looked smaller than I'd ever seen him.

Jeremy's eyes caught mine from across the yard, a silent confirmation that we'd both clocked the same thing. That wasn't just a casual exchange — it was an opening gambit, and Harley had been the one made to react. In a place where control was everything, that mattered.

## THE SMILE THAT BROKE

I didn't hear the exact first word Lisa used — she kept her voice low enough that only Harley would catch it — but I saw the change hit him. One second his smirk was intact, sharp and rehearsed like always, and the next, the edge slipped. It wasn't gone entirely, but it cracked just enough for me to know the remark had landed where she meant it to. "What did you just say?" Harley asked her, quiet but tight, his hands still buried in his pockets. Lisa leaned in slightly, her eyes level with his, and replied, "Just an observation. You've been slipping lately." She didn't blink when she said it. Harley chuckled, loud enough for the kids nearby to hear, as if he'd been handed a harmless joke.

"That's cute," he said, shaking his head. "You think you know my game?" He stepped half a pace closer, enough to let his shadow fall across her. But Lisa didn't step back. "I don't think," she said, her tone flat, "I watch." She let that settle between them before adding, "And you're easier to read than you want to believe." The corner of Harley's mouth twitched like he was about to fire something back, but instead he glanced over her shoulder toward his friends. They were watching but saying nothing. That silence was part of the sting — she'd drawn his audience into the moment without inviting them to speak.

"Careful, Lisa," Harley said finally, lowering his voice again. "You might forget where you're standing." Lisa smiled in a way that wasn't friendly, but not outright hostile either. "Oh, I know exactly where I'm standing," she said, her eyes cutting sideways toward the hopscotch lines, "and who's watching." Her gaze lingered there before returning to him. The way she held eye contact wasn't a challenge in the usual sense — it was a steady, patient hold, the kind you only break when you've decided you've won.

He laughed again, but this time it was thin. "You've got a mouth," he told her. "You're going to find out that's not always a good thing." Lisa tilted her head just slightly, the same way someone might when they're about to explain something to a child. "Depends who's listening," she said, and then, almost casually, "and who's tired of hearing you." Harley froze for a second — just a fraction too long for anyone not paying attention to notice — then turned his body away from her, signalling the conversation was done. But it wasn't, not really.

When she walked off, Harley stayed put, eyes fixed on a point in the distance that wasn't anything in particular. "She's fishing," Leo whispered beside me, though I hadn't realised he'd come up. "Yeah," I murmured back, "and she's already got a line in him." Harley eventually rejoined his group, but his laugh didn't have its usual weight. It was too quick, too forced, the kind of laugh you give so people don't ask if something's wrong.

From where I stood, I could see Lisa a few yards away, talking to another kid with that same surface-level friendliness she'd used earlier. But her eyes kept cutting back to Harley, not in a rush, not needing the next move right now. She'd done enough in a single pass to shake him, and she knew it. Harley must have known too — because every time her gaze landed on him, he looked somewhere else.

"I'm telling you," Jeremy said, leaning just enough toward Leo and Alex so Harley couldn't hear, "it's not her size that gets to him." He kept his eyes on the spot where Lisa had been, tracking her without needing to move. "It's the way she talks. She doesn't swing first with her hands — she swings with words, and she's good at hitting where it hurts." Leo nodded, arms folded, his gaze locked on Harley, who was still pretending to be fully invested in whatever his group was talking about. "He's not scared she's gonna push him," Leo added, "he's scared she'll say something that makes him look small." Alex gave a low whistle, not out of admiration, but out of understanding. "That's worse than getting hit," he said quietly. "If she cuts him down in front of the right people, he won't be able to walk it back."

Jeremy shrugged, but his eyes were sharp. "That's what makes her dangerous. She doesn't rush. She waits until she knows the exact spot to press." He tapped his temple lightly, the kind of gesture that wasn't just about brains but about calculation. "Harley's used to people coming at him head-on. She doesn't do that. She moves sideways, then gets you when you're not looking." Leo leaned a little closer, lowering his voice so only we could hear. "And the thing is," he said, "once she's got you like that, she never lets it go. She'll keep poking at it until it sticks in your head."

I could see Harley glance over toward Lisa again, not long enough to be obvious, but enough to prove Jeremy's point. He wasn't tracking her movements — he was tracking her mouth, like he was waiting for the next dart to fly. Alex smirked faintly, though it wasn't friendly. "She's got him marked," he said. "It's just a matter of when she decides to follow through." Jeremy's jaw tightened. "And when she does," he said, "it won't be in a corner where no one's watching. She'll pick her stage."

The three of us stood there a moment longer, watching Harley try too hard to seem unbothered. It was in the way he laughed — quick bursts with no follow-up, like he was filling silence rather than enjoying himself. Lisa, on the other hand, was across the yard, leaning on the fence and talking to a younger kid like she didn't have a care in the world. But every so often, she'd glance our way, and each time, Harley's shoulders would shift, his posture tightening just slightly.

Leo caught the movement too. "See that?" he muttered. "That's not just tension. That's him keeping himself ready in case she comes back." Jeremy nodded once. "Yeah," he said. "He's bracing. Problem is, when you brace for someone like her, you give away you're already hit." Alex's brow furrowed at that, but he didn't argue. He knew it was true. We all did.

From where I stood, I couldn't tell if Lisa was smiling because of the kid she was talking to or because she'd caught Harley looking again. Either way, it didn't matter — she was in his head now, and once she was there, she wasn't leaving. Jeremy saw it as plain as I did, and when he finally looked away, it wasn't because the moment was over. It was because the moment was just starting.

It was during the lull between the bell and the shuffle into line that one of the younger kids, a wiry fifth-grader named Mason, wandered too close to the wrong conversation. He wasn't trying to stir anything — just curious in the way kids are when they sense something they can't name. He glanced from Harley to where Lisa stood on the far side of the yard, then back again. "So… are you two, like, friends or something?" he asked, his voice carrying farther than he probably meant it to.

Harley's head snapped around so fast it was a wonder his neck didn't give out. "We're not," he said sharply, the words out before he'd even formed the thought. There was no pause, no shrug to soften it — just that flat, hard tone that made the air between us tense in an instant. Mason blinked, stepping back a little, as if the answer had been more for self-protection than information. It wasn't the kind of denial you give when you don't care. It was the kind you give when you care far too much about what people think.

Jeremy, standing to my left, caught my eye and didn't even bother to hide the flicker of understanding. He leaned just close enough to murmur, "Too fast. That's how you know." Leo, who'd been watching without comment, gave the smallest of smirks, not aimed at Harley but at the slip-up itself. Alex shifted his weight, glancing toward Lisa, who hadn't heard the question but seemed to sense that her name had been in play. She didn't move toward us — she didn't have to. Her attention was a weapon, and Harley knew it.

Harley tried to patch over the reaction with a laugh that came out too brittle, too quick, and it fooled no one. "Just saying," he added, forcing a shrug. "We don't hang out." But the damage was already done. That first answer — the raw, unfiltered one — had shown more than the second could ever cover. Mason gave a slow nod, not really convinced but smart enough not to push. He stepped away, tucking his hands in his pockets like the exchange had left him colder than the spring air.

From where I stood, I saw Harley's jaw tighten as he watched Mason go, as if he regretted the outburst almost as soon as it happened. But regret in Harley never came with apology. It came with overcompensation. He turned his body toward his own group, throwing himself into a half-hearted joke about someone's sneakers, loud enough to carry, desperate to drag the focus back where he thought it belonged.

Lisa hadn't moved, but her eyes were on Harley now, her posture relaxed, one shoulder against the fence. If she'd heard Mason's question, she was storing the answer for later. That was the trouble with someone like her — she didn't need to attack in the moment. She could wait. And when she finally decided to use that slip, it wouldn't matter if it had been ten minutes or ten days.

Jeremy's voice was quiet beside me, but it landed like a truth we all knew. "She's already got more on him than he's got on her." I didn't answer, but I could feel it in the way Harley kept his back too straight, his voice too loud, his eyes flicking toward Lisa every time he thought no one was watching. And I knew — he'd just given her the first real crack to work with.

Lisa didn't rush to respond, and that was the first sign she'd already decided how to use the moment. She lingered at the fence for another beat, arms loose at her sides, letting Harley's voice drift over the yard without so much as a flinch. Then, without turning fully toward him, she started to walk away. Her pace was unhurried, every step measured, as if she were strolling toward some private appointment only she knew about. Harley's eyes tracked her — not openly, but in those sideways flickers you catch when someone's pretending not to care.

Just as she reached the edge of the basketball court, she tilted her head slightly, enough that the faint sunlight caught the curve of her jaw. "Careful what you say too fast," she called back, not loud enough for the whole yard, but clear enough to find his ears. The words hung in the space like a loose thread, daring him to tug at it. She didn't wait for his answer. She didn't even slow down. That was how she kept control — by making sure there was never an opening to grab it back.

Harley had been mid-step toward his group, some retort half-formed, when her voice cut through. He froze. Not dramatically, not enough for most to notice, but his foot hesitated on the asphalt and his shoulders squared without moving forward. It was the pause of someone replaying the line in his head, searching for the insult buried under the calm. And the longer he stood there, the more obvious it became that she'd hit her mark.

Jeremy, Leo, and Alex caught it immediately. Leo raised his brows at me, as if to say, She just took that round without lifting a hand. Alex shifted closer, his voice low. "She's telling him she heard," he murmured, the faintest grin tugging at the corner of his mouth. Jeremy didn't even grin — he just watched, eyes sharp, like someone cataloguing cause and effect for later use.

Lisa never turned back to confirm his reaction, and that was the brilliance of it. Her authority came from never needing to witness the sting to know it landed. She slipped between two clusters of students, sliding back into her corner of the yard as though nothing had been said at all. By the time she leaned against the far railing, she had already drawn another small crowd, her attention shifting with surgical precision to whatever conversation suited her next move.

Harley finally broke the stillness with a small shake of his head, muttering something under his breath, but his stride toward his group was slower now. Whatever quip he'd been about to use was gone, replaced with a silence that didn't fit him. He forced a smirk when he rejoined the others, but it didn't hold. His eyes kept darting past them, back toward the place where Lisa now stood laughing at something he couldn't hear.

Jeremy leaned toward me just enough to speak without the others catching it. "That wasn't just a comment," he said. "That was a warning." I didn't answer. I didn't need to. We both knew that a line like that, delivered in passing and without a second glance, was never just words. It was the planting of a flag — and Harley, whether he'd admit it or not, had just lost ground.

Leo leaned toward Jeremy just enough that his voice wouldn't carry past us. "I've seen him scared before," he said, eyes still on Harley, "but never like this." It wasn't the usual tension you'd get before a fight, not the hot, ready-to-swing kind of fear. This was quieter, stranger — the kind that comes from knowing you're outmatched in ways you can't punch your way out of. Harley stood with his group, but the way his head kept angling toward Lisa gave him away. He wasn't just watching her. He was measuring distance, planning exits.

Jeremy nodded slowly, his arms folded like he was weighing the words. "It's not her size," he muttered, "and it's not her friends. It's her." The way he said it made me think he'd been watching her longer than today, taking note of how she operated. Lisa didn't use the playground rules Harley had mastered — the shoves, the teasing, the public dominance. She played a longer game, one that didn't need an audience to hurt.

Leo's brow furrowed, his gaze flicking between them. "I think it's because he doesn't know the rules she's using. That's what's getting to him." Harley was leaning on the fence now, pretending to listen to something one of his friends was saying, but his eyes stayed fixed in Lisa's direction. Every time she laughed, even faintly, his mouth tightened just enough to notice.

"You can't fight someone who doesn't take the bait," Jeremy said, glancing at me before looking back to Leo. "If he pushes, she won't push back. She'll just move the ground under his feet." There was a kind of respect in his tone — not admiration, but an acknowledgment of skill. It made sense. Jeremy had always been the one to read the deeper currents under people's actions, the things you miss if you're only watching the surface.

Leo smirked faintly. "So she's the kind who doesn't need to win loud." He kicked at the edge of the blacktop, his sneaker scraping against the painted line. "That explains why he's not charging in like usual. He's waiting for her to play his game." And as we all knew, waiting wasn't his strength. The longer he stood still, the more obvious the cracks became.

We watched in silence for a moment. Lisa was still across the yard, her back to him now, talking with a smaller group of kids who looked like they'd follow her anywhere. She leaned in, whispered something, and one of them glanced over at Harley before quickly looking away. Whatever she'd said, it was enough to shift the air between them without her taking a single step closer.

Jeremy tapped the side of his notebook — the one he carried for reasons he never explained — as if he were logging this exchange for later. "He's not just scared of her," he said quietly, "he's scared of what she might do without him knowing." Leo didn't argue. We'd all seen bullies who needed an audience, but it was rarer to find one who could win by staying invisible.

By the time Harley finally moved, pushing off the fence to rejoin the flow of the playground, there was something different in the way he walked. He was trying to look casual, but his eyes kept sweeping the space like someone checking for tripwires. And maybe, just maybe, he'd realised Lisa had already set a few.

The bell rang with its usual blunt note, herding us toward the doors in a restless shuffle. Harley slipped inside first, shoulders squared, but his stride had the overdone precision of someone trying to prove nothing had rattled him. I followed with Leo, our steps syncing in the easy rhythm of habit, though my eyes kept darting past Harley toward the back of the hall. Lisa was coming in at her own pace, her coat half-slipped from one shoulder, her expression unreadable. She wasn't in a hurry; she never was.

Inside the classroom, desks scraped against the floor in their uneven chorus, the sound of thirty kids settling into seats. Harley took his usual place near the window, draping his arm over the backrest like he owned the view. It was a performance as much as a posture, but the cracks showed in the way his fingers tapped the metal bar in short, staccato beats. Then Lisa stepped in. She didn't scan the room like some kids did, didn't need to. Her path was direct — three rows over, two seats back — the perfect angle to see him without having to turn her head much at all.

She slid into her chair with the kind of grace that didn't ask for attention but drew it anyway. Her bag landed softly on the floor, her notebook appearing on the desk with deliberate quiet. She didn't speak, didn't so much as nod in Harley's direction, yet there was a pause in her movements that told me she was aware of him. It was the kind of pause that says, I know you're there, and I don't need to acknowledge you to keep you thinking about me.

Harley, for his part, tried to keep his focus on something in the far corner of the room — the flag, the bulletin board, anything that wasn't her. But human eyes are traitors, and his flickered toward her desk in a glance so quick most people would miss it. I didn't. Neither did she. That glance was all she needed to confirm he was still watching. She didn't smile, didn't frown, but her hand paused on the pencil she was about to pick up, a stillness sharp enough to catch his attention and hold it for a beat too long.

Leo leaned toward me just enough to murmur, "She's not saying a word, but he's already hearing her." I gave the faintest nod, watching Harley's jaw set harder, his knuckles whitening as he gripped the edge of his desk. Lisa finally moved again, flipping open her notebook as though the moment hadn't happened. It was subtle, surgical, the kind of move you couldn't fight without looking like you'd just admitted it worked.

The teacher entered, the shuffle of papers and the scrape of chalk breaking whatever unspoken tether had been stretched between them. Still, Harley didn't relax. His arm came down from the backrest, folding over his desk in a posture I'd never seen him take before — one that closed him in instead of spreading him out. Lisa's gaze drifted once more in his direction, this time disguised as a casual scan of the room. When her eyes passed over him, they lingered for the barest fraction too long before moving on. It was enough to plant the seed that she could do it again anytime she wanted.

# THE SMILE THAT BROKE

I watched Harley exhale slowly, the way you do when you've just dodged something you're not sure you actually avoided. His fingers started tapping again, but this time it was slower, less certain. The rest of the class was already sliding into the day's lesson, pens scratching, whispers fading, yet I knew Harley wasn't hearing a word of it. Neither, I suspected, was Lisa. She was playing her own lesson plan, one that didn't need a blackboard to make its point.

Group work had always been Harley's stage. It didn't matter if the subject was math, history, or drawing a map of Canada — he'd position himself in the centre, talk the loudest, and decide whose idea counted as "good." Usually, the others let him, not because he was right, but because it was easier than wrestling the role away from him. Today, though, the edges of his control frayed before the pencils even touched the paper.

We were splitting into clusters of four, desks dragged together in uneven squares. Harley landed with his usual followers, but instead of leaning in with that commanding posture, he sat just off to the side, eyes flicking across the room. It wasn't the restless scanning of someone who's bored — it was the sharp, repeat glance toward Lisa. She was two groups away, her head bent over her page, saying something low to the girl beside her. It shouldn't have mattered, but for Harley it clearly did.

When the first question landed on the table, Harley gave a vague shrug, offering half an answer before his gaze slipped back toward her again. The boy next to him — Kyle — tried to steer things back on track, but the rhythm was already broken. Normally, Harley would have cut him off, maybe teased him into silence, yet now he just let Kyle finish, his mind elsewhere. It was the first time I'd seen someone in his group talk for more than a sentence without him jumping in.

Across the table, one of his other allies, Ben, nudged him with a pen. "You've got an answer for this, right?" Harley blinked, nodded like he'd been listening, then muttered something that didn't quite fit the question. Ben frowned but let it pass. Harley didn't notice — or maybe didn't care — because Lisa had just tilted her head enough to see over the heads between them. Their eyes didn't meet, but the proximity was close enough to make his shoulders rise a fraction higher.

Leo, sitting in my group, leaned toward me with that knowing smirk. "He's losing the room," he whispered. He wasn't wrong. Harley was holding his pen like it might break, tapping the side of his paper in short bursts, as if writing something down would pull his attention away from her. It didn't. Every time Lisa shifted in her seat or moved her hair behind her ear, his eyes darted back. She never looked directly at him, but I could tell she knew. She was letting him chase her attention without offering it.

By the second question, Harley had spoken less than everyone else at his table. Kyle took the lead, the others following, and the shift was so quiet, so unceremonious, that it might have gone unnoticed if not for the stiffness in Harley's jaw. He caught me watching once, and I didn't look away. His glare lasted only a second before he glanced back toward Lisa, almost like checking to see if she'd noticed his lapse. If she had, she gave no sign.

The teacher made a slow circuit of the room, pausing to glance at Harley's group. Normally, he would have seized that moment to present an answer, to make himself look like the unspoken leader. Instead, he stayed quiet, letting Kyle respond. It was another small surrender, one most kids wouldn't even register, but in the chain of small shifts happening today, it was another link broken.

By the time the group work wrapped, Harley had spoken maybe a quarter of what he normally did, and half of that was filler. Lisa closed her notebook with a soft snap, standing with a deliberate ease. She didn't glance his way as she crossed the room, but the way Harley's eyes tracked her, you'd think she had. He tried to speak to his group as they shifted their desks back, but his words were swallowed by the scrape of chair legs. It was the sound of someone used to leading who'd just been quietly replaced — and the worst part was, he knew it.

Alex had a way of watching people that made you feel like he was building a map in his head — a map with paths, dead ends, and secret routes no one else noticed. We'd just finished shoving the desks back into neat rows when he leaned slightly toward me, keeping his eyes on Lisa. "She's not just confident," he said quietly, his voice low enough that only I could hear. "She's calculating."

I followed his gaze. Lisa was walking toward the pencil sharpener, not in a straight line, but weaving just enough to pass a few desks she had no real reason to pass. She didn't speak to anyone, but each stop of her steps felt intentional — a tilt of the head toward one kid, a passing glance at another, then nothing. It wasn't random movement; it was placement. "What do you mean?" I asked, though I already felt the answer forming.

"She decides when she's visible," Alex continued, his tone even, like we were discussing the weather. "And when she's not. Most kids don't think like that. They're either trying to be seen all the time or hiding all the time. She does both, on purpose." He tapped his notebook lightly against the desk as if to mark the rhythm of her choices. "It's the kind of thing that keeps people off balance. One minute you forget she's in the room, the next she's in your head."

I glanced at Harley. His posture was stiff, his eyes darting toward Lisa's slow progress across the classroom. He didn't want her near, but he couldn't ignore her either. It was like he was waiting for her to choose which version of herself he was going to get — the one that faded into the edges, or the one that stepped into the centre and owned it. Alex saw it too. "He hates that," he murmured. "Not knowing when she's going to make her move."

Lisa finally reached the sharpener, cranked it twice, and returned to her seat without a word. She didn't even look at Harley on the way back, but the tension in him stayed. Alex raised an eyebrow at me as if to say, *See? That was the point.* She'd crossed the room for nothing more than a dull pencil, but somehow, she'd made the trip feel like an inspection.

"She's patient," Alex added, leaning back in his chair. "That's the part that makes her dangerous. She doesn't need to win every second. She just needs to be the one you remember when the day's over." His voice stayed calm, but the weight in his words was heavier than most warnings I'd heard from kids our age. He wasn't just guessing — he'd already seen enough to be sure.

The rest of the class settled back into quiet work, but I kept replaying Alex's description in my head. Lisa wasn't chasing control the way Harley did. She was setting traps without moving the bait. And the more I thought about it, the more I realized Harley wasn't the only one keeping her in sight. The difference was, I wanted to know what she'd do next. Harley just wanted her gone.

When the teacher glanced up from her desk, Lisa had her head down like she'd been working the whole time, her pencil moving in a slow, steady line. Alex smirked at me as if we'd just watched a trick no one else had caught. "Told you," he whispered, and I didn't argue. Some things didn't need debating — not when you'd just seen them unfold right in front of you.

By the time lunch rolled around, the air in the hallways had changed. It wasn't loud gossip — no one was throwing out bold claims or pointing fingers — but the undercurrent was there. Small knots of kids leaned closer together when Lisa or Harley passed, the way people do when they're trying to decide if what they've noticed is worth saying out loud. I caught fragments in the shuffle between classrooms: "Did you see his face?" "She just stared him down." "He didn't even talk back." They weren't accusations, not yet, but they were seeds, and once seeds get planted, they don't just disappear.

Harley came out of math with his shoulders set a little too square, like he'd already heard enough to know the whispers were about him. He didn't snap at anyone, didn't shove, but there was a current in his movements, a restlessness that had no place to go. Lisa, on the other hand, looked entirely unaffected. She strolled out behind two friends, chatting easily about something that had nothing to do with him — at least, that's how it looked. But I knew her by now. She didn't have to steer the conversation toward him for it to still end up there.

Leo slid in beside me as we headed toward the lockers. "You hear it?" he asked without lowering his voice. "Everybody's talking about those two, but nobody's saying it straight." His grin was quick, almost satisfied, like he'd been expecting this moment since the first time he noticed Harley flinch at her name. "It's like watching two storms circle each other," he added. I knew what he meant. They hadn't collided yet, but the pressure in the air promised they would.

At the lunch tables, the pattern held. No one outright declared a side, but glances travelled like notes being passed. Harley sat with his regular crew, yet their laughter felt thinner, their attention not entirely his. A couple of them even leaned back to catch a glimpse of Lisa across the room. Harley noticed. He didn't mention it, but the way his jaw tightened each time her name floated by said enough.

Lisa's table was just as telling. She wasn't holding court in a way that demanded the whole room's attention; she didn't need to. Every so often, someone would lean in close, she'd speak a few words, and then they'd glance — not subtly — in Harley's direction. Whatever she was saying, it didn't have to be overheard to work. It was the reaction she wanted spreading, not the content.

I tried to piece together if she was fuelling the whispers or simply letting them grow on their own. Alex, sitting across from me, chewed slowly and said, "Doesn't matter which. Either way, she wins." I couldn't argue with that. The school wasn't split down the middle yet, but the idea of there being a "Lisa camp" and a "Harley camp" had begun to take shape.

Even the teachers seemed to notice the strange energy. Mr. Clarke stood by the door, scanning the tables more than usual, as though he was taking a quiet headcount of who was gravitating where. If he suspected what was behind it, he didn't say. But I could tell from his eyes that he understood this wasn't about a single spat or one mean comment. It was about two people who both hated losing control — and the fact that, right now, neither had it completely.

By the time the bell rang to send us back to class, the whispers hadn't grown louder, but they'd spread wider. And in my experience, that was worse. Loud rumours burn fast; quiet ones sink in and stay. Walking back down the hall, I caught Harley's reflection in the display case glass. He wasn't smiling. Not even pretending. That, more than anything, told me this was just getting started.

The hall between lunch and the next bell was crowded, a steady tide of backpacks and sneakers and voices that bounced off the lockers. I was halfway down the corridor when I saw Lisa coming from the opposite direction, her pace steady, her gaze straight ahead. Harley was leaning near the water fountain, talking with two boys from his class, though his eyes kept tracking the movement in front of him like he was watching for trouble. That's when Lisa shifted just enough in her stride to pass closer to him than necessary. Her sleeve grazed his arm — not hard, not even enough for someone else to notice — but I saw the way he froze in that split second.

It was the stillness that gave him away. Harley wasn't someone who paused in the middle of a hallway unless he meant to, and this wasn't that kind of pause. This was a glitch — like his mind stalled before his body remembered to keep moving. Lisa didn't look at him, didn't slow down, didn't do anything to acknowledge what had just happened. That was what made it so pointed. Her power wasn't in the touch; it was in denying him the satisfaction of a confrontation. She was already past him before he'd figured out how to react.

When he did, it was immediate overcompensation. He pivoted toward one of the boys he'd been talking to and barked out a laugh loud enough to make three kids at nearby lockers turn their heads.

"Yeah, right, like I'd believe that!" he shouted, though no one had actually said anything worth yelling about. The words didn't matter — the volume did. He was reclaiming the air around him, reasserting that this was his stretch of hallway, his audience. But the crack was visible.

I caught Leo watching the whole thing from farther down, leaning against a locker like he'd been waiting for it. When I reached him, he muttered under his breath, "That was deliberate." He didn't have to explain who he meant. "She's in his head now," he added. I could see it. The loud joke, the too-wide grin, the way his shoulders squared after she passed — all of it was armour being pulled up too late.

Lisa, by then, had melted into the crowd near the far door. She didn't look back, but she didn't need to. If she wanted to know whether her move landed, all she had to do was listen for the volume spike behind her. Harley was practically shouting his way down the hall, tossing comments to people who weren't even part of his conversation. The sound was forced, a shade too bright, the kind of tone you use when you're trying to drown out the echo of something you'd rather not hear.

The rest of the hallway moved on like nothing had happened. A couple of kids brushed past me, chattering about a science quiz, oblivious to the undercurrent. But for those who caught it — and I know there were more than just me and Leo — it was the kind of moment that would stick. Not because it was dramatic, but because it wasn't. That tiny brush had done what bigger clashes couldn't: it had pulled Harley off his footing without ever knocking him down.

When the bell rang, Harley was still talking too loud, his words spilling over into the stairwell. I didn't have to look at Lisa to know she'd noticed. You could feel it in the way she'd left the scene entirely on her terms.

That morning, Lisa's absence felt like an empty space in the middle of the room, though no one said it aloud at first. Harley came in later than usual, hair uncombed, moving with the aimless pace of someone who'd already decided the day was a write-off. He slumped into his seat, drumming his fingers against the desk, glancing toward the doorway every time it opened. When it became clear Lisa wasn't coming, his rhythm slowed, his gaze dropping to the scuffed floor tiles. The teachers didn't keep it quiet for long. Their voices carried from the hallway — not hushed, not guarded, just plain enough for any passing ear to catch.

"Hospital," one of them said. "It's bad." The words didn't land like a hammer; they slid in sharp and cold, cutting before you could brace. I watched Harley's head lift at that, his posture tightening as if the air itself had gone wrong. His face stayed neutral for a beat too long, but then the control cracked — his eyes glossing over with something I'd never seen on him before. He blinked fast, like maybe no one would notice if he kept his chin level. They noticed. We all did.

By lunch, he was pacing the edge of the yard like a caged thing, muttering about going to see her. It didn't sound like an idle idea — it sounded decided. No one stopped him from leaving the grounds, though a few of us watched him slip out the gate. He was gone less than an hour, and when he came back, he wasn't moving like someone who'd found answers. His jaw was set, his hands jammed deep in his pockets, and his eyes were locked somewhere far beyond the building.

Later, we learned why. The family hadn't let him past the reception desk. No polite explanations, just a clear wall between him and her. That might have been the end of it, but then one of Lisa's relatives came forward with an envelope. His name was written on it in blocky letters, the kind she used on her homework when she didn't care about neatness. He stood under the shade of the maple tree in the corner of the yard and tore it open, scanning the page once, then again.

The note was short. No apologies, no threats, no grudges — just a handful of sentences in her looping script:

Harley,

I have to start this with the truth, because if I wait until the end to say it, I'll talk myself out of it. I'm already in love with you. Not the kind of love people at our age joke about, not the shallow crush that fades as fast as it came. This is the real kind — the kind you can't shake even when you try, the kind that stays in your chest no matter how much noise is around you. You've been in my head and my heart since the first day we both walked through those school doors, and it's only grown stronger since.

You need to know it's not because of how you stand in the playground or the way people make space for you when you walk past. If anything, those things are the surface, and I've always wanted more than the surface. I love you because I see the boy underneath all that armour. I see the way your eyes change when you think no one's looking, the way you carry things that most people couldn't even imagine, and the way you still keep moving. You remind me of myself, only you've had to fight even harder.

I've acted tougher than I needed to around you, and maybe you've wondered why. It's because I didn't want you to think I was weak, and I didn't want to give anyone else the satisfaction of seeing me soft. But every time I looked at you, I wanted to drop all of it. I wanted to talk to you without the walls, without the act. I wanted you to know me, not just the version I show the school. I wanted you to see that I understand you — the real you — better than anyone else here.

We grew up in the same kind of world, didn't we? One where you learn early that no one is coming to save you, so you have to save yourself. Where you pretend you don't care so the hurt doesn't show. Where you make your own rules because the ones you were given never worked for you.

That's why I think we could have been something different together. Not perfect, not easy, but real. We could have been the people who held each other up when no one else even knew we were falling.

I love the way you're still here, even with everything you've had to carry. I love the way you try to hide when you're hurting, but the truth leaks out anyway. I love that you don't realise how much you matter. And maybe you'll never believe me when I say this, but you deserve more than just surviving, Harley. You deserve someone who sees you exactly as you are and doesn't turn away. I would never turn away from you.

If I could, I'd tell you all of this face to face. I'd stand right in front of you and make sure you couldn't look away until you heard every word. But I've waited too long, and now this letter will have to do. You don't have to say anything back. You don't even have to keep it. But I hope you read it more than once, because every word is the truth.

If you ever wondered if someone could love you without asking you to be someone else, you have your answer now. It's me. It's been me since day one.

With all my Love.
Love always.
— Lisa

He read it so many times that the paper went soft in his hands. When he finally folded it, his mouth pressed tight like he didn't trust what would come out if he spoke. For someone who lived on words — sharp, loud, constant — his silence was louder than anything else on that playground.

Rumours filled the gaps before facts did. By mid-afternoon, the truth had made its way through the building: Lisa hadn't just stayed home sick, and this wasn't some accident from a clumsy fall. She'd been jumped off school grounds, near the park where the older kids hung out after dark. It wasn't a stranger, but no one could agree on names. What was certain was that she'd been hurt badly enough to end up in the hospital, and badly enough that the teachers had stopped pretending this was just another absence.

In the hours that followed, Harley didn't pick a fight. He didn't even bother to hold court at his usual locker spot. He sat through the rest of the day like someone waiting for a verdict, the folded note a small square in his hand that he never put away. And for the first time, no one dared interrupt his quiet.

Fear doesn't always come from the biggest fists or the loudest voice. Sometimes it lives in the quiet power of knowing someone can touch a part of you no one else can reach. That's what I'd always thought about Lisa when it came to Harley — that she scared him because she could get under his skin without ever laying a hand on him.

But today wasn't that. Today, whatever fear he had of her was buried under something else, something heavier. It was grief, raw and unfamiliar, stripping him of the armour we all thought he was born wearing. The tough, unshakable Harley was gone, replaced by someone who looked like him but moved as if every step cost more than he had to give. I was by the lockers when it happened. One second, he was still upright, still holding that note like it might explain something if he read it one more time. The next, his knees buckled as if the ground had stopped holding him.

It wasn't dramatic, not the way movies make it look — it was worse. Quiet, slow, and real. His shoulders sagged first, then his hands dropped, the paper slipping between his fingers before Ty caught it. Ty didn't hesitate, just stepped in and caught him mid-fall, arms closing around him in a grip meant to hold someone together when they're sure they're about to split apart.

Harley didn't fight it. Didn't push away. Didn't try to cover his face or hide behind his sleeve. He let himself lean into Ty's chest, his forehead pressing against the fabric like he was trying to find a place to breathe that wasn't full of the noise in his own head. The tears came fast, and not the kind you can blink away before anyone sees. These were the kind that run hot and unrelenting, the kind that drag the breath out of you on their way down. No one moved to make a joke. No one muttered a comment. For once, the hallway was still.

Ty said nothing, his only movement the slow, steady press of his palm against the back of Harley's head. He didn't try to tell him it would be all right — that would have been a lie, and we all knew it. He just stayed there, solid and unmoving, letting Harley's grief have a place to go. The note was still in Ty's other hand, the paper damp and crumpled, Lisa's words smudged but still visible. It might as well have been burning a hole through him, the weight of what it meant sitting between them. I realised then that Harley wasn't crying because he was afraid of Lisa. He was crying because she'd reached him, in ways he probably hadn't let anyone else in years. And now she was hurt, maybe because of the same sharp edges that had kept people at a distance for so long. He cried for her without apology, without shame, in full view of anyone who cared to look. That alone said more than any fight or insult ever had.

As the moment stretched, I caught myself memorising the scene — Ty standing firm, Harley folded into him, the note clutched between them like some fragile truth neither could say aloud. This wasn't the Harley we knew, the one who used fear as a shield. This was someone stripped bare, someone who'd been hit in a way no bruise could show. And maybe that's the thing no one ever admits about fear — it's not always about what someone might do to you. Sometimes, it's about what you stand to lose.

When Ty finally eased them both upright, Harley didn't look around to see who had been watching. He didn't wipe his eyes. He didn't put the mask back on. He just walked beside Ty toward the end of the hall, his steps slower but steadier, the note folded small in his pocket. No one stopped him. No one dared. And as I followed a few paces back, I knew this was the kind of day that doesn't fade. Not for him. Not for any of us. Harley let Ty read the letter from Lisa.

## CHAPTER 4: SHADOWS IN THE HALL

The last weeks before summer always carried a strange rhythm — the days seemed shorter but felt heavier, as if the clock resisted letting the school year end. The light poured longer through the classroom windows, warming the floors and making the dust in the air shimmer, yet there were still corners of the building where the light didn't quite reach. Nico noticed them most in the hallways, where clusters of students lingered between classes.

Harley was one of them, moving with a steadier pace than he had two weeks ago, though there was still that restless flicker in his eyes. He often glanced at the main doors as if expecting someone, his gaze snapping away just as quickly when caught. Across the hall, Ty sat at his usual place at the far library table, hunched over a thick psychology book whose title most kids would never bother trying to read. There was a kind of weightlessness to him — not absent, not distracted, but grounded in a way that made him almost untouchable.

Ty didn't need an introduction. He was known in every corner of the school, and not in the way loud students were known. His presence was one of quiet permanence. Full Japanese heritage, both parents born and raised in Japan before settling here, he carried his family's calm dignity like a second skin. His father's job — RCMP investigator — was common knowledge, though Ty never leaned on it to earn respect. He didn't need to. His reputation had been built on something harder to describe: an unwavering instinct to stand between the weak and the ones who might hurt them. This wasn't the kind of fame you earned in a week, or even a year. It had been six long years of simply being Ty. The ones who had been here since primary knew this without explanation. They didn't need to ask where he was from, what he could do, or why his opinion carried weight.

For the new students, though, there was always that moment of curiosity, usually followed by a quiet acceptance once they realised he wasn't a mystery to be solved but a person whose edges you only understood if you earned the right. There was a balance in him, like the calm surface of deep water. Harley had crossed paths with Ty often, yet Nico had noticed that Harley never tested him the way he tested others. Even in Harley's worst days, when his smirk was sharpened into something meant to cut, he seemed to recognise that Ty wasn't a target. Not out of fear — or at least not just fear — but because there was no weakness to be exploited.

The hallway today was the same as ever, humming with footsteps, slamming lockers, and conversations that tangled and overlapped. The air felt warmer, closer, carrying the smell of paper, pencil shavings, and the faint trace of lunch that had been served hours ago. The chatter shifted slightly when Ty passed through, not because he demanded attention but because the group's rhythm unconsciously adjusted to him. Nico watched this happen more than once and never saw Ty notice. Or maybe he noticed everything and just didn't show it. That was just as likely. His psychology books weren't for show; he absorbed them, stored them, and applied them in ways no one saw coming.

Harley, meanwhile, was different now than in the cold two weeks. His voice carried less bite, though not gone entirely. The sharp comments still slipped out when he felt cornered or mocked, but the frequency had dulled. Nico suspected the shift had less to do with sudden self-awareness and more with certain people's watchful eyes. Ty's, for one. And now, with summer on the horizon, there was a question floating quietly in the air — whether Harley's recent steadiness would last once the structure of the school year was gone.

Nico caught a glimpse of movement near the doors — Harley's eyes darting there again — and then followed his line of sight. It was empty now, just a couple of younger students hurrying past. Whatever or whoever Harley was expecting hadn't arrived. It gave Nico the odd feeling that the hall itself was waiting for something. Waiting for someone to walk through and change its shape. That thought stayed with him, even as the bell rang.

Ty didn't rise immediately. He turned a page in his book, let his eyes sweep it once, then closed it in one fluid motion and slid it into his bag. There was no hurry to his movements, yet he still reached the door before most. His pace was deceptively efficient — quiet, but exact. The kind that told you he'd been trained in something beyond school hallways and classroom etiquette. Nico had heard fragments of stories about his father's work and Ty's own training, but they never came from Ty himself. They came from others who had watched him react in situations where most kids froze.

The crowd in the hall thinned, yet Ty and Harley's paths crossed briefly. They didn't speak, but Harley gave a half-nod, the kind that was almost respectful but still held an edge of caution. Ty didn't return it. He just walked on. Nico thought it was interesting — that small gesture from Harley. It wasn't submission, but it wasn't defiance either. More like an acknowledgment of rules unspoken.

Nico leaned against the wall for a moment longer, letting the scene imprint itself in his mind. The hall was a living thing — shifting, breathing, adjusting to the people who filled it. And Ty, without trying, was one of the few who could change its pulse simply by being there. As the last of the stragglers vanished into classrooms, the silence in the hallway deepened. Somewhere in that silence, Nico was certain, there was a shadow already stretching toward what was coming next.

Ty was the kind of student whose name didn't need repeating when it was spoken in the hall. In a building filled with voices trying to be louder than each other, his was never raised — yet somehow it carried. He wasn't the class clown or the top athlete or the loud debater who always won arguments; he didn't need to be. His presence came from somewhere deeper, the kind of confidence that didn't demand attention but earned it all the same. People remembered Ty because he made them feel safe in ways they didn't even notice until they needed it. It wasn't safety through strength alone, though he had that too. It was in the way he listened when others spoke, and how his answers felt like they'd been shaped carefully, never thrown out carelessly.

His Japanese heritage was not just a fact about him — it was part of the calm that seemed to settle around him wherever he went. Both of his parents were from Japan, carrying their traditions and quiet values into the home Ty grew up in. It showed in him, in the small, deliberate movements, in the respect that coloured his tone, in the way he could make even restless students slow down without saying a word. Teachers saw it. Students felt it. Ty didn't talk much about his family, but everyone knew his father was an RCMP investigator. That piece of information had passed through the school years ago and stuck, not as a badge of intimidation but as something that added weight to Ty's already steady character.

The truth was, Ty's authority didn't come from his father's job at all. It came from the way he handled people. He had the patience to let someone talk themselves into calmness, the skill to guide an argument away from a fight, and the quiet courage to step in when stepping in was necessary. He never shoved himself into a problem to show off. He did it because he couldn't stand by and watch someone hurt another person — and that was all anyone needed to know about him. Even the kids who thought they could push anyone around didn't test Ty for long. They learned quickly that his stillness wasn't weakness.

Harley, for his part, had been slow to trust anyone since the walls around him began to crack. But with Ty, the trust seemed to build without him noticing. It wasn't a loud moment, no dramatic scene where one declared loyalty to the other. It was small gestures stacking quietly over time — Ty sitting beside him when others avoided him, Ty asking the right question without making it sound like an interrogation, Ty understanding without Harley needing to explain every scar. Harley wasn't used to people understanding him without judgement first. Ty did. And it mattered more than Harley ever admitted out loud.

One of the first things Harley realised was that Ty's interest in psychology wasn't an academic hobby. It was a tool. Ty understood what made people tick — their fears, their habits, their triggers — and he didn't use that knowledge to manipulate. He used it to dismantle tension before it could explode. It was almost surgical, the way he could strip the heat out of a situation without making anyone feel cornered. For Harley, who had always been surrounded by people who either pushed too hard or left too soon, Ty's measured approach felt different. Safe, even.

Nico watched the shift happen like someone noticing a plant turning toward the sun. Harley didn't change overnight, but there was a visible easing in his shoulders when Ty was around. He stopped flinching at certain remarks. He stopped meeting every glance with suspicion. It was as though Ty's presence acted like a shield, not in the sense of blocking all blows, but in giving Harley enough space to stand without constantly bracing for the next one. The kind of friendship forming between them wasn't about shared jokes or similar hobbies — it was about an unspoken agreement that they could rely on each other in ways no one else could provide.

Even for the kids who didn't know the details of Harley's struggles, it was easy to see that something was different when Ty was near. The edges of Harley's temper dulled, his voice lost some of its bite, and he no longer prowled the hallways looking for friction. Ty didn't tell him to change. He didn't lecture or make speeches. He simply stood beside him, and that seemed to be enough. The steadiness of Ty's presence said what words couldn't: You're not alone in this anymore.

It was strange, Nico thought, how friendships sometimes formed without ceremony. There was no handshake, no agreement, no label slapped onto it. Yet here it was — Harley trusting someone enough to let his guard down in small but noticeable ways. Ty didn't take advantage of that. He didn't push for more than Harley was ready to give. That patience was part of what made him trusted by nearly everyone, even those who had crossed him in the past. Ty seemed to know that the slow road was the only road worth taking when it came to change.

It wasn't just Harley who benefited. Ty's quiet watchfulness extended to others in the circle — Leo, Jeremy, even the younger students who sometimes trailed behind. He didn't announce that he was looking out for them, but Nico could see it in the way his eyes swept the hallway, catching small shifts in body language others missed. He was as much a part of the school's unspoken structure as the teachers, and maybe even more effective in certain situations.

The remarkable thing was how few people realised the depth of his influence. To most, Ty was simply "the good one" — the student who never got in trouble, who could be counted on to help with events, who earned the trust of adults without seeming to try. But Nico, who paid attention to the undercurrents, knew that Ty was more than just a model student. He was a quiet strategist, mapping out relationships, knowing who to step between and when, and letting people believe they'd arrived at peace on their own.

Harley was starting to see it too. In their conversations, Ty would drop a question or a comment that made Harley think long after the moment had passed. Sometimes, those thoughts unsettled him, forcing him to consider why he reacted the way he did, or why certain people seemed to set him off without warning. It was work — hard work — to face those truths, but Ty never left him to do it alone. That made all the difference.

The rest of the school might have seen them as an unlikely pair — Harley with his rough edges and history of conflict, Ty with his unshakable calm — but Nico thought they fit in a way that didn't need explaining. They balanced each other out. Ty didn't try to smooth Harley's edges away entirely, and Harley didn't try to make Ty louder or flashier. They let each other be exactly who they were, and somehow that made them stronger.

Nico also noticed that Ty didn't just focus on Harley's present; he was quietly nudging him toward the kind of future that didn't involve repeating old mistakes. It was subtle, built into casual talks and moments that seemed ordinary. That was Ty's way — working change into the fabric of daily life until it became impossible to tell where it started.

By the time the lunch bell rang, Nico could see that the bond was no longer tentative. It was there, solid enough that Harley no longer hesitated to seek Ty out in a crowded room. It was something Nico suspected Harley would guard fiercely, even if he didn't yet realise just how much it meant to him.

When the two of them walked out together, Nico caught a glimpse of Harley's expression — not quite a smile, but not the guarded scowl he used to wear. It was the look of someone who'd found an anchor in the middle of uncertain tides. And in the quiet way he always had, Ty simply matched his pace and kept walking.

The truth of Ty's upbringing was never spoken of in the way secrets are, but in the way facts settle into the air and simply become part of the room. There was no whispered speculation, no half-heard tales traded in corners. Everyone knew, though most couldn't have told you where they'd first heard it. His father's work as an RCMP investigator was the easy part to name, the badge and authority giving it shape. The harder part — the part people felt without quite understanding — was the way Ty carried himself, a quietness that wasn't meekness, a stillness that wasn't hesitation. There was a discipline there, in the way his eyes tracked the movement of a hallway, in the way he seemed to register the shift in a room's mood before anyone else even knew it had changed. It was the kind of presence that made you feel safer without quite knowing why.

Harley spotted him near the end of the corridor, half in the shadow of the lockers, his head bent over another thick-bound psychology book. Ty didn't fidget or glance up at passing noise. He absorbed words the way some people breathed, as if each sentence was a measured draw of air that steadied him for whatever came next. Harley didn't call his name. He didn't make a sound at all until his own shoes scuffed against the linoleum close enough for Ty to lift his gaze. No words passed between them — not yet — because sometimes speaking too soon ruins what needs to be felt before it's explained.

The hug happened in a single, unbroken movement. Harley stepped in and closed the distance, arms wrapping fully around Ty's shoulders, chest meeting chest in the kind of hold that left no doubt about its meaning. This wasn't a side squeeze, wasn't a polite half-measure that fathers sometimes give their sons as a stand-in for affection. This was the full weight of gratitude, pressed into a gesture that asked nothing in return. Ty returned it without hesitation, his arms locking around Harley with the kind of firmness that told you he understood exactly what was being given, and exactly what was being asked for in return.

It wasn't the sort of scene that drew a crowd. A few students passed without slowing, their chatter about homework or lunch plans filling the air between the two boys like harmless static. But for those who happened to notice, there was something in the stillness that made them avert their eyes, not out of discomfort, but out of respect. You didn't intrude on a moment like that. You didn't break the quiet between two people who had decided, without ever needing to say it, that this was a safe place to stop carrying the weight alone.

Harley didn't pull back quickly. He stayed in the hold longer than anyone might have expected from a boy who had spent so much of his time in the armour of bravado. His hands gripped the back of Ty's shirt, not tightly, but with the same steadiness as a man holding a rope in the dark, certain that letting go would leave him lost. Ty didn't speak. He didn't ask questions. He simply held on, the steady rise and fall of his breathing giving Harley something to match, something to anchor himself to.

When they finally stepped back, it wasn't with awkwardness. There was no embarrassed shuffling of feet, no quick glance away to pretend it hadn't happened. Harley met Ty's eyes with the unguarded clarity of someone who had decided this was a friendship worth protecting. His voice didn't come, but it didn't need to. The thanks had already been spoken in the way his shoulders had eased, in the way the tension had bled from his jaw, in the way his eyes no longer darted toward the exits as if searching for escape.

Nico, watching from the far end of the hall, recognised it for what it was. He had seen hugs before — careless ones between friends, dutiful ones between parents and children, fleeting ones exchanged at the end of a school day. But this was different. This was the kind of hug that told a story no one had dared write down yet. It was a beginning, but it was also an answer — proof that sometimes, when you meet the right person, you don't need to ask them to stand with you. They already are.

Ty closed his book after Harley stepped back, not marking the page, not caring that the line he'd left behind might be lost. "Come on," was all he said, his tone even, carrying no demand, no instruction. Harley nodded once, falling into step beside him without hesitation. There was something in that silence — not the heavy kind that follows an argument, but the kind that says we understand each other now.

As they walked, the hum of the hallway returned around them, lockers opening, doors shutting, the dull ring of a bell in the distance. But it didn't touch the space between them. Ty's calm presence seemed to push the noise outward, making room for Harley to breathe without the constant press of eyes or expectations. For someone who had spent so long being watched for the wrong reasons, it was a rare relief.

Nico trailed behind at an easy distance, knowing this wasn't the time to insert himself. He'd tell the others later — not in a way that cheapened it, but in the way you speak of a turning point you've just witnessed. Because that's what this was. Not a dramatic rescue, not a grand speech, but a quiet, undeniable shift in the way Harley carried himself. A shadow warrior's son didn't need to raise his voice or throw a punch to make a difference. Sometimes all it took was being there when no one else was.

By the time they reached the library doors, Harley's stride had changed. It wasn't lighter — not yet — but it was steadier, each step matching Ty's in unspoken rhythm. If you didn't know what had just happened, you might have missed it. But for those who did, it was impossible to unsee. And for Harley, it was impossible to forget.

Ty's taste in books had always set him apart from most kids in the sixth grade. While others tore through comic volumes or traded the latest action paperbacks, Ty preferred weightier titles — psychology textbooks, case studies, even dense academic articles that most adults would have skimmed past. His father never had to push these onto him; the interest had been Ty's from the beginning, sparked by a fascination with why people did the things they did. It wasn't curiosity for curiosity's sake, either. He read with purpose, mapping out the way people's choices connected to the places they had been, the hurts they had carried, and the victories they had claimed along the way. To Ty, no action was random. Every word, every look, every pause had a root if you knew where to dig.

That skill — and it was a skill — shaped the way he moved through school. While other students reacted to what they saw on the surface, Ty noticed the undercurrents. He could see a joke land wrong and trace the ripple effect across the room before anyone else had realised the shift. He recognised when a laugh was genuine and when it was a mask. He watched body language like some people read sheet music, noting the tempo changes and subtle shifts until he could predict the next beat. To him, hallways weren't just corridors; they were case studies unfolding in real time.

It was no surprise, then, that when Harley had first slipped that folded letter into his hand, Ty had read it the way a professional might handle a statement from a witness — not just for what was written, but for what was between the lines. He'd read it twice that first day, once to take in the surface meaning, and again to feel the weight beneath the words. But now, days later, he was re-reading a photocopied copy of it, sitting at the far end of the library with the kind of focus that made even Leo hesitate before sitting down beside him.

Lisa's handwriting was quick and slanted, the sort you'd expect from someone who'd written more with urgency than with the goal of neatness. Ty's eyes followed each loop and slash of ink as though the strokes themselves might reveal more than the sentences did. It wasn't the declaration of love that held him — though it was there in every line — it was the layers of self-awareness, the way she had measured her words like someone who knew exactly how they would land on the person reading them. Ty could see the restraint, the choices she'd made to omit certain details, to soften others, and to sharpen the truths she wanted to cut through.

Leo leaned back in his chair, studying Ty more than the paper in his friend's hands. "You've read that a dozen times," he said, not accusing, just observing. Ty didn't look up. "And I'll read it a dozen more," he replied evenly, his voice as calm as if they were discussing a homework assignment. But Leo could tell there was more to it — the way Ty's fingers tightened just slightly on the edge of the page, the way his eyes lingered on certain sentences before moving on.

Leo had always felt a responsibility toward Harley. Not in the way you feel responsible for someone younger or weaker, but in the way you take it on yourself to keep them from tipping over the edge when they've already been standing there too long. Seeing Ty take that role so naturally didn't surprise him, but it did make him feel less alone in carrying it. Between the two of them, maybe Harley had a real chance at staying on level ground.

Ty finally folded the photocopy, sliding it back into the inside cover of the thick book in front of him. It wasn't a place-marker so much as a safeguard — the letter hidden in plain sight, between pages on cognitive behaviour theory that most people wouldn't bother opening. "It's not just what she says," Ty murmured, more to himself than to Leo. "It's how she says it. She's telling him she understands him, down to the way he pretends not to care."

Leo nodded slowly, though his eyes stayed on Ty. "And?" he asked. Ty's gaze flicked up then, just briefly, meeting Leo's. "And," he said, "that's why it matters. People don't get to Harley like that. She did. That means someone else could try — for worse reasons."

They sat in silence for a moment, the low hum of the library filling the space. Ty turned his psychology book a fraction, the way he always did when he was shifting from thought to action. "If he loses her, or if she's kept away from him, he's going to start making decisions based on protecting himself instead of growing. That's when people get stuck." His tone was matter-of-fact, but the weight of it wasn't lost on Leo.

Leo didn't pretend to understand all the theory behind Ty's words, but he understood the outcome. A Harley with walls up was a Harley no one could reach — and a Harley no one could reach was a Harley who would start slipping back into the habits everyone had worked so hard to break. Leo wasn't about to let that happen, and he could see Ty wasn't either.

The book on the table was thick enough to serve as a shield, but Ty didn't need it. He'd learned early on that information was a weapon, and he'd armed himself well. Each chapter he read gave him another angle, another way to anticipate what might come. And if reading people like open pages meant he could see trouble before it arrived, then he'd keep doing it, even if it meant spending hours under the quiet fluorescent lights of the library while the rest of the world moved on without him.

When the bell rang, Ty didn't rush to pack up. He placed the photocopy back into its place, shut the book with care, and only then looked at Leo. "We keep an eye on him," he said simply. Leo didn't need to ask who "him" was. He just nodded, the weight of the task settling over him like it always did — heavy, but not unwelcome.

Ty slid the book under his arm as they left the library, his stride as even as ever. But Leo knew his friend well enough to see the change. Ty wasn't just watching anymore; he was planning. And when Ty planned, it meant things were about to shift — not with noise, but with the kind of quiet precision only someone raised in shadows could manage.

There was something different in the way Ty looked at Harley, and once you noticed it, you couldn't unsee it. It wasn't the open stare of someone waiting for a spectacle, nor the quick glance of a friend making sure you hadn't drifted too far. It was a steady, patient kind of watchfulness — the kind you only give to someone you know might stumble at any moment, even if they appear steady on their feet.

Nico caught it first, standing at his locker one morning while Harley joked too loudly with a cluster of kids by the water fountain. On the surface, it was normal — Harley was back in his element, his voice carrying like it always had. But Nico saw Ty in the corner of the hall, leaning against the frame of the trophy case, eyes fixed not on the crowd, but on Harley's hands. He wasn't listening to the words. He was watching the small tremors that came when Harley tried too hard.

It wasn't suspicious, that watchfulness. If anything, it looked like responsibility made visible. Ty had a way of noticing when Harley's voice tipped into false bravado, when the laughter came half a beat late, when the shoulders squared too stiffly to be natural. Nico realised Ty wasn't waiting for Harley to fail; he was waiting for the exact moment he could step in before the fall happened. And that was something most kids wouldn't even think to do.

Harley didn't seem to catch it, not at first. He was too busy building up his new rhythm, trying to prove — to others or himself, Nico couldn't tell which — that Lisa's absence hadn't broken him completely. But there were cracks. Sometimes his eyes darted toward the empty desk in the classroom before settling back to his book, or he'd lose his thread mid-sentence when the wrong song drifted from someone's headphones. And every time, Ty noticed. He wouldn't say anything aloud. He wouldn't even move, not unless he had to. But his gaze followed, quiet and precise, as if each slip was another piece in a puzzle only he was working to complete.

Nico thought about the letter then, the one Ty had read and re-read until it looked worn in his hands. He wondered if Ty's constant watch wasn't only about Harley's safety but about honouring what Lisa had put into words. Maybe Ty had decided — silently, without fanfare — that her trust in Harley meant something worth guarding. If Harley crumbled now, then her voice, her declaration, would be wasted. Ty wasn't about to let that happen.

The strangest thing was how unobtrusive it all was. Ty didn't hover, didn't crowd Harley with overbearing concern. He stayed at the edges, blending into the background like he always did, letting Harley believe his steps were his own. But Nico could see the invisible net stretched tight, ready to catch him if he slipped. It was the same way Ty read his psychology books — not loud, not obvious, but with the kind of patience that turned chaos into patterns.

One afternoon in the yard, Harley went too far. His joke carried an edge sharper than it should have, and the laughter that followed had the brittle quality of kids laughing because they felt they had to. Harley's grin faltered when he saw the shift, and for a moment it looked like he might double down, push harder until the balance broke entirely. That was when Ty moved. He didn't say much — just called Harley's name and tossed him a ball from across the yard, breaking the tension like it was nothing. Harley caught it, surprised, then used the excuse to jog over, leaving the crowd behind. Nico watched as Ty simply shrugged, as though the timing hadn't been surgical. But Nico knew it had been.

Harley probably thought he'd escaped embarrassment on his own. That was fine. Ty wasn't looking for credit. What mattered was that the hallway didn't turn against Harley that day, that the spiral never started. That was the point of the watchfulness — not to control, but to redirect when the edge grew too sharp. It wasn't flashy, but it was effective.

By now Nico had made a habit of watching Ty watch Harley. It fascinated him, the way Ty's eyes flickered at just the right moments, the way his body shifted as though he was calculating outcomes in advance. It was almost like seeing someone play chess with pieces no one else realised were on the board. And the more Nico studied it, the more he understood why Harley had started to trust Ty so quickly. Ty didn't need to say, "I've got you." He showed it in the way he was always already there.

It wasn't that Ty saw Harley as weak. Quite the opposite. He saw him as someone who had been forced to be strong for too long, someone who had built armour so heavy that even a moment of genuine feeling could throw him off balance. Ty's job wasn't to tear that armour off — it was to stand nearby in case it cracked. Nico thought that kind of loyalty was rare, rarer than most people ever realised.

At times, Nico wondered whether Ty's father had taught him this quiet vigilance, or if it was something Ty had shaped himself from hours of reading about human behaviour. Maybe it was both. Whatever the case, it was clear Ty wasn't just a boy with a stack of heavy books. He was someone who could read a room faster than most teachers, someone who could sense danger in silence before it even formed into words. And Harley, without even knowing, had become Ty's case study — not to dissect, but to protect.

It didn't escape Nico that Ty's vigilance extended to Lisa as well, even in her absence. Her shadow hung over Harley's every move, and Ty seemed to understand that protecting one meant protecting the other. If Harley faltered, it wasn't just his fall. It was hers too, her words, her trust, her love folded neatly into his pocket. Ty was watching for both of them.

The day Lisa finally returned, walking slowly through the front doors with her books clutched tight, Ty was the first to notice Harley's reaction. Harley stood a little straighter, his laughter lost for a beat, his face caught between relief and fear. Ty didn't move, didn't interrupt, but Nico could tell he was braced — ready to steady Harley if the flood of emotions pulled him too far. That was the kind of watchfulness no one else could name, but Nico saw it clearly: Ty was guarding not just Harley's body, but the fragile ground his heart was finally learning to stand on.

In time, Nico realised that Ty wasn't just a watcher. He was a mirror too. By watching Harley so carefully, he made Harley reflect on himself, forcing him — without a word — to see when the act no longer matched the truth. That was perhaps the quietest power Ty held. And Nico, who had spent much of his life narrating the stories of others, couldn't help but respect it.

For all the noise that filled the halls, it was this silence that mattered most. Harley was changing, little by little, and Ty was there for every step, the unseen presence making sure the change was real. And Nico, ever the observer, stood just behind, taking note of the watcher who refused to let Harley slip back into the shadows he'd finally begun to leave.

The day Lisa returned to school began like any other, the hallways buzzing with the usual chatter of students rushing to lockers and comparing notes for the morning's quiz. Yet beneath the ordinary rhythm, something different lingered, something only a few of us understood. Lisa's absence had stretched across two long weeks, and though the teachers gave their usual half-truths about illness and rest, the silence around her absence spoke louder than any official word. Those who knew what had really happened waited with a tension that never found its release bell. When the front doors finally opened and she stepped through, the hallway stilled, as if every sound was caught on the edge of her presence.

Lisa carried herself differently. The same sharp confidence lived in her stride, but there was a caution now, a shadow of pain veiled by her straight back and lifted chin. She didn't seek attention; she never had to. Heads turned without her asking, whispers followed without her trying. But instead of feeding off it, she cut straight through the crowd with her eyes set on one person, as though the rest of us weren't even there. She wasn't here to reclaim her place. She was here for Harley.

Harley, for his part, froze at the first glimpse of her. The smirk he'd been wearing mid-conversation slipped right off his face, replaced by something rawer, quieter. He didn't move toward her — not because he didn't want to, but because it was the first time anyone had seen Harley unsure of his own steps. For weeks he had carried her letter folded tight in his pocket, pulling it out when he thought no one noticed, rereading each line until the paper had grown soft and creased. And here she was, living proof that those words weren't just comfort from a distance, but a truth she'd chosen to walk back into his life and stand behind.

Ty saw the shift instantly. He had studied Lisa's letter more carefully than even Harley had, searching for any hint of exaggeration or misplaced emotion. But line after line had told him the same thing: she had meant every word. Her love for Harley wasn't shallow or borrowed from teenage fantasy — it was carved deep, rooted in shared scars and mirrored battles. Ty knew the difference between infatuation and recognition, and Lisa's writing had bled the latter. He had guarded that knowledge quietly, waiting to see if her actions would match her words. Now, watching her cross the hall with unwavering purpose, he knew they did.

When she reached him, Lisa didn't hesitate. She dropped her books against her hip, stepped into Harley's space, and wrapped her arms around him in a hug that was nothing like her usual defences. There was no hardness in it, no mask of strength — only gentleness, as if she knew just how much he needed that kind of touch to hold him steady. For a heartbeat, Harley stiffened, unused to being received with tenderness rather than challenge. But then his arms moved, cautious, mindful not to press against the places where she was still healing. It was the first time anyone had seen Harley cradle instead of grip.

The kiss came next, unexpected in its simplicity. Lisa leaned up just enough to close the space, pressing her lips to his with a careful grace that quieted the entire hall. It wasn't a show, wasn't performed for the audience that lingered along the lockers. It was a statement, one meant only for him, though the rest of us couldn't help but witness it. Harley's hand hovered for a moment, then found its place against the side of her face, fingers trembling slightly with the weight of it all. For once, he wasn't performing. He was present.

Nico, watching from the corner, felt the charge ripple through the hallway. It wasn't the spark of gossip or scandal — though those whispers began almost immediately — but something heavier, something truer. For months, Harley had been a storm always on the verge of breaking. Now, in Lisa's arms, that storm softened, not gone but quieted, the eye of it finally showing itself. And in that silence, we all saw the truth: Lisa wasn't afraid of his edges. She had chosen to step straight into them.

Ty kept his gaze steady, observing the way Harley handled the moment. He'd been waiting for proof that Harley could let down his guard without falling apart, that he could accept love not as a weakness but as strength. And here it was, in the open hall where everyone could see. Lisa didn't just heal her own reputation by walking back into school; she began healing Harley by making it clear he was worth more than his armour. Ty tucked the image into memory like another note in his silent study of human behaviour.

Harley's friends hovered nearby, caught between awe and uncertainty. Some shifted awkwardly, pretending to rummage through lockers, while others whispered into cupped hands. But none of it mattered. The only thing that did was the way Harley exhaled into Lisa's shoulder after the kiss, like a weight he hadn't realised he was carrying had finally lifted enough for him to breathe again. For once, his body didn't buzz with the need to prove himself. It rested, however briefly, against someone else's strength.

Lisa stepped back after the kiss, but only slightly, her hand lingering against Harley's arm as if to remind him that she wasn't vanishing this time. The bruise near her collarbone peeked out from under her sweater, a silent reminder of what she'd endured, but her eyes didn't carry shame. They carried fire — fire aimed at anyone who thought her return marked defeat. Harley seemed to read it too, his jaw tightening not with anger, but with resolve. Whatever had happened to her, it wasn't just her fight anymore. It was his too.

Ty noted the way Harley's posture shifted as Lisa's hand slipped down to hold his. There was no false bravado now, no swagger. Just quiet steadiness. It was the kind of shift Ty had hoped for, the kind that meant the change wasn't only external but rooted deep where it mattered. He knew enough to understand that one kiss didn't erase old patterns, but it was a start — and a powerful one at that.

The teachers, who had been watching from a distance, exchanged glances that carried a thousand unspoken worries. But even they didn't step in. For all their authority, they knew better than to interrupt a moment that was shaping something larger than classroom order. Lisa and Harley had chosen each other in front of everyone, and that choice would ripple through the hall long after the whispers died down.

As the crowd began to shift again, the noise of the school creeping back into motion, Ty remained where he was, leaning lightly against the wall, his book tucked under his arm. He didn't smile or frown, but there was a quiet satisfaction in his eyes. Lisa had meant her words, and Harley had accepted them. For Ty, who lived in the details of people's hearts and habits, this was more than affection on display. It was a turning point — one that meant the boy he had been watching so closely was finally stepping into the possibility of something beyond survival.

For Harley, the hallway would never look the same again. The place that had once echoed his bravado and bruises now held the memory of a hug that melted his guard and a kiss that gave him permission to be seen. And for those of us who witnessed it, the shadows in the hall shifted that day. They didn't disappear, but they were no longer his to carry alone.

When Lisa and Harley finally walked away together, the space they left behind wasn't empty. It pulsed with the knowledge that something had changed, something real and unshakable. Nico found himself replaying it in his head even as he moved to class, knowing that this was the kind of moment that wouldn't fade into memory. It would anchor itself, not just in Harley's story, but in all of ours.

And for Ty, watching from just behind the lines, it was confirmation of what he had believed all along: sometimes the quietest gestures carry the sharpest truth. A hug, a kiss, a letter meant in full — these were the things that broke through armour thicker than fists ever could. Lisa had returned, not as a shadow, but as the light Harley didn't even know he'd been waiting for.

It didn't happen with fireworks or some grand announcement, but with a simplicity that cut sharper than spectacle ever could. By the end of that week, no one needed to whisper or speculate; the truth was written in the way Lisa and Harley walked side by side, hands brushing until one of them gave up the hesitation and clasped the other's firmly. There was no denial, no attempt to play coy. They were together, and the hallways adjusted accordingly. Where once Harley had prowled with his entourage, daring others to meet his gaze, now he moved at Lisa's pace, the two of them orbiting one another like opposite poles of a magnet finally finding rest. The oddest part wasn't that it happened. It was how natural it felt once it did.

To most, they seemed an unlikely pair. Harley with his sharpened edges, known for a temper that turned classrooms into battlegrounds, and Lisa with her fierce independence, a girl who carried scars she refused to show as weakness. Yet when they stood together, something softened in both of them. Harley's voice, always pitched to carry above the noise, lowered when he leaned toward her. Lisa's posture, usually coiled tight against anyone who dared get close, loosened whenever Harley brushed her arm. Their contradictions didn't cancel out. They balanced.

Ty, more than anyone, understood the precariousness of that balance. He had spent weeks quietly watching Harley fight himself in silence, piecing together the boy's fractures as if they were lines in one of his psychology books. He knew how easy it would be for old patterns to return, for Harley's walls to slam back into place the moment he felt vulnerable again. But he also knew Lisa's letter had struck something deeper, and her return had sealed it. What Ty had witnessed when Harley broke down into his arms wasn't weakness. It was the raw beginning of change. And Ty wasn't about to let that slip away.

Harley seemed to understand, in his own rough way, what Ty had done for him. One afternoon, between classes, he approached Ty without a word, no audience, no attempt at bravado. He simply stepped into Ty's space and wrapped his arms around him in a full-bodied hug — the kind that fathers give sons when words are insufficient. It wasn't the quick clap on the back boys sometimes used to mask affection, but something deeper, tighter, his chin pressed into Ty's shoulder as if he were returning the strength Ty had given him. For Harley, who never lowered his guard willingly, that hug was an act of gratitude too honest to mistake for anything else.

Ty didn't flinch or look surprised. He closed his arms around Harley with equal measure, not as a rescuer this time, but as a friend who understood the weight of what he was being given. There was no need for words; Harley's grip carried more truth than any thank you could. It was the kind of exchange Nico, watching from down the hall, knew he would remember long after the sound of their footsteps faded. In that moment, Harley acknowledged something rare — that he needed, and that someone had answered without turning away.

Lisa had been walking toward them when it happened. She stopped just short, watching with an expression that flickered between awe and disbelief. This was not the Harley she had known, the boy who used to wield arrogance like a blade. This was someone unmasked, someone who could accept help without crumbling. The sight brought a sting of tears to her eyes before she could hide them. She pressed her knuckles to her mouth, as though steadying herself against the sudden flood of emotion.

When Harley stepped back at last, Lisa moved in. Her arms went around Ty in a hug as genuine as the one Harley had just given, her cheek pressed briefly to his shoulder. For Lisa, who trusted few and allowed even fewer close, that embrace was no small gesture. It was an offering, a thank you carried not in words but in presence. Ty accepted it quietly, his hand resting lightly between her shoulders, grounding her the way he had grounded Harley. Nico noticed how easily he held space for both, not demanding anything, not drawing attention — simply steady, simply present.

Afterward, Lisa wiped at her eyes, laughing softly at herself for the tears she couldn't quite disguise. "You caught him," she said to Ty, voice unsteady but sincere. "When I couldn't be there… you caught him." Ty didn't offer a speech. He only nodded, the faintest smile brushing across his face, the kind that said everything without the clumsiness of too many words.

The three of them stood together for a long moment, not needing to fill the silence. Harley shifted closer to Lisa, his hand slipping into hers again, his thumb brushing lightly over her knuckles. It was such a small thing, almost unremarkable, but in its quietness it spoke volumes. For once, Harley wasn't performing for the hallway. He was simply choosing to hold on. Ty, watching with the careful eye of someone who studied more than words on a page, noted the subtle change. It wasn't for show. It was real.

Their pairing became official not because someone declared it, but because it was lived in the open, in gestures too clear to mistake. By the next morning, the school buzzed with whispers that Harley and Lisa were together, but the two of them seemed unaffected by the talk. If anything, the rumours only hardened the resolve in the way they carried themselves. Harley still bristled at glances he didn't like, but now his anger was redirected. He didn't lash out at shadows anymore. He saved it for anyone who dared test Lisa.

Ty knew this was only the beginning. Love, especially in its first fierce blaze, could burn as much as it healed. But he also knew that with Lisa beside him, Harley had a chance at learning something he'd resisted for years: that being cared for wasn't weakness. It was survival. It was growth. Ty would remain watchful, as always, but for now he allowed himself the rare satisfaction of knowing he had played his part well.

Nico, narrating from the edges, saw the trio for what they had become. Harley and Lisa, opposites who somehow balanced their fire and steel, and Ty, the quiet sentinel, the bridge that kept them steady. It wasn't dramatic, wasn't the stuff of legends — but it was real, and in the hallways of our school, real was rare enough to matter more than anything else.

For Harley, the hug given and the hand held marked a turning point he wouldn't fully understand until much later. For Lisa, the tears shed openly meant she no longer had to stand alone. And for Ty, the observer and protector, the one who caught a boy when he fell apart, the reward was not in thanks but in knowing he had helped alter the course of two lives. Together, they carried on, not lighter exactly, but stronger — bound by the kind of truth that no amount of rumour or ridicule could erase.

By the end of that day, it was clear to anyone paying attention: Harley and Lisa were no longer two storms circling separate skies. They had collided, and in their collision, found calm. And at the centre of it all stood Ty, watchful, steady, content to remain the shadow that made sure the light held.

The first thing you noticed about Jarod wasn't his size, though he was taller than most of us and carried himself with the bulk of someone who had long since stopped being mistaken for a boy. It was the air around him, the sharp-edged tension that seemed to cling to his shoulders and radiate into the space he entered. When he walked down the hallway that first Monday, the sound of conversation dipped for just a breath, as though everyone had inhaled at the same time and forgotten to exhale. Nico, standing near the lockers with Ty and Leo, saw the ripple for what it was — not awe, not admiration, but recognition of something unwelcome. This wasn't just a new student arriving near the end of term. This was a storm finding its way into a building that had only just begun to settle.

He was in the seventh grade, one year older than Ty and Leo, though his presence made it feel like the gap was wider. His eyes, dark and restless, moved across the hall with a predator's patience, lingering on faces as if marking which ones would be worth his time. Jarod didn't bother with introductions. He didn't flash a smile or extend a hand. His arrival was marked only by the way his backpack slammed into the side of the lockers when he dropped it, the metal shuddering as though it had been struck on purpose. The silence that followed wasn't total, but it was telling. Students lowered their eyes, suddenly interested in shoelaces and textbooks. No one wanted to invite his attention.

Harley was the first to break the stillness, though not with his usual bravado. He leaned against the wall, arms crossed, studying Jarod as though sizing up a reflection of what he might have been six months ago. The resemblance wasn't perfect — Harley's sharpness had always been tempered by wit, a quick tongue that could cut deeper than fists. Jarod radiated something colder, less nuanced. He looked like someone who didn't need words to make his point. Nico saw Harley's jaw tighten, and for once, it wasn't out of a need to prove dominance. It was recognition. He knew Jarod's type. He'd worn that armour himself.

Ty didn't look away. He rarely did, even when others thought it safer to disappear into the background. His gaze followed Jarod's movements with the steady patience of someone cataloguing every detail: the way Jarod's hands curled into fists even when he wasn't threatened, the way his steps echoed heavier than necessary, the way he seemed to test the boundaries of the hall with each turn of his head. To Ty, it was a study in behaviour, a pattern revealing itself before the first word had been spoken. To Nico, watching from the side, it looked like two shadows circling the same room, waiting to see which one would claim the space.

When Jarod finally spoke, his voice was rougher than expected, carrying the gravelled tone of someone who had been yelling long before this morning. He didn't introduce himself; he made a comment about the size of the lockers, about how small the school felt compared to what he was used to. The words weren't much, but the delivery was laced with disdain, and that was enough. A few younger students shuffled back, as if the remark had been aimed at them directly. Jarod smirked, satisfied, and Nico realised then that this wasn't someone who would need weeks to settle into a role. He already knew exactly what part he intended to play.

Lisa's eyes found him almost immediately. She had just returned, still bearing the quiet strength of someone healing, and her reaction was different from the rest of us. There was no hesitation, no flicker of confusion. Recognition lit her features, sharp and sudden. She froze in place, her hand tightening on Harley's arm. For a moment, it seemed as though she might walk straight out of the building again, but instead she stayed where she was, staring at Jarod with a gaze that could have cut glass. It was clear she knew him, and just as clear that whatever history lay between them was not one she had asked for.

The hallway shifted in response, the unspoken tension thickening into something almost visible. Students whispered, teachers glanced over with the weary expressions of people already anticipating trouble. Jarod didn't notice, or if he did, he welcomed it. He adjusted the strap on his backpack with deliberate slowness, then began walking again, each step daring someone to cross him. He wasn't just a new student finding his place. He was a storm announcing its intent to break.

Ty moved slightly closer to Harley and Lisa, not enough to draw attention, but enough to make it clear he had marked the threat. His silence was not passive; it was preparation. Nico caught the subtle shift and understood what it meant. Ty wasn't looking for a fight, but he was ready for one if Jarod forced it. And from the way Jarod's eyes had flicked toward Ty when he entered, brief but telling, it seemed he already recognised something in the boy that unsettled him.

Leo, usually quick to crack a joke and ease the tension, said nothing this time. His younger brother Jeremy, trailing at his side, looked up at the older students with wide eyes, sensing the weight of the moment even if he couldn't name it. For the younger ones, Jarod was simply an unknown. For the rest of us, he was something we had seen before, only sharper, heavier, more dangerous.

By the time the bell rang, the hallway had not yet returned to its usual rhythm. The chatter was thinner, the movements quicker, everyone careful not to linger near Jarod as he made his way toward the classroom doors. Nico closed his locker with deliberate calm, but inside he carried the same unease as the others. This wasn't just a boy transferring schools. This was a force walking in under a borrowed uniform, and none of us knew yet what damage he was prepared to leave behind.

The teachers noticed too, though they tried to keep their voices light as they urged students to move along. Their glances at Jarod weren't casual; they were calculating, wary. They had been through their share of difficult students, but this was different. This was a boy who carried with him the kind of reputation that didn't need to be spoken aloud to be felt. He was harder than he looked, and he looked hard enough already.

For Harley, the arrival of Jarod was less a surprise than an inevitability. He didn't say it, but his silence carried the weight of someone who understood exactly what kind of trouble had just walked through the door. For Lisa, it was something far worse: the return of a shadow she thought she'd escaped. And for Ty, it was the beginning of another watch — one he knew would demand more of him than observation alone. The rest of us? We simply braced ourselves. Because when a storm arrives, you don't question whether it will break. You only wonder when.

The first chance she had to breathe away from the crowd, Lisa pulled Ty aside. It wasn't dramatic; she didn't march across the hall or make a show of demanding his attention. She simply waited until the hall thinned enough that their voices wouldn't carry, then leaned in with the kind of urgency that didn't need volume to be heard. Her voice was steady, but the undertone betrayed something sharper, something unsettled. "You need to know about Jarod," she said, eyes fixed on Ty as if making sure he understood she wasn't speaking out of rumour. She was speaking out of history.

Ty listened without interrupting, the same way he always did, his gaze never drifting from her face. Lisa didn't hesitate. "He isn't just mean. He isn't just another kid trying to push his way to the top. He can hurt people. Really hurt them." Her tone was flat, stripped of exaggeration, stripped of anything that could be dismissed as gossip. The words were delivered with the cool finality of a fact, not a warning, though the weight of it landed just as heavy. Nico, close enough to hear, caught the tremor beneath her calm — the sound of someone speaking from scars, not speculation.

Leo and Harley arrived midway, drifting into the quiet pocket Lisa had carved out, and she didn't flinch at their presence. If anything, her eyes hardened. "You've seen his size. That's not the dangerous part. The dangerous part is that he knows what he's doing with it." Her fingers tightened around the strap of her backpack, knuckles whitening as she forced herself to continue. "He doesn't just lash out when he's mad. He plans it. He chooses it. And when he does, he doesn't stop until he's made sure you won't get up again." The silence that followed was thick, every word hanging like a blade above us.

Harley tilted his head, arms crossed, his usual smirk absent. He didn't question her. That alone told Nico how serious it was. Harley, who never missed a chance to test strength or authority, didn't press for details. He didn't ask what Jarod had done or when. He simply watched Lisa with the wary respect of someone who knew when a truth was too sharp to touch. His eyes flicked to Ty, as if silently measuring how much weight the other boy would give to Lisa's words. Ty gave no outward sign, but the stillness in his face suggested he was absorbing every syllable.

Lisa's voice dropped lower, almost a whisper now, though no one would mistake it for weakness. "I know because I've been on the other end of it." Her eyes flickered toward the floor, just for a moment, before she forced them back up. She wasn't asking for pity. She wasn't asking for comfort. She was stating evidence, making sure it was recorded in the minds of those who needed to hear it. Ty's hands curled loosely at his sides, the only break in his otherwise steady composure. Nico felt his own breath catch. The meaning was plain, and yet none of us rushed to fill the silence that followed.

Leo broke it first, his voice firm but not loud. "If that's true, then we're not letting him corner anyone." The conviction in his tone wasn't youthful bravado. It was loyalty, shaped by the unshakable instinct to protect those he counted as his own. Lisa gave a single, sharp nod, as if to say she hadn't expected anything less. But even with Leo's words hanging in the air like a shield, the shadow of Jarod's presence didn't lift. It lingered, stretching over us like the stormcloud it was.

Nico noticed Lisa's hands trembling slightly, not with fear but with restrained fury. Her warning wasn't about spreading panic. It was about making sure none of us mistook Jarod for just another schoolyard bully. She wanted us to understand the difference — the difference between someone who postures for power and someone who weaponises it without hesitation. That kind of difference was often invisible until it was too late. Lisa wasn't going to let that happen again, not here, not to Harley, and not to anyone standing within reach.

Ty finally spoke, his voice low and measured, the way he always delivered his thoughts. "Thank you." Nothing more, nothing less. It wasn't dismissal, and it wasn't sympathy. It was acknowledgment — the kind of acknowledgment that promised he had heard her, that he had filed the truth away where it would not be forgotten. Lisa exhaled sharply at that, relief mixing with the tension still wound tight in her shoulders. She hadn't been sure how much to say, but she had said enough. The rest, she knew, Ty would piece together on his own.

For Harley, the weight of her words landed differently. He already carried Lisa's letter like a stone in his chest, her declarations of love still raw in his mind. Now, hearing her admit that Jarod's violence wasn't a theory but a lived truth, he seemed caught between anger and helplessness. He didn't shout. He didn't plan revenge out loud. Instead, he pressed a hand against the locker behind him, steadying himself as if the metal could ground the storm swirling inside. The change in him was subtle, but Nico saw it — the tightening of his jaw, the flicker of heat in his eyes. He had a reason to care now, one that went deeper than pride.

Lisa's warning spread quickly among the small circle. She didn't repeat it to the whole class, but those who had heard would not keep silent. Whispers began to move, low and careful, shifting the way students looked at Jarod even before he had a chance to prove her right. And maybe that was the point. Lisa wasn't just protecting herself. She was shifting the narrative before Jarod could build his throne of fear. She had put her truth out first, and in doing so, she had undercut his power before it had a chance to bloom unchecked.

But even as her words moved among us, Nico could see the toll it had taken on her. Every sentence had been a blade pulled from her own skin, and though she held herself steady, the cuts were fresh. She leaned back against the wall for just a moment, her gaze unfocused as though she was remembering every detail she had forced herself to put into words. Then she straightened, shook her shoulders as if shaking off the weight, and pressed forward. That, too, was part of her warning — not just the danger Jarod posed, but the strength it took to name it.

The rest of the day carried on in outward normalcy, but beneath the surface, Lisa's words worked like an undertow. Every laugh sounded sharper, every glance toward Jarod lingered longer, every quiet conversation carried an edge of caution. We weren't just students navigating a hallway anymore. We were witnesses holding knowledge that demanded we act differently. And whether Jarod realised it or not, he was already standing in a hall that no longer welcomed him with blind ignorance.

Ty's eyes followed Jarod when they crossed paths again that afternoon. Nothing outward had changed — Jarod still walked with the same heavy stride, still scanned the room as though measuring who he could bend first. But Ty's watch was different now. It was no longer simple observation. It was defence, sharpened by Lisa's warning, fuelled by the unspoken promise he had made by listening. Nico, noting the exchange, felt the air tighten again. This wasn't over. It had only just begun.

Lisa ended the day quieter than usual, her smile reserved, her eyes distant. But when she passed Harley in the stairwell, she touched his hand lightly — not enough to draw attention, just enough to remind him of what she had already said in her letter: that she was with him, even when it cost her. He nodded once, no words needed, and in that gesture Nico saw the shift. Harley wasn't standing alone anymore. And neither, for that matter, was she.

By the time the final bell rang, Lisa's warning had rooted itself into the bones of the day. It wasn't something that could be undone by jokes or distractions. It was a truth spoken aloud, and once truth is spoken, it can't be returned to silence. We carried it with us as we left the building, and though no one said it directly, we all knew the same thing: shadows don't fall without reason. And Jarod's shadow was only beginning to stretch.

The first time Jarod showed his teeth, it wasn't in the yard with kids half his size, but inside the classroom where authority was supposed to hold ground. It happened on a Tuesday morning, the kind of morning when everyone expected the usual rhythm of lessons and scribbled notes, but Jarod had no interest in rhythm. He came in late, his chair scraping across the floor with a sound that pulled every eye toward him, and when the teacher reminded him about punctuality, he didn't offer an excuse. He laughed — not loudly, not in a way that invited others to join — but with the low, cutting tone of someone who found the rules beneath him. The teacher tried again, firmer this time, and Jarod leaned back in his chair, arms crossed, smirk growing wider with every word he ignored.

By mid-morning, the tension broke. The science lesson stalled when Jarod decided the questions on the board were beneath him. Instead of answering, he muttered under his breath, and when pressed, he let the words spill out — sharp, crude, laced with a vocabulary that had no place in a school corridor, let alone a classroom. It wasn't the casual swearing of a kid trying to look tough in front of his peers. It was venom, delivered with precision, each word chosen to cut deep. The room froze around him, not because no one had heard profanity before, but because of the sheer force with which he wielded it. It wasn't rebellion. It was contempt.

The teacher, a man who had managed rowdy groups for decades, stood his ground. His voice grew stern, commanding Jarod to leave the room until he could speak respectfully. Most kids would have backed down at that point, if only to avoid the consequence that would follow. But Jarod didn't budge. He stayed planted, arms hooked behind his head, grin sharp and unshaken. When the teacher moved closer, hoping proximity might press him into obedience, Jarod leaned forward just enough to make the moment feel dangerous. He didn't shout, but the weight of his words was enough to suck the air out of the room: "You don't scare me. None of you do."

The silence that followed was heavier than any noise could have been. Even the clock ticking above the chalkboard felt louder than the teacher's next words. The order to report to the principal's office was clear, but Jarod only stood when he was ready, dragging his chair deliberately back into place, making sure every sound of resistance carried. He walked down the hall without hurry, daring anyone to believe he was being punished rather than choosing his own pace. The younger students watched from doorways as he passed, whispers starting before he was even out of sight. Fear didn't need time to build. It had already arrived.

The meeting with the principal was supposed to reset the balance, but Jarod had no intention of being reset. When asked to explain his behaviour, he leaned back in the office chair as though it were his living room couch, tossing out replies dripping with insolence. Each reprimand rolled off him without effect, his grin widening at every attempt to draw contrition from him. The principal, a woman known for her ability to quell even the fiercest tempers, tried to meet him with steady calm, but Jarod only laughed again — louder this time, the kind of laugh that sounded like a dare. Profanity followed, sharp and ugly, spat with the kind of force that stripped the room of its authority.

Nico heard about it not from the teachers directly, but through the network of whispers that always ran faster than official reports. By the time the last bell rang, the story had stretched through every hallway: Jarod had cursed at the principal, not in panic, not in mistake, but with deliberate malice. And the worst part — he hadn't been suspended. Not yet. The punishment was still being weighed, and that delay alone was enough to seed the idea that maybe, just maybe, Jarod was untouchable. If the principal couldn't scare him, who could?

Lisa caught Nico's eye when the news reached their group, her expression a mix of fury and confirmation. Her warning hadn't been taken seriously enough, and now Jarod had demonstrated, in full view, the truth she had already lived. Ty's face remained unreadable, but his silence carried weight. He had seen students test boundaries before, but never like this. This wasn't about attention or bravado. This was about dominance, about Jarod staking his claim on the very structure of the school itself.

Leo muttered something under his breath, something about the lines being drawn now whether the teachers liked it or not. Jeremy, only half understanding the depth of what was unfolding, looked up at his brother with wide eyes, sensing that something larger than him was shifting. Nico noted it all — the way fear spread not through Jarod's fists but through his refusal to bend. It was the kind of defiance that didn't just shake the rules. It shook the ground under them.

The next day, Jarod returned to class as if nothing had happened. He strode into the building without apology, without hesitation, his presence filling the hall like smoke after a fire. No teacher confronted him outright. Not then. Not with the memory of his profanity still echoing in their ears. Instead, they adjusted — subtly, but noticeably. Instructions came with more caution, corrections delivered with softer edges. It wasn't submission, not entirely, but it was close enough to send the message: Jarod had shifted the balance of power, even if only by a margin. And for someone like him, a margin was enough.

Nico couldn't shake the image of Lisa's warning when he saw it unfold. Jarod didn't need to throw punches to prove himself dangerous. He only needed to show that authority meant nothing to him. That was the beginning of true fear, the kind that seeped into every corner of the school, leaving students and teachers alike questioning what line he might cross next. And the worst part was, no one could be certain how far he was willing to go.

In the days that followed, whispers replaced laughter in the halls. Where there had once been chatter about summer plans and weekend games, there was now speculation about Jarod's next move. Some thought he'd pick a fight with a student. Others thought he'd go after a teacher again, maybe push further this time. No one agreed on the details, but everyone agreed on the truth: Jarod wasn't just another troublemaker. He was something else entirely, something harder to name, harder to contain.

Ty watched him closely, his gaze sharp, his patience unshaken. He didn't confront Jarod directly, not yet. That wasn't his way. Instead, he studied the patterns — the way Jarod chose his words, the way he baited authority, the way he seemed to thrive on the tension he created. Nico could see it in Ty's expression: he was cataloguing Jarod the way he had catalogued others before. Only this time, it wasn't about understanding. It was about preparing.

Lisa, meanwhile, carried herself with even more guarded strength. She didn't flinch when Jarod passed her in the hallway, but her jaw tightened every time his shadow fell across her path. She had lived his danger once already, and she wasn't about to be blindsided again. Harley, standing closer to her now than ever, picked up on every change in her posture. And though he said little, Nico could sense the storm brewing in him — the kind of storm that would not settle easily.

The teachers tried to pretend that order had been restored, but it was a hollow act. Their authority had been tested in front of everyone, and they had failed to make it stick. That kind of failure doesn't fade quietly. It lingers, feeds, grows. Jarod walked the halls with the easy stride of someone who knew the rules didn't apply to him, and for the moment, he was right. That was the part that unsettled Nico the most — not just Jarod's defiance, but the silence that followed it.

In that silence, every student knew the same truth: if the teachers couldn't stop him, then it would fall to someone else. And whether we were ready or not, that someone was already watching from the edges, measuring every move, waiting for the right moment to act. Ty, the shadow warrior's son, hadn't spoken of it yet, but Nico could see it written in his stillness. Jarod's reign of defiance would not go unanswered. Not forever.

For all of Jarod's swagger, for all the venom in his voice and the ease with which he tore through classroom order, something subtle changed whenever Ty drew near. It wasn't obvious to most — the average glance would still see the same smirk, the same broad shoulders set like stone — but to those who knew how to watch, the cracks were visible. His arms would tighten just slightly against his chest, his jaw would flex with the faintest hesitation, and his eyes — sharp and predatory with most — would shift, just briefly, to measure the boy he pretended not to see. Ty wasn't loud, he wasn't boastful, and yet Jarod seemed to recognise something in him that unsettled his balance. It was the kind of recognition that doesn't need words: a predator catching sight of another predator, one who moves in silence and knows exactly when to strike.

The principal had been watching, too. Days of Jarod's defiance had eroded her patience, and though she had decades of experience handling difficult students, this one was different. She called Ty into her office with a gravity that made even the air feel heavier. The request she made of him was unlike anything she had asked of another student before: to help. To be the quiet counterforce to the storm Jarod had brought into their halls. It wasn't a burden she gave lightly, but Ty accepted it without hesitation. He didn't see it as a challenge for his ego or a chance to rise above his peers. He saw it as responsibility, the kind his father had trained him for since he was old enough to balance on his own two feet.

Still, Ty understood the weight of such a task could not rest on him alone. That evening, he called his father, laying out the situation in calm, measured detail. He spoke not with the flustered urgency of a child seeking rescue, but with the clarity of one who had already analysed the danger and was preparing to act.

His father listened without interruption, the kind of silence that meant every word mattered. By the time Ty had finished, the decision was made: his father would come to the school. Not to intimidate Jarod, not to publicly assert authority, but to stand beside his son and ensure the responsibility he carried was matched with protection.

When Ty returned the next morning, there was a shift in his posture. He walked with the same quiet composure as always, but there was steel in his stride, a certainty that had not been there before. The other children felt it, though they could not name it. Jarod felt it most. When he rounded the corner and found Ty standing at the far end of the hallway, there was no exchange of words, no challenge spoken aloud. Yet Jarod's smirk faltered, just slightly, before he pulled it back into place. It was a fleeting thing, but Nico caught it — the unmistakable sign of someone meeting a wall he hadn't expected to find.

Permission had been given, too, in a form no one could contest. Ty had been authorised to act, not as an aggressor, but as a protector. If Jarod's violence ever crossed the line toward the smaller children, Ty was allowed to intervene. The knowledge of that authority gave him no thrill, no swell of pride, only a deeper calm. It meant his instincts, honed through years of practice under his father's guidance, could finally have a place. He was no longer just a student in the hall. He was the quiet shield waiting for the moment it became necessary to rise.

Few knew the depth of Ty's training, though. They saw the boy with the books, the one who read psychology with the intensity others reserved for novels, but they didn't know about the hours spent in dojos, the sweat-soaked evenings practicing stances until his muscles trembled. They didn't know about the way he studied forms of Kung-Fu, learning not only how to strike but when not to. They didn't know about the fluid strength of Tai-Chi, the control it demanded of every breath, every shift in balance. To Ty, martial arts weren't about fighting — they were about discipline, about readiness, about the art of becoming still even in the face of chaos.

Jarod didn't know the details either, but he sensed it all the same. Predators recognise when they are being watched by someone who does not flinch. Ty never stared him down or puffed his chest, never spat challenges or tried to outdo him in noise. He simply stood where he needed to stand, his gaze steady, his silence louder than any insult. And that was what made Jarod restless. He couldn't measure him, couldn't provoke him, couldn't find the edge that would let him push Ty into revealing weakness. The absence of reaction was more threatening than any show of force.

Nico saw the unease bloom in Jarod's movements over time. When Ty entered a classroom, Jarod shifted his weight. When Ty lingered at the lockers, Jarod walked faster. It wasn't fear in the traditional sense — not the wide-eyed terror of someone shrinking from danger — but a deep wariness, the kind that creeps into the spine and whispers caution. Jarod might have towered over smaller children, might have barked obscenities at teachers, but when Ty was near, the bravado never quite landed with the same weight. Something in him hesitated, and in that hesitation lay the truth.

The smaller children noticed, too. They clustered a little closer to Ty in the yard, their instincts recognising safety even if they couldn't explain why. Ty never made promises aloud, never declared himself their protector, but the message was carried in every movement he made. He was present, he was steady, and when Jarod prowled the edges of the group, Ty's calm presence drew an invisible line no one dared cross. Even Harley, who had rarely leaned on anyone, felt that line and trusted it. He had been caught by Ty once before when he fell apart, and he knew — beyond words, beyond doubt — that if the moment came again, Ty would be there.

The principal kept her watch from the sidelines, noting how quickly Jarod's fire dimmed in Ty's shadow. It was not victory yet, not a resolution, but it was something to build upon. Authority had failed when it came from her voice, but it seemed to hold when carried by Ty's silence. She understood then that control is not always won by the loudest presence in the room, but by the one who refuses to bend. And in Ty, she saw a steadiness that might hold the balance of the school in place.

Jarod tried to test it, of course. He shoved shoulders in the hallway when Ty was only a few feet away, waiting for a reaction that never came. He spat insults that rolled off Ty like water, frustration mounting when his usual tools failed. Each failed attempt chipped at his power, a fact that only deepened the wariness in his eyes when he met Ty's gaze. And though Jarod never admitted it, everyone who watched understood: the fear he carried was not of being hurt. It was of being seen — measured and known by someone who could dismantle him without lifting a hand.

Nico carried that truth quietly, his eyes always drifting to Ty when Jarod tried to make noise. The storm in the hallways had not passed, but its path had shifted. There was a new centre of gravity now, and though most didn't realise it, Jarod already knew he wasn't the only force casting shadows in the hall. Ty stood there, unyielding, the weight of his training hidden in every calm breath, and Jarod's fear — however carefully he tried to mask it — betrayed him every time.

Ty and Leo had been close for years, the sort of friendship that didn't need constant words to prove itself. They moved together in the halls with the ease of brothers, their shoulders almost brushing, their strides naturally falling into rhythm. It wasn't forced, nor was it something they had to announce. It was simply there — a current that carried them both through the chaos of the school day. Nico noticed it often, how one would glance across a room and the other seemed to understand exactly what was meant without the need to speak. Their connection wasn't loud, but it was undeniable, built on a foundation of loyalty and an instinct to protect each other at all costs.

Leo was no fighter by nature, but he carried his strength in other ways — a steadiness of heart, a willingness to stand by his friends even when it was uncomfortable. That was what Ty valued most. He didn't need another version of himself; he needed someone who could hold ground in different ways. When Jarod arrived, Ty never had to explain his concerns to Leo. A single look across the cafeteria was enough. Leo knew. He always knew. And when the moment came to act, it was never a question of if Leo would stand with him, only how. That certainty bound them more tightly than blood ever could.

There was a way Leo trusted Ty that others struggled to. Most students saw the calm, book-reading boy who sat quietly at the far end of the library. They didn't grasp the depth of his awareness, nor the discipline that shaped him into something much stronger than appearances suggested. Leo did. He saw the way Ty observed, the way he carried responsibility without complaint, and he never doubted that strength. For Leo, Ty wasn't just a friend; he was a constant. That certainty shaped his every choice, especially when Harley faltered or Lisa pulled away from the group. Leo knew Ty would steady things, and Ty knew Leo would keep people close.

Their bond wasn't built on grand gestures but on countless small ones. Passing notes in class that said more with a single word than a whole page of explanations. Sharing lunches without needing to ask who was hungriest. Staying late after school, not because either had pressing work, but because the other wasn't leaving alone. They were brothers in practice long before they ever said it aloud, and even then, they didn't say much. It was simply understood. A truth woven into the fabric of their friendship. Nico, who watched closely, often felt like an outsider looking in on a language made of gestures, silences, and the smallest of smiles.

When Harley collapsed in the hallway weeks earlier, Ty had been the one to catch him, but Leo had been the one who steadied the space around them. He had turned his body toward the rest of the students, daring anyone to make light of what was happening. His posture alone spoke volumes — not a word needed, not a fist raised, but an unspoken command: leave them be. Nico saw it all unfold, recognising that the strength of Ty and Leo's bond lay not just in what they did for each other, but in how they instinctively supported what the other was already doing. One stepped forward, the other held the line. Together, they were unshakable.

The teachers noticed it too, though they rarely admitted it aloud. When Ty offered to keep watch over Jarod, the principal gave him that authority in part because she knew Leo would never let him carry it alone. She saw how they moved as a pair, one reinforcing the other. It gave her a kind of relief, knowing that responsibility this heavy wasn't resting on a single student's shoulders. If Ty was the blade, sharp and precise, then Leo was the shield — strong, reliable, and always placed exactly where it was needed. The metaphor was imperfect, but it was the closest she could come to capturing what they were together.

The friendship also had its lighter side. They joked in ways that made no sense to anyone else, building humour out of half-remembered lines and private references. Nico often watched them burst into laughter over nothing more than a raised eyebrow or a slight tilt of the head, and though he didn't always get the joke, he understood the importance of it. Those small sparks of humour weren't just about fun — they were about relief. They were the release valve that kept the pressure of their responsibilities from breaking them down. And when things grew heavy, as they often did with Harley and Lisa and now Jarod, those moments mattered more than anyone realised.

There were times when Ty seemed older than his years, weighed down by the discipline and expectations his father had instilled in him. In those moments, Leo's presence was a reminder that he was still just a boy, still allowed to laugh, still allowed to carry the world a little more lightly. And when Leo grew overwhelmed by the drama of their peers, by the constant pull between loyalty and frustration, Ty's calm grounded him. It was a balance, each steadying the other, a rhythm of give and take that never needed to be spoken aloud. Nico saw it as a kind of partnership few people ever found, even as adults.

When Jarod first clashed with a teacher and the school trembled with his defiance, Ty and Leo exchanged one look across the crowded hall. Nico caught it — a flicker of understanding that passed in less than a second. To most, it was nothing, but to them, it was a strategy. Ty's silent promise to keep the danger in check, Leo's unspoken commitment to stand beside him. No words were necessary. By the time Jarod looked their way, both were already in position: Ty steady at the edge of the crowd, Leo anchoring the rest, their presence a quiet but undeniable resistance.

Even Jeremy, Leo's younger brother, felt the ripple of their bond. He often trailed after them, not quite old enough to be part of every conversation but always included in spirit. Ty never dismissed him, never made him feel like an annoyance. He let Jeremy tag along, and Leo made sure he never felt out of place. To Jeremy, it was like being pulled into a circle far stronger than he could have imagined on his own. He often told Nico in whispers that Ty felt like another brother, someone who would never let him down. Nico never argued; he agreed completely.

The schoolyard itself seemed to bend around their friendship. Smaller kids, sensing the quiet safety they created, often played closer to wherever Ty and Leo were standing. They weren't bodyguards, weren't patrolling the yard, but their presence alone was enough. Nico wondered sometimes if even they realised just how many people looked to them for steadiness. They didn't ask for the role, didn't seek it out, but they carried it with a grace that came from knowing who they were and what they stood for. In a way, their friendship had grown beyond themselves — it had become a pillar for others too.

When Lisa returned and leaned on Harley, Ty and Leo both noticed the shift it caused. They didn't need to discuss it, but their eyes met more than once, sharing unspoken questions about what it meant for the group. Ty saw the potential for healing, Leo saw the risks of more pain, and between them they carried the responsibility of balancing both. Their brotherhood wasn't just about laughter or protection; it was about carrying each other's burdens and, by extension, those of the people they cared for. Nico admired it deeply, knowing it was the kind of strength most friendships never reached.

There were cracks, of course, as with any bond. Moments when one pushed harder than the other, when silence turned heavy instead of easy. But even those cracks were temporary, smoothed over by a shared understanding that nothing could truly divide them. They didn't hold grudges. They didn't need apologies spelled out. One would show up at the other's door the next morning, and everything would be as it had been. Nico often thought of it as a kind of resilience, the ability to bend without breaking, to carry both the storms and the silences with equal strength.

When Jarod prowled the edges of the schoolyard, throwing sharp words at smaller children, Ty and Leo both moved without hesitation. Ty stepped closer to the danger, calm and watchful, while Leo widened his stance behind him, catching the nervous glances of the younger ones and holding them steady. Nico watched the scene unfold and realised that this, more than anything, defined their bond. They were not separate forces — one did not move without the other. And together, they created a line no one dared cross.

Nico narrated it all with a mix of awe and certainty. To him, Ty and Leo weren't just friends; they were proof that loyalty could be something unshakable, something that didn't fracture under pressure. He had seen friendships crumble over less, seen bonds collapse under the weight of pride or misunderstanding. But Ty and Leo stood firm. In their brotherhood, Nico saw a kind of truth that could stand even in the shadow of someone like Jarod. And as long as they held together, the rest of the school had a chance to stand too.

The hallways held many shadows now — Lisa's quiet return, Harley's fragile healing, Jarod's looming presence — but Ty and Leo's bond was a light that cut through it. They didn't seek the role of protectors, didn't demand recognition or thanks, but they carried it all the same. Nico closed his notes in his head with a kind of reverence, knowing that this was the bond everyone wished they had: unshaken, unbreakable, and entirely their own. Whatever storms lay ahead, Ty and Leo would face them side by side, brothers in every way that mattered.

Jeremy was younger, smaller, and still carried the wide-eyed look of a boy just beginning to understand the unwritten rules of school life. Yet, within the gravity of Ty and Leo's orbit, he was never out of place. Though only in fourth grade, he was pulled into their bond naturally, like a younger brother welcomed without ceremony. It was not a matter of age or strength; it was a matter of trust. Jeremy knew, without ever having to ask, that standing near Ty and Leo meant he was safe. And for a boy still navigating hallways where taller shadows often loomed, that safety mattered more than anything else.

Jeremy looked up to Ty differently than he did to Leo. Leo was family by blood, the older brother who had guided him through scraped knees, forgotten lunches, and the sting of careless words. Ty was family by bond, the steady presence who carried the same protective energy but wore it with calm, deliberate control. Together, the two older boys created a wall that Jeremy leaned against, a certainty that no matter how chaotic the day became, he would not face it alone. That bond, though unspoken, was written in every moment they shared, in every look of reassurance, in every subtle act of care.

Nico often saw Jeremy following a few paces behind them, not clinging, not begging for inclusion, but moving with a quiet assurance that he belonged. There was never a question of whether he was allowed. He simply was. Ty treated him with the same respect he gave Leo, never brushing off his questions, never making him feel small for his age. It gave Jeremy a kind of confidence rare for a boy his age, the assurance that his presence was not a burden but a strength to the circle. And in return, Jeremy's loyalty was fierce, as unwavering as if blood tied them all together.

That loyalty showed itself in small, significant ways. When Jarod barked insults at the smaller children, Jeremy was often among the first to shift closer to Ty and Leo, not to hide, but to stand with them. His shoulders squared in imitation of Leo's, his gaze steady in reflection of Ty's. He didn't have their size or their skill, but he had their courage, and he made sure it was visible. The teachers noticed it too, though they rarely commented. Jeremy was learning what true brotherhood looked like, not through lectures or stories, but through the daily example set by the two who stood before him.

Leo watched carefully, guiding Jeremy in ways only an older brother could. He reminded him to temper his bravery with caution, to understand that courage was not recklessness but measured strength. Yet even he knew that Jeremy's courage grew stronger in Ty's presence. Ty, though never one to give long speeches, had a way of grounding Jeremy with a single glance, a quiet nod, or a hand placed gently on his shoulder. It was not grand, but it was powerful, enough to make Jeremy straighten his back and believe that he could stand against anything.

Their dynamic was not without its humour. Jeremy often brought a levity that Ty and Leo sometimes forgot was necessary. He made faces at lunch, cracked jokes that didn't always land but still drew laughter, and carried a spark of energy that lightened the gravity of the older boys' responsibilities. In that way, he balanced them. When Ty grew too serious or Leo too protective, Jeremy's presence reminded them that they were still boys, not just shields against the storm. His joy, though small, was a gift — a constant reminder that even in the shadow of danger, laughter had its place.

Jeremy was also fiercely observant. Nico realised this quickly, catching the boy's eyes lingering on conversations, studying body language, memorising details. He was learning not only from his brother but from Ty, piecing together an unspoken education in strength and awareness.

It made him sharper than most children his age, less naïve, and more attuned to the undercurrents that shaped their days. When Lisa returned, Jeremy was among the first to notice how Harley's posture shifted around her, how Ty's eyes lingered longer, assessing. He did not fully understand the complexities, but he understood enough to recognise that something important was happening.

At times, Jeremy's age betrayed him, and his emotions ran ahead of his reason. There were moments when anger flared, when he wanted to charge into confrontations with Jarod or defend a classmate too recklessly. In those moments, Ty's quiet hand and Leo's firm voice anchored him. They reminded him that strength was not only about standing tall, but about knowing when not to strike. Jeremy learned quickly, humbled not by harsh correction but by the respect with which his mistakes were handled. It deepened his trust, binding him tighter into their circle.

To Nico, watching from the outside, it was remarkable how seamless the dynamic was. Jeremy was not an accessory to their friendship, not a younger tagalong tolerated out of obligation. He was integral, woven in as naturally as if he had always been part of the bond. Blood made him Leo's brother, but bond made him Ty's. Together, they formed a trio that balanced strength, caution, and spirit, each element as necessary as the others. It was not a hierarchy but a harmony, one that gave Nico hope for what loyalty could be at its best.

Even the other students began to recognise it. Whispers in the hallway acknowledged not just Ty and Leo as a unit, but Jeremy as part of it too. Smaller children gravitated toward him, sensing the protection that flowed from his place within the circle. Older ones, even those who mocked at first, gradually stopped. There was something about the way Jeremy carried himself with Ty and Leo that discouraged ridicule. It was clear he was not alone, and that made him untouchable in ways he couldn't have managed on his own.

The teachers, too, adjusted their perspective. They saw Jeremy's closeness to Ty and Leo not as a distraction, but as a stabilising force. His behaviour improved under their watch, his confidence growing stronger with each passing week. In conferences, they spoke of his maturity, his surprising steadiness for his age, though none could quite place the reason. Nico knew it was simple — he was learning from two of the most grounded boys in the school, and their example had become his education.

There were moments of vulnerability too, moments when Jeremy's young age was most apparent. When rumours of Lisa's attack spread, Jeremy had clung to Leo's arm, eyes wide with fear he could not hide. He had asked questions no one wanted to answer, and it was Ty who crouched to meet his gaze, offering only the truth he could bear: that she would heal, and that Harley would not face it alone. Jeremy had nodded, his trust intact, though Nico saw the way his small hands trembled. In those moments, the bond of brothers — by blood and by choice — carried him through what his years could not yet handle alone.

Jeremy's loyalty was perhaps most clearly displayed when he defended Ty and Leo in small but powerful ways. When older kids muttered doubts or questioned their choices, Jeremy was quick to speak, his voice small but steady. He didn't need to win arguments; his conviction was enough to silence most. It was the conviction of someone who had seen loyalty lived out every day, who had experienced it firsthand and believed in it fully. Nico admired it, recognising that loyalty, when tested in small moments, was what made it unbreakable in larger ones.

The strength of their bond showed itself not only in conflict, but in the quieter parts of daily life. Walking home together, sharing snacks, even doing homework side by side — these moments built a foundation of trust stronger than any single act of defence. For Jeremy, it was proof that brotherhood was not just about facing storms, but about living in the calm between them too. And for Ty and Leo, it was a reminder that their responsibilities extended beyond each other, shaping the life of someone still growing into his own strength.

As weeks turned into months, Jeremy's place within the bond grew unquestioned. He no longer lingered at a distance or waited for permission to join. He simply stepped into place, confident in the knowledge that he belonged. To Nico, watching all this unfold, it was a testament to the truth of brotherhood. Blood might begin it, but bond completed it. And in the case of these three — Ty, Leo, and Jeremy — it was clear that bond was stronger than anything else.

The school, with its shifting shadows and storms, often felt like a battleground. But within that space, the brotherhood of these boys stood as a constant — a shield, a light, and a reminder that strength is not measured in size or age, but in loyalty. Nico saw it all, recorded it silently in his memory, and understood that what he witnessed was rare. Brothers not by blood alone, but by bond. And that, he realised, was the kind of brotherhood that could stand against anything.

The hallways had always carried a hum of restless energy, but with Jerod's arrival, the rhythm had shifted into something heavier. Nico felt it every morning, the way glances darted between students and conversations thinned when Jerod's steps echoed down the corridor. It was as though the entire school had been forced into a new pattern, each movement calculated, each silence deliberate. And yet, within that uneasy shuffle, certain players had begun to show themselves more clearly. Harley and Lisa had grown closer, their movements synchronised like pieces that now belonged on the same square. Ty, however, stood apart — not as a bystander, but as the one who watched the entire board, seeing every angle.

Lisa had warned them all, her voice low and steady, about Jerod's danger. Nico could tell she wasn't exaggerating. There was a weight behind her words, the kind that came from lived experience, not speculation. Harley, for once, didn't laugh it off. His posture had shifted since Lisa's return, less about bravado, more about protection. He wasn't trying to be the loudest voice in the room anymore — not when Lisa was watching, and not when Ty was silently measuring every move Jerod made. For Nico, it was like watching pawns reshuffle into new positions, each one trying to guard the other.

Ty's attention was constant. He rarely confronted Jerod outright, but the air between them was taut whenever they crossed paths. Nico had seen it firsthand: Jerod tossing an insult across the lockers, too close to Lisa for it to be accidental, his smirk sharp with challenge. Ty didn't need to raise his voice. He simply moved closer, his presence alone cutting through the tension. The effect was instant. Jerod's bravado faltered, not vanishing, but cracking just enough to reveal the unease he tried so hard to bury. It was a small victory, but Nico could see it mattered.

One afternoon, though, the balance nearly broke. Jerod's swagger carried him too far when he decided to shove past one of the teachers in the hallway — a mistake that set every pair of eyes on him. Teachers were not sacred to everyone, but in this school, they carried a bond with the students that extended beyond the classroom. To shove one was to shove at the foundation of the place itself. Ty had been standing just a few steps away, and for the first time, Nico thought he saw the shadow of a strike ready to land. Ty's hand had moved, quick and precise, chest-level, ready to drive Jerod back before his arrogance could grow roots.

It was not an empty threat. Nico had seen enough of Ty's discipline in martial arts to know that if he had wanted to strike, Jerod would have felt it in every breath that followed. But Ty stopped just short, his palm hovering inches from contact, steady and controlled. It was a warning more powerful than any blow could have been. Jerod saw it too — the calculation in Ty's eyes, the restraint that made it clear this wasn't about temper but about principle. For the first time, Jerod looked as though he had collided with something immovable, a wall he couldn't intimidate.

The teachers noticed as well, though none dared call Ty out for it. They knew his father's reputation, the discipline instilled at home, and the responsibility that came with it. Instead, their gazes flicked between the boys, acknowledging silently that Ty had done what they could not: he had drawn the line. Nico marvelled at it, realising this was no longer about boys posturing in hallways. This was about a quiet guardian stepping forward when the school itself had been challenged. Ty had reminded them all that there were boundaries Jerod could not cross without consequence.

In the days that followed, Nico kept watching, piecing together the shifts like a puzzle. Harley had grown more subdued, but not weaker; his energy had redirected toward Lisa, their connection sealing into something more permanent. Lisa herself moved differently now, less concerned with protecting her own reputation, more willing to let her affection for Harley show. Every hug, every glance, was a counterweight against the chaos Jerod threatened to bring. And Leo, steady as ever, moved like Ty's second shadow, reinforcing his friend's watchful stance without needing instruction.

Jeremy's role, though smaller, was just as crucial. He stayed close to Leo, mirroring his brother's awareness, learning the rhythm of danger without fully understanding the depth of it. To Nico, it looked like a younger knight on the board, positioned carefully, still learning the moves but already contributing to the defence. The circle was tightening, each piece leaning into its role, and Jerod — whether he admitted it or not — was finding fewer gaps to exploit. It was, in every sense, a chess game in motion, and Nico could not look away.

He noticed Jerod's eyes often scanning the room, testing for weaknesses, for places where fear still lived. But more often than not, his gaze caught Ty's, and in those moments, his swagger faltered. It wasn't a collapse, not yet, but it was enough to prove that even storms had places they couldn't reach. Ty wasn't playing the same game as Jerod. He wasn't a piece on the board at all — he was the one who saw the whole thing, the strategist who never moved without purpose. And Jerod, for all his size and fire, couldn't match that kind of control.

The hallway, once ruled by loud voices and heavy steps, had become quieter in its tension. Students walked with sharper awareness, their conversations clipped as if waiting for the next move. Nico wrote it into memory like a story unfolding: Harley, tempered by love; Lisa, steady with her warning; Ty, unflinching in his vigilance; Jerod, dangerous but not invincible; and the rest, caught in between, learning the shape of resilience in real time. The school was a board, the pieces alive, and every day was another match waiting to be played.

It wasn't that Ty had solved the problem of Jerod — far from it. Jerod's presence still loomed, his threats still whispered in corners, his temper still unrestrained. But Nico saw clearly that the balance had shifted. Jerod was no longer unchecked. His words did not land with the same force when Ty was near. His actions carried the risk of consequence, even if only in silence. And perhaps that was enough for now: to know that someone was watching, always steady, always ready to act.

When Nico later replayed the image of Ty's hand almost striking, he realised it was more than just a moment of restraint. It was proof of something deeper — that true strength was not in the blow itself, but in the choice not to deliver it. Ty had shown that discipline could be louder than aggression, that fear could be instilled not through violence but through control. And that, Nico thought, was the lesson Jerod had not yet learned: that storms burn themselves out, but those who stand like stone endure.

The board shifted once more as the weeks unfolded, but the memory of that almost-strike lingered. For Nico, it became the anchor of the chapter they were all living — a reminder that even in the chaos of adolescence, some moments revealed truths too sharp to fade. Ty had revealed his truth that day, and Jerod had been forced to see it. The game would continue, of course, but the pieces were set. And Nico, always the watcher, would not forget the shape of the board as it stood.

The balance of power in the hallways was fragile, yes, but it was also undeniable. With every move, with every glance, the story deepened. And though Nico knew storms were still coming, he also knew that within the shifting pieces, there were players who understood the stakes better than anyone else. Ty most of all. And as long as he stood watch, the game — though dangerous — was not lost.

The word "shadows" had always meant something different to each of them. To Ty, it meant vigilance — the silent presence he carried with him wherever he went, watching, measuring, never allowing harm to move unseen. To Jerod, it was menace — the looming outline of a storm that crept into every corner he occupied, casting fear before his fists ever rose. And for Lisa, shadows were memories — inescapable stains from the night at the park that had carved itself into her bones. When she spoke of it, it was not loud, not meant to dramatise, but whispered with the kind of weight that silences a room more effectively than any shout.

It happened in fragments, late in the afternoon when the halls were half-empty, and the light from the high windows threw long streaks across the floor. Lisa leaned against the wall, her arms folded, her eyes fixed not on anyone in particular but on a space somewhere far away. The conversation had drifted naturally, the way things sometimes do when guards are lowered, and then, as if a dam cracked, she let it slip. Not all of it. Just enough. The park. The circle of kids. The hands that shoved, the laughter that burned. And then the sharp cut of truth that no one had fully admitted before: Jerod had been there.

The words dropped like a stone into water, sending ripples through the small group that stood within earshot. Ty did not flinch; he simply absorbed, his gaze steady, his breathing unchanged. He had suspected as much — Lisa's earlier warning about Jerod had carried too much conviction to be guesswork. But to hear it confirmed was different. It wasn't a matter of speculation anymore. It was history made present, the shadow of that night stretching directly into their hallway. For Ty, shadows could be studied, understood, confronted. For Harley, however, the revelation was fire.

The anger lit his face immediately. His fists clenched so tightly that the tendons in his wrists bulged, his chest rising and falling with the uneven force of breaths pulled too fast. His voice broke out, sharp and raw, demanding explanations, demanding revenge, demanding action in the way only Harley could — loud, forceful, unwilling to contain the storm inside him. To him, the shadows had names, and Jerod's was the clearest of all. It was not enough to know the truth; he wanted to tear into it, to make Jerod feel even a fraction of the terror Lisa had endured.

Ty moved before Harley could. His hand closed on his shoulder, firm but not cruel, a weight meant to steady rather than restrain. He knew Harley's type of rage — explosive, consuming, quick to destroy the one carrying it as much as the one it was directed at. He positioned himself in front of Harley, not as a shield but as a barrier to his fury, his voice calm and level. He didn't tell Harley to stop — that would have only fuelled the blaze. Instead, he told him to breathe. Simple words, spoken in a low rhythm, until the sharp edge of Harley's temper dulled enough for sense to return.

Lisa, watching, understood more than anyone what Harley was feeling. Her own eyes watered, but she shook her head at him, quietly refusing to let him fight her battles. "It doesn't matter," she whispered, her tone steady despite the tremor beneath. "Boy or girl, they'll get you if they want. That's what I learned that night." Her words weren't defeatist — they were a statement of reality, carved out of lived fear. She was not excusing Jerod, not forgiving him, but telling Harley that the fight wasn't his to wage, not in this way.

Still, Harley trembled under Ty's hand. His lips pressed thin, his jaw grinding as though his teeth were holding back the words his tongue wanted to throw into the air. Ty kept his hand firm, not squeezing, not forcing, but grounding him. His other hand hovered just slightly, a subtle readiness that Nico, standing nearby, caught immediately — the stance of someone who was prepared to intercept more than just anger if Jerod himself appeared. Ty wasn't reckless with his protection. He carried it like a discipline, one shadow cast against another.

Jerod's name hung in the air like a curse. The fact that he had been involved in Lisa's night of terror was not a secret that could be retracted, not a rumour that could be brushed aside. It was truth now, written in Lisa's voice, her eyes fixed on the floor as though she could still see the broken pavement of the park beneath her. Nico felt it too, the way the hall seemed colder, the way every passing footstep outside their circle suddenly sounded louder, as though the building itself recognised the shift in the story.

Ty asked nothing of Lisa in that moment. He didn't pry for details, didn't demand a retelling she clearly wasn't ready to give. Instead, he gave her silence — a silence that meant she had been heard, that her truth was enough without performance. That was the difference between Ty and the rest of them. He didn't need more to act. He already understood what shadows did when left unchecked: they spread. And Jerod's shadow had already stretched far enough.

Harley finally sagged, his fists loosening at his sides, his shoulders heaving with the release of a breath he hadn't realised he'd been holding. His anger hadn't gone, not fully, but Ty's presence anchored it, pulled it back from spilling over into something that would have left scars of its own. Lisa stepped closer, her hand brushing against Harley's arm, reminding him with her touch that her strength was her own, that she wasn't broken, even if Jerod had tried to make her feel that way.

The three of them stood in a triangle of unspoken resolve, each carrying a shadow of their own. Lisa's shadow was memory, raw and lingering. Harley's was rage, fierce and unyielding. Ty's was protection, disciplined and immovable. Nico saw it with clarity — how those shadows overlapped, how they stretched across the wall like shapes cast by a single unseen flame. Together, they were heavier than Jerod's menace, but only because Ty's steadiness held them together.

Jerod's presence loomed even without him being there. Everyone knew it now, though few dared say it aloud. His danger was no longer theoretical — it was carved into Lisa's scars, etched into Harley's fury, measured in Ty's discipline. The hallway felt different for it, a place where the shadows had names and the truth had finally stepped out of silence. Nico knew it would not end here. Shadows never did. They clung, they shifted, they followed. But at least now, they had been seen for what they were.

In the quiet that followed, Ty finally spoke, his words low enough that only Harley and Lisa could hear. "Shadows don't win unless you let them." It wasn't comfort, not a false promise. It was a truth, the kind Ty lived by, and one that Lisa needed more than sympathy. Harley's nod was stiff, reluctant, but real. Lisa's eyes shone with unshed tears, but she held her chin high. For that moment, the three of them weren't victims of shadows — they were the ones casting them.

The wall behind them stretched long with their silhouettes, tall and overlapping in the fading light. Nico, from his corner, held the picture in his mind like a memory worth keeping. The shadows on the wall told their story better than words: fear, anger, protection, and resolve, all bound into one shape. Jerod's shadow might have started it, but it would not be the only one remembered.

And so the title of the chapter took on its form — not abstract, not symbolic, but real and breathing. The shadows had been named, and in naming them, the first step toward their undoing had begun. For the first time since Jerod's arrival, Nico felt that even in the darkest stretches of the hallway, light could still carve outlines strong enough to fight back.

The school had grown quieter in ways that were not natural for the final weeks before summer. Usually by now, laughter spilled in waves down the corridors, voices lifted with the anticipation of freedom, the air heavy with the scent of grass carried in through open doors. But this year, the atmosphere was taut, strung too tight, every moment stretched thin like thread waiting to snap. Jerod's arrival had not been forgotten, nor had Lisa's truth. Both lived in the air like static, making even the sound of footsteps echo sharper than before. The waiting was not passive — it was a coil, wound and ready, though no one admitted aloud what they were waiting for.

Jerod had his own way of shaping the silence. His presence in the halls was enough to pull conversations shorter, to make eyes shift toward the ground, to pull teachers to their thresholds in wary glances. He never needed to strike first. His words, rough and vulgar, carried their own violence, a language that cut before hands ever lifted. The Principal's warnings had not softened him. Detentions only thickened the wall around him. Each new rule he ignored was a step closer to a breaking point everyone could sense but could not name.

Ty remained the counterbalance, though even his steady shadow could not erase the unease. He carried himself with the same calmness as always, but there was a sharpened edge to it now — the kind that comes when patience is measured against duty. His eyes followed Jerod without being obvious, his movements deliberate, his gestures controlled. To the casual observer, it might have seemed as though nothing had changed, but Nico noticed it. The stillness was not peace; it was readiness. Ty wasn't waiting for trouble. He was preparing for it.

Lisa's return had brightened the hallways, but even her presence could not completely dispel the tension. Her strength was visible, the scars unseen but deeply felt. She stood close to Harley now, walking beside him as though their pairing were armour forged from their differences. Yet she, too, understood the game being played. She had warned them all, her voice carrying the conviction of lived fear: Jerod was not a storm that passed without consequence. He was one that built quietly until the first strike tore everything open.

Harley, for his part, wore his fury beneath his skin like a second pulse. Ty's hand had steadied him once, but no one was certain it would work again if Jerod pushed too far. The thought lingered among them like a whispered rumour: what happens when Harley decides he cannot wait? He was not built for patience. Every day he walked the halls without exploding was a small miracle, a measure of restraint that could not last forever. His loyalty to Lisa was both anchor and fuel, and Jerod was tinder waiting for the spark.

Nico, the quietest of them, became the watcher of all watchers. He saw how the pieces aligned, how Ty's stillness played against Harley's volatility, how Lisa's resolve stood like glass — fragile in places, but shining with its own resilience. He even saw how Jerod thrived on the tension, feeding off the atmosphere like a predator scenting fear. Nico could not predict the exact moment of collision, but he knew it would come. Every story has a centre, and theirs was spiralling closer with each passing day.

Teachers noticed too, though they pretended otherwise. Their tones grew sharper during lessons, their eyes flicking toward Jerod with a frequency that betrayed their unease. Even the Principal's office seemed to hum with the anticipation of confrontation, as if the building itself could not stand still under the weight of what was coming. Students carried the same sense, though they expressed it in avoidance — choosing hallways that kept them out of Jerod's path, lowering their voices when he passed, watching the walls more than the people around them.

In those final days of the term, time seemed to bend strangely. Hours dragged in the classroom, every tick of the clock like the drag of a blade across stone, yet afternoons dissolved in a haze of restless energy. By the lockers, whispers curled like smoke, speculating not if but when. Some thought Harley would break first. Others placed their quiet certainty in Ty. A few even imagined Lisa would step forward again, her voice sharper than any teacher's authority. None of them considered the possibility that Jerod himself might spark the fire — but Nico knew better. Jerod was built for ignition.

Even moments of normalcy felt staged, as though everyone was acting in a play they didn't believe. A soccer game in the yard drew cheers, but eyes flicked toward the fence whenever Jerod wandered past. A joke in class earned laughter, but shoulders tensed the moment the door opened unexpectedly. Every smile was half-shadowed, every laugh tinged with restraint. The waiting game wasn't about silence; it was about how noise itself became dangerous.

Ty did not name it aloud, but his actions told the truth. He walked the halls with deliberate routes, placing himself where Jerod would not have full control of a crowd. He spoke to teachers in calm tones, giving advice disguised as casual observations. He trained after school, his martial arts sharper, his breathing slower, his discipline honed in preparation. To those who knew him best, it was clear — Ty was not planning for the possibility of confrontation. He was preparing for its inevitability.

Lisa carried her warning like a torch, never repeating it, but never needing to. The way she moved when Jerod entered a room, the way her jaw set when his laugh cut through the hall, told everyone what words could not. She didn't have to convince anyone of his danger anymore. They had seen it. They had felt it. The only question left was how far it would go before someone stopped it.

Harley's patience was stretched thinner with each day. He clung to Lisa's hand, his grip sometimes more forceful than he intended, his eyes tracking Jerod with a predator's focus. Ty noticed it, Nico noticed it, Lisa noticed it — but no one could undo it. The anger had been planted too deeply, fed by the truth Lisa had spoken aloud. The waiting game wasn't just between Jerod and Ty anymore. It was inside Harley himself, a battle between restraint and eruption.

Nico often thought of the shadows on the wall, the overlapping shapes that had defined their hallway days ago. Those shadows had lengthened, darker now, stretching far across the tiles. They weren't just reminders of what had been revealed; they were promises of what was still to come. He didn't know who would strike first, but he knew the wall would not stay empty for long.

So the days closed one after another, each ending with the same lingering quiet. No fists yet. No shouts that shook the windows. Just silence, heavy and full, pressed down on them like the weight of an unseen storm. It was not peace. It was not safety. It was the edge of something they all recognised but refused to name aloud.

The chapter itself ended on that silence — no resolution, no false calm, only the certainty that waiting had an end, and it was drawing closer with every step Jerod took down the hall. The waiting game was not about patience anymore. It was about bracing for the sound of the first break, the first crack in the wall that would open the flood none of them could contain.

## CHAPTER 5: THE OLD WOUNDS OF LEO AND ALEX

The bell had not yet finished its echo when I asked our class to sit closer, not because I am in charge but because today is not like the others. Leo stood by the windows with his hands folded as though the glass could steady him, and Alex kept his eyes on the floor like the tiles were reading back his thoughts. I told them both I would start, and then I breathed so the words would land where they should. "We are going to talk about who we used to be," I said, and I meant all of us, not just the two who agreed to speak. The room made a small hush that felt older than our grade, older than the posters that tell us to be kind and then forget to watch. I did not turn this into a lesson; I turned it into a doorway. "When I'm finished," I said, "Leo and Alex will take their turn, and we are going to let the truth sit where it belongs."

I reminded them that we are two months out from summer, which is when people like to pretend the school year can be folded away clean. That is not how it works, and you know it; whatever we do not face now will follow us to the bus stop and climb aboard like it paid a fare. I said this gently because gentleness keeps people from hiding, but I did not cover the hard edges. "You already know how words break a person," I said, and a few faces changed because last year's book taught us that much. "Today is about what hands can do, and what eyes can dare, and what a hallway can become when nobody thinks to stand." I did not raise my voice. I raised the meaning.

Leo lifted his chin and gave me a nod that said I could go one step farther. "You see Leo the way he is now," I told the class, "but I have the map of who he was before he came home to us." I said "home" because that is the only word that makes sense when a brother is pulled out of the storm and kept warm on purpose. I did not decorate it with sorrow; Leo does not need charity, he needs truth. "He learned cruelty the way other children learn scales for a piano," I said, and Leo's mouth moved as if he were counting each note. "But he is here to put the instrument down and tell you what the noise cost." The room did not shrink away. It leaned in.

Alex stood beside him, not shoulder to shoulder but near enough to prove he would not run from himself. "If you want to know how gaslighting sounds," I said, "ask Alex how he made people question their own feet." Alex gave a small, dry laugh that did not hide, and then he pressed his palm flat against the desk to show it would not shake. I told the class that Alex once turned apologies into tools and silence into a leash. I told them he could shape a story until the victim thought they had written it. No one interrupted. Interruptions are what fear does when it is frightened of finishing the sentence.

I said Harley's name next, and every head moved a little, not in worry but in habit, the way a field turns toward the wind. "He is listening," I told them, "and he is safe to listen because he is not the bad guy here anymore." Harley had come through the door without swagger, and he took a chair by the far wall where the light makes soft edges. His smile was quiet and did not pretend to be anything else. He has had nights that do not sleep, and mornings that ask for courage at the sink. Lisa came in after him and stood behind his chair, not to guard him but to share the place where she now stands. I did not call them examples. I called them proof.

Because someone would wonder, I said it plain: "Jerod is the one causing harm." I said it without heat so no one could mistake anger for a plan. Jerod is not in this grade, but the grade above does not make him taller where it matters. His name has been turning up where bruises turn up, and in the spaces where laughter stops too fast. I told the class we are not here to judge him before the sun goes down; we are here to keep the sun from setting on the same injuries again. "There is a difference between a person and a pattern," I said. "Today we break the pattern." The desks felt less like barriers and more like anchors.

"Before Leo speaks," I told them, "I want you to know why he trusts me to hold the first thread." Leo is my brother by adoption, but the paperwork did not teach us how to belong; the hugs did, and the dinners, and the way we say goodnight with both arms. I said, "When I hug him, it means I love you," because that is what it means, no secret code, no performance. Those hugs are a harbour, and harbours do not brag when storms turn away. Leo's breath evened out while I spoke, not because I protected him but because love steadies a man better than armour. "We will not decorate the past," I said. "We will put it on the table and look it in the face."

I reminded everyone of the library morning when Mr. Clark told the truth about Myles, and how the truth changed the air in our hallways. I did not retell it; I carried its weight forward like a banner we are not permitted to drop. The point was not to make the room cry; the point was to make the room ready. Ready for Leo to say what his hands once did and what his voice once broke. Ready for Alex to admit how he trained the doubt in other people's eyes. Ready for Harley and Lisa to sit still while the past is named and the present is set in order. The clock on the wall sounded like a reminder, not a threat.

I set simple rules and called them courtesies because that is what they are. We do not clap when someone admits the worst thing they have done, because applause confuses the wound. We do not whisper to the person beside us, because whispers make a person stand alone when they have just come in from the cold. We keep our eyes on the speaker so the speaker knows they are not in a dark room. We welcome silence when it arrives, and we do not race to fill it. We breathe like people who plan to be brave for more than a minute. Then I nodded to Leo.

He did not begin with excuses. He began with a time and a place, the way a map begins with a north arrow. He said there was a boy who dropped his books, and he made a joke that the boy still remembers. He said he enjoyed the way the laugh made the air throb, and he hated himself for enjoying it only much later. He told us how he learned to tilt a story until the guilty person looked like a mirror. He told us how quickly a crowd becomes a useable tool if you're willing to waste it. I kept my mouth closed and let the sentences stand on their own feet.

Alex took the thread without my asking and tied it to his own. He said he liked the feeling of being the smartest person in the room even when he was wrong. He said he could edit a memory with three words and a tilted eyebrow. He said he discovered how to turn kindness into a lever by making it rare. He admitted that he pushed Leo into becoming harder, then watched his reflection and felt the awful truth of it. He called it wicked, and he did not flinch from the word. The room had no coughs in it.

I spoke again only to keep the doors open. "If any of this sounds familiar," I said, "it is because cruelty repeats itself like a song on a broken player." I did not point, and I did not scan the faces for confessions. That is not how trust is built. I said gaslighting is not a clever word; it is a theft of reality, and that is worse than a bruise because a bruise knows where it hurts. I said manipulation smiles while it arranges your feet where it wants them. I said intimidation can be silent and still count as shouting. The pencils on our desks looked like small, straight promises.

Lisa stepped forward, not to steal the floor but to confirm it. She said, "I used to hit first and decide later," and it moved through the room like a cold wind that belonged here. She told how she learned to keep her face calm so teachers would believe anything she said. She said there were days when she respected no one, including herself, and those days were the easiest to ruin someone else's morning. She admitted she liked the moment a target understood who held the leash. Then she looked at Harley and said, "That isn't me anymore," and her voice had the weight of a sworn oath. Harley did not smile. He bowed his head a fraction, which is sometimes stronger.

I named what the class could see so they would not miss it. "People can change," I said, "but change is not a costume; it is a scar." Leo has them, Alex has them, and Lisa does too, though not all of them live on skin. The scar, I told them, is the proof that something cut you once and you refused to keep bleeding. We are not here to praise the cut. We are here to praise the stopping. If Jerod ever stands in this room to do the same, we will make a chair for him. Until then, we will make a wall where he expects a door.

I spoke of witnesses, because truth needs them, and of timing, because rescue has a clock. I said when hands go up in the back of a yard and nobody sees, that is the school's failure, not the victim's shame. I said walking away is noble only if the danger walks away too. If it follows, then someone must step in, the way adults are paid to do and students are brave enough to try. I told them Mr. Clark has not forgotten Myles because forgetting would be a second death. We are not repeating that lesson here. We are building the memory into policy.

Leo cleared his throat and asked to add one more piece, and I waved him forward with my palm open. He said the worst part of being a bully is how easy it becomes to treat people like furniture. Move them, sit on them, ignore them, kick them by accident and call it clumsy. He said the second worst part is how long it takes to admit that is what you did. He thanked the class for not flinching while he took the lid off. He said if any of them needed to name a hurt, he would stand there and listen without defence. Alex said, "Me too," and it sounded like a plank laid across a gap.

I drew the room back to the present so nobody got lost in the past. "We are not here to write apologies on the board and call it solved," I told them. "We are here to make certain the halls do not become a place where smiles go to die." I said the title of our work out loud because names are anchors. "When a smile breaks," I said, "we treat that like a siren." We do not ask the smile to fix itself. We bring tape, and hands, and yes, sometimes we bring the kind of defence that stops a fist mid-flight. Even then, we step back the second safety returns. That is the rule Ty taught us and the rule we keep.

I looked at Harley then, because he earned the truth as much as anyone. He has been the storm and he has been the shelter, and he knows the cost of both. He did not shift in his chair when I said his name; he let it sit in the air like a weight he can now carry. Lisa's fingers brushed the back of his shoulder the way a lighthouse touches water. Neither of them needed to speak. Their silence said: we are not hiding, and we are not finished learning. That is all any of us can promise in a place like this.

I ended my part the way you close a gate you plan to open again. "You have heard enough from me," I said. "Now you are going to hear from the two who knew how to break people and chose to stop." I told them to keep their eyes up and their hearts steady. I told them to take notes if words needed a place to land. I told them not to fear the tears that sometimes come when truth gets told with both hands. Then I sat, because that is what you do when the floor belongs to someone else. And I nodded to Leo, because beginnings deserve a witness.

I will not decorate it for you. The first time I mocked someone, there was no grand reason, no wound to avenge, no noble story hiding behind my tongue. I did it because I could, because the room was noisy and I knew how to make the noise point in one direction. A boy dropped his binder and the papers burst like birds, and I laughed a split second before anyone else so my laugh became the cue. That is all it took—half a heartbeat—to claim authorship of the moment. I said something small and sharp about clumsy hands, and the class smiled as if I had handed out permission slips. He bent to gather the pages, and I stood a little taller, astonished by how easy it was to move the air with nothing but a smirk. Power can be a whisper; the room hears it anyway.

You want to know why it snowballed; it begins with the applause you cannot hear. It happens when the teacher doesn't look up, when the clock decides not to tick, when your friends glance over with that quick approval that says, do it again. I learned that cruelty does not require volume; it only requires timing. I began to speak a fraction before the moment arrived, shaping the laugh the way a conductor lifts a hand before the first note. A raised eyebrow became a lever; a shrug became a verdict; an eye-roll became a stamp. None of it left a bruise you could see. All of it left a mark you could feel. I told myself it was harmless because no one cried in front of me.

After that I started choosing my scenes like a director. I picked doorways where a person had to squeeze past me, not because I needed the space but because authority likes tidy lines and I knew how to stand just off centre. I learned that a shoulder can say "move" without touching, that a sigh can say "you don't belong" without a word. I ran little experiments: a joke on Monday, a nickname on Tuesday, a correction on Wednesday that sounded helpful but wasn't. By Thursday the group would repeat my cadence for me, which is how you know you've stolen the room. By Friday the target would plan their path around desks as if I had laid ropes on the floor. I pretended not to notice. I noticed everything.

Gaslighting arrived like a tool I had always owned but never named. I discovered that if I denied the obvious with enough calm, I could make a person rehearse their memory until it came apart. "That didn't happen," I would say inside a larger sentence—never alone, always tucked into something that sounded reasonable. "You're taking it the wrong way," I would add, and then I would tilt my head as if I were the patient one. If they pushed back, I called it drama; if they retreated, I called it maturity. Either way, I won the headline. I learned to force people to ask me what I meant when I knew exactly what I meant. The worst part is how quickly it became fluent.

I lied by subtraction more than by invention. I left out the nudge before the stumble, the stare before the mistake, the dare before the poor decision. Adults love a simple report, and I became very good at offering one. "We were just joking," I'd say, and that word "we" was a net I threw over the crowd so no one would want to cut free. I learned to put compliments in front of insults so teachers heard the compliments twice. I learned to speak softly when I was most at fault, because softness is the liar's armour. If you measure harm only by volume, you will never catch someone like I used to be.

It did not feel like evil. That is important for you to understand. It felt like competence, like being quick with the right line, like walking down the centre of the hallway because you know where you belong. I told myself I was teaching weaker kids to be tougher, that my jabs were practice for the world outside the brick walls. I even dressed it up as honesty: better they hear the truth from me than from someone cruel. The mind is good at furnishing excuses when the rent is paid in attention. I paid that rent every day and called it earned. The boy from the first day stopped making eye contact. I named that progress.

When you get good at manipulation, kindness becomes a ration card you stamp for effect. I could turn friendly in a breath and the room would sigh with relief, which made my next turn of the screw easier. I offered help with homework that I had no intention of giving; I offered seats I didn't surrender; I offered advice that pivoted to embarrassment at the punch line. By then I knew how to make an audience complicit—lower the voice, widen the eyes, share the secret. People want to be near the current because the current feels like life. I used that want like a handle. And when someone asked if we had gone too far, I made them feel greedy for even asking.

Physical intimidation is not all fists. It is posture and placement and pretending you don't see who is trying to pass. I practised the slow step that forces someone else to stop. I stood an inch closer than courtesy allows and called it friendly. In gym, I brushed shoulders harder than the game required and apologised louder than sincerity allows so the teacher would hear my performance. I did not push first; I engineered second pushes. I claimed accidents like a collector. I slept well, which is the most terrifying sentence I can offer you from that season of my life.

The first time I saw fear land because of me, it made my stomach turn—but I misread the reason. I thought the turn was thrill; it was shame knocking. I told myself the boy deserved it for being slow, the girl for being proud, the group for being gullible. I baptised my own behaviour with their imagined faults. I wrote private scripture: if people get hurt by small things, they will never survive the large ones; I am training them. This is how a lie dresses as a favour. This is how you forget that training is supposed to build, not break.

You are wondering where the adults were. Some were right there, doing the impossible arithmetic of thirty needs and one voice. Some were tired, and I built my small empire in the gaps between their blinks. A few noticed and pulled me aside, and I performed contrition like a seasoned actor until the bell freed us both. "You're a leader," one told me, and I wore the word like armour. If leadership means deciding who gets to breathe easy, then yes, I was one. The title kept me from looking in a mirror for longer than I will admit.

You want the moment it began to change; I owe you that. It did not start in a speech or a punishment. It started in a tiny hallway where Jeremy put his arms around me for no reason at all. There was no audience to impress, no bargain to strike, no deal to close. He didn't say "I've got you." He said "I love you," and he said it with his ribs and his breath and his warm, ridiculous insistence that I was worth more than the noise I could make. A person who intends to control you does not offer that kind of contact. My body knew the difference before my mind did.

At home the weather was fists made into words and words made into rules. You learn obedience to storms when storms decide whether dinner is quiet. You learn how to read the room by morning light, how to fold your rage into a pocket and call it a coin for later use. I carried those coins to school and spent them where I could get change. That is not an excuse; it is a map. If you have lived under thunder, you come to believe the only way to be safe is to become a little thunder yourself. The lie tastes like safety because it tastes like home.

The snowball did not look like a snowball while it rolled. It looked like a clever morning, a good comeback, a crowd gathered not by force but by orbit. I told myself I was simply better at the game everyone was playing. The snowball grows because it gives you small rewards every few feet—laughter here, deference there, the teacher who trusts your version first. By the time you notice the hill, the mass is heavy enough to flatten whoever stands in front of it. I built that weight with grins and shrugs. The crash was inevitable. I would like to tell you I jumped out of the way; the truth is Jeremy pulled me.

# THE SMILE THAT BROKE

Shame is a better teacher than pride, but only if you let it speak. At first I tried to silence it by doubling down. If a joke stung, I made another. If a face fell, I rolled my eyes harder. You escalate not because you are brave but because you are frightened of the quiet where your name might be called. My turning began the day Ty looked at me like a man who has measured worse storms and still chooses a door over a wall. He told me what defence is supposed to look like. I had been practising offence and calling it preparation. I had been wrong.

You ask about the first apology; I did not deliver it well. I tried to make it clever, which is to say I tried to keep control even while giving ground. The boy I had nicknamed nodded like a person humours a child, and I felt smaller than I had ever felt while towering over a joke. That is when it struck me that every laugh I had collected was borrowed. It could be returned in a heartbeat, and I would be left holding nothing but the bill. I went home and stared at the ceiling and finally understood what interest means.

What did it cost the others? I cannot measure it, but I can name the shapes. Some began to speak less, which is a kind of theft. Some changed their routes, which is a kind of leash. Some learned to smile before they felt like it, which is a kind of bruise that never shows. I did that to them with ordinary tools any of us can reach for: timing, tone, and the hunger to be taller without growing. If you see yourself in my sentences, do not flinch away. Flinching is how the next cruelty finds room.

So here is the first confession, the one that matters: I liked the feeling of control more than I liked being a person. I built a version of myself that could not love anything he could not arrange. I was not a monster; monsters are rare and easy to spot. I was a boy who discovered leverage and mistook it for worth. I cannot undo the mornings I rehearsed other people's hurt into a routine. I can put my hand up now and say, I did it, and I will not do it again.

And here is the second confession, which is not an excuse but a ledger entry: I did not stop because someone shamed me in public. I stopped because someone loved me in private, and love made the power taste stale. Jeremy's hugs are not strategies; they are declarations. Ty's steadiness is not theatre; it is law. I stand here with my mouth telling the truth because their lives left me no believable lie to step into. If you are carrying a snowball down the hill, the only honourable work is to let it melt in your hands and accept the cold. Then you start sweeping the path you ruined, one plank at a time.

I am not going to stand here and make my story sound smaller than it is. If Leo tells you he mocked others because it gave him control, then I must tell you that I mocked him because it gave me something colder—satisfaction. I wasn't just another bully in the crowd; I was the one who decided Leo's own armour had cracks, and I was the boy who pressed my fingers into them until they split. The irony is hard to swallow now: he and I wore the same mask, yet I found it easier to spit on his than to look at my own. I knew his jokes before he told them, and I cut his voice short with sharper ones. I saw the relief on his victims when I turned my blade on him instead. But it wasn't kindness that moved me; it was vanity. I wanted to prove that even the loudest bully could be silenced.

The first time I called him out in front of others, it was not premeditated. He had delivered a line about someone's walk, slow and slouched, and the laugh was circling back to him like a boomerang. I interrupted with, "Better than your crooked grin," and the class broke into a new kind of laughter, the kind that stings the giver instead of the receiver. That was the day I discovered I didn't have to be quick to wound—only crueler. The look in his eyes then was a mix of disbelief and fury, and I carried it with me like a trophy. For weeks I hunted him in the hallways with that same crooked-grin line, reshaping it, sharpening it, making sure no day passed without the reminder. The crowd loved it, and I loved the crowd's love.

I will not pretend my words were harmless. Words are heavier than fists because they leave echoes. A bruise fades, but a phrase is portable; it follows you into your dreams, it leans over your shoulder in the mirror. I knew that, even then. I saw the way Leo's smile faltered when he was not on stage, the way he checked the room before speaking, measuring whether I might be nearby. My words became his leash, and I yanked it whenever I pleased. I told myself it was balance—that he deserved what he had given others. But balance was a lie; I enjoyed the spectacle of power turned against itself. That enjoyment made me worse than him.

I discovered that humiliation carries more weight than pain. I could flatten him with a sentence while he still thought of a comeback. If he raised his voice, I lowered mine, and the room leaned in to hear me, not him. If he tried to laugh, I made the laughter brittle by pointing at the crack. He grew angrier, and anger made him clumsier, which fed my arsenal. I did not need fists because I had rhythm and diction, and both are weapons if you decide to use them that way. Watching him stumble under words was like watching a man sink in shallow water—everyone can see he is drowning, but no one knows how to throw a rope.

Teachers saw the arguments but rarely the precision. They saw two boys trading remarks, not one boy carving the other open by inches. I made sure my insults were wrapped in plausible cloth: "just teasing," "just friends," "just playing around." That word "just" is poison—it minimizes cruelty until it sounds edible. I handed it out so often that adults repeated it for me. Every time they said, "It's just words," I smiled. They had no idea they were sharpening my knives for me.

There is no pride in telling you that I perfected the art of isolating him. I made him feel ridiculous in front of people who once admired him. When he mocked others, I mocked his mockery. When he strutted, I pointed out the limp in his posture that wasn't even there. I made him question the ground beneath his shoes. It is easy to destroy a bully's confidence; they depend on it like oxygen. What I didn't expect was how much damage I was doing to myself in the process. Each cut I made on him was mirrored inside me, though I ignored the bleeding.

What made it worse was that I knew where to strike because I shared his scars. I knew what it was to feel small at home, to hear the walls shake with voices that should have been calm. I knew what it was to wake with a jaw tight from grinding teeth all night. And still, I chose to use that knowledge not for solidarity but for sabotage. I weaponized our similarities to magnify his suffering. That is cruelty in its most deliberate form: seeing yourself in another and deciding to wound them where you are already wounded.

We fought once, not with fists but with silence. He stopped talking when I entered a room, and I let the silence hang like smoke. Students noticed, teachers noticed, but no one intervened. They thought it was rivalry, a typical boyish contest. It wasn't. It was me squeezing the last breath from his sense of authority. I made his silence my applause, and I mistook the emptiness it left in me for victory.

Looking back, the worst thing I ever said was not the sharpest insult or the loudest mock. It was quiet. It was when I leaned toward him in the middle of lunch and whispered, "They laugh at you, not with you." That sentence drained him faster than any public humiliation. His eyes dimmed in real time, and I pretended I was proud of myself. But later, lying in bed, the echo of that whisper returned, and for the first time I wondered if I had crossed a line that couldn't be uncrossed.

When Jeremy came into the picture, he didn't take sides. He didn't crown me victor or victim. He stood between us and forced the silence into something else—a pause, not a punishment. The day he hugged Leo, I saw the difference between possession and love. My words had possessed Leo; Jeremy's arms loved him. I realised then that I had never offered love to anyone without attaching strings. That realisation hurt worse than any insult I had ever delivered.

Ty watched me too. I could feel his eyes the way a man feels a shadow at his back. He never accused, never mocked, but I sensed the quiet judgment that came with his patience. It unsettled me more than Leo's anger ever had. Leo could fight me with noise; Ty fought me with stillness. And in that stillness, I started to hear the cruelty of my own voice. Silence became my mirror, and I did not like what I saw reflected.

I tried to excuse myself with stories about home, about hardship, about survival. But excuses are scaffolding for a house that should never have been built. The truth is, I bullied Leo because it was easy, because it distracted me from my own pain, because cruelty is a quick currency in a world that feels bankrupt. I am telling you now so no one else has to bear the weight of my denial.

Leo and I were two halves of the same wound, tearing each other open to keep from healing. I thought making him smaller would make me larger; it only made the room colder. I thought silencing him would make me heard; it only made the echoes sharper. And when I finally understood that, I had to face the shame of admitting I had not just bullied others—I had bullied the one person who might have understood me best.

If you want to know why words cut deeper than fists, listen to the silence that follows them. Fists bruise flesh; words bruise memory. Flesh heals quicker. Memory carries scars for decades. Leo bears mine. And I, in turn, bear his. This is the knot we tied together, the knot we must untangle aloud if we want anyone else to be free of it.

So here I stand, not excusing, not disguising, but confessing: I was his bully, and I was proud of it then. I am ashamed of it now. And if my words once carved him open, let these words stitch a little of him back. Let the scar remain, because scars remind us of our failures. But let no more wounds come from me. I will not be the boy with knives for teeth anymore. I will be something else. Someone who chooses to speak life instead of carving death into another's day. That is my confession, and it burns to say it. But fire cleans, and I am tired of living in the smoke of what I once set ablaze.

Gaslighting, Leo said, was never about the shove in the hallway or the laughter that followed a cruel remark. Those things stung, yes, but they healed. What did not heal so easily was the bending of reality until another child no longer trusted their own eyes or ears. He explained to the class that he could make a boy trip over a desk, laugh about it, and when that boy told a teacher what had happened, Leo would insist he had imagined it. "You're clumsy," he would say, with such calmness that the victim began to believe it. That was the weapon: not fists, not strength, but certainty. Whoever held the most certainty in their voice became the one others believed, and Leo wielded that certainty like a shield. He could paint the victim as clumsy, weak, or oversensitive, and the teachers—too busy, too distracted—would nod in agreement.

Alex followed by admitting his own tactics were worse. He didn't just deny an action; he created an alternate story so convincing that others doubted themselves. If he broke a pencil that wasn't his, he would insist the owner had done it first. If he shoved Leo, he'd claim Leo had tripped on his own. He learned to layer lies so thickly that the truth was smothered. The victim's voice became quieter because it no longer seemed reliable. "The trick," Alex explained, "wasn't to make someone believe me. The trick was to make them doubt themselves." He told the room that once a person doubts their own memory, their own worth, it becomes easier to control them. The silence in the room as he spoke was heavy—students shifted uncomfortably in their chairs, because they recognised the echo of such tactics in their own lives.

Jeremy leaned forward at that point, making sure the weight of the lesson sank in. He told the students that gaslighting is not always loud or violent. It often arrives disguised as concern, as a friend's reassurance, or as a joke that goes too far. He reminded them that when someone insists, "It didn't happen that way" again and again, they are not always correcting—they may be erasing. And erasure of truth, he warned, is a dangerous theft. He told the children to trust the memories that make their hearts pound, because those are the ones bullies try hardest to erase. When the class nodded, Jeremy pressed further: "Gaslighting," he said, "is a bully's most dangerous weapon, because it doesn't just bruise your body—it rewires your mind."

Leo described how he would use the smallest mistakes to prove his point. If a boy mispronounced a word in class, Leo would mock him for hours, then later insist he had never mocked him at all. The child would question himself, thinking, Maybe I'm too sensitive. That small seed of doubt grew into a forest of silence. Alex added that when they did this often enough, children stopped reporting it, stopped trusting teachers, and sometimes stopped speaking altogether. "That," Alex admitted, "was the moment I knew I had broken someone's spirit. Not when they cried. Not when they yelled. But when they stopped trying." He looked at the floor after saying it, the shame written across his face.

Jeremy pointed out to the class that bullies use gaslighting to isolate their targets. If a victim questions their own memory, they stop reaching for help. He warned the students to be careful when they hear someone repeat, "You're overreacting," or, "You're too sensitive." Those are not always harmless phrases—they are tools to dismiss pain. He said if they ever feel like their truth is slipping away under someone else's words, they should anchor it by speaking to someone they trust. "Because truth is heavy," he said, "but lies are heavier, and bullies will always try to make you carry both."

Leo confessed that he sometimes felt like a puppeteer. By twisting stories, he could make classmates turn on one another, and he never had to lift a hand. "I didn't even need to throw a punch," he said, "because I could make someone else believe they deserved one." His voice cracked as he admitted it, the cruelty of those words echoing back against him. Alex, too, said he could ruin friendships with a single whispered lie. He could tell one boy that another had insulted him, and when the fight began, Alex stood back, clean and untouched, while his lie did the work.

Gaslighting was not about power, Jeremy explained—it was about control. Power fades when you leave the playground, but control lingers. He told the students how damaging it is when someone makes you question whether you're worthy of kindness. That wound does not fade quickly. Jeremy warned that when you allow someone to twist your reality, you lose pieces of yourself, and reclaiming them takes years. He looked around the room at the faces of children who had perhaps already felt that theft, and he said gently, "You are not crazy. You are not too sensitive. You are not overreacting. Those words are lies meant to keep you quiet."

The students grew restless, shifting in their seats, because they understood now that the battlefield wasn't the playground but the mind. One girl raised her hand to ask if laughing along to avoid embarrassment counted as giving in. Jeremy told her that sometimes laughing is survival, but survival should not be mistaken for agreement. He said it was never too late to speak the truth afterward. Leo added that he once heard a classmate laugh with him only to see the same classmate's eyes fill with tears later. That memory haunted him, he confessed, because he realised laughter can hide pain but cannot erase it.

Alex admitted he used the same method at home. He would deny breaking a rule so strongly that his parents doubted themselves. "Maybe we didn't tell him," they'd whisper, second-guessing their own authority. Gaslighting, he explained, doesn't just hurt peers—it corrodes trust between parent and child, teacher and student. It makes everyone question what is real. He said it was the ugliest part of himself, and speaking it aloud made him feel exposed, but also relieved.

Jeremy closed the section firmly, telling the class that they must never underestimate words. "A fist can make you stumble, but gaslighting can make you lose yourself entirely," he said. He urged them to remember that truth needs no rehearsal; lies always do. And if someone repeats a lie often enough, it begins to sound rehearsed. He warned the students to pay attention to patterns, because repetition is the mark of manipulation.

The silence after his words was profound. Students were not only thinking of their classmates; they were thinking of their own homes, their own families, their own lives. They recognised gaslighting not as a distant term but as something that lurked in familiar shadows. Some shifted uncomfortably; others stared straight ahead, unwilling to meet Jeremy's eyes.

Leo finished with a final confession: "Gaslighting was my favourite weapon, because I didn't get caught. But it was also the weapon that made me the most ashamed, because it didn't just hurt someone—it erased them." Alex nodded, agreeing that the scars of lies are far deeper than those of fists. Jeremy reminded them that this was why they were speaking today—to drag such hidden cruelties into the light where they could no longer thrive. The students were left with a truth that would not easily be forgotten: that the mind, not the body, is the true battlefield of bullying. And on that battlefield, the sharpest blade is not a fist, not a shove, but the deliberate twisting of truth itself.

Leo began this part of the talk with his voice lower, as if ashamed to even shape the words. He said the cruelest weapon he had ever used was not his fist, not even his lies, but his smile. A smile, he explained, could be sharper than a blade when wielded the wrong way. He recalled how he would sit beside a boy at lunch, offering a bite of his sandwich or an invitation to play soccer, pretending warmth that was never there. The victim would light up, thinking they had finally found a friend, and that glow of trust was exactly what Leo wanted. He admitted he felt powerful knowing he could raise someone's spirits just to break them later. The betrayal that followed was not just humiliation—it was demolition of trust.

The class listened in silence as Leo described how he once lured a quiet boy into his circle by calling him "brother" in front of others. For a week, that boy believed he was included. Then, when enough classmates were watching, Leo turned on him, ridiculing his shoes, mocking his speech, and laughing until others joined in. The boy walked away crushed, and Leo still remembered the way his shoulders bent under the weight of that betrayal. "That," he admitted, "was worse than any shove. I built him up so I could watch him collapse." The shame in his voice was heavy, and he did not hide it.

Alex nodded slowly before adding that he did the same, often with even less conscience at the time. He confessed that he enjoyed pretending to care about someone because it gave him access to their secrets. Once those secrets were shared, Alex weaponised them. He would spread whispers about crushes, fears, or mistakes, ensuring that when he finally mocked the person, the insult cut deeper because it was personal. He told the class that the cruelest laughter is the laughter born from betrayal, and he had caused plenty of it. He lowered his head when he said it, because even now he could see the faces of the children he had tricked.

Jeremy made sure the students understood: manipulation in friendship is not harmless joking. It is a trap. He told them that false friendship is dangerous because it weakens a person twice—first by opening them up, and second by slamming the door shut in their face. He said that a bruise may fade in a week, but humiliation born from betrayal can last a lifetime. He reminded them that real friendship is proven not by words or smiles but by consistency, by the way someone treats you when no one is watching. "A true friend doesn't disappear when laughter comes at your expense," he said firmly.

Leo went further, admitting he sometimes played the long game. He would act kind for weeks, building trust, then choose the perfect moment to humiliate his "friend" in front of others. It was not just cruelty; it was performance. He treated betrayal like a stage play, with the victim as the main act. The audience, he admitted bitterly, often cheered. That laughter, he said, made him feel invincible. Only later, as he grew older, did he realise that every cheer was hollow and every joke poisoned his own spirit. The applause of cruelty, he confessed, was nothing more than an echo of emptiness.

Alex said he once had a boy tell him, "You're my best friend," and instead of honouring that trust, he used it as a setup. Days later, he mocked the boy publicly, repeating something he had been told in confidence. The boy looked at him not with anger but with heartbreak. That moment haunted Alex more than any punch he had ever thrown. "It's one thing to make someone mad," he said, "but it's another to break their heart." The room shifted with unease; students glanced at each other, thinking of their own friendships and wondering who truly stood beside them.

Jeremy paused then, letting the silence work. He told the students that betrayal disguised as friendship is why some children stop trusting altogether. He warned them not to mistake friendliness for friendship, because the two are not the same. A bully can be friendly when it suits them, but a friend will never disappear when you need them most. "If you feel like someone only smiles at you when others are watching," he said, "be careful. That smile may not be meant for you—it may be meant for the show."

Leo admitted that sometimes the manipulation was subtle. He would give a compliment and follow it with an insult, confusing his target. "Nice shirt," he would say, "too bad it looks like your grandma's curtains." The victim would not know whether to smile or frown, caught between hope and humiliation. That, Leo said, was the point—to keep them off balance. Alex added that he too would dangle kindness like bait, offering it in one breath and stealing it away in the next. This unpredictability, he confessed, made children cling even harder, desperate for the rare moments of real kindness. It was a cruel cycle, and they both knew it.

Jeremy leaned into this point, warning that fake friendship can sometimes feel addictive. A victim will hold onto even scraps of kindness because they are starved for it, not realising those scraps are poisoned. He urged the students to guard their hearts against such games. "A real friend doesn't make you guess," he said. "They don't confuse you with kindness one day and cruelty the next. That's not friendship—that's manipulation." The nods across the room showed his words were understood.

Alex looked across the classroom and admitted that he used to study his classmates like a hunter. He knew who was desperate to belong and who could be tempted with a smile. Those were the ones he targeted, because their trust was easy to earn. He spoke with regret, saying he now understood how dangerous it is to treat someone's hunger for friendship as a weakness. "It wasn't their weakness," he said, "it was my cruelty." His voice trembled when he said it, because the truth of his past finally stung him as much as it had stung his victims.

Leo added that sometimes he manipulated teachers as well. He would sit beside a lonely student during class so that adults thought he was kind. The teachers praised him, which only made the eventual betrayal sting more for the victim. He admitted this gave him a rush, because he had fooled not just a child but an adult too. The students gasped at this, realising that betrayal can extend far beyond peers—it can corrupt the trust of authority figures as well.

Jeremy told them that false friendship is especially cruel because it robs a person of the very thing they need most: trust. He reminded the children that trust is not just about believing someone—it is about feeling safe enough to be yourself. When that safety is shattered, it is difficult to rebuild. He urged them to remember that no smile is worth the price of their dignity. "If a friend makes you doubt yourself," he said, "they are not a friend at all."

The lesson grew heavier as Leo recalled how he used to enjoy watching someone's face crumble when he turned on them. "The worst part," he admitted, "is that I thought it was funny." He looked at the class with eyes that seemed older than his years, eyes that carried the weight of too many wrong choices. Alex, sitting beside him, nodded in agreement. "I thought so too," he whispered, almost ashamed to raise his voice. The two of them sat in silence for a moment, united in their regret.

Jeremy broke that silence by reminding the class why they were listening. "We are not telling these stories to glorify them," he said. "We are telling them so you will see the traps before you fall into them. So you will know the difference between a friend who stands beside you and a bully who pretends." His words landed with the weight of a promise.

The students sat straighter now, recognising the difference between the warm laughter of true friendship and the cold laughter of betrayal. They realised that smiles can deceive, but truth never does. The lesson of that moment was clear: manipulation in friendship is no friendship at all, and those who wield it only betray themselves in the end.

Leo leaned back slightly, his arms folded, as if his body itself was ready to demonstrate the lesson he was about to give. He told the class that sometimes he never needed to lift a hand. A glance, a tilt of his head, or the way he stepped into someone's space could silence them more effectively than a slap ever could. He admitted that he had perfected the art of looming—standing just a little too close, towering over a smaller child until their back touched the wall, forcing them to shrink without a word spoken. It wasn't the strike that mattered, he explained, but the possibility of it, the silent threat that hung in the air like a storm cloud.

He described how a hallway could be turned into a stage. By walking down the centre with his shoulders broad and his stride deliberate, he forced others to press themselves against the lockers, giving him the right of way. It was theatre, he confessed, a show of dominance designed to remind everyone that he was the one in control. No punches were thrown, but dignity was bruised every time someone stepped aside. The memory made him wince now, but at the time, it felt like victory.

Alex followed, his voice carrying its own weight. He admitted that he was worse in some ways, because he knew how to make sudden movements—jerking his fist forward, only to stop inches from a face. He laughed then, bitterly, not at the memory but at the cruelty of his own satisfaction. He said he liked the way children flinched, the way their eyes widened, because that reaction gave him power without consequence. No teacher could punish him for a punch that never landed, but the fear it created was punishment enough for his victims.

The class sat still as he spoke, the silence proof that they understood. Alex explained that the threat of violence lingers longer than the violence itself. A bruise fades, but the memory of flinching every time someone raises a hand can last for years. He confessed that he had shaped people's instincts, turning laughter into tension whenever he entered a room. "Fear," he said, "is a leash. And I held it tightly." His voice cracked as he admitted the shame of carrying that leash for so long.

Jeremy stepped in then, clarifying the point so it could not be missed. He told the students that intimidation does not require fists—it requires presence. He warned them that posture, tone, and silence can become weapons just as sharp as words. "When someone takes up space they don't need, when they force you to move, when they raise a hand and stop short," he said, "that too is bullying. Don't think you are safe simply because no one touched you. Fear leaves scars you cannot see."

Leo added that sometimes all he had to do was stand behind someone quietly, letting them feel the weight of his shadow. He described how his victims would quicken their steps, stumble over their words, or even drop their books, all because of his looming presence. He confessed that he found it funny once, but now he understood how it stripped children of their peace. "You should never make someone feel small just because you can," he said, his voice low with regret.

Alex admitted that he often paired physical intimidation with whispers. He would lean close, his breath hot against someone's ear, and mutter a threat so softly that no one else could hear. The victim would freeze, paralysed by fear, and Alex would step back with a smile, looking like nothing had happened. He explained that this gave him the cruel satisfaction of control without the evidence of wrongdoing. It was, he said, cowardice disguised as power.

Jeremy warned the class that these tactics often go unnoticed by teachers and parents because they leave no marks. He told them that bruises are easy to spot, but the fear of walking down a hallway, the dread of hearing footsteps behind you, is invisible. "That is why intimidation is so dangerous," he said. "It hides in plain sight, and sometimes the only proof is the way a child lowers their eyes or quickens their pace."

Leo shook his head as he recalled how he would sometimes slam his fist into a locker beside someone's head, never touching them, but leaving their ears ringing and their hearts racing. He admitted that the sound was louder than any shout, a crash of metal that echoed through their bones. He said he did it because he could, because fear was easier to spread than kindness. The shame of that confession weighed heavily on his shoulders as he spoke.

Alex told the class that the cruelest part of intimidation was how it lingered long after he left the room. Students would watch him carefully, waiting for the next sudden move, the next looming stance. He explained that fear does not end when the bell rings—it walks home with you, sits at your dinner table, and follows you into your dreams. He admitted that he had stolen peace from children without laying a hand on them, and that theft was unforgivable.

Jeremy let that settle before reminding everyone that bullies often thrive on silence. He told the students that intimidation only works if the victim does not speak up. "If you feel fear without bruises," he said firmly, "tell someone. Do not wait for the punch to land. Fear itself is enough proof that something is wrong." His voice carried authority, and the children listened with wide eyes.

Leo added that he sometimes intimidated not just children but teachers too. He recalled staring down an adult, refusing to break eye contact until the teacher looked away. That small victory, he admitted, fed his ego for weeks. He said now that such moments were not triumphs, but failures—failures to respect those who were trying to guide him. His voice softened as he apologised for those moments, not to the teachers, but to the students listening, so they would never repeat his mistakes.

Alex confessed that he used height as his greatest weapon. Being taller than most of his classmates, he exaggerated his size by standing on his toes, puffing his chest, or raising his chin. He said it was ridiculous looking back, like a child pretending to be a giant, but at the time it worked. His classmates cowered, and he felt powerful. Now, he admitted, that false sense of power was nothing but weakness in disguise.

Jeremy told the class that real strength is not measured in inches or posture but in restraint. "Anyone can take up space," he said. "The real question is what you do with it. Do you make room for others, or do you push them out?" The students nodded, some shifting in their seats as if suddenly aware of their own posture.

Leo ended his account by saying that intimidation had been his shield, his way of hiding his own insecurities. He admitted that he only stood tall because he felt small inside. Alex agreed, saying that every sudden movement, every looming stance, was nothing more than a mask. Together, they told the class that masks can fool others for a time, but they always crack. The truth, they said, is that no bully is as strong as they pretend to be.

The classroom stayed quiet as Jeremy closed the lesson, reminding the students that fear without touch is still fear, and scars without bruises are still scars. He said the bravest thing anyone can do is to see intimidation for what it is and refuse to let it define them. With that, the silence became heavier, not with fear, but with understanding.

Leo's voice dropped lower than it had all afternoon, so quiet the students leaned forward to catch every word. He said that when he looked back on his worst days, he could see now that they were never about the kids in front of him. The cruel jokes, the threats, the intimidation— none of it had to do with the victims at all. It had everything to do with what he carried home each night. He explained that behind his anger was shame, and behind that shame was the heavy hand of a father who believed pain was the only language worth teaching. He told the class that cruelty was the only inheritance he thought he had been given, and he wore it like a suit of armour.

He paused, letting the silence breathe, before he confessed that his father never struck him in anger alone—he struck him with purpose, as if discipline meant breaking a boy until he could no longer feel. Leo said he learned quickly that showing weakness meant another blow, another lecture, another reminder that he was never good enough. He admitted that it made him furious, a fire that burned with nowhere to go. And so, the easiest path was to turn it outward. If he could not fight the man who towered over him at home, he could at least tower over someone smaller at school. He could reclaim a fragment of power in a world that otherwise left him powerless.

Jeremy stood nearby, his gaze never leaving Leo. When Leo's voice caught, Jeremy moved closer and placed a hand firmly on his shoulder. It wasn't a hug, not a gesture of pity, but an anchoring presence that told Leo he wasn't standing alone anymore. The room grew still as students saw the small moment unfold, realising that even the strongest-looking boy could tremble beneath the weight of his own history. That hand on his shoulder said more than words could: I see you, I acknowledge you, and I will not let you fall while you speak your truth.

Leo drew in a slow breath before continuing. He said that his father's words cut deeper than fists. Being told he was worthless, lazy, or soft became a chorus that followed him into every classroom, every recess, every sleepless night. He admitted that he believed those lies for years, and the only way he knew how to silence them was to prove to others he was the opposite. If his father said he was weak, then at school he would become the strongest. If his father said he was pathetic, then he would make others look smaller than him. Bullying, he explained, was nothing more than his shield against a father's shadow.

The students shifted uncomfortably, their young faces drawn in thought. Some recognised the pattern without ever having lived it; others seemed to connect dots in their own homes. Leo told them he never wanted anyone to feel sorry for him. He said he was not sharing his story for sympathy but for understanding—that bullies are rarely what they appear to be. "We don't start out mean," he said. "We learn it, the way I learned it. And sometimes the lessons come from the people who are supposed to protect us." His honesty cut through the air with a sharpness that could not be ignored.

Jeremy spoke then, not to explain away Leo's actions but to frame them. He told the class that hurt passed down is still hurt, no matter who carries it next. He reminded them that Leo's past did not excuse his bullying, but it explained the shame beneath it. "You see," Jeremy said gently, "anger is loud, but shame is quiet. Anger wants to be seen, but shame wants to stay hidden. That is why so many children like Leo lash out—they would rather be feared than pitied. And yet, pity is not what they need. What they need is for someone to notice, someone to steady them when they finally speak."

Leo nodded slowly, acknowledging Jeremy's words, and went on to admit that he hated himself during those years. Every time he made another child cry, a piece of him whispered that he had become exactly what his father said he was. He confessed that bullying gave him temporary relief but left him hollow when the laughter faded. He said he carried that hollowness like a stone in his stomach, heavy and cold, and that shame turned into anger all over again. It was a cycle he did not know how to break until someone like Jeremy noticed him and cared enough to intervene.

He described nights when he would lie awake replaying the day in his head, remembering the faces of the children he had frightened. He admitted that the shame of those memories kept him awake longer than his father's punishments ever did. The shame was quieter, but it was sharper, because it was his own. "I was living under two bullies," he said softly. "One at home, and one inside me." The classroom hung on every word, and for the first time, they did not see Leo as a boy who had once been cruel, but as a boy who had survived cruelty and carried its scars.

Jeremy pressed his hand once more against Leo's shoulder, grounding him in the moment. He told the students that everyone carries burdens, but what matters is how they choose to carry them. He explained that Leo's mistake was believing that pain could be passed along like an heirloom, when in truth, pain must be broken, not handed down. He told the class that courage is not found in fists or threats, but in speaking the truth, even when that truth is soaked in shame.

Leo's eyes lowered as he admitted that the hardest part was forgiving himself. He explained that it is easier to hate the bully he was than to accept that he was a scared boy hiding behind anger. He said he was still learning how to live without shame, and every day was part of that lesson. He reminded his classmates that no one is beyond change, but change demands honesty, and honesty demands facing the shame you've hidden. He looked up then, meeting their eyes, letting them see that his shame was not gone but no longer in control.

The classroom remained still, but not in fear—in respect. The students understood now that Leo's story was not simply about cruelty, but about survival, shame, and the way anger masks wounds too deep to name. Jeremy lifted his hand from Leo's shoulder only when he felt the boy's voice steady, and then he let the silence carry the lesson the rest of the way. It was a silence not of discomfort, but of recognition, the kind that leaves its mark long after the words have ended.

Alex leaned forward in his chair, elbows on his knees, and stared at the floor as though the words were carved into the wood beneath him. He admitted to the class that for a long time, mocking Leo had been his favourite weapon. It gave him control, a feeling that he was cleverer, sharper, and untouchable. But there came a day when it stopped working. He remembered the exact moment: he had hurled a line meant to cut Leo deep, one of those cruel remarks that usually left him looking wounded. But that time, Leo didn't flinch. He didn't fight back. He just stood there with eyes that had gone flat, eyes that had grown too used to pain to care anymore. Alex said that moment scared him more than any punch ever could.

He told the students that Leo's silence was not strength, not the kind that made you proud—it was armour. It was the kind of armour forged by years of blows, insults, and fear, and when he saw it, Alex realised he had been hammering at that armour himself. He described how the victory he once felt evaporated. Instead of triumph, he felt a sickness in his stomach, because in that moment he saw that Leo had become what Alex himself was shaping him to be: hard, cold, unreachable. And the truth hit him like a strike to the chest. He was no different from the father Leo had just described.

Jeremy kept his eyes on Alex, giving him the same quiet steadiness he had given Leo earlier. The class leaned in, watching Alex wrestle with the memory. He confessed that for weeks after that moment, he couldn't shake the image of Leo's empty stare. It followed him into classrooms, into his bed at night, into every corner where silence lived. He admitted that he began to ask himself the question he had always avoided: What kind of person have I become? And for the first time, he had no excuse to hide behind. He couldn't blame it on friends, or on jokes, or on wanting to fit in. He had to face that he was responsible for the look in Leo's eyes.

He told the class that realisation was like looking into a mirror and finally recognising the monster staring back. He explained that when you're a bully, you convince yourself it's just teasing, that everyone laughs eventually, that words don't leave scars. But he had proof they did, right in front of him, in the boy he had torn down piece by piece. Alex said that was the day he understood cruelty does not just pass through you—it stays, and it builds walls in others. And when he saw the wall in Leo, he could no longer lie to himself about what he was doing.

Jeremy interjected, softly framing the moment for the students. He told them what Alex had found was a mirror, the kind that does not flatter, but exposes. He reminded them that bullies often hide from mirrors because they fear seeing their own cruelty reflected back. But Alex, whether he wanted to or not, had been forced to see. That turning point, Jeremy explained, is one of the hardest steps a person can take: admitting that the pain in another is your own doing.

Alex nodded and carried the story further. He explained that he tried, at first, to brush it aside, but the weight grew heavier with every passing day. The laughter that once gave him satisfaction now sounded hollow. Even his own voice began to disgust him. He said he started noticing how others looked at him when he joked at someone's expense—not with admiration, but with unease. He realised people weren't laughing with him, they were laughing out of fear. That revelation struck deeper than he expected. It was one thing to be feared by someone weaker, but another to be distrusted by everyone.

He described one afternoon when he caught his reflection in a window after sneering at a younger student. He said he didn't see a strong boy staring back—he saw someone who looked almost desperate, almost begging for control he didn't actually have. He admitted that was the first time he truly hated himself. "You can't outrun a mirror," Alex told the class. "Sooner or later, you have to face it." His voice shook, but he pressed on, determined not to lose the thread of honesty he had finally found.

Jeremy reminded the class that turning points rarely look dramatic. They don't always happen with a fight or a big moment. Sometimes they come quietly, in silence, when you realise your weapons no longer work, and instead of victory you feel only emptiness. He explained that Alex's moment with Leo was exactly that: the end of one kind of power and the beginning of a very different understanding.

Alex's tone grew heavier as he confessed that recognising the truth didn't make him better overnight. He said he still carried the habit of cruelty like a reflex, snapping at others before thinking, pushing boundaries just to see them break. But each time he did, he saw Leo's stare in his memory, and it broke him a little more. "It's hard to admit," he said quietly, "but I realised I was shaping people to hate themselves, the way I hated myself. And that was the ugliest truth of all."

He turned to Leo then, his voice gentler, and admitted that in a strange way, Leo's resistance—his hardened silence—saved them both. It forced Alex to confront himself in a way nothing else could. He told the students that sometimes it takes seeing the damage you've done to another person before you realise how damaged you are yourself. That, he explained, was the moment he began to change—not because he wanted to, but because he couldn't stand the sight of who he was anymore.

Jeremy placed a hand briefly on Alex's arm, the same gesture he had used with Leo, acknowledging him, anchoring him. He told the class that confession is never easy, and reflection even harder. But in Alex's honesty lay a lesson: change does not come from pretending you were never cruel. It comes from facing cruelty, owning it, and refusing to live in its shadow anymore.

Alex's eyes lifted at last, meeting the gaze of his classmates. He admitted he still struggles with shame, just as Leo does, but now he fights against it instead of feeding it. He told them that was his turning point, the day he stopped enjoying power and started seeking something different: respect. And respect, he explained, could never be earned through fear.

The room stayed quiet, not with discomfort, but with recognition. Jeremy allowed the silence to rest there, heavy but necessary, letting Alex's words sink in. The class understood that turning points are not sudden escapes from the past, but painful beginnings of a harder path. And for the first time, they saw Alex not as the boy who once delighted in cruelty, but as someone who had chosen to face the mirror and not look away.

Jeremy stood slowly, his eyes moving across the classroom, and he told the students that what they had just witnessed from Leo and Alex was not a performance. It was not staged for sympathy or crafted to make them look better. It was the cost of truth, laid bare for all to see.

He explained that most people think bullying is only about what happens to the victim, about the bruises, the tears, the fear left behind. But the damage doesn't end there. It digs into the bully too, leaving behind guilt, shame, and regret that do not wash away easily. He reminded them that cruelty stains both sides, and even when the victim heals, the bully is left haunted by the weight of what they've done.

Leo shifted uncomfortably in his chair as Jeremy spoke, his jaw clenched. He admitted aloud that Jeremy was right. He said the hardest nights of his life were the ones when he lay awake replaying the faces of kids he had mocked or cornered, faces that looked back at him long after the moment was gone. He said he couldn't count the number of times he tried to convince himself it wasn't serious, that they forgot, that kids bounced back. But the truth kept gnawing at him, because deep down he knew words stick longer than bruises. He said the guilt became a shadow that followed him everywhere, heavier than any punishment a teacher could give.

Alex spoke next, his voice lower, almost subdued. He told the class that the fallout of bullying was not just guilt—it was self-loathing. He explained how the more he hurt others, the more he despised himself. It became a vicious cycle: the worse he felt inside, the more cruel he became, as if punishing others might distract him from punishing himself. But it never worked. He described nights where he couldn't look in the mirror, because every reflection reminded him of what he had done to Leo and others. He said the weight of regret never really left him, and even now, standing in front of the class, he could still feel it pressing on his chest.

Jeremy placed a steady hand on the back of Alex's chair, grounding him, and spoke to the class again. He told them that people rarely talk about this side of bullying because it forces us to admit bullies are not monsters—they are people. They are broken in their own ways, and though their choices are wrong, the scars they leave on themselves are real. He explained that regret is not a quick punishment. It is a lifelong reckoning, and the only way to ease it is through honesty and change. "What you're hearing today," Jeremy said firmly, "is the price of cruelty. It doesn't disappear when the laughter ends."

Leo lifted his head then, his eyes tired but clear, and he told his classmates that the guilt still choked him sometimes. He said he could be walking down the hall and suddenly remember a boy he once shoved against a locker, or a girl whose books he knocked to the floor, and the shame would hit like a punch to the stomach. He admitted that sometimes he still wanted to run from it, to bury it under excuses, but he knew that if he did, it would only grow worse. Speaking the truth, as painful as it was, was the only way he had found to quiet the guilt, even just a little.

Alex added that guilt alone wasn't enough to change someone. He said plenty of bullies carry guilt but never speak of it, never admit it, and so it festers. He told the class that admitting it out loud was the hardest step of all, because it meant no longer hiding behind the mask of toughness. "When you admit what you've done," he said, "you strip yourself bare. You lose the armour. And it's terrifying." He paused, then looked directly at the students. "But it's the only way you can start again."

Jeremy nodded at Alex's words and expanded on them for the students. He said that shame can rot a person from the inside if it's left unspoken. It eats away until the bully is no longer lashing out at others—they are lashing out at themselves. He reminded the class that what Leo and Alex had just done was not weakness but courage. By speaking, they were choosing not to be defined forever by their cruelty. They were choosing to confront the fallout instead of hiding from it.

Leo confessed that there were times he thought he would never escape the shadow of his father, that he would always carry the anger passed down to him. But by admitting the shame, he said, he had finally felt a crack of light in the wall that trapped him. He explained that while he still lived with guilt, he no longer lived chained to it. Speaking gave him a way forward, a way to turn regret into something useful instead of destructive.

Alex's hands tightened on his knees as he admitted that he still hears the voices of kids he taunted, still feels the sting of words he can't take back. But he told the class he no longer runs from them. He lets them remind him who he never wants to be again. He said the fallout doesn't vanish, but it can be reshaped into resolve. "Every time I remember what I did," he said, "I use it to remind myself why I have to do better."

Jeremy circled the two boys with his gaze, then addressed the class once more. He told them this was the truth about bullying that too few understood: it destroys everyone involved. Victims bear scars of fear and doubt. Bullies bear scars of regret and shame. And those scars do not disappear because time has passed. They remain until someone decides to face them, to acknowledge them, and to turn them into something better.

Leo leaned back, closing his eyes briefly, and admitted that sometimes he still dreams about the kids he hurt. In those dreams, he said, the faces look at him, silent and accusing. He said waking up from them feels like drowning. But he explained that talking now, in this moment, gave him a chance to breathe again. He urged his classmates never to carry such a burden, never to let cruelty take root, because the weight of regret would never leave them once it settled in.

Alex looked around the room and said he wanted his classmates to understand something clearly: bullies don't get away clean. Even if no teacher punishes them, even if no one else remembers, the bully remembers. He told them the regret lives inside, and it becomes a chain dragging you down every single day. He admitted that standing here today was not easy, but it was better than living chained forever.

Jeremy concluded the section with a quiet warning. He told the students that the emotional fallout of bullying is real, and it doesn't care about intentions or excuses. "It will scar you," he said, "whether you are the one who suffers it, or the one who causes it. And the only way forward is honesty, the kind you've just witnessed." He let the silence linger, heavy but necessary, until the students shifted in their seats, each one grappling with the truth that cruelty leaves no one untouched.

The classroom door creaked open with the kind of hesitation that drew every pair of eyes toward it. Lisa stepped inside without asking permission, her small frame hardly filling the doorway, but her presence making the space feel suddenly sharper. She crossed the room with the casual confidence of someone who had nothing to prove, yet everyone knew there was more beneath the surface. Jeremy didn't move to stop her. He understood immediately that she belonged in this conversation, and the students seemed to hold their breath, waiting to see what she would do. Harley's glance followed her, his shoulders taut, though not out of fear anymore—out of the recognition of someone who could unmask him once upon a time.

Lisa leaned against the chalkboard, arms folded, her expression unreadable. She didn't waste time with greetings or excuses. Instead, she said plainly that she wasn't about to stand in front of everyone and pretend she regretted everything she had ever done. She admitted there were moments she cherished, moments when her fist connected with someone's jaw, and the satisfaction felt like justice. "Sometimes," she said with a voice as sharp as glass, "knocking someone down felt like the only way to shut them up." Her words landed like stones, jarring the students who expected remorse wrapped neatly in apology. Instead, Lisa gave them something raw, stripped of the polite polish others had attempted.

A ripple moved through the class, half shock, half curiosity. Some students shifted uncomfortably, others leaned forward as though drawn to the honesty of it. Lisa didn't flinch at their reactions. She explained that in those moments, she hadn't thought of herself as a bully. She thought of herself as someone cutting through arrogance, someone refusing to be underestimated. To her, fighting was survival, and survival had a taste she wasn't willing to spit out. She tilted her head toward Leo and Alex, smirking faintly, saying that while they spoke of guilt and shame, she could not say the same for every bruise she had left behind.

Jeremy didn't interrupt. He allowed the words to settle, his silence giving Lisa the space she clearly demanded. She continued, her voice steady but edged with something darker, confessing that power thrilled her. She admitted that in those moments, watching someone stumble, watching them lower their eyes, she felt untouchable. The class listened in wary silence, realising that this was the truth bullies rarely admit aloud—the intoxicating pull of dominance. Lisa delivered it without apology, daring them to deny the temptation of that rush.

Leo broke the silence first, his voice firm but not confrontational. He told Lisa that he understood the feeling, but he had also learned the cost. He reminded her that the satisfaction never lasted. The faces of those hurt came back later, twisting in memory, leaving stains that even victory couldn't erase. He said the bruises faded from their skin, but they carved scars into their hearts, scars that remained invisible but permanent. His words were not an accusation; they were a reflection of his own journey. He wanted her to see the shadow that followed triumph, even when it seemed deserved.

Lisa's gaze lingered on him, and for the first time her smirk wavered. She admitted quietly that maybe he was right—that maybe the satisfaction had faded quicker than she ever let herself admit. But she also argued that sometimes the damage went both ways. She reminded the class that she never picked fights with children who couldn't defend themselves. She chose equals, sometimes bigger, sometimes louder. To her, those fights had balance. Yet when Leo pressed further, asking whether she believed her punches had left no scars, she faltered. The classroom fell into another hush as Lisa seemed to weigh her answer, caught between defiance and reluctant recognition.

Harley finally spoke, his tone unusually soft. He told Lisa that he used to believe the same thing, that his fists were simply a way of surviving or proving himself. But he reminded her of the night she ended up in the hospital, when all her bravado cracked and she left him that letter. He said he knew then that beneath her armour was someone who longed for something other than fights. The students turned at once toward Lisa, waiting for her reaction. She didn't speak immediately, but her jaw tightened, and for once, she looked away.

Jeremy seized the pause and explained that Lisa's honesty mattered. He told the class that admitting she still felt the thrill, that she didn't regret everything, was not weakness. It was truth, and truth was where change could begin. He said pretending to regret every action would have been a lie, and lies offered no lessons. By speaking openly, Lisa had shown them the other side of bullying—the side where the bully convinces themselves they are right, even when they're not. It was a rare glimpse into the mind of cruelty that most victims never hear spoken aloud.

Lisa's voice cut through again, this time quieter, but still firm. She confessed that Leo's words had struck her harder than she expected. She admitted that maybe she had convinced herself those fights were fair, when in reality, fairness was never the point. She realised, standing there in front of her classmates, that she had carried a lie even to herself: that hurting others was only ever survival. The truth, she admitted, was that sometimes it was simply about control, and admitting that was harder than any fight she had ever won.

Alex leaned forward then, his voice steady as he told Lisa that he too had once convinced himself the cruelty had balance. He explained how easy it was to lie to yourself when you wanted to believe you were justified. But he reminded her that no justification erased the impact. "The hurt is still the hurt," he said. Lisa didn't argue this time. She lowered her eyes briefly, then lifted them again with a spark that wasn't defiance but something closer to acceptance.

Jeremy watched the shift and pointed it out for the class. He told them that this was how change began—not with polished speeches, but with raw truth, with the courage to admit not only guilt but the stubborn pride that hides behind it. He said Lisa's confession was proof that honesty was not always comfortable, but it was always necessary. The students nodded slowly, some visibly unsettled, but all taking in the weight of what had just unfolded.

Lisa stepped away from the chalkboard then, standing closer to Leo and Alex. Her arms were still crossed, but her posture had softened. She admitted that she wasn't ready to say she regretted everything, because she wasn't there yet. But she promised she would start listening—to Leo, to Alex, to Harley, even to Jeremy. And though her words were laced with hesitation, they carried a sincerity that the room felt. It was not a confession of innocence; it was the first step toward honesty.

The room seemed lighter for a moment, though the heaviness of truth still lingered. Students exchanged glances, whispering softly, processing what they had heard. Jeremy let the moment rest before concluding the section with a reminder: "The hardest truths," he said, "are the ones that make us squirm, the ones we'd rather bury. But those are the ones that need to be spoken." Lisa gave a faint nod, as if conceding that she understood. For the first time that day, her expression softened—not into a smile, but into something almost vulnerable.

Harley had been standing near the window the entire time, his long frame outlined against the light that spilled through the glass. His silence was different from the others' voices, louder in its refusal to join the conversation. The students noticed it; they always noticed Harley. Taller than most, his presence was sharp, his posture carried like a wall built out of years of learning to be seen but never truly known. Jeremy let the silence linger, observing Harley as much as the rest of the room, and he made sure the students understood that the absence of words sometimes spoke more clearly than the boldest confession.

Harley shifted his weight, the creak of the floorboard beneath his shoes cutting into the hush. His arms were folded across his chest, his gaze lowered not out of shame but out of careful calculation, as if measuring every syllable spoken by Leo, Alex, and Lisa. He hadn't spoken once since the start of the session, and the restraint felt heavy, deliberate. The students, some of whom remembered his old temper, sat taut with unease, waiting to see if he would eventually break his silence. Jeremy's eyes caught the boy's for the briefest moment, but Harley didn't hold it. He turned his focus back toward the glass, letting his silence thicken the air.

Jeremy finally addressed it, though not with accusation. He told the class that Harley's stillness was important. "Not every bully is ready to speak," he explained gently, his voice steady, "and silence can sometimes be its own form of honesty." The words drew the attention back to Harley, though Jeremy carefully steered it away from cornering him. He explained that when wounds are too fresh, when battles are still being fought inside, words don't always come quickly. He reminded the class that forcing confession before it is ready often drives the truth deeper into hiding.

Harley's shoulders lifted faintly as though he meant to breathe in a defence, but he let it fall away instead. He didn't argue. He didn't offer excuses. He remained where he was, framed by sunlight that seemed almost at odds with the shadows he carried. Students whispered faintly, the tension of his quiet standing out more now that Jeremy had named it. It wasn't fear in their eyes, not anymore—it was curiosity and perhaps a trace of respect for the boy who once frightened them but now seemed locked inside his own silence.

Jeremy reminded them that silence did not equal softness, nor did it equal hardness. It was simply silence. "Some of us," he said, glancing again toward Harley, "aren't ready to untangle the words yet. And that's all right. What matters is knowing that silence itself is not a shield forever. It is only a pause." His words carried a weight that pressed gently on Harley's frame, though the boy remained still, his jaw clenched, his eyes trained firmly away. The class understood what Jeremy was doing: giving Harley room to stand without pressure, while still acknowledging that his shadow loomed.

Leo leaned forward from his seat, speaking softly as though to himself but clearly meant for Harley's ears. He said he used to think silence was strength, that it made him untouchable. But he admitted that it had been weakness in disguise, fear of being seen for what he really was. The admission hung in the air, pointed but not sharp, an invitation rather than a challenge. Harley's head shifted slightly at the words, though his mouth remained closed, his eyes still on the window. It was a flicker, but it was noticed.

Alex followed with his own observation, recalling the times Harley's silence in the past had frightened others more than words ever did. "You didn't need to say much," Alex confessed openly, "because people saw the height, the glare, the folded arms. That was enough." He wasn't accusing, only naming the memory. Harley's jaw tightened once again, and for the first time, the room saw the boy's silence not as absence, but as a weight that carried echoes of the past, echoes that were louder than he could yet admit.

Jeremy told the class that shadows often remain even after the light has shifted. He explained that Harley was standing now in his shadow, visible for everyone to see, but not ready to step out. "It doesn't mean he won't," Jeremy added calmly. "It only means that today, this is where he stands." The phrasing eased the students, who had grown tense waiting for Harley to either speak or erupt. They began to understand that the shadow itself was a stage of the process, not a failure of it. The silence became less threatening, more understandable.

Lisa, still perched near the edge of the chalkboard, tilted her head toward Harley with a faint smile, not mocking but steady. She reminded him, gently but firmly, that she too had once stood in silence, refusing to admit what was inside her. "You don't have to say anything now," she told him, "but don't think we don't see you." Her words reached him with the familiarity of someone who had walked alongside his silence before, and though Harley didn't turn to face her, the faintest flicker crossed his expression—a shadow stirred by recognition.

The students leaned back then, no longer waiting for an outburst but accepting the stillness for what it was. Harley's shadow remained stretched across the floor, his frame unbroken against the window's glow. Jeremy wrapped the moment by telling the class that not every voice comes at the same time. Some confessions spill like water, immediate and rushing. Others gather slowly, like rain behind a dam, waiting for the right moment to break. "What matters," he told them, "is that we do not mistake silence for nothingness. Sometimes it means more is coming than we expect."

The day's session continued with Harley still at his post, still unspoken, but his presence had been acknowledged, his silence given weight and meaning rather than suspicion. The students carried this awareness forward, no longer pressing him to speak, no longer fearing the unspoken. Jeremy let the class close on that note, trusting that Harley's shadow, though long, was not endless. In time, words would come, but for now, his silence was allowed to remain exactly what it was—part of the truth.

Jeremy leaned against the corner of the desk, hands folded loosely, his voice quieter than usual as he addressed the room. "Did you notice it?" he asked, eyes shifting between rows of expectant faces. "Did you notice how the things Lisa and Harley described… sound nearly identical to what Leo and Alex admitted to?" The students stirred uneasily, some whispering, some nodding, as though the question struck something they had not wanted to say aloud. Jeremy held their silence for a moment, then added, "That's what I want you to see. Patterns. Because bullies don't invent new tricks every time—they repeat what they know."

The students shifted in their seats, recalling the confessions from earlier. Leo's stories of mocking, Alex's descriptions of cruel words, Lisa's blunt honesty about her fists, and Harley's looming silence all began to braid into something unnervingly familiar. A boy in the second row murmured that it sounded like different faces wearing the same mask. Jeremy picked up the thought, repeating it for the class: "Different faces, same mask." He explained how cruelty disguises itself in different forms—sometimes laughter, sometimes fists, sometimes silence that waits for the right moment—but beneath it, the patterns all share the same hunger for control.

Jeremy drew a piece of chalk across the blackboard, making four short columns: Leo. Alex. Lisa. Harley. He underlined each, then turned to the class. "What did they all do?" he asked. Slowly, answers came: mocking, gaslighting, intimidation, pretending to be friends. Each answer he wrote beneath the names until the board filled with a list of cruelties, overlapping so heavily that the columns began to blur together. "Do you see it now?" he asked. "How none of these things belonged to just one of them?" The class murmured in agreement, faces grim with the recognition that the differences they once believed separated each bully were far thinner than they imagined.

A girl in the back raised her hand cautiously. She admitted she had always thought Lisa was different, because Lisa fought with her fists, not her words. But now, she said, it didn't feel so different—because the damage was the same. Jeremy nodded, explaining that wounds wear many disguises, but they bleed the same. He told the class that recognising these disguises is the first step in stopping them. "Bullies count on you not noticing," he said. "They count on you believing each act is unique, or too small to matter. But when you connect the dots, you see the cycle."

Jeremy let his words sink in, then invited Leo to speak again. Leo admitted that he thought his cruelties had been clever, original even, when in reality he was just recycling patterns he'd endured himself. Alex added that he too thought his tricks were his own, but now, hearing Lisa's words, he realised he had only repeated what someone else once used against him. The realisation unsettled them both, but Jeremy seized on it, pointing out how this was proof that cruelty is contagious—it passes from one to another until someone chooses to break it.

Lisa frowned as she listened, arms crossed, but her expression softened into something less guarded. She confessed that she had once thought her fists were her own weapon, her way of being stronger than the ones who hurt her. But hearing Leo and Alex talk about gaslighting and fake friendships made her realise she had leaned on patterns too—different in shape, but the same in purpose. "It's all the same game," she muttered, shaking her head. The students absorbed the words, the image of a game making them see how bullies play for power rather than fairness.

Harley did not speak, but Jeremy included him anyway. He told the class that even silence could be a pattern: the posture, the folded arms, the glare. "Fear doesn't always need sound," he explained. "Sometimes the quietest bully is the loudest in the room." The statement sent a shiver through the class, because they all remembered moments when Harley's silence had been enough to make them falter. Jeremy reminded them that seeing the pattern doesn't mean condemning the person forever. It means recognising the truth so the cycle can be stopped.

The students began naming other behaviours they had seen: the "fake smile" before a punch, the casual shove in the hallway, the whispered rumour meant to stain someone's name. Jeremy wrote these on the board too, clustering them beneath the four names. When he stepped back, the blackboard looked like a spider's web of tactics, no one strand belonging to just one bully. "Do you see?" he asked again, his voice firmer. "This is why we can't excuse it. Because the moment we excuse one strand, the web stays intact." The class stared at the board, no longer able to separate the bullies by their methods.

Jeremy told them that patterns are dangerous because they hide in plain sight. "If you think a bully has to look or act a certain way," he explained, "you miss the truth right in front of you." He gestured toward Lisa, who looked far too small to have carried such a reputation, and toward Harley, whose silence disguised his storms. "They don't come with labels. They don't look like villains in a storybook. That's what makes recognising the patterns so important." His words stripped away the last comfort of believing cruelty could be spotted easily.

The students grew restless, shifting uneasily, as though seeing too much of themselves reflected in the patterns on the board. Jeremy didn't let them retreat into silence. He reminded them that recognising patterns isn't about blame—it's about prevention. "You see it," he said firmly, "so now you can stop it. That's the difference between letting it repeat and breaking it." The air in the room grew taut, not with fear but with the weight of responsibility. They could no longer claim they didn't know what to look for.

Leo leaned back, running a hand across his face, muttering that he wished someone had shown him the patterns when he was younger. "I thought I was clever," he said bitterly, "but I was just a copy." Alex nodded beside him, his voice low but clear. "And so was I." Their words rang with a hard kind of regret, a truth that stung more than the confessions themselves. Jeremy told the students to remember those regrets, because they were warnings written in real voices, not in lessons pulled from books.

Jeremy ended the section with one last question, his eyes sweeping the room: "Now that you can see the patterns... will you let them repeat, or will you be the ones to break them?" The question landed heavily, leaving no escape. The students didn't answer right away, but their silence was no longer avoidance—it was recognition. They had seen the threads, and they knew they could not unsee them.

Leo drew a breath, shoulders tense, before he faced the rows of waiting students. His voice carried a different weight now, not the sharp edge of confession but the tired resolve of someone desperate to be understood. "We're not saying all this so you feel sorry for us," he began, steady though his eyes betrayed a storm. "We're not telling these stories to make excuses, or to make you think what we did was somehow okay. It wasn't. It will never be. We're saying it because if you don't see how it starts, if you don't see what it turns into, then you'll repeat it. And I don't want that for any of you." The room went still, the students leaning forward as though afraid to let a single word fall unheard.

Alex shifted beside him, crossing his arms, then dropping them again as though holding them tightly only locked the guilt deeper inside. "Leo's right," he said, his tone lower, measured. "We don't gain anything by admitting this. If anything, it makes us look worse than you already thought. But honesty is the only way out. It's the only way to step away from the cycle. Because as long as we keep secrets, as long as we pretend we weren't as cruel as we were, it still owns us. We don't want to belong to it anymore." His words echoed against the silence, unpolished and raw, but strong in their simplicity.

Jeremy let them stand in that truth for a moment, his gaze moving across the class, watching the unease settle into thoughtfulness. He knew the power wasn't in perfect speeches—it was in the visible struggle of those standing before them. Leo and Alex weren't actors reciting rehearsed lines; they were boys dragging their worst shadows into the open, daring to let their classmates see them for what they were. That vulnerability was a weapon turned against the cycle itself. Jeremy pointed at them gently and told the students, "They share because keeping it inside would only let it fester. This is what breaking looks like."

Leo rubbed his hands together, his eyes flicking toward the floor. He admitted that for years he carried the memories alone, convinced that silence would bury them. "But silence doesn't bury anything," he said flatly. "It only makes the weight heavier. I thought if no one knew, it would disappear.

But it didn't. It haunted me. Every laugh, every shove, every lie—I carried them until I thought I'd choke on them. Talking about it now doesn't erase it, but at least it stops it from choking me." His honesty cracked something fragile in the room, reminding them all that secrecy was not strength but suffocation.

Alex followed, his expression grim, as though Leo's words had unlocked his own. "When I bullied Leo," he said, glancing at his friend with shame and resolve, "I told myself it wasn't serious. I told myself it was normal. That everyone did it. And that lie kept me in it. That's what lies do—they give you a shield to hide behind so you don't have to face the truth. I see that now. And that's why I'm telling you. So you don't fall for the same lies I did. Because once you believe them, you can justify anything." His tone hardened on the last words, and the students flinched slightly, feeling the sting of what he admitted.

A girl in the front row raised her hand, her voice tentative as she asked why they were brave enough to share now, when they hadn't before. Leo gave a sad smile, almost rueful. "Because before, we thought it would make us weak. We thought it would ruin us. Now we know keeping quiet ruins you more. We share because we want something better than the silence that owned us. We share because we don't want you carrying that same silence." The words trembled with sincerity, and the students seemed to understand that confession wasn't weakness—it was resistance.

Jeremy stepped in then, reinforcing their point. "Do you see?" he asked the class. "This isn't about excuses. It's about refusing to stay trapped. Bullies don't talk because they're afraid the cycle will lose its grip once exposed. That's why honesty matters—it's the first cut against the chains." His tone sharpened, drawing their attention back to the fact that truth-telling isn't comfortable, but it is necessary. "The cycle feeds on silence. They're breaking that silence now." The students nodded slowly, some folding their arms across their chests as if to guard themselves from the weight of the lesson.

Alex looked around the room, his gaze meeting faces that avoided his at first, then cautiously held it. "We're not proud of who we were," he admitted, voice rough. "But if telling you helps even one of you stop before it gets worse, then maybe it means what we went through has a purpose. Maybe it won't all be wasted." His words drew a murmur of agreement from the students, many of whom had never considered that regret could be reshaped into something useful, something that might spare others the same mistakes.

Leo added, his voice steadier now, "We've done damage we can't take back. That's the truth. We'll always carry it. But carrying it doesn't mean dragging it forward into more harm. It means standing still long enough to say, 'No more.' That's why we share. Because this is the only way to stop it from repeating." He pressed his lips together, then exhaled heavily, as if the act of saying it aloud finally loosened some of the iron wrapped around his chest. His eyes were brighter, though tired, the face of someone finally allowing air into a long-locked room.

Jeremy folded his arms, surveying the class with quiet insistence. "Do you hear them?" he asked, his tone a mixture of pride and solemnity. "This is what courage looks like—not in fists, not in shouts, but in facing your own worst mistakes and refusing to hide from them. They're not here to earn sympathy. They're here to show you that change is real, but only if you're willing to tell the truth." His words sealed the moment, giving it a finality that demanded respect rather than pity.

The students sat in stillness, their faces thoughtful, some troubled, some inspired, as though the lesson had carved a new space in their understanding. The message was unshakable: stories told in honesty do not excuse, they redeem. Patterns are broken not by silence, but by naming them. Leo and Alex's voices carried not the pride of survival, but the heavy dignity of repentance. That dignity filled the room, pressing into every corner, leaving no room for denial.

The silence that followed wasn't awkward or fearful—it was reverent. Students recognised that what had just been given to them was not a performance but a gift, fragile and heavy, carrying the weight of lived mistakes. And in that silence, Jeremy closed the session, reminding them all that the act of sharing is not the end of the story, but the beginning of change.

The silence in the room broke like glass under a cautious hand. A boy near the back cleared his throat, not to speak but to steady himself, his eyes red though no tears had yet fallen. A girl in the front row blinked rapidly, pressing her palms against her desk as if bracing herself from being swept away by the tide of what she had just heard. The classroom had shifted into something heavier than instruction, something more raw than storytelling. It was the kind of silence that comes after a truth is laid bare, a silence that demanded everyone wrestle with it before they could breathe again.

One student raised her hand with hesitation, though her voice wavered before she found the strength to speak. "I…I remember when Lisa pushed me against the lockers," she said softly, glancing quickly at Lisa, who now sat pale, biting her lip. "It wasn't hard, but it made me feel like I was invisible. Like no one would stop her, and no one cared." The admission fell into the air like a stone into still water, ripples spreading across the classroom. A boy nearby nodded slowly, the recognition in his eyes betraying his own memory. For the first time, it felt safe enough to admit what had been endured.

Another boy leaned forward, fists clenched on his desk, his voice shaking with restrained anger. "I used to think Harley was my friend," he said, the words spilling faster now. "He would laugh with me, then trip me in the hallway so everyone else could laugh too. I didn't know what to do—if I told, I was weak, if I didn't, I was a joke. And I hated myself for falling for it every time." His eyes met Harley's across the room, and Harley shifted uncomfortably, his jaw tight, his silence louder than any denial. The boy sat back, his face red but relieved, as though naming it had freed him.

A girl at the far side whispered something under her breath before daring to raise her voice. "It happened to me, too," she said, softer still. "Lisa told me she was my friend, then made me stand alone at recess while she told everyone I smelled bad. I went home and washed until my skin hurt." Her words brought a gasp from another student, who muttered quietly, "I remember that day." The ripple grew, and for the first time, Lisa's chin dropped, her shoulders curling inward. She was listening not to accusations, but to echoes of her own cruelty finally spoken aloud.

The tears began then, quiet at first. A younger boy buried his face in his arms, and Jeremy noticed how others patted his back, silent comfort for something too heavy for him to confess in words. The anger too, was palpable. A tall student muttered, "I wanted to fight back but didn't know how." His jaw quivered, though his fists remained pressed flat against the desk. The stories weren't rehearsed, and they weren't polished—they were unfiltered bursts of memory, each one a wound held shut for too long, now bleeding into the open.

Lisa lifted her head, her voice cutting softly through the heavy air. "I remember doing that," she admitted, her tone trembling. "I thought it was funny. I didn't know it hurt that bad." Her words didn't erase the harm, but they cracked something inside the wall she had built. She didn't defend herself or twist the truth—she simply acknowledged it, and in that acknowledgment, the room shifted again. Students stared at her with disbelief, anger, and some faint relief that at least she did not deny it.

Jeremy watched closely, allowing the stories to flow but guiding gently when needed. "This is why we speak," he said firmly. "Not to humiliate, not to retaliate, but to reveal. When you tell the truth, the power bullying has over you weakens." His words steadied the room, reminding the students that what was happening wasn't about revenge. It was about finally saying aloud what silence had protected. The children looked at him, then back at each other, sensing that what was unfolding wasn't a classroom exercise but something far more sacred.

A boy who had remained silent until now leaned forward, eyes brimming. "I never told anyone, but…Harley shoved me into the coat rack once," he admitted, his voice almost a whisper. "I told my parents I tripped. I didn't want anyone to know." His confession was followed by a pause so long it seemed the entire room inhaled together. Then another student murmured, "I've done that too. Pretended it was nothing." One by one, silent nods began, the quiet acknowledgement that the harm had spread farther than anyone realised.

The relief was visible, though tangled with pain. Shoulders loosened. Tears flowed freely from some, while others sat straighter, as though unburdened. For many, it was the first time their truth had ever been heard. The classroom had become a confessional, not of sins only, but of wounds unacknowledged. Jeremy knew what they had entered was dangerous ground—truth could heal, but it could also burn. Yet he allowed it, because silence was worse.

Lisa sat rigid now, her hands folded tightly, staring at the floor. She did not defend herself, and perhaps that silence was her own first step. Harley, taller and sharper, stayed near the wall, his face unreadable. But Jeremy noticed the flicker in his eyes—the recognition that his own name had been spoken more than once. He didn't deny it either. That silence, thick with consequence, was its own kind of admission.

A girl near the window whispered, "I thought I was the only one." Several others nodded. That one sentence broke through the last layer of isolation. The class realised that the pain wasn't private—it was collective, a web of unspoken stories finally seeing daylight. The relief of not being alone rippled like a second silence, softer but no less powerful.

Jeremy stepped forward then, summing up what they all felt. "You see now why these stories matter," he said, his tone steady. "When you hide them, they eat at you alone. When you share them, you see you're not the only one, and you take back the ground you lost." His words struck with finality, offering direction to the mess of emotions swirling in the room. He did not tell them what to feel, only that they were not alone in feeling it.

The students wiped eyes, exchanged glances, and some even leaned toward one another in tentative gestures of comfort. For once, the classroom wasn't divided into victims and aggressors, but joined in a fragile community of witnesses. It was not forgiveness yet, nor reconciliation, but it was the first moment the old wounds were truly named. And that naming changed the air itself.

The anger, the tears, the relief—they existed together without drowning each other out. Students left their desks carrying truths that had lived in silence for too long. And though Jeremy knew this was only the beginning, he also knew they had crossed a threshold. What had been hidden was now spoken, and what had been endured in isolation was now shared.

Jeremy remained standing at the front of the classroom, his eyes sweeping across the rows of faces that seemed at once older and younger than they had been at the start of the day. Every child carried a look that had been reshaped by what had been said—eyes swollen with tears, jaws tense with anger, shoulders bent with the sudden weight of memory. He allowed the silence to linger, refusing to rush into it. Some silences are heavier than words, and this one demanded respect. Then he drew a long breath, his voice steady but solemn. "You've seen now what happens when we stop pretending," he said. "When the smile breaks, the truth steps through. And truth will always step through, no matter how carefully someone paints their mask."

He leaned slightly against the edge of the desk, not as a teacher commanding authority but as a peer willing to stand beside them. "I want you to think about those smiles," he continued. "The ones you've seen on bullies, on classmates, maybe even on yourselves. You know the kind—forced, tight, sometimes even wide, but with nothing behind it. That is not a real smile.

That is a warning. A sign that someone is covering up what they're about to do, or hiding what they've already done." He paused, letting the students replay the countless moments in their minds. "A smile like that can be more dangerous than a scowl, because it tells you nothing until it's too late."

The students were quiet, but he could see the gears turning. He did not rush to fill the space. Instead, he pressed further. "When Leo and Alex told you their stories, when Lisa admitted hers, when Harley stayed silent—you saw the cracks in the masks. You saw how false strength breaks down when truth is spoken aloud. That is why you must learn to recognise those smiles. A painted smile is armour for cruelty. It hides shame, or fear, or anger. But it cannot last forever. Sooner or later, it breaks." His words fell slowly, like stones on glass, each one leaving a mark.

Jeremy shifted, folding his arms as if steadying himself. "I'm not telling you this so you become suspicious of everyone who smiles," he said, gentler now. "Real smiles are easy to see. They soften faces, they reach eyes, they make you feel lighter even if you don't know why. But painted ones—those stay rigid. They sit on the surface. You can feel the difference if you pay attention." Several students nodded faintly, recalling their own encounters, their bodies remembering the unease that always accompanied such smiles.

He glanced toward Harley, who leaned against the far wall, arms crossed, expression unreadable. "Even Harley had one of those smiles," Jeremy said plainly. "Many of you saw it. And some of you still remember how it felt when that smile was aimed at you. But here's the thing—Harley doesn't wear it now. Not in the same way. Because once truth cracks a smile like that, the person underneath has to decide: do I keep pretending, or do I step out into the light?" The weight of his gaze lingered on Harley just long enough to acknowledge him without cornering him.

Lisa shifted uncomfortably, her hands gripping the desk edge, but Jeremy did not let the silence cover her either. "Lisa, too," he said. "Her smile was sharp once. You've heard her admit it. But today, you heard something else—her voice when she realised her actions left marks she hadn't thought about. That wasn't a painted smile. That was a moment where she finally stopped holding the brush." Lisa lowered her eyes, but for the first time she did not tense against the words. She allowed them to rest where they landed.

Jeremy returned to the class, drawing them all back in. "What I'm saying is simple: learn to see. Learn to notice when a smile doesn't match the eyes. Learn to notice when someone laughs too loudly after hurting another, or grins while someone else shrinks. That's the moment you must pay attention. Because that is when cruelty hides itself best." He let his words hang heavy. The students stared back, their expressions shifting with realisation, discomfort, and a cautious sort of understanding.

A boy in the second row raised his chin. "So…if we see it, what do we do?" His question was hesitant, as though asking might bring more than he wanted to hear. Jeremy answered slowly, firmly. "You don't always have the power to stop it in that moment. But you can remember it. You can speak it later. You can refuse to carry the silence that gives it strength. And sometimes, if it's safe, you can call it out directly. What matters is you see it, and you don't pretend it isn't happening." The boy nodded, relieved that noticing itself could be an act of resistance.

Jeremy looked over the room, seeing how the truth had settled like dust after a storm. "This isn't just about bullies," he continued. "It's about all of us. We all wear masks sometimes. We all try to hide when we're hurting, or when we've hurt someone else. But hiding doesn't make it go away. Only truth breaks the mask. And only when the smile breaks can you see what's really there." The words echoed, and in that echo was a warning wrapped in hope.

He paced slowly across the room, each step deliberate. "So remember this day. Remember what Leo and Alex admitted. Remember what Lisa confessed. Remember Harley's silence. These are not stories meant to shame them—they are lessons meant to teach all of us. Because what happened here is rare. Most people never hear bullies speak like this. Most people never get to see the truth behind the painted smile. But you have. And now you can't ignore it."

The students shifted uneasily in their seats, some leaning toward each other as if to seek comfort, others folding arms to keep themselves from trembling. Jeremy didn't let them retreat. "The hardest part is not seeing the smile," he said. "The hardest part is knowing what it means, and still facing it. That's why we're here. Not to run from it, not to bury it, but to face it together."

His voice softened, but it carried no less weight. "You may still feel anger. You may still feel hurt. That's natural. But you've also seen something else today—the possibility of change. Leo and Alex are proof of that. Lisa, too, is taking her first steps. And Harley…" He glanced toward the boy again. "…Harley has a choice. Just like Jerod will have a choice when his day comes. Every bully does." The class followed his gaze, the truth sharp in their eyes.

Jeremy stood tall now, drawing the conversation to its edge. "So don't be fooled by a smile. Don't be silenced by it. Learn to see it for what it is. And when you see it, remember today—remember that a painted smile can break, and when it does, the truth cannot be hidden anymore." His voice carried the certainty of a promise, a vow that what had been spoken here would not vanish into the air unnoticed.

He let his arms drop to his sides, his posture easing but his expression still solemn. The classroom remained silent, but this was no longer the silence of shock. It was the silence of thought, of students carrying the words inward, weighing them against their own memories. Jeremy let that silence linger, knowing it was doing the work his words could not finish.

Finally, he looked around once more, steady and sure. "We've opened the old wounds today," he said. "But wounds, when treated, can heal. They don't heal by being hidden. They heal by being seen." The students absorbed it, some blinking back fresh tears, others staring at their desks as if carving the words into memory. Jeremy knew he had given them something to hold onto, something heavier than the day before but necessary all the same.

The bell had not yet rung, but he closed his eyes briefly, drawing in a long breath. This was the reflection they needed, not for closure but for clarity. The painted smiles had been broken here. Now, it was up to each of them to see what remained.

The bell finally broke the silence, but it did not shatter it. Instead, the sound echoed strangely, as if reluctant to intrude upon what had just unfolded. No one leapt from their desks as they usually did, eager to escape the classroom and spill into the hall with chatter and laughter. The students rose slowly, their movements hesitant, like children who had stumbled into a church they did not expect to find. The air was heavy, and every shuffle of a book bag or scrape of a chair felt louder than it should have. Jeremy remained by the desk, his arms loosely crossed, watching them file out with a measured calm. He had no intention of sending them off with a smile or a joke; this moment needed to end in quiet, because quiet was the only vessel strong enough to carry the weight of what had been said.

Leo stayed near the back, his face drawn but not ashamed. Alex lingered beside him, their steps more deliberate than usual, as though they had walked through a storm and were still learning how to move in sunlight. The class parted around them, some students casting glances of respect, others still unsure what to feel. Yet no one mocked, no one laughed, no one sneered. For once, even the whispers had been stolen from the room. That absence spoke more than any confession had. It was as though the very act of admitting their pasts had pulled the venom out of the air, leaving behind an ache that would take time to heal.

Lisa walked with her arms folded tightly across her chest, her head lowered. The bluntness of her earlier words still lingered in the minds of her classmates, and no one dared to confront her about them. Yet, in the subtle way she kept close to Harley without touching him, there was a change—something almost fragile in its restraint. She did not radiate her usual defiance. She carried something heavier now, something she had not expected to carry when she first spoke. If anyone noticed, they kept it to themselves, perhaps recognising that silence was the greatest kindness they could offer her in this moment.

Harley stood still for a time, waiting until the crowd had thinned before moving. His height gave him presence, and his silence gave him mystery. The younger students watched him carefully, unsure whether to fear him or pity him. He did not break his mask, nor did he speak, but Jeremy noticed the way his jaw had tightened, his knuckles flexed, his shoulders drawn closer together. It was not anger that lived in him now, but the uncomfortable burn of being seen. Harley had not spoken a word, but his silence had already said more than he wanted it to. In that quiet, Jeremy recognised a boy at war with himself.

The hallway outside was uncharacteristically subdued. Instead of the rush of footsteps and bursts of conversation, there was a hush, as though the school itself was holding its breath. Pairs of students leaned close, not daring to raise their voices, trading half-finished sentences and unfinished thoughts. They carried the heaviness of confession like an invisible book clutched to their chests. No one wanted to be the first to dismiss it, no one wanted to break the spell too soon. For once, silence followed them down the corridor, and silence was stronger than noise.

Jeremy stayed in the room until the last of them had gone. He looked over the rows of empty desks, each one a witness to what had been spoken. He imagined the echoes of voices lingering there—Leo's confession, Alex's admission, Lisa's sharp honesty, the unsaid words from Harley that weighed as much as any truth. He walked between the desks slowly, placing his hand lightly on one, then another, as though grounding himself in the reality of the moment. Every surface seemed to hum with memory, and he knew that this day would not be easily forgotten.

He stopped at the window, watching the courtyard where students moved quietly toward their next class. It struck him that old wounds had been opened today, not just for those who spoke, but for those who listened. There had been pain in those stories, shame in those memories, but also something else—possibility. The possibility that healing could grow in the space left behind, if only the lessons were carried forward. He pressed his palm against the glass, his reflection faint, almost ghostly, and whispered under his breath, "Let them remember." It was not a command, nor a plea, but a hope.

Leo and Alex lingered just outside the classroom door, speaking softly to one another. They were not joking or roughhousing as they might have months ago. Instead, their words carried a new timbre, the sound of boys trying to shoulder responsibility instead of shrugging it away. Jeremy watched them for a moment before turning back into the room, letting them have their space. They had earned it. They had faced the class not as tormentors but as men willing to be seen for what they had done. That was no small thing, and it would take time to settle into their bones.

Lisa and Harley did not wait. They moved further down the corridor, side by side but not touching. Their silence was different from Leo and Alex's—it was raw, unfinished, the silence of two people whose wounds had only just been named. Jeremy could tell from the way Lisa's head remained bowed and Harley's shoulders remained rigid that they were not ready to face each other, not fully. But time has its own way of working on silence, and sometimes silence is the first step toward understanding.

Inside the classroom, the quiet was nearly complete. Jeremy lowered himself into a chair, resting his elbows on his knees, staring at the floor. The session had taken more from him than he realised, pulling energy from the deepest parts of his resolve. He thought of the faces of the students as they listened—some stricken, some angry, some relieved—and wondered what those faces would look like tomorrow, or the day after. Would they harden again? Would they carry on unchanged? Or would they begin to see, really see, the painted smiles when they appeared? That question lingered heavier than any answer he could give.

He remembered the boy who had asked what to do if they saw it. That question echoed now, louder than before. Jeremy knew he could not be everywhere, could not stand as shield for every student, but he could arm them with awareness. He could show them that silence is not neutral, that noticing is not weakness. That knowledge itself could become protection. It was a thin kind of armour, but armour all the same. He hoped it would be enough.

The clock on the wall ticked steadily, its sound amplified in the empty room. Each second stretched out like a reminder that life would continue, that routine would resume, that the world outside the classroom would keep spinning regardless of what had just taken place. And yet, Jeremy knew the shift was real. Something had cracked today, and cracks are not so easily repaired. They spread, they deepen, they change the shape of what they touch. That was the quiet aftermath: the sound of something broken refusing to return to what it once was.

He stood at last, gathering his notes without really looking at them, and placed them neatly on the desk. The act was simple, but it steadied him. He turned off the light, leaving the room in dim half-shadow, and stepped into the hallway. The school seemed quieter than usual, its hum softened, its edges dulled. As he walked, he felt the weight of both hope and burden pressing down on his shoulders. Hope that they had heard. Burden that they might forget.

As he made his way down the corridor, Jeremy thought of the faces of Leo, Alex, Lisa, and Harley, and of the many faces still waiting to speak. Old wounds had been opened, but wounds were not death sentences. They were beginnings, if tended to properly. That truth gave him enough strength to keep walking, even as the silence clung to him like a shadow. He did not break it. Some silences are meant to remain.

By the time he reached the stairwell, the noise of the school had begun to return in distant echoes—lockers slamming, laughter bubbling, the ordinary chaos of youth resuming its place. Yet even within that noise, he sensed an undertone of quiet. The aftermath lingered, not erased, not forgotten. The session had ended in silence, but silence is not absence. It is a seed. Whether it would grow into healing or harden into walls would depend on what they chose to do with it.

Jeremy descended the steps slowly, one hand brushing the railing, the other clutching nothing but his own thoughts. The heavy silence had not left him; it walked with him, a companion both stern and necessary. Healing was possible, yes—but only if the lessons held. Only if silence turned into memory, and memory into change. The quiet aftermath was not the end. It was the fragile beginning of something yet unseen.

## CHAPTER 6: THE UNSEEN FIGHTS

I always knew when Jarod was about to hurt somebody, because he wore the same smile every time. It wasn't like the smiles we gave each other when a joke was funny or when a game went right. His was stretched too big, like his face didn't fit it. His eyes never laughed with it, never matched. They stayed flat, almost empty, like he'd already made up his mind about what came next. That smile meant trouble. I'd watch kids stiffen when they saw it, like they were waiting for the hit before it even came.

When Jarod smiled like that, I felt my stomach twist. You could almost count the seconds before he shoved somebody, tripped them, or said something sharp enough to cut right through. The grin came first, like a warning signal, though most of the kids never caught on. They thought maybe he was joking, or maybe he just wanted to join in. I knew better. I'd seen it too many times. The grin was never about joining. It was about owning. Owning the space. Owning the moment. Owning whoever was unlucky enough to be standing close.

I tried to explain it once to Ty. I told him, "That grin is fake. It's not real. It's the same one right before he hits." Ty just looked at me the way he does when he's thinking too much. He nodded once, but he didn't say anything. He didn't have to. He'd seen it too. Ty sees everything. He doesn't miss a single move. But I was the one who noticed the grin, the way it always slid across Jarod's face like he was putting on a mask before the blow.

Sometimes I wondered if Jarod even knew he was doing it. Maybe it was like a switch he couldn't turn off. His mouth went one way, his eyes went another, and his hands balled into fists soon after. Maybe he thought it made him look calm, like he had control. But to me, it made him look dangerous. You can't trust a smile that doesn't reach the eyes. My mom says that. But with Jarod, it wasn't just untrustworthy. It was a weapon.

The first time I noticed it was back in gym class. We were lined up for dodgeball. Jarod smiled wide at the kid across from him, the kind of smile that made you think he was just playing around. Then the whistle blew, and he slammed that ball so hard into the kid's chest that he crumpled to the floor. The grin never left his face. He didn't laugh, he didn't shout like the rest of us. He just stood there, grinning, while the teacher rushed to check if the kid could breathe again.

From then on, I started watching closer. It was like reading a book where the ending was always the same. Jarod grinned. Jarod struck. Over and over. Kids stopped wanting to be near him, but sometimes you couldn't help it. Hallways are tight. Classrooms are tighter. He'd flash that grin, and you just hoped you weren't the target. I started thinking maybe I was the only one who could see it for what it was, a mask before the hit. But deep down, I knew others saw it too. They just didn't say anything.

# THE SMILE THAT BROKE

Leo said once, "That's not a smile. That's his warning." He knew, because he used to have one too. His was different, but it was still a mask. He told me he used to smile before he tore someone apart with words, just to make them doubt what was coming. Hearing him say that made me shiver. It meant Jarod wasn't just cruel. He was practiced. It meant he knew exactly what he was doing.

Even Alex admitted he'd seen it. He said, "That grin means you're about to bleed, one way or another." He didn't mean it as a joke. He never joked about Jarod. Neither did Lisa. She said she hated that grin most of all, because it tricked people. "He makes it look like he's safe," she told me, "but really, it's the last safe thing you'll see." She wasn't wrong.

The teachers never noticed. They saw a boy smiling, maybe even thought it was nice. They didn't look at the eyes. They didn't see how stiff his jaw was, or how he tilted his head just slightly, like he was already sizing you up for the blow. I tried to tell one teacher, but she only smiled back at me and said, "At least he's trying to be friendly." I wanted to yell, "No, that's not friendly! That's his weapon!" But I didn't. I knew she wouldn't believe me.

Once, Harley caught him grinning at a smaller kid by the lockers. Harley stepped in, taller, stronger, not afraid anymore. He looked Jarod straight in the eye and said, "Not this time." Jarod's grin wavered, just for a second. But then it came back, tighter, meaner. The little kid slipped away while the two of them stared each other down. I remember thinking that maybe Harley, who used to be a bully himself, was the only one who could break that grin. But even he didn't always win.

The worst part was how quiet it could be. No shouting, no warning. Just that grin. Then a shove into the lockers, a trip in the hallway, a fist to the stomach when no one was looking. The smile told you what was coming, but it didn't stop it. It was like hearing thunder and knowing lightning was already on its way. You couldn't stop the storm. You just braced for it.

I think the reason it scared me most was because I started seeing it in my sleep. Dreams where Jarod's grin followed me through hallways, across the playground, even into my own house. I'd wake up sweating, heart pounding, like he was waiting right there in the shadows with that same stretched grin. My mom said it was just bad dreams, but I knew better. It wasn't just dreams. It was the truth of who he was.

Sometimes I wondered if he ever smiled for real. If he did, I never saw it. I only ever saw the mask. And masks break eventually. Leo says that. He says the mask cracks when someone finally stands up to it, when the truth is too loud to ignore. But we weren't there yet. Not with Jarod. His grin was still strong, still cutting through the hallways like a knife no one wanted to touch.

I hated that grin. Not because it fooled me, but because it didn't fool anyone else enough to stop it. Everyone saw it, even if they pretended not to. But no one wanted to say the words out loud: Jarod was dangerous. Jarod was waiting for his next target. Jarod's grin was the flag that told us war was coming, and we weren't ready for it.

I wanted to tell him once, face to face, "Stop smiling. We all know what it means." But I never did. Maybe I was scared. Maybe I knew it wouldn't matter. Maybe I thought if I said it, he'd just grin wider, like he'd won again. So I stayed quiet. And every time that grin came back, my chest tightened, because I knew what was next. And I hated being right.

That grin is burned in my mind. Too wide. Too polished. Never real. It's the mask before the blow, the storm before the strike. And every time I see it, I know someone's about to get hurt. Sometimes it's me. Sometimes it's not. But the grin never lies.

It started with a low murmur that spread across the room like ripples in water. A few students leaned into one another, eyes shifting to the doorway as if Jarod might appear even when he wasn't there. Jasmin spoke first, her voice barely above a whisper, "I've seen that grin before." Her hands tugged at the edge of her desk as though she could hide inside the wood. Beside her, Ella nodded slowly, chewing at her lip, adding, "He did it right before he shoved me against the lockers. I thought maybe I was in his way, but no… he wanted it." The words carried weight, heavier than the air itself, pressing on every ear in the room.

Sophie clenched her fists tight on her lap, her eyes fixed on the floor tiles as she whispered, "He laughed after it. But it wasn't laughing, not like a joke. It was mean. He smiled and then he laughed like I wasn't even a person." The class shifted uncomfortably, a shuffle of shoes and a creak of chairs that made the silence afterward feel sharp. Nico glanced around, his face tense, and said aloud what others had been holding back: "That grin isn't just a face. It's a warning. We all know it." The statement lingered, no one rushing to disagree, because every student there carried a memory of it.

Jeremy leaned forward, his voice calmer but steady, "He did it to me too. Back when he thought he could corner me by the water fountains. That grin came first. Then he shoved me hard enough I smacked my shoulder against the tiles." He rubbed his arm, the echo of pain clear in his tone. Leo set his hand on Jeremy's shoulder, a brother's steadiness in his touch, and said firmly, "That's why we're talking about it. If you see the grin, you need to know what it means. He isn't joking. He isn't playing. He's planning."

Ty, quiet until then, raised his eyes. They were sharp, focused, and he spoke with the calm of someone trained to watch carefully. "I've studied people," he said simply, "and I can tell you Jarod's grin is his signal. It's his mask. It means he's already chosen someone. You don't wait for it to happen. You step back. You stay aware." The class listened closely, the authority in his voice cutting through the fog of fear. He didn't raise it, didn't sound angry, but when Ty spoke, students leaned in.

Miss Kara, standing at the back of the classroom, folded her arms tight, her face pale. She had been listening quietly, but finally said, "I've seen that smile in the hallway too. I thought maybe it was mischief, but now I realise… it's worse."

Mr. Clarke adjusted his glasses, his jaw tight, and admitted, "I missed it. I thought he was trying to be friendly." The honesty in his voice carried the same sting as the students' confessions. Teachers were supposed to know better, yet here they were, caught in the same shadow.

Mrs. Dunlop, usually composed, shook her head slightly. "That's the danger of a mask," she murmured. "It looks harmless until it isn't." She looked at the students, her expression firm. "You were right to speak up. Don't ever think your voices aren't enough." Nico caught the words and repeated them softer, like he needed to hear them himself. "Don't ever think our voices aren't enough." It was the kind of echo that settled deep, planting itself in the room like a seed.

From the far side, Mila, small and usually quiet, lifted her hand shakily. "He smiled at me once," she admitted, her voice cracking, "and then he tripped me in front of the whole playground. Everyone laughed, and I just wanted to disappear." Her eyes watered, and she ducked her head. Lisa, sitting only a desk away, clenched her jaw. She had been silent, but now she said bluntly, "That's exactly what he wants. He wants you small. He wants you scared. I used to do that too. And I hate that I did." Her words cut like a knife, because she didn't spare herself either.

Alex, leaning against the side wall, crossed his arms. "Fear is his game," he said. "He doesn't need fists to hurt you. The grin does half the work already. The rest comes after." He paused, meeting eyes across the room. "Don't lie to yourself and think it's harmless. It's not." The students shifted again, the truth heavy in the air. Some nodded, some bit their lips, but all of them knew he was right.

Mrs. Locke cleared her throat, her voice softer than usual. "I've taught long enough to see patterns," she admitted. "I should've seen this one. Smiles are supposed to bring comfort. His doesn't. It breaks it." The words echoed the book's title without her meaning them to, and Nico felt a chill as if the room itself understood the weight of what was being uncovered. The truth had been spoken now, no taking it back.

From the corner, Mrs. Haller spoke low. "We must remember this," she said. "Not brush it away, not excuse it. You've all described something dangerous, and ignoring it only helps him." Her gaze swept over the students, landing firmly on the teachers. Nico noticed how Mr. Arnett, the principal, shifted uneasily at that. He had been quiet through it all, but even he couldn't deny what was now laid bare.

At last, Sophie's small voice broke the silence again. "So what do we do when we see it?" Her question hung like smoke. Jeremy answered quietly, "We remember what it means. And we don't let him win." Leo added, steady and unshaken, "And we don't stay quiet anymore. Not about this. Not about him." The room grew still again, the sound of breathing louder than usual, every student suddenly aware of how close truth and fear lived together.

Mrs. Henley, the counselor, spoke with care, "What you've all shared today matters. Naming it is the first step. Don't ever think courage is only in standing up to a fist. Sometimes, it's in saying the words aloud." She gave a small nod toward Nico, Jeremy, and Leo. "And you've all done that here." The students let that sink in, the tremor of unease shifting slightly into something firmer, a small stone of strength at the center of their fear.

Still, none of it erased the chill that ran through them. The grin wasn't gone. Jarod wasn't gone. He would be back, in the halls, in the classrooms, on the playground. And each of them would see that grin again, sooner or later. But now, at least, they had spoken the truth of it. Now, they knew what it meant. And knowing was its own kind of power, even if their hearts still raced when they remembered it.

Leo stood up slowly, not rushing, his eyes fixed on the group of students who were all leaning forward as if waiting for him to drop something heavy on the floor. He rubbed his palms together once and said, "You don't need to shout to scare somebody. You don't even need to push. Sometimes your face does the job for you." His voice had no pride in it, no grin of his own, only the sound of someone who remembered too much. "That smile you're talking about? I used it before Jarod ever thought of it. It's not a smile—it's a warning." He paused, looking at Nico, then Jeremy, then back to the class. "When you see it, you're already the target."

Nico swallowed hard, the silence sharp around them. "You mean…" he started, but Leo cut in, his tone steady, "Yeah. It means you're next. And I don't care if it's your shoulder, your stomach, or the back of your head—you're already marked. Jarod doesn't pick by accident. He decides. And that smile is his promise." The room shifted, shoes scuffing faintly against the floor, but no one spoke. They knew Leo wasn't making it up, because the weight in his voice was too real.

Sophie's small voice broke through, trembling but brave. "You… you did that too?" Her question floated in the room. Leo nodded once, slow and firm. "I did. I wore that smile. I thought it made me strong. But really, it just made me mean. I used it when I wanted someone scared before I even touched them. And it worked." He looked down, jaw tight. "That's what makes it so dangerous. By the time you see it, your body's already braced for the hit."

Ty leaned forward, his arms resting on his knees. "So it's not just a face—it's strategy." His tone wasn't accusatory, just sharp in observation. Leo turned toward him. "Exactly. He's already won half the fight before he lifts a hand. You don't forget that grin once it's turned on you." He drew in a breath. "And Jarod's worse than I ever was. He doesn't stop at a shove. He'll punch you in the back of the head when you don't see it coming. Or right between your shoulder blades where it shocks your whole body. I've seen kids drop just from that."

Ella hugged her arms around herself, nodding nervously. "That happened to me once. I thought it was an accident." Leo shook his head, his eyes locking with hers. "No accident. Never with him. If it feels like it was on purpose, it was. Bullies don't waste effort. Every move is chosen. Every grin is timed. That's what I'm warning you about—don't excuse it. Don't tell yourself it was nothing. It's everything." His words carried a cold clarity, one that couldn't be brushed aside.

Jeremy, younger but no less fierce, piped up, "But you stopped. You don't do it anymore." His voice was insistent, almost demanding that the point be made. Leo's mouth softened for a moment. "Yeah, I stopped. Because people saw through me. Because Jeremy hugged me when I thought no one would. But Jarod's not there yet. He's still living in that grin. And until someone breaks it, he'll keep on hurting."

Mr. Clarke cleared his throat, his face pale but firm. "Leo's right. I've taught for years, and I've seen that same grin on boys who thought they ran the halls. We told ourselves it was mischief, but no—it was menace." His voice faltered, and Mrs. Locke added quietly, "We missed it too many times. Not this time." The teachers exchanged looks that spoke louder than words: they couldn't afford to pretend anymore.

Alex, leaning against the wall, arms crossed, finally spoke up. "You know what makes it worse? Jarod doesn't just grin at the small kids. He does it at anyone. Doesn't matter if you're big, older, stronger. He'll still do it. Because he wants to prove he can." He tilted his head, his voice dropping low. "That's the difference between him and me. I picked targets I thought I could control. Jarod doesn't care. He'll swing at anyone. That makes him dangerous in a way even I wasn't."

Nico shifted, feeling the weight of the words. He glanced at the students nearest him and saw the fear in their eyes. They weren't imagining it. They had seen that grin, and they had felt its sting. He took a breath and repeated softly, "So when he smiles, it's not a smile at all. It's a threat." The words settled into the room like dust, impossible to ignore.

Jasmin's voice cracked when she added, "He grinned at me before he shoved me into the mud last week. Everyone laughed. I didn't." Her eyes welled, but she didn't look away. Leo's gaze softened as he looked at her. "That's the truth. It's not about the shove. It's about breaking you in front of everyone else. The grin makes them laugh first. The hit makes them remember it."

Mrs. Haller folded her arms, her eyes narrowed. "We cannot allow this to continue unchecked. If that grin is his weapon, then naming it is ours." Her words carried a weight of finality, as though the adults in the room were finally stepping in where before they had been blind. But still, the students knew the fight wasn't over. It was only being seen.

Mila, quiet and hesitant, spoke last. "So… if we see the grin, we know something's coming. What do we do then?" She looked at Leo like he held the answer. Leo exhaled slowly, shaking his head. "You don't stand alone. You call someone. You stay with people who'll stand beside you. Because bullies like Jarod want you cornered. Don't give him that."

Ty's voice carried the steadiness of his father's training. "Strength isn't about standing alone. It's about standing together." He looked around the room, his eyes meeting each student. "That grin only works if you're alone with it. But we're not alone." Heads lifted slightly, the weight of his words building a fragile strength among them.

Nico's thoughts curled around what he'd just heard. Leo's warning wasn't just about Jarod. It was about all of them, about what they let slip by as "nothing." Every grin remembered, every laugh ignored, every bruise excused—they were all pieces of the same game. And Leo, once the master of it, was now standing here to expose it.

The silence that followed was sharp, not empty but heavy with understanding. Everyone in that room—students and teachers alike—had seen the grin. Now, no one could pretend they hadn't. The mask was off, the promise exposed, and the truth spoken aloud. The next time Jarod smiled, it would not be met with confusion. It would be seen for what it was: a weapon waiting to strike.

Alex leaned back against the wall, his arms folded tight, but his eyes were fixed on the group like he was carrying a stone in his chest that he couldn't put down. He let out a slow breath and said, "You know what? I used to stand in front of my bedroom mirror and practise it. Not a smile. Not really. More like a smirk. The kind that looks like you know something the other person doesn't. I'd tilt my head just so, curl my lip a bit, and watch myself until I got it right." The words came out heavy, and the room went quiet in a way that pressed into everyone's shoulders.

Nico swallowed hard, hearing the honesty in his voice. Alex didn't sound proud. He sounded ashamed, like dragging old bones out into the open. "I thought it made me powerful," Alex continued, his tone flat. "Like I didn't need to lift a hand, because one look could tell them what was coming. It made kids shrink away before I even touched them. That was the point. I wanted them scared before I ever laid a finger on them." He looked down at his shoes, unable to hold the weight of his own admission.

Ella shifted in her seat, frowning as she pulled her knees up a little, resting her chin on them. "So you… practised it? Like, on purpose?" Her question was soft, but it carried disbelief. Alex nodded, slowly, eyes still down. "Yeah. On purpose. Every night for a while. I practised being the guy people crossed the hallway to avoid. It was stupid, but it worked." His voice cracked slightly at the last word, the truth catching in his throat.

Leo gave a slow nod beside him, his voice steady but sad. "I did it too. Just not in the mirror. I knew how my face felt when I wanted to scare someone, and I used it. But Alex… yeah, he perfected it." The admission wasn't cruel, just plain, as though two guilty friends were trading scars in front of everyone. Jeremy pressed closer to Leo, sliding his arm around his brother's waist without saying a word, the hug enough to hold him steady.

Jasmin shook her head, eyes wide. "That's… creepy. Like, scary creepy. Practising how to be mean." She hugged her arms tight around herself. "I don't get why anyone would do that." Alex finally lifted his head, his eyes wet but fierce. "Because I didn't want to be small. I didn't want to feel like I was nothing. I thought if I scared everyone else first, they couldn't scare me." His words dropped heavy, and a murmur passed through the students, some nodding because they understood, others shuffling uncomfortably because they'd felt the sting of that smirk before.

Sophie leaned forward, her voice low but strong. "It still hurts, though. Even if it's just a look. It makes you feel smaller than you are. It makes you feel like you're about to get shoved, even if it doesn't happen." She bit her lip, her eyes locked on Alex. He nodded slowly. "I know. And I hate that I did that to people. It wasn't strength—it was fear, twisted into something ugly." His shoulders slumped, the fight gone from his posture.

Mr. Clarke rubbed the bridge of his nose, sighing. "I've seen that look on boys for years, and I told myself it was attitude, just bravado. I never thought about it being practised." His voice sounded weary, like the admission hurt him too. Mrs. Locke added quietly, "But it makes sense, doesn't it? How else does something become that sharp unless it's been sharpened?" The teachers exchanged glances, faces lined with the realization of things they'd missed.

Ty broke the silence, his voice calm but cutting. "That's the thing about training. Doesn't matter what it is—good or bad—it makes you stronger at it. You practised cruelty, Alex. You got strong at cruelty. But you stopped. You chose something else." He leaned back, folding his arms across his chest, his gaze steady. "Jarod's still training. Every day he practises that grin, whether he knows it or not."

Mila, who had been quiet the whole time, whispered, "So… every time he does it, it's not random. It's practiced." She shivered, her hands clenched in her lap. Alex looked at her, his face drawn tight. "Yeah. It's rehearsed. And that's why it works." His tone held no pride, only warning. The truth in his voice left no room for doubt.

Mrs. Dunlop, the vice principal, leaned against the doorway, her arms crossed, eyes sharp. "This is why we can't call it mischief. It's method. It's intentional. That changes everything." Her words carried the kind of weight that made the students straighten in their seats. For once, the adults weren't brushing it off. They were finally seeing it for what it was.

Jeremy tugged gently at Leo's sleeve, his small voice clear. "But he's not alone now. Alex isn't alone either. That's the difference." His eyes turned to the group, wide and sure. "Jarod doesn't get to win just because he practises. We can practise too. We can practise standing up together." The room stirred, small nods passing among the students like a ripple.

Alex blinked hard, his lips pressed tight, then gave Jeremy the smallest smile. "You're right," he said, his voice soft. "I practised the wrong thing for too long. Maybe now it's time I show you how to practise the right thing." His eyes swept the room, lingering on the students who looked most afraid. "Because if I can stop, if Leo can stop, then Jarod doesn't get to say it's impossible."

Mrs. Henley, the counsellor, finally spoke, her tone firm but kind. "And that's the truth we need to hold on to. Not just the fear, not just the grin, but the fact that it can end. That it has ended before." Her gaze rested on Alex, then Leo. "You two are living proof." The words didn't erase the discomfort in the room, but they gave it a direction.

Nico shifted in his seat, feeling the pulse of tension soften just a little. The story wasn't pleasant, and no one felt good hearing it, but maybe that was the point. Sometimes truth hurt more than lies, but it healed in ways nothing else could. He knew that by the way his classmates' eyes glistened—some with fear, some with anger, some with quiet relief.

And as Alex lowered his arms and leaned forward, his elbows on his knees, he muttered, "Don't ever fall for that smirk. Don't ever laugh at it. Call it what it is—a weapon." His words weren't loud, but every single person heard them, and no one dared to argue. The smirk had been unmasked, and now its shadow stretched across the room, undeniable, but no longer invisible.

Lisa shifted her weight, her chin lifting with the same defiance that once made kids back away before she'd even opened her mouth. Her eyes flicked toward the classroom windows, catching her own reflection for a moment, and then she turned to the others with a voice steady enough to cut through the hush. "That smile of Jarod's doesn't scare me," she said, the words plain but sharp. "You think I don't know it? I do. Because I wore it myself. Mine wasn't fake. Mine was a grin that meant I was ready. Ready to swing, ready to knock someone down. It dared people to push back, and most didn't." Her voice rang clear, filling the silence with the truth of who she had been.

The class tensed. Jasmin's mouth hung open for a second, then she shut it fast, eyes darting to Sophie as if to ask if she had heard the same thing. Sophie's arms tightened across her chest, her eyebrows drawn down. "You mean… you liked it?" she asked, her tone heavy with disbelief. Lisa didn't flinch. "No," she replied firmly, "I didn't like it. I needed it. There's a difference. I needed to be mean before anyone else got the chance. So I smiled the way Jarod does now, because I knew the second someone saw it, they'd know what came after. And I made sure of it."

Nico felt the air press heavy, his stomach turning. He wanted to look away, but Lisa's words pinned him where he sat. Jeremy, small but solid, shifted closer to Leo, clutching his brother's hand tight. Leo reached across with his other hand and touched Lisa's shoulder, steadying her with a glance that said he understood. She exhaled and squared herself again, as if his touch had given her permission to continue.

Ella raised her hand, her voice trembling. "But Lisa… weren't you scared? Like, even a little?" The question seemed almost childlike, but it hung in the air like a plea. Lisa's lips curled, not in a smirk, not in defiance, but in something sadder. "Of course I was scared. Every single time. But you think I'd show that? No. Fear doesn't keep you safe in places like this. Anger does. That grin? It was my armour. If they thought I was ready to hit, then maybe they wouldn't try."

Ty leaned forward, his eyes narrow but calm. "That's a warrior's mask. Only you weren't protecting yourself. You were picking fights. You turned it outward." His words weren't cruel; they were measured, almost analytical. Lisa nodded slowly, her jaw tight. "Yeah. I did. And I won't stand here and lie about it. I was cruel. I wanted people to flinch. I wanted to see them fold. Jarod's not new to me. He's familiar. He's me—just with more rage than control."

Alex shifted where he sat, his face pale, remembering his own mirror-practised smirk. "So you're saying you'd walk into a room smiling like him, and everyone knew what was coming?" Lisa looked him dead in the eyes. "Yes. Exactly that. And if they didn't know, they learned fast." Her voice caught for a moment, softer now. "I don't feel proud about it. But I won't hide it either. Someone has to say it plain. Jarod's grin is a warning. I know, because mine was too."

Mrs. Locke's lips pressed into a thin line. She didn't interrupt, though her eyes glistened with something between sorrow and anger. Mr. Clarke's hand hovered over his desk as though he wanted to speak, but he didn't. The silence was left for Lisa to fill, and she did. "If you think bullies always look the same—loud, shouting, obvious—you're wrong. Sometimes it's just a smile. A smile that breaks you before a fist ever does."

Mila whispered, almost to herself, "But that's worse. Because smiles are supposed to mean good things. Not that." Her words barely carried across the room, but Lisa heard them and gave a small nod. "That's the point. It's a trick. A weapon. And it works because no one wants to believe a smile could hurt."

Jeremy let out a shaky breath, his small hand still locked in Leo's. "But you're not like that now," he said firmly, his voice rising to steady her. Lisa's gaze softened, her posture losing some of its hardness. "No," she admitted, "not now. But I need you all to know that I was. Because if you think Jarod's the only one, you'll miss the signs. And missing the signs means someone gets hurt."

Mrs. Dunlop stepped forward, arms crossed, her expression stern. "Lisa's telling you something valuable. Don't dismiss it because it makes you uncomfortable. This is the truth of how intimidation grows." Her voice carried the authority of years in charge, and even the restless students stilled.

Nico watched the faces around him. Some were pale, some flushed with anger, some just tired with the weight of what they were hearing. He realised, with a sharp clarity, that no one in that room could ever look at Jarod's grin the same way again. It had been unmasked, laid bare, turned inside out by someone who had once used it as her own shield and sword.

Leo cleared his throat, speaking low. "And you stopped. That matters, Lisa." She gave him a half-smile, one without menace, without armour. "I stopped because someone cared enough to pull me out of it. That's what broke me. Not a fist. Not a fight. A letter. And a hug I didn't think I deserved." She turned briefly toward Harley, and his cheeks flushed red, but he didn't look away.

Alex whispered, "So Jarod's still trapped in it." Lisa nodded once, firmly. "Yeah. And until someone pulls him out, he'll keep smiling that way. And people will keep flinching."

Ty straightened, his calm voice carrying a weight beyond his years. "Then we don't flinch. Not anymore. We've seen it. We know it. His weapon isn't hidden anymore." His words lingered, steady as stone, and the room seemed to draw a collective breath.

The tension held, thick and sharp, but no one broke it with nervous chatter or laughter. They all sat in it, letting the truth settle into their bones. Lisa's confession had stripped the grin of its disguise, leaving nothing but the dangerous shadow it truly was. And in that silence, the class began to understand—sometimes the fight starts before fists ever fly.

Harley stood against the wall, his arms folded tight, shoulders heavy as though carrying more weight than his frame could bear. His eyes tracked the room slowly, not with the swagger he once carried, but with a stillness that drew attention anyway. When Lisa's words settled and the silence stretched too long, he gave a single nod, almost reluctant, but strong enough to be seen. "She's right," he said quietly, his voice lower than most expected. "I've done it too. That grin. You don't need fists when you've got that. Sometimes the look alone is enough to stop someone cold." His admission drew the room's gaze, the honesty disarming in its bluntness.

Jeremy shifted on his chair, staring at him with wide eyes. "You mean… you didn't even have to hit them?" he asked, his voice steady but sharp with disbelief. Harley shrugged, his jaw tight. "No. Sometimes I didn't. A grin, a step closer, and they froze. They'd stand still like rabbits do when they think a fox is near. Afraid if they moved, they'd get worse. So they stayed. They let me have control without me ever needing to touch them." His words dripped with shame, and for once his tall frame looked smaller.

Ella's breath caught, and her hand went to her mouth. "But that's awful," she whispered, her voice breaking. Harley's eyes flicked to her, and he nodded once. "It is. I'm not saying it's not. I knew what I was doing. I knew they were scared. I liked it." The words burned the air, heavy with guilt. His fists clenched against his chest, not in threat, but in memory. "And every time, that grin made it worse. Because it wasn't just fear. It was me showing them I was enjoying it."

Leo leaned forward, his tone low but steady. "That's the truth of it. You don't need to swing a punch. Just a look will do. You freeze them in place and make them feel trapped. That's worse than a hit sometimes. Because a bruise fades, but that memory doesn't." He met Harley's eyes, and for a moment the two boys, once mirrors of each other, shared the weight of knowing what they had been. Harley's chin dropped slightly, his agreement silent but absolute.

Mila raised her hand, her face pale but determined. "So you both… liked seeing the fear?" she asked, her voice trembling. Harley's throat tightened as he answered. "Yeah. At the time, I did. Because it meant I was winning. It meant I had power. And when you've never had power before, it feels like air when you're drowning." His voice cracked at the last word, and the room stilled as the confession lingered.

Ty, calm and sharp-eyed, spoke softly. "But that's not winning. That's taking. Taking what doesn't belong to you." His gaze pinned Harley, not with judgment, but with truth. Harley nodded again, rubbing the back of his neck. "I know that now. I didn't back then. Back then, all I knew was that smile worked. They'd see it, and I'd own the room. Even teachers noticed, and most of the time they let it go because I wasn't hitting anyone." His voice was bitter, the taste of old habits still in it.

Sophie frowned deeply, her voice rising louder than usual. "But you scared kids who never did anything to you! That's not power. That's cruelty." Her anger quivered, but it was honest. Harley turned toward her, his eyes weary. "I know," he said again, the words scraping. "I can't undo it. But I can say it out loud so you all know the signs. If you see that grin, you'll know it's not real. You'll know someone's about to get hurt."

Mrs. Locke pressed her hand against her desk, her knuckles white. She didn't interrupt, but her eyes fixed on Harley as though she was memorising every word. Mrs. Dunlop's lips parted as if to speak, but she let him continue, letting the moment carry itself. The adults didn't lead here. The children did.

Jeremy let out a breath he didn't know he was holding. "So the smile's like… a warning?" Harley met his younger friend's gaze and gave a slow nod. "Yeah. A warning. And if you ever see someone grin like that, don't believe it's friendly. It isn't. It's a mask. The meanest kind of mask." His voice had gone soft again, but it carried to every corner of the room.

Jasmin leaned forward, her brows knit together. "And you'd use that at recess, in the halls… anywhere?" she asked carefully. Harley's lips pressed thin, and he answered without hesitation. "Everywhere. The playground, the hallways, even at the bus stop. That smile was mine, and I wore it like armour. And every time, I thought I was proving I was strong." He shook his head, regret weighing his words. "But really, I was proving I was scared."

Alex exhaled, his voice quieter than usual. "That's the part they don't tell you. Being a bully doesn't mean you're brave. It means you're too scared to show weakness." His glance toward Harley wasn't cruel, but knowing. Harley clenched his fists, then let them fall open. "Yeah. That's it. I was too scared to show I was broken, so I made sure everyone else looked broken instead."

The class shifted, restless but subdued. Nico felt the pulse of the truth pounding through the room. These weren't excuses. They were confessions, laid bare by voices that once used the same weapons Jarod now carried. He realised, as did the others, that the grin wasn't just Jarod's. It had been theirs too, and it had already left scars.

Mrs. Henley leaned against the back wall, her eyes glistening. She said nothing, but her hand brushed against her notebook as though she might write it down to remember later. Mr. Clarke's gaze swept the room, settling briefly on Harley before moving back to the students. The silence belonged to the children, and he didn't take it from them.

Ella whispered almost to herself, "So… a smile isn't always safe." The words were barely audible, but they echoed through every ear. Harley heard them most of all, and for the first time, his tall frame seemed to shrink as he nodded in agreement. He looked down at the floor and let out a breath that carried the weight of every false grin he had ever given.

In that quiet, the truth stood taller than any bully could. The mask of a grin was broken, its sharp edges laid out for everyone to see. And Harley, stripped of bravado, left it there on the floor, never to be picked up again.

I've seen a lot of smiles in this school, but Jarod's isn't one of them. His grin is like a fist before it ever swings, the kind that makes your stomach hurt because you know it's not for fun. Most teachers walk past it, thinking it means nothing, just a boy showing teeth, but every kid in this room knows better. We've all felt it. That grin is a promise. It's the warning before the punch to the back of your head or the shove that knocks you into lockers. It's louder than words, and it burns into you so deep that you carry it home even after the bruise is gone. Adults don't see that fight, but we live it every day.

Ty leaned forward on his desk, his hands folded like he was ready to spring if he needed to. "It's a battle before the first move," he said softly, but I think every one of us heard him. His voice cut through the quiet like it was meant to be there.

# THE SMILE THAT BROKE

Ella rubbed her arms and glanced at Sophie, and they both nodded without saying anything. They knew what he meant. You could feel Jarod's grin from across the playground, and it still felt like you'd been pushed. That's what I was trying to say.

Leo shifted in his chair and met my eyes. "I used that look too. When I wanted control, I didn't need fists right away. The grin did it first." He wasn't proud, but he wasn't hiding either. I nodded back at him, because I believed him. And that's why Jarod scares us all. He knows exactly what that grin does. It's like he practised it the same way Leo and Alex once did, except Jarod isn't interested in control. He wants damage. He wants you down on the ground before you can think.

Alex tapped his desk with his knuckles, slow and steady. "It's the kind that hurts before it even hits you. You see it, and your body braces. You already feel the blow before it comes." His words made Jasmin flinch, like she had remembered one herself. She turned her eyes down, but not before I caught the shake in her shoulders. I hated seeing that, hated that Jarod could make her feel small just by smiling. It proved everything I was trying to explain.

Jeremy, my little brother, leaned closer to me. "So… it's like the fight starts in your head before it starts on your body?" he asked, his voice carrying enough for everyone to hear. I put my hand on his desk and nodded firmly. "Exactly. And that's the worst part, because no adult believes you. You can't point to a bruise yet, but it's already there inside you." Jeremy's eyes dropped to his desk, and he didn't say another word. He didn't need to.

Mrs. Locke adjusted her glasses and opened her mouth like she was going to speak, but she didn't. She just watched us. Mr. Clarke, too. His jaw was set, but he stayed back, letting us carry it. For once, they weren't filling the silence with teacher talk. They let the weight stay where it belonged. I think they finally understood that kids can explain it better than any handbook.

Lisa crossed her arms, her chin lifting high. "Jarod's grin is different from mine ever was. Mine was for a fight I could control. His is for pain, plain and simple. He doesn't want to prove himself. He wants to break someone." Her honesty made Harley glance at her, then at the rest of us, and he nodded slowly. "She's right. That's why it feels worse. It's not just a warning—it's him enjoying the thought of it before he even lifts a hand." His voice was rough, the truth dragging out of him.

Mila raised her hand but didn't wait to be called on. "So it's like an invisible fight? Everyone knows it's happening, but no one says anything?" Her question hit exactly what I was thinking. "Yes," I said, loud enough so no one missed it. "That's what I've been trying to say. These are fights you can't see, but every kid feels them. And by the time someone finally gets hit, it's too late. The damage was already done the moment he smiled."

Mrs. Dunlop shifted uneasily in her chair, but she didn't cut in. Ms. Henley, the counselor, scribbled something in her notebook, but her eyes were wet. She'd probably heard hundreds of stories, but maybe this was the first time she really heard it from us, not through reports. Maybe now she'd remember the way our voices shook when we said it out loud.

Sophie let out a shaky laugh, but it wasn't happy. "Adults always say to ignore it. But you can't ignore a grin like that. It sticks to you like glue." Her laugh faded quick, and silence took over again. No one corrected her, because she was right. You can't ignore it. You carry it even when you try to walk away.

Harley leaned forward, his elbows heavy on the desk. "That's why Jarod scares everyone more than they admit. Because we all know what comes next." He didn't smile, not once. For him, the grin was something he had left behind, and now it made him sick. The look on his face said he wished he could erase every time he had ever used it.

I looked around at my classmates, at Ty's steady eyes, Jeremy's small frame, Leo and Alex's sharp edges dulled by honesty, Lisa's defiance, Sophie's pale face, Jasmin's lowered eyes. Every single one of them knew. They didn't need me to explain anymore, but I did anyway, because the truth matters more when you say it twice. "These smiles are invisible fights. They sting just as much as a punch. And if you see it, you should know what it means—because it means the punch is already coming."

The room stayed quiet after I said it, but I saw nods, slow and heavy. Even the teachers didn't argue. They knew the fight wasn't just in the fists. It was in the grin that started it, and now that we'd put words to it, no one could unsee it again.

When Leo stood up from his chair, there was no hesitation in him. He didn't look at Mr. Clarke or the principal for permission, he simply stepped into the open space at the front of the room and crooked his finger at Alex. Alex grinned, not the good kind, but the one every kid recognised—the grin he had spoken of earlier, the one he had trained in front of a mirror long ago. A ripple of unease rolled through the students, a shuffle of feet, a few nervous coughs. They already understood what was coming, even before Leo squared his shoulders and dropped his chin slightly, that predator's angle that made him look larger, older, sharper than his eleven years. I felt my stomach tighten, because even though they weren't going to hurt anyone, the memory of what those postures meant was still strong.

Alex mirrored him with slow precision. His back straightened, arms loose at his sides but with fists curled just enough that the knuckles whitened. His grin widened into something that dared everyone to deny the fear creeping in. Sophie pressed her hand against her desk, fingers digging at the wood. Jasmin whispered something to Ella, but her eyes never left Alex. It wasn't the threat of a fight—it was the certainty that one could happen at any second. That was the weight these two carried with nothing but stance and a look.

Jeremy leaned close to me, whispering into my sleeve. "They don't even have to move, Nico. It feels real already." His voice cracked, and I nodded because he was right. It was real, even if no punch landed. The air grew heavy, and even the teachers didn't interrupt. They knew this demonstration was worth more than a thousand words. Mrs. Dunlop crossed her arms but stayed in her chair, letting the lesson unfold.

Leo lowered his shoulders and took a single step forward, and I swear half the class pulled back in their seats. It was instinct, pure and simple. Sophie's breath caught loud enough that I heard it. That one step carried the history of all the kids he'd ever cornered, all the threats he had ever made. And now Alex tilted his head, grinning wider, that same look that had once made Leo himself a victim. The two of them weren't touching anyone, but the room was caught in their web just the same.

"See?" Leo's voice was steady, but it cut through the silence. "This is how we did it. We didn't need words, because your own body tells you what's coming. You freeze before the first shove." He straightened, pulling himself back from the posture, letting the class breathe again. Shoulders eased, but the memory didn't. Alex followed suit, shaking out his arms, as though letting go of a shadow.

"That grin," Alex added, pointing to his own mouth, "was enough to make someone fold. That's why Jarod's grin scares you. It's the same language. It's the same trap." A hush followed, and I could see every student take those words and pin them to Jarod in their minds. They couldn't deny it anymore.

Lisa stepped forward then, arms crossed, her eyes narrowing at both boys. "That's child's play compared to him," she said flatly. "You two know how to scare kids. Jarod knows how to hurt them. I've seen it." She looked around the room and added, "Leo and Alex use it like a game, but Jarod… he enjoys it." Her words landed heavier than the demonstration itself.

That's when Leo glanced at Alex, something unspoken passing between them. He took a breath and said, "We found out something yesterday. Jarod's not just a schoolyard bully. He trains. He's been at the dojo downtown." The class stiffened, waiting for more. Alex's grin was gone now, his face sharp with seriousness.

"He's a purple belt in Kung Fu," Alex said, his voice carrying to the back of the room. "That means he's not guessing. He knows how to hit you in ways that can do damage. He's not just swinging fists, he's trained." A murmur broke across the room—Ella gasped, Sophie whispered, "That's why it hurts so bad," and Mila pressed her hand to her chest.

Ty finally spoke, calm but firm, his words carrying the weight of knowledge. "A purple belt isn't a beginner. It means discipline, technique, and speed. If Jarod uses it the wrong way, he can hurt more than bones. He can leave scars no one sees." He looked at Jeremy, then at me, then around the class. "This isn't just intimidation anymore. It's real danger."

Mr. Clarke adjusted his tie, looking troubled, but even he didn't interrupt. The adults let the current of our words keep flowing. Mrs. Locke scribbled notes, her lips pressed into a line. The principal tapped his pen against his notebook but said nothing. For once, no adult tried to water down what we already knew.

Leo stepped back from Alex, running a hand through his hair. "This is what we mean when we say fights aren't always seen. You think it's just a smile or a step forward. But with Jarod, it's training behind it. It's a strike waiting to happen." He wasn't boasting, he wasn't preaching. He was warning. And the class took it like a truth they'd needed spelled out.

Jeremy raised his small voice. "So, if he grins… that means he's already picked someone?" The words made everyone fall silent. Even the teachers exchanged looks, because it was the kind of question only a nine-year-old would dare to ask, and it was the one everyone else had been thinking.

Harley, leaning back in his chair with his arms folded, finally broke his silence. "That's exactly what it means. He's already decided. He's just waiting for you to flinch, and then he strikes." The honesty in his tone hit harder than any grin could. Lisa looked at him, and for once she didn't argue.

Alex let out a long breath. "That's why you all needed to see it. So the next time you catch that grin, you'll know you're not imagining it. It's real. And it means get ready, because he's not smiling at you—he's smiling at the thought of hurting you."

The room stayed heavy, every word pressing down, every kid clutching the truth tighter. No one looked at Jarod's empty chair, but we all thought of it. His presence was there even without him. That's how much power that grin carried, and that's why this demonstration mattered.

When Lisa stood, it wasn't sudden or noisy, but everyone in the room seemed to feel it. She didn't need to say a word. She had that way about her, that heavy presence that made people slide their chairs back without even thinking. She didn't look at Mr. Clarke, didn't look for permission, just crossed her arms and tilted her chin, that grin stretching slow across her face. It wasn't friendly. It wasn't meant to be. It was the same grin she once used when she wanted to make someone sweat before she threw the first punch. I knew it wasn't real anymore—she'd changed—but the echo of who she used to be filled the air.

Harley followed her lead, pushing back from his desk with a scrape of chair legs that made Sophie wince. He didn't talk either. He didn't need to. He was taller than most of the class already, sharper in the shoulders, his shadow spilling over the nearest desks. When he took two steps forward, that alone was enough to make three students lean back, hands gripping the sides of their chairs. He didn't sneer, but the grin he wore had the same weight Leo had spoken of earlier. A mask. A threat. A promise that pain was waiting.

Ella whispered to Jasmin, "They're not even doing anything," her voice cracking with nerves. Jasmin nodded, eyes wide, hugging her notebook close to her chest as if it might shield her. Mila twisted a strand of hair around her finger, whispering prayers under her breath that Lisa and Harley weren't about to turn on someone. The fear in the room wasn't because they thought a fight would break out. It was because every one of us remembered what it was like when that grin meant a fight was about to break out.

Jeremy's small voice cut through the hush. "This is what it felt like before. Every time." He didn't lift his head. He didn't need to. The tremor in his words said enough. He'd seen Harley do this before, long before Ty pulled him back from that life. Jeremy's voice carried weight because it was memory, not just lesson.

Lisa leaned just a little closer to Sophie's desk, her grin widening. "Feels heavy, doesn't it?" Her tone was calm, but it made Sophie sink into her chair. "That's all it takes. Just standing here. No fists, no words. You can feel it crawling under your skin." She pulled back then, arms still crossed, letting her words do the bruising instead of her hands.

Harley added, his voice lower than usual, "It freezes you. Doesn't matter if you're smaller or bigger. That grin tells you you've already lost." He looked at Leo, then Alex, then down at Jeremy. "We used it all the time." He wasn't proud. He wasn't boasting. He was laying it bare, and every student in the room believed him because we'd all felt it before.

Mr. Clarke shifted in his seat, but he didn't move to stop them. None of the adults did. They recognised this was a teaching moment, even if it left their stomachs knotted. Mrs. Locke scribbled something in her notes, her face pale. Miss Kara tapped her pen against her notebook, restless but silent. Even the principal just watched, lips pressed tight. They let the lesson play out because this wasn't theory—it was reality, alive and standing right in front of us.

Ty finally spoke, voice steady as ever. "That grin is a weapon." His eyes flicked from Lisa to Harley, then to the rest of us. "Don't fool yourselves into thinking it's harmless. It's the first strike before the strike." His words didn't scold—they explained. But even Ty's calm couldn't ease the heaviness pressing down.

Lisa's grin faded, her expression hardening. "I used to love this feeling," she admitted. "The way people sank into their seats when I stood like this. The way no one dared look me in the eye. It gave me power." Her honesty chilled the room more than her grin had. It wasn't past tense in her voice—it was a confession that this power still lingered in her, waiting to be chosen or denied every single day.

Harley shook his head, his grin slipping into something tighter, almost ashamed. "It eats at you though. After a while, it doesn't just scare them—it scares you too. Because if you can control a room with nothing but a look, you start to wonder if you even know who you are without it." He rubbed the back of his neck, breaking eye contact with everyone. For the first time since standing, he looked small.

The students whispered among themselves, voices weaving through the heavy air. "That's what Jarod does," one said. "That's the same grin." Another added, "But his is worse. He really means it." Their words fluttered like broken leaves, scattered but true. Even the teachers heard them and didn't silence them. Everyone knew the truth.

Jeremy leaned forward, his voice steady this time. "And that's why we're showing you this. So you can see it for what it is. A lie. A mask. And when you know it's a mask, you don't have to give it your power anymore." His words, though small, carried like a bell in the stillness.

Lisa and Harley stepped back then, their grins fading, their shoulders dropping. The room let out a breath it didn't know it had been holding. Jasmin unclenched her fists, Sophie wiped her palms against her skirt, and Mila finally let her hair fall from her hands. The silence after their retreat was almost as powerful as the moment itself.

No one doubted the lesson. No one doubted the truth. The menace of their presence had shown us all that bullying didn't always need fists or names or even words. Sometimes it was just a smile—a smile that broke the air like a storm before lightning struck. And every student in that room knew they'd seen it before, and that they would see it again.

The room had gone still, and you could hear the scratch of a pencil rolling off one desk to the floor like a pin dropping in a chapel. No one moved to pick it up. Shoulders tightened, bodies shrank in on themselves, and eyes stared at anything but Lisa or Harley. That's the thing about intimidation—it doesn't need fists, it doesn't need shouting. It crawls under your skin and makes you fold into yourself as if you can somehow make yourself smaller, invisible. And even though no one had been touched, the air felt heavy, pressed down on our chests like something waiting to explode.

I glanced around the room, watching the way Jasmin kept her head down, hair falling like a curtain to shield her face. Ella chewed the edge of her lip until it was nearly raw, clutching her pencil so tightly it looked like it might snap. Sophie sat stiff, hands flat against her desk, her eyes locked on the grain of the wood as though memorising every line would save her from glancing up. These weren't bruises you could photograph, but they were bruises all the same. Fear doesn't always show itself in colours on the skin—it shows itself in the way your voice disappears.

Leo shifted in his chair, his jaw tight, as though every moment was pulling memories out of him he didn't want to face. Alex leaned forward with elbows on his knees, his eyes narrowed, nodding faintly as if saying to himself, See, this is exactly what we used to do. Jeremy sat with his hands gripping the edge of his chair, his knuckles pale, trying not to let his voice tremble if he spoke. We all knew the truth: this silence wasn't peace. It was pressure. It was the pause before a blow.

Harley looked down now, his grin gone, his shoulders dropped. You could see it in his face—he recognised what he'd just stirred. Maybe he'd forgotten what it felt like to stand there in the middle of the room, making people shrink away. Maybe he hadn't realised how much it still lived inside him, even though he wasn't that person anymore. Lisa folded her arms again, no longer grinning, her lips pressed together, eyes hard as stone. She didn't enjoy what she saw reflected back in the class. That was the sting, wasn't it? Power feels different when you're standing on the other side of it.

Ty finally broke the silence, his voice steady and low. "No one here got hit. Not a scratch, not a bruise. And yet look around you." He gestured slightly with his hand, sweeping across the room. "You all felt it. That weight? That's the fight before the fight. That's what a smile can do when it's not real." His words didn't rise above normal, but they carried sharp enough to cut through the stillness. Heads lifted just enough to glance at him, then quickly lowered again. He had spoken the truth we'd all been choking on.

Mr. Clarke leaned back in his chair, fingers pressed against his lips, as though he wanted to step in but knew better than to interrupt. Miss Kara scribbled quickly into her notebook, her eyes darting back and forth, watching every reaction. Mrs. Dunlop and Mrs. Locke exchanged a glance, and Mrs. Haller simply folded her arms tight, her mouth a grim line. Even the adults felt it—that reminder that fear didn't always need to be loud to leave its mark.

Mila raised her hand halfway, hesitated, then dropped it again. "It feels like…" she whispered, not sure if anyone would listen, "…like we're waiting to be picked." The words cut deeper than anything else. A few heads nodded slowly, as though she'd spoken for everyone who had ever sat in that very spot, waiting for the bully's eye to land on them.

Jeremy finally spoke, voice quiet but clear. "That's why it matters. Because nobody sees this. Teachers don't see it, parents don't see it. But we do." He swallowed hard, his eyes on Leo. "And sometimes, it's worse than the hit." Leo nodded once, firm, his eyes darker than usual, and Alex gave the smallest grunt of agreement. They knew, more than anyone, that intimidation was the first wound, the invisible one.

I leaned back slightly, letting the weight of the silence settle before adding my own thought. "This is what we mean when we say unseen fights. It's not fists flying in the hallway. It's not shouting across the playground. It's this. Shoulders hunched. Eyes down. Breathing stuck in your throat. And even if no one touches you, you walk away already hurt." My words weren't meant to scare them more. They were meant to name what was already there.

The counsellor, Ms. Henley, folded her hands, her eyes softer than the rest of the teachers. She didn't say anything, but the way she looked at us said she knew exactly what had just happened. Mrs. Takashi, calm as always, simply nodded at her husband, as though they'd both agreed silently that this lesson didn't come from them—it came from us. And that was the only way it could work.

Lisa finally spoke again, her voice firm. "That grin isn't a joke. It isn't just a face. It's a threat. And the truth is, when I wore it, I meant it. Every time." She let the words hang in the air. No excuses, no softening. Just the truth. And the truth was heavy enough to keep us all quiet for a long while after.

No one clapped. No one thanked her. That wasn't the point. The point was, every single person in that room now understood something they hadn't put into words before: intimidation leaves marks. Fear doesn't need fists to bruise you. And the hardest battles are often fought in silence, before the first punch is ever thrown.

The door creaked open, and everyone in the room froze as if the air itself stopped moving. Jarod stepped inside with that same grin, stretched too wide across his face, sharp as glass. He didn't say a word, but the way he held his shoulders back, his chin lifted, told everyone he didn't need words. That grin carried its own voice, and it spoke louder than anything else. I felt my stomach twist, because I'd seen what came after that look, and so had plenty of others in the room.

Ella's chair squeaked as she shifted, pulling her feet closer under the desk, trying to vanish. Jasmin gripped her pen so hard her fingers trembled. Sophie let out the smallest breath, like she'd been holding it since the door opened. Even Mila, who rarely showed nerves, tilted slightly back, her eyes following Jarod's every step as though bracing for something to snap. That's what fear looks like when no one admits it out loud—it's written in the way bodies move, or don't move at all.

Leo's jaw clenched, and I saw him glance toward Jeremy, as if to say, This is it. This is what I warned you about. Alex sat back, folding his arms tight, his eyes narrowed but steady, though the flick of his foot against the floor gave him away. Lisa's face hardened, but her hands had gone still in her lap. Even Harley, taller than most, shifted his weight as though something about Jarod's grin scraped against an old memory he couldn't shake.

Jarod stopped near the front of the room, his grin never slipping. He didn't raise his fists, didn't shout, didn't throw a single punch. But the silence grew louder, thicker, until you could almost hear hearts beating faster. That was the thing about him—he didn't need to touch you to own the moment. He knew the weight of his presence, and he used it like a weapon sharper than any fist.

Mr. Clarke sat straighter, his lips parting, but he didn't speak. Mr. Arnett's hand hovered near the edge of his desk, knuckles pale. Mrs. Dunlop looked from student to student, her eyes wide, searching for something she could do to stop the pressure building in the room. Miss Kara's pen tapped quickly against her notebook, her own nerves showing in the rhythm. Mrs. Locke glanced toward Mrs. Haller, whose brow furrowed as if calculating what might happen next. Even Ms. Henley, calm as she always tried to be, leaned forward slightly, as though bracing herself.

Ty didn't flinch. He sat quietly, watching Jarod the way his father once told him to study a shadow—never turning away, never breaking eye contact. His stillness was a different kind of defiance, one Jarod noticed. For just a moment, the grin twitched, his eyes narrowing, as if he didn't like that someone so much smaller refused to shrink back. Ty's silence wasn't fear. It was a challenge without words.

Jeremy's small voice broke through, softer than I expected. "Why do you smile like that?" The room held its breath. Jarod tilted his head, his grin widening, but he said nothing. That silence was louder than any answer, and Jeremy lowered his eyes quickly, his hand gripping the edge of the desk until his knuckles turned white.

I could feel my chest tighten, because we all knew the truth: Jarod didn't need to prove himself in that moment. He had already done it. Every flinch, every lowered eye, every clenched jaw was proof enough. He had owned the room the moment he walked in, and he knew it. That grin wasn't just for us—it was for himself, feeding on the fear he stirred.

Mrs. Takashi's gaze met her husband's, both of them silent but sharp-eyed. They weren't fooled. They'd seen this kind of grin before, the kind that promised violence was never far behind. But they didn't interrupt, because this wasn't their fight. It was ours. And that truth made the weight in the room even heavier.

Jarod finally shifted his gaze across the room, letting it rest on one student after another, lingering just long enough for each to feel the burn of being seen. He never raised his fists, but everyone felt them anyway. His grin was a weapon, and it left bruises no one could see. And in that moment, every single heart in that room raced faster, waiting for what might come next.

Ty stood up slowly, his chair scraping across the floor in a way that made the entire room freeze. He didn't look afraid, not even a little. His voice came steady, like it belonged to someone far older than eleven. "Jarod doesn't mess with words. He doesn't twist things around like Leo and Alex once did. He uses fists. He uses kicks. He uses that grin to warn you what's about to happen. And he doesn't care if it hurts." His eyes stayed fixed on Jarod's, calm but unflinching. "That's why he's dangerous."

A ripple went through the class, a mix of shock and relief. Shock that someone dared to say it out loud, relief that at least one voice was brave enough to name what everyone else had only whispered. Ella's hand fluttered near her desk, her pencil rolling off and clattering to the floor. Sophie drew in a sharp breath but kept her eyes low, as though afraid Jarod might notice her agreement. Jasmin looked between Ty and Jarod, her lips parted, caught between fear and admiration for Ty's courage.

Jarod's grin twitched, but Ty didn't falter. He lifted his chin slightly, not in pride, but in readiness. "I'm not scared of you," he added, his tone flat, not raised, not trembling. "Because I've trained for people like you." His words landed in the silence like small stones dropped into still water, rippling outward until every student in the room shifted. Jeremy's wide eyes fixed on Ty, the younger boy gripping the table edge as though anchoring himself to the moment.

Leo leaned forward, elbows on his knees, studying Ty with something close to surprise. He hadn't expected the quiet one to be the first to rise. Alex crossed his arms tighter, his expression unreadable, though his eyes flicked back and forth between Jarod and Ty like he was measuring the odds. Lisa gave a small nod, approving, while Harley tilted his head just enough to show respect for the boy who dared.

Mr. Clarke adjusted his glasses, but he didn't interrupt. Mr. Arnett straightened in his chair, his hand sliding away from the desk edge, letting the tension play out. Mrs. Dunlop's lips pressed into a thin line, her knuckles white on the arm of her chair. Mrs. Locke's pen stopped moving across her page, frozen mid-sentence, while Mrs. Haller's jaw tightened. Ms. Henley's fingers curled together as though holding back the urge to intervene. The adults, for once, sat silent, listening, letting the truth come from the students themselves.

"My father," Ty continued, his voice even, "is a Master of Taoist Tai Chi and Kung Fu. And I train with him. I hold a black belt in Tai Chi, and a brown belt in Kung Fu. I study in two different dojos. I know exactly how someone like you fights. And I know how to stop it." The words weren't a boast—they were a declaration, the steady truth of someone who had lived every motion on the mat, every strike and block carved into his muscles.

Jarod's eyes narrowed, his grin faltering just slightly, but his body stayed loose, as if testing whether Ty was bluffing. The silence thickened again. Mila whispered under her breath, "He means it," and though the words were soft, they carried across the room. Nico swallowed hard, his chest tightening with the weight of Ty's calm honesty. I felt it too—Ty wasn't looking for a fight, but he wouldn't back down from one either.

Jeremy shifted forward on his desk, his small voice rising, "He's telling the truth." The boy's loyalty burned through his fear. Leo gave a slow nod, backing Jeremy's words. "Yeah," he added, "I can see it. Ty isn't pretending. He doesn't need to."

Mr. Takashi, standing at the back, finally spoke, his tone level but heavy with meaning. "My son doesn't lie about his training. And he doesn't use it to show off." His eyes locked on Jarod, not with anger, but with warning. "He uses it only to protect." Mrs. Takashi, at his side, remained silent, her eyes sharp, but she folded her arms as though to anchor the room with quiet strength.

Jarod shifted his weight, and for the first time, the grin cracked, his lips pressing together before curling again, smaller, thinner. He scanned the room, perhaps hoping to find fear still alive in the corners, but what he found instead was a room waiting—not for him, but for Ty. The balance had shifted. The silence no longer belonged to Jarod.

Sophie whispered, "He's not the same as the others," and Jasmin nodded quickly. Ella dared a glance at Ty, her shoulders straightening a little, as though she had borrowed some of his courage just by watching. Leo's voice cut in low and certain, "That grin isn't enough anymore, Jarod." Alex leaned forward with him, adding, "Not when the truth's been spoken out loud."

I felt my own heart pounding, because Ty had done more in one calm statement than anyone else had managed in days. He had ripped the mask off Jarod's grin and showed everyone in the room that it wasn't magic, wasn't power—it was just a signal of fists and pain. And now, everyone knew it.

It started with Jasmin's voice, small but steady, rising from the corner of the room. She didn't look at Jarod when she spoke, but her hands twisted at the hem of her shirt. "He shoved me against the lockers last week," she said. "No reason. He just wanted to see if I'd fall." The words cracked something open in the air. For a moment, nobody breathed, and then the silence gave way to more voices.

Ella leaned forward, her cheeks flushed with both fear and relief. "He pinned me by the shoulders near the stairwell," she added, her voice sharper, louder, but trembling at the edges. "He told me if I told a teacher, he'd make sure I couldn't walk home without bruises." Her words drew a ripple through the class. Eyes darted to Jarod's grin, but now it wasn't working—it was losing its shine in the face of open truth.

Sophie swallowed hard, her voice thin but unbroken. "He whispered things to me," she admitted. "Not… names, not teasing. Just promises. Promises that if I looked at him wrong, I'd regret it." She shivered as the memory brushed her skin like a cold hand, and the room felt it too. Chairs creaked, shoes scraped against the floor, as though every student needed to adjust under the sudden heaviness of recognition.

Mila shifted uncomfortably in her seat, but her eyes flashed with a quiet courage. "He told me once that nobody would ever stop him," she said, her voice flat. "And he laughed about it. Like it was a joke. But it wasn't. It was real." She crossed her arms tightly, like she was holding herself together, but her words struck harder than any punch.

Leo nodded, his jaw tightening as the voices built. "That's what I'm talking about," he said firmly, looking around the room. "It's not the fists first—it's the promise of them. It's that look, that grin, that says he's already chosen you, and you just don't know when it's coming." He shifted his gaze to Jarod, not afraid to meet it head-on. "And we all know it now. Every one of us."

Alex uncrossed his arms and leaned forward, his voice carrying more weight than before. "When you've been on the other side, when you've been the one making that smile, you know exactly what it does. It keeps people quiet. It makes them carry the bruise before they even get hit." He swept his eyes over the room, landing briefly on Jarod. "But it only works until people start speaking."

Jeremy's small voice cut in, surprising everyone. "He scared me too," he admitted, his nine-year-old tone fragile but ringing true. "I didn't want to walk past him in the hall. I thought if I did, he'd push me or trip me. And I didn't want to be on the floor again." His words fell heavy, because if even the youngest was carrying the fear, then none of them were free of it.

Mr. Clarke cleared his throat, but he didn't interrupt. Mr. Arnett's eyes tightened, his hand curled into a fist against the desk, but he remained silent. Mrs. Dunlop's expression hardened, her lips pressed thin. Mrs. Locke's pen hovered again, but she didn't write. Mrs. Haller looked toward Ms. Henley, who sat very still, her hands folded in her lap. The adults had heard the whispers before, but now it was no longer whispers—it was confessions, truth spoken in front of everyone.

Ty's gaze never left Jarod. "See?" he said simply, his voice calm. "You don't even need to swing. You've already left them carrying the weight." He didn't raise his tone, didn't boast. He just pointed to the truth everyone had shared. Nico felt it too, the way the air shifted—every student stiff, shoulders tense, breaths shorter. The room wasn't just listening anymore; it was remembering.

Jarod's grin flickered, still there but thinner, stretched tighter. His eyes darted, scanning faces that refused to stay silent. He shifted his stance, one foot tapping once against the floor, not in boredom but in unease. The cracks in his mask were beginning to show, even if he forced the smile to stay. And I knew then, every kid in that room knew then—fear had changed sides. It wasn't hiding in us anymore. It was standing in him.

I noticed something strange that morning, something none of the teachers thought we'd catch. When Jarod shifted his weight and leaned against the back wall, still grinning, none of the adults looked at him straight on. Mr. Clarke, who never backed away from eye contact with anyone, kept his gaze on the floor, shuffling his papers like they suddenly mattered more than what was happening in front of us. Even Mr. Arnett, our principal, stared at the wall above Jarod's head, not at his face, like looking at him might spark something dangerous.

Jasmin caught my eye, tilting her head slightly toward Mrs. Dunlop. The vice principal had her arms crossed, but her shoulders weren't stiff with authority the way they usually were—they looked small, folded in, like she wanted to shrink away. When Jarod glanced her way, she didn't move, but her throat tightened and her lips pressed flat. Jasmin whispered, "See? Even she won't look at him." Her words stuck like glue. If teachers couldn't stare him down, what chance did we have?

Ella shifted in her chair, clutching the edge of the desk. She whispered, "They're scared too." I thought about that, about how every time Jarod moved his head, the teachers flinched just slightly. Even Miss Kara, who could handle the loudest kids without breaking a sweat, adjusted her chair so she was angled away from him. That tiny movement told us more than any words could—she didn't want his eyes on her.

# THE SMILE THAT BROKE

Sophie leaned forward, her eyes darting from teacher to teacher. "They're pretending they don't notice him," she said, almost in disbelief. "But we do." Her voice trembled, but her words were steady enough to hit the point. It wasn't just the grin that worked, it was the silence that followed it. The kind of silence that stretched long and heavy, like every adult was waiting for something to happen but praying it wouldn't.

Leo's fists clenched against his knees. He wasn't angry at us this time; he was angry at them. "If even they won't stop him," he muttered, his teeth gritted, "then how are we supposed to?" His words carried a sting that made the room colder. It wasn't rebellion—it was disappointment. The adults we thought were supposed to shield us were doing the same thing we were: hoping Jarod wouldn't pick them.

Alex leaned back, his jaw tight, his voice low but strong. "This is how bullies get their power," he said. "Not because they're strong, but because everyone—even the ones with more power—pretends not to see them." His eyes cut toward Jarod for only a moment, enough to make the point, then back to us. "If they won't stand up, then we've got to."

Jeremy's small voice broke through, sharper than before. "That's not fair," he said. His face was red, not from fear but from anger. "We look at the teachers to stop things. But they don't even want to look at him. That means they're scared too." He swallowed hard and looked down, hugging his arms around himself. It wasn't a complaint. It was a realization none of us wanted to admit.

Mila's voice rose next, cool and controlled. "Fear's contagious," she said. "We're catching it from them." She lifted her chin, her eyes meeting Jarod's for the briefest second before darting away. Her hands curled into fists on the desk, as if to fight against the urge to copy the adults. "And if we keep catching it, he's already won."

Ty's calm voice carried across the room, steady like always. "That's why it has to stop," he said. "Jarod's power isn't his fists. It's the way everyone lets that grin grow bigger because they look away." His eyes didn't leave Jarod's face, not once. And for a flicker of a moment, Jarod's grin faltered before snapping back into place. But we saw it. Ty saw it most of all.

Mrs. Locke tapped her pen against her notebook, the sharp sound breaking the air. But she didn't speak. Mrs. Haller shifted her chair, eyes fixed on the window. Ms. Henley crossed her legs tightly, lips pressed thin. And Mrs. Takashi, sitting near the back, finally shook her head, her voice only a whisper: "Even now, the shadow's too long." It wasn't to us. It was to herself. But we all heard it.

That was when it clicked for me—Jarod didn't just make kids afraid. He made adults afraid. And when kids see adults afraid, the fear doubles, because it proves the danger is real. Nobody had to tell us. We already knew. But seeing it, right there in the way our teachers avoided his eyes, made the weight heavier than ever.

And so the room sat in silence again, heavy and fragile, every one of us knowing the truth: Jarod wasn't just another bully. He was the kind that even the grown-ups weren't sure how to stop.

Jeremy's voice broke the silence, smaller than Jarod's shadow yet heavier than the weight pressing over the room. "He's not bluffing," he whispered, eyes fixed on his desk. Nobody moved. "Jarod's different. He doesn't fake it. His fights are real. His hands… they're weapons." The words settled on us like cold rain. Nobody laughed, nobody argued. We all knew Jeremy was right, and that was the scariest part—he had said the thing we all thought but were too afraid to admit.

Mr. Arnett straightened, adjusting his glasses, but his face betrayed something none of us expected: agreement. "Jeremy's right," he said finally, voice low but firm. "Jarod is dangerous." His words sent a ripple through the classroom. For once, a teacher wasn't covering it, wasn't softening it. "That's why we've already been in talks with the board. Measures are being taken." He looked at Ty, and for a moment, silence held us again.

Ty sat taller, calm even under the weight of every eye in the room. Mr. Clarke stepped forward, placing a hand on Ty's shoulder. "The board understands," he said carefully. "Ty has training. He's disciplined, and he doesn't provoke. But if Jarod escalates—if anyone is in danger—Ty has permission to act." A collective gasp spread among us. We weren't used to hearing adults give a student permission to fight, not like this. But there it was.

Leo's jaw dropped, his eyes flicking from Ty to the teachers. "You're saying…" He stopped, shaking his head. "You're saying Ty can fight him? Like… really fight him?" His voice was half disbelief, half relief. For the first time, it felt like the adults weren't helpless.

Ty's face stayed steady, his voice measured. "I won't fight unless I must," he said, calm as always. "Violence isn't a game. But Jarod doesn't understand limits. If he pushes too far, I will stop him." His words weren't a threat—they were a promise, and that made them stronger than any grin Jarod could pull.

Sophie shifted in her seat, biting her lip. "But what if he comes after you outside school?" she asked, her voice trembling. "What if he waits?" The question made the air tighter, because we all knew Jarod wasn't the type to keep things in the playground.

Mrs. Dunlop glanced at Mr. Arnett, who gave a slow nod. "If Jarod takes this beyond school property, it becomes a matter for law enforcement," she said, her tone flat. She didn't name who, but every head in the room turned toward Mr. Takashi, sitting quietly in the back. His eyes met Jarod's for the first time, and something in that steady look cut sharper than words.

Jarod's smirk flickered. Just for a second, it broke. He didn't like being reminded that Ty wasn't just a boy with training—he was the son of a master. And that master was already here, watching.

Later that day, after the last bell rang and the playground had emptied into the quiet of the street, Jarod made his move. He stepped into Ty's path, fists clenched, grin wide. "No teachers now," he sneered. "Let's see what you do without them." His voice was laced with confidence, but there was a tremor buried deep beneath it.

Ty stood calm, his bag still slung over one shoulder. "You don't want this fight," he said, his voice steady. But Jarod lunged forward, steps heavy against the pavement. That's when a second shadow fell over him. Mr. Takashi stepped from the corner, silent until Jarod froze mid-step.

"You think you're a fighter," Mr. Takashi said, his voice low, sharp as steel. "But a fighter without discipline is only a danger to himself." His eyes never left Jarod's, and the air between them crackled with something none of us had words for. Authority. Power. The kind that couldn't be faked.

Jarod stiffened, caught between his pride and the realization that he was cornered. His fists twitched at his sides, but he didn't swing. Not with Ty steady before him and Mr. Takashi behind. For the first time, his grin faltered and didn't come back.

Jeremy's words hung in the back of our minds even then: Jarod isn't bluffing. His fights are real. But now we'd seen something else too—that there was someone stronger watching, someone who wouldn't let Jarod's violence go unanswered. The dangerous truth was out, spoken aloud and proven on the street. And Jarod, for the first time, had been stopped before the fight could even begin.

The air inside the classroom hung heavy, a weight none of us could name but every one of us carried. Jarod leaned against the back wall with that grin again, wide and empty, stretching across his face like a crack in glass. It wasn't joy, it wasn't humour. It was a mask that promised pain without saying a word. Eyes dropped quickly, shoulders curved in, and no one dared laugh. The silence told its own story. Everyone understood. This was not a joke. This was not an accident.

Leo's fists tightened in his lap, the sound of his knuckles popping loud in the stillness. He knew that grin better than anyone—he had worn it once himself, but never like this. His own had been a shield, a bluff, something to hide behind. Jarod's was different. His was a blade. I watched Leo lean forward slightly, his jaw clenched, as if ready to snap back at any moment. But he didn't. He knew if he did, Jarod would only feed on it.

Sophie pressed her palms flat against her desk, her lips trembling without words. She glanced at Jasmin, then at Ella, who both sat frozen, their eyes fixed on the floor as though it might open and swallow them whole. They had seen that grin before—everyone had. On the playground, in the hall, in the washroom doorway. Always followed by something that hurt. The grin was a warning label, and no one needed to be told twice.

Mr. Clarke's throat cleared, but even he hesitated, his eyes narrowing on Jarod's posture. He didn't speak, not right away. He simply looked at Mr. Arnett, who sat at the back, stiff in his chair, lips pressed into a line so tight they turned white. Teachers weren't supposed to show fear. But when even they avoided his eyes, we all felt the truth of Jeremy's words earlier—Jarod wasn't bluffing.

Jeremy's hands fidgeted at his sides, restless and small, yet his eyes never left Jarod. At only nine, he seemed to carry the awareness of someone much older. He leaned toward me and whispered, "He's daring us to breathe wrong." His words made the hair on the back of my neck rise, because he was right. Every inhale felt dangerous, every exhale too loud. That was the power Jarod carried.

Lisa, though, sat forward in her chair, her chin tilted high, her dark eyes locked on Jarod without blinking. She didn't flinch, didn't fold, though I could see the fire in her hands—ready, but restrained. Harley shifted next to her, taller, sharper, his chest rising as though daring Jarod to look at him directly. For once, Jarod didn't. His grin stayed steady, but his eyes flickered briefly to Ty.

And Ty, calm as always, stared back without anger, without fear. Just steady. His silence was a wall Jarod couldn't climb, and the grin cracked again, just faintly, before returning like a shadow sliding back into place. But we saw it. We all saw it.

The silence didn't break when the bell rang. It carried into the hallways, into the shuffle of shoes and the scrape of lockers. Students walked with shoulders high, glancing behind them more than ahead, waiting for a sudden hand on their back, waiting for the grin to return. This was the unseen fight—the one without fists, the one that bruised from the inside out.

Later that evening, the story took a turn no one expected. Ty and his father walked into Jarod's dojo, the faint ring of the bell above the door announcing their presence. Students sparred on mats, the sound of strikes echoing against padded walls. Jarod's master looked up, puzzled but respectful, bowing slightly at the sight of Mr. Takashi, whose reputation stretched far beyond this room. Ty held a small black case in his hands.

Inside the case were discs and files pulled from the school's security system. Audio, video, timestamped and clear. Jarod's grin on camera. His fists raised. His threats spoken in a voice impossible to mistake. It was evidence, not rumour. Proof that his violence had stepped onto school grounds and become part of the record.

When Jarod entered, his grin faltered instantly. The dojo wasn't his domain anymore. His steps slowed as his eyes darted from Ty to the case, then back again. For once, the weight shifted. It wasn't Jarod who carried the invisible strike, it was Ty, calm and silent, the evidence heavy at his side. The dojo master frowned, his gaze narrowing on his student. He had been lied to.

"You used what you learned here to harm," the master said slowly, disappointment thick in his voice. His words cut more sharply than any blow, because Jarod had never been shamed in front of his peers before. The room quieted as every student on the mat turned to look at him. The grin was gone now, stripped away like a mask that had been ripped off.

At school the next morning, though, the tension hadn't lifted. Jarod sat in the back again, eyes darker than before, lips pressed tight. He didn't grin this time, but the silence around him spoke louder than words. We knew better than to relax. A cornered shadow was still dangerous.

The battle lines were invisible, yes, but they were real. They stretched across every desk, every hallway, every glance at Jarod. No chalk marked them on the board, no teacher declared them. But every one of us carried them in our chests, waiting for the next move. And Jarod, staring at Ty with quiet fury, swore his revenge—not just on the students, not just on the teachers, but on anyone who dared to strip away his grin.

## CHAPTER 7: LINES CROSSED

I remember the moment clearly, as though the air in the school itself had shifted and grown heavier with the weight of something none of us had asked for. It began not with whispers, not with rumours that trailed down the hallways like smoke, but with paper—crude flyers pressed against the notice boards, stuffed into lockers, fluttering down from the staircase railings as though the very wind had agreed to carry the message. Jarod had written his challenge in bold, uneven letters, daring Ty to face him at the citywide martial arts championship. No more hiding behind schoolyard taunts or cornered scuffles. This was official, loud, impossible to ignore. It was meant to draw us all in, and I knew before the end of that morning, it had succeeded.

Jeremy found one of the flyers near the library doors, his small hands trembling as he lifted it. I could see the way his eyes widened, not in disbelief but in a stunned sort of realisation that everything he had feared about Jarod's hunger for violence was now walking straight into the public light. "He's not just trying to scare people anymore," Jeremy muttered, his voice carrying further than he thought, and already three others leaned closer to hear him. "He's putting it on a stage." His words cut through the usual chatter, and for once, no one laughed. No one called him dramatic. The air was too tense for that.

Ty, however, was calm—always calm. He took the flyer from Jeremy's hands and studied it like a teacher examining a careless essay. His dark eyes lingered on the jagged letters, the sharpness of the words that Jarod had chosen. There was no trace of fear in him, no spark of anger either. He folded the paper neatly, slipped it into his pocket, and simply said, "So, he has made it official." That was all. No speech, no bluster. The strength of Ty's silence was enough to make even Leo shift uncomfortably, because silence in Ty's mouth was never weakness—it was preparation.

By lunchtime, the entire school knew. Students clustered in corners, voices low, trading predictions as though it were a match already set to be wagered on. Some doubted Jarod, whispering that his arrogance might finally snap his back. Others defended him, saying that he had never lost, not once, and that Ty had made a mistake in stepping into the ring at all. But I watched Ty sit with his friends—Jasmin, Ella, Sophie, and Mila—his composure unbroken. He ate his meal without rushing, he laughed when Sophie teased him about being "too polite" to ever throw a punch, and when Leo asked outright if he was ready, Ty only nodded. That nod carried more power than any boast Jarod could have made.

Teachers were not blind to it either. By afternoon, Mr. Clarke had already plucked one of the flyers from the wall and delivered it straight to the principal's office. I followed as far as the hallway outside, catching glimpses of Mr. Arnett frowning deeply, Mrs. Dunlop shifting uncomfortably in her chair, and Ms. Henley pacing with arms crossed. They knew this was beyond school walls now. A citywide championship was not a playground, not a space they could patrol or suspend. This was public, sanctioned, yet still carrying the danger of spectacle. And they knew too well what Jarod's kind of spectacle meant.

Ella's voice broke the tension in the classroom later that day. "Why would he want Ty?" she asked, her hands twisting the hem of her shirt. "Why not pick someone else? Why not someone older, or bigger?" Ty looked at her kindly before answering, his words slow, steady, like water smoothing stone. "Because he thinks size and anger will win. He does not see what lies beyond them." Ella frowned, but she nodded, perhaps not fully understanding but sensing the truth tucked into his tone. Even at eleven years old, Ty carried an authority that could silence a room without raising his voice.

Leo was less gentle. He slapped the desk with his palm and leaned forward. "Jarod wants blood," he said flatly. "He's looking to humiliate you, Ty, and you know it. He'll try to take you apart in front of everyone." The room stiffened at the harshness of his words, but Ty only tilted his head. "Then he will learn that humiliation can turn back on the one who seeks it," Ty replied. His voice was neither cruel nor mocking. It was simply certain, and I could feel the shiver that passed through the others at hearing it. Ty was not stepping into this fight for pride, nor for victory. He was stepping in for something larger.

That evening, the flyers followed us home. Some were tucked into backpacks, others crumpled at the bottom of waste bins, but none of us could escape them. Even Sophie admitted to dreaming of Jarod's grin pasted across her pillow, a grin too wide, too smug, daring her to stop staring. "He's trying to get into our heads," she said the next morning, rubbing her eyes. "And it's working." Yet Ty only smiled, a small, knowing smile, and said, "Let him. The mind that breaks first is already defeated." That answer unsettled Sophie, but it planted a strange calm in the rest of us.

Mr. Takashi, Ty's father, addressed it bluntly at dinner. "This is no game," he said, his voice heavy with the authority of both a parent and an investigator. "Jarod is not entering this for respect. He is entering this for spectacle. That makes him dangerous." Ty met his father's gaze without flinching. "Then I will not play his game," he said. His mother, quiet as she painted in the corner, added softly, "Show them what control looks like, Ty. Not just fists, but control." The words settled over the room like a mantle. Even Jeremy, sitting at the far end, straightened in his chair.

By midweek, the tension at school had shifted into something sharper. No one teased Jarod openly anymore, no one dared push his patience, because his grin had grown darker, too wide, a mask stretched thin across his face. He thrived on the attention, yet beneath it, I could see the crack—the desperation in his eyes, the need for this fight to confirm everything he told himself in the mirror. Ty, by contrast, moved through the halls as if nothing had changed. His stillness was louder than Jarod's grin, and the more the students saw it, the more their whispers turned from doubt into cautious hope.

Sophie said it aloud one afternoon: "Maybe Ty will win. Maybe he can actually beat him." And no one laughed. No one called her foolish. Even Alex, who usually scoffed at optimism, muttered under his breath, "If anyone can, it's him."

Those words spread faster than Jarod's flyers. Hope has its own way of moving through walls, and in that week, I saw hope become louder than fear. But Jarod, of course, noticed it too. He ripped down one of his own flyers in anger, muttering something about "cowards and fools," his knuckles white as he clenched it into a fist.

The teachers knew they could not stop it. Mr. Clarke gathered us before the last bell that Friday, his expression stern, his voice carrying no softness. "This is not a joke," he said. "This is not something to cheer for as though it were theatre. This is a moment where respect will be measured, where control will matter more than power. You will remember that when you watch." His eyes lingered on me, perhaps because he knew I would carry those words into my narration. And so I do.

Jarod wanted blood. Ty wanted discipline. And in that difference, we all felt the clash building, not just fists against fists, but two worlds colliding—the world of violence against the world of restraint. I knew, even then, that something irreversible was about to happen. And though my voice trembled as I told this story to the class, I made sure to end with the truth: "This isn't about who wins. It's about what will be remembered."

The room fell silent after that. Flyers still hung crookedly on the boards, still slipped out from lockers, still waited to be crumpled by nervous hands. But we all understood. The line had been drawn. The challenge was announced. And there was no going back.

I will never forget the look on Jeremy's face that morning when the weight of it all landed on his shoulders. He was the first to say aloud what many of us had been whispering, though none dared to voice it so clearly. His small fingers clutched the paper, that crude flyer with Jarod's dare printed in ink that smudged against his skin, and his eyes flickered with disbelief before fear rose behind them. "It's real," he breathed, his voice trembling just enough to silence the chatter around him. "This isn't just playground talk anymore. He's really going to fight Ty." The room, which moments before had hummed with ordinary school noises, fell into a stunned stillness. Even the scraping of chairs seemed suddenly loud.

Jeremy's voice broke again, louder this time, as though he was trying to convince himself more than anyone else. "The invisible fight… it's not invisible anymore. It's on paper. It's official." I could feel the shiver in his tone, the same one that passed through the class like a draft beneath the door. Jasmin leaned forward, her brows drawn together, as though she wanted to reach out and take the flyer from him, to prove it was only some cruel joke. But Jeremy held it tightly, refusing to let it slip from his grasp. His nine-year-old face, so often full of light-hearted mischief, was pale now, weighted with the heavy truth of what we all knew: Jarod's challenge was no game.

Ty remained still at his desk, as though nothing had been said, but Jeremy's eyes searched the room desperately for confirmation, for someone to tell him it was false. Sophie, usually the first to laugh off rumours, didn't laugh at all.

Instead, she murmured, "If it's on flyers... he means it." Ella nodded slowly, her lips pressing together in a thin line, while Mila simply stared at the words on the page as though they were carved into stone. Even Alex, who normally met these moments with cold amusement, shifted in his seat. Jeremy saw all of it and grew more unsettled, because no one—absolutely no one—was contradicting him.

He pressed on, unable to leave the silence unchallenged. "Don't you all see?" Jeremy said, his voice rising with urgency. "If Ty says yes, it won't just be here. Everyone will see it. The whole city. What if Jarod—what if he—" His voice faltered, catching in his throat, and for a moment his words dissolved into a tremor he could not control. His hands shook, and the paper rattled like a dry leaf caught in the wind. I wanted to reach out, to steady him, but it was Ty who finally looked up and spoke. "Jeremy," he said evenly, his voice deep with calm, "it is not the fight that matters. It is how it is faced." Those words seemed to anchor Jeremy, though the tension in his shoulders did not fade.

Mr. Clarke, watching from the corner, stepped forward then. "Jeremy," he said gently, but with a firmness that made it clear he took him seriously. "You're right to be shaken. This isn't just schoolyard rumour. But you're also right to speak it aloud. We cannot pretend this doesn't matter." Jeremy blinked quickly, fighting the sting of tears, and Leo leaned back in his chair with a low exhale. "He's scared because he's smart," Leo muttered, his voice gruff but strangely protective. "We should all be scared." That admission hung heavy in the air, carrying a weight that pressed down on every student.

Jeremy finally sat, folding the flyer into careful creases, as though taming its power by containing it in smaller pieces. "I just... I don't want this to be another story we read later," he whispered. "Another story where we say we all saw it coming and didn't do anything." His words were quiet, but they struck harder than any shout. Sophie's eyes darted to me, and I felt the same chill she did—Jeremy wasn't just frightened for Ty. He was frightened for what might happen to all of us if Jarod's violence spilled past the ring. He had voiced the unspoken fear we all carried: that once this line was crossed, there was no pulling it back.

The teachers who had gathered outside the door didn't hide their concern either. I caught a glimpse of Mrs. Locke whispering to Mrs. Dunlop, their faces pale, their hands tight against their notebooks. Ms. Henley, the counselor, watched Jeremy with visible worry, her lips pressed tightly as though she wanted to intervene but knew she couldn't undo what Jarod had set into motion. Even Principal Arnett, so often unreadable, looked grim as he passed the flyer between his hands like evidence in a case. They weren't just teachers anymore—they were witnesses to something spiralling beyond their reach.

Jeremy looked around the classroom again, his eyes darting from face to face, and when no one answered, he stood abruptly, chair legs scraping against the floor. "You're all just sitting there," he said, his voice breaking between anger and fear. "He's dangerous! Ty, you know what he's like. You've seen what he does when no one's looking!" Ty's calm eyes lifted to meet Jeremy's, steady as stone, and he nodded once. "I have seen," Ty said softly. "And that is why this must be done. Not for me. For everyone who has seen and stayed silent."

Jeremy's breath hitched, his chest rising and falling too fast for words to catch up. He pressed the folded paper against his chest as though it were proof of his own voice. Jasmin finally spoke, leaning toward him with an intensity rarely seen from her. "Jeremy, we believe you," she said firmly. "We know what he's like. And we're not laughing, we're not ignoring it. But Ty's right—this isn't about who's strongest. It's about who shows what strength really is." Jeremy looked at her, and for a flicker of a moment, I thought I saw some of the fear in his face ease, though his hands did not stop trembling.

I, too, felt the pull of his fear, and as a friend, I could not deny the truth in his words. The invisible fight had been dragged into the light. No longer hidden in whispers or in the back corners of the playground, it stood before us in ink and paper, in trembling voices and steady eyes. Jeremy was shocked, yes, but in his shock lay the raw truth none of us could escape: Jarod's challenge was not simply about fists and mats. It was about what we were willing to see, and whether we would dare to face it.

The classroom remained heavy with silence after his outburst, as though even the air was bracing for what was to come. Jeremy lowered himself back into his chair, but his small body looked weighed down by a burden too large for his nine years. I saw him fold the flyer again, his fingers deliberate now, as if he were sealing away his fear one crease at a time. Yet I knew—and he knew too—that no amount of folding could erase what had been written. And so we sat, the shock hanging in the room like a bell's echo, knowing that the sound of it would follow us all the way to the day of the fight.

I will always remember the way Ty rose to speak, not in anger, not in haste, but with the calmness of still water. Where Jeremy's voice had shaken, Ty's was steady, as though no storm could rattle him. He stood in front of the class, eyes meeting ours without flinching, and in that gaze was not pride but a deep, unshaken purpose. "I will face him," he said simply. His words were quiet, but they carried across the room like a bell tolling in the night. No one doubted him. No one could. It wasn't bravado—it was certainty.

Jeremy gasped, his small frame tensing as if Ty's acceptance had knocked the air out of him. "Ty, no! You don't have to prove anything. He's just trying to drag you into his world!" Jeremy's voice trembled with urgency, his eyes darting to each of us as if begging someone to stop Ty. But Ty raised a hand, not to silence him but to reassure him. "This is not about proving myself," he answered softly, his voice low and steady. "This is about showing what honour looks like. Jarod fights with rage. I will fight with respect."

Leo shifted uneasily in his seat, his fists clenching as though he too wanted to intervene. "You're only eleven, Ty," Leo muttered, shaking his head. "He's bigger, meaner, and he doesn't play fair. You know he'll use every dirty trick." Ty met Leo's warning with a calm nod. "That is why this must happen. Not for me. For everyone who has seen his cruelty and believes it cannot be stopped." The weight of his words pressed into us, and even Leo, hardened by his own past, fell silent. Ty was not asking for approval. He was declaring truth.

Ella spoke next, her voice wavering. "But… what if he hurts you? He's not like other fighters, Ty. He doesn't care about rules." Ty turned to her, and I saw the gentleness in his eyes soften her fear. "Ella," he said, "the strength to hurt is not the same as the strength to protect. If I fall, I will fall with honour. But if I do not stand, then his violence wins before the match even begins." The quiet conviction in his tone made her bite her lip and lower her eyes, knowing there was no argument that could unseat him.

I felt the room hold its breath when Sophie leaned forward, frowning in that sharp way of hers. "You talk about honour like it's a shield, Ty," she said. "But shields break. What if it breaks on you?" For the first time, Ty's lips curved into the faintest smile. "A shield of respect cannot be broken," he replied. "It is not armour you wear on your body. It is what you carry in your heart. Jarod cannot take that from me." Sophie's frown loosened, though she crossed her arms as if hiding the way his words reached her.

Mr. Clarke finally stepped in, his voice low but measured. "Ty," he said, "you must understand what you're taking on. This is not a playground scuffle. This is a public arena, a championship. You'll be under lights, in front of judges, your peers, and your community. Do you truly accept this?" Ty bowed his head slightly, the gesture respectful, and replied, "Yes, sir. I do. Because it is not about winning. It is about exposing what Jarod calls strength for what it really is—dishonour."

Jeremy shook his head furiously, unable to let it go. "But why you, Ty? Why not just let the teachers stop him? Why do you have to be the one to fight?" Ty crouched slightly to meet Jeremy's eye, his voice warm but unwavering. "Because Jeremy," he said, "I am the one he challenged. If I refuse, he will not stop. He will keep pressing, keep hurting, until someone else pays the price. If I step forward, then no one else has to." Jeremy's lip trembled, but he didn't speak again. He only clutched the folded flyer tighter.

Jasmin, who had been quiet, finally spoke, her voice careful but full of strength. "Ty's right," she said, looking around the room. "This isn't about him versus Jarod. It's about showing everyone what kind of fighter Jarod really is. If Ty walks away, Jarod gets stronger. But if Ty stands, then maybe—just maybe—everyone else will see the truth." Her words, like Ty's, carried weight. Jeremy looked at her helplessly, but she didn't back down. She believed in Ty's calm, and slowly, so did we.

I watched it all unfold, and in that moment, I realized the difference between them. Jarod wore his violence like a crown, daring anyone to knock it from his head. Ty wore his honour like quiet armour, invisible yet unbreakable. One thrived on fear, the other on discipline. And though Jarod's strength seemed monstrous, Ty's stillness had a gravity all its own. It pulled us closer, steadied us, reminded us that violence was not the only answer. Respect itself was a weapon—and Ty knew how to wield it.

Even Alex, whose scepticism rarely wavered, leaned back and muttered, "Kid's got more guts than half the adults I know." His words were laced with a reluctant admiration, and though he didn't say more, we all heard the truth behind them. Ty's calm wasn't naivety. It was choice. A deliberate stand against the chaos Jarod brought. And that choice, more than any punch or kick, was what set him apart.

Mr. Arnett appeared in the doorway, his expression unreadable, but his silence spoke volumes. The principal, who so often clamped down on every rumour and every outburst, said nothing now. He let Ty's words hang in the air, let them root themselves into us. And in that silence, I felt something shift. It wasn't fear anymore, not exactly. It was a strange mix of dread and faith, bound together by Ty's certainty.

When Ty finally sat, the class remained hushed, not because they doubted him, but because they knew the stakes had changed. His acceptance had made it real. The fight was no longer Jarod's alone—it belonged to all of us. We were tied to it now, bound by the knowledge that Ty's honour would stand for more than his own pride. It would stand for every one of us who had ever been shoved, mocked, or broken by Jarod's cruelty.

I breathed deeply, steadying myself, for I knew as a friend that my words must capture the truth of that moment. Ty didn't gloat. He didn't hesitate. He didn't burn with the false fire of rage. He stood in calm defiance, declaring that dishonour would not win. And in that stillness, in that quiet agreement, he became something Jarod could never be: untouchable.

The lesson was clear to all of us, even if Jeremy's heart still quaked with fear. Strength was not fists, nor was it fury. It was honour, respect, and control. And as Ty's voice lingered in the room, I realized that even before the match began, Jarod had already lost something. He had lost the dignity that Ty carried effortlessly, the dignity that made us see which one of them was truly stronger.

When I stepped through the wooden gate into Ty's home, the world seemed to quiet itself. His father's garden lay spread before us, raked gravel in straight deliberate lines, smooth stones placed where they seemed both accidental and inevitable, and a tall plum tree swaying with patience in the breeze. Mr. Takashi stood with his arms folded, watching Ty with a gaze so steady it felt sharper than any blade. "Again," he said calmly, and Ty obeyed without question. His small frame bent, hands flowing through a pattern so precise I almost forgot he was only eleven. Each motion blended the softness of Tai Chi with the sharp edges of Kung Fu, a language of control written across his body.

I watched the way Ty breathed as he moved. Every exhale seemed timed to the sweep of his arms, every inhale rooted him deeper to the earth beneath his bare feet. His stance widened, heels biting into gravel, and with a twist of his waist the slow grace of Tai Chi suddenly snapped into the fast cut of Kung Fu. His father's voice, low but exacting, guided him. "Balance before speed. Patience before strike. You do not meet violence with violence. You meet it with truth." Ty nodded without breaking rhythm, his eyes locked on an invisible opponent.

Jeremy sat on the step beside me, knees pulled to his chest, whispering in awe. "It's like he's dancing, but… but scarier." His words trembled with both admiration and fear, because we knew this wasn't just practice. This was preparation for Jarod, a boy who had never moved with anything but brute force. Ella leaned closer, her eyes wide. "No, not scarier," she corrected softly. "Stronger. Jarod throws punches. Ty… Ty is weaving something." Her words made sense, though I didn't fully grasp it until I kept watching.

Mr. Takashi's own movements mirrored his son's, though slower, deliberate, demonstrating rather than competing. His posture was like a mountain, unshaken by wind, while Ty was the flowing river carving through stone. "The body is not the fighter," Mr. Takashi instructed. "The mind is. Control your thoughts, and your opponent's body will follow yours." He shifted into a quick strike, hand cutting through the air, and Ty mimicked him, his palm slicing the air with sudden sharpness. Gravel leapt from the ground at the power of it.

Jasmin leaned forward, gripping her hands together, whispering to Sophie, "I didn't know Tai Chi could look like that. I thought it was slow stuff for old people." Sophie smirked, but her voice stayed hushed, as though the air itself demanded reverence. "It's only slow when you don't need it. Look at him. Ty's turning it into armour." I caught Jeremy staring, lips parted, not with disbelief but with the heavy realisation that Ty's training wasn't for glory. It was survival with dignity.

Mr. Takashi suddenly barked, "Stop!" and Ty froze mid-strike. His father circled him, testing balance with the light push of a hand against his shoulder, his hip, his knee. Ty did not stumble. He stood firm, breathing even. Mr. Takashi gave a small approving nod. "Now again. But faster. Imagine Jarod before you. Imagine his fury. Let him waste his strength while you wait." Ty's eyes hardened, and he launched back into motion, this time quicker, sharper. His hands moved like water flowing into stone, redirecting invisible blows I could almost see.

Mila whispered behind me, almost as if afraid Jarod could hear. "He looks like he's already fighting him." Alex grunted from where he leaned against the wall. "That's the point. He's beating him before the fight even starts. Jarod won't even know what he's looking at." Alex's tone carried no mockery, only respect. For a boy who had once believed fists solved everything, his eyes now shone with a new understanding. He, better than anyone, recognised the difference between power that broke and power that built.

Mrs. Takashi emerged from the house then, carrying a jug of water and placing it carefully on the steps. She did not interrupt, but her quiet presence seemed part of the rhythm itself. Her gaze was softer than her husband's, but no less proud. She spoke gently when Ty paused for breath. "Remember, Ty. Your art is not about hurting. It is about harmony. Even when you strike, you are reminding the world of balance." Ty's lips curved into the smallest of smiles, the kind that carried both humility and assurance.

As the evening wore on, the training grew more intense. Ty moved through reversals, throws, sweeps that sent invisible foes crashing into the gravel. His father corrected only sparingly, as though the lessons had already sunk deep into Ty's bones. Watching him, I realized Jarod's brute force would look clumsy in comparison. Where Jarod lunged, Ty flowed. Where Jarod struck, Ty redirected. Where Jarod laughed at pain, Ty would show silence, stillness, and control. It wasn't about crushing an opponent. It was about teaching them they had never truly been strong.

Leo exhaled slowly, his arms crossed, his brow furrowed. "I used to think fighting was about who hit harder. But look at him. That's not hitting. That's… it's teaching." The word slipped from Leo like a reluctant confession, and I felt its truth. Ty's every move seemed to carry a lesson meant for Jarod: that violence without control is weakness disguised as strength. And soon, Jarod would have to face that truth in front of everyone.

The moon began to rise, silver light catching on the gravel, and still Ty moved. His father finally lifted a hand, signaling the end. Ty bowed deeply, sweat dripping from his brow, his chest rising and falling with steady breath. Mr. Takashi's voice, calm but resonant, broke the silence. "You are ready, my son. Not because you can win, but because you can endure. Remember—victory is not breaking him. It is showing him what cannot be broken."

Jeremy whispered to me as we left, his voice trembling with awe. "I didn't know training could look like that. It's not fighting… it's something else." I placed a hand on his shoulder, steadying him. "It is the difference between chaos and control," I murmured. "And tomorrow, Jarod will finally see it."

We walked away quietly, none of us daring to shatter the weight of what we had just witnessed. Ty had trained not to defeat Jarod's fists, but to unravel Jarod's pride. And in that garden, under the watchful eyes of his parents, he had already begun to win.

I noticed Jeremy hadn't moved from the garden steps, even when the rest of us had started to drift back toward the gate. His small hands clutched the railing, knuckles pale, eyes still locked on the space where Ty had been training moments before. He whispered so faintly I almost thought it was the breeze. "I always thought martial arts was… just hitting. You know, blocks and kicks and stuff. But that wasn't hitting. That was…" His voice trailed off, and he looked down at his shoes as though the words were buried somewhere in the dirt between them.

Ty approached quietly, wiping the sweat from his brow with the edge of his sleeve, his breathing steady and calm as though the hours of drills had been no more tiring than a walk. He crouched so his face was level with Jeremy's, his expression soft, his tone clear. "The fight is never with fists first," he told him. "It begins here," he tapped his temple gently, "and here," he touched the centre of his chest. "Your mind, your breathing, your control. That decides everything before a strike ever lands."

Jeremy's wide eyes blinked at him, trying to absorb each word as though they were too heavy to balance all at once. "So… it's not about being the strongest?" His question broke into the air with such earnestness it stilled the rest of us. Ty didn't laugh or shake his head. He only drew in a long, calm breath and let it out slowly, demonstrating the very lesson he was teaching. "Strength without control is just chaos. And chaos always destroys itself."

Leo muttered from the side, folding his arms across his chest. "Wish someone had told me that a long time ago." His eyes flickered with memories he didn't share, but the regret lingered in his voice. Alex gave a small nod, his tone sharp but carrying a hint of respect. "Control. That's the word Jarod doesn't even know how to spell." There were faint chuckles from Sophie and Jasmin, but they faded quickly, replaced by silence as Ty's words carried deeper than any joke could reach.

Mrs. Takashi placed a gentle hand on Jeremy's shoulder, her voice quiet, almost like the rustle of the plum tree in the wind. "Discipline doesn't make a fighter less fierce, Jeremy. It makes them unbreakable. Remember that when you watch tomorrow." Jeremy lifted his chin slowly, his cheeks flushed, and gave a small nod, though his lips still pressed together in confusion and awe. I could see him wrestling with the idea that victory wasn't measured in bruises or knockouts.

"Let me show you," Ty said softly, rising to his feet. He motioned for Jeremy to step into the gravel circle with him. Jeremy hesitated, his small frame trembling with both nerves and curiosity, but Ty's calm presence steadied him. They faced each other. Ty lifted his arms in slow motion, guiding Jeremy's hands into mirrored positions. "Breathe," Ty instructed. "Not from your throat. From here." He tapped Jeremy's stomach gently. Jeremy inhaled shakily, then exhaled, eyes still locked on Ty's.

"Now push me," Ty said. Jeremy frowned but pressed forward with both hands, leaning into the effort. Ty shifted his stance, redirecting the push with a simple turn of his hips. Jeremy stumbled past him, wide-eyed, before catching his balance again. Ty smiled faintly, almost invisible. "See? It wasn't about strength. You gave me all you had. I didn't fight it. I let it go where it wanted to go. That's control."

Jeremy looked down at his hands, then back at Ty, and for the first time in a long while, his voice steadied. "So it's… it's not about beating someone down. It's about… teaching them they can't control you?" Ty nodded, the smallest tilt of his head, his eyes glinting with pride. "Exactly. And if they cannot control you, they cannot defeat you."

Ella whispered to Sophie, her voice tight with awe. "Jarod's not ready for this. He doesn't even know what Ty's talking about." Sophie nodded, leaning closer, her voice sharp with certainty. "That's the point. Tomorrow he's going to learn in front of everyone." Jasmin hugged her knees tighter, adding, "And for once, it won't be the little kids paying the price. It'll be him."

Jeremy turned back to the group, his small chest rising with a new sort of confidence. "I thought fighting was about who got hurt the most. But... maybe it's about who learns the fastest." His words hung in the air, fragile but true, like a lesson none of us had expected him to be the one to say aloud. Ty placed a steady hand on Jeremy's shoulder and gave a single nod, the gesture quiet but powerful, as though to say: you've begun to understand.

Mr. Takashi finally broke the silence, his voice measured but heavy with authority. "Tomorrow, you will all witness the difference. Jarod has trained his fists. Ty has trained his spirit. That is why this battle will not belong to fists." He turned back toward the house, leaving us to sit in the cooling night, the lesson settling deeper into our bones than the gravel beneath our feet.

As we walked away, Jeremy whispered again, this time not in fear but in wonder. "The fight isn't fists first. It's... everything before that." I squeezed his shoulder gently, steadying him. "And now you know what Jarod will never understand," I murmured. The night closed around us, and though tomorrow promised a storm, Jeremy's small smile told me the truth had already begun to shift him.

I remember the night clearly, because while Ty's home glowed with the warmth of calm voices and patient teaching, Jarod's dojo carried a storm of its own. The room smelled of sweat and leather, the mats scuffed deep from years of collisions. Jarod struck the heavy bag with a fury that made the chain creak above him. Each punch was less about form than force, each kick a thunderclap echoing against the walls. His breathing was ragged, nothing like Ty's steady rhythm; this was an engine that burned until it sputtered.

His master, a wiry man with silver streaking his hair, stood with arms folded, watching. He had trained countless boys into disciplined fighters, but Jarod was different. Every strike came too fast, too wild, as if the point wasn't to control the movement but to destroy whatever stood in its way. "Again!" Jarod barked at himself, driving his fist into the pad so hard that sweat flicked from his forehead. His eyes narrowed, teeth clenched, his body a knot of anger barely held together.

"You will not last three rounds if you fight like this," the master finally said, his voice even, but cut sharp as a blade. Jarod spun on him, sweat dripping, lips curled in defiance. "Then I'll end it in one. I'll crush him. I'll crush Ty." The words hissed out, low and venomous, and he threw another kick into the bag as if punctuating his vow. The bag swung wildly, the chain rattling in protest.

The master shook his head slowly. "Do you hear yourself? You speak like a brawler, not a martial artist. Anger is heavy. It will sink you before the fight even begins." His words should have cooled the boy, but Jarod only squared his shoulders, chest heaving, eyes hard. "I don't need calm. Calm doesn't win fights."

"Control wins fights," the master replied sternly, stepping forward now, his presence filling the space. "Without it, your strength is wasted. Your rage blinds you." Jarod's jaw tightened, but he refused to answer, only pounding the bag again and again until the sound drowned out the master's voice. The strikes blurred into a frenzy, each one louder, faster, but less precise.

The master finally stepped between him and the bag, stopping its wild swing with a firm hand. "Enough." Jarod froze, panting, his fists trembling inches from striking his teacher. That pause lingered, dangerous and long, before Jarod finally dropped his arms to his sides, chest heaving. "I'll win," he muttered, voice dark. "I don't care how."

"Listen to me, boy," the master said, eyes locking onto his. "Win or lose, if you shame this school, you shame yourself. Remember that when you step onto that mat." His tone held no malice, only warning, but Jarod turned away, his silence heavy with defiance. His hands clenched into fists again, knuckles white. He didn't want wisdom. He wanted blood.

I watched the tension coil inside him, and even from the edges of that memory, I knew the truth—Jarod wasn't preparing for a competition. He was preparing for a war, one only he believed could be won by force alone. The others trained for honour, for growth, for balance. But Jarod trained for destruction. And even his master's words, sharp and final, seemed to find no soil in which to plant.

When he picked up his bag at the end of the night, shoulders rigid and steps heavy, his master sighed softly, his gaze following him out the door. "If he does not learn tomorrow," the master whispered to himself, "he may never learn at all." The dojo fell silent again, but the echoes of Jarod's fury clung to the air, restless, like a storm that would not pass.

I could see Lisa's face before she said a word, and I knew something wasn't sitting right with her. Her usual sharp stare softened when she sat beside Jeremy, fiddling with the edge of her sleeve, not wanting anyone else to notice the tremor in her fingers. She wasn't afraid of fists, not her. She'd stood up to kids bigger than her without blinking, but this was different. The thought of Ty stepping into a ring, cheered and jeered by a crowd, churned something in her chest she hated to admit out loud.

"Jeremy," she whispered, just low enough for me to catch it from where I sat, "do you know what it feels like when people clap for you after you've hurt someone?" Jeremy shook his head, eyes wide, waiting. Lisa swallowed hard. "It feels good. Too good. That's why I don't like these things. Because I know how easy it is to mistake cruelty for strength when people cheer." Her voice didn't crack, but I could hear the weight dragging on every word.

Jeremy leaned closer, his brow furrowing, the way he does when he wants to shoulder someone else's hurt. "But Lisa, you're not that girl anymore," he told her firmly, though his tone trembled just a little. She looked back at him, and for a second her eyes darted away, ashamed, almost angry at herself. "Doesn't matter," she murmured. "It's still in there. When the crowd roars, you don't hear right from wrong. You only hear them telling you to do it again."

Ty sat across the room, tying the strings of his training gi, silent as ever. His calm didn't need words, but Lisa's eyes flicked toward him like she couldn't look away. "See him? He's got control," she said, almost as though she wanted to convince herself. "But me? If I went in there, I don't trust myself not to slip back." Her voice dropped lower, her nails biting into her palm. "That's what scares me."

Jeremy didn't argue this time. Instead, he nodded, lips pressed tight, respecting her honesty. I spoke then, my voice steady over the hum of the classroom. "Lisa," I said, "fear doesn't mean weakness. It means you've seen what's inside and you don't want to go back to it." She looked up at me, startled for a moment, then exhaled through her nose, almost like she'd been holding her breath all morning.

Jasmin, who had been listening quietly, chimed in with a voice softer than Lisa expected. "You're brave for saying that out loud. I mean, bullies don't admit when they liked the power. But you just did." Lisa shot her a half-smile, lopsided, and shook her head. "Don't call me brave. I'm just being honest." But I could tell the words landed in her chest, sitting there like a seed that might grow.

Across the room, Sophie nudged Ella and muttered, "See, even Lisa's scared of what cheering can do. Maybe that's the real fight, not the one in the ring." They didn't mean for Lisa to hear, but she did, and for once she didn't snap back. She only nodded faintly, agreeing with words she didn't have the strength to repeat.

Leo, arms folded, spoke next, his voice surprisingly gentle. "Crowds don't make you cruel. They just clap for whatever they see. If you show them something different, something worth clapping for, you'll teach them too." Lisa blinked at him, as though unsure if she should laugh or thank him. Instead, she settled on crossing her arms, muttering, "Easy for you to say." But I caught the tiny curve in her lips that betrayed the faintest hint of relief.

Ty finally raised his head, his dark eyes calm, unreadable. "Lisa," he said, voice steady as stone, "if cruelty could be cheered, so can discipline. It is not the crowd who decides who you are. It is you." His words were not dramatic, not loud, but the silence that followed told me everyone felt the ground shift just a little.

Lisa's jaw clenched, her teeth pressing together as if holding back another confession. She shook her head, almost laughing at herself, and muttered, "Still doesn't make me like it." Ty gave her the faintest nod, as though he respected her unease as much as any courage she'd shown before.

Jeremy glanced between them both, whispering under his breath to me, though the whole room could hear it. "That's the difference, isn't it? Jarod fights for cheers. Ty fights for respect. Lisa knows which one is poison." I didn't correct him. He was right.

When the bell rang, the room shifted into motion, books shutting, chairs scraping. Lisa lingered behind, her eyes following Ty again as he packed away his gi. She looked back at Jeremy once more and said quietly, "Promise me something. If the crowd cheers for blood, don't clap. Not even once." Jeremy nodded without hesitation, his answer simple. "I won't."

And as she left the room, shoulders squared but stride a little slower, I could feel the ripple her words had left behind. Unease, yes, but also truth. The kind that sticks to your ribs, the kind you can't unhear once it's been spoken.

I watched Leo shift in his seat, leaning forward with his elbows on his knees, his voice carrying that steady mix of regret and hard-earned wisdom. He didn't raise his tone, but he didn't need to; everyone in the room leaned in as if he had tugged them closer with invisible strings. "You think the ring changes anything?" he began, his gaze sweeping the class. "It doesn't. It just makes everything louder. The crowd, the cheers, the gasps—none of it's different from the whispers in the schoolyard. It's just more eyes on the same fight."

A hush fell as his words weighed on us. I could feel my own chest tighten because Leo wasn't talking about Ty or Jarod alone—he was talking about himself too. He rubbed his knuckles together as if remembering fists he'd once swung, then shook his head. "A bully doesn't need a black eye to win. Most of the time, all they want is for you to believe you're beaten before they've even touched you." His eyes flicked briefly toward Harley, who didn't flinch but shifted ever so slightly, as though acknowledging the sting of truth.

Jasmin, her notebook clutched close, tilted her head and asked softly, "So the bruises aren't the worst part?" Leo gave a short laugh, bitter but honest. "No. The worst part is when you believe the voice that says you're smaller than you are. When you start carrying that weight even when no one's looking." He tapped his chest with two fingers, firm. "That's the scar. Right here."

Alex, sitting beside him, nodded, though his jaw was tight. "He's right," he added. "I used to push kids around just to see if they'd fold. Sometimes they didn't even fight back—they just lowered their heads. And I thought I'd won. But that wasn't strength. That was me stealing something from them without laying a finger." His voice cracked, but he pressed on.

Sophie raised her hand, more out of instinct than need, and whispered, "But Ty won't fight like that." Leo's eyes softened, and he nodded toward her. "Exactly. Ty's fight isn't about beating Jarod bloody. It's about standing so strong that Jarod's fists don't change him. That's how you beat a bully—by showing they can't shape you, no matter how hard they try."

Jeremy, wide-eyed, leaned closer to me and muttered, "That's what Myles never got the chance to prove, right? That he couldn't be shaped by them." His voice broke, and I steadied my breathing, because even repeating the boy's name set the air trembling. Leo gave a small nod of respect, as if he'd heard Jeremy's words across the silence.

Ty, still composed as ever, tied his belt with deliberate calm. "A fight," he said, his tone measured, "is never won on the mat first. It is won here"—he tapped his temple—"and here." His hand touched his chest. "If Jarod makes you hate yourself, then he has won. But if you stand without changing, then you are the victor, even if you fall." His words dropped into the room like stones into deep water, leaving ripples everywhere.

Ella whispered to Mila beside her, "So, what Leo's saying is, we've all been in the ring already. Every time someone sneered at us, every time someone pushed us, that was it. Just smaller crowds." Mila gave a thoughtful nod, murmuring, "And maybe every time we said nothing back, we taught them they were winning." The realisation seemed to sting, but also to steady them.

Leo folded his arms then, speaking slowly. "I don't stand here because I'm proud of who I was. I stand here because I want you to know there's another way. I saw my reflection in Alex's cruelty, and it broke me. The ring is no different—it's a mirror. Jarod will see himself if he dares to look, and I hope to God he hates what he sees." His voice carried a finality that hushed every whisper in the room.

I could feel the air grow heavy, the kind of silence that wasn't empty but filled with thought. Mr. Clarke adjusted his glasses and said quietly, "Leo's right. We treat the schoolyard as small, but it holds the same lessons as the arena. Respect or cruelty—those are the only two choices." Even Mr. Arnett nodded solemnly, the usual firmness of a principal tempered by something almost like sorrow.

Lisa crossed her arms, staring hard at the floor before admitting, "If the schoolyard was a ring, then I was cheered more than once. And I liked it." Her words cut across the stillness, but no one snapped back. Instead, Leo's gaze softened as he said, "That's why you understand better than anyone why it can't happen again." She didn't argue, only nodded stiffly, as though swallowing a truth she didn't want but knew she needed.

Jeremy, his small frame tense, asked in a fragile voice, "But what if Jarod doesn't learn? What if he just gets worse?" Ty turned toward him, expression unreadable but steady. "Then he will carry his loss louder than any win. Sometimes the greatest punishment is knowing you were defeated not by fists, but by someone's unbroken spirit." His words gave Jeremy a strength he hadn't known he was reaching for.

As I looked around the room, I realised Leo's reminder wasn't just for the fight ahead. It was for every one of us. The ring, the schoolyard, the classroom—different places, same choice. Who you let shape you, and what you become when the cheers grow loud. And in that moment, even before the tournament, I think we all understood Ty had already won something Jarod could never touch.

The day broke with a sharpness in the air that made me feel as though the whole city had been holding its breath for what was to come. I sat with the others on the bus ride in, the rumble beneath our feet echoing louder than usual, or maybe it was just our nerves making everything feel heavier. When we arrived at the arena, the sight of it struck me first: a building larger than any school gym, banners strung high, doors thrown open wide. Crowds spilled inside, a mix of eager students, protective parents, and teachers who looked more like chaperones to history than simple supervisors. I caught sight of Mr. Clarke already deep in conversation with Mrs. Locke, their faces drawn, as if even they knew this was no ordinary competition.

We found our seats in the bleachers, the wooden rows creaking under the weight of bodies and anticipation. My friends clustered around me, Jasmin clutching her bag so tightly her knuckles had gone white, Ella whispering furiously to Sophie about whether Ty would be safe. Jeremy sat forward, small fists balled in his lap, eyes darting everywhere as though searching for proof that this was still just another school trip. But it wasn't. Not today. This wasn't a science fair or a field day. This was Jarod's challenge thrown into the open, and Ty's calm acceptance standing tall in reply.

Parents lined the lower seats, voices buzzing like a restless hive. I spotted Mr. and Mrs. Takashi sitting side by side, their presence more than parental—it was solemn, protective, like guardians watching the ground itself. Mr. Takashi's sharp gaze scanned the room with the precision of the investigator he was, but Mrs. Takashi's hands never stopped moving, sketching with a pencil across a small pad she had brought, as though catching the mood before it could vanish. Behind them, Mrs. Dunlop and Ms. Henley leaned in close, their words soft but serious, as if debating whether what was about to unfold belonged in a school at all.

Then the announcer's voice rose, echoing through the hall, and silence swept across the bleachers like a tide retreating. All eyes turned to the front where mats stretched in a wide square, polished, waiting. And stepping into that silence was a man whose very presence seemed to still the restless air: Sho Kazushi, a Japanese grandmaster whose name alone carried respect. He was not tall, not broad, but something in his poise filled the space larger than any frame could. His bow was deliberate, his posture unshaken, his words steady. "Today is not about fists," he said, his voice low but carrying. "Today is about respect."

The words seemed to cling to the walls of the arena, refusing to fade. I leaned forward, caught in the weight of them. Around me, even the younger children stilled, as if they sensed something sacred had been declared. Ty lowered his head respectfully from where he stood, a calmness radiating from him that felt unshakable. Jarod, across the mat, smirked with that familiar grin of his, but for the first time, the grin seemed out of place, almost childish under the gaze of Sho Kazushi.

Beside me, Leo murmured to Alex, "That man's already won this match. Jarod just doesn't know it yet." Alex gave the faintest nod, his eyes fixed not on Jarod but on Ty, as if he had placed every ounce of hope he had in the boy who stood there with quiet strength. Ella clutched Sophie's hand tightly, whispering prayers under her breath not to any god but to Ty himself, as though his balance alone might steady the whole world.

Mr. Arnett stood near the front, arms folded, his expression unusually tense. I could tell even he, who often bristled at being drawn into our world of schoolyard dramas, understood this had become something larger, something that would spill beyond the mats and into the lives of every student watching. And as Sho Kazushi's eyes swept the crowd, I felt for the first time that we were not spectators at all—we were participants in a lesson being written before us.

Jarod rolled his shoulders, bouncing lightly on the balls of his feet, his impatience visible even at a distance. He wanted the fight. He wanted the roar. But Ty stood with his hands folded in front of him, feet planted, breathing steady. No rush, no grin, no glare. Just balance. And I knew then, as surely as the sun had risen, that something was going to break today—and it wasn't going to be Ty.

The arena held us all in its grip, hearts pacing to the rhythm of unspoken fear and hope. Jeremy whispered, almost to himself, "This is more than a match." And I nodded silently, because he was right. This was the day lines would be crossed, and none of us would walk away unchanged.

I could feel it before Jeremy even opened his mouth. The tension had a scent, thick and sharp, like the mats themselves that gave off the faint rubber smell of sweat and effort. Every breath tasted of that mix of dust and polish, as though the arena had been scrubbed down too many times but could not erase the ghosts of fights before this one. Shoes echoed against the wooden floor as spectators shuffled into their seats, each step bouncing back into the silence that followed the grandmaster's opening words. It was not an ordinary hush; it was the kind that pressed down on the chest, the kind that told you something irreversible was about to begin.

Jeremy leaned forward, his small frame trembling with an energy he couldn't contain, and his voice—though low—was enough to pull the eyes of everyone around him. "It's not just a tournament," he said, staring at the mats as though they were something more than stitched canvas.

"This is judgment day for Jarod." His words seemed to cling to the rafters, drawing nods from Leo and Sophie, who both shifted uneasily as if acknowledging that none of this was sport. Even Mr. Clarke, seated nearby, tightened his jaw as though he couldn't argue with the boy's declaration.

The announcer's voice droned names of early contenders, each one followed by the shuffle of fighters stepping onto the mats, but no one in our group truly paid them mind. The air around us vibrated with anticipation, each strike and block from the first matches serving only as a backdrop to what loomed ahead. The smell of mats grew stronger as competitors began to sweat under the lights, and the sharp thuds of contact rattled into the bleachers. Still, Jeremy's words anchored us. He wasn't dramatizing it. He was stating what we all felt in our bones.

I shifted in my seat, watching Ty, who sat cross-legged at the side of the ring, calm as water. His breathing was steady, eyes half-lidded, and yet his presence filled the room. Jarod stood on the opposite side, pacing, fists clenched, shoulders rolling as though every moment without a fight was torture. Their contrasts painted themselves so clearly: one boy still, the other a storm contained only by the boundary of the mat. Ella nudged Jasmin, whispering, "Look at him. He doesn't even blink." She meant Ty, and Jasmin's wide eyes reflected the same awe.

Behind us, parents murmured, some clapping politely at the ongoing bouts, but most stealing glances toward Ty and Jarod. They knew too. The teachers along the row, Mrs. Locke with her brow knitted, Mrs. Dunlop wringing her hands, Mr. Arnett stern and silent—all of them carried the same unspoken recognition. This was no longer a matter of schoolyard grudges. This was a collision of two forces: violence unchecked and discipline embodied.

Jeremy pressed on, his voice cutting into the heavy air once more. "You smell that?" he asked softly. "That's fear. Not just theirs. It's his." He nodded toward Jarod, who smirked but whose jaw twitched in a way I hadn't noticed before. "He knows it, even if he won't say it." Sophie's fingers dug into the wood of her seat, and Leo muttered something about how he'd seen that grin too many times in the halls, the one that came before fists. But here, in this ring, with Sho Kazushi watching, it didn't look so invincible anymore.

The crowd shifted uneasily as the early matches ended and names began to fall closer and closer to those we were waiting for. Each echo of the announcer's voice felt like a hammer striking an invisible bell, vibrating through the bleachers, through our ribs, through the very air. My heart kept pace with that rhythm, quickening, waiting for the moment when the call would come. Ty did not move, did not flinch, but every student who had ever felt Jarod's cruelty seemed to sit a little straighter, as if preparing themselves for a reckoning they'd waited for far too long.

The silence deepened once again, heavier this time, pulling us all inward. Jeremy's small whisper rose one last time: "When he walks onto that mat, Jarod won't just be fighting Ty. He'll be fighting the truth." And with those words, I knew the hush in the arena wasn't simply the quiet before a match—it was the quiet before a storm that none of us would forget.

The first pair of fighters bowed to each other, their movements precise and respectful. I watched as they circled, their stances rooted yet fluid, every strike measured, every block calculated. The sound of their feet on the mat was steady, almost rhythmic, as though they were dancing to a hidden beat only they could hear. Gasps and claps rose from the crowd each time a strike landed clean, and the air filled with admiration rather than fear. It was martial arts as it should be—discipline and control wrapped in grace. Ty leaned forward slightly, eyes sharp but calm, as if he were studying scripture written in movement.

The matches went on, and I found myself leaning with him, my eyes following each contestant's posture and breath. There was no waste in their movements. Every step, every extension of a fist or snap of a kick had purpose. The Japanese grandmaster Sho Kazushi watched from his seat with a serenity that mirrored Ty's, nodding faintly at each respectful bow, each exchange of points. It was clear that in this space, victory meant more than landing the most blows; it meant holding yourself with dignity. I could feel the younger students absorbing this lesson, their eyes wide, their hands gripping the edges of the benches as though clinging to the idea that this was what strength truly looked like.

Then Jarod entered the ring. The difference was instant and violent. His feet stomped against the mat rather than glided. His fists clenched too tightly, knuckles whitening, and when the bow came, it was shallow, rushed, almost mocking. The crowd seemed to stiffen as he lunged forward with his first strike, wild and hard. His opponent staggered back, caught off guard by the raw aggression, and the gasp from the bleachers was not admiration this time—it was fear. Jarod attacked with reckless speed, ignoring the flow of the fight, battering forward until the referee called a halt. His grin was wide, too wide, and the cheers that followed were hesitant, brittle.

Jeremy's whisper carried to those of us closest to him. "That's not martial arts. That's just… hitting." His small fists balled at his sides, and I saw Sophie nod quickly, her face tight. "He's not learning anything," she murmured, and Leo, shaking his head, muttered, "He doesn't want to. He just wants to break things." Even the teachers seemed uneasy, Mrs. Locke exchanging a troubled glance with Mr. Clarke, as though wondering how a child so young could already have mastered violence without mastering respect.

Jarod's next match played out the same way, but harsher. His opponent was quicker, sharper, but every time he moved with clean technique, Jarod answered with brute force. He shoved, slammed, and forced his way through every defense until the boy crumpled. The referee stepped in, voice sharp, warning Jarod to respect the rules, but Jarod only smirked, bowing with a mocking flourish that earned him no applause this time. The silence from the audience was louder than any cheer could have been.

Meanwhile, Ty remained seated, watching with a stillness that unsettled me more than Jarod's rage. He did not frown, did not twitch, but his eyes followed every move with precision. When Jarod's opponent fell for the last time, Ty breathed out softly, as though filing the lesson away, not of what to do, but of what never to become. Beside him, Alex leaned over and muttered, "He's wasting his energy. He thinks he's winning, but he's only burning himself out." Ty gave no reply, only the faintest nod, his expression unreadable.

Ella leaned against me slightly, her whisper low but urgent. "It's scary... not because he's strong, but because he doesn't care." I wanted to tell her she was wrong, that Jarod cared too much about winning, but I knew what she meant. There was no joy in his victories, no lesson in his movements. He cared for nothing but the domination, the look on his opponent's face when they realized they could not withstand him. It wasn't strength; it was hunger, and hunger like that could devour anyone if left unchecked.

The contrast grew clearer with every match. Fighters who bowed with grace, who helped their opponents up, earned applause and respect from the crowd. Jarod, who stomped and sneered, drew silence and frowns. It became a rhythm, one the students began to notice and whisper about. Jasmin nudged Mila, whispering, "Do you see? It's different. They're respected. He's just feared." Mila nodded, her small hands gripping her knees tightly. Even she, who rarely spoke much, understood the difference.

By the time Jarod crushed his third opponent, tossing the boy to the mat with a reckless throw that made the referees rush forward, the crowd had stopped clapping altogether. His grin faltered for a moment as he glanced up at the bleachers, realising the cheers had dried up, but he shook it off, rolling his shoulders as though he did not need anyone's approval. Ty's gaze never wavered. He did not look away from Jarod even once, as if waiting patiently for the storm to reach him.

I could feel the hush spreading again, different from the silence that had filled the room before. This was not the silence of respect, nor of awe—it was the silence of dread. Everyone knew Jarod would face Ty soon, and the early matches had shown us all the truth: Jarod was powerful, but he was careless. Ty was patient, but he was sharp. And when patience meets recklessness, the outcome is not in doubt. The only question left was how far Jarod would fall when he finally collided with the lesson Ty had come to deliver.

The referee called the names, his voice echoing across the gymnasium like a bell tolling before battle. "Takashi. Jarod." Every head in the bleachers snapped forward, and in that instant, the noise of shuffling feet and low chatter died away into a silence so sharp I could almost hear my heartbeat. Ty rose smoothly, adjusting his gi with calm hands, and when he walked to the mat, his steps were measured, steady, like a river flowing where it meant to go. Across from him, Jarod strutted forward, shoulders rolled high, his grin stretching too wide for his face. He cracked his knuckles loudly as though the sound itself were meant to intimidate, but if Ty heard it, he gave no sign.

The air was thick with something that pulled the breath from our lungs. Jeremy clutched the railing so tightly his knuckles paled, his wide eyes fixed on the mat. "It's starting," he whispered, and though his voice trembled, it carried in the quiet. Ella leaned into Sophie's side, her voice soft but certain. "Ty's not afraid." And she was right—his face was unreadable, not stern, not cold, but simply clear, as though he had emptied himself of every distraction except the moment before him. Jarod, in contrast, buzzed with restless energy, bouncing on the balls of his feet, his grin flashing in every direction as if begging for attention.

They faced each other, and the referee gestured. Jarod gave the shallowest of bows, his eyes never leaving Ty's. Ty's bow was full, low, precise, the kind that carried centuries of respect in its angle. The contrast was so stark that murmurs ran through the crowd, parents shifting, teachers nodding to one another as if the fight had already spoken its truth before a single strike had been thrown. I caught Mr. Clarke's gaze across the room, his arms folded, his jaw tight, but his eyes steady with trust in Ty.

The grandmaster, seated like a mountain at the edge of the mat, gave the faintest nod of approval at Ty's bow. Jarod missed it entirely, too caught in the swell of his own bravado. Jasmin whispered near me, "That's the difference. Ty's already won the respect. Jarod's still chasing it." Her words rang louder in my mind than the crowd's hush, for they cut straight to the truth. Respect was never something you seized; it was something you embodied.

The referee raised his hand, and in that heartbeat before the match began, I noticed Ty's breathing. It was deep, controlled, his shoulders rising and falling like waves steadying themselves against a storm. Jarod, meanwhile, puffed air through his nose, sharp and uneven, his chest heaving with the impatience of a boy who believed power lay only in the strike. The moment froze there, two boys mirroring the oldest of lessons—discipline against fury, balance against chaos, silence against noise.

"Begin!" The call rang, and Jarod surged forward immediately, his fists flying. The bleachers erupted with gasps, but Ty didn't flinch. He stepped lightly, his body bending like a reed against wind, redirecting Jarod's charge without matching force to force. The room filled with the sound of feet skidding on mats, but no blow landed. Jarod's grin widened, certain he was only warming up, but I could see the edges of it twitch—nervous, almost strained. Ty's eyes stayed clear, his movements so fluid that even the teachers leaned forward, whispering in awe.

Leo muttered near me, "He's not even fighting yet. He's waiting." His words settled over us all like a cloak. Ty wasn't rushing, wasn't reacting with panic. He was showing us something else, something hidden in the rhythm of stillness itself. Every dodge, every block was not just defense—it was patience. Jarod's strikes grew wilder, louder, but with every miss, every redirection, it became clear that brute force would not be enough.

Jeremy's voice cracked, but he spoke anyway, his eyes locked on Ty. "He's… teaching him. Even now." The truth of it tightened my chest. This was not about fists or even about victory. This was about exposing Jarod's violence, laying it bare so that everyone could see it for what it was—dishonour dressed as strength. Ty's calm was the mirror, and Jarod's fury only showed itself more distorted with every attempt to shatter it.

In that moment, even before the first clean strike landed, I knew the match had already been set—not in points, not in belts, but in the lesson everyone here would carry out of the room. Ty wasn't there to win. He was there to show us all what winning really meant.

The instant the referee dropped his hand, Jarod exploded forward like a cannonball loosed from its chain. His fists flew wild, thick arms pumping with every ounce of rage he had stored, each strike a promise to destroy rather than to spar. His sneakers squealed against the mat, the air between him and Ty tearing apart under the force of his charge. I held my breath, because for a heartbeat, it looked as though the storm he carried would swallow everything before it. Yet Ty didn't meet it head-on. He shifted one step to the side, light as wind through tall grass, and Jarod's fist cut the air where his jaw had been a moment before. The crowd gasped, but Ty's face never broke calm.

The sound of skin slapping against arm guards filled the room as Jarod threw another punch, then another, each louder than the last. Ty moved in rhythm, not faster, not slower, but perfectly placed, redirecting every strike with a palm that carried no anger. Jeremy clutched my sleeve so hard it pinched, his whisper escaping in shock. "He's not even hitting back." And it was true—Ty was turning the fight into a mirror, forcing Jarod to see himself flailing. Every time Jarod swung, he met only emptiness or his own momentum thrown off course.

Leo leaned forward in the bleachers, his voice edged with something between awe and old memory. "That's not defence—it's control. He's steering him." It looked like water slipping around stone, only here the stone was roaring, spitting, trying to crush the river, yet every lunge only deepened his imbalance. Jarod stumbled, caught himself, then bellowed and came again. His grin faltered, and in its place came a twisted snarl. That mask he had worn in hallways, that smirk that ruled over kids too small to fight back—it had no power here.

Sophie's breath caught audibly. "He's too fast." She was right. Ty's speed wasn't the frantic kind that wasted energy. It was precise, efficient, so quick it seemed like he was already there before Jarod finished moving. A block with the forearm. A sidestep with barely an inch of space. A redirection that sent Jarod spinning a half turn, his back exposed. Ty didn't take the chance to strike. He simply let him reset, a quiet lesson sharper than any punch.

Jarod roared and came with a kick, clumsy in its power. Ty raised his leg, intercepted it with a gentle angle, and shifted. The kick collapsed into nothing, Jarod hopping back with a snarl.

The bleachers rumbled with murmurs, students looking at each other as if they'd never seen Jarod before. Mila whispered across Ella's ear, "He's losing. Look at him." But it wasn't just the fight he was losing—it was the image of invincibility he had built stone by stone in our hallways. Each miss cracked it wider.

Mr. Clarke's jaw tightened as he watched, arms folded hard against his chest, but his eyes gleamed with something close to relief. He knew what this meant. Ty wasn't humiliating Jarod. He was exposing him. And the more Jarod lunged, the more desperate it all appeared. Sweat dripped down his brow, his breathing jagged now, while Ty's chest rose and fell with the slow cadence of someone still in practice, still in training, never once pulled out of balance.

I found myself whispering even though I hadn't meant to. "It's like watching him fight air." My words surprised me, but Jasmin nodded fiercely. "No, Nico—it's worse for him. Air doesn't send you stumbling back." Her words clung to me, because she was right. Ty wasn't hurting Jarod's body, but he was breaking the armour he had wrapped himself in, piece by piece, in front of the whole school.

Jarod swung again, wild, reckless, desperate to land a hit. This time Ty ducked low, his body flowing under the arc of the fist, and in one motion, he tapped Jarod's arm aside and stepped behind him. The crowd gasped in unison. Ty could have ended it right there. He could have driven a strike into Jarod's ribs or dropped him with a sweep. Instead, he simply let him stumble forward, humiliated by his own momentum.

Jeremy's voice cracked again. "He's… he's showing everyone. Jarod's not strong. He's out of control." And those words mattered. They mattered because, for years, Jarod's strength had been the truth none of us could deny. But now, right here, under the eyes of grandmasters, teachers, parents, and classmates, that truth was crumbling. All that strength, all that rage—it meant nothing against balance, patience, and respect.

The first exchange was over before the crowd even understood it had begun. Jarod huffed and puffed, sweat streaking his brow, his fists trembling not with exhaustion but with humiliation. Ty stood unmarked, unbothered, his breathing steady as if he had simply walked across the mat and back. The referee's eyes flicked toward the grandmaster, who nodded silently. And in that stillness, I realised what had been taught without a word: the fight wasn't fists. It was control. And Ty had it.

The moment shifted, and I could feel it in my bones before my eyes caught up. Ty no longer waited, no longer stepped aside like drifting mist. His father's training moved through him now, every inch of discipline he had absorbed brought into the light. One instant he was water, flowing around Jarod's fist with effortless grace, the next he snapped forward with the precision of iron, his palm cutting like a blade into Jarod's chest. The sound echoed, sharp and final, and Jarod reeled backward as if he had slammed into a wall no one else could see.

Jarod snarled and stormed back, swinging high and low, his arms flailing like clubs meant to smash stone. But Ty met him with reversals I barely understood. His wrist turned, his elbow cut a line, his leg slid under Jarod's stance, and before anyone realised what had happened, Jarod's body was airborne. He hit the mat with a crash that sent shivers through the floor. The crowd gasped in unison, the sound rising and falling like one massive breath torn from their lungs. Jeremy squeezed my arm hard, whispering through clenched teeth, "He's not just fighting him. He's rewriting him."

The referee stepped closer, but Ty had already backed away, steady, calm, his breathing untouched. Jarod staggered up, eyes blazing with fury, only to charge again, reckless. Ty caught his momentum as though it had been handed to him on a platter. A turn of the shoulder, a shift of the hips, and Jarod spun in midair, hurled like a ragdoll across the mat. He tumbled, scrambled, his arms clawing at the ground to catch himself, but even his pride could not disguise the fact that he had been thrown.

Leo leaned in, his voice dark but certain. "That's Tai Chi inside Kung Fu. It's not about crushing—it's about teaching." He was right. Ty's movements weren't chaotic. Every strike had intention, every throw carried a lesson. Jarod had built his strength on fear, but Ty's strength was balance itself, an anchor no storm could uproot. Jarod swung again, his jaw clenched, but Ty blocked him with a single hand, redirected the fist, and with a sudden pivot, brought him to the ground again. This time Jarod's breath whooshed out, the sound pitiful in its emptiness.

Sophie's eyes widened, her voice rising above the murmurs. "He can't win. Look at him—he's out of control." And she was right. Jarod's fury had burned past the point of sense. His strikes had no aim, no shape, only noise and speed. But Ty's discipline cut through it like a blade through cloth. Every counter was clean, every reversal a declaration. With each throw, Jarod lost not just footing but image—the smirk, the grin, the mask he had worn at school now shattered into fragments scattered on the mat.

I felt my own chest rise with awe and fear together. "He's showing him what fighting really means," I whispered to no one and everyone at once. Jasmin nodded fiercely, eyes never leaving the ring. "It's not fighting—it's teaching." Her words stuck like nails. That was what it was. Ty wasn't here for victory. He was here for correction.

Jarod roared again, his voice breaking, his fists lifting high as though rage alone could repair what was slipping. He lunged, but Ty stepped inside the arc, his palm guiding the blow wide. In the same motion, Ty's leg hooked under Jarod's, and with a sharp twist, Jarod flew sideways, his body spinning like paper caught in a gale. He hit the mat outside the boundary, rolling until the ropes stopped him. The arena gasped. Teachers leaned forward. Parents clutched hands together. And for the first time, Jarod's eyes widened with something that looked a lot like fear.

Jeremy's voice trembled as he whispered, "He knows. He knows he can't beat him." And I could see it. The flush of rage had given way to the pallor of realisation. Jarod had met someone he could never dominate.

No threat, no punch, no roar would grant him power here. Ty stood with his shoulders steady, his head bowed slightly, as though the fight belonged to something greater than himself. His silence spoke louder than Jarod's screams: violence without discipline is nothing.

The crowd murmured, some rising to their feet, others clutching their mouths. Mr. Clarke's voice rumbled low where he stood among staff, "They're all seeing it. Every student in this room will remember this." And he was right. It wasn't just Jarod who was learning. It was all of us. Ty's strikes, his reversals, his throws—they weren't just tactics. They were truths given shape.

I looked at Ty and saw him not as a boy my age but as something larger, something that had been waiting for this moment. His fists were weapons, but not of violence—of control, of honour, of balance. Jarod had mocked respect his whole life, sneered at discipline, scorned patience. And now every one of those virtues was standing in front of him, unmoved, unbreakable. Jarod stumbled back to his feet, panting, his chest heaving, but even he seemed to know. This was no fight he could win. This was a lesson he could not escape.

I could feel the air shift before Ty even moved. The tension had stretched thin, snapping across the arena like a string pulled too far, and then Ty stepped into it. He didn't rush, didn't flinch, didn't even harden his face. He waited until Jarod's charge came crashing toward him, all muscle and rage without thought, and then he answered with a single, precise strike. It wasn't the kind of blow that snapped bones or scattered blood—it was sharper than that, cleaner. His fist cut across Jarod's momentum with the speed of lightning and the certainty of stone, halting him in his tracks as if an invisible wall had risen between them.

Jarod staggered, the shock written across his face more than the sting of impact. His eyes widened, his mouth half-open as though his body had betrayed him by failing to follow through. For years, he had been the storm—loud, heavy, impossible to ignore—and in that single motion Ty had revealed him for what he was: noise without substance. The crowd gasped all at once, the sound filling the bleachers and pouring back into the ring. The arena seemed to draw in its breath and hold it.

Jeremy leaned forward, his voice barely more than a whisper, yet strong enough to carry through the silence. "He's not just fighting him—he's teaching him." The words landed heavy, truer than anything I'd heard all day. Jarod was being reshaped before our eyes. This wasn't punishment for punishment's sake. It was a lesson in its purest, most painful form.

Jarod stumbled back, clutching his chest where Ty's strike had found him. He growled, forcing his body upright, but even his steps betrayed the tremor that had taken root in him. His strength had met something greater—not greater in size, not greater in volume, but greater in purpose. He swung again, a desperate lunge, but Ty's response came like a whisper. He sidestepped, redirected the force, and with no more than a twist of his wrist, sent Jarod spiralling off balance. The boy crashed to the mat once more, his pride breaking louder than the fall itself.

# THE SMILE THAT BROKE

I had seen Jarod smile before. It was never pleasant. It was the smile of someone who knew he could take what he wanted, that his fists would silence protests before words ever began. But now his grin was gone, replaced by something that looked uncomfortably like confusion. He hadn't prepared for this—hadn't even known this kind of fight existed. His strength was bared for what it truly was: blunt, shallow, hollow. And Ty had peeled it away without even raising his voice.

Jasmin clutched the edge of her seat, her knuckles white, her eyes wide. "He's breaking him apart piece by piece," she murmured. She didn't mean broken bones. She meant the deeper cracks, the ones carved into pride and arrogance. Ella nodded, not even blinking, her lips pressed tightly shut. None of us could look away.

Ty stood still again, waiting, his chest rising evenly, calm as a steady tide. His face betrayed nothing—no gloat, no scorn, not even triumph. It was that restraint that spoke loudest of all. It told Jarod, and all of us, that mastery had nothing to do with rage, and everything to do with control. The silence in the room pressed close, so close I could hear the soft scrape of Jarod's shoes as he pulled himself upright, panting, furious, desperate not to be seen as small.

But small he was. For the first time, Jarod looked smaller than Ty, though his shoulders were broader and his frame heavier. His presence had always been oppressive, a shadow that swallowed every hallway he walked through. Now it flickered like a candle threatened by the wind. And Ty, without lifting his voice or rushing his movements, had become the wind itself.

Jeremy's hand tightened into a fist at his side. His whisper came again, this time steadier, as though he needed to hear it just as much as Jarod did. "He's teaching him." It wasn't only Jarod who needed to learn. We all did. Respect was louder than violence. Control was stronger than chaos. And a single, precise strike, delivered with purpose, could undo a hundred fists thrown with hate.

Jarod came at Ty as though the floor itself would open if he didn't keep swinging. His arms snapped like whips, his fists hammering the air, each punch fuelled with desperation more than skill. Sweat poured down his forehead, his teeth clenched, his chest heaving with the weight of pride crumbling before the crowd. I could see it in his face—the realisation that he was no longer the predator here, but prey cornered in a ring where the whole world could see him falter. Still, he kept flinging himself forward, reckless, blind, unwilling to accept what everyone else already knew.

Ty didn't move at first. He stood as still as a tree rooted in the earth, letting Jarod's rage blaze around him like a wildfire that had already burned out its strength. His eyes didn't flicker, his breathing stayed level, and his arms rose only when needed—to redirect, to block, to let Jarod collapse under the weight of his own fury. He was patience personified, holding his ground with the calm of someone who knew there was no chance, no crack, no opening Jarod could exploit. It was a quiet certainty that rattled Jarod more than any blow.

The crowd shouted now, a mix of voices rising with every clash. Some wanted Jarod to win, others whispered for Ty, but all leaned forward, pulled to the centre where the two of them circled. I could hear Sophie's breath quicken beside me, see Leo's fists clenching on his knees, as if willing Ty to hold his balance. Jeremy was trembling, not from fear but from awe, his wide eyes locked on Ty's every move. It wasn't a fight anymore. It was something more, something deeper.

Jarod's arms grew heavy, his strikes losing form, his breath breaking in jagged gasps. His once powerful frame sagged beneath exhaustion, his rage having eaten itself alive. Ty moved at last, a ripple in water disturbed by the final stone. His body flowed like silk, effortless, almost tender, and then it shifted into steel. One sweeping motion, a single perfect arc of balance and strength, and Jarod was stripped of his momentum, his fist twisted out of line, his legs swept from beneath him.

The sound of his fall shook through the floorboards, a crash that silenced even the loudest voices in the bleachers. He sprawled across the mat, his arms spread wide, his pride broken in every angle of his posture. His chest heaved, but his eyes refused to lift, fixed on the ceiling above as though looking anywhere but at Ty could undo the shame burning through him. For the first time, Jarod's silence was louder than his fists.

Ty did not advance. He didn't press his advantage, didn't raise his hand for the finishing strike. He simply stood tall, his body still as calm water, then bent at the waist and bowed. The gesture was deliberate, a blade sharper than any punch, a reminder that dignity didn't come from bruising another boy's skin—it came from restraint. Ty's silence spoke volumes. Violence had its chance and failed. Respect had won.

The bow hung in the air, unchallenged, undeniable. Every student, every teacher, every parent who had gathered here knew what they had just witnessed. Jarod had come with fury, Ty had answered with discipline, and the gulf between them had been laid bare for all to see. The lesson wasn't hidden in words; it was painted across the mat with each strike, each fall, each breath. Ty had taught without cruelty, had corrected without hatred, and in doing so had shown the strength Jarod had always pretended to have but never possessed.

Leo leaned closer to me, his voice hushed but steady. "That's it. That's how you stop someone like him. You don't just beat them—you show them they were never strong to begin with." Ella nodded at his side, her eyes shining with the reflection of the moment. Jasmin wiped her palms on her skirt, whispering, "He's making Jarod feel what he made others feel. Small. Powerless. Only now it's real."

Jeremy, though, had no words. His hands were clasped in front of him, pressed so tightly that his knuckles turned white. His lips trembled, but his eyes never left Ty. There was something holy in the way he looked, as though he had witnessed not just a fight but a truth he would carry for the rest of his life. For him, the lesson wasn't just for Jarod—it was for all of us.

Jarod rolled onto his side at last, coughing, his face pale and blotched with humiliation. The jeers didn't come. The crowd didn't mock him, didn't shout, didn't cheer. They simply waited, their silence more cutting than any insult. The weight of shame filled the arena, pressing down on him until his broad shoulders seemed smaller than they ever had before. He had been exposed, stripped of the mask he wore, and all that was left was a boy out of breath and out of excuses.

Ty turned from him without another glance. That choice cut deeper than any strike could. By refusing to look down at Jarod, by refusing to celebrate his fall, Ty showed what true strength was. Strength wasn't about reminding the fallen of their weakness. It was about proving you never needed to push them down in the first place. The bow had already ended the fight. Anything more would have been cruelty, and Ty would not indulge it.

Mr. Clarke adjusted his glasses from the staff row, his eyes soft but proud. I caught the faintest shake of Mrs. Locke's head, her lips pursed as if to say finally. Even Principal Arnett, who so rarely betrayed emotion, leaned forward, his jaw tightening as though he, too, understood the significance of what we had seen. Every adult knew this wasn't simply a children's tournament anymore. It had become a classroom far larger than any they had taught in.

I let the air back into my lungs, not realising I had been holding it all this time. Ty's bow still echoed in my mind, sharper than the crash of Jarod hitting the floor. It was the kind of memory that would never leave us, a moment where silence carried the greatest weight. Jarod had tried to build his world on violence, but in that ring, Ty had shown him—and shown us all—that such a world collapses under the lightest hand of discipline.

The lesson was delivered. Not shouted, not written, not even spoken. It was delivered in the pause, the bow, and the refusal to strike again. And I knew as surely as I knew my own name that none of us would ever forget it.

The mat was still vibrating beneath Jarod's fall when silence spread through the arena like a tide swallowing every sound. The chatter of parents, the laughter of classmates, even the rustle of programs being folded in nervous hands—gone. It was as though the air itself had been told to hold its breath. I felt my chest tighten with it, the weight of quiet pressing on my ribs. This wasn't the silence of confusion or of indifference. This was the silence that follows truth when there is nothing left to argue.

Sho Kazushi, the grandmaster flown in from Japan, stepped forward with a poise that belonged more to a mountain than a man. His hands folded neatly in front of him, his eyes steady on Ty, then briefly on Jarod. His voice, when it came, cut clean through the silence without raising its tone. "The victor of this match," he announced, "is Ty Takashi." His words carried no flourish, no exaggeration, no crowd-pleasing rhythm. They carried only fact, as sharp and final as the crack of a gavel.

The crowd stirred at his declaration, but Ty didn't shift, didn't lift his arms, didn't allow triumph to twist his face into the smirk Jarod so often wore. He simply stood, shoulders square, eyes forward, his silence louder than the cheers that wanted to rise. And then, in a voice clear and unyielding, he spoke words that would brand themselves into us: "No. Respect is the victor. Violence has no place here." The statement cut deeper than Jarod's fists ever could, clean and simple, stripping victory itself of glory and leaving only the lesson.

Jarod's head fell. His chest heaved, not with the strength of a fighter catching his breath, but with the hollow collapse of someone who realised the audience no longer feared him. His shoulders curled inward, shrinking a frame that had once looked so large. His eyes, usually sharp with arrogance, flickered to the floor. The shame lit his face in blotches of red, his lips pressed thin against words he couldn't summon. The grin, his weapon of choice, was gone. He had no mask left.

Jeremy, seated two rows from me, leaned forward until his small hands clutched the rail. His lips trembled, but the whisper that escaped him was steady enough to carry: "Lines were crossed today… now we all know the difference." He said it not for us, but for himself, as if he needed the words to anchor what his eyes had witnessed. I glanced at him, saw his wide eyes glistening, and knew those words would never leave him. He had seen too much cruelty in Jarod's reign not to mark this moment as its end.

Leo sat back, his hands clasped in front of his mouth, not speaking, not moving, only nodding. Sophie's jaw was tight, her brows furrowed, but her eyes shimmered with something close to relief. Ella's breath caught in short bursts, her hand resting on Jasmin's arm for balance. Mila leaned forward, her gaze fixed not on Jarod, but on Ty, as if trying to memorise his stillness, his refusal to be moved by victory. Even Alex, older and harder in his usual stance, looked down at Jarod with something close to pity.

The adults were no less affected. Principal Arnett adjusted his tie with slow fingers, but his eyes never left Ty. Mr. Clarke's face carried both pride and warning, as if silently praying that Ty would not let this burden weigh too heavily on him. Mrs. Locke pressed her hand against her cheek, and I caught the faint trace of moisture on her skin. Even Mrs. Dunlop, so stern in every assembly, sat with her arms crossed not out of disapproval, but to hold herself together.

I breathed in, trying to steady my own heart, and found the smell of the mats sharp in my nostrils, a mix of rubber and sweat that felt heavier than ever. The silence did not crack. It did not ease into cheers. It grew denser, thicker, until it filled the hall with something close to reverence. This wasn't a victory that could be clapped away. It was a revelation, and revelations demanded silence.

Jarod shifted on the floor, his palms pressing against the mat as if to rise, but even in that small movement he looked diminished. His hands trembled, his back curved, his breath whistled with exhaustion. No one moved to help him. No one needed to. The weight wasn't his fall—it was the silence that told him plainly that the crowd had seen through him. He could rise, but he could not stand taller than the truth anymore.

Ty finally stepped back, bowing once more, this time toward Sho Kazushi. The grandmaster bowed in return, his head lowering with respect. It was not just for Ty's technique, but for his words, for the refusal to let violence define what strength meant. That exchange—silent, graceful—reignited something in me. It wasn't about winning. It was about reshaping the very idea of what it meant to fight.

Beside me, Jasmin murmured under her breath, "He didn't just win. He changed it." Her voice was barely audible, but Sophie nodded beside her, adding softly, "Jarod can't come back from this. Not here. Not with us." I knew they were right. Something fundamental had shifted, and no matter what Jarod did in the future, this silence would always linger in the memory of his name.

The students around us—some who had once cheered Jarod's violence—sat still, their faces pale, their bodies tight. They weren't just quiet. They were unsettled, shaken to the core. I wondered if they too were realising that they had fed his fire with their fear, and that silence now was not only for Ty but also for themselves, for the recognition of their part in this tournament.

Ty's words still echoed, impossible to dismiss: "Respect is the victor. Violence has no place here." They hung above us like scripture, rewriting every cheer, every whisper, every memory of Jarod's strength. Even Jeremy's whisper had joined them, adding a child's fragile truth to a fighter's solemn declaration. Together, they sealed the moment so firmly that even the loudest crowd could never erase it.

And so, we sat, all of us, in that silence that followed. Not as spectators anymore, not as students or teachers, but as witnesses to something that had broken through the usual noise of fights and feuds. The silence itself was the aftermath, the bow, the verdict. It was the lesson carved into air so heavy no one dared break it.

I knew then that the fight had ended long before Jarod fell. It ended here, in this silence, where every student, every teacher, every parent had been forced to confront the difference between power and respect. And as I sat there, breathless, I understood: this was no ordinary lesson. It was a wound cut open in public, but it was also the start of its healing.

The silence after the match had weight, but what came next bent the silence into something even heavier. Sho Kazushi held out the polished trophy toward Ty, a glint of gold catching in the overhead lights. The crowd leaned forward, eager to see the moment of victory sealed, expecting Ty to claim what he had already earned with skill and grace. My own breath caught, waiting, but I knew Ty well enough to sense he would not take this in the way everyone assumed.

Ty bowed once, deeply, respectfully, but his hands did not move toward the trophy. Instead, he raised his head and spoke clearly, each word carrying as though carried on the mats themselves: "There is one here tonight who deserves this more than I do." The sentence dropped into the silence like a stone into still water, ripples spreading instantly. Murmurs began in pockets of the bleachers, quick exchanges of disbelief, questions muttered between parents and students alike. Ty's eyes scanned the room, steady, unwavering, before they found the boy who had fought earlier with remarkable discipline but had been eliminated before the final.

The boy—slender, with dark hair plastered against his forehead with sweat—sat on the edge of his seat, frozen. His hands gripped his knees as if to keep himself from floating away. Ty lifted his arm and pointed directly at him, not accusingly, but invitingly. Gasps escaped from the crowd. The boy's eyes widened, his lips parting in shock. He mouthed a silent me? as though no one in the world would ever have chosen him in this moment.

"Yes, you," Ty said, his voice calm, steady, generous. He gestured with one hand, beckoning the boy to come forward. The boy stood awkwardly, almost stumbling over the legs of those seated beside him, his feet clumsy in his disbelief. He looked back once, perhaps to find a parent, perhaps to make sure he wasn't dreaming, and then stepped onto the mat with hesitation thick in each stride. The murmurs in the hall rose to a buzz, the surprise thickening like a storm.

When the boy reached him, Ty did not wait for a speech or a thank you. He simply pressed the trophy into the boy's hands with quiet authority. The boy tried to resist, shaking his head quickly, but Ty closed his fingers firmly around the base of the trophy, making it impossible for him to decline. "You fought with discipline," Ty said softly but firmly. "That deserves respect more than victory does."

The boy's mouth trembled with words he couldn't find. His eyes darted across the crowd, then back to Ty, then down at the shining trophy in his hands. He swallowed hard, cheeks burning red, and finally nodded once, quick and almost desperate, as though agreeing not with Ty's words but with the impossibility of rejecting such a gift. His chest rose and fell with sharp breaths as he clutched the prize that minutes ago had seemed unreachable.

The crowd, for a heartbeat, stayed hushed, trying to understand what had just happened. Then the whispers turned into small claps, polite at first, then swelling into something louder, a roar of approval not only for Ty's victory but for his refusal to let the trophy define it. Parents stood, applauding. Teachers exchanged stunned glances, some nodding, some simply shaking their heads in awe. Students shouted his name, but Ty kept his face calm, his bow directed not at himself, but toward the boy still trembling with the weight of the award.

Jeremy leaned toward me, his mouth hanging open, his words barely escaping. "He gave it away… he actually gave it away." His tone was half disbelief, half wonder, as though Ty had done something both impossible and obvious at the same time. Ella clapped slowly, then faster, her eyes locked on the boy with the trophy. Jasmin whispered, "That boy will never forget this," and Sophie added, "Neither will Jarod." Her words hung heavier than she realised.

For Jarod, still crouched near the edge of the mat, the moment was salt on an open wound. To lose was humiliation enough, but to watch his rival not only claim victory but cast it aside in favour of another boy's discipline—that was devastation. His face flushed darker, his jaw tightened, his fists clenched at his knees, but he had no ground left to stand on. He could not protest without further exposing the emptiness of his own approach to fighting.

Leo caught my eye across the row, his expression not smug but sober. He mouthed quietly, "This is the end of him." I nodded, understanding. Not the end of Jarod as a person, but the end of his reign of fear. He had relied on strength without respect, violence without discipline. And tonight, Ty had shown in front of everyone that such strength would always collapse when weighed against honour.

The grandmaster, still standing tall, folded his hands once more and bowed to Ty, his expression unreadable but his eyes glinting with quiet pride. For all his decades of teaching, he too knew he had witnessed something rare: a lesson that transcended training halls and trophies, one that could never be forgotten by those present. Ty's gesture was more than humility. It was defiance against everything Jarod had embodied.

The boy with the trophy clutched it tight, as though afraid it would vanish if he loosened his grip. He looked at Ty with a mix of awe and disbelief, tears shining in his eyes though he tried to blink them away. He whispered something, too soft for me to hear, but Ty nodded in return, placing a hand briefly on the boy's shoulder before stepping back, leaving him in the centre of the mat, bathed in the echo of applause that had once belonged to him.

I realised then that this wasn't about giving away a prize. It was about rewriting the meaning of winning. Ty had refused to let the trophy stand as proof of victory, instead choosing to elevate respect above recognition. And in doing so, he had shifted the lesson away from himself, ensuring that everyone—Jarod, the students, even us watching—would remember the day not as Ty's triumph but as the night respect defeated violence.

The applause carried on, filling the gymnasium with a sound that could not be silenced, a sound louder and more lasting than Jarod's fists had ever been. And as I watched the boy trembling with the weight of the trophy, I thought to myself: this is what it means when someone refuses to let victory be about themselves. This is what it means to draw a line, to cross it, and then to show everyone else the way back.

I could feel the air change the moment Ty placed his hand on the boy's shoulder. His grip wasn't forceful, just steady, carrying the kind of weight that words could never reach on their own. His voice rang out clear, not shouting, not trembling, but certain, as though it had been waiting in him all along. "You are an excellent fighter. That is what deserves respect. Not winning. Respect." The crowd answered not with silence but with an eruption that shook the rafters. Applause thundered, cheers rose, and for a moment the entire hall forgot itself, giving way to the sound of respect being applauded as fiercely as victory itself.

I scanned the faces around me, every teacher, every parent, every student caught in the force of what Ty had just done. Mrs. Locke had both hands clasped together near her chin, her face soft with something that almost looked like relief. Mr. Arnett, usually unreadable, stood with his arms crossed but his eyes glimmering with approval he couldn't mask. Even Mr. Clarke, with his usual stiffness, was clapping so hard that his palms must have stung. The applause wasn't polite—it was powerful, a wave rolling across the room until no one could resist adding their hands to it.

But as the roar grew, my eyes moved to the one person who couldn't join it. Jarod sat low, his shoulders hunched, his face shadowed by the weight of his own defeat. His fists dug into his knees, knuckles pale, but he didn't rise, didn't protest, didn't move. The message had already been carved into the night, and everyone knew it. Strength without respect had been stripped bare for what it truly was—emptiness. His grin, once so wide it filled every room he walked into, was gone. His lips pressed tight, his eyes burning with humiliation that no one else could erase.

Sophie leaned forward in her seat, her voice tight but certain as she whispered, "He's finished." Ella nodded beside her, her hands clapping softer now, eyes narrowed as she watched Jarod with a kind of cold recognition. "The mask is off," she said, not to anyone in particular, but the words landed heavy all the same. Leo glanced my way, lifting his chin in the smallest gesture of agreement, as though even he could see the final nail being driven into Jarod's throne of fear.

Jeremy's small hands clapped, but his eyes never left Ty. "He's not just our friend anymore," he whispered, almost like he was confessing something sacred. "He's… he's the kind of person everyone's going to remember." His voice cracked, and I felt it too, the realisation that this wasn't just a match, wasn't just a school rivalry—this was history, being written right in front of us.

Then, in the middle of it all, something happened none of us could have predicted, though perhaps it had been waiting all along. Jasmin rose from her seat, her steps quick, her face flushed not with embarrassment but with resolve. She crossed the space between the crowd and the mat as though pulled forward by something greater than herself. For a heartbeat the clapping slowed as people turned, wondering what she was doing, but she didn't stop. She reached Ty, who looked at her in surprise, his calm composure finally shaken by something he couldn't anticipate.

Without hesitation, Jasmin leaned in and pressed her lips to his. It was quick, unplanned, but filled with a year of waiting, a year of unsaid words, a year of love that had been silently carried. The sound of applause faltered into gasps, whispers, and then returned with even greater force, laughter and cheers mingling with the shock. For Ty, it was his first kiss, a moment that left him blinking, stunned, as though this battle had given him more than just honour—it had given him a piece of life he never expected.

I felt my breath catch. Sophie covered her mouth, her eyes wide. Ella burst out with a laugh that carried no malice, only delight at the boldness of it. Jeremy's jaw dropped, his small hands frozen mid-clap as though time itself had stopped. Even Alex, usually too cool to react, muttered a low, "Finally," with a grin that betrayed how long he'd seen it coming.

Jasmin pulled back slowly, her cheeks flushed, her eyes locked on Ty's. For the first time that night, his calm cracked into something else—astonishment mixed with a smile so faint it could have been missed if you blinked. She whispered, just loud enough for those close to hear, "I've loved you since day one." Her voice didn't tremble. It was clear, certain, stronger than the cheers of the crowd.

The arena swelled with more noise, but this time it wasn't for the fight, wasn't for the trophy, wasn't even for the grandmaster's words. It was for a boy who had chosen respect over victory, and for a girl who had chosen love over silence. The two threads wove together in front of us, unstoppable, undeniable. I sat there knowing I had just witnessed not one, but two victories that night—one over violence, and one over fear of the heart.

Jarod's humiliation deepened, though he tried to hide it. No longer was he the centre of whispers, the one who held attention through force. The spotlight had shifted completely, and not even his anger could pull it back. For the first time, he was irrelevant. For the first time, his shadow was gone.

I leaned back, letting the roar of the crowd fill me. Respect had been made public. Love had been made public. And Jarod's downfall had been made public. It was a night no one would forget, a night when lines were not just crossed but rewritten before our eyes.

I felt the air bend as the applause thinned into murmurs, a hundred conversations sparking at once in whispers and glances. Teachers leaned into one another, their eyes wide with a mixture of disbelief and awe, as though they had not prepared for a lesson so public and so unshakable. Mrs. Dunlop pressed her hand to her chest, her face pale with the weight of it, whispering something to Mr. Clarke, who nodded slowly, his mouth set in a grim line. The fight had ended, but the memory of it was still swinging through the rafters, heavy enough to reshape the air in the room.

The parents scattered through the bleachers carried the same stunned look, eyes darting between Ty, Jasmin, and Jarod. Some clapped again, the sound hesitant, others simply watched, as though what they had just witnessed would take years to fully settle. Respect had been demanded, displayed, and then sealed by the choice of a boy barely twelve years old. For the first time, the adults seemed to realise that the children were not only learning from them but teaching them too. That realisation shook them, a ripple that ran deeper than applause ever could.

My classmates exchanged glances of their own, none louder than Sophie's. She leaned forward, her eyes burning with a sharp kind of joy, whispering to Ella, "Do you see him now? Jarod isn't untouchable. He's just a boy who lost." Ella nodded, her voice low but firm. "No, not just lost—he's been unmasked. We've all seen it. He can't hide behind fear anymore." Those words were heavy, not spoken as children teasing a rival, but as judges handing down a verdict.

Leo leaned back in his chair, his eyes fixed on Ty, his jaw set with respect he didn't bother to hide. "That's how it's done," he muttered, almost to himself, but I heard it clearly. Alex crossed his arms, nodding once with quiet agreement, his usual smirk softened into something closer to admiration. Even they, who had once wielded fear like a weapon, now bowed inwardly to the power of respect Ty had placed before everyone's eyes.

Jeremy tugged at my sleeve, his small voice breaking through the sea of whispers. "He changed everything, didn't he?" he asked. I nodded, though I wasn't sure I had the right words. It wasn't just a fight. It wasn't even just a kiss. It was a rewriting of how this school would remember its own halls, how Jarod would be spoken of in corners, and how Ty would be measured in every retelling from now on. Jeremy's eyes widened with the kind of awe only a child could hold, his belief in heroes suddenly made flesh.

Jarod himself sat lower than I had ever seen him. His grin, once the sharp edge he carried into every room, was gone, carved away by humiliation. He looked smaller somehow, his shoulders hunched, his fists slack against his knees. For the first time, the fear he had fed on was no longer his to command. His classmates' eyes slid over him differently now, not with the dread he had counted on, but with pity, with scorn, with the recognition that he was not a monster, only a boy stripped of his throne. That was the deepest wound, and he knew it.

The grandmaster's words lingered in the silence: Respect is the victor. It wasn't just Ty who had delivered the lesson; it was the entire arena that had borne witness, and in bearing witness, had changed. The students whispered to one another, their voices tinged with a new courage. Ella's laugh rang out, not cruel, but certain: "He's done." Sophie's nod sealed it, her eyes never leaving Jarod as if she were holding him accountable with every glance.

Teachers exchanged looks, the kind they would carry back to staff meetings, the kind that said something irreversible had happened here tonight. Mr. Arnett's jaw worked as though chewing over words he would not speak in front of us, but his silence said enough. Miss Kara wiped her glasses, her eyes bright, as though she were both proud and chastened by what she had just seen. For them, it was a reminder that lessons could come unannounced, written not on chalkboards but in the sweat and resolve of a child who refused to bow to violence.

Jasmin stayed near Ty, her cheeks still red, her head high in defiance of the whispers trailing her boldness. She didn't flinch under the looks, didn't regret what she had done. If anything, her stance only made the moment more unshakable, her courage paired with his. She had kissed him not for the crowd but for herself, and in doing so, gave Ty's lesson a seal no one else could replicate. Love had walked onto the mat that night, hand in hand with respect.

I caught Sophie glancing at me, her eyebrows raised, as if to ask silently, Did you see that? Did you feel it? I nodded once. How could anyone not? The ripple of it was too strong, shifting everything we thought we knew about our place, our school, our stories. It wasn't just Ty standing taller now—it was every one of us who could see that fear wasn't the only crown worth wearing. Respect, love, and truth held more weight than any grin Jarod could muster.

The applause softened into murmurs again, but those murmurs were different now, not the chatter of idle spectators but the beginnings of a retelling. Parents leaned toward their children, children leaned toward one another, each word carrying the memory forward already. It would be told again and again, how Jarod was unmasked, how Ty refused the prize, how Jasmin kissed him. The fight was already legend, growing in the room before our eyes.

Jarod's shadow shrank as the ripple spread. He was no longer the figure towering in the hallway corners, no longer the name whispered with dread in classrooms. His story had been rewritten in a single night, his power dissolved not by fists alone but by something far greater. He looked foolish now, small, even childish, and no matter how he tried to recover, those watching eyes would never unsee what they had witnessed.

I leaned back against the wooden bleacher, drawing in a slow breath. For me, the ripple wasn't just in the room; it was inside me. I felt the lesson brand itself into my memory. Fear fades. Respect remains. Love endures. That was what I would carry away from this night, what all of us would carry, whether we admitted it or not.

And as the crowd settled, as Ty stood calm with Jasmin beside him, and as Jarod sat smaller than ever, I knew this wasn't just an ending. It was the kind of ripple that would keep moving, reshaping hallways, classrooms, and lives far beyond this gym. The school's memory had been rewritten, and nothing Jarod did could ever reclaim it.

I heard the whispers spread before the night was even over. Jarod had not only been beaten in the ring, but word was already circling among the parents, the teachers, and the older students: his own master had spoken. I could still hear the voice in my memory, cold, clipped, merciless in its finality—"Don't come back." It was harsher than any blow Ty had landed, a dismissal not of effort but of worth. Jarod, once paraded as a prodigy, was being shut out of the very place he thought had made him strong.

The story leapt from that one voice into many. Other dojos heard of the disgrace, and the judgment spread like wildfire. One by one, doors that Jarod had walked through with his belt tied proud and his chin lifted were closed to him. They saw not a disciplined fighter, not a boy learning the path of martial arts, but a danger—a storm with no control. Their verdict was quiet but unyielding: no place for him here. What had once been a world of belonging was now nothing but exile.

I watched him that night as the truth sank in. The belt tied at his waist looked heavier than it ever had, not as a mark of honour but as a chain. He pulled at the knot, his fingers trembling, until at last he let it fall slack around him. For all his bluster, Jarod looked broken, not by fists but by shame. And I knew in that moment that Ty had won something greater than a fight—he had dismantled the illusion Jarod had built around himself.

Ty stood calm at Jasmin's side, her hand brushing his sleeve, steady as ever. He didn't gloat, didn't sneer, didn't even look at Jarod now. That silence was more cutting than any victory speech could have been. Jarod was left alone, his shoulders hunched as if the entire room pressed against his back. No allies came to lift him. No friends leaned near. Even those who had once cheered his victories stared at him with eyes that said they were finished following his lead.

Leo whispered under his breath, words I caught clearly. "That's worse than any beating." His face was grim, his voice carrying not triumph but a kind of weary understanding. He knew, perhaps more than any of us, what it meant to be marked by shame that would not wash away. Alex nodded beside him, his arms crossed, his smirk absent. For once, even he found no pleasure in Jarod's fall—only the recognition of what happens when power is built on fear alone.

Jeremy tugged on my sleeve again, his wide eyes still shining with the need to understand. "Is he really finished?" he asked, his voice hushed like he was afraid Jarod could still hear him. I leaned down, my answer low but certain. "Yes. Because no one will stand with him anymore." Jeremy bit his lip, nodding slowly, and the words seemed to settle deep inside him like a lesson etched into stone.

Teachers whispered among themselves, though their faces betrayed the weight of what had happened. Mrs. Locke shook her head, her voice carrying in fragments. "It's the exile that breaks him. Not the fight." Mr. Clarke gave a solemn nod, his jaw tight, as though he too saw the lesson echo far beyond the mats. Miss Kara pressed her books tighter to her chest, as though carrying away something fragile yet unforgettable. They knew as well as we did: respect builds. Violence destroys.

I glanced back at the parents in the stands. Some held their children closer, as though the sight of Jarod's downfall was more frightening than his violence had ever been. Others wore expressions of relief, almost gratitude, that a line had finally been drawn, that someone had stood up and shown what strength truly meant. The ripple Ty had created wasn't only for us students; it was spreading through generations, reshaping how parents would speak to their children about what it meant to fight.

Jasmin stood tall beside Ty, her chin lifted, her face flushed but unflinching. The kiss she had given him earlier had not been undone by whispers; instead, it seemed to mark her with a courage that mirrored his. Ella and Sophie exchanged glances of pure pride, their eyes bright with the unspoken certainty that this was a night none of us would forget. Even Mila, usually quiet, leaned forward with a small smile, her gaze never leaving Ty's calm figure.

Jarod, however, seemed to sink deeper into himself with every passing moment. His eyes darted from face to face, searching for one person, anyone, who might look at him with loyalty. But there was none. He was no longer the leader of whispers, no longer the shadow cast across our halls. He was alone, and he knew it. That knowledge struck him harder than Ty's precise strike, harder than the fall to the mat. Alone was the one place Jarod never thought he'd be.

The grandmaster remained silent now, his earlier words still hanging in the air like banners. Respect is the victor. He did not need to say more, for the exile had spoken louder than any speech could. Jarod had been taught, but not in the way he had expected. He had been taught that power without respect crumbles, and that once it crumbles, nothing can rebuild it.

As I looked around the gym, I realised the lesson wasn't just his. We all carried it. Sophie leaned close to me, her voice low but firm. "We'll remember this, won't we?" I nodded, because there was no choice. We had seen what it meant to build and to destroy. We had seen the cost of violence when it has no heart, no discipline, no respect.

Even as the crowd began to disperse, even as the echoes of applause gave way to the shuffle of feet and the murmur of departing voices, the lesson held steady in the air. Jarod's exile wasn't just from a dojo. It was from the power he had claimed over us, from the fear he had once ruled with. That crown was gone, and it would not return.

And as we stepped down from the bleachers, filing out into the cool night air, I carried the thought with me like a promise. Ty had shown us something greater than victory. He had shown us that respect endures where violence withers. Jarod's exile was the proof. Respect builds. Violence destroys. And we, the witnesses, would never forget it.

## CHAPTER 8: JAROD'S HOMELIFE

I remember the first time I followed Jarod home, not because I wanted to spy, but because something in his walk betrayed him. He carried himself like a fighter in retreat—head low, shoulders braced, hands curling and uncurling like he was waiting for another blow. From the outside, his house looked ordinary, a dull grey siding with windows that didn't open, but the sound that spilled out when the front door cracked open was anything but ordinary. I heard the shouting before I saw him step inside. It wasn't the raised voice of a parent correcting a child. It was sharp, violent, venom pressed into every word, like knives scraping across glass. I froze at the gate, listening longer than I should have, and that is when the crash of something breaking echoed through the yard.

Jarod came back outside a moment later, and I knew then that the shouting wasn't finished—it was only paused. His arms were crossed, but not in defiance. He crossed them as though to shield himself, his sleeve slipping back just enough to show a bruise. His skin was mottled purple and blue, the kind of mark you couldn't mistake for falling off a bike. I didn't ask him about it that day, not yet. I just watched as he picked up the broken shards of what had been a ceramic bowl, stuffing them into the trash before returning inside. I wanted to turn away, to pretend I hadn't seen, but the truth has a way of rooting you to the ground.

Ty was the first one I told. He didn't look surprised, not even for a second. "I already knew," he said quietly, his voice steady in a way that almost frightened me. "I can tell the difference between playground bruises and home bruises." He didn't say how, but I understood later. His father had trained him to read signs, to see things most people ignored. "We can't tell him we know, not yet. He won't trust us," Ty added. I hated it, but he was right. Jarod was still a boy who wore armour made of anger. If we pierced it too soon, he would only strike harder.

The next day, in class, I watched Jarod flinch at the smallest sound. When Mr. Clarke closed a book too hard, Jarod's shoulders jumped. When Mrs. Locke's pen dropped from her desk, his hand twitched like he was ready to duck. I realised then that violence followed him everywhere, even in silence. He was a storm contained in a boy's frame, and it was not of his own making. Every cruel word he flung at others was born out of the cruelty he was steeped in at home. I wanted to despise him, I had despised him—but now, I found myself staring at the edges of his brokenness instead.

At recess, Jeremy tugged at my sleeve. "He's not just mean, Nico. He's scared." Jeremy was only nine, but sometimes he saw things with sharper eyes than any of us. "Look at the way he doesn't sit down, like the bench will hit him back." And Jeremy was right. Jarod didn't sit with the others. He leaned against the fence, always standing, always ready. Like an animal taught never to rest. I nodded but didn't say much. How could I explain to Jeremy that fear, when it festers, grows into claws and teeth?

The shouting from Jarod's house carried farther than he realised. Sophie, who lived two streets over, told Ella that she had heard it from her window at night. "It's like thunder," she whispered, "but it doesn't stop." Ella shivered at the telling, and Jasmin turned away, pressing her lips tight. The girls didn't gossip about it the way others might have; they carried it like a secret too heavy for them to name. I knew then that Jarod's suffering was not hidden—it was simply ignored. Neighbours closed curtains. Teachers looked at the marks and nodded politely. Only Ty, and now us, chose to keep our eyes open.

Leo sat with me later, his arms folded across the desk. "Do you see it?" he asked. "The cycle?" He didn't need to explain. He had lived it under his own father's hand. "It doesn't excuse him. But it explains him." His eyes were dark with the kind of understanding that hurts. I could see Alex listening from the side, chewing on his lip, for once not offering sarcasm. The three of us knew what was happening, but the question was, what could we do without shattering the fragile shell Jarod lived inside?

When Mr. Clarke stepped into the classroom that afternoon, he studied Jarod longer than usual. The boy had pulled his sleeves down, but teachers with sharp eyes always notice what children hope to hide. Mr. Clarke didn't say anything, though; he only adjusted his glasses and began the lesson. Later, I overheard him speaking to Ms. Henley in the hall, his voice low and tight. "It's not playground scrapes. Those are welts. Someone needs to step in." But even then, the school moved cautiously, afraid of saying too much without proof. Proof. As though the child's silence wasn't proof enough.

That night, when I lay in bed, the sound of Jarod's house replayed in my head. The shouting. The crash. The silence that followed. I thought of him lying awake in his room, staring at the ceiling, waiting for the next storm. It wasn't hard to imagine why he came to school full of fists and fury. When your world is made of blows, you carry them with you. I whispered to myself, "Behind closed doors." Because that's where the truth lived—not in the classroom, not in the yard, but in the house where no one dared to look too closely.

Ty came to me the next morning before class began. He looked sharper, colder, his jaw set. "We'll wait," he said simply. "But not forever." And I understood what he meant. We could not rescue Jarod by force, not yet, but one day those doors would open. And when they did, the truth would come spilling out, and none of us could claim we hadn't known. Until then, I would keep speaking, keep watching, keep remembering. Because silence is complicity, and I refused to be complicit.

When Jarod walked into the classroom that morning, even the air seemed to pause. His face was framed by two bruises so dark they resembled ink stains beneath his eyes, and his right shoulder sloped unnaturally low, the arm hanging loose as though it didn't belong to him. The room stirred with whispers, the kind of hushed tones children use when they don't want to be caught staring, but can't turn away either.

I watched Mrs. Locke glance up, pen frozen mid-mark, then look quickly back at her papers. Teachers notice everything, yet they often choose silence, as though speaking would break something more fragile than glass. But the truth was already broken.

Ty leaned forward at his desk, eyes narrowing, his breath steady. He didn't whisper like the others. He didn't pretend not to see. He saw more than the bruises; he saw the limp, the uneven steps, the way Jarod's good arm hugged his body as if trying to hold the rest together. "That's no bike fall," Ty murmured to me under his breath, his words as sharp as blades. I didn't answer. I didn't need to. Ty's certainty left no room for argument.

At recess, Jarod didn't join the group that lingered by the swings. Instead, he made for the far side of the schoolyard, where the fence met the shadow of the gym wall. He stood alone, back pressed to brick, eyes fixed on the ground. His silence dared anyone to come close, and most didn't. But Ty did. Quietly, deliberately, he peeled away from the others, crossing the yard with a calm that masked his intent. I followed at a distance, my chest tight, because I knew Ty wasn't going to let this moment pass.

Jarod's jaw clenched when Ty stopped in front of him. His bruises caught the light, blue turning to yellow at the edges. For a long moment, neither boy spoke. Then Ty lowered his voice. "Those aren't from falling," he said, the words neither cruel nor soft. Just true. Jarod flinched, as though the truth itself had struck him. He lifted his good shoulder in a shrug, muttering something about a bike accident, but Ty didn't look away. He held the gaze, steady as stone. "No accident does that," Ty added, pointing gently toward Jarod's eyes.

I could see the storm building in Jarod. His lip curled, not in anger but in defence, the mask he always wore when cornered. "You don't know anything," he hissed, shifting his weight as if to leave. Ty didn't block him, didn't raise a hand, didn't threaten. Instead, he stayed still. "I know what it looks like," Ty replied quietly. "I've seen it before. My dad's taught me to recognise it. You're not fooling me." The words were sharp, but behind them was something else—something Jarod hadn't heard before. Not pity. Not accusation. Recognition.

Jarod's throat worked as though swallowing stones. His eyes flickered, caught between fight and flight, but then Ty did something unexpected. He opened his arms, not wide, not forced, just enough to make the offer. The gesture was so simple it stunned me. For Jarod, it was as if someone had spoken in a language he had never known but somehow understood. He froze, chest heaving, hands curled into fists at his sides. He had never been offered this before. Not safety. Not comfort. Certainly not an embrace.

At first, Jarod shook his head. "No," he muttered, voice rough. But his body betrayed him. The tension that locked his shoulders faltered. His fists loosened. He swayed as if gravity itself was pulling him forward. Ty didn't move, didn't rush. He just waited. And slowly—so slowly it broke my heart—Jarod stepped into the space. His forehead pressed against Ty's shoulder, his bruised eyes hidden at last. Ty wrapped his arms around him with the quiet strength of someone who knew this was not weakness but survival.

I felt my throat tighten watching them. Around us, the playground still moved: children shouted, swings creaked, balls bounced. But in that shadowed corner, everything else seemed to still. For once, Jarod wasn't the boy who struck first. He wasn't the bully everyone feared. He was simply a child, hurt and desperate, clinging to the only person who dared to see him. Ty didn't say, "You're safe now." He didn't say anything. His embrace spoke louder than any words could.

When Jarod finally pulled back, his face was wet but his eyes were harder to read. He muttered, "Don't tell anyone," voice thick with the remnants of tears. Ty nodded once, a pact made in silence. But I could see it—something had shifted. The bruises were still there. The fear still burned. Yet for a brief moment, Jarod had been held, and that memory would not leave him.

Leo later said to me, "That's the first crack." He didn't mean Jarod was fixed. He meant the armour had been tested, and the boy inside had let someone touch it. Alex, listening nearby, nodded grimly. "He'll fight it. He'll deny it. But he can't un-feel it now." And I knew they were right. Something had changed, even if Jarod himself didn't understand it yet.

That night, as I wrote my notes in the margins of my journal, I couldn't shake the image of Ty holding him. It was so brief, yet so powerful. And I thought of Myles, of the story Mr. Clarke had told, and I whispered into the dark, "If only someone had held you too."

The next morning, Jarod shuffled into the classroom wearing his story like a coat. His bruises had deepened into purple shadows, the kind you couldn't hide no matter how many excuses you stitched together. He didn't sit right; his shoulder still hung low, and his steps were uneven. Yet when Mrs. Dunlop raised her eyebrows at him, her lips tight with a question she didn't ask, Jarod spoke first. "Bike fall," he muttered, eyes locked on the floor. "Slipped on the curb. That's all." His tone was flat, rehearsed, like a script he had memorized in front of a cracked bathroom mirror.

I caught Sophie's eyes across the room. She frowned, just slightly, the way she always did when something didn't sit well with her. Jasmin leaned over and whispered to Ella, but even their whispers didn't carry belief. They had seen Jarod play soccer last week, sprinting across the field like a storm. They had seen him lift a boy by the collar without hesitation. That boy didn't trip over curbs. He didn't fall off bikes. But none of us spoke the contradiction aloud. We all knew the game: his lies weren't for us to believe. They were for him to survive.

Mrs. Locke set her chalk down, her gaze lingering a fraction too long on his blackened eyes. But instead of pressing, she said only, "Sit down, Jarod." Her voice was steady, her hands folded tightly on the desk, as though by pretending not to see she could wish the truth away. That's what adults often did, I realised—pretend. They called it giving space, but in reality, it was fear. Fear of what the truth demanded of them if they admitted they saw it.

Jarod slumped into his chair, dragging his bag across the floor with a deliberate scrape. He leaned back, smirking faintly, as though daring anyone to challenge his story. "Clumsy me," he said, forcing a laugh that scraped like sandpaper. Nobody laughed with him. Even Alex, who once would have twisted the moment into a cruel joke, kept his eyes lowered. Leo studied him too, but his expression wasn't anger—it was recognition. The kind you see between mirrors, one cracked and one whole.

Ty didn't say a word, though his fists curled on the desk. His silence wasn't disbelief—it was restraint. He knew pressing Jarod now would only harden the walls. Instead, he waited, the way he always did, storing the truth until Jarod was ready to hear it. I could see Ty's eyes dart to the shoulder hanging limp, to the faint line of red where the shirt collar rubbed against bruised skin. He saw what the rest of us saw, but more than that, he understood it. Those weren't playground marks. Those were household wounds.

At recess, Jarod repeated the lie to Mila when she asked if he was all right. "Bike fall," he said again, sharper this time, snapping the words before she could question him further. Mila frowned, lips pressed tight, but she didn't push. She turned away with a look I recognised—helplessness mixed with anger. We wanted to help, but every time we reached out, Jarod's walls slammed higher. His lies weren't just excuses; they were armour. And like armour, they weighed him down, but they kept him standing.

Later, in geography, Mrs. Haller asked him to write on the board. He rose slowly, moving stiffly, each step betraying pain he couldn't mask. "Trip on the curb," he muttered again when she glanced at him. The class exchanged looks. No one said anything, but the silence itself grew thick, heavy, alive. The lie hung in the air, stretched so thin it was ready to tear, but still no one pierced it. We let him hold it, because we knew if it fell, the truth beneath might crush him.

Sophie whispered to me at lunch, "It's not true." Her eyes glistened with frustration. I nodded, because I couldn't lie to her. "I know." She leaned closer, her voice trembling, "Why don't the teachers say something?" I looked over at Mr. Clarke in the staff yard, watching the children with hands folded behind his back. His eyes followed Jarod, but he didn't move to confront him. Maybe because he'd seen this before, too many times. Maybe because he knew the lie was the only shield Jarod had left.

Jarod sat at the edge of the yard, staring at his sandwich without eating. His jaw moved, clenching and unclenching, as though rehearsing the story over and over. A bike fall. A slip. A curb. Each word was a stone stacked on top of the last, building a wall around the bruises no one dared name. But walls have cracks. And in the way his hand shook when he lifted the bread, in the way his good shoulder hunched forward as if bracing for another blow, the truth leaked through.

I watched him for a long time, writing the scene into my memory like a note in my journal. And in that silence, I thought of Myles again. He, too, had stories around him—children who had seen but not spoken, teachers who had turned away. Lies and silences alike had wrapped around him until it was too late. And I whispered to myself, though no one heard: not again.

Ty joined me later, his voice low and sure. "He'll keep saying it. But one day, he'll stop." I asked him how he knew. He looked at me with steady eyes and answered, "Because lies can't heal. They only hide. And sooner or later, even Jarod will need more than hiding." His words echoed long after the bell rang, louder than Jarod's lie, louder even than the silence of those who refused to challenge it.

That afternoon, Mrs. Henley passed by Jarod in the hall. She didn't say anything, but she rested her hand lightly on his shoulder, the uninjured one. He flinched, then froze, then walked on. I caught her expression—pained, knowing. She saw through him too. But just like the rest of us, she let him keep the lie. For now.

By the end of the day, the words had worn grooves in Jarod's voice. "Bike fall. Curb. Clumsy." He said it so often he almost believed it. Almost. But the eyes of his classmates told another story. We didn't laugh. We didn't tease. We didn't call him clumsy. We only watched, waiting, carrying the truth he wasn't ready to carry himself.

And in the silence of that waiting, something shifted. His lie remained intact, but for the first time, it looked fragile. And fragile things, I knew, cannot last forever.

I watched Ty that morning more carefully than anyone else. He didn't flinch at Jarod's excuses, didn't frown like Sophie, didn't whisper like Jasmin or Ella. Instead, he studied the boy the way his father had taught him to study a case file—quiet, observant, taking in details no one else wanted to see. Ty didn't argue when Jarod said "bike fall." He didn't laugh when Jarod called himself clumsy. He only looked at the set of Jarod's jaw, the way his eyes refused to meet anyone's gaze, and the way his shoulder dragged forward as though it belonged to someone else entirely.

Ty had been raised differently from the rest of us. While most of our parents told stories about homework and chores, his father told him stories about investigations. He taught Ty that patterns never lie. "A bruise from a fight," his father had said, "is almost always on the knuckles, the shins, the elbows. But a bruise from home…that leaves shadows in places no playground scuffle would ever touch." Ty remembered those lessons now as his eyes swept over Jarod's frame, measuring the difference between a punch thrown in anger by a classmate and a strike delivered behind closed doors.

I leaned toward him and whispered, "You don't believe him, do you?" Ty shook his head, not to me but to himself, as though dismissing the thought of arguing with Jarod's lies. "Not a bike," he murmured under his breath, voice low enough that only I caught it. "That's not what this is."

I wanted to ask how he knew, but I already saw the answer in his eyes. Ty carried a catalogue of hurts he'd studied secondhand, the bruises his father had traced in old reports, the photographs he'd glimpsed when he wasn't supposed to. He knew the look of violence that came from inside the house, not outside.

Jarod, sensing Ty's stare, bristled in his seat. He turned sharply, snapping, "What are you looking at?" Ty didn't reply. He didn't back down either. He just let his gaze linger for a moment longer, calm, steady, unthreatening, before lowering his eyes to his notebook. That silence unsettled Jarod more than any insult could have. Bullies thrived on resistance, on noise. But Ty offered neither. He offered recognition, and Jarod didn't know how to handle that.

Across the room, Leo crossed his arms. He recognised something too, though his recognition came from memory, not training. "It's the same silence I used to keep," Leo said later when we were alone. "When I went home with marks I couldn't explain. When I lied to the teachers because I knew no one wanted to hear the truth." He didn't say it loudly; he didn't need to. The words carried their own weight. Alex nodded beside him, a guilty acknowledgement that he'd seen those marks once and ignored them, choosing instead to twist the knife with words.

But Ty was different. He leaned back in his chair, listening as Jarod repeated the lie again to Mrs. Locke during English. "Tripped. Just clumsy." Ty's pencil stopped moving, his knuckles whitening around it. He didn't write another word that period. I could almost see the calculations running through his head—angles, impacts, weight distribution, all the things his father had once broken down at their kitchen table when explaining why some stories never matched the evidence. Ty didn't need to speak; his silence was already building the truth.

At lunch, Ty followed Jarod into the yard, careful not to crowd him. Jarod dropped onto the bench near the fence, muttering to himself while picking at the crust of his sandwich. Ty sat a few feet away, eyes on the ground. He didn't accuse, didn't question. He only spoke when Jarod finally looked at him and spat, "It was a fall, okay? You think you know better?" Ty's voice was soft, too soft for Jarod's anger to bounce against. "I know it wasn't a fall," he said simply. "But I'm not here to prove you wrong."

Jarod blinked, caught off guard. His anger faltered. "Then what are you here for?" Ty turned his gaze to the yard, watching the others play. "To make sure you don't break someone else the way you've been broken," he answered. The words were matter-of-fact, not cruel. That was Ty's strength. He could deliver truth without wrapping it in pity, and that truth lingered in the air long after Jarod stood and stomped away.

Later that afternoon, I noticed how Ty positioned himself differently in the classroom. He didn't shadow Jarod in a threatening way, but he sat where he could see him clearly, a quiet sentinel. It wasn't about suspicion anymore. It was about recognition. He had placed Jarod in a category that no one wanted to speak of aloud—a child bearing the marks of home's betrayal. And once Ty had recognised it, he would not unsee it.

When the final bell rang, Ty lingered behind, waiting near the door. Jarod brushed past him, muttering another excuse under his breath. Ty didn't respond, didn't move, but his eyes followed him out. "It's always the same," Ty said to me quietly. "The bruises tell the truth, even if the boy never will." His words sank into me, heavy as stone, and I realised then that the silence of recognition was more powerful than all the noise of disbelief.

That night, as I lay awake, I thought of what Ty had seen in Jarod's eyes. Not just pain, but a pattern. A cycle. And I wondered how many teachers, how many classmates, how many friends had seen that same pattern before in others, and chosen to look away. Ty would not. And because of that, neither would I.

I could feel the shift in Jarod even before the others noticed it. The bruises he carried into class were not slowing him down; they were fuelling him. Every insult that slipped from his mouth was sharper, every shove in the hallway carried an edge of fury he could not contain. It was as if the violence at home was spilling through his skin, pouring out onto anyone unfortunate enough to cross his path. I had seen bullies before, but Jarod's cruelty had a different weight to it—it wasn't just about control. It was a storm seeking release, a storm that had no safe place to break.

Ty knew it too. He shadowed Jarod without ever making it obvious, stepping into his path at just the right moment, sliding between him and the smaller students Jarod tried to corner. Ty never raised his voice. He never made threats. He simply stood there, shoulders squared, eyes calm, like a wall Jarod could not move. I remember the first time it happened, when Jarod lunged toward Sophie for a remark she hadn't even made. Ty slipped in front of her, took the brunt of the shove, and held his ground without flinching. Jarod's fury fizzled out the moment it met resistance he couldn't shake.

Jarod snarled, "What's your problem, Takashi?" Ty's voice was steady, measured, the kind of calm that only angered someone already in chaos. "You're my problem when you hurt people." The words didn't carry a shout, but they held more power than Jarod's growl ever could. The class had grown used to this pattern—Jarod's explosion followed by Ty's silent intervention—but no one said a word. They just watched, waiting to see which side would break first.

Later that day, I caught sight of Jarod by the lockers, pinning Jeremy's shoulders back with one arm, teeth clenched as he spat insults into his face. Jeremy didn't cry or shout—he just stared straight through him, as if daring Jarod to see his own reflection in those eyes. Before I could move, Ty was there again, gripping Jarod's wrist firmly and pulling him back. "Enough," Ty said, voice low but final. Jarod twisted, trying to wrench free, but Ty's grip wasn't born of anger—it was born of control. And control always wins over rage.

For a moment I thought Jarod would strike him. His fist curled, his chest rose, his breath came ragged. But then something unexpected happened. His hand loosened, his arm fell, and he just stood there, breathing hard. Ty's other arm opened slightly, an invitation no one expected.

"You don't have to fight me," Ty said softly. "You don't have to fight at all." Jarod's face contorted, torn between pride and desperation. For a second he refused, shaking his head violently, but then the fight drained from his eyes. His body leaned forward almost involuntarily, and he pressed against Ty's chest, shoulders trembling.

The schoolyard around them went silent. A boy everyone feared, the same boy who had left bruises on so many, stood clinging to the one who had stopped him. Ty didn't make a scene. He didn't say a word to the crowd. He just wrapped his arms around Jarod and held him there until the trembling slowed. To anyone else it might have looked like weakness, but I knew better. That moment was the first crack in Jarod's armour, the first sign that maybe, just maybe, he wanted something more than rage.

When Jarod finally pulled away, his face was blotched with shame and confusion. He muttered, "Don't think this means anything." Ty didn't argue. He only nodded and stepped back, letting Jarod have his space. It wasn't victory Ty was after—it was survival. Not just for himself, but for the boy who had been told all his life that fists were the only language worth speaking.

Afterwards, during math class, Miss Kara pretended not to notice the heaviness between them. But Jeremy leaned toward me and whispered, "Did you see it? He took the hug." I nodded, because it wasn't the kind of thing you ignored. It was a turning point, not a triumph, but the sort of moment that plants itself in the soil of memory and waits to grow. The others had seen it too—Jasmin biting her lip, Ella watching with wide eyes, Leo lowering his gaze as though remembering his own first crack. Even Alex looked shaken, as if realising for the first time that someone as violent as Jarod might still be reachable.

Jarod didn't stop bullying that day. If anything, the outbursts came more frequently, like waves crashing harder after a dam has been weakened. But every time, Ty was there, catching him before the impact could land on someone else. And each time, Jarod's resistance faltered a little more. His punches hit less often, his insults dragged with less venom, his eyes carried a flicker of something no one dared to name—something like longing.

That night, when I closed my notebook, I thought of the way Jarod had leaned into Ty's chest. It wasn't surrender. It wasn't forgiveness. It was need. And need, I realised, was the root of all storms. What he needed most wasn't power. It wasn't fear. It wasn't victory. It was the simple proof that someone could stand before him and not flinch, not break, not turn away. And Ty, without a word, had given him that proof.

I could feel it before the blow even came. Jarod's whole body trembled with fury, a fire that no words could soothe. His fists were balled, his jaw set tight, his chest rising like a storm breaking its banks. I braced myself, because I knew what was about to happen: Jarod wasn't just going to shout this time. He was going to release every ounce of pain he carried, and Ty—always the steady one—was the one standing in his path. The air in the gym stilled as if everyone knew it too.

# THE SMILE THAT BROKE

Jarod lunged first, a wild swing meant to crush, not to scare. Ty did not strike back. He tilted his body, letting the punch slide past him, his open hand guiding Jarod's arm away instead of meeting it head-on. Jarod roared, launching again, faster this time. Ty moved with calm precision, each deflection like water redirecting a stone. He did not hit. He did not shove. He simply redirected, over and over, teaching with silence what no lecture could ever carve into Jarod's mind.

"Fight me!" Jarod shouted, voice cracking between rage and desperation. His fists slammed toward Ty's ribs, his shoulders shaking with each strike. Ty breathed evenly, pivoting, redirecting, his every move born of training and patience. "I'm not here to fight you," Ty answered quietly. "I'm here to stop you from fighting yourself." The words hit harder than any punch. Jarod's face twisted, furious, but his punches grew sloppier, his body heavier. He was burning himself out, caught in a war against someone who refused to be his enemy.

The others stood frozen around the edges—Nico's wide eyes, Ella clutching Sophie's sleeve, Leo shifting uncomfortably as memories stirred, Alex muttering under his breath, "He's gonna drop." Even Mr. Clarke and Mrs. Dunlop, who had come running at the sound of shouts, did not interfere. They knew, somehow, that what was unfolding could not be interrupted. This was no schoolyard scuffle. This was a battle between rage and restraint, between destruction and discipline.

At last Jarod's swings faltered. His arms sagged, his breath came ragged, his knees buckled beneath him. Ty didn't hesitate. He stepped in, not with a block this time, but with both arms open. He caught Jarod's collapsing frame, locking him into a hold that was not victory but refuge. Jarod fought against it for a moment, chest heaving, teeth clenched, but then the last of his strength dissolved. His fists unclenched. His forehead dropped against Ty's shoulder. And the sound that broke out of him wasn't a growl—it was a sob.

It wasn't quiet. It wasn't neat. It was raw, loud, the kind of crying that comes when the dam has broken after years of pressure. His body shook violently in Ty's arms, and Ty didn't flinch. He tightened his embrace, steady as stone, whispering words that cut through the storm: "I'm here. You're safe now. You are loved." No lecture. No judgement. Just truth, offered with the weight of a brother's promise.

For a moment, the room didn't know how to breathe. Jeremy's small voice whispered, "He's holding him like family." And it was true—Ty wasn't restraining Jarod anymore. He was cradling him the way an older brother would, shielding him from a world that had only taught him pain. Nico wiped his eyes, Jasmin reached for Ella's hand, and Leo turned away, unable to watch but unable to leave. Even Alex, the cynic, muttered, "That's… that's what I should've done for him before."

The adults exchanged looks, but no one moved. They understood instinctively that Ty had stepped into a place no authority could reach. No suspension, no detention, no lecture could have brought Jarod to this point. Only love in the form of absolute strength could do it, and Ty had given it without hesitation. He didn't need a classroom or a counselor's chair. He needed only his arms, his patience, and his refusal to let Jarod drown alone.

When the sobs finally slowed, Jarod didn't let go. He clung tighter, face pressed against Ty's shirt, voice muffled but breaking. "Why… why would you do this for me?" he asked. Ty's hand rested firm on the back of his head, guiding him like a parent would a child. "Because no one ever did it for you," Ty said simply. "But I will. And I'm not letting go until you believe me."

And Ty didn't let go. Not when Jarod's knees gave out fully and he sagged against him. Not when the watching crowd began to stir. Not when the teachers whispered about whether to step in. He held him until the fight was gone, until the tears softened into shallow breaths, until Jarod's body accepted that—for the first time in his life—he wasn't alone in the battle.

I wrote it down in my notebook that night: rage collapsed where control endured, and in the wreckage of a fight, a hug rebuilt what fists could never touch. Ty had proven what we all needed to see—that even the toughest bully can break, not from punishment, but from love that refuses to back down.

The gym was quiet now, the echoes of Jarod's sobs still lingering in the air like smoke after a fire. Ty didn't rush him, didn't loosen his grip too quickly, because he knew that letting go too soon would feel like abandonment. He simply held him, steady and calm, until Jarod's breathing slowed into something less jagged. Around us, not one of us dared move. Even the teachers who were normally quick to step in gave Ty the space to finish what he had started. When Jarod finally lifted his head, his eyes swollen and red, Ty gave him the smallest nod—as if to say, you're still here, and that's enough.

I could see Jarod's confusion etched deep on his face. He wasn't used to this. He had thrown everything he had at Ty—his fists, his fury, his pain—and Ty hadn't thrown it back. He hadn't humiliated him, hadn't punished him, hadn't made him feel small. Instead, Ty had given him something Jarod couldn't understand yet: a brother's embrace, not as a prize for good behaviour, but as a lifeline in his worst moment. And now, Ty was about to give him something else entirely.

Ty stepped back only enough to look Jarod in the eyes. His voice was soft, but every word landed with weight. "If you want to be strong, you have to learn discipline. Hitting without thinking—that's not strength. That's losing control. If you want to fight, then fight the right way. Strike, defend, stand tall. But never to destroy. Always to protect." The words weren't from a textbook. They were lessons carved into Ty by his father, an RCMP investigator who had taught him the Shadow Warrior discipline from his own lineage. Now Ty was passing it down, not as an authority, but as a gift.

Jarod wiped at his face with the back of his hand, his voice cracked and small. "Why would you… why would you want to teach me?" His tone wasn't aggressive anymore—it was bewildered, almost childlike. Ty didn't hesitate. "Because no one taught you how to stop hurting. You think fists make you strong. I'm here to show you what real strength looks like." He stepped back, squaring his shoulders, and demonstrated a stance—feet planted, fists raised, calm and balanced. He motioned for Jarod to mirror him. For a moment, Jarod only stared, but then, slowly, he copied.

It wasn't perfect. Jarod's arms trembled, his legs staggered into place. But Ty nodded anyway. "That's the beginning," he said. "Hold your ground. Don't swing. Don't lash out. Just breathe. Balance means you won't fall." Jarod tried to steady himself, the tremor in his shoulders more from emotion than weakness. Watching him, I realised that this wasn't about fighting at all. It was about teaching Jarod how to stand without fear. How to exist without flinching at every shadow.

Jeremy whispered from beside me, his young voice solemn. "He's teaching him to fight so he doesn't have to." Leo, arms crossed, added quietly, "That's what none of us figured out when we were bullies. We only knew how to tear down. He's showing him how to build up." Alex nodded in agreement, for once without sarcasm. "That's the difference. Discipline. That's what we never had." The students in the room, even the ones who had feared Jarod the most, leaned forward, drawn to something they hadn't expected to see: the hardest boy in school learning, for the first time, what strength truly meant.

Ty stepped forward again, placing his open hand against Jarod's raised fist. He pressed gently, enough to test balance. Jarod's arm shook but didn't fall. "See?" Ty said softly. "You're not as weak as you think. You've just been fighting the wrong way." Jarod's eyes filled again, not with rage but with something heavier—grief, relief, maybe both. His fist slowly unclenched, his hand dropping as his body sagged forward. Ty didn't let him collapse this time either. He caught him in another embrace, tighter, firmer, leaving no room for doubt.

The silence was broken only by Jarod's voice, trembling and barely audible at first. "Thank you," he whispered. Then louder, choking back the tears that hadn't finished falling: "Thank you. I… I really needed that." His words weren't to the crowd, not to the teachers, not to anyone else. They were to Ty alone. And Ty, calm as ever, only nodded and whispered back, "You'll always have it. Every time you need it."

I knew in that moment that something had shifted. Jarod wasn't fixed—not yet, maybe not for a long time—but the cycle had cracked. He had tasted the difference between fear and love, between rage and discipline, between breaking and healing. The rest of us stood in silence, watching not a fight but a beginning, and I wrote the words in my mind: A bully still burns, but even fire can be taught where to rest, if someone dares to hold it.

The teachers exchanged glances, some with tears in their eyes, some simply stunned into silence. Mr. Clarke leaned on the doorframe, shaking his head slowly, and muttered, "That boy just saved him without lifting a fist." Even Mr. Arnett, the principal, whose job it was to discipline, stood humbled. He whispered to Mrs. Dunlop, "This is the lesson we could never write into policy."

The class didn't move until Ty finally stepped back, resting a hand on Jarod's shoulder. "This is where we start," he told him. "Not with fighting. With standing." Jarod didn't answer, but he didn't need to. His whispered thanks still hung in the room, heavy with the truth that—for the first time in his life—someone had given him more than fists or fury. Someone had given him the chance to begin again.

The house was too quiet when Jarod stepped inside. The kind of silence that doesn't mean peace but danger. He shut the door carefully, hoping the click wouldn't be heard, but he knew already it was too late. His father's voice erupted from the living room, slurred and sharp, demanding to know why his son had been late. Jarod froze in the hallway, his breath caught in his throat. He had walked this corridor a thousand times before, every step usually ending with a blow. But this night was different, and though his stomach twisted with fear, Ty's words echoed in his mind: stand tall, breathe, balance.

His father emerged, the smell of alcohol heavy on his breath, his frame towering in anger. "Think you can sneak around me, boy?" the man growled, grabbing at Jarod's arm. The old reflex rose—flinch, cower, collapse—but something inside shifted. Jarod remembered Ty's stance, the way his feet had been planted firm. Instead of shrinking, he stepped back, raising his arms the way Ty had shown him. His father sneered, "You want to fight me now?" and swung wildly. But Jarod blocked. For the first time in his life, the blow didn't land.

The shock of resistance lit his father's eyes with fury. Another strike came, clumsy, uncoordinated, fuelled by rage instead of control. Jarod lifted his shoulder, deflecting, his breath steady. He didn't want to hit back—Ty had told him fighting wasn't about destroying—but when the man lunged forward, Jarod pushed, striking with just enough force to send him stumbling into the wall. The sound echoed through the house, glass rattling in the frames. For the first time, it was his father who recoiled, not him.

The man staggered, eyes narrowing, trying to summon his authority, but the look in Jarod's face stopped him cold. The boy who had once cowered was standing upright, fists clenched, shoulders steady, eyes unbroken. "I'm not scared anymore," Jarod whispered, his voice trembling but firm. His father swore, spat words too ugly to repeat, then swung once more. Jarod deflected again, this time shoving the arm aside and planting his feet exactly as Ty had taught him. The man stumbled a second time, rage dissolving into something else—hesitation. For the first time in years, Jarod had forced him to back down.

The silence that followed was heavier than the blows. His father glared at him, panting, chest heaving with drink and rage, but he didn't move closer. He muttered something under his breath and staggered back into the living room, slamming the door behind him. Jarod stood frozen, heart hammering, every nerve on fire. His hands shook, not with fear anymore, but with the rush of survival. His knees buckled, and he knew he couldn't stay another moment.

He ran. Down the hallway, through the door, across the dim street where shadows stretched long. His lungs burned, his arms felt heavy, but he kept going until he spotted Ty waiting on the corner as though he had known Jarod would come. Ty saw the state of him—the trembling arms, the bruised face, the broken strength holding him together—and didn't say a word. He just opened his arms. Jarod collapsed into them, every ounce of exhaustion spilling out at once.

I watched from the edge of the street with Leo, Alex, and Jeremy beside me. It was quiet except for the sound of Jarod's sobbing against Ty's shoulder. Ty's embrace was different this time—no lesson, no stance, no discipline to show. Just the arms of a brother holding someone who had finally fought back against the nightmare of his own home. Ty rested his chin lightly against Jarod's hair and whispered, "You're safe. You did it. You stood."

Jarod couldn't answer at first. His body trembled too hard, his breath rattled out in jagged pieces. But slowly, through the gasps, came his words. "He tried… I stopped him… I'm not scared anymore." His voice cracked, but it carried the weight of victory. Ty tightened his hold, pulling him closer, refusing to let him slip back into the darkness of his father's house.

Jeremy shifted beside me, his small hand squeezing mine. "That's what it takes," he whispered. "One stand. One choice." Leo nodded, his expression heavy with memory. "I wish someone had given me that chance earlier," he said softly. Alex crossed his arms, shaking his head, but his voice betrayed him. "That kid's tougher than he knows. Tougher than I ever was."

The teachers caught up moments later, Mr. Clarke and Mr. Arnett stepping into the street, their eyes taking in the scene—the broken boy in Ty's arms, the courage it had taken to stand, the exhaustion that followed. Mr. Clarke's voice wavered. "He defended himself," he said. "For the first time, he didn't just take it." Mr. Arnett nodded grimly, his jaw tight. "Then tonight is the night everything changes."

Jarod clung to Ty as though letting go would mean being dragged back into the storm. His tears soaked through Ty's shirt, but Ty didn't move. He just whispered again and again, "You're safe now. You're safe." Around us, no one dared interrupt. It wasn't pity that held us silent—it was respect. Respect for a boy who had finally faced the wrath of his father and walked away standing.

When Jarod finally looked up, his eyes were swollen but clearer than I had ever seen them. "He can't break me anymore," he said quietly. His words trembled, but they carried more truth than anything he had spoken before. Ty nodded, gripping his shoulder firmly. "No. He can't. Not now. Not ever again."

The night air wrapped around us, heavy but strangely freeing. For the first time, Jarod's story was no longer about survival alone. It was about defiance. About finding the strength not to destroy, but to endure. As Ty guided him down the street, his arm still around him, I knew the cycle had cracked wide open. The boy who had once been the storm was learning how to weather it—and for the first time, he wasn't facing it alone.

I never forgot the look in Ty's eyes that night—fierce and unyielding, but steady like the calm before a storm. He stood close to Jarod, one arm firm around him, as if to declare he would not let anyone pry the boy from safety again. When Mr. Takashi arrived, his steps were measured, each one carrying the weight of duty and of fatherhood. He scanned the scene quickly: Jarod trembling but standing, Ty refusing to let go, the teachers hovering uncertainly, and the rest of us watching in silence. The air felt heavier than ever, because we all knew this was the moment the truth could no longer be hidden.

"Jarod," Mr. Takashi said softly, his voice stripped of authority, lowered to something human. "I need you to tell me the truth. No more lies about bikes or accidents." His words were not a demand but an invitation, one that gave the boy a chance to step out from behind the shield he had built for years. Jarod swallowed hard, his lips trembling, and for a long moment I thought he would break into another excuse. But then he looked at Ty, at the brotherly arm holding him steady, and shook his head. "It's him. My dad. He won't stop."

The words dropped like stones into the quiet street. Mr. Clarke's face fell, his hand tightening around his notebook. Mr. Arnett closed his eyes as though he had waited years to hear that confession. And Mr. Takashi—though a seasoned investigator—let out the smallest sigh, the sound of a man hearing the truth he already knew but dreaded confirming. He crouched down so his eyes were level with Jarod's. "You did not deserve that," he said clearly. "And it ends tonight."

Jarod's knees buckled at those words, not from fear but from release. He had spoken it, and for the first time the law was not abstract but present—standing right there in front of him in the form of Ty's father. Ty drew him close again, holding him tight, no lesson in his stance this time, just the pure weight of family. Jarod's sobs came heavy, his forehead pressing into Ty's shoulder, his body shuddering as years of silence finally cracked open. I watched as Ty tightened his arms, whispering low, "You're not going back there. Not now. Not ever."

The others gathered close, but not too close, each of us sensing that this was not ours to interrupt. Jeremy's face was pale, his fists curled as though holding back anger he couldn't yet name. Leo shifted uncomfortably, guilt flickering across his features, remembering too clearly the days he had been someone else's tormentor. Alex muttered under his breath, "No kid should have to say that," his voice sharp, almost bitter, though his eyes betrayed sorrow. Ella, Sophie, and Jasmin stood together, their eyes shining with tears but their silence honouring Jarod's courage.

Mr. Takashi rose again, his frame strong, and turned to the staff. "I'll be filing the papers tonight. The man will be arrested. No child goes back to that kind of home, not under my watch." His words were not empty—they were steel, forged in years of service and responsibility. But then he turned to Ty, softening. "Until then, he stays with us. Is that what you want?" Ty's answer came without hesitation. "Yes, Dad. He needs us."

And so it was settled. Jarod looked up at Ty with wet eyes, his voice barely a whisper. "You mean it? I can stay?" Ty hugged him again, pulling him close without restraint, the kind of embrace that stripped away the difference between protector and brother. "Of course you can," Ty said firmly. "You're family now." Jarod buried his face into Ty's chest, his voice breaking apart. "Thank you… I really needed that."

The teachers exchanged glances, relief mingling with sadness. Mr. Arnett placed a hand on his chest as though steadying his own heart. Mrs. Locke brushed her eyes with a handkerchief, while Ms. Henley, the counsellor, whispered, "This is what healing begins with." None of them spoke louder than that, because to raise their voices would have been to intrude on a moment that belonged entirely to Jarod.

I took it all in—the sight of a boy once feared now trembling, not in violence but in release. It struck me then how quickly a bully's fire could turn to ash when the roots of their pain were finally seen. Jarod was no monster, not truly. He was a boy who had been shaped by cruelty, and tonight, for the first time, someone had stood between him and the storm. Ty had become more than his shadow; he had become his shield.

Jeremy stepped closer, speaking in a low voice that carried like a promise. "You're not alone anymore, Jarod. We won't let you be." Jarod's lips moved as if to answer, but he was too choked to form words. Still, the look in his eyes said it all—he believed him. And maybe, for the first time in his life, he trusted that belief would hold.

The night deepened, but none of us moved quickly. We lingered, knowing history had shifted under our feet. Mr. Takashi's presence meant more than law; it meant Jarod's suffering had been named, confronted, and dismantled. Ty's arms meant more than protection; they meant family. And Jarod's tears were no longer the silent ones of fear but the open ones of a boy learning he could let go.

When the group finally began to move, leading Jarod towards the Takashi home, I stayed behind for a moment. I needed to see the empty street, to memorise the silence after such a storm. It was the quiet that follows truth—the quiet that meant something had ended, but something new had also begun.

I stood in the street that morning watching Jarod walk with his head down, his steps dragging as though every footfall carried the weight of years. Mr. Takashi had spent the night arranging the arrest, and by dawn, the house that had once held only shouting and fists was silent. Yet it was not the silence of peace; it was the silence of emptiness.

The door to his home hung ajar, left unlatched by the officers who had taken his father away. Inside, there was nothing welcoming—no mother's voice, no warmth, no sense that anyone had ever cared who lived within those walls. Jarod stopped at the threshold and didn't step in. He just stared at the broken frame, as though he could still hear the echoes of his father's wrath.

His mother had left when he was seven. No goodbye, no explanation, just gone. The house had been crumbling ever since, one nail at a time. The neighbours whispered that she had gone north to start over, but to Jarod it felt like she had simply erased him. Now, with his father in handcuffs and facing charges, the boy had no one. No mother's embrace, no father's guidance, no home that could shield him. The truth weighed on him in a way no fists ever could: he belonged nowhere. The system loomed in his mind, the words "foster care" circling like vultures, ready to strip away even the last fragments of stability he thought he had.

We gathered around him quietly, each of us sensing the hollow air inside that house. Jeremy stood closest, his small hand brushing Jarod's arm. "You don't have to go back in there," he said firmly, his voice sharp for someone so young. Jarod's lips trembled, and he shook his head. "There's nothing in there for me. Not even a bed that feels like mine. It's just walls." His words struck deeper than he realised, because in that moment we all understood: the building was not a home, it was a shell. And Jarod, for all his rage and cruelty, was simply a boy who had been caged in it too long.

Mr. Clarke exhaled slowly, adjusting his glasses as though trying to steady himself. "This isn't just about punishment anymore," he said softly. "This is about survival." Ms. Henley, the counsellor, nodded, her eyes trained on Jarod. "He has nothing to return to. We cannot send him back into emptiness." Her words carried the kind of conviction that teachers and counsellors hold when they know a child is standing on the edge of despair. Still, the reality of what came next loomed over us like a shadow—forms, hearings, temporary housing. Foster care was a safety net, yes, but it was also a place of strangers, of uncertainty, of being shuffled from one door to another. Jarod knew it, and fear tightened his shoulders as the thought crept in.

Ty stepped forward, his voice calm, steady, unshaken by the fear in Jarod's eyes. "You're not going into that system," he said. "Not while I'm here. You'll stay with us." Jarod looked at him sharply, disbelief written across his face. "They'll never allow it," he muttered. But Ty's father spoke then, his tone resolute. "The courts will listen. I'll fight for it myself if I must. No boy who has already endured this deserves to be lost in the shuffle of the system." Jarod's body sagged at those words, the tension momentarily giving way to something rawer—grief. He turned toward Ty, his voice breaking. "I don't want to go to strangers. I don't want to pack a bag and disappear again."

Ella stepped closer, her tone soft but her words clear. "You don't have to. We're not strangers. We've seen you at your worst, and we're still here." Sophie added quickly, "And maybe, just maybe, you can start again with us. But not in that empty house. That place doesn't deserve you." Jasmin, standing behind Ty, whispered, "Home isn't walls anyway. It's people." Those words landed, because Jarod flinched as though someone had struck a nerve. For years, his house had been nothing but walls, and in one sentence, she had undone the lie he'd been forced to live with.

Mr. Arnett, the principal, stood tall at the edge of the group, his arms folded but his face soft. "The system has rules, but rules can bend when justice demands it. I will not see this boy vanish into a foster roster. Not while I'm principal here." His words, like Mr. Takashi's, carried authority—the kind of weight that meant promises would not dissolve in the morning sun. Even Mrs. Dunlop, usually stern and procedural, muttered, "It would break him, sending him there. I've seen too many like him come back hollow. We can't let that happen."

Jarod's knees wavered, and Ty caught him again, holding him steady. This time Jarod didn't resist. His arms hung at his sides, but his head fell against Ty's shoulder, eyes wet, face pale. "Why do you care?" he asked in a voice so thin it barely carried. Ty answered with no hesitation, "Because you're my brother now, whether you want it or not." The words were simple, not rehearsed, not polished, but they struck with the force of truth. Jarod closed his eyes, his breath catching. "I don't know what that feels like," he whispered.

Nico, who had stayed silent until then, finally spoke, his voice low but firm. "It feels like this. Like people refusing to give up on you. Like arms that hold you when you're too tired to stand. Like a house full of voices that want you there." He stepped forward and touched Jarod's shoulder lightly, not intruding, just reminding him that this was not pity—it was solidarity. Jarod shuddered again, the words sinking into him like water on dry soil. For the first time, he did not shake them off.

Inside the house, the silence remained, unbroken and heavy. But outside, around him, there was a different kind of silence—one full of presence, full of promises not yet fulfilled but already believed. Jarod turned his back on the doorway, making his choice clear without words. The house behind him would not define him anymore. It was empty, and so he left it empty.

As we walked him away, the truth settled over all of us: the system might loom, the paperwork might pile, but Jarod would not vanish into it. Not while we stood around him. The walls of that house had crumbled, but around him now rose something sturdier—not brick, not wood, but arms and voices and truth. And for the first time in years, Jarod let himself lean into it, the faintest spark of safety flickering in his eyes.

I remember the stillness that settled after Jarod turned his back on that empty house. We all stood there, uncertain of what the next step would be, but unwilling to leave him to the silence he had known for so long. It was then that Mr. Arnett, who had been watching with folded arms and sharp eyes, took a step forward. His voice, when it came, carried both authority and warmth.

"Jarod," he said, "the courts will want to send you into foster care. They'll want to find a placement, a temporary bed, someone to keep you until the system decides where you belong. But I won't have it. You've had enough of being passed around, enough of being broken down. If you'll allow it, I'll open my home to you. Not for a week. Not until papers are signed. Permanently."

The words hung in the air like a bell that would not stop ringing. I saw Jarod freeze, his eyes wide, his breath catching in his throat. He searched Mr. Arnett's face for a trick, some hidden clause, some condition that would strip away the promise. But there was none. Only resolve, deep as bedrock, in the principal's steady gaze. "You don't mean that," Jarod whispered, his voice cracked and uncertain. Mr. Arnett stepped closer, not bending down, not speaking as though Jarod were smaller than he was, but speaking to him as an equal. "I mean every word. A boy like you doesn't need another cold bed and another stranger's face. You need family, and I'm offering mine."

Ty shifted then, moving closer so that his shoulder pressed against Jarod's. "See?" he said quietly. "You're not going to be thrown away. Not while I'm here, not while he's here. You've got me, no matter what happens." He didn't need to add the rest, but Jarod knew it: Ty's arms would always be open. The memory of the last embrace lingered, that moment when Jarod had finally collapsed and let himself be held. Now, in the face of this new offer, he wanted to believe it could last. But his lips trembled with doubt, and his eyes darted nervously to the rest of us.

Jeremy stepped forward, his young voice clear and steady. "You don't have to be scared of this, Jarod. Not everyone leaves. Some people stay, even when you don't think they will." He glanced at Leo, who stood nearby, quiet but strong, his arms crossed not in defiance but in protection. Leo gave a single nod, as though sealing Jeremy's words with a promise of his own. Alex followed with a blunt honesty that only he could deliver. "Don't mess this up, Jarod. You don't get chances like this twice. But if you grab it, if you really hold on, it can change you."

Jarod swallowed hard, his voice barely carrying. "What if I ruin it? What if I make it worse, like I always do?" Mr. Arnett answered without hesitation. "Then we face it together. Family doesn't mean perfect. It means you don't walk away when it's hard. You've lived under discipline without love. Now you'll learn what it feels like when the two stand side by side." His words carried something more than comfort—they carried structure, and Jarod needed that as much as he needed affection. A house without rules had no shape, but rules without care had no mercy. Mr. Arnett was offering both.

Ms. Henley, the counsellor, spoke next, her tone both cautious and approving. "This will not be easy, for either of you. But I have seen what happens when children like Jarod are left to the system. They become ghosts in their own lives. Mr. Arnett, if you're truly prepared for this, then you may be the one person who can anchor him." Mr. Clarke added quietly, "The boy deserves more than statistics and case files. He deserves someone who will still be here tomorrow." Their words, though measured, held encouragement that gave weight to Mr. Arnett's vow.

Jarod pressed his hands to his face, his voice muffled but raw. "I don't know what family is supposed to feel like anymore." Ty placed a hand on his back, firm but gentle. "It feels like me standing right here, not moving. It feels like him," he pointed toward Mr. Arnett, "saying you can stay forever. That's what family feels like." The tears came then, slow at first, then unstoppable. Jarod shook as though the idea itself were too heavy to hold. But when Ty slipped an arm around his shoulder, he didn't resist. He leaned into it, desperate for proof that he wasn't dreaming.

Sophie, standing with Jasmin and Ella, spoke softly but clearly. "You don't need to believe it all at once. Just take today. Believe today." Her words cut through the storm inside him, giving him something smaller, something manageable. Not a lifetime, not forever, just today. Jarod nodded weakly, clinging to that fragment of hope. Leo added, his voice strong, "Every bully I've known was just a broken boy waiting for someone to see him. You've been seen, Jarod. Don't turn away now."

Mr. Arnett extended his hand, not forcing, not rushing, just holding it out. "The choice is yours, Jarod. But know this: my door will stay open, whether you take the step now or later. This is not a trick. It's a promise." For a long moment, Jarod stared at that hand, frozen by years of mistrust. Then, with a trembling breath, he reached out and took it. His grip was weak, uncertain, but it was there. A connection formed, fragile but real.

The silence that followed was not heavy, not empty, but full. Full of something new, something none of us dared name too loudly for fear it might vanish if spoken. Jarod stood between Ty and Mr. Arnett, and for the first time, he was not caught between violence and fear, but between protection and choice. His eyes lifted, meeting ours, and though his smile was faint, it was real. In that fragile curve, I saw what we had all hoped for: a boy beginning to believe that family could still be found.

I spoke quietly to the class as though reliving that day, because it is not one I will forget. After Mr. Arnett offered his home to Jarod, the room felt almost too still, as though we had stepped into a place where words themselves mattered more than air. But Mr. Arnett, being the man he was, did not let promises float without weight. He straightened his shoulders and looked at Jarod with the same mixture of firmness and care he gave every student. "There will be one condition," he said, his voice calm but unshakable. Jarod flinched at first, expecting punishment, expecting the rules to come with chains. But Mr. Arnett continued before fear could settle. "This is not a condition meant to hurt you, but to strengthen you. If you live in my home, you will attend anger management sessions with me. Not once, not for a short while, but as a steady journey. We will walk it together."

Jarod blinked in confusion, his lips parting, but no protest came. I could see his mind fighting between suspicion and hope. "Anger management?" he asked finally, his voice dry, almost defensive. Mr. Arnett nodded, unshaken. "Yes. Because your anger is not something to be ignored. It's not something to bury until it erupts again. It's something we'll face, together. You will not face it alone." His words had weight because they were not spoken like a threat. They were spoken like a lifeline. I saw Jarod's eyes flicker with doubt, but also with the faintest ember of relief.

Ty was standing close by, his expression steady, his arms loosely crossed as though he had already guessed what was coming. He had been through the same kind of lessons with his father, though not out of necessity for himself, but out of preparation to read people and protect them. When Jarod turned toward him, uncertain, Ty simply gave a short nod and said, "He means it. It's not about rules. It's about building something inside you that no one can break again." That sentence landed heavy, not only on Jarod but on all of us. We knew how true it was.

Jeremy, though the youngest, was never shy in moments like these. He tugged at Jarod's sleeve and whispered just loudly enough for us to hear, "If it helps you not hurt anymore, then it's worth it. It doesn't make you weak to go. It makes you smart." Jarod glanced at him, startled that a nine-year-old could speak with such certainty, but he didn't argue. Instead, he looked back at Mr. Arnett, waiting. That waiting was a kind of answer on its own.

It was then that something unusual happened, something that broke a line none of us had expected to see crossed. Jarod, trembling and still shaking from the storm inside him, stepped forward as though he couldn't hold himself back any longer. He reached for Ty and clung to him first, burying his face in Ty's shoulder as though afraid the offer of family would vanish if he let go. Ty wrapped his arms around him without hesitation, holding him in that steady way that always said, "I'm here, you're safe."

But Jarod didn't stop there. His hand reached out blindly until it found Mr. Arnett's sleeve, tugging him closer. It might have been against rules, might have been against the walls schools built to keep things proper and professional. Yet in that moment, none of that mattered. Mr. Arnett hesitated for the briefest second, his hand hovering as though bound by invisible law, when Mr. Takashi, Ty's father, stepped forward from where he had been standing. His voice was calm, carrying the authority of both a father and an RCMP investigator. "Let him," he said. "There are rules, yes. But there is also honour. A teacher who protects a child does no wrong."

With that quiet permission, the hesitation fell away. Mr. Arnett bent down and embraced Jarod alongside Ty, his arms steady but careful, as though cradling not only a boy but the fragile hope that had just been born. Jarod wept then, not the muffled cries he had tried to hide before, but the full release of someone who had carried too much for too long. And in that circle, Ty's arms were the bridge, linking student and principal, child and father figure, making it possible for Jarod to believe he belonged.

I remember seeing Mr. Clarke's eyes glisten at the edge of the room, his normally stern face softening. Mrs. Dunlop covered her mouth with her hand, and Miss Kara turned slightly away to wipe her eyes. Even Mrs. Locke, who was seldom moved by anything in class, lowered her gaze as if humbled by what unfolded. It was not a display of weakness but of strength, a moment that proved care was stronger than cruelty.

Jarod pulled back at last, sniffling, his face blotched with tears but his eyes clearer than I had ever seen them. He managed a shaky laugh, embarrassed by the attention. "I didn't think… I didn't think anybody would ever do that for me." Mr. Arnett gave him a firm but gentle squeeze on the shoulder. "Get used to it," he said. "Because this is what it will be now. Not always easy, not always neat, but never alone."

Ty added quietly, "We'll walk into those sessions together. I'll sit with you if you want. You don't have to be afraid of what it means." Jarod swallowed hard and gave a small nod, still uncertain but no longer fighting it. He leaned against Ty once more, this time not from collapse but from choice. That choice was what mattered.

Sophie leaned toward Jasmin and Ella, whispering, "I've never seen him cry like that. Maybe he's really changing." Jasmin nodded, her hand pressed against her chest, while Ella's eyes lingered on Jarod as though watching for proof that it would last. Leo, however, simply muttered, "It'll take time. But at least he's started." Alex agreed with a grunt, but his gaze was softer than his tone.

I told the class then, in my narration, that this moment was not about rules or exceptions. It was about survival, about finding the one crack where light could finally enter. "Jarod may not have believed in family before today," I said, "but standing between Ty and Mr. Arnett, with Mr. Takashi's word to protect it, he felt what family meant. It wasn't about being perfect. It was about being held when you could no longer stand."

That day was the start of his anger management—not the sessions that would follow in neat classrooms, but the first, truest session: admitting that his anger was only the shadow of his hurt, and that hurt was finally being met with something stronger than fists.

I told the class that silence filled the room long after the embrace broke apart, silence that seemed to weigh heavier than words. Jarod stood there, his fists half-clenched, his shoulders hunched as if he expected everything to vanish with the next breath. For a boy who had been taught that promises always came before pain, hesitation was carved deep into him. He looked from Ty to Mr. Arnett, then down at his shoes, as if the ground itself might open and swallow him rather than let him decide. And then it came—soft, uncertain, but real. "Yes," he whispered, his voice breaking as though the word itself was too fragile to live. That "yes" was not just agreement; it was the first crack in the walls he had built around himself, the first sign that he was willing to believe someone might not abandon him.

Mr. Arnett did not rush forward, did not crush the moment with celebration. Instead, he crouched down so his eyes met Jarod's level. "Thank you for trusting me," he said steadily, the way only a man with patience could. "Now, if you're going to live under my roof, you get to choose what to call me. That's your right." The room leaned in, almost as if holding its breath. Jarod blinked, caught off guard. "Call you?" he asked. Mr. Arnett nodded. "Yes. You can keep calling me Mr. Arnett if that feels safest. You could call me Dad if you want, or Ted, if you'd rather use my first name. Or…" he smiled faintly, letting a little humour slip through, "if you prefer something old-fashioned, you can call me Sir."

The word hung in the air like a dare. Jarod's lip twitched first, then his shoulders shook, and before anyone knew it, a small laugh escaped him. "Sir?" he repeated, almost choking on the sound, as if laughter was a foreign language. The class watched, stunned, because none of us had ever heard him laugh like that before. Mr. Arnett chuckled too, shaking his head. "Yes, Sir," he teased back, matching the tone. And for the first time, Jarod smiled, not the crooked smirk he wore when he was cruel, but a nervous, shy grin that broke through the hardness of his face like sunlight through storm clouds.

Ty stepped forward, clapping a hand on his shoulder. "Well, I guess that's settled. No knight in armour here, just a Sir with paperwork." That sent another ripple of laughter around the room, softer this time, not mocking but warm. Jasmin giggled, covering her mouth, while Sophie nudged Ella, whispering, "He actually laughed. Did you hear that?" Ella only nodded, her eyes wide, as if witnessing something she thought she'd never see.

Jarod's smile wavered as quickly as it had come, but he didn't retreat from it. Instead, he looked at Mr. Arnett and whispered, "Maybe… maybe Ted. I don't know if I can call you Dad yet." His honesty cracked something in all of us. Mr. Arnett didn't flinch, didn't pressure. He only said, "Then Ted it is. And when you're ready for something else, you'll know." His voice held no demand, only patience.

Leo leaned back in his chair, his arms folded but his expression softer than usual. "That's how it starts," he muttered. Alex gave a short nod. "Not with threats, not with lectures. With choice." Their words carried weight, for they knew better than most what forced obedience felt like, and how different it was to be offered freedom.

I turned back to the class and told them plainly, "That laugh mattered more than all the fists Jarod ever threw. Because it meant he finally believed he wasn't trapped anymore. That yes was the smallest word, but it was the biggest step." Jeremy, sitting cross-legged on the floor near Leo, whispered so quietly that I almost missed it, "It's like the smile that came back." And though the title belonged to the future, not the present, in that moment it felt like a promise.

The teachers exchanged glances, most of them wiping their eyes in quiet motions. Mrs. Locke cleared her throat as if to hide her tears, while Miss Kara murmured something about never underestimating children. Even Mr. Takashi, who had seen more broken homes than any of us could imagine, looked moved. His arms were crossed, his expression unreadable, but his eyes were gentler than I had ever seen them.

Jarod stood straighter after that, still nervous, still carrying shadows, but no longer drowning. When Ty nudged him toward the group, he didn't resist. When Nico teased him lightly about "Sir Jarod of the Black Eye," he even smirked instead of snarling. It was awkward, messy, unsteady. But it was change.

That afternoon, when we walked out of the classroom, I told the others, "We just saw the first brick come loose in a wall that's been standing for years. Don't underestimate it." And though I knew harder days were ahead, that fragile "yes" kept ringing in my mind. Not pity. Not charity. Partnership. That was the word Mr. Arnett gave him, and that was the word that finally made Jarod laugh.

I told the students that the paperwork was signed quicker than anyone expected, and for the first time in Jarod's life, the word home meant something other than fear. He stepped into Mr. Arnett's house with his shoes muddy from the walk over, his bag hanging loose off one shoulder, and his eyes darting as though every corner might still hold a trap. But it didn't. No shouting greeted him, no fists followed him inside. Instead, there was order, calm, and rules that carried weight without cruelty. "You'll help with dishes after supper," Mr. Arnett said gently, not as a punishment but as a rhythm. "And homework gets finished before television. That's the way it works here." Jarod only nodded, testing each word, but no storm followed. The walls didn't shake. His body didn't tense for a blow. For the first time, the rules steadied rather than crushed him.

Ty came by that evening, quiet as always, and stood with him in the backyard where the air was cooler. "Strange, isn't it?" Ty said, his hands tucked into his pockets. "Silence that doesn't feel dangerous." Jarod looked at him for a long time before answering, "I don't know if I'll ever get used to it." Ty nodded once. "You will. It just takes time." The boy who had spent years flinching at footsteps now stood in a space where footsteps didn't mean pain. That alone was a miracle too fragile to touch, but too real to ignore.

Jarod shifted, his voice low, almost ashamed. "You were right… about aggression." Ty tilted his head. "Which part?" Jarod's jaw tightened. "The tournament. I came at you with everything. I wanted to break you, to prove I was stronger. But you barely moved. You didn't even fight like I expected. And still, you beat me." The words burned coming out, but they were the truth he couldn't bury anymore. "I thought rage was strength. But you showed me it just makes you lose faster." His eyes watered, not from weakness, but from finally letting honesty breathe.

Ty's reply was steady, unshaken. "Aggression always beats itself. It collapses under its own weight. I didn't win because I was better than you, Jarod. I won because I didn't let rage control me. That's the difference." Jarod swallowed hard, his throat working against the ache of understanding. "Thank you… for showing me. And for not letting me destroy myself." His voice cracked, the gratitude raw, unpolished, but real.

Without another word, Ty reached forward and pulled Jarod into a hug, the kind that carried no judgment, no victory, only brotherhood. Jarod stiffened first, then sank into it, pressing his forehead against Ty's shoulder as though leaning against something unshakable for the first time. "Through everything," Ty whispered, his tone quiet but fierce. "I'll be here." And Jarod believed him, because Ty had already proved it with actions stronger than words.

When they pulled apart, Ty added with a faint grin, "And if you ever want to spar again, I'll be waiting. Not to fight you down, but to keep you sharp. Kung Fu isn't about tearing people apart—it's about knowing when not to. And if you want, I'll teach you Taoist Tai Chi. It slows the storm. Teaches you balance." Jarod gave a half-smile, unsure but curious, his eyes narrowing as if weighing whether such calm could ever belong to him. "Balance," he repeated, the word foreign on his tongue, but not unwelcome.

Nico leaned against the doorway, arms crossed, and spoke up for the first time. "You should take it. Ty's got more patience than the rest of us put together. And Tai Chi? It's like learning how to breathe properly all over again." Jasmin, standing beside him, nodded. "You'll see yourself differently when you move like that. It's not about fighting anymore—it's about not needing to fight." Her words carried a softness that Jarod wasn't used to hearing. He stared at the ground, cheeks reddening, not from shame, but from something he didn't quite understand yet—hope.

Jeremy piped up from the stairs where he sat cross-legged, his voice as steady as a nine-year-old could muster. "Jarod, don't forget—you don't have to carry everything alone anymore. You've got us, and you've got Ted now." At the sound of the name, Jarod looked toward the kitchen where Mr. Arnett moved about with quiet steadiness. The boy's eyes softened. "Ted," he whispered again, as if testing it, finding it fit better than expected.

That night, when Jarod lay in the small room Mr. Arnett had prepared for him—sheets crisp, walls plain but peaceful—he stared at the ceiling longer than he slept. He listened, waiting for the slam of a door, the stomp of boots, the thunder of fists. None came. Only the sound of the clock ticking in the hall and the faint laugh of Ty and Nico talking in hushed tones down the street. He realised then that silence could be safety. And that was the beginning of a new kind of strength.

I told the class that morning began softly, with sunlight spilling into Jarod's new room through curtains that didn't bear holes from fists or stains from beer. He lay there awake long before the alarm clock rang, listening not for danger but for the gentle clatter of dishes in Ted's kitchen.

He was still learning what quiet meant when it wasn't sharp with threat. At first, he doubted his own senses, thinking perhaps the night had been an illusion, a pause before the storm returned. But the storm was gone, and so was the man who carried it. Jarod rose with a heaviness in his chest, not of fear but of something even harder to hold—relief.

His steps down the staircase felt different, not as hesitant, not as fearful, yet still careful, like testing ice that might break. He passed Nico sitting at the table scribbling in a notebook, Jasmin leaning against the counter sipping orange juice, and Jeremy bouncing his legs as he read a book upside down. None of them looked at him with suspicion, none of them whispered as he entered. Instead, Nico just looked up and said, "Morning," as if Jarod had been part of their mornings forever. That was enough to crack the armour Jarod still carried, and he lowered his gaze quickly so no one would see the tears already gathering.

But Ty noticed. Ty always noticed. He moved quietly, like someone who never needed to announce himself, and waited until Jarod's eyes flicked up, searching. Without a word, Ty tilted his head toward the back door, and Jarod followed, grateful for the chance to escape the stares he imagined were heavier than they truly were. They stepped outside, into the yard where the grass was still damp, the air sharp with the scent of morning. Jarod stopped near the fence and turned, his fists clenching and unclenching, his throat fighting against words that refused to come easily.

Then suddenly, as if ripped from his chest, the words spilled. "Ty… I love you. You're my brother." His voice broke, but the truth of it thundered through the quiet yard. The boy who had once swung fists at Ty now opened himself with nothing but trembling honesty. For a moment, the silence that followed felt endless, until Ty's own tears slid down his cheeks. He didn't hide them, didn't wipe them away. Instead, he stepped forward and wrapped Jarod in his arms, full-bodied and without restraint. No half-hugs, no cautious touches—just the kind that meant family, permanent and unshakable.

Jarod buried his face against Ty's shoulder, gripping as though afraid he might vanish if he let go. Ty held on even tighter, whispering through the thickness in his throat, "I love you too, Jarod. You're my brother now, forever." They stood there long enough that the others, peeking from the kitchen window, grew quiet. Jasmin touched Nico's arm and whispered, "Do you see it? That's what breaking the cycle looks like." Nico nodded, scribbling a single sentence into his notebook: Hugs are unlimited for family.

When they finally pulled apart, Jarod's cheeks were wet, his eyes swollen, but his back stood straighter than it ever had. He laughed, a shaky sound that surprised even him. "I didn't think I could ever say that," he admitted, "not to anyone. But with you, it's different. You fought me. You stopped me. And then you stayed. No one ever stayed before." Ty smiled softly, shaking his head. "I didn't stay because you needed fixing. I stayed because you mattered." The words landed heavier than any punch ever had, and Jarod nodded, unable to reply.

Jeremy darted out the door then, unable to keep still. "You said it, didn't you? You told him!" His little brother's grin stretched wide as he launched himself at Jarod's side, hugging him too. Jarod stiffened, then looked down at Jeremy's arms wrapped tight and sighed with something close to joy. "Yeah, I told him." Jeremy only squeezed tighter, declaring, "That means you're my brother too, whether you like it or not!" Jarod let out a short laugh and ruffled his hair, something he'd never dared do before.

By the time they all gathered inside again, the weight in the room had shifted. Even Ella and Sophie, who had once whispered nervously about Jarod in the hallways, now sat closer, their eyes softer. Lisa leaned against Harley and whispered, "See? Even the hardest ones can change." Harley nodded, his arm resting protectively across her shoulders. For once, no one argued, no one doubted.

Nico closed his notebook, looking around the table. "What we just saw—remember it. Because this is what matters more than all the old wounds we've been talking about. It isn't the fights, or the bruises, or even the punishments. It's the moment when someone says 'I love you' and means it. That's the break in the cycle. That's the start of something new."

Ty and Jarod exchanged a glance then, the kind brothers share without needing words. They didn't need to prove anything anymore. The hug had already said it all, the tears had sealed it, and the truth had anchored it. From that morning on, the bond was no longer a fragile thread— it was steel. And though the road ahead would still be hard, it would be walked side by side, without fear of walking it alone.

I told the class the shift came quietly, without fireworks or loud applause, but with the kind of stillness that tells you something sacred has taken root. That evening, Mr. and Mrs. Takashi sat Ty and Jasmin down at their long wooden dining table, a place where many difficult talks had been had, but this time their voices were warm, softened by approval. Mrs. Takashi folded her hands, smiling the gentle smile of an artist who sees the picture before anyone else does. "We've seen the way you look after each other," she said. "And we trust you. From today, you may call yourselves what you already are—boyfriend and girlfriend. But with respect, always." Jasmin blushed, Ty lowered his eyes with a rare grin, and the rest of us sat hushed, knowing this was not small news. It was permission born of trust, and no permission weighs more heavily than that.

Mr. Takashi, careful as always, slid an envelope across the table. Ted Arnett had written it himself, a letter addressed to both families, granting his full approval for Ty and Jasmin to be seen openly as a couple. It was simple, written in Ted's steady hand, but its weight carried more than ink could hold. "I've watched them long enough," Ted had written. "This is not childish affection—it is loyalty, respect, and care. I give my blessing." Jasmin held the letter close to her chest, her fingers trembling slightly, and Ty reached out, steadying her hand in his. The room filled with something brighter than pride—it was belonging, the kind that makes even the coldest days seem easier to bear.

Jarod watched from the corner of the table, his fragile smile flickering in and out like a candle learning how to stay lit. He didn't interrupt, didn't draw attention to himself, but we all noticed the way his eyes followed every word, every gesture, as if measuring whether this kind of peace could ever truly include him. Ty reached across the table, squeezing his shoulder without words, and Jarod's chest rose with the weight of a breath he hadn't realised he was holding. For the first time in his life, he wasn't outside looking in—he was part of the circle.

That night, the house moved into its usual routines. Nico scribbled more notes by lamplight, Jeremy fell asleep mid-sentence with a book spread across his chest, Sophie and Ella whispered under blankets, and Jasmin wrote Ty's name in the margins of her homework with a smile. But Jarod lingered downstairs, staring at the hallway that led to his new room. His hand brushed the wall as if testing whether it might vanish if he touched it too roughly. Ted Arnett approached quietly, holding two mugs of cocoa, one for himself and one for the boy who had been more storm than child for so long. He didn't force a conversation; he simply placed the mug in Jarod's hands and sat beside him on the couch.

Minutes passed before Jarod finally spoke. "No one's ever told me I could stay before. It was always… temporary. Always waiting to be sent back." His voice cracked, more confession than statement. Ted nodded slowly, resting one large hand on the back of the couch, careful not to crowd him. "You're not waiting anymore, son. This is your home. And I'm not going anywhere." The word "son" caught Jarod like a strike to the chest. His eyes flooded instantly, and before he could stop himself, he leaned forward, wrapping his arms around Ted in a hug that held nothing back. It was desperate, trembling, but real.

Ted embraced him in return, strong but gentle, no hesitation. "I love you, Jarod," he whispered, steady and clear. The words broke something open in the boy, who clutched tighter, his face buried against the man's chest. Tears streamed freely from both of them, but neither pulled away. For Jarod, the moment sealed what no court order or official paper ever could. This was family—not forged by blood, not handed down by name, but made in the raw truth of choosing one another.

The others peeked from the hallway, silent witnesses to the bond being sealed. Ty placed a hand on Jasmin's shoulder, his steady grip grounding her as her own tears slid down. Leo whispered, "That's it—that's what saves us." And Alex, for once without bravado, simply nodded, eyes wet. Even Jeremy stood still, his usual chatter caught in his throat, whispering instead, "He's got a dad now."

Jarod pulled back at last, wiping his eyes with his sleeve but unable to stop smiling. "I never thought I'd hear those words," he admitted. Ted brushed a hand across his hair, not with the roughness of discipline but with the gentleness of care. "And I'll say them again tomorrow, and the day after, until you believe it without doubt." Jarod nodded, clinging to the promise as if it were the first real rope thrown to him while drowning.

That night, when Jarod climbed the stairs to his room, the house felt different under his feet. It was not a place to escape from, not a space to fear, but a home that would wait for him at the end of every day. He paused at the top of the staircase, looking back toward the living room where Ted still sat, reading quietly. The words replayed in his head—I love you, Jarod. They would echo for years, steady as heartbeat, steady as hope.

And when he finally lay down, pulling the blanket over his chest, the smile that spread across his face did not flicker. It held. Fragile, yes, but real. And for the first time since he could remember, Jarod believed he was safe. The cycle had not only broken—it had been rewritten. Then tomorrow morning, a new student arrives at school, his name is Tom.

## CHAPTER 9: WHEN JEREMY DECIDES

The small group of third and fourth graders gathered on the carpeted floor of the multipurpose room, their legs crossed, eyes lifting with the curiosity that only children carried when the world still felt enormous. The teachers stood at the back, letting Jeremy take the space. At nine years old, he looked far younger than the authority his posture demanded, but when he clasped his hands in front of him, the hush fell across the room. "You know," Jeremy began, his voice steady, "a bully doesn't always wear the same face. Sometimes they smile wide, open doors for you, or even sit beside you at lunch. But that smile doesn't always mean they're your friend. Sometimes it hides storms." His tone was blunt, not cruel, and the younger children leaned closer, sensing truth being poured out rather than a lecture being stacked upon them.

Sophie whispered from the back row, her hand half-raised as though testing if questions were allowed. "Do you mean like… when someone laughs too much, but then they shove you later?" Jeremy nodded, acknowledging her courage to speak. "Yes. Exactly like that. They'll make you think you're safe, but then they twist it. And it hurts more because you believed the smile." The silence that followed was not empty; it was filled with the weight of recognition. The younger children knew the patterns, even if no adult had ever named them so directly. Jeremy's honesty painted the room in sharper colours, and the teachers exchanged glances, quietly astonished at how clearly he spoke without stumbling.

Nico leaned against the wall near Ty, his arms folded, listening without interrupting. "He's right," Nico said suddenly, his voice cutting through. "I've seen it too many times. The smiles that break are the ones that trick you. That's why you can't just look at the face. You have to look at the actions." A ripple of agreement passed through the older students nearby, and even the adults stiffened a little, the truth pressing against them as well. Jeremy looked back at Nico briefly, grateful, before turning his eyes to the small faces waiting for more. "So, if you ever feel that storm hiding behind a smile," Jeremy said, "don't tell yourself you're imagining it. Trust what you feel. Because you're probably right."

Ella raised her hand more boldly this time. "But what if the teachers don't see it? What if the bully's nice when they look, but mean when they're gone?" Jeremy's lips tightened. "Then you keep saying it. You tell them again and again. You don't stop until someone listens. Bullies love silence because silence keeps them strong." His words were sharp but not harsh, and the room grew still again. Jasmin spoke up next, softer than the others. "What if… it's your friend? What if you don't want to get them in trouble?" Jeremy's eyes met hers, unwavering. "Then you ask yourself if a real friend would make you feel small. If they did, then maybe they weren't your friend at all." The truth landed hard, but no one argued.

At the back, Mr. Clarke folded his arms, his chin lowering as he watched. He had spoken of bullies many times in his career, yet there was something different in the way Jeremy commanded the room. He wasn't handing out warnings or rules; he was planting truths like seeds, and the younger students were grasping them as though clutching something solid in their hands.

Mrs. Locke leaned toward Mrs. Haller and whispered, "He speaks like he's been carrying this for years." The other teacher only nodded, her expression unreadable. For a moment, the adults felt they were listening to something larger than a nine-year-old boy — they were listening to someone who had chosen to protect.

Ty finally stepped forward, his voice calm and even. "Jeremy's right. Sometimes bullies act because no one ever stopped them early. If you feel unsafe, you say so. Don't wait for tomorrow. Don't hope it will disappear. It won't." His tone was precise, his father's investigative clarity echoing faintly in his words. The younger children's eyes widened; Ty's presence was steady, a weight that held them. Jeremy glanced at him, the unspoken gratitude clear between them. "That's why we talk about this now," Jeremy added, "before it grows bigger. Because once it grows, it's harder to stop."

Mila raised her hand hesitantly. "What if the bully says it's your fault?" Her question trembled. Jeremy's reply was immediate. "That's the oldest trick. They'll blame you to make themselves feel powerful. But it's never your fault that someone chooses to hurt you. Never." Leo, who had been listening quietly by the doorway, nodded and muttered, "He's saying what we should have said years ago." Alex leaned closer to him and murmured, "And he's saying it better." They shared a look heavy with memory, knowing that scars still lived inside them, but also recognising the strength in seeing someone younger rise without fear.

The bell outside rang faintly, signalling transition, but no one moved. The children were still locked into the gravity of the moment, and the teachers gave no order to stand. Jeremy exhaled slowly, gathering his final words. "So here's what I want you to remember," he said, lowering his voice until the silence pulled everyone in. "If someone breaks your smile with cruelty, you do not stay quiet. You don't carry it alone. Because bullies are only strong when no one else knows. And you deserve better than silence." His words lingered as if carved into the air, and when he stepped back, there was no applause, no chatter. Just the hush of young minds turning inward, already carrying the lesson with them.

The room emptied slowly, the younger grades filing out in small lines, their faces quiet and thoughtful as they moved back toward their classrooms. Jeremy stayed behind, folding the newspaper clipping he always carried, placing it carefully in his pocket as though it were glass. He didn't notice Leo and Alex until they stepped closer, their shadows long against the pale floor. "You didn't even shake," Leo muttered, his tone half incredulous, half admiring. Jeremy blinked at him, startled. "I thought I did," he answered softly. Alex shook his head, lowering his voice so only they could hear. "No. You didn't. Not once. You stood there like… like you'd been doing it for years." The truth of it left Jeremy quiet, but his shoulders lifted, as though the weight he carried had not crushed him but strengthened him instead.

Leo rubbed his temple, his mouth tightening as his thoughts churned. "When you spoke about the smiles… I saw myself. Not just the words, but the way you said them. That was me, Jeremy. I used to put on that fake grin, every single day, just to cover the storm I was throwing into other people's lives."

His tone grew raw, thick with regret. Jeremy stepped closer, looking him square in the eye. "And you're here now," he replied simply. "That's what matters. You're not hiding behind it anymore." The bluntness of Jeremy's answer caught Leo off guard, silencing him into reflection.

Alex folded his arms, leaning against the wall as his eyes narrowed, not in anger but in memory. "He's right," Alex said. "When you talked about silence, I remembered how I used it. I would push Leo down, laugh at him, make him doubt himself, and then I'd stand there, daring him to say a word. He never did, because I had him convinced it would only make things worse." His voice was sharp, unflinching. "I heard my own words in yours, Jeremy. It felt like being caught all over again, except this time I wasn't the one holding the chain. I was the one hearing it break." His confession settled heavy between them, and for a long moment the three just breathed, the stillness broken only by faint footsteps down the hall.

Jeremy pressed his hand against his pocket where the article rested. "That's why I spoke the way I did. Because silence almost killed Myles. If no one listens, if no one says it out loud, then the bully wins. You both know that better than anyone." Leo swallowed hard, nodding once. "Yeah," he whispered. "We do." Alex shifted uncomfortably, then leaned closer, his eyes fixed on Jeremy. "You're younger than us, but you're stronger in ways we weren't. When I bullied, I thought power came from being louder, being meaner. But you… you stand steady without shouting. That's what scares bullies. That's what makes them fold."

Ty, who had stayed nearby without interrupting, finally spoke, his tone calm and deliberate. "You saw yourselves in his words. That means you've already changed. A bully who hasn't changed wouldn't feel anything listening to him. But you did." The truth struck deep, silencing Leo and Alex again, their gazes lowering as if Ty had cut through every excuse they might have held onto. Jeremy didn't smile; instead, he stepped back toward the centre of the room, his small frame standing firm. "It isn't about me," he said evenly. "It's about Myles. It's about making sure no one else breaks because we stayed quiet. If I sound strong, it's only because I remember him every time I speak."

Leo's hand twitched as if he wanted to reach for Jeremy's shoulder, but instead he let the words sit, his chest tight with something he couldn't name. Alex muttered quietly, almost to himself, "Maybe this is what it means to grow past what we were. Not speeches, not punishments. Just truth. Simple, hard, and steady." Jeremy looked between them both, his voice low but unyielding. "Then carry it with me. Don't let it die here." The air thickened with meaning, the weight of scars and lessons pressing into the three of them, binding them not by past wounds but by the choice to face them together.

I walked Jeremy to the door and watched the younger grades trail away in their quiet line, then turned back to find Leo and Alex waiting with that look they wear when a truth has landed too close to home. "Stay a minute," I said, keeping my voice low so it wouldn't echo down the corridor, and the two of them drifted in beside me like brothers who knew the weight of closed doors.

Ty stood farther down, hands in his pockets, watchful without hovering, and Mr. Clarke's reflection moved in the glass of the library case like a patient tide that never quite reached the shore. "There's someone new," I told them, and I could feel my jaw set the way Jeremy's does when he refuses to flinch. "His name is Tom, thirteen, taller than most, and the hall listens when he walks." I didn't raise my voice; I didn't need to. The truth filled the space between our feet.

Leo's eyes narrowed, not in anger, not yet, but in the slow study he learned the hard way, and Alex shifted the way he always does when memory presses on an old bruise. "New how?" Leo asked, and I could hear the careful gate he puts on every word now, because once upon a time he let words gallop. "New like Jarod," I said, and Ty's head tipped from the far end as if a chord had been plucked that only the four of us could hear. "Only worse. Ninety percent worse by what I've seen in two days—less talk, more pressure, like he's holding a storm behind his teeth." Alex breathed out through his nose, and Jeremy, small as he is, came back to lean on the doorframe, listening without interruption, because he knows the difference between chatter and the sound a fuse makes.

"I don't want panic," I told them, and my voice stayed even, because fear is food for boys who hunt it. "But I saw him in the stairwell after lunch, hand flat against another kid's chest, not shoving, not yet, just measuring out the inches like a ruler he owned." Leo's mouth tightened, and he nodded once; it was the nod of someone who remembers owning that ruler. "Did he smile?" Alex asked, not looking at me but at the pattern he knows too well. "No," I said, "and that's the part that bothers me. Jarod smiled before he struck, like a theatre curtain before the show. Tom doesn't bother with curtains." Ty took a step closer at that, not dramatic, just enough to say he'd heard what mattered.

Jeremy folded his arms the way he does when he's bracing for a cold wind, and his eyes found mine like a question posted on a wall. "You're sure?" he asked, and he didn't have to say of what. "Yes," I answered, and the word landed with the quiet of a stone in clear water. "I'm watching the corridor bend around him. Kids shift before he arrives. Teachers call his name twice instead of once. He cracks his knuckles but never laughs. He doesn't need to." Leo glanced toward the library tables where the younger ones had sat, and I knew he was counting faces he promised himself he wouldn't let disappear between bells. "Where did he come from?" he asked, and I shook my head. "Not sure yet. Ms. Henley knows more than she's saying. Mr. Arnett's tone changed when he said Tom's last name."

Alex rubbed at the seam on his sleeve, a nervous habit honesty gave him. "Jarod pretended he was fine until he wasn't," he said, and the air around his words tasted like old iron. "He loved an audience; he wanted the world to clap when he broke someone." I held his gaze. "Tom doesn't need applause," I said. "He needs air and space and the kind of silence that lets a fist decide the argument." Ty's eyes tracked a shadow along the floor as the door swung and settled. "How many saw him in the stairwell?" Ty asked. "Three," I said. "Two fourth-graders and a sixth. They looked away like they'd been taught manners by fear."

# THE SMILE THAT BROKE

Mr. Clarke crossed the threshold, heard just enough to understand the shape of what we were building, and he paused at the case where the old yearbooks lived like quiet witnesses. "We're not forecasting doom," I told him without looking, because he dislikes prophecy when what he needs are plans, "but we're not going to pretend the wind is nothing but air." He nodded once and passed, his footfalls a measured count that steadied the corridor. Jeremy shifted closer to Leo and Alex as if choosing where to plant his flag. "If he's worse than Jarod," Jeremy said, steady as truth, "then we don't wait for the first break."

"I'm not calling for a fight," I said, and both Leo and Alex lifted their hands, palms open, to show they understood the difference between readiness and hunger. "Good," Leo said, and there was an echo of the boy who once took pride in looming; now he uses height to shelter the small. "But you're saying we prepare." I nodded. "We prepare to stand. We prepare to speak before the silence teaches the younger ones to swallow pain like it's homework they forgot to hand in." Alex looked toward the window where the winter light lay thin as paper. "What did he do after the stairwell?" he asked, and my answer was not a story, just a fact. "He smiled at Ms. Kara and held the door. Polite. Empty. Mechanical as a clock."

Ty came fully in then, the set of his shoulders telling me his father's discipline had already been laid across his thoughts like a ruler on a map. "Silence is a lid," he said, and the room seemed to draw a breath. "If he's holding it down, the steam builds. Lids blow." Jeremy looked up at him, small and fierce, and said what none of us were willing to leave unsaid. "I don't want any more names on paper." He meant the clipping in his pocket. He meant the boy whose first name we keep close like a prayer spoken without candles. Leo's hand hovered over Jeremy's shoulder and settled there, grounding us both.

"We watch patterns," I said, and I listed them the way Mr. Takashi taught Ty to list a scene: arrival routes, chosen corners, the way people clear space without knowing they've done it, the jokes that land too hard and then dry up when a shadow crosses them. "Tom doesn't test with words," I added. "He tests with reach. He places objects and people the way some boys arrange chess pieces, and then he stares long enough to teach them not to move." Alex swallowed, and I heard the rasp of regret leave his throat. "That used to be me," he said, and he didn't hide from it. "Not anymore," Jeremy answered, flat as a gavel. "That's the point."

Mr. Arnett's door clicked open down the hall, and Mrs. Dunlop's voice carried something warm through the thin light, but it didn't reach us; some conversations don't let other sounds in. "If he's ninety percent worse," Leo said, rolling the number like a stone in his palm, "then the ten percent is our window." I met his eyes and let the agreement show. "That ten percent is the moment before the chair flies, the inch before the push becomes a fall, the breath before the shout becomes a swing." Ty nodded once. "Then we hold the ten," he said. "We live in it. We build a wall out of presence."

"Jarod learned to perform his rage," I said, and my voice didn't accuse; it simply placed a marker on the trail. "Tom doesn't perform. He conserves. That means he'll look small until the moment is large." Alex's jaw tightened. "Conserve and explode," he muttered, and Jeremy's mouth pressed into a thin line. "So we don't give him a room to explode in," Jeremy said, and there was the edge that saves, the simple plan that refuses to be clever when steadiness will do. Leo's hand left Jeremy's shoulder and found mine for a heartbeat, not a plea, not a vow, just contact that said the ground beneath us was shared.

"Who has he marked?" Ty asked, and I answered with the names of two boys from Grade Four who carry too many library slips because the stacks let them vanish, and a girl from Grade Six whose voice goes quiet when taller feet enter a room. "We put them near the front of the line," Leo said. "We walk the same corridors they do." Alex glanced at the clock and then at the ceiling, and I knew he was mapping the next bell against the next corridor. "Ms. Henley needs to know what we see," he added, and no one flinched at the word need. We've all learned the difference between snitching and saving a Wednesday afternoon.

Mr. Clarke returned long enough to slide a book onto the desk and leave a note with his tight, square printing: Eyes open, voices ready. He didn't wait for thanks; he trusts us to read what is laid down. "There's one more thing," I said, and my voice dropped the way it does when I don't want the hall to own what belongs to the four of us. "Tom's eyes went dead when a seventh grader bumped him at recess. No shove, no words, just that flat look, like a door closing on light." Jeremy's breath caught, small and sharp. Ty's head tilted as if to let the description settle exactly where it belongs in his mental file.

"Dead eyes before action," Leo repeated, tasting the pattern. "Jarod lit up before he hit; Tom goes dark." Alex exhaled a single syllable of agreement, not a curse, just the sound a boy makes when he recognises a road sign he hoped never to see again. "Can we reach him early?" Jeremy asked, and the whole room seemed to lean toward the answer. "Maybe," I said, and I refused to lie to a nine-year-old who has seen more truth than most men. "But we don't begin with speeches. We begin with closeness. We begin with witnesses who refuse to blink." Ty's eyes softened, and for a heartbeat he looked eleven, not older than the year allows.

"We loop the adults," Alex said, and he counted them off like prayer beads: Mrs. Locke for watchful eyes, Ms. Henley for quiet doors, Mr. Arnett for the calls that matter, Mr. Clarke for the angles of the building that muffle sound. "And my parents," Ty added, steady as a cord that won't snap. "When presence needs weight, we borrow it." Jeremy nodded, and I could see the article folded like a small square of iron against his heart. "No one else breaks," he said, and the words did not seek drama. They sought work. We all said yes without moving our mouths.

I stepped to the library door and looked down the long run of lockers shaped like a throat that could swallow smaller names if we let it. "Tom stands in the gap between bells," I said, and I didn't mean the schedule; I meant the breaths between choices. "So, we stand there too."

Leo slipped his pack higher on his shoulder. "I'll walk the east hall before last period," he said. "Alex takes the stairwell. Ty does a slow pass by the art room where the fourth-graders stage their hiding." Jeremy lifted his chin. "I'll stay near the doors," he added. "Small doesn't mean soft." No one laughed; no one ever laughs when Jeremy says the obvious thing that adults forget.

"Tell me the one thing we do not do," Ty said, and his father's profession braided itself into the rhythm of his words. "We do not corner him," I answered. "We do not make a show; we do not hand him a stage. We take away the echo instead." Leo gave a single tap of his knuckles on the table, not habit now, but signal. "And if the chair flies?" he asked, because pretending is a luxury children cannot afford. "We pull the room back," I said. "We call the names that calm him if we can find them. We lift, not strike. We get the little ones to the edge and we give the adults the lane."

Alex's eyes moved to Jeremy, then back to me, and for a heartbeat his old shame tried to speak, but he didn't let it. "This is not a story we watch," he said. "This is a Wednesday we change." Jeremy's mouth softened, but his spine didn't, and he stepped in close so our shoulders nearly touched. "I don't care if he's worse than Jarod," he said. "I care that the ten percent is still there." I put my hand on the cool frame of the library door and let the wood ground me. "Then we live in the ten," I said. "Until it widens."

The corridor breathed once, long and low, and the four of us took that breath with it, not as a promise, not as a threat, but as the simple air required for boys who refuse to let silence teach. Mr. Takashi passed at the far end, a brief nod, the kind a man offers when he recognises a watch being set without anyone telling him the time. Mrs. Takashi's paint-stained cuff flashed by the art-room window like a small flag of colour in a winter field. The school resumed its ordinary hum, but beneath it the chord we had struck kept vibrating. "We'll walk," Leo said. "We'll stand," Alex added. "We'll see," Ty finished. I looked at Jeremy, and he looked at me, and neither of us blinked.

The library felt heavier when the three of them sat together at the wide oak table, light slanting through tall panes and catching dust like secret signals. Jeremy kept his fingers flat against the folded article about Myles, but his words leaned in another direction. "Do you remember Jarod?" he asked, his voice calm but weighted, and the mention of the name made Alex shift in his chair as though an echo had crossed his back. Leo's eyes narrowed in the way they do when memory forces its way forward. Ty, who had been silent at the corner, lifted his chin in acknowledgment. The room drew tight, the hum of pages turning fading to a quiet expectancy. "Jarod had signs," Jeremy pressed, not accusing, just reminding. "I saw them late, but you saw them too."

Leo leaned back, staring at the ceiling tiles as though they carried a chalkboard of regret. "Jarod smiled before he hurt someone," he said, almost clinically, but the heaviness in his tone betrayed the history stitched beneath his words. "That grin was his curtain, his way of enjoying the moment before the storm."

Alex ran his hand across the surface of the table, slow and deliberate. "I used to think it was funny," he admitted, voice low. "I laughed when he teased kids for tripping, when he mocked them into silence. But the grin… the grin told us when to step back. We knew it meant something was about to snap." Jeremy listened, chest rising steady, and noted how both brothers described not the strike itself but the ritual that came before it. "That's the difference with Tom," he said at last. "There's no grin. Just the silence."

Ty's voice entered then, smooth as water over stone. "Silence is worse," he said, and everyone leaned toward him without realising they had. "Jarod's anger was noisy, like thunder. But thunder warns you it's there. Tom's quiet is like a blade sheathed. You don't hear it until it's drawn." His father's training laced the words, but Ty spoke as a boy who had lived through the corridor wars of the previous year. Jeremy turned his head toward him, eyes wide with the recognition of wisdom coming from someone only two years older. "So what broke through?" Jeremy asked. "What cut the blade before it swung?" Ty took a breath and let it out slow, as though measuring truth. "Not words," he answered. "Not rules. A moment when he realised someone was still standing there, not afraid, not moving away."

Alex folded his arms and looked down. "That was you," he said plainly, his voice directed at Ty. "You didn't run when the rest of us did." Ty gave a small nod, the kind that dismisses pride but confirms reality. "I held his wrist," Ty recalled. "Not to fight him. To stop the swing. He looked at me, and for the first time he saw someone wasn't going to disappear." Leo let out a breath that sounded half like relief, half like shame. "I should've been the one," he admitted. "I was taller, stronger. But I didn't step in. I let fear hold me." Jeremy looked between them, sensing the weight of the confession, and his voice dropped. "Maybe that's why Jarod broke through," he said. "Because finally someone didn't flinch."

The three sat with the silence until Jeremy broke it again. "Tom doesn't smile. He doesn't taunt. He waits." His hands pressed the folded paper tighter, as if anchoring himself to another boy's name. "It feels worse. Like Jarod was the storm you saw coming, but Tom's the earthquake you don't hear until the walls shake." Alex winced at the image but nodded. "I don't want to face another earthquake," he muttered. Leo pressed his palms flat to the table. "But we might have to. If the signs are there, then we can't pretend not to see them. Jarod taught us that." Jeremy swallowed and glanced at Ty. "And you taught us that sometimes one hand can stop a storm."

Ty leaned forward, elbows on the table, eyes sharp but steady. "Don't confuse bravery with luck," he said firmly. "Jarod could've hurt me worse than he did. But it worked because he saw something he didn't expect. He saw resolve." Jeremy tilted his head, curious. "Resolve?" Ty nodded. "The kind that says, 'You won't scare me off.' Jarod thrived on scattering people like leaves. When one didn't scatter, he cracked." Alex let out a hollow laugh, though there was no humour in it. "Cracked… that's a polite way of saying he lost it." Jeremy lifted his chin. "But losing it was the beginning of change. He couldn't go back to pretending after that."

Leo sat straighter, eyes fixed on Jeremy. "Do you think Tom can be broken the same way?" Jeremy hesitated before answering. "I don't know. I don't want to believe everyone breaks the same way. But if he's worse—ninety percent worse, like I said—then maybe we need something stronger than resolve." Ty exhaled slowly, considering. "Stronger doesn't mean louder. Sometimes stronger means steadier." Jeremy thought about this, turning the phrase over, and found his voice softer when he answered. "So, steadier. Not scattered leaves. A wall." Alex tapped the table once, the sound sharp in the quiet. "Then we build a wall," he said. "This time, before the swing. Before someone else carries scars we can't erase."

The library door clicked open, and Nico, Jasmin, and Sophie drifted in with books in their arms, their chatter dying when they sensed the heaviness in the room. They didn't ask what had been said, not yet, but the pause in their steps spoke volumes. Jeremy turned to them briefly and then back to the older boys. "Jarod's path was warnings ignored until they screamed," he said. "Tom's path… I think it's warnings whispered. And whispers can drown kids before anyone realises." Leo rubbed his temple, the old regret clear. "We missed the whispers last time. We can't miss them now." Ty's eyes narrowed just slightly, the weight of his father's lessons settling in his tone. "Then we listen harder than the silence."

Alex leaned across the table, his voice a low thread. "What if Tom doesn't want to be reached? What if he's not Jarod—what if he's worse?" Jeremy met his gaze, his small frame steady despite the weight. "Then we still stand. Even if it doesn't work, even if it breaks us, we stand. Because not standing is what gave Jarod room to grow." For a long moment, the three of them held that truth in the air, heavy and unmovable. The folded article under Jeremy's palm grew heavier still, the silent testimony of another boy who had not been saved. And in that silence, the question none of them wanted to ask pressed into the walls: was history about to repeat itself, or could this time be different?

Jeremy leaned back in his chair, legs barely touching the floor, his hands balled in his lap as if keeping something from spilling. His voice, usually clear, now came out in a tremble that carried through the quiet library. "I'm nine," he said, the words sharp but heavy. "How am I supposed to stand up to someone like Tom? He's taller, stronger… louder even when he's silent. I can feel it." Leo leaned forward, elbows on his knees, shaking his head slowly. "Don't measure yourself in inches, Jeremy. Courage doesn't care how tall you are." The words were kind, but Jeremy's eyes stayed fixed on the floor, doubt swimming in them like shadows under glass. He had seen what Tom carried in his silence, and it made even the memory of Jarod's old grin seem like child's play.

It was then that Jeremy turned, almost desperately, toward Jarod, who had been quiet on the edge of the group. "Jarod," he said, voice cracking but steady enough to be heard, "you changed. You know what it feels like to walk out of the darkness. What do we do with Tom?" The name made Jarod flinch, just slightly, as if a door from his past had been shoved open without warning.

For a long moment he didn't speak, his gaze fixed on the row of books lining the far wall. When he finally lifted his head, his expression was carved out of seriousness that none of the others had seen in him before. "You don't know him," Jarod said, his tone low, each word deliberate. "Not the way I do. Not the way I wish I didn't."

The silence that followed was jagged. Even Ty, who rarely let surprises register on his face, shifted in his seat. "What do you mean?" Leo asked cautiously, leaning closer. Jarod's eyes dropped, his fists tightening on his knees. "Tom wasn't just gone for a while," he said. "He was locked up. Juvenile detention. Kid jail." The words struck the table like dropped stones, and even Jeremy sat straighter, his breath catching. "What?" Jeremy whispered, almost as if saying it too loud might make it worse. Jarod nodded once, his jaw hard. "Nobody knows. Not the students, not the teachers, not even you, Ty. Only me. I knew him before he went in. And I know what he became in there."

The room pulled tighter, every student listening without daring to shift. "He wasn't just a bully," Jarod continued. "He was mean in ways that didn't make sense. Even the other kids at detention—kids who weren't scared of anything—were terrified of him. Some teachers were too. His temper… you can't measure it. It's not a storm, it's an explosion, and you don't always see the fuse." Alex exhaled sharply, shaking his head. "You're saying he's worse than you ever were?" Jarod met his eyes without hesitation. "Ninety percent worse. Maybe more. I pushed, I lied, I hurt people—but Tom? Tom doesn't stop. He doesn't think. His uncle made sure of that."

Jeremy blinked, confusion mixing with dread. "His uncle?" Jarod nodded grimly. "The one who trained him. Taught him how to use his strength like a weapon. Taught him that fear is respect, and pain is power. His parents… they're scared of him. Both of them. They don't control him. He controls them. That's what makes him different." The words hung, sharp and ugly, over the group, and Nico's hand fidgeted against the spine of a book as though trying to hold onto something steady. "So he's not just angry," Sophie whispered, her face pale. "He's dangerous."

Leo pressed his palm flat against the table, the grain digging into his skin as he tried to make sense of it. "Dangerous how?" Jarod's reply came fast, without hesitation. "He's thirteen, but his strength is closer to a twenty-year-old's. You can't push him, can't restrain him the way you could me. If he loses it, people get hurt." Ty's eyes sharpened at that, and for the first time he sat forward, shoulders squared. "Strength isn't everything," Ty said, but even he sounded cautious, as though measuring the challenge before him. Jarod looked at him directly. "It will be if no one stands against him. And you're the only one who can."

The declaration sat heavy in the room. Jeremy's heart pounded in his chest, his earlier words echoing louder in his head—I'm only nine. But now he saw the fear on faces older than his own, and something inside him twisted.

"Why didn't anyone say anything?" he asked, his voice strained. Jarod shook his head. "Because no one knows. Not the principal, not the teachers. I never told them. I thought maybe Tom would stay quiet. Maybe he'd change. But I can see now… I was wrong." The confession carried shame, but also urgency. For Jarod, silence had once been survival. Now, breaking it was the only way forward.

At the far side of the room, Principal Arnett had entered quietly, unnoticed by most, and stood just inside the door. His expression was grave as Jarod's words filled the space. He didn't interrupt, didn't reveal himself, but each word carved deeper into his responsibility. Juvenile detention. Trained by an uncle. Parents terrified of their own child. The pieces fit too neatly to ignore. When Jarod's voice faltered, Arnett turned and left without sound, heading back to his office with the knowledge heavy in his chest. If Jarod's words were true—and he suspected they were—then the school had been blindsided by a danger no one had prepared for.

Meanwhile, Jeremy's hands trembled against the article folded in his pocket. Myles' name pressed like a brand against his palm. He looked at Leo, at Alex, at Jarod, and then finally at Ty. "So what do we do?" he asked, and the question sounded far older than nine years. Leo leaned toward him, voice calm but urgent. "We don't run. We don't pretend we don't know. We stand. Just like with me, just like with Alex, just like with Jarod. We stand." Jeremy swallowed hard, his voice just above a whisper. "Even if it breaks us?" Leo nodded once, steady. "Especially then."

The room carried silence after that, but it wasn't empty. It was thick, a silence that carried the weight of confession, warning, and the edge of a battle none of them had chosen. And in the middle sat Jeremy—small, afraid, yet unwilling to look away.

Alex leaned back in his chair, arms crossed, his jaw set in that way he always had when he was trying not to sound like he cared too much. His eyes, however, betrayed him; they carried a nervous sharpness as they swept the group. "Listen," he said, his voice firm but low, "you need to understand something about bullies like Tom. They don't start at the top. They test the waters. They build up. And then, when they think no one's paying attention, that's when they snap." Jeremy frowned, his small hands pressed flat on the table as if to ground himself. "Snap how?" Alex's eyes met his, unwavering. "Snap in a way you can't take back. The kind that leaves someone on the ground before anyone knows what happened."

Leo shifted uncomfortably, rubbing the back of his neck. "Alex is right. I used to think I was tough, but even I never had that look Tom carries. It's the silence that gets you. He doesn't joke, he doesn't warn, he doesn't play. He waits. And then—" Alex cut in sharply, "—he follows." Jeremy blinked at him, his voice quiet. "Follows?" Alex leaned forward now, his voice dropping lower so only their small circle caught the weight of his words. "This morning, at recess, I saw him. He wasn't playing tag, wasn't kicking a ball. He was following a fifth grader, step for step. Not close enough to touch, but close enough that the kid kept glancing over his shoulder. And it wasn't playful."

The air in the library thickened. Sophie and Ella exchanged a look, their faces pale. Nico's hand tightened around his pencil until it almost snapped. Ty tilted his head, expression unreadable, though his eyes sharpened like blades catching light. "Did anyone else notice?" Ty asked. Alex shook his head firmly. "No. That's the problem. Everyone was too busy. Teachers chatting. Students distracted. I kept my eye on him because it didn't feel right. That wasn't a walk. It was a hunt." Jeremy's throat went dry, and he whispered, "So he's already choosing someone." Alex nodded once, his face grim. "He is."

Jarod's face tightened, his jaw clenching. "That's exactly how it starts," he muttered. "He watches, he circles, he finds the weak spot. He doesn't just lash out blind—he makes sure his target feels it first. The fear. The trap." Mila shifted uncomfortably, folding her arms. "That fifth grader… do we even know who it was?" Alex shook his head. "Didn't catch his name. Smaller boy, dark hair, nervous steps. Could've been any of them, really. But Tom noticed him. That's enough." Jeremy's stomach turned, the folded article in his pocket pressing harder against his side. Myles' story was right there, a reminder that silence and shadows were never innocent.

Leo spoke, his voice breaking the tension just slightly. "We can't panic. That's what he wants. Fear gives him ground to stand on." But Alex wasn't finished. His eyes swept across the group again, steady and cold. "Fear also tells us what's coming. And if you think Tom's silence means safety, you're wrong. It means he's getting closer to his breaking point. He hides behind it, waiting. And when it cracks—" He snapped his fingers sharply, the sound echoing in the quiet library. "—someone gets hurt." The room fell into stillness again, but the message was sharp enough to slice through every student listening.

Jeremy leaned toward Alex, his voice shaking but determined. "So what do we do? Watch him all the time? That's impossible." Alex's expression softened only slightly. "Not all the time. But enough. When you see patterns, when you see someone shadowing another like that, you don't ignore it. You say something. You act. That's the difference between a warning and a regret." Ty's gaze lingered on Alex, reading him, then nodded once in agreement. "That's why I watch shadows," he said quietly. "They tell the truth before people do." His words carried a calm weight, one that landed heavily on Jeremy's shoulders.

Mrs. Locke, standing a few feet away with a pile of returned books in her arms, glanced over, sensing the seriousness in the children's voices. She didn't interrupt, but her brow furrowed slightly, her teacher's instinct warning her that something larger than a schoolyard squabble was being whispered here. She moved on, though slower than before, keeping a discreet ear turned toward them. Meanwhile, Jeremy pressed his small fists against the table, frustration building. "Why does it always feel like we're already too late?" His voice cracked, and Leo quickly reached out, steadying him with a hand on his shoulder. "Because we know what to look for now," Leo said softly. "That's not being too late. That's being ready."

Alex leaned back again, his eyes narrowing. "Ready's good. But don't fool yourselves. Tom isn't like me. He isn't like Leo. We were cruel, but we still wanted attention, still wanted to be seen. Tom doesn't care. He wants control, and he'll take it however he can. And that makes him worse." Jeremy swallowed hard, his voice trembling. "Then we stop him before he gets to that fifth grader." Alex nodded firmly. "Exactly. Because once he chooses, once he breaks cover, there's no undoing the damage." The tension held, thick and suffocating, the knowledge that something dangerous was already moving through the hallways settling heavily on them all.

Even Jarod, who had once been the storm himself, looked shaken. "If he's already started shadowing, then he's closer than I thought," he said quietly. "He won't wait long." The group exchanged glances, the unspoken truth hanging in the air. Myles' name, though unsaid in that moment, pressed against Jeremy's thoughts like a warning bell. This was how it began—with whispers, with shadows, with teachers too distracted to notice. And Jeremy, nine years old but carrying more weight than he should, knew Alex was right. Silence was the mask before the explosion. And Tom's silence was deafening.

The library had been hushed only moments before, the sound of pages turning and pencils scratching filling the air with a steady rhythm. Mr. Clarke moved quietly among the rows, rearranging books and whispering a reminder now and then to keep the voices low. Jeremy sat with Leo, Alex, and Ty at the long table near the back, papers spread out before them, though no one was really working. They were watching, waiting, because the silence that Alex had described earlier carried a weight that was hard to ignore. And then it cracked open. The doors swung in sharply, and Tom stormed inside, muttering under his breath with a voice that carried even when he wasn't shouting. The sound of it alone broke the calm, each syllable edged with something sharper than anger—something dangerous.

The students lifted their heads one by one, shoulders tightening, backs straightening, every body in the room sensing the same shift. Jeremy caught Nico's wide eyes across the room, the boy frozen with his pencil mid-stroke, not daring to move. Jasmin leaned closer to Ella and Sophie, whispering something hurried that only they heard, but her face said everything: this was not normal. Tom's heavy steps echoed against the floorboards, each one deliberate, dragging the air with him like a stormcloud pressing into a summer sky. His eyes flicked left, then right, catching the glances that darted away as quickly as they had landed on him. He smirked—not with humour, but with menace—before slamming a hand down on the nearest table. The books jumped, and so did the students sitting there.

Jeremy felt the article in his pocket pressing again against his side, as though reminding him that this was exactly the kind of moment Myles' story was meant to warn against. He looked at Leo, who was watching Tom with narrowed eyes, his jaw tightening, his posture rigid as though he'd already decided to stand up if things worsened. Alex wasn't far behind, his hands clenched into fists under the table. But Ty was different. Ty did not tense, did not lean forward or back. His gaze locked onto Tom the moment he entered, sharp and steady, like a shadow hunter waiting for his prey to reveal itself. "He's unsettled," Ty said softly, almost to himself, but Jeremy heard it clearly. "Something broke before he even came in here."

Mr. Clarke approached cautiously, his calm, even voice carrying across the tense room. "Tom," he said gently, not raising his tone but grounding it, the way an adult sometimes does when testing if a storm will listen. "This is study hour. If you need to speak, I can step outside with you." Tom turned, eyes blazing, muttering words under his breath too quickly for anyone to catch, then louder: "I don't need anything from you." He shoved past a chair, the wooden legs scraping loudly across the floor. Mrs. Locke appeared from between the shelves at that moment, startled by the noise, her arms full of books. She froze, instantly aware of the tension hanging heavy in the air.

Mila whispered to Nico, her voice sharp with fear. "Why does it feel like he's looking for someone?" Nico didn't answer, but Jeremy did, though his words caught in his throat. "Because he is." Alex's words from earlier about the fifth grader replayed in his mind, each syllable hammering like a drumbeat. Tom's eyes flicked from table to table, pausing just long enough to make students drop their gaze. He didn't move toward the shelves or the tables of younger children yet—he lingered in the centre, his chest heaving with the kind of controlled fury that looked seconds away from erupting. It wasn't loud, not yet. But every heartbeat in the room was waiting for it.

Sophie tugged gently at Ella's sleeve, whispering, "Why doesn't someone stop him?" Ella whispered back, "Because no one knows how." Their exchange was short, quiet, but heavy with the helplessness every student felt in that moment. Ty's eyes never left Tom, his breathing even, his posture still. Leo leaned closer to Jeremy, muttering low. "It's the same look I used to wear. Like the world owed me something. Like hurting someone was the only way to remind myself I was strong." Jeremy's small voice replied, steady despite his fear. "But you changed. He hasn't. Not yet." Leo nodded, though his eyes stayed locked on Tom, the memory of his old self pressing against the reality of the boy storming before him.

Mrs. Haller entered through the side door just then, pausing as her eyes took in the tension. She knew something wasn't right, though no one had spoken above a whisper. The air itself was loud. "Back to work, everyone," she tried, but her voice trembled, betraying her concern. Tom turned toward her, his muttering cutting off, his silence heavier than before. He stared at her for a long second, long enough to make the entire row of students lower their heads again, waiting for whatever came next. Mr. Clarke moved another step closer, carefully placing himself between Tom and the rest of the class.

Ty spoke then, his voice calm but carrying just enough strength to slice the air in half. "Tom." The name itself hung like a warning. Tom's head jerked toward him, his eyes narrowing. The muttering returned, words spitting out like sparks, though still too broken to catch. Jeremy gripped the edge of the table tighter, his small hands trembling but steadying themselves with force. He had seen fear before, had felt it in moments when bullies circled, but this was different. This was fury without a leash, something deeper than teasing or intimidation. It was the silence Alex had described, now cracking wide open before their eyes.

Ella leaned into Jasmin, whispering, "Why's he so angry?" Jasmin shook her head, her voice hushed. "Because he doesn't want to be seen. But Ty sees him." The truth of it rang heavy. Tom hated being watched, hated the idea that anyone could read him, and Ty's steady gaze was slicing through his mask. Jeremy whispered again, mostly to himself, though Leo caught it. "This is how it starts. The silence, the muttering, the waiting. It's all the same." His words trembled with memory, with the image of Myles in his mind, though he never spoke the name aloud in that moment. Leo placed a hand firmly on his arm, steadying him, grounding him the same way Jeremy always did for him.

Mr. Arnett stepped into the library just then, his presence filling the doorway like an anchor dropped in a storm. His sharp eyes scanned the scene quickly: the tense students, the rigid teachers, Tom's heaving chest. He didn't speak yet, but his silence wasn't like Tom's. It was control, authority, a reminder that someone was watching with intent. Tom noticed it instantly, his muttering faltering for just a second. But that second was enough to confirm what everyone already knew. Something was about to happen. And when it did, the room would never be the same.

The moment arrived without a breath of warning. Tom's muttering stopped mid-sentence, silence crashing down like the pause before thunder. Then, with a sudden roar of movement, his hands seized a wooden chair and flung it across the library. The crack of wood against the floor and table rang like a gunshot, and the air erupted into screams. The chair missed Nico by less than a foot, splintering the calm into chaos. Books leapt from their piles, scattering like startled birds, some sliding across the floor, others thudding against walls. Students bolted from their seats, their bodies colliding in the narrow aisles, panic feeding panic until the noise was deafening.

Ella clutched Sophie's arm, pulling her down low behind a row of shelves, her breath sharp and shallow. "He nearly hit Nico!" she gasped, her voice trembling. Nico stood frozen, staring at the wreckage where the chair had landed, his face pale and eyes wide, unable to step away. Jasmin darted toward him, yanking at his sleeve. "Move, Nico! Please move!" Her shout cracked with desperation, and only then did he stumble backward, his legs nearly buckling beneath him. The chaos swelled, young voices breaking into cries that echoed far beyond the library walls.

Jeremy felt the air hammering in his chest as though the strike had been aimed for him, the noise of it all drowning his thoughts. He ducked down, pressing himself close to Leo's side. "He wasn't aiming," Jeremy whispered, his small voice trembling. "That means he doesn't care who it hits." Leo's jaw tightened, his eyes following Tom's every step. "That makes it worse," Leo muttered, his hand gripping the edge of the table, ready to push himself forward. Alex hissed beside him, his tone sharp. "Don't rush in. You'll only make it bigger." But Leo's eyes betrayed the storm brewing in his chest, a storm he was trying to leash for Jeremy's sake.

Mr. Clarke was the first adult to move. He lunged across the room, arms spread in a firm attempt to corral Tom before the boy could reach another chair. "Enough!" he shouted, his voice breaking across the chaos. But Tom spun sharply, his face blazing with fury, his fists clenched. Mrs. Locke abandoned her stack of books, rushing to Mr. Clarke's side. "Stay back!" she barked to the students, her voice cutting through the screams. They scattered toward the corners, huddling behind shelves and tables, some pressing their hands over their ears to drown out the sound, others simply crying quietly where they crouched.

Mila's voice cracked as she huddled against Jasmin and Sophie. "They said in the paper—four students in hospital. Six blocks from here. Everyone saw it this morning." Her words trembled into the air like a curse. "It could happen here too." Jasmin pulled her closer, whispering, "Not if Ty steps in. Not if he does what he always does." But her eyes betrayed fear, because even she knew this was different. This wasn't a game of shoves in the hallway or sneers at recess. This was violence breaking open in a place meant to be safe.

Ty stood motionless at the far end of the room, his gaze locked on Tom with an intensity that froze the air. His calm, steady breathing was the opposite of Tom's ragged fury. "He's beyond listening right now," Ty said under his breath, though those nearest him heard it clearly. "But that doesn't mean he's beyond stopping." Jeremy turned toward him, his voice cracking with urgency. "Then stop him, Ty! Please!" Ty's eyes narrowed slightly, his posture unshifting. "Not yet. If I move too soon, it'll only feed his fire. Let him show his hand fully."

Meanwhile, Tom seized another chair, dragging it across the floor, the legs screeching like metal against glass. He raised it above his head, his chest heaving, eyes scanning the room as if daring someone to move. Mr. Arnett stepped forward now, his voice sharp, commanding, honed by years of authority. "Put it down, Tom!" The sound cracked like a whip, pulling even the panicked students into silence for a breath. Tom sneered, spitting words that none could decipher, then slammed the chair back onto the ground, the wood rattling the very floor beneath them. He kicked it aside with one violent strike, sending it skidding into a shelf, books tumbling down in cascades.

Jeremy squeezed Leo's arm tightly, whispering hoarsely. "This is worse than Jarod ever was." Leo nodded once, his jaw firm. "Jarod scared us with words. Tom terrifies us with silence and rage." Jarod himself stood near the back wall, his face pale, lips pressed into a thin line. He had once been the shadow that frightened others, but even he now looked shaken, as if seeing in Tom something he never wished to become. He leaned toward Alex, whispering low. "You don't know him like I do. If he's not stopped now, someone's going to leave this room in an ambulance." Alex stared at him, his face grim, but said nothing.

Mrs. Dunlop arrived at the doorway, her eyes widening at the chaos, her voice sharp as she called out, "Evacuate the younger ones! Now!" Teachers quickly herded children toward the back exits, but not fast enough for Jeremy's comfort.

He could see Tom's eyes scanning again, searching, restless, unfocused, but filled with a raw hunger to strike. "He doesn't even know who he wants to hurt," Jeremy whispered to Leo, his heart pounding. Leo's hand pressed firm on his shoulder, grounding him. "That's the most dangerous kind," he said. "The ones who don't care where the damage lands."

Tom roared suddenly, the sound reverberating against the library walls, and shoved another chair onto its side. The legs snapped with the impact, one jagged piece of wood spinning across the floor. Nico yelped as it skittered close to his shoes. Jeremy flinched, his breath catching in his throat. He looked at Ty, waiting, hoping, desperate for the boy to move. But Ty stood unmoving still, eyes like steel, his every sense honed in. "Almost," Ty murmured, his words lost to the air but clear to himself. "Not yet. But almost."

The library was no longer a place of learning. It had become a battleground, every corner filled with trembling voices and wide, frightened eyes. And in the centre of it all stood Tom, wild, furious, his shadow stretching long across the wooden floor, ready to fall upon whoever dared move next.

Mr. Clarke lunged first, his arms wide as though he could catch Tom by sheer force of will. Mrs. Locke followed close, her voice sharp as a blade cutting through the noise. "Put it down! That's enough!" she barked, but Tom spun, his shoulder slamming into Mr. Clarke with the force of a battering ram. The older man stumbled backward, colliding with a desk that groaned under the impact before toppling. Papers flew like startled doves, drifting to the floor in chaos. Mrs. Locke reached for Tom's arm, only to be flung aside as he twisted, her glasses sliding off her face as she caught herself against the edge of a shelf. The students gasped, some screaming anew, others frozen in stunned silence.

Desks scraped across the floor as Tom pushed them aside, his raw strength tearing the room apart faster than the teachers could react. A heavy dictionary toppled from the shelf and struck the ground with a thud, echoing through the tension. Older students—ones nearly as tall as Tom—hovered at the edges, fists clenched, yet none dared step forward. Fear pinned them in place, their muscles locked with the knowledge that stepping in might mean a broken nose or worse. Even Alex, who had faced fists before, bit down hard on his lip, his body leaning forward but never crossing the invisible line of terror.

Principal Arnett strode into the fray, his presence commanding silence even amid the screams. His voice boomed with the authority of years in service: "Stand back!" The teachers froze, even Mrs. Locke pausing mid-motion, breathing heavily, strands of hair clinging to her damp face. Arnett's gaze swung to Ty, sharp and unyielding, a silent command behind the words that followed. "Now, Ty. Do what you were trained for. End this before someone is hurt." The words cut through the air, and every eye in the room shifted to the quiet boy who had been standing so still.

Ty stepped forward, his calm movements in stark contrast to the storm raging around him. His eyes locked on Tom, who spun toward him with a growl, fury radiating from every muscle. "Stay back!" Tom bellowed, his voice cracking with rage. But Ty's voice was calm, low, measured, the tone of a boy who had seen storms before. "I'm not here to hurt you," he said, moving with deliberate slowness. "I'm here to stop you." His hands lifted slightly, open palms, yet his feet slid into a stance so subtle only his father watching from the doorway recognized its discipline.

Tom lunged, his fist swinging like a hammer meant to crush whatever it struck. Ty shifted barely an inch, his shoulder rolling away from the strike, and in that instant his fingers pressed sharply into a nerve along Tom's arm. Tom's body jerked, the punch faltering mid-motion as though his strength had been stolen. Ty stepped in close, his hand striking another point along Tom's side, then a third along the back of his neck. Each motion was fluid, precise, trained—not the wild thrash of a fight, but the controlled discipline of a boy schooled in ancient skill.

Tom staggered back, his eyes wide in shock. His breath hitched as a strange numbness spread through his arm, then down into his legs. "What—what did you do to me?" he spat, his voice breaking into panic. He tried to raise his fist again, but it trembled, sluggish, refusing to obey his fury. Ty's eyes never wavered, his voice steady as stone. "You can still breathe. You can still move. But you can't hurt anyone else." The room, still buzzing with fear, fell quieter now, the students staring in disbelief at the sight of the strongest bully they had ever seen stumbling like a puppet with cut strings.

Mrs. Locke caught her breath, adjusting her glasses with shaking fingers as she watched Tom falter. Mr. Clarke pushed himself up from the toppled desk, his chest heaving, his eyes wide with both fear and relief. "Dear Lord," he whispered under his breath, though no one paid him mind. The students shifted slowly from their hiding places, their eyes huge, mouths parted in shock. They had expected fists to clash, expected blood or bruises, but what they saw was stranger—a battle fought with precision, ending without a blow ever truly landing.

Jeremy clutched Leo's arm so tightly that his knuckles whitened, his young voice barely audible. "He… he stopped him. Just like that." Leo, his jaw set firm, nodded once, his voice low. "That's why Ty's different. He doesn't fight with anger. He fights with control." Alex leaned in, his eyes darting between Ty and Tom. "I've never seen anyone shut someone down like that. Not even adults. Ty… he's eleven. And Tom looks like he could break through walls." His words carried awe, but also unease, for power like that held weight far heavier than most could understand.

Tom staggered again, his legs betraying him, the strength he relied on slipping away with each step. His chest heaved, his breaths sharp, furious, but his fists no longer obeyed his rage. The paralyzing tingles spread like a current, stealing his dominance inch by inch. His eyes blazed at Ty, filled with fury and fear all at once. "You can't do this to me! You don't get to stop me!" he shouted, though his words rang hollow, his voice cracking. Ty stepped closer, his presence calm, unshaken, and whispered back, "I already did."

The silence that followed was deafening. Students stared, wide-eyed, their fear mingling with something else—relief, respect, awe. Teachers slowly stepped forward again, their movements cautious, as though afraid that breaking the stillness might reignite Tom's fury. Principal Arnett's eyes lingered on Ty, the weight of responsibility heavy in his stare, yet he gave the boy a single firm nod. The moment had been dangerous, wild, close to disaster, but the storm had been stayed, if only for a moment. And in that silence, every student understood: this battle was far from over, but they had just seen the first sign of how it could be fought.

Jeremy's small hands clenched into fists at his sides, though he knew they were useless against the storm raging only feet away. His eyes followed Tom's thrashing frame, the toppled desks, the gasps of frightened students pressed against the shelves, yet his legs wouldn't move. His mind screamed to run, to push through the doorway and find safety in the hallway, but his body betrayed him, frozen as though rooted to the floor. His breath came shallow, his heart hammering in his chest, every beat loud in his ears like the pounding of a drum. The weight of fear pressed down on him, heavier than anything he had carried in his short nine years.

Leo's voice cut through the noise like a lifeline. "Jeremy, listen to me. Don't run. Walk. Slowly. Like it's just another day." His hand brushed Jeremy's shoulder, steady and firm, grounding him in the moment. Jeremy turned his wide eyes up to his brother, and though fear still gripped him, he nodded faintly. He could hear the chaos still, the sharp commands of Mr. Arnett, the rustle of teachers trying to regain control, but Leo's calm tone anchored him in the storm. Jeremy knew Leo had lived through fear before—fear of fists, fear of anger—and if Leo said walk, then that's what had to be done.

Jeremy swallowed hard, his throat dry, his lips parting with effort. He shifted one foot back, testing his balance, and then another, each movement stiff and deliberate. His mind screamed to hurry, to bolt for the door, but he forced himself to obey Leo's command. "One step at a time," he whispered under his breath, the words so soft they were only for him. Each step away from the chaos felt like climbing a mountain, but still he moved, his small frame steady against the invisible weight that tried to hold him still.

Nico's whisper reached him next, sharp and urgent but quiet enough to avoid Tom's notice. "Don't look at him, Jeremy. Just keep walking. Eyes forward." Jeremy obeyed, fixing his gaze on the doorway, the sliver of light spilling from the hallway like a beacon. He felt Tom's presence like a shadow pressing at his back, but he did not turn. Each desk he passed, each student crouched low in fear, became part of a tunnel that led him out. His steps slowed the pounding in his chest, turning terror into resolve.

As he neared the door, Mrs. Locke's voice rose again, firm and strained. "Everyone stay calm! Keep low!" She caught sight of Jeremy, her eyes wide with a mixture of fear and pride. He was only nine, yet here he was, walking as though he had been told this was a drill, not a moment of crisis. Her lips tightened, but she gave the faintest nod, an unspoken encouragement that he was doing the right thing. Jeremy's fingers brushed against the frame of the door, the cool wood beneath his palm grounding him again.

Outside, the hallway stretched empty and silent, the echo of chaos muffled now behind the library doors. Jeremy exhaled, a long breath he hadn't realized he'd been holding. His knees trembled, threatening to buckle, but he forced them straight, remembering Leo's words. He didn't sprint. He didn't collapse. He walked, steady and deliberate, until he reached the wall and leaned against it, his forehead pressing into the cool paint. His hands finally unclenched, the ache in his knuckles sharp now that the immediate danger was behind him.

Leo's voice echoed in his memory—walk, don't run. The wisdom of that instruction sank deep into his chest. Running would have drawn eyes, drawn Tom's fury. Walking meant calm, meant control, even if fear still boiled beneath the surface. Jeremy closed his eyes and breathed, each breath deeper than the last, until the pounding in his chest dulled into a steady thrum. He wasn't free of fear, but he had not let fear control him. And for a nine-year-old boy, that truth carried a weight he could not ignore.

When Leo and Alex slipped out moments later, their faces pale but determined, they found Jeremy standing straight, his fists unclenched, his jaw tight. Leo gave him a small nod, a silent approval only brothers could share. Alex's voice, quieter than usual, carried something closer to respect. "Not many grown men could've done what you just did, Jeremy. You didn't run. That means something." Jeremy didn't answer, his voice still caught somewhere between fear and pride, but the faintest spark lit in his chest. He had been tested, and though he trembled still, he had not broken.

Behind the doors, Tom's voice roared again, mingled with Ty's steady tones, the clash of chaos and calm locked in battle. Jeremy pressed his ear to the wall, listening, his small frame trembling with the knowledge that this was far from over. But for now, he had obeyed, he had survived, and he had shown a kind of courage that even he hadn't known he carried. And as his breath steadied, one thought pulsed steady in his mind: courage didn't always look like fists or shouts—it sometimes looked like walking away, one calm step at a time.

Jeremy pressed his back against the wall, the faint vibration of Tom's rage still trembling through the air, when Leo bent low beside him. His brother's breath was quick, but his voice was sharp and clear, cutting through the fear like a blade. "This is your moment, Jeremy. Decide who you're going to be." The words landed heavy, not as a command but as a truth Jeremy could not avoid. For a moment, his nine-year-old body wanted to shrink, to let others carry the weight, but something in Leo's eyes held him steady. Beside him, Jarod stood solid, his hand resting on Jeremy's shoulder, not pushing him forward, not pulling him back—just anchoring him. The cycle of fear and violence pressed on every side, and Jeremy knew it would either swallow him or force him to stand taller.

Jarod's low voice rumbled with the certainty of someone who had walked this path before. "You don't have to do it alone," he said, his gaze locked on the doors ahead. "I'm right here, every step." Jeremy glanced at him, remembering all the times Jarod had once been the storm in these halls, the one others feared.

But now, the boy who had nearly destroyed so much stood at his side, calm, watchful, ready to lend his strength. It wasn't just words—it was living proof that change was possible. Jeremy's chest tightened, not from fear now but from the weight of choice. This wasn't about fists or running. It was about whether he would speak, whether he would refuse to let Tom's shadow consume the school the way others once had.

Leo leaned closer, his voice quieter, almost a whisper for Jeremy's ears alone. "If you walk away, nothing changes. If you step forward, even if your voice shakes, you break the cycle." Jeremy's breath caught, and his small fists clenched again, not with panic this time but with resolve building in his bones. He could hear the clash of desks, the sharp call of Mr. Clarke trying to restore order, the steady, measured tone of Ty facing the storm inside. Yet in that hallway, everything narrowed to this moment, this choice. Jarod shifted slightly, standing at Jeremy's back like a shield, and Jeremy felt his own spine straighten.

Nico, peeking out from behind a row of lockers, whispered sharply, "Jeremy, you don't have to prove anything!" His voice cracked with worry, but Jeremy shook his head slowly. "Yes, I do. Not to anyone else. To myself." His voice surprised even him, steady despite the storm still pounding in his chest. He glanced up at Leo, then over his shoulder at Jarod, and saw the faintest glimmer of pride in their eyes. No one could make the decision for him. The library door loomed ahead, the shouting behind it louder now, but Jeremy no longer looked at it with the eyes of a child about to flee. He looked at it as a wall he would not allow to stand.

Leo's whisper returned, urgent but gentle. "Then do it, Jeremy. Walk back in. Speak. Show him you won't be silenced." Jarod's hand tightened briefly on Jeremy's shoulder, a wordless promise that he would not be left to face it alone. Together, the three of them stood just outside the threshold, the chaos mere feet away, the choice pressing heavier by the second. Jeremy inhaled deeply, the folded newspaper article about Myles tucked in his pocket brushing against his fingers, a reminder of the truth he had carried since that first chapter. If no one stood, the story would repeat itself. He could not allow that.

And so, with Leo's words still burning in his ears and Jarod's steady presence like a wall of protection at his back, Jeremy set his jaw and placed his hand on the door. His voice did not tremble when he spoke, though his body quaked. "I know who I'm going to be," he whispered, the words meant for himself but carrying out into the hall nonetheless. Leo and Jarod exchanged a glance, silent but certain. In that instant, Jeremy's choice was made—not just to survive this moment but to stand in it, to claim it, and to become the kind of boy who refused to let fear dictate the fate of his friends.

Jeremy's voice cracked as he spun toward Leo and Alex, urgency etched into every syllable. "Ty has to step in. He's the only one who can do it. If anyone's going to stop Tom before he breaks someone, it has to be Ty." His small fists clenched as though holding onto a rope for dear life, eyes darting from one friend to the other, demanding agreement.

Leo hesitated, biting his lip, but Alex frowned, arms crossed. "Jeremy, Ty isn't a weapon. He's a person. Do you even understand what you're asking of him?" Jeremy shook his head sharply, almost stomping his foot, desperation bleeding into his tone. "I'm not asking him to fight. I'm asking him to stop what's coming. None of us can stand against Tom. Ty is the only one who can."

Ty, standing at the edge of the chaos, shifted his weight and finally looked back at them. His dark eyes carried no fear, only a depth of knowing that cut deeper than Jeremy's frantic pleas. "You think I can stop him because I know how to move faster than he does. Because I can press the right nerves and force his body down." His voice stayed calm, but there was steel beneath it. "But you don't understand. Tom isn't like Jarod. Jarod could be reasoned with. Tom's mind… it's fractured. He doesn't only need discipline or restraint. He needs something no school, no classroom, can give him. He needs to be locked away somewhere safe—for his sake, and everyone else's." The words landed heavier than the toppled desks still rattling on the library floor.

Jeremy's chest tightened, eyes widening at the blunt honesty. "An institution?" The word burned in his mouth. "Like—like a prison?" Ty shook his head slowly. "Not prison. But not freedom either. A place where doctors can help him. Where he can't hurt anyone else. His uncle trained him to break people, Jeremy. That's not something you talk out of a boy in the middle of math class." His voice sharpened just slightly as his gaze flickered to Leo and Alex. "You two should understand. You know what rage looks like when it's been fed. Tom's rage is fed by more than playground grudges. It's bred into him."

Leo looked at his shoes, the truth cutting deeper than he wanted to admit. Alex's jaw tightened. "You mean he can't change?" Ty's silence lasted too long, but finally he spoke again, quieter this time. "I mean he can't change here. Not like this. Not in a place with so many to hurt and so many to fear him." The weight of the words made Jeremy's knees wobble. His dream of standing tall, of saving Tom the way Leo and Jarod had once been saved, bent under the force of reality. Still, Jeremy's stubborn heart refused to yield completely. "But we can't just give up on him." His whisper trembled, defiant even as his eyes watered.

Jarod stepped forward then, his voice heavy with memory. "Jeremy, you wanted my truth. Here it is. Tom was feared even in juvie. Bigger kids wouldn't go near him. Teachers avoided him. They couldn't restrain him. He doesn't just lash out—he plans it. He wants control. That's worse than I ever was." The words turned Jeremy cold, but they carried the kind of conviction only someone who had lived through it could share. Mr. Arnett, listening quietly from the doorway, rubbed his forehead with a hand that shook faintly. His eyes shifted from Ty to Jarod, weighing both accounts against the reality he knew he would have to face as principal.

The room seemed smaller now, air tight and suffocating. Jeremy's voice cracked again as he pushed against the weight pressing him down. "But he's still just a kid." Ty crouched low so his eyes met Jeremy's, steady as stone.

"So were the others he hurt, Jeremy. So was Myles." The name dropped like a stone into water, the ripples stretching through every face in the room. Jeremy's breath hitched, the article's folded corner digging into his pocket like a thorn. He wanted to fight back, to say something that could undo the inevitability of Ty's truth, but the words refused to come.

Instead, Leo placed a hand on Jeremy's back, grounding him. "It doesn't mean we stop caring about him," he said softly. "It just means we stop pretending we can fix what's broken beyond us." Alex nodded grimly. "If Ty's right, then the best way we protect everyone—including Tom—is by making sure he gets taken somewhere safe." Jeremy blinked at the word safe, hating how it sounded more like exile than protection. But when his eyes fell back to Ty, he saw no malice there, only a boy who had already measured the weight of violence too many times for his young age.

The argument fell into silence then, broken only by the distant echo of a chair leg skidding across the floor. Outside, students whispered nervously, waiting for the verdict none of them wanted to name. Ty finally stood tall again, his shoulders squared like a boy carrying a man's burden. "I'll do what I can right now. But don't mistake this—I can't cure him. All I can do is make sure no one else bleeds today." Jeremy nodded slowly, the fight draining from his eyes, though his heart still screamed against the truth. It was not the ending he wanted, not the hope he clung to—but it was the only path forward.

Ty stood with his arms folded across his chest, his expression calm but unreadable, the kind of quiet that carried more weight than shouting ever could. The others looked to him as if he already held the answer in his hands, but he shook his head slowly, refusing to let their hope tie itself too tightly to him. "You want me to step in," he said, his voice steady but firm, "but you don't understand what that means. Breaking through Tom's rage isn't like holding back a shove or dodging a fist. When someone's anger runs this deep, you don't just risk yourself—you risk everyone in the room." His eyes swept across Jeremy, Leo, Alex, and then Jarod, each of them frozen under his gaze. "If I try and fail, someone is going to get hurt. Maybe worse."

Jeremy opened his mouth to argue, but Ty raised a hand, stopping him before the words even formed. "Listen. Jarod could be reached. I knew he could, because underneath the anger was fear, guilt, and a need for someone to pull him back. Tom doesn't give those signs. Not yet. All I see in him is pressure building with nowhere safe to go. If I make the wrong move, if I push him too hard, he won't crumble—he'll explode. And when he does, the people closest to him will pay the price." The library air thickened around his words, a silence no one wanted to break.

Leo frowned, trying to anchor Ty with the conviction he always leaned on. "But you've done it before, Ty. You broke through Jarod. You stopped fights before they went too far. You've trained for this your whole life." Ty's jaw tightened, but he did not soften. "And every time, it was a gamble. You think I'm fearless, but I'm not. Every fight could end with someone on the floor who doesn't get back up. You all believe I can just switch something off in Tom. But what if I can't? What if I push too far and it becomes another tragedy that no one here can erase?"

The weight of his words landed hard, and Jeremy's shoulders slumped as though the air had been stolen from his lungs. Ty crouched down then, looking Jeremy directly in the eye. "You remember what you said about Myles?" The boy's name alone silenced even the soft shuffling of feet around them. Ty's voice dropped lower, almost a whisper. "Do you understand what it means if I fail? It means we could be standing in a hallway one day, just like those teachers back then, too late to save someone. Another child. Another story told too late. Another Myles Neuts." Jeremy's chest tightened, his eyes stinging as the meaning struck deeper than he wanted to admit.

Alex rubbed the back of his neck, his usual boldness gone. "So you're saying we just stand back and wait for Tom to do something?" His voice carried frustration, but Ty shook his head again. "No. I'm saying you need to understand the cost. Intervention isn't a game. It isn't just stepping in like some hero in a story. It means risking blood on the floor, maybe worse than bruises. It means if I'm wrong, there won't be time to undo it." His hand pressed lightly against the table beside him, steadying himself as though the truth itself was heavy to carry.

Jarod stepped forward, arms crossed tight. "Ty's right. Tom isn't like me. I had a line I wouldn't cross, even when I was at my worst. I didn't want to see someone die. Tom doesn't have that line. He'd drag anyone down with him if it meant proving he was stronger." The others shifted uncomfortably, Jarod's words echoing the tension already coiling in their minds. Jeremy's small hands clenched at his sides, but his voice wavered. "So what are we supposed to do? Just let him keep scaring everyone? Let him throw chairs and hurt people until someone gets carted away?" His frustration spilled out, but Ty didn't flinch.

"I'm saying," Ty replied quietly, "that we plan with our eyes open. That we stop pretending Tom is just another angry kid. He isn't. He's dangerous, and not just because he's bigger or stronger. He's dangerous because he doesn't care what happens next. That's the kind of storm you can't just walk into without being ready to get torn apart." His calmness cut sharper than shouting could have, each word deliberate, each syllable an anchor in the storm. "If I move too quickly, if I try to break through when he isn't ready to listen, we'll end up with another headline no one here ever wants to read."

Nico, who had been silent until now, finally found his voice. "So you're saying this could get as bad as that story? As bad as Myles?" His tone was hushed, but it carried the weight of the unspoken fear everyone else shared. Ty's eyes softened, but his reply was mercilessly honest. "Yes. If we're not careful, it could be exactly that. A boy cornered, a room too late, teachers helpless. And no one is ready for that—not you, not me, not the school." The truth hung between them like smoke, choking and undeniable.

Jeremy's heart hammered against his ribs, but his voice cracked through the silence. "Then what do we do, Ty? If you won't act, who will?" Ty rose to his full height, his shoulders squared, his eyes steady on Jeremy's trembling form.

"I will. But not until I know I can do it without pushing him over the edge. That's the difference. It's not about being brave—it's about being careful enough to make sure no one pays the price of my mistake." He glanced around the room, letting every student and teacher present feel the gravity in his words. "Because I won't let this school become another story whispered the way Myles's is. Not on my watch."

The silence that followed was heavier than shouting, heavier than fear. And though Jeremy hated every word, he knew Ty's reluctance wasn't weakness—it was the kind of strength that understood the cost of getting it wrong.

Jeremy stood straighter than usual, his small frame trembling but his voice steady, as though every word had been carved out of the silence that Ty had left hanging in the air. "If no one does anything," he said, his tone sharper than his age suggested, "Tom will never stop. He'll keep breaking chairs, he'll keep scaring kids, and he'll keep hurting people until one of us is gone." The room hushed, even the teachers who had been whispering fell silent, watching the nine-year-old speak with the conviction of someone far older. "You think you're protecting us by waiting," he pressed, eyes locked on Ty, "but waiting won't save anyone. It just gives Tom more time to make someone else's smile break."

Ty exhaled, calm but guarded, and started to shake his head, but Jeremy raised a hand, mimicking the same motion Ty had used earlier. "No, let me finish," Jeremy insisted, his small fists clenched at his sides. "I don't want Tom destroyed, Ty. I don't want him locked away forever if there's another way. I just want him helped. Even if that means he can't stay in this school, even if that means he has to go somewhere else, I don't care. What I care about is that he has a better life than the one he's living right now. Someone has to stop him before he stops himself. And you're the only one who can do it." His blunt honesty cut through the air, leaving no one in doubt that the words came from his heart and nowhere else.

Leo shifted in his seat, watching his younger brother with something between pride and fear. "Jeremy," he muttered, almost warning, but the boy shook his head. "I know what I'm saying," Jeremy replied firmly, his voice breaking with raw emotion but never softening. "I've seen this before. I saw it in Leo, when he thought no one could love him. I saw it in Alex, when he tried to hide behind lies. I saw it in Lisa and Harley, when they thought fists and anger could hide their pain. And I saw it in Jarod, when he was so close to becoming something he never wanted to be." He turned his gaze back to Ty, his eyes burning. "I've seen too many of you saved to believe Tom can't be. But not if we wait. Not if we just sit here and hope."

Alex leaned forward, nodding slowly, his usual arrogance humbled by Jeremy's fire. "He's right, Ty. We were all a mess, every one of us. And it took someone younger, smaller, and braver than us to pull us back." His words echoed through the classroom, drawing murmurs from students who remembered their own wounds. Jarod stepped closer, his presence silent but powerful, his eyes flicking from Ty to Jeremy. "If he could save me," Jarod said quietly, "then maybe he can save Tom too. But only if you step in, Ty. Because none of us can do what you can." His voice carried no pride, only the heavy truth of lived experience.

Jeremy's fists trembled harder now, his breath uneven, but he pressed forward, speaking with the same brutal honesty he had used the day he stood in front of Leo to protect him. "Do it for Myles Neuts," he said, his voice breaking at the name but refusing to falter. The sound of the boy's name silenced every shuffle, every breath in the room. Jeremy's words sharpened with grief and determination. "He didn't get saved. Nobody stood in front of him. Nobody stepped up in time. And now his story is all we have left. Don't let Tom's story end the same way. Do it in memory of Myles, so no one here has to see that happen again."

Ty's eyes narrowed, his calm expression cracking at the edges as Jeremy's plea pierced deeper than he wanted to admit. He turned away for a moment, staring at the bookshelves that lined the library, as though the answers might be written in their spines. His silence stretched long, but Jeremy didn't waver. "You tell us to see the signs," Jeremy continued, his voice rising in a way that startled even the teachers. "Well, we see them, Ty. We see Tom the same way we once saw Leo, Alex, Lisa, Harley, and Jarod. The only difference is, if we ignore them now, it's not just Tom who's going to pay the price. It's one of us. And I won't let that happen. Not again."

Nico stepped forward hesitantly, his usual quiet voice barely louder than a whisper. "Jeremy's right. If we don't do anything, Tom will just get worse." Ella nodded, her hand clutching Sophie's tightly. "We can't let another Myles happen. Not here." Their voices joined Jeremy's, building a chorus of agreement that filled the air, pulling even the hesitant into the weight of the moment. The students looked at Ty, their faces pale but determined, waiting for his answer.

Mr. Clarke cleared his throat quietly, his voice solemn. "Jeremy speaks the truth, Ty. We failed Myles once. I don't want to see another boy lost because we hesitated. You're right to be cautious. But maybe he's right too—waiting won't save us." His words gave weight to Jeremy's plea, showing the adults were no less haunted by the truth. Mrs. Dunlop wiped her eyes quietly at her desk, and Mr. Arnett leaned against the wall, his face pale as though Jeremy's words had struck deeper than any lecture ever could.

Jeremy looked back at Ty one last time, his voice no louder than a whisper but heavy with resolve. "If you can't do it for us, then do it for him. Do it for Myles. Because if his story meant anything, it should mean that no other kid dies because we were too afraid to try." His words hung in the air, heavier than any silence before, demanding an answer Ty wasn't sure he could give.

The library had not yet settled from Jeremy's plea when Leo leaned in close, his hand resting firmly on his younger brother's shoulder. "You're right, Jeremy," he said, his tone measured, "but we have to be smart. We can't just run at Tom and hope he listens. That will only drive him deeper into his rage." Alex folded his arms, pacing in a tight circle before adding, "We don't fight him, we don't corner him. We surround him. Not with fists, but with presence. If he tries to break the world apart, he'll have to look every one of us in the eye and see that we won't let him." The words seemed to steady Jeremy, who nodded quickly, eager but trembling. Ty watched the exchange quietly, the lines in his young face betraying a maturity carved out of discipline and long practice.

Jarod stepped closer, his voice low but determined. "I know Tom. He doesn't back down from strength, but he does freeze when he realises he can't scare someone. If we stand there together, not budging, not afraid, then maybe he'll feel that wall and not know what to do." He clenched his fists, but Jeremy caught the motion and shook his head. "No fists, Jarod. Just stand with us. That's the plan." It was a strange picture—boys who had once been bullies themselves now speaking about unity, about drawing a line with courage instead of violence. The younger students watched in silence, their faces pale but wide-eyed, understanding that something real was forming in front of them, something more than just another lecture about "being nice."

Mr. Arnett, standing near the doorway, listened carefully, his arms folded across his chest. His stern gaze swept across the room, then dropped onto Jeremy, who had become the unlikely centre of all of it. "Jeremy," he said, his voice deep but calm, "if you're going to stand in this, you need to know exactly what you're up against. I won't allow you to walk into this blind." His words made Jeremy's stomach twist, but the boy lifted his chin anyway. "Then tell me," he said bluntly, "because I'd rather face it than pretend it doesn't exist." The room shifted again, teachers exchanging wary glances, but Mr. Arnett didn't look away. Instead, he reached for his office key and gestured for Jeremy to follow.

The corridor was quiet as the principal led Jeremy away, with Leo, Alex, and Ty trailing close behind. When they entered the office, the blinds were drawn, the air heavier than before. Mr. Arnett pressed a button on the intercom, summoning Tom's parents to join them. Jeremy sat uneasily, his small hands folded tightly in his lap, watching the principal move with a deliberate weight that spoke of secrets too heavy for ordinary classrooms. Ty stood at his side, silent but protective, while Leo whispered quietly, "Stay steady, Jeremy. You wanted the truth. You'll get it now."

When Tom's parents arrived, they looked worn and hollow, as though years of exhaustion had been carved into their faces. His mother's eyes darted nervously around the room, while his father's shoulders slumped, his gaze fixed on the floor. Mr. Arnett wasted no time. "We're not here for pleasantries," he said firmly. "We're here because your son nearly hurt someone badly today, and because Jeremy has asked to help him. Before I allow that, he needs to know who Tom really is." Jeremy's stomach flipped, but he didn't look away. He braced himself, gripping the edge of his chair.

Tom's mother finally spoke, her voice trembling. "You don't understand what it's like at home. We… we're terrified of him." The confession fell into the air like a stone into still water, sending ripples across the room. Jeremy's eyes widened, but he forced himself to remain calm. "Terrified of your own son?" he whispered, but the woman nodded quickly, her eyes filling with tears. "He isn't just angry, Jeremy. He destroys things. He breaks doors off their hinges, he's thrown knives, he screams until the walls shake. And it isn't always when he's provoked. Sometimes… sometimes it's for no reason at all."

Her husband added quietly, his voice low and ashamed. "It's his uncle. That's where it began. Tom's uncle raised him like a weapon—taught him to fight, to lash out, to never show weakness. We thought we could undo it, but the truth is…" His voice broke, and he swallowed hard before finishing. "We can't control him. He's stronger than us now. We live in fear of our own child." Silence filled the office. Even Ty, who was usually steady, lowered his eyes, the weight of their words pressing against him.

Mr. Arnett turned toward Jeremy, his tone solemn. "This is the truth I wanted you to hear. You're brave, Jeremy. Braver than most adults I've known. But bravery without knowledge is dangerous. Tom isn't just another student with a temper. He's a boy trained to destroy. If you step into this, you must know you're stepping into something darker than anything you've faced before." Jeremy clenched his fists in his lap, his voice trembling but firm. "I'd rather know the truth than live a lie. If we don't help him, then he'll keep hurting people until no one can stop him. I don't care how hard it is. I want to try."

Leo leaned forward, pride and fear mingling in his eyes. "That's my brother," he said softly, though his voice carried through the room. Alex shook his head, not in disagreement, but in awe. "Nine years old, and you're already saying what most of us couldn't even admit when we were twelve." Ty finally looked up, meeting Jeremy's gaze with a heavy steadiness. "If this is the path you choose, then I'll stand with you. But you must know—it may not end with smiles."

Tom's parents exchanged a broken glance, torn between shame and gratitude, as Mr. Arnett closed the folder on his desk. "Then it's settled," he said, his voice deep and final. "The plan is not to fight Tom, not to corner him, but to surround him—with presence, with truth, and with the one thing his uncle never taught him: care. Jeremy, this is the weight you've chosen to carry. And I will not stop you. But I will make sure you are never carrying it alone." The room grew quiet again, heavy with what was now decided. And in that silence, Jeremy's resolve burned brighter, a child's fire daring to face a storm grown far too strong.

The office felt colder after Tom's parents left, their words still hanging in the air like a shadow no one could shake off. Jeremy sat at the small wooden chair near the corner, the folded newspaper article trembling in his hands. He had read the story of Myles Neuts more times than he could count, but tonight it seemed heavier, as though every word pressed against his chest. The faces around him blurred for a moment — Ty's calm, Leo's watchful, Alex's restless — yet all Jeremy could see was the boy from 1998 who never had a chance to grow up. His fingers tightened around the article until the crease deepened, his knuckles pale.

Ty crouched down in front of him, his steady eyes narrowing. "Jeremy," he said softly, "you don't have to take this on yourself. You're only nine. It isn't your fight alone." Jeremy lifted his gaze, his voice firmer than Ty expected. "But if I don't take it on, who will? If I stay quiet, if I just wait for someone else, then Tom keeps breaking people. And I can't live with that." Ty exhaled slowly, recognising the same fire that had once driven him to stand in front of Jarod. "Your courage scares me sometimes," he admitted, almost like a confession. Jeremy shook his head. "It scares me too, but I still have to use it."

Leo slid onto the edge of the desk, arms crossed, but his eyes were softer than usual. "I used to think being tough meant controlling people, making them bend to my anger. But seeing you now, Jeremy… I realise I never knew what strength really was. You're showing it. Not me. Not Alex. You." Jeremy gave a faint smile, though his lip quivered. "Strength isn't shouting, Leo. It's holding steady when everything tells you to run." Alex grunted but leaned closer. "And you're doing that better than any of us ever did. Even I can admit that."

Mr. Arnett adjusted his glasses, his face stern but not unkind. "Jeremy, you asked for the truth, and I gave it. Tom is more dangerous than most adults realise. But if you're going to stand in this storm, you'll need to remember that you're not alone. These friends around you, this staff, even I—none of us will let you carry it all." Jeremy nodded once, folding the article neatly as though sealing a promise inside it. "I know," he whispered. "But this paper reminds me what happens when people wait too long to act. I don't want another Myles. Not ever again."

Nico, who had been sitting quietly at the side, finally spoke, his voice trembling. "Jeremy, do you really think you can stop him? Tom's older, bigger, stronger…" Jeremy turned to him with a steady look. "He's all those things, yes. But he's not unbreakable. Nobody is. And sometimes, the thing that breaks you isn't fists or fear. It's someone refusing to give up on you." Nico blinked, caught off guard by the certainty in Jeremy's words. He wanted to argue, but instead he found himself nodding slowly, almost against his will.

Jasmin, Ella, and Sophie exchanged nervous glances before Jasmin leaned forward. "Jeremy, you can't carry Myles' story like it's a sword. It's a wound. Doesn't it hurt you to think about it all the time?" Jeremy lowered his gaze to the folded paper, running his thumb across the edge. "Of course it hurts," he admitted, his voice quieter. "But the hurt is what makes me remember. If I let it fade, then Myles fades. And if he fades, then the warning fades too. I won't let that happen." The room grew heavier again, the silence pressing in as though daring anyone to break it.

Mrs. Locke, who had been standing near the doorway, finally moved closer. "Jeremy," she said carefully, "sometimes children shouldn't have to hold these kinds of truths. It's too much weight for someone your age." Jeremy looked up, his small frame straightening as if every word lifted him taller. "But I already know the truth. I've seen what bullies do. I've seen how people suffer. Pretending I don't see it won't protect me. It just leaves others unprotected. I won't do that." His words silenced the room once more, every teacher realising they were staring at a child speaking with the gravity of someone far older.

Mrs. Dunlop wiped at her glasses, her tone soft but solemn. "Then we'll stand with you, Jeremy. But you must promise us one thing: never face Tom alone." Jeremy nodded quickly. "I won't. But if I can be the first one to tell him he doesn't scare me, then maybe… maybe that's where it starts." Leo squeezed his brother's shoulder gently, a silent confirmation that he would never let Jeremy stand without him. Alex crossed his arms but shifted closer, his usual smirk gone. "If you go down, we go down with you," he said flatly. Jeremy almost smiled. "Then we're not going down at all."

Mr. Clarke stepped forward, his face lined with something between sorrow and pride. "Jeremy, you remind me of why I told Myles' story in the first place. It wasn't to reopen wounds. It was to make sure his life, and his death, meant something. You've taken that into your hands, and I can see now it was worth the risk." Jeremy lifted the folded paper to his chest and whispered, more to himself than anyone else, "No one else is going to break if I can stop it." The words hung in the air, quiet but unshakable.

The office fell into silence, but it wasn't the silence of fear anymore. It was the silence of resolve, heavy and sharp, the kind that pressed into every heart and left its mark. Outside, the school bell rang, but no one moved. The sound only deepened the weight of what had been decided. Jeremy stood slowly, his fists still tight around the article. He was only nine years old, but in that moment, even the adults in the room felt smaller beside him.

Ty placed a hand on Jeremy's shoulder, his voice calm. "Then it begins here. Whatever comes next, we're in it together." Jeremy nodded once, his jaw set, his eyes brighter than before. For all his fear, for all his trembling, he felt the fire inside him burn steady. Tom was dangerous, yes, but Myles' story had already written itself into his bones. He would not let another child fall into silence. He could not.

Leo moved closer, wrapping his arm around his brother. "Then we'll make sure no smile breaks again. Not while we're here." Jeremy let himself rest against him for a brief moment, his small frame leaning into the warmth of family, before stepping back with a firmness that startled even Alex. "Then it's settled," Jeremy said simply, his voice carrying through the room. "Tom may think he's the storm, but he hasn't met us yet."

The adults exchanged quiet looks, torn between fear and hope, but none dared to speak against the boy who now carried the folded truth of Myles Neuts against his chest. As Jeremy walked out of the office, the words still whispered in his head: No one else is going to break if I can stop it. And for the first time, he believed it might be true.

## CHAPTER 10: THE FIRST SPARKS

The meeting had been called swiftly, and the teachers gathered in the staff room with the unease of those who knew something unpleasant was about to be laid before them. Mr. Clarke leaned back in his chair, hands folded tight, while Mrs. Locke tapped her pen against the table, betraying her nerves. Principal Arnett stood near the window, his arms crossed, the posture of someone already bracing for bad news. No one spoke until Mr. Takashi cleared his throat, his voice steady, precise, and utterly without excess. He had not come to speculate, nor to soften truths. His job, his duty, was to lay bare the reality they were now facing.

"Tom is not a rumour," he began, his eyes cutting across the table one by one. "He is not a story passed among frightened students. He has a documented record with the police, and it is my responsibility to make sure you understand that this is not hearsay. This is fact." The room went still. Chairs stopped creaking. Pens stopped tapping. The silence felt heavy, as though the air itself grew thicker around them. It was Mrs. Haller who first lowered her gaze, as if ashamed that the truth was worse than what they had whispered among themselves in private.

He placed a thin folder on the table, the weight of its presence greater than the papers inside. "These reports detail incidents of violence — not scuffles, not the ordinary mischief of childhood. I am speaking of deliberate, targeted attacks that left lasting harm. Some involved weapons improvised from objects lying within reach. Others were his fists alone, and those were often worse. You will notice the consistency: every time he was confronted, he escalated. He does not back down when cornered. He feeds on it." His voice had the ring of finality, each word falling like stone upon still water.

Mrs. Dunlop shifted uncomfortably, her fingers tightening on the arms of her chair. "You're saying we can't treat him like the others. That he isn't just another boy acting out?" The vice principal's voice wavered between question and statement, but the answer was clear before it came. "Correct," said Takashi, firm but calm. "He cannot be handled with the same assumptions. He is more dangerous, not because of size alone, but because of training he has given himself through rage. He has studied the reactions of those he hurts, and he repeats what works. He is learning violence as others learn arithmetic."

Ms. Henley, the counselor, leaned forward with a mixture of disbelief and pity clouding her expression. "But he's still a child. Surely—" "Children can be dangerous," Takashi cut in, not harsh but immovable. "Do not mistake youth for harmlessness. I have seen boys younger than him take lives, simply because no one wanted to believe they could. If you underestimate him, you will put other students at risk." His words hit harder than any raised voice might have, for they carried not speculation but lived authority, the weight of an investigator who had already walked through the wreckage left by other boys like Tom.

Principal Arnett finally spoke, his voice quieter than expected. "What do you propose we do? Suspend him again? Remove him outright? We cannot manage a student by fear alone." Mr. Takashi shook his head slowly.

"Suspensions mean nothing to him. Removal without intervention only drives him deeper into hostility. What must be done is vigilance — constant observation, immediate response, and above all, no denial. The moment you see signs of escalation, you intervene. Do not wait. Delay is what he feeds upon."

The teachers shifted, some uneasy, others reluctantly nodding. Mrs. Locke looked across the room toward Mrs. Haller, both women exchanging a glance that spoke of sleepless nights to come. "And what of the students?" asked Mrs. Kara softly. "What do we tell them? They already whisper that he's worse than Jarod. Do we deny it, or do we admit it?" At that, Takashi's gaze grew harder, though his tone remained measured. "You do not feed their fear, but you do not lie to them. Children recognize dishonesty faster than most adults care to admit. Tell them that steps are being taken, and mean it. If they see you standing firm, they will stand firmer themselves."

Jeremy's name came up next, though he was not in the room. "What about Jeremy?" asked Clarke, his hand unconsciously tapping the folder. "That boy has a way of sensing trouble before it breaks. He's nine years old, yet he speaks with more clarity than some of us. If anyone can read Tom's intent, it will be him. But I fear for him too. Tom may see his insight as a threat." Silence met his words, each teacher realizing that Jeremy's courage made him both shield and target.

Leo and Alex were mentioned too, their pasts as bullies recalled not as shame but as strange preparation. "They understand the language Tom speaks," said Mrs. Locke. "Perhaps better than we do. They've wielded it themselves, once." Mr. Takashi gave a single nod. "And because of that, they may be his first chosen opponents. Watch them. Protect them. But also, use their understanding. Sometimes only those who have walked through fire know where the flames will rise next."

The staff sat heavier in their chairs, the weight of the meeting pressing down. Nico, Jasmin, Sophie, Ella, and Mila were not named directly, but each teacher knew the smaller ones, the quieter ones, the children who shone brighter because of their gentleness. They would be the first tested by Tom's cruelty. They always were, boys like him choosing their prey not by strength but by the very light he could snuff out. That knowledge sickened them, though no one dared speak it aloud.

Mrs. Haller broke the silence, her voice brittle. "So this is what we face. A boy with a history, a boy who already carries a record thicker than most adults will ever have. And yet, here he is, walking our halls." Mr. Takashi answered with the finality of a gavel striking wood. "Yes. And he will either be broken by truth or break others in its absence. Which it is will depend on how quickly we act."

The meeting ended without the scrape of chairs or chatter of closing conversation. They filed out in silence, each lost in thought, each replaying the folder in their minds though none had dared open it fully.

# THE SMILE THAT BROKE

The air of the school shifted that day, heavier, denser, the kind that settled over the shoulders like an invisible weight. For the first time, the teachers realized they were not simply teaching lessons of grammar, numbers, or maps. They were standing guard over something far more fragile — the safety of every child within those walls.

Even Ty, only eleven years old, listened from the hallway where his father's words reached him through the crack of the door. His dark eyes did not widen with fear, nor narrow with anger. Instead, they held stillness — the calm before a storm, the silence of a boy who understood that his own strength might soon be tested in ways even his father could not predict.

And so the warning was shared, its weight now spread across more shoulders than one. Yet the truth was plain: Tom was not like the others. He never had been. And from that day forward, no one inside the school could afford to forget it.

The classroom was alive with the faint scrape of pencils and the soft hum of voices reading in pairs, yet Ty heard little of it. His attention was drawn elsewhere, fixed on Tom, who sat near the back with his chair tilted slightly, as though claiming his space without permission. Ty did not study him like the others did, waiting for the bursts of noise, the obvious outbursts. No, Ty's eyes were sharper than that. He watched the small signals, the tiny betrayals of control. A jaw tightening at the smallest correction. Fingers tapping against the wood of the desk, not in rhythm but in agitation. Eyes that darted before settling, measuring the room not for lessons but for threats. These fragments built themselves into a map, each piece telling Ty something others failed to see.

Nico leaned forward in his seat, whispering to Jasmin about a missed line in the book they shared, unaware that Tom's glance had already cut their way like a blade. Ty noted it. He marked how Tom's lips curled faintly, not into a smile but something closer to possession, the kind of look that claimed control before the moment came to act. Most would dismiss it as nothing, but Ty's mind captured it, stored it, and added it to the growing ledger he was keeping silently in his head. Tom wasn't unpredictable. He was a pattern, dangerous only to those unwilling to notice.

Sophie and Ella laughed briefly over a shared mistake in their worksheet, the sound bright and quick. Ty saw Tom's shoulders stiffen. Not from disapproval of the laughter itself, but from the attention it gave them. Ty had seen this before — the way resentment built not in sudden bursts but through moments stolen from him, as though every sound of joy in others chipped away at his control. Ty wrote it in his mind: Tom reacts to joy like insult. That was a dangerous seed, one that would sprout quickly if left unchecked.

Jeremy sat close to Leo, humming faintly as he doodled in the margin of his notebook. Tom's gaze swept toward him more than once. Ty caught it each time, subtle but unmistakable. Jeremy, the smallest in the group, was marked already. Tom measured him, not for strength but for vulnerability, and Ty knew such calculations well. They were the silent math of bullies — who is easiest, who will break fastest, who offers the cleanest display of power. Ty's jaw clenched, though no one saw. He added another note to the map: Jeremy will be tested first.

Leo, though older and broader, gave little attention to Tom, choosing instead to help Jeremy with a sentence he was stuck on. Ty saw the irony — the boy once feared as a bully himself now leaned in to protect another. But Tom did not know that history, and so he looked at Leo differently, not with fear but with curiosity. Ty wrote it down in silence: Leo will not be avoided. He will be challenged, but later. Tom preferred to build dominance layer by layer, starting with the weakest, saving the largest for when victory would carry more weight.

Miss Kara moved about the classroom, glancing at workbooks and giving nods of approval. When she neared Tom's desk, Ty's eyes never left him. Tom's hand stilled, jaw shifted, and his eyes rose too quickly, too sharply, as though bracing against correction. When Miss Kara only offered a mild compliment, he gave a nod far too slow, like a predator allowing a passerby to escape. The other students never saw it. Ty did. Another line was drawn on the map: authority is tolerated, not respected. That meant every teacher was a temporary obstacle, not a boundary.

Mrs. Locke came in briefly, her voice carrying across the class as she spoke with Kara about an upcoming event. Ty saw Tom's hand press against the edge of his desk, knuckles whitening for a moment, then loosening just as quickly. His control was surface-level. It cracked at interruptions, even small ones. Ty noted the fragility, the way restraint wasn't strength at all but a mask. This boy lived on the edge of fracture, and it was only a matter of time before someone touched the wrong chord and the mask shattered completely.

Jasmin caught Ty watching, her brows furrowed as though to ask what he saw. Ty only shook his head slightly, returning his gaze to his page, yet his ears remained open to the rhythm of Tom's movements. He knew no one else read it the way he did, but he also knew they trusted him, even when they did not understand. Ty was their unspoken guard, though only his father and Jeremy truly sensed the depth of it.

Nico passed a note to Mila, making her stifle a laugh. Ty caught Tom's stare at that moment. The narrowing of the eyes. The tightening of his mouth. The sudden, harsh rub of his palm against the wood as though trying to grind the joy from the table itself. Ty felt the shift ripple through the air, so slight no one else seemed to notice. The map sharpened further: laughter provokes aggression. And once provoked, he doesn't forget. He will find a time.

Mr. Clarke entered then, holding a sheaf of papers for Kara, his warm voice briefly brightening the room. "Good progress today, everyone," he said. Tom's eyes flicked up once, not with respect but with calculation. Clarke had authority, yes, but not the kind Tom feared. Ty filed the observation carefully. It was clear Tom recognized power only in forms he could not break. Clarke would be tested eventually, but not yet. Tom was waiting, studying, just as Ty was studying him.

The bell rang and chairs scraped, voices lifting in chatter as students packed their books. Ty did not join the scramble. He stayed seated, his eyes still fixed on Tom. He watched how Tom moved, how he pushed his chair back with deliberate slowness, how he glanced at the others with something colder than irritation, closer to possession.

Ty mapped the walk, the posture, the small gestures that betrayed more than words ever could. Each line he drew in his mind became part of a plan, the shape of what was coming, the proof that Tom was already circling for a fight.

Ella brushed past Tom on her way out the door, smiling politely as she excused herself. Ty saw the flicker in his eyes — not anger, not yet, but the storing of it. He would remember her too. Every slight, every contact, every smile. They were all debts in his ledger, waiting for the day he decided to collect. Ty saw it clearer than anyone. The map was filling fast.

By the time the room emptied, Ty remained at his desk, still, calm, but awake in every nerve. His father's words from earlier replayed in his mind: "He will either be broken by truth or break others in its absence." Ty believed them, but he also believed something more. He would not allow Tom's breaking to come at the cost of another child. Not Jeremy, not Nico, not any of them. If Tom had to be stopped, Ty was ready. His silence was not weakness. It was preparation.

The last glance came as Tom walked out the door, shoulders straight, jaw tight, his head turning just enough to catch Ty's gaze. For the briefest instant, the air between them hardened, two sets of eyes meeting in quiet challenge. Tom's lips curled faintly, the echo of a smirk. Ty's face did not change. His stillness was louder than any reply. And in that moment, the map was sealed. The battle would not be loud when it came. It would be precise. It would be inevitable.

Ty gathered his books slowly, letting the others walk ahead. He wasn't racing them. He was shadowing the storm, step for step, until the day it broke. And if no one else could stop it, he would.

By the time the lunch bell rang, the corridors felt alive with something heavier than the usual chatter of children looking for a place to sit. Fear has its own sound, and that sound is sharper than laughter, quicker than footsteps, a murmur that slides from one pair of lips to another. "He's worse than Jarod ever was," one voice said near the lockers, pitched low but not low enough to escape Ty's ear. The name of Jarod still lingered like a shadow over the school, and to be compared unfavourably with him was enough to change the very air. Ty kept walking, silent, his tray balanced in his hands, though his eyes shifted just enough to catch the faces. Fear travels faster than truth. He had known that since the first day his father taught him how words could wound without ever raising a fist.

Nico, Jasmin, and Mila clustered at the far end of the cafeteria table, their voices subdued for once. "I heard he's been arrested before," Mila said, eyes wide, as though repeating it aloud might make her brave for saying it. Nico shook his head, pushing food around his tray. "Doesn't matter if it's true," he muttered. "People believe it, so it'll spread." Jasmin leaned closer, whispering, "He stared at me in math. Not like normal staring. Like he was deciding something." Her words set a tremor between them, one neither of them knew how to quiet. The unease was not in what was confirmed but in what might be. Possibility became its own prison, trapping them in fear they could not measure.

Jeremy sat beside Leo, his small frame hunched, eyes darting around at every passing rumour. "They keep saying it louder," he whispered, tugging lightly at Leo's sleeve. "Why are they all saying it louder?" Leo, calm in his new strength, patted Jeremy's back but said nothing. It wasn't his job to silence fear. His job was to recognise what was real and what was smoke. Still, the weight pressed down on the table, settling into Jeremy's chest. He tried to chew, but every bite tasted like ash. His brother's steady presence was his only anchor, though even Leo's eyes were more alert than usual, watching Tom from across the room.

Tom sat two tables away, alone yet not alone, because silence surrounded him like armour. No one dared sit within three seats of him. He chewed slowly, methodically, his jaw set with precision, as though eating was another performance of control. Ty watched him closely from the corner of his eye. Tom's ears picked up every rumour too — Ty could see it in the twitch of his cheek, the slight tilt of his head. Yet he gave no outward sign of anger. He let the whispers grow, let them turn the hall into an echo chamber of his reputation. Ty marked it carefully: this boy doesn't fight the rumours. He feeds them by silence.

Ella and Sophie sat across from Jasmin and Mila, their voices sharper, urgent. "I saw him shove a seventh grader near the water fountain," Sophie whispered. "No one said anything because he just looked at them." Ella added quickly, "My cousin said someone told their parents already, but the teachers can't do anything unless he's caught." They nodded, each retelling of the story adding more weight to the legend forming around Tom. Fear inflated him larger than his frame, painting him as untouchable before he even moved. Ty's hands rested flat on the table. He knew how dangerous this was — when fear builds faster than truth, it creates an opponent more dangerous than reality itself.

Mr. Clarke moved through the cafeteria, clipboard tucked beneath his arm, his keen eyes glancing across tables. He paused briefly near Tom, but Tom didn't look up. The room shifted with tension. Students watched that small moment like an audience at the edge of their seats. Clarke continued on, but whispers reignited as soon as he left. "Even Clarke doesn't want to mess with him," a boy muttered, passing behind Leo's table. Ty stiffened. Clarke had done nothing of the sort, yet the rumour reshaped the truth instantly. It was another line added to the story Tom's silence allowed to flourish.

Ms. Henley, the counselor, sat quietly at the edge of the cafeteria, observing as she often did. She saw groups shifting closer together, voices lowered, eyes wide. Yet even she did not see what Ty saw: the lines of the map forming, the ledger of fear Tom was cultivating without effort. Ty knew that once fear became currency, it was almost impossible to strip it away without confrontation. His father had said it clearly: "Power unearned is the most dangerous kind. It builds without cost." Ty kept that truth in mind, watching every detail as students filled their plates and found seats, the hum of unease rising higher than the clatter of trays.

Leo leaned closer to Jeremy, voice firm but quiet. "Don't listen to it all. Not everything they say is true." Jeremy nodded, though his small hands clutched his juice box too tightly, nearly crushing it. "But some of it might be," he whispered, eyes darting to Tom's still figure. Leo said nothing further. He knew that fear wasn't logical. Once planted, it grew regardless of evidence. And this fear was being watered with every passing sentence, every nervous glance toward the boy who hadn't needed to lift a hand.

At another table, Alex crossed his arms, his sharp eyes narrowing at Tom. "They're letting him win without him even moving," he muttered, half to himself, half to Ty. Ty nodded once but didn't look away from Tom. "That's the point," Ty replied softly. "Fear moves faster than fists." Alex sat back, lips pressed tight, as though chewing on words he could not spit out. He had once thrived on fear himself, and now he recognised its dangerous simplicity. But seeing it return in someone else lit a fire in his chest he couldn't easily quiet.

Near the far wall, Jasmin heard another whisper travel down the line of students waiting for lunch. "My brother said he's been kicked out of schools before." Whether it was true or not, it was already believed by those who repeated it. Ty's father had said facts were fragile things; rumours survived far longer. Ty knew that truth could not walk alone anymore. It had to be guarded, explained, proven again and again, or else it would be devoured by the whispers now shaping Tom into something more than human.

Mrs. Dunlop, the vice principal, stepped into the cafeteria briefly, her stern eyes scanning the room. For a moment the whispers dropped to a hush, as though authority itself had pressed its hand down. But the silence broke the instant she turned her back, replaced again by the hiss of rumour. Ty took note: even adults with power couldn't stop it. Not unless they spoke directly, decisively, tearing rumour apart with fact. Dunlop had not, and so the cycle continued. Tom's legend grew unchecked.

Ella's voice trembled when she leaned toward Jasmin again. "What if he really is worse than Jarod? Jarod hurt people, but this one—this one doesn't even need to. He just looks, and everyone feels it." Ty heard it, even across the table. He knew it wasn't the look alone — it was the story the whispers had built around it. Tom understood that silence could be louder than shouting, and he was playing it with precision. The hallways throbbed with fear that had no anchor, yet was treated as solid as stone.

Leo's eyes cut across the cafeteria and found Ty's, the unspoken question clear: Is it true? Is he really this dangerous? Ty gave no reply, no shake of the head, no nod of confirmation. He knew the map was still forming. But what he did know was enough: the fear was real, and it was spreading faster than fact could keep up. And once fear became the heartbeat of the room, it took more than reason to silence it. It took strength.

As trays were emptied and voices rose again, the corridors filled with fragments of rumour. Students carried them from one corner of the building to the other, feeding Tom's shadow with every step. "He's untouchable." "He's worse than Jarod." "Even the teachers are scared." None of it proven, all of it believed. Ty walked with the others, silent, listening. His eyes fixed forward, yet his ears caught every echo. The truth would be slower to spread, but Ty was patient. He always was.

By the time the lunch period ended, the air itself seemed charged. Students glanced over their shoulders more than once, laughter dying too quickly, smiles breaking under the weight of whispers. And through it all Tom walked calmly, his silence untouched, his steps steady, feeding on every fear left behind in his wake. Ty watched him leave the cafeteria, a calm shadow stalking ahead. Fear had already crowned him king, and not a single word had been spoken.

Jeremy sat low in his chair, his knees drawn close beneath the desk, his eyes darting between Tom and Ty as though measuring a space that could not be crossed. His small voice barely rose above the shuffle of papers, but Ty heard it clearly enough. "Are the rumours true?" Jeremy's lips trembled around the words, not because he was afraid of Ty's answer but because he already knew that asking would change something. It was not a question of curiosity. It was a question of safety. Ty turned his head slowly, his face unreadable, his dark eyes fixed on Jeremy with the calm of a pond that concealed depth far too deep to measure. He didn't speak, but Jeremy felt the answer all the same.

Nico leaned in, hearing the whisper, his brow furrowed. "You really think so?" he muttered, glancing toward Tom's seat at the far edge of the room. Jeremy nodded faintly, his throat dry. "He's not just a story," he said, more to himself than to Nico. The others caught the edge of his tone, enough to stiffen Jasmin's shoulders and draw Ella's eyes down to her desk. It wasn't the sort of truth that needed words. Ty's silence said more than any reassurance could. When Ty didn't deny something, it meant the danger was real.

Sophie shifted in her seat, uneasy. "But he hasn't done anything here yet," she whispered, half-defiant, half-hopeful. "Maybe the stories are just that—stories." Leo, calm as ever, set his hand on Jeremy's arm, grounding him with the steady weight of a brother. "Some names aren't just names," he said softly, his voice a low anchor. "Some names carry the storms with them." Jeremy looked back at Ty, still searching for an answer, but the boy's gaze held steady, unblinking. The silence tightened the air like rope pulled taut.

Across the classroom, Tom shifted his chair slightly, the scrape of wood against the floor a sound that seemed too loud. Every head turned instinctively, though he had done nothing more than adjust his posture. The weight of his presence pressed into the room without effort. Jeremy whispered again, "He's dangerous, isn't he?" But Ty still gave no reply. Instead, he leaned forward, his elbows resting on the desk, his gaze fixed on Tom with quiet calculation. That gaze was enough. Jeremy's chest tightened; he understood. He wished he didn't, but he did.

Mrs. Locke continued writing on the board, unaware of the storm building in the minds of her students. Equations filled the chalk, neat and precise, but none of the children were following. They were watching Tom, watching Ty, and holding their breath for the sound that would break the uneasy stillness. Mila pressed her palms together on the desk, glancing at Jeremy. "If Ty won't say it out loud, it means it's serious," she murmured. Jeremy nodded, his small fingers tightening on the pencil he hadn't lifted for minutes.

Mr. Clarke passed the doorway, clipboard in hand, catching the tense posture of the children within. He slowed, observing, but he did not enter. His eyes flicked briefly to Tom before moving on, and even that was enough to stoke the quiet fire of rumour. "Even Clarke's watching him," someone breathed from the back. The sentence rolled forward like a wave, unsteady and quick, another piece of Tom's legend added without proof. Ty heard it, stored it, and stayed silent. Silence was its own weapon, but so was knowledge, and Ty was already mapping every piece.

Alex, taller than most, leaned back in his chair, his arms folded, his eyes narrowed at Jeremy. "Don't waste your breath asking him," Alex said, nodding toward Ty. "If Ty doesn't answer, it's because he knows we won't like the truth." Jeremy frowned, his lips pressed thin. He wanted to argue, but the weight of Ty's unbroken stare toward Tom cut the words from his throat. He had his answer. It wasn't the one he wanted, but it was the only one he was going to get.

Mrs. Haller, moving between rows, caught the unsettled posture of her students and paused. "Is there something on your minds?" she asked, her tone soft but searching. No one spoke. Jeremy ducked his head, pretending to work, while Leo's hand pressed once more on his shoulder. Even silence was safer than confirmation. Haller waited a beat longer, then moved on, chalk tapping rhythmically against her palm. Ty's eyes never left Tom. He didn't blink. He didn't need to.

The minutes dragged like hours, the weight of the name itself pressing into every breath. Tom wasn't a story whispered anymore. He wasn't a shadow passed down by rumour. He was here, in their classroom, his name written in the attendance roll, his body present in the seat at the far side of the room. Jeremy thought of Myles, of Mr. Clarke's voice in the library days before, of the word deceased spoken without apology. He felt a chill climb his spine. Names could break more than smiles. They could end lives. And now, Ty's silence made it clear: Tom's name was not one to forget.

Sophie scribbled on her paper but kept glancing up, her eyes flickering between Ty and Tom. She saw the same thing Jeremy did: Ty's focus was not anger, not fear, but preparation. He was watching the smallest movements, every flick of Tom's hand, every shift of his shoulders. "Why does he keep staring?" she whispered, though no one answered. Everyone knew the reason without saying it. Ty was not staring out of curiosity. He was readying himself.

Ms. Henley, seated quietly in the back, noted the posture of the room, the tension running like a thread between the children. She saw Jeremy's hunched shoulders, Leo's protective watch, and Ty's unwavering gaze. She didn't know the whispers that had carried into the cafeteria, didn't know the weight of Tom's record whispered by his father the night before. But she saw the fear and she felt it deepen. Children rarely hide what they feel. They wear it on their faces until it stains the air itself.

Jeremy leaned close to Leo, his voice barely a thread. "It's true, isn't it?" Leo didn't look away from the front of the room, but his grip on his pencil tightened until the wood creaked. "It doesn't matter if it's true," he said. "What matters is that Ty knows, and Ty's never wrong." Jeremy closed his eyes briefly, his stomach heavy. He thought of Ty's silence, the way it spoke louder than words, and he realised that some answers are heavier than any child should ever have to carry.

When the bell rang at last, the sound jolted the room as though waking it from a long, tense dream. Desks scraped, chairs pushed back, voices rose quickly in chatter meant to disguise the fear that still lingered. Tom stood slowly, deliberately, his movements controlled. He left the classroom without a word, and yet every eye followed him until he was gone. Jeremy turned to Ty once more, searching for any sign of relief, but Ty's expression never shifted. He was still watching, still listening, still mapping the boy no one could ignore.

Out in the hallway, rumours picked up again, louder now, but Jeremy barely heard them. He had his answer, though Ty had never spoken a word. Tom was not a story. Tom was not a rumour. Tom was a danger — one whose name would not be forgotten, not in this school, not in Jeremy's mind, not in the silence that Ty left behind. The weight of it followed him down the hall, a shadow that could not be shaken.

The playground was alive with its usual hum, balls bouncing, voices carrying, laughter and noise all tangled together into the sound of freedom between classes. Yet beneath it, as always, there were currents unseen by most, patterns invisible unless you knew how to look. Ty knew. He didn't waste time on the noise, didn't let the distractions blind him. His eyes stayed trained on Tom, who carried himself not like a boy in school but like someone constantly measuring distance, checking territory, waiting for the smallest spark to strike. Ty saw the flicker in his steps, the way his fists already hung too tight at his sides.

The shove came sudden, without ceremony. A smaller boy, no more than a head shorter, had brushed too close in the press of the crowd. Tom's arm shot out, not careless, but precise, slamming into the boy's chest with a force that sent him stumbling backward. The laughter and shrieks of play around them faltered into silence for a heartbeat. The boy caught himself, blinking wide-eyed, unsure whether to speak or run. Tom didn't follow with words, didn't add insult to the strike. He simply squared his shoulders, his chin tilting upward, his stance widening — not play, not accident, but readiness. The message was clear: come closer and see what happens.

Jeremy had seen boys shove before, and he knew the difference. This wasn't teasing, wasn't the clumsy push of boys chasing each other across the field. He pulled at Leo's sleeve, his whisper sharp. "That wasn't nothing. That was a warning." Leo didn't argue. His eyes narrowed, watching the set of Tom's jaw, the quiet threat woven into his posture. Beside them, Sophie gripped her hands together, her voice low. "He's waiting for it. For someone to give him a reason."

Ty moved no closer, but he shifted his weight, his stance calm but ready. It wasn't his place to leap in yet, not when no fight had broken, but he wouldn't miss a single detail. He memorised the tightening of Tom's back, the way his shoulders rolled forward as though carrying armour invisible to everyone else. He saw the smaller boy freeze, his arms hugging his chest, his eyes darting not for a teacher but for escape. That was what fear looked like when it had been earned, not imagined. Ty knew the difference, and so did Tom.

Nico stepped forward as though to intervene, but Jasmin caught his wrist, shaking her head. "Not yet," she hissed. Nico looked at her, frustrated, but stopped. It wasn't cowardice. It was recognition. You didn't run at a storm when it was still gathering. You waited, measured, prepared. Jeremy's heart pounded, but his eyes stayed locked on Ty, searching for any sign of what to do. Ty gave him none, only the stillness of a boy who had already made his choice: to wait, to map, to step in only when the fire threatened to consume.

Mr. Clarke had stepped onto the playground at that moment, clipboard in hand, scanning the children with the tired but steady gaze of long years in classrooms. He didn't catch the shove, but he caught the silence that lingered afterward, the way the smaller boy slipped away quickly, head down, his face pale. Clarke's brows drew tight. He knew what silence meant on a playground. It meant fear had walked through and left its scent. He looked toward Ty briefly, catching the boy's still posture, and nodded once before moving on. Clarke trusted Ty's eyes more than most.

Ella tugged at Sophie's sleeve. "That was just one shove," she whispered, trying to dismiss it. But Sophie shook her head firmly. "No. That was the first sign of fire. You don't wait until it burns to admit the smoke." Her words hung between them, truer than she realised. Alex crossed his arms, his jaw set. He had been the one who used to shove for fun, to watch fear bloom like bruises without ever laying a fist. He saw too much of himself in Tom's stance. It unsettled him more than he would admit.

Mila, sharp-eyed, leaned close to Jeremy. "He's testing everyone. He wants to see who'll stand up and who'll look away." Jeremy swallowed hard, his eyes flicking to Ty again. Ty's calm didn't break. But in his silence, Jeremy read more than words: Tom wasn't testing them anymore. He was preparing. Jeremy hugged his arms tight against his chest, the weight of Myles's story echoing in his memory. A shove, a stall, a hook — it all began with something small. And if no one stopped it, the fire would spread until it couldn't be put out.

The bell rang, but the tension didn't fade with it. Children scattered back toward the building, their voices louder, trying to push noise over the silence Tom had left behind. He lingered, letting the others move ahead, his chin still high, his eyes sharp. Ty didn't follow the crowd either. He stayed until Tom finally turned toward the doors. They didn't exchange a word, but their eyes met once, steady and unflinching. Tom's smirk was small, but Ty caught it — the smirk of someone who had shown his teeth and found no one bold enough to bite back. For now.

Inside, the others whispered again, louder this time. "Did you see him shove?" "He didn't even smile after. Not once." "He wanted a fight." "He's worse than Jarod." Jeremy sat at his desk, his pencil still untouched. He had no words to chase the whispers. He only had Ty's gaze burned in his memory, still locked on Tom, still calm, still ready. It wasn't over. The first spark had been lit, and the fire was waiting.

The dangerous thing about Tom was not his fists, though they carried weight enough. It was the speed with which rage seemed to climb into him, fed by the smallest embers of imagined insult. He sat at his desk one morning while the class worked through Miss Kara's math problems on the board. A laugh broke out across the room, careless and innocent, two boys chuckling over a crooked line drawn by mistake. But Tom's head snapped toward them as though the sound had been fired at him. His eyes narrowed, jaw tightening, the red flush creeping from his neck upward. The laugh wasn't his, and therefore it must have been about him. That was how his mind worked — every sound a threat, every smile a weapon turned sharp.

Ty, from two rows back, caught the shift instantly. He watched the way Tom's shoulders rolled forward, how his pencil snapped in two between restless fingers. He did not look at the boys who laughed — they weren't his interest. His eyes never left Tom, because Ty understood what others didn't: it wasn't the big fights that ruined classrooms, it was the smallest slights that lit the matches. Nico leaned close to Jeremy, whispering, "He looks ready to fight over nothing." Jeremy whispered back, his voice thin, "It's not nothing to him." Both boys quieted when Ty turned his head just slightly, reminding them silence was safer when a fuse had been lit.

At recess, it was the same pattern. Ella had glanced across the playground, not even at Tom, but in the direction of a bird perched on the fence. Tom caught it, misread it, and his voice thundered across the yard, "What are you looking at?" Ella froze, startled, her hand still raised toward the bird. Sophie stepped beside her, steady but cautious. "She wasn't looking at you, Tom," she said, her tone firm. But Tom's eyes burned with certainty, convinced all gazes were aimed at him. It was the same story every hour: a word said too loud, a laugh shared too close, even the shuffle of shoes he thought meant someone had whispered his name. Every detail twisted inside him until it became disrespect.

Mrs. Locke, walking past in the hallway later, had corrected his spelling on a worksheet. She had circled one word in neat red ink, meaning nothing more than guidance. Tom's face darkened as though she had carved insult into the page.

He shoved the book back across the desk so hard it slid nearly into the next row. "It's fine," he muttered, his voice low but sharp enough to sting. Mrs. Locke, steady after years of such storms, placed the book back without raising her tone. Yet she saw it, the way his fists tightened, how his chair legs ground against the floor as if he were anchoring himself to stop from rising.

The invisible truth was that Tom did not wait for open insult. He thrived on the quiet corners of everyday life, twisting them into proof that the world hated him first. Mila once tapped her pencil three times, a nervous habit she barely noticed herself. Tom's head whipped around, his eyes narrowing. "You mocking me?" he snapped. Mila blinked in confusion, her lips parting but no words coming. Alex stepped between them with an even stare, his voice steady. "She wasn't mocking you, Tom. She does that all the time. You just don't notice because you're too busy watching for enemies." For a moment, Tom's nostrils flared, his chest heaving. Then he turned sharply away, his silence more threatening than any reply.

Ms. Henley, watching from the corner of the lunchroom, scribbled notes furiously in the margins of her folder. She knew the signs of paranoia, of an anger that sought roots where none had grown. Yet even her trained eyes could not break through the wall Tom had built. He was both hunter and hunted, convinced of his own persecution, using it as permission to strike before anyone else could. Students began whispering more quietly now, not because the rumours had stopped, but because they feared even the sound of their breath might draw his wrath. Fear spread quicker than truth, and in Tom's presence, truth itself bent under his glare.

Ty never let a moment slip. He didn't write notes or whisper with others. He studied Tom like a map, each trigger drawn and marked, each reaction catalogued. A laugh here, a glance there, a correction, a nudge, a word — each spark measured, each flame noted. He knew it was only a matter of time before one spark grew too wild to contain. And when it did, Ty would have to step forward. Until then, he kept his silence, his eyes sharp, his heart steady, while Tom lived like dry wood waiting for the match.

Ty never declared what he was doing, and he never asked permission. He simply began to move when Tom moved, keeping a distance that felt natural but never distant enough to lose sight. If Tom walked toward the drinking fountain, Ty adjusted his pace, arriving at the lockers nearby just in time to lean against them. If Tom pushed open the door to the yard, Ty's shadow stretched across the same threshold seconds later. It wasn't intimidation in the loud sense; it was something subtler, heavier. The quiet certainty that one pair of eyes would always be there. Students noticed. They whispered in corners, saying Ty had turned into Tom's shadow, not hounding him, but never letting him slip free of watchful sight.

Nico caught it first, tugging at Jeremy's sleeve as they lined up after recess. "Look," he whispered. Jeremy's eyes followed, and he saw it plainly: Tom shifting his shoulders, trying to walk with swagger, while Ty simply mirrored the rhythm half a pace behind.

"He doesn't even have to say anything," Jeremy murmured, his young voice filled with something close to awe. Leo, listening from the other side, smirked faintly. "That's how you do it," he said under his breath. "You don't challenge the storm; you follow it, make sure it never hits someone else." Even Alex, usually quick with sharp commentary, stayed quiet, his eyes locked on the unspoken duel of presence.

On the playground, Ty stood where Tom stood. If Tom leaned against the fence, Ty leaned against the corner post. If Tom crossed the field, Ty angled across the same stretch, his steps unhurried but always precise. Tom noticed, of course. How could he not? His eyes darted often, testing the distance, testing whether Ty would look away. But Ty never did. He didn't glare, didn't smirk, didn't taunt. His silence was more deliberate than words, and that silence unsettled Tom more than jeers ever could. Students huddled in their own groups, murmuring, "Even when he doesn't talk, Ty's louder than the rest of us combined."

Mrs. Dunlop noticed it too, from her place near the staff doors. She tilted her head, watching how Ty planted himself, balanced, steady. "He doesn't hover," she murmured to Mrs. Locke. "No, he never hovers. He just is there." Locke nodded, her lips pressed thin, her eyes shifting between Tom's restless movements and Ty's calm frame. "That's what unnerves him," Locke replied. "Ty doesn't play by Tom's rules. He doesn't rise to the bait, doesn't step back either. He leaves Tom trapped between reaction and restraint." The teachers shared the look of those who understood that control was sometimes quieter than chaos.

Inside the classroom, the pattern repeated. Tom hunched low over his desk, scribbling too hard, and Ty sat angled just right, his chair turned slightly as though studying the window. But his gaze, sharp and unbroken, lingered on Tom's hands. When Tom tapped his pencil in irritation, Ty shifted his own fingers, mimicking calm rhythm on the wood of the desk. When Tom slammed his eraser down, Ty's hand hovered, steady, not as challenge but as reminder. Tom felt it. He felt every silent note of resistance, every unswerving eye. He twisted in his seat once, muttering, "Stop looking at me." But Ty didn't answer. Silence was his reply, and silence carried deeper weight than any argument.

At lunch, Jasmin asked softly, "Why does he do that? Why not just tell Tom to stop?" Ella, thoughtful, answered, "Because talking won't work. Tom hears everything as a fight. Ty's showing him instead." Sophie leaned forward, her voice quieter than usual. "It's like he's saying: I see you. You're not hidden. You're not free to hurt someone when you think no one's looking." Mila added, almost to herself, "That's scarier than yelling. Because it means Ty will never miss it." The girls exchanged a glance, realizing Ty's silence carried a language they all understood without translation.

Tom, however, hated it. Every step reminded him that his freedom was checked. Every pause in Ty's presence told him his movements were mapped, judged, contained. He snarled once, under his breath, when Ty blocked the hallway door for a heartbeat too long.

But Ty only tilted his head, his eyes level, his lips never parting. Tom shoved past with more force than necessary, muttering about respect, but the tremor in his voice betrayed the unease growing inside. For bullies like Tom, fear was currency. Ty had stripped it from him, not with fists, but with presence. Students saw it plainly: for the first time, Tom was not the one in control of the silence.

Even Mr. Clarke, who had weathered many years of schoolyard storms, saw the pattern forming. "It's like he's a guardrail," Clarke told Ms. Henley. "Not pushing, not dragging, just there to keep the car from veering off." Henley nodded, her eyes fixed on Tom's restless scowl. "Yes, but remember," she whispered, "guardrails don't stop the car from trying. They just absorb the impact. Ty's brave, but he's only one boy. And Tom… Tom doesn't like being cornered." Clarke agreed, though he also knew the truth: in the balance of presence, Ty was heavier than Tom's fury. And that balance mattered.

So the day passed, the halls filled with whispers, the classrooms stiff with tension. Wherever Tom's shadow fell, Ty's shadow followed, quiet, patient, relentless. And by the last bell, it wasn't Tom the students remembered most. It was Ty — the boy who said almost nothing, yet spoke louder than any voice in the school.

The commotion began the way most trouble does—small, sharp, and sudden. A shove too hard, a muttered insult that cut deeper than intended, and then the scrape of shoes against gravel as Tom squared himself against a boy barely half his size. Within seconds, a circle began to take shape. Students, hungry for something to watch, pressed closer, their shouts rising like a fire fed with dry tinder. The noise wasn't cheer yet, not quite, but it carried the same raw pulse. Tom thrived on it. His shoulders broadened as though the air itself had swelled his lungs, and his jaw set with grim satisfaction. He had an audience, and that was enough to give his anger shape.

Nico pulled at Jeremy's sleeve, his young eyes already sharp with worry. "It's happening," he hissed. Jeremy, smaller but unwilling to shrink, pushed forward just enough to see. The boy opposite Tom looked pale, his hands curled but trembling, his mouth twisting as if he wanted to speak but couldn't find breath. Leo, standing taller behind them, muttered low, "This is bad. Tom's not bluffing this time." Alex's silence told the same story; his eyes, narrowed and grim, followed Tom's every twitch as though preparing for the moment things collapsed.

The circle grew tighter. Feet shuffled in the dirt, sneakers crunching stones, elbows pressing closer as children jostled for position. Jasmin grabbed Ella's wrist, whispering, "We should call someone." Ella shook her head, eyes locked on Ty across the yard. "Wait," she murmured. "Ty's already moving." And indeed he was, slow and deliberate, threading through the gaps in the crowd with a calmness that unsettled more than if he'd charged in. Students shifted, sensing that calm, whispering his name under their breath. The crowd that had gathered for chaos suddenly found itself watching for balance instead.

Tom snarled at the boy in front of him, "You think you can laugh at me? You think I don't see it?" His words cracked sharp in the air, each one rising in volume to match the swelling noise of the circle. The boy stammered something inaudible, but Tom didn't wait to hear it. He stepped forward, his chest puffed, his fists curled with dangerous intent. Jeremy gasped aloud, ready to lunge in blind defiance, but Leo caught his arm. "Don't," Leo whispered. "Not yet. Ty won't let it happen." His words were steady, but his knuckles were white against Jeremy's sleeve.

Mrs. Dunlop had stepped into the yard, her eyes narrowing as the circle caught her attention. She began to push her way through the crowd, but the noise drowned her calls for space. Mrs. Locke followed just behind, her sharp voice carrying only halfway before it vanished under the roars of "Fight!" and "Hit him!" Students were no longer individuals in that ring; they were a single creature, one with a pulse and breath of its own, demanding a spark to ignite the blaze. Tom's chest rose and fell faster. He could feel their energy feeding him. He needed to swing. He wanted to swing.

Ty's steps cut through the noise. He did not rush. He did not shout. He simply walked, a straight line of calm weaving between restless bodies. Sophie, pressed to the front of the circle, felt it first. She whispered to Mila, "Do you feel that? The air—like it's waiting for him, not Tom." Mila nodded, biting her lip, her fingers tightening around Sophie's wrist. Tom caught sight of Ty then, and his expression faltered just for a moment. The crowd didn't see it, but Ty did. The shift of the eyes, the sudden hitch in the breath—the recognition that someone had stepped into his fire who wasn't afraid of the flames.

The boy Tom had shoved stepped back further, his heels scraping against the dirt. He looked not at Tom, but at Ty, relief flickering across his face as though he knew salvation had arrived. Tom growled low, trying to drag the eyes back onto himself, but the balance was already shifting. Students murmured louder now, not cheers but questions: "What's Ty going to do? Did you see him last time with Jarod? He stopped him without a punch." The murmurs spread like a current under the louder chants, dulling them, twisting the energy. The crowd was no longer hungry for blood—they were waiting for an answer.

Mr. Clarke, having spotted the circle from across the yard, began to hurry over. He glanced at Mr. Arnett near the doors, motioning sharply for backup. Arnett nodded, already breaking into a run. But even as the adults closed in, it was Ty who commanded the air. His silence pressed heavier than their shouted warnings. He was not bigger than Tom, not stronger, but he was steady, unshaken. And that steadiness cut through Tom's fury like cold steel.

By the time Ty reached the inner ring, the noise had ebbed into uneasy quiet. Tom, standing rigid, chest heaving, fists trembling, felt the eyes of the entire yard on him. Not just the eyes of children urging him forward, but the eyes of Ty, clear and unwavering, stripping the power from his posture. The crowd leaned inward, breaths held, waiting not for the strike they had once craved, but for the stillness that only Ty could deliver. The fight hadn't begun, but the circle already knew who held its center.

The moment stretched thin, fragile as glass. Tom's rage burned bright in his stance, but Ty's calm stood taller, heavier, unbroken. And in that fragile space between strike and silence, the whole yard balanced, watching, listening, waiting.

The air around the circle felt brittle, as though the faintest motion could shatter it into chaos. The smaller boy facing Tom held his chin up, though his knees shook beneath him. His fists were curled, not out of confidence but out of desperation, the kind that drives a child to stand even when he knows he cannot win. Tom, sensing the fear, prowled forward with slow, deliberate steps. His fists were clenched tight at his sides, the veins at his temples visible. He didn't need to swing yet—every inch of his body was already a threat. The crowd pressed closer, their voices dimming into a low hum, as though even the students sensed this was no longer play but the edge of something dangerous.

Nico tugged Jeremy's sleeve again, whispering fast, "He's going to do it, he's going to hit him." Jeremy's wide eyes darted between Tom and Ty, who stood only a few paces away. "Not if Ty gets there first," Jeremy muttered, though his voice trembled. He knew what Tom's fists could do. He had seen the rage in him before, the sudden, merciless outbursts that left bruises not only on skin but on spirits. Beside them, Jasmin bit her lip hard, her hands pressed against her chest as if to steady the pounding within. "Someone has to stop this," she whispered, though her eyes never left Ty.

The boy opposite Tom swallowed hard, his Adam's apple jerking visibly in his throat. He wanted to run. Every nerve in his body screamed for him to turn and flee. Yet some quiet stubbornness kept him planted, his sneakers rooted to the dirt. Perhaps it was pride, perhaps the knowledge that if he ran now, Tom would chase him forever. His refusal to step back was both bravery and peril. Tom smirked at that, stepping closer, his shadow falling across the boy like a storm cloud blotting the sun. "Go on," Tom growled, low enough for only those closest to hear. "See what happens when you don't move."

At the edge of the circle, Mrs. Locke had reached the throng. She called out sharply for the children to make way, but the crowd was too tight, too breathless, too hungry for the outcome to let her through quickly. Mr. Clarke, taller and firmer, tried to push in from the opposite side, but even his voice was swallowed by the tension. Behind them, Mrs. Dunlop's eyes widened as she caught the shape of Tom's raised shoulders, the way his arm began to tense. She turned and shouted to Mr. Arnett, who had just reached the playground edge, "Now! We need you now!"

Still, the moment had not yet broken. The boy in front of Tom lifted his chin again, his lips trembling but set. He did not speak, but the refusal in his eyes was louder than any words. Tom snarled, baring his teeth like an animal cornered, and stepped so close their shoes almost touched. His fists rose just enough to make his intent clear. The crowd gasped as one, a single, sharp intake of breath that carried across the yard. It was the moment before thunder, when the sky holds its breath and the air quivers with what is about to come.

Ty's eyes locked on Tom, unwavering, unflinching. He had measured this boy carefully for days now—the triggers, the postures, the sparks. And now he knew. This was the strike point, the split second when the wrong move would unleash all the violence bottled inside Tom. But Ty didn't tense. He didn't rush. He simply stepped closer, his body angled not to confront but to intercept. That calm, deliberate motion carried more force than any shove could. Students near the front felt the balance shift and whispered, "He's here, it's Ty, he won't let it happen." The whispers spread, stealing the air Tom had been feeding on.

Sophie reached for Mila's hand and gripped it hard. "He's going to hit him," she whispered, almost sobbing the words. Mila shook her head, not out of certainty but out of hope. "No. Ty won't let it happen." Their voices joined the hum of the crowd, a low, expectant chorus that seemed to sway the energy in the ring. No longer was it solely Tom's stage. Ty's presence was reshaping the circle, dragging the eyes away from fists and toward the boy whose silence carried more weight than the roar of a hundred voices.

Mr. Takashi had arrived at the schoolyard's edge, his eyes narrowing as he read the scene with an investigator's precision. He saw the way Tom's arm shifted, the angle of his wrist, the muscles twitching in preparation for the swing. He had seen men twice Tom's age make the same mistake. His jaw set, but he did not move. He knew Ty had already chosen his place, and this was Ty's test to meet. Behind him, Mrs. Takashi's hand flew to her mouth, her eyes wide with fear for her son. But she, too, stayed still. She had seen the way he carried himself, the way discipline steadied him like a blade honed to perfection.

The crowd hushed. The teachers strained forward. The boy opposite Tom clenched his fists tighter, even as tears burned at the corners of his eyes. He would not move, he could not. And Tom's arm rose just slightly higher, enough that every student knew the strike was seconds away. The playground seemed to tilt, every breath balanced on that fist. And in that unbearable stillness, with storm about to break, it was not Tom's roar or the boy's fear that held the yard—it was the calm shadow of Ty, stepping in at the perfect moment, carrying with him the certainty that the spark would not catch.

The fist never landed. Before Tom could drive it forward, Ty slid into the narrow space with such precision it seemed he had been standing there all along. His movement wasn't hurried, not panicked, not the frantic scramble of someone afraid. It was deliberate, measured, and carried the silence of a shadow that had simply chosen to step into the light. Tom's fist, once filled with raw momentum, hung suspended in the air as though the weight of Ty's calm presence alone had stalled it. The crowd gasped, then hushed in an instant. Even the boy facing Tom forgot his fear long enough to blink in astonishment.

Tom snarled, caught off guard, but Ty did not flinch. His hands did not strike, yet his body spoke louder than fists. Shoulders squared, stance grounded, Ty placed himself directly between Tom and the smaller boy.

His eyes were locked, not wide with warning but steady with unbroken focus. He spoke no threats. His silence was its own form of command. Tom's chest heaved, breath sharp and fast, yet his fist lowered fraction by fraction under the invisible weight pressing against him. The crowd leaned forward, drawn to the strange power of calm set against fury.

Nico tugged at Jasmin's sleeve and whispered, "Did you see that? He didn't even touch him." Jasmin nodded, eyes wide, as though she had witnessed something impossible. "He doesn't have to," she murmured. "Tom can feel it." Her voice held the awe of a child who had seen control without violence, strength without the need for blows. Even Ella, who normally tried to defuse tension with a nervous laugh, was quiet, her lips pressed tight as though she dared not disturb the fragile balance Ty had created.

Tom stepped forward again, testing the stillness. Ty did not move back, nor did he block aggressively. He merely shifted his weight, enough to remind Tom that any reckless lunge would collapse under its own force. "Step aside," Tom hissed, low and dangerous, but Ty did not yield. He answered not with words, but with a tilt of his head, the faint narrowing of his eyes, a signal clearer than any shouted command. It said simply: No. And in that one refusal lay a fortress Tom could not breach.

The smaller boy behind Ty clutched his hands to his chest, relief flooding his face as he realised he was no longer alone. For the first time, he could breathe. His knees wobbled, but he stayed upright, shielded by Ty's presence. Around them, the ring of students no longer crackled with the thrill of impending violence. Instead, it shifted into reverence, as though they all understood something significant was unfolding. Some whispered Ty's name under their breath, as if invoking it was enough to keep Tom's rage at bay.

Mrs. Locke and Mr. Clarke had nearly reached the front of the circle when they, too, stopped. Their instinct had been to intervene with words, with authority. But seeing Ty planted there, silent and immovable, they realised any interruption might fracture the delicate line he held. Mr. Clarke swallowed hard, his voice caught in his throat, and for the first time in his years of teaching he understood what it meant to witness discipline in its purest form. Ty wasn't fighting Tom. He was neutralising him without a single blow.

Tom's jaw clenched, teeth grinding audibly. His nostrils flared as he searched Ty's face for weakness. None was there. No mockery, no fear, no bait to provoke him further. Only quiet certainty. That absence of reaction unnerved him more than any threat could have. Rage thrived on resistance, on the satisfaction of seeing fear reflected back. Ty offered none. Instead, his stillness drained the fire, leaving Tom's fury burning without fuel. It was suffocating him, turning his own strength inward until it trembled uselessly in his clenched fists.

Jeremy edged closer to Leo and whispered, "He's not even scared." Leo shook his head, a faint smile flickering on his lips. "That's the point," he replied. "Ty isn't fighting him—he's teaching him without saying a word." Jeremy frowned, puzzled.

"Teaching him what?" Leo's gaze stayed fixed on Tom as he answered softly, "That rage can't touch someone who refuses to give it power." The truth of those words resonated in the hushed circle, seeping into ears that would remember them long after the day ended.

Sophie squeezed Ella's hand so tightly it turned pale. "He's going to stop him," she whispered, and Ella nodded, though her eyes never left Ty's stance. "He already has," she replied. They both exhaled, a collective breath that carried into the crowd like a ripple across water. Mila, standing with her arms folded, studied Tom's trembling hands with a hard expression, silently daring him to test Ty one more time. But even Mila, who often spoke in blunt truths, found no words sharp enough for the scene. Ty's silence had already said them all.

Tom's fist finally lowered, hanging limp at his side. His chest still rose and fell in ragged bursts, but the tension in his shoulders cracked, loosening against his will. He tried to mutter something, but his voice broke into a strained growl that carried no weight. Ty did not respond, nor did he smile in triumph. He simply held the space until Tom took a single, grudging step back. That small retreat, invisible to some, felt monumental to the students watching. They had just witnessed the impossible: Tom backing down.

Mr. Arnett and Mrs. Dunlop reached the scene at last, ready to intervene, but found the danger already diffused. They exchanged a glance, both recognising Ty's intervention had achieved what no adult order could have. Mr. Takashi, who had stayed at the edge, allowed a slow breath to escape, his sharp eyes softening. He had seen his son trained for moments like this, but watching it unfold in the chaos of a schoolyard was something different entirely. He felt the pride deep in his chest, though he kept it hidden behind his usual stern composure.

The circle of students slowly dissolved, their voices hushed but buzzing with wonder. "Did you see how he didn't even touch him?" one whispered. "He just stood there, and Tom… he stopped." Another shook his head in disbelief, muttering, "Not even Jarod ever froze like that." The comparisons spilled out, but all led to the same conclusion: Ty had shown them a kind of power no bully could own. Not power to hurt, but power to prevent harm. That was rarer, stronger, and infinitely harder to break.

Tom glared at Ty one last time, his eyes burning with the promise of unfinished battles. But he did not swing. He turned sharply, shoving through the circle and storming away across the yard, his steps heavy and uneven. The crowd parted quickly, the echo of his anger trailing behind. Yet no one followed him. Their eyes stayed on Ty, who had not moved, had not spoken, and yet had already rewritten the story of that fight before it could begin.

The boy Ty had shielded lingered behind, shaking but safe. His lips parted, trying to form a thank you, but no sound came. Ty glanced back once, a faint nod enough to steady the boy's trembling knees. Then, without a word, Ty walked away, blending back into the crowd as though nothing had happened. He did not seek praise, nor did he invite questions. His silence was the lesson, and those who saw it understood.

For long minutes after, the yard carried a quiet hum, not of fear but of awe. Teachers spoke in hushed voices, students whispered what they had seen, and the playground felt different—safer, though no rule had been written, no punishment delivered. It was the stillness left in Ty's wake, a reminder that sometimes the most powerful intervention is not the loudest, but the calm shadow that steps in when no one else dares.

The bell finally rang, pulling the children back to class. Yet the silence lingered, woven into the air like an invisible thread. Tom's fists had not landed. The smaller boy was unhurt. And the lesson remained, etched into every pair of eyes that had watched: a fight had been stopped before it could begin, not by force, but by the unshakable presence of one boy who knew exactly when to move.

Tom twitched as if to throw his fist again, the fire in him refusing to dim, but Ty moved with the clarity of instinct. His hand darted, not in violence but in precision, two fingers pressing into a tendon at Tom's wrist while his opposite palm settled lightly on the crest of Tom's shoulder. The effect was immediate. Tom stiffened, his arm folding against his will, muscles clenching but refusing to obey his rage. It was not pain that stopped him—it was control, sharp and exact, a command written into the body itself. The crowd gasped softly, sensing the invisible line that Ty had drawn.

Tom's eyes went wide, the fury there strangled by shock. He strained, but the more he pushed against the hold, the more his own body betrayed him, trembling and weak under the measured pressure of Ty's touch. The yard fell into a strange hush, as though everyone knew they were seeing something both dangerous and merciful at once. No bruise would form, no mark would linger, but the message was carved deeper than any blow: Ty had chosen to spare him, but not to release him.

The smaller boy behind Ty stood frozen, uncertain whether to run or collapse. It was Leo who stepped forward, guiding the boy gently by the shoulder, whispering something steady into his ear. Jeremy darted to his side, hands flapping nervously but voice firm enough to say, "Come on, let's go." Together, they steered him away from Tom's looming shadow, toward the path that would lead into the safety of the office. Each step he took away from the circle was a victory measured not in bruises avoided, but in breaths still his to draw.

Tom let out a guttural growl, his jaw locked, face flushed. He wanted to scream, to lash out, to prove he wasn't trapped, but Ty's stillness hollowed him out. The pressure wasn't cruel, it wasn't crushing—it was calm authority, a reminder that raw strength was nothing when placed against skill and restraint. Tom's knees bent slightly, betraying the tremor in his legs. Students leaned closer, some holding their own wrists unconsciously, feeling in phantom what Tom was enduring.

Mr. Clarke, halfway through the crowd, paused mid-step. He had taught many lessons in his years, but never had he seen one written so clearly on a boy's face. "Controlled without cruelty," he muttered, almost to himself, and Mrs. Locke beside him nodded, her lips pressed tight.

They both recognised that what Ty had just done was beyond any rulebook. It was discipline delivered in silence, the kind that left no scar but altered the heart, if the heart chose to listen.

Jasmin tugged Ella's sleeve, whispering in awe, "He can't move." Ella's reply was barely a breath. "It's not just his arm. Look at his eyes. He doesn't know what to do." Sophie pressed her palms together nervously, staring as though she were watching a storm fold in on itself. To them, it wasn't just technique—it was the impossible made real, the proof that someone could halt fury without feeding it.

Nico stood straighter, his fists curling at his sides, not in challenge but in pride. He understood the depth of what Ty was risking. One slip, one ounce of pressure too hard, and Tom would be hurt. One release too soon, and the fight would reignite. But Ty walked that line with the balance of a boy who had been taught not just how to fight, but when to stop. Nico swallowed the lump in his throat, realising how rare it was for someone their age to bear such a burden.

Tom strained again, his shoulder jerking, but the tremor collapsed into stillness once more. His breath came in heavy bursts, nostrils flaring, but he could not deny the truth his body was screaming: he was trapped. He glared at Ty with all the venom he could muster, but Ty's gaze did not flinch. The silence between them stretched long, filled with a hundred unspoken words: I see you. I won't let you harm him. I won't let you harm yourself either.

Behind them, the boy being led away glanced back once. His eyes met Ty's steady form, and for the first time since Tom had squared his fists, he no longer felt small. He wasn't saved by luck, nor by chance. Someone had chosen to stand between him and violence, and that choice carried more weight than anything Tom had tried to prove. His steps grew firmer as he disappeared toward the office, his shoulders lifting from their slump.

Mrs. Dunlop finally broke through the circle with Mr. Arnett. They saw the hold, saw the fury bound within it, and hesitated. There was nothing in the manuals, nothing in the codes of conduct that told them how to respond to a child who could immobilise another without harm. Mr. Arnett raised his hand to speak, but lowered it again, realising his voice would only fracture the delicate control already at play. The safest path was silence, at least until Ty chose otherwise.

Tom's knees buckled slightly, the fury draining from him with every ragged breath. His shoulders sagged against Ty's hand, but the boy before him did not press harder. He simply held the line until Tom realised his fight was already over. The humiliation burned hot across Tom's face, but it was laced with something else—fear, not of Ty's strength, but of Ty's restraint. Rage knew how to battle rage. It had no weapon against calm.

Jeremy pressed against Leo's side, whispering anxiously, "What if he snaps again?" Leo's arm wrapped protectively across his younger brother's shoulders, his voice low but sure. "He won't. Ty's got him. Watch." And Jeremy did, eyes wide, heart thudding, as he saw what it meant for someone to control not with fists, but with presence. It was a lesson he would carry, though he barely understood it yet.

Mila leaned forward, her brow furrowed. She was not easily impressed, but the sight of Tom, the boy who terrified others with a single glare, frozen under Ty's touch made even her exhale in disbelief. "That's power," she muttered, but Nico shook his head softly from her side. "No—that's discipline." His correction hung between them, sharp and undeniable. Mila said nothing more, letting the truth settle in the pit of her chest.

Tom finally sagged fully, the fire in him smothered by exhaustion. Ty eased his hand from the wrist, then the shoulder, with the same precision he had applied when placing them. Tom staggered back a step, glaring, rubbing his arm as if to shake off the invisible weight still clinging to him. But he did not attack again. Ty straightened, silent, his eyes calm but unyielding. He had not bruised Tom. He had not shamed him with words. He had simply shown him a boundary that no anger could cross.

The students stared, breath held, waiting for the crack of violence to erupt once more. It didn't. Instead, Tom shoved past the outer edge of the circle, muttering under his breath, and stormed off. His shoulders trembled with fury, but his fists remained unclenched. The other boy was safe, and the fight was gone. Ty stood there a moment longer, ensuring the storm had passed, then finally turned, his silence louder than any cheer.

And when the circle dissolved, when whispers rose like wind again, no one spoke of Tom's strength. They spoke of Ty's restraint. They spoke of the boy who had stopped fire without burning. It was a memory they would carry, one that would outlast bruises, one that had shown them the rarest kind of victory.

The confrontation did not end with Tom's retreat across the yard. His rage simmered beneath the surface, restless and unresolved, and it was only a matter of time before it found another target. That moment came sooner than expected, when Mrs. Locke stepped forward, trying to guide the boy inside before another scene could unfold. Tom's posture stiffened at the sight of her hand reaching toward his shoulder, and his fury flared like sparks on dry kindling. His eyes narrowed, jaw tightening, and the crowd sensed the danger before the teacher did. One wrong move and his anger would spill directly onto her.

Ty saw it instantly. He did not move like someone rushing to stop an accident. He moved like someone who had already anticipated it, his small frame gliding across the grass in silence until he was standing directly behind Tom. Tom raised his arm, the muscles in his wrist twitching with the intent to lash out, but he never made contact. In one precise motion, Ty's hand pressed into the tendons of Tom's wrist while his other palm anchored firmly against the joint of his shoulder. The effect was immediate. Tom froze, the fire in his muscles locked in place, his body refusing to obey his rage.

Students gasped softly, watching the shift in power ripple through Tom's body. It wasn't a strike. There was no bruise, no pain sharp enough to draw a cry. It was control, delivered through precision. Tom's chest rose in ragged bursts, but his arms would not swing.

His shoulders trembled, and for the first time his strength was useless against something he could not see nor understand. It wasn't fear of being hit back. It was the bewildering realisation that his own body would not answer him. His fury was caged inside, thrashing with no way out.

Mrs. Locke stumbled back, startled, but she caught the look in Ty's eyes and understood. This was not an attack. This was restraint designed to protect her. She steadied her breath, her hands gripping the papers against her chest, and let the boy guide her toward the safety of the office door. Every step she took away was matched with Ty's quiet focus. He held Tom steady, not long enough to humiliate him, only long enough to ensure she was clear of harm. Once she reached the threshold of the building, Ty loosened his grip, releasing Tom's arm with a precision equal to the hold.

Tom staggered, clutching his wrist as though unsure what had just happened. His breath tore out of him in short growls, frustration gnawing at his pride. He spun toward Ty, eyes blazing, but the crowd saw the truth before Tom could admit it—he had been disarmed without a blow. His rage had been silenced by something beyond fists, beyond brute force. It was a kind of strength he could neither match nor comprehend, and the confusion cracked through his fury like a fissure in stone.

Mr. Clarke, who had reached the scene, nodded once at Ty, a gesture of both gratitude and awe. He had been teaching for years, but never had he seen a child prevent violence with such mastery, with such calm. Mr. Arnett, standing at his side, rubbed his chin, troubled by the thought that it had taken an eleven-year-old boy to do what the adults had failed to manage. Still, he knew better than to interrupt. This was not recklessness. It was discipline of the rarest kind, and it had spared them a scene that could have ended in disaster.

Nico leaned closer to Leo, his voice trembling with excitement. "He stopped him again. Did you see that?" Leo nodded slowly, his eyes never leaving Ty. "It's more than stopping him," he whispered. "Ty knows exactly where to touch, where to move. He could hurt him, but he doesn't. That's control." Jeremy, standing shorter among them, frowned as he tried to process what he had just seen. "It's like Tom's body just… stopped working," he said. "How can he do that?" Leo glanced at him and answered, "Because Ty was taught not just how to fight, but how not to fight."

The whispers spread like wildfire through the students. "He froze him," one said. "Did you see his arm? He couldn't move!" Another shook their head in disbelief. "He didn't even hurt him. He just… stopped him." The awe carried across the playground, a chorus of voices retelling the moment before it had even ended. To the children who watched, it was no longer about Tom's anger or Mrs. Locke's near danger. It was about Ty, the boy who had shown them a different kind of strength—one that defended without striking, one that commanded without cruelty.

Tom, humiliated but too shaken to admit it, shoved through the thinning crowd. His movements were jagged, unbalanced, his pride dragging him forward while his body betrayed him with every uneven step. He growled low under his breath, the sound more of a wounded animal than a victorious fighter. The students parted quickly, none daring to block his way. Yet the fear that usually followed him was gone. In its place hung a silence, heavy and knowing. They had all seen that Tom was not untouchable.

Ty stood still, his hands dropping back to his sides, his face calm as though nothing unusual had occurred. He did not revel in the moment, did not seek recognition from the students staring at him in open wonder. Instead, he turned quietly and began to walk toward the doors, his stride unhurried, his presence still carrying the weight of discipline. Behind him, the whispers grew into a low hum, the schoolyard buzzing with the memory of what had just happened. Mrs. Locke was safe, Tom had been stopped, and not a single blow had been exchanged.

Mrs. Dunlop approached Ty as he neared the steps, her eyes filled with questions, but she held her tongue. She saw the steadiness in his expression and chose silence over interruption. Some lessons, she realised, were not meant to be explained in words. They were meant to be witnessed. Mr. Takashi lingered near the edge of the yard, his sharp eyes softening as he gave the faintest nod of approval. His son had acted precisely as trained—calm, decisive, and without excess. Pride filled him, though he showed it only in the subtle curve of his jaw.

The bell rang again, pulling the children back to their routines, though none returned the same as before. They carried the image of Tom halted in mid-rage, his fury trapped beneath Ty's quiet hand. For some, it was reassurance. For others, it was a challenge. But for all of them, it was unforgettable. Even Lisa, usually sharp-tongued, muttered under her breath as she passed Nico, "Now that's control." And Nico, for once, didn't argue. He simply nodded, his mind replaying the moment over and over, a reminder of the difference between violence and mastery.

Inside, the teachers gathered briefly in the hall, murmuring among themselves. Mrs. Locke's voice shook as she explained how close it had been, how easily Tom might have lashed out if not for Ty. Mr. Clarke placed a steadying hand on her shoulder, his expression grim. "He's different," he said quietly, glancing toward Ty. "Not just Tom, but Ty as well. We need to be careful how we handle both of them." The staff nodded, the weight of the morning pressing into their thoughts. They had been reminded that danger walked their halls, but also that discipline lived among their students.

The day pressed on, but the shadow of that encounter stretched long into the afternoon. Students carried it into whispers at their desks, teachers carried it into hushed conversations behind closed doors. Tom's fury had been halted, Mrs. Locke had been spared, and the memory of Ty's steady hands lingered like an imprint on the air. It was not the end of conflict, not by any means, but it had set a tone. There were new rules in the schoolyard now, unwritten yet deeply felt: rage could be stopped, violence could be restrained, and sometimes the quietest boy carried the strongest touch of control.

The moment Ty released Tom, there was no speech, no lecture, no scolding to fill the air. Instead, silence hung like a blade suspended over the circle of children, sharper than any insult or shout could ever be. Ty stood still, his eyes steady, his breath controlled, and the quiet pressed down on everyone who had gathered. Tom shifted on his feet, rubbing at his wrist, his lips parted as if to spit an insult, but nothing came. The silence stripped him of words before he could even form them, leaving him naked in the centre of a crowd that watched not with mockery, but with a wary kind of awe.

Tom's pride demanded action—another swing, another shove, anything to prove he still held power. Yet his body refused. The calm he had felt under Ty's touch still lingered in his muscles like a phantom weight, and that stillness terrified him more than any blow. He knew how to rage against fists, how to spit against shouts, but he had no weapon for this kind of restraint. His eyes darted, scanning the circle for jeers, for laughter, for the smallest opening to rebuild his crumbling authority, but all he found was silence reflected back at him.

The students waited, breaths caught in their throats. They expected Ty to speak, to condemn Tom, to declare his dominance, but Ty's refusal to say a word carried more force than anything else. His quiet meant judgment without insult, power without arrogance, and for Tom it was unbearable. He tried to laugh, to snort, to cover his unease, but the sound cracked halfway through, swallowed by the pressure in the air. He looked smaller then, not in height, but in presence, as though the crowd no longer saw the brute but the boy fumbling behind the mask.

Jeremy gripped Leo's sleeve tightly, whispering, "Why isn't he saying anything?" Leo shook his head, his gaze never leaving Ty. "Because he doesn't have to," he answered, his voice hushed with reverence. And in that answer, Jeremy began to understand that sometimes words only fed the fire, but silence starved it until it collapsed under its own weight. Even Nico, who had often believed in strength as proof, folded his arms and nodded once, admitting to himself that this kind of control was greater than any fight he had trained to win.

Tom's chest rose and fell sharply, his breath loud in the void left by Ty's silence. His fists clenched, then unclenched. He stepped forward once, daring himself to try, but Ty's gaze caught him mid-step. The younger boy did not move, did not threaten, did not prepare to strike. He simply looked at him, calm and unshaken, and Tom's step faltered into nothing. The silence had reached deeper than fear. It had crawled into his rage, reminding him that no scream, no threat, no punch could reclaim what Ty had already taken from him: the illusion that he could not be stopped.

Jasmin's hand covered her mouth as she whispered to Ella, "It's like he froze him without even touching him." Ella nodded slowly, her eyes fixed on Tom's trembling hands. "That's worse than being hit. He can't fight it." Sophie shivered, not from cold but from the invisible weight that pressed on them all. It was the kind of silence that made the heart pound louder than words, the kind that demanded reflection rather than retaliation.

Mrs. Dunlop exchanged a look with Mr. Arnett, both of them recognising what had just been done without being written into any policy or manual. "He's teaching them," she whispered, and Mr. Arnett's jaw tightened as he replied, "And teaching him too." Their eyes fell on Tom, who shifted back another step, his pride bleeding out into the ground beneath him. They had seen bullies tamed by detention, by suspension, by shouted authority. Never by this.

The counsellor, Ms. Henley, observed carefully from the edge of the yard. She did not miss the way the other students stared at Ty—not with fear, but with respect. His silence had created a new balance, one where power did not belong to the loudest or the strongest, but to the calmest. It unsettled her, but it also filled her with hope. Perhaps, she thought, there was a lesson here greater than any punishment could provide.

Tom spat on the ground, a hollow attempt at defiance, but even that fell flat in the quiet. The circle began to dissolve slowly, students breaking off into small clusters, whispering in voices too low for him to hear. He stood there, left in the gap Ty had created, and for the first time he felt what it was to be seen and yet stripped of control. His scowl returned, but the heat in it had cooled, replaced with a twitch of doubt that even he could not smother.

Ty turned away at last, still wordless, his shoulders squared but his pace calm. He walked as though nothing had happened, as though holding back a storm was ordinary, leaving Tom to stew in the emptiness left behind. That choice was its own punishment. The fight had not ended with fists, nor with victory declared. It had ended with silence, and the silence followed Tom more closely than any shadow ever could.

When the teachers finally moved, it was not to scold or to threaten, but to usher the remaining students back toward class. They did not speak either, understanding that words would only fracture the lesson. And so the silence stretched further, trailing into the hallways, into the classrooms, into the uneasy corners of Tom's mind. For all his snarls and fists, it was silence that conquered him that day.

And when Jeremy later sat at his desk, still shaken, he whispered only one thought to himself: "That silence was louder than anything I've ever heard."

By the time the students were ushered back inside, the whispers had already begun weaving their way through every corner of the school. Children spoke in hushed tones, glancing over their shoulders, their voices filled with awe rather than fear. Some said Ty had frozen Tom in place with nothing but a single hand. Others swore that it wasn't the grip at all, but his silence, his stare, the stillness in his body that carried more weight than fists ever could. The truth was simple enough—Ty had stepped in, measured and calm—but the retelling of it grew, magnified by the way the crowd had felt it, how every child had walked away certain they had witnessed something extraordinary.

Jeremy, sitting at his desk, leaned close to Leo and whispered, "They're already calling him a shadow." Leo's brow furrowed, his voice low in reply. "He doesn't like that kind of attention. He's not looking to be a hero." But even Leo knew it was too late; the myth had already begun to grow legs. Once a whisper starts to move in a school, it does not stop. It travels faster than truth, sharper than reason, and in Ty's case, it carried a reverence that no adult could manufacture with speeches or rules.

Nico, who sat across from them, picked up fragments of chatter from the row behind. "He didn't even say anything," one boy muttered. "He just looked at Tom, and Tom froze." Another girl added, "My brother said Ty's dad is an investigator. Maybe he taught him things." Their voices carried wonder rather than judgment, and Nico glanced toward Ty, who sat calmly writing notes in his book, as if none of it mattered. That composure only added to the legend forming around him. He looked untouched, unmoved, and the more he ignored the talk, the larger it grew.

At the lunch tables, Jasmin leaned across to Sophie and Ella. "Do you think he's dangerous?" she asked in a whisper. Sophie shook her head, though her eyes remained cautious. "Not dangerous like Tom. Ty's different. He doesn't scare people. He just… stops them." Ella's voice was softer still, but certain. "That's why Tom hates him already. He's not afraid of fists, but he doesn't know what to do when someone doesn't fight back." Their words, meant to remain private, were overheard by half the table, and soon those ideas slipped outward, reshaped into new versions of the same truth.

Ms. Henley, walking quietly past the cafeteria door, caught enough of the whispers to understand the shift. She saw how the students' faces had changed. They no longer spoke of Tom as the unmovable force; now their fear had fractured, redirected toward curiosity about Ty. She paused, considering how myths are made—not from facts, but from the way people feel when they cannot find words. She knew this would follow Ty now, and though she respected the boy's strength, she worried about the weight of such expectations on his young shoulders.

Up in the staff room, Mr. Clarke and Mrs. Locke spoke in low voices. "The children are already talking," Mrs. Locke said. "They're making him into something more than a student." Mr. Clarke's jaw tightened as he stirred his tea. "That's because they felt safe for the first time today. Safe because of a boy, not an adult. They'll hold on to that." He sighed, knowing well that safety in a school should never depend on a child's ability to confront danger. But he could not deny what he had seen either, nor could he silence the story that now had a life of its own.

Tom heard the whispers too, though no one spoke them directly to him. They lingered behind his back, slipped around corners, grew louder whenever he entered a room. Every mention of Ty's name burned him like a fresh wound, every retelling of that silence made his stomach knot. He clenched his fists and muttered curses under his breath, but nothing he did erased the memory of the crowd circling him, watching his fury collapse under Ty's calm. The more the students talked, the smaller Tom felt.

Jeremy noticed it immediately. He watched how Tom's steps grew heavier, his eyes sharper, his face more guarded than before. The whispers that exalted Ty were the same whispers that chipped away at Tom's mask, and Jeremy, though still only nine, understood how dangerous that could become. He leaned close to Leo again and said, "He's going to snap. The more they talk, the worse it will get." Leo nodded grimly, because he knew from experience how shame and pride can tangle into something violent.

Mila, who rarely spoke during such moments, finally whispered to Alex, "He'll try again. He won't let it go. Bullies never do when they feel small." Alex didn't answer at once, but his eyes flicked toward Ty, who sat with his usual composure, unbothered by the storm brewing around him. Alex exhaled slowly and muttered, "That's why he has to stay calm. If he slips, even once, Tom will think he's won." It was less a warning than a truth carved from the old wounds of his own past.

And so the myth of Ty grew, not because he wanted it, but because silence is louder than noise, and restraint heavier than fists. By the end of the day, even the teachers had overheard at least one version of the story: that Ty could stop anyone, that his silence was a weapon, that his shadow was enough to bend a storm. It was only one moment in a long day, but the school had already changed. Tom had been seen for what he was, and Ty had been seen for what he could be. The balance had shifted, and though the whispers made Ty larger than life, the boy himself remained steady, his eyes watching, his silence speaking louder than any rumour could.

The walls of the staff room held a heaviness that had not been felt in years, as though the air itself recognised danger lingering in the halls. Mr. Clarke set his cup down with a sharp clink, the sound breaking the silence that had spread between the teachers. "We've had fights before," he said, his voice low but edged with worry, "but this—this feels different." Mrs. Locke nodded, her folded hands tightening until her knuckles paled. "It is different. The children aren't just whispering about a boy with a temper. They're speaking of Tom like he's a storm they expect to hit again." Across the table, Mrs. Dunlop shifted in her chair, her eyes flicking toward the closed door as if expecting the boy's shadow to slip under it.

Miss Kara leaned forward, her brows knitted tight. "What frightens me isn't only Tom," she admitted. "It's that the children have already built Ty into something larger than himself. They're clinging to him for protection." She sighed heavily. "That isn't fair to him. He's only eleven. We cannot let this rest on his shoulders." Mrs. Haller glanced at her with quiet severity. "Fair or not, it already has. Children do not ask for heroes, they create them when they feel unsafe. And today, they saw Ty step where none of us reached in time." The remark landed hard, making Mr. Clarke's jaw tighten as though she had struck him personally.

Ms. Henley folded her arms, her tone steadier than the rest. "We can't ignore what Ty did, nor can we encourage it. He's skilled, yes, but what if Tom escalates? What if the next fight is worse, or if Ty feels cornered into using more force than he intends?

These are children, not soldiers." The weight of her words made several nod, yet no one dared speak against her. Mr. Arnett, the principal, finally cleared his throat, his voice solemn. "We cannot have our school become a battleground. If Tom is truly as dangerous as it appears, we must intervene decisively before the next spark."

At that, all eyes turned to Mr. Takashi, who sat at the end of the table with an unreadable expression, his hands steepled beneath his chin. His pause was deliberate, allowing the silence to press until each teacher felt it fully. When he spoke, his voice carried no panic, only certainty. "You are right. This is only the beginning. Tom is not finished, because boys like him rarely are. What you saw today was the surface. Beneath it is a fire waiting for air." He let his words settle, his gaze sharp enough to still any doubts. "Ty understood that, which is why he moved the way he did. But make no mistake—this will happen again."

Mrs. Locke exhaled, shaking her head slowly. "So what do we do? Suspend him? Call the police?" Mr. Takashi's eyes flicked toward her, calm yet firm. "You do not wait for violence to demand reaction. You prepare for it. You anticipate it. And when it comes, you must act swiftly and without hesitation. Hesitation costs children their safety." He leaned back, his tone cooling into something almost weary. "I have seen this pattern too many times outside of schools. Once the spark catches, the fire spreads quickly. If you think today was frightening, brace yourselves—worse is coming."

The teachers absorbed his words with unease. Mrs. Haller rubbed her temples, muttering, "We are teachers, not enforcers. This is beyond our calling." But Mr. Clarke spoke sharply in response. "And yet the children still look to us. If we cannot answer, then who will?" He looked toward the door, his thoughts no doubt on the students scattered through their classrooms, unaware of the gravity of this conversation. "We've already been late once today. We cannot afford to be late again." His words echoed with an unspoken guilt, a shadow of his memory of Myles' story still haunting him.

Mrs. Dunlop glanced around the table, her voice quieter but firmer than before. "If Mr. Takashi says sparks will fly again, we have to trust him. He has seen more than we ever will. But how do we stop Tom without lighting that fire ourselves?" Her question hung heavy, unanswered, because no one truly knew. The staff shifted uncomfortably, recognising the truth of their helplessness.

Finally, Mr. Arnett placed both hands flat on the table, his voice steady though his eyes betrayed the weight he carried. "Then we prepare. We stay vigilant. And if Tom forces our hand, we act together. No child, not even Ty, will face this alone." He looked across at Mr. Takashi, who gave the smallest nod of approval, as though acknowledging that the principal had at last spoken with the firmness the moment demanded.

The room fell into silence again, not the calm of resolution, but the silence of bracing for impact. They all knew it—the boy called Tom was not finished. He was a fuse already lit, and no amount of whispered rumours or watchful eyes could extinguish him yet. All they could do was wait, sharpen their resolve, and hope their unity would be enough when the fire finally broke loose.

The classroom carried the uneasy hush of children who had seen too much outside and were now pretending that numbers on a chalkboard or words in a textbook could smooth over what lingered in their minds. Mr. Clarke's voice, steady as it usually was, sounded thinner now, as though even he could not pretend the day had not shifted something in the air. Students bent their heads over their work, but every so often their eyes flicked to Tom. He sat near the middle row, his back straight, his hands resting too still on his desk, and his eyes fixed on Ty. It was not the casual glance of curiosity, nor the wary look of someone chastened. No, it was sharper, colder—a glare that carried the promise of unfinished business.

Tom's gaze did not wander. He studied Ty with the intensity of someone memorising every movement, every breath, as though planning how to strike when the time was right. His jaw tightened, his cheek twitched once, and though he made no sound, the silence around him felt louder than the rustle of paper or the scratch of pencils. Ty, for his part, seemed unfazed. His shoulders remained even, his pen gliding in steady strokes across his notebook, but his eyes did not lift. He did not need to meet Tom's stare to know it was there. Calm was his armour, and he wore it deliberately.

The narrator—unseen, unnoticed—watched the exchange as though time itself had slowed, catching the hidden lines of battle that most children could not yet read. Tom's glare was more than anger; it was calculation. He was not thinking of the moment that had just passed, where Ty had stepped between him and violence. He was imagining the next one, a place where he might not be stopped, where the crowd might not whisper with awe but cry out with fear. The difference between today and that day lived only in his planning, and the thought alone made the room feel smaller.

Jeremy shifted uneasily in his chair, sensing it though he could not name it. His pencil tapped once against the desk before he stilled it, glancing at Leo beside him. Leo caught the motion, frowned, then turned his eyes toward Tom. Recognition passed across his face like a shadow. He had seen that look before—in his own reflection years ago, when cruelty had been his shield. He whispered nothing, but his hand clenched into a fist beneath the desk, as if bracing for something he could not yet stop.

Nico, sitting behind them, leaned forward slightly, his keen gaze flicking between Ty and Tom. He was no stranger to tension—his own quick wit had made him a target before—but this was heavier. Beside him, Jasmin's brow furrowed, her eyes narrowing as though trying to pierce through Tom's thoughts.

She whispered something to Ella, who only shook her head, unwilling to let the worry take root aloud. Even Sophie, usually quick to chatter, sat stiller than usual, her book open but her eyes fixed not on the page but on the boy whose presence drew the air taut.

Ty's calm presence anchored the others. He did not raise his eyes, did not falter in his writing, but there was a subtle stillness about him, the kind that comes before deliberate action. He was aware, always aware, yet he chose not to respond. His silence was not ignorance—it was strategy. The more Tom glared, the less satisfaction he found in seeing fear reflected back. And that, more than any spoken warning, left Tom unsettled. Yet in his unsettling, his anger only deepened, curdling into something darker, more patient.

From the staff table at the side, Mrs. Locke watched carefully. Teachers often pretended to focus on their papers, but she had been an educator too long to miss the silent duels that played out among children. She saw Tom's glare, and she saw Ty's deliberate calm, and she pressed her lips together in concern. In her mind, she heard Mr. Takashi's warning again: This is only the beginning. The words had sounded grave in the staff room. Now, looking at Tom's eyes, she believed them entirely.

The invisible narrator held the moment in memory: one boy's glare, one boy's silence, and a room of children who felt the storm tightening around them. Tom was not finished. He was planning, and every beat of the clock brought him closer to the moment he would try again.

The final bell rang, its sharp tone carrying through the halls like the release of a held breath. Students gathered their books with a quiet haste, as if eager to step away from the heaviness that lingered after the midday clash. The usual rush of voices did not rise. Instead, lockers shut with muted thuds, shoes scuffed against the floor, and whispers carried like fragile threads. Everyone knew the school day had ended, yet something unspoken had begun. The air still felt charged, as though the echoes of Tom's glare followed them into the corridors.

Ty remained steady, walking calmly beside Nico and Leo as they filed toward the exit. Jeremy trailed behind, his small frame lost in the crowd but his sharp eyes fixed on Tom. He could not let go of the picture of Ty stepping forward, paralyzing Tom without anger. It had been controlled, almost frightening in its quiet precision, and Jeremy knew that was the very thing holding Tom back—for now. Still, he worried. He had seen enough to know that fire never dies after the first spark. It smoulders, waiting for air.

Teachers moved more deliberately too, their eyes scanning the groups of children with unease. Mr. Clarke paused at the doorway of the library, speaking low to Mrs. Locke, who nodded with her arms folded tight against her chest. Mrs. Dunlop whispered something to Principal Arnett, and his frown deepened. They all felt it: today had drawn a line, and though the fight had not come, it nearly had. That nearly was enough to keep them wary. For them, duty meant being ready for when Tom tested the line again—and he would.

# THE SMILE THAT BROKE

Tom himself walked stiffly through the throng, his shoulders squared, his face expressionless. Yet his silence did not feel like surrender; it felt like calculation. He carried no bruise, no mark, nothing visible to say he had been checked. But the memory of Ty's hand pressing against him, stopping him cold, was carved into his pride. His steps were too quick, his jaw set too hard, the unspoken promise in his glare carried with him down the hall. Others moved aside instinctively, as though the storm still swirled about him.

Outside, the playground lay quiet, emptied of laughter that usually carried at dismissal. Groups of students gathered close, whispering to each other as though recounting a ghost story. Mila leaned in to Sophie and Jasmin, her brow furrowed. "He's worse than Jarod," she muttered, and though Sophie shook her head, her silence betrayed she feared it might be true. Alex, taller than most, walked beside Leo and Jeremy, saying nothing but scanning the edges of the crowd. Old instincts made him wary of what others might do when fear had already taken root.

Ty remained calm, walking with his usual measured steps, but his mind never rested. Every detail of Tom's movements, every glance and silence, he stored carefully. His father had taught him that shadows reveal as much as daylight, and Tom's shadow was stretching long. Nico noticed his friend's focus and nudged him lightly, as though to remind him he wasn't alone in this watch. Ty responded with the smallest nod, never breaking his calm stride, but the gesture spoke volumes. They were all alert now.

The invisible narrator lingered over the scene as the sun dropped lower in the sky, painting the windows in gold. It was not a day marked by blows or blood, but it was marked all the same. A line had been drawn—not in chalk or ink, but in silence, glares, and the weight of things left unsaid. Students carried it home with them, tucked between their books and their uneaten snacks. Parents would ask about their day, and they would shrug, saying little, but in their eyes the truth would live: something dangerous had begun at school.

The first sparks had not yet burned into flames, but everyone could feel the tinder waiting. Ty knew it. The teachers knew it. Even the youngest of the students, barely old enough to tie their shoes without fumbling, sensed it. And as the schoolyard emptied, and the last footsteps faded into the streets, the silence that settled over the building did not feel like peace. It felt like the pause before the fire finds its fuel. This was not an ending. This was only the beginning.

## CHAPTER 11: SHADOWS OF THE UNCLE

The corridors were never quiet, but today the sounds carried differently, as though the walls themselves bent to hold the rumours tight. Teachers huddled near doorways, voices lowered, words slipping between the shuffle of books and the slam of lockers. They spoke of shouting after dark, of doors slamming with enough force to rattle windows, of broken dishes left uncleaned until morning. Students, always quick to echo what adults whispered, repeated it in fragments, weaving it into stories heavier than they understood. I listened, unseen, uncounted, a shadow among them, recording their unease. It was not the parents, they said. His mother and father had no such history. The trouble was older, taller, harder. It was the uncle — eight years older than Tom's father, and far meaner.

The younger children carried the words like stones in their pockets, each rumour making them walk heavier, slower, afraid of looking over their shoulders. Nico leaned into Jasmin, his whisper hurried and sharp, "They said his uncle once threw a chair across the yard. Split it in half." Jasmin's eyes widened, but she said nothing, her lips sealed by the chill of the thought. Ella added her part soon after, repeating what she had overheard from her own sister: "He drinks. That's when it starts." Fear, once loosed, needs no proof to flourish. It simply spreads, filling corners with shadows until no light is trusted.

Teachers knew more, though not all. Mr. Clarke, steady as stone in most matters, carried lines across his brow deeper than before. He had seen the folder, or so the children believed, and his silence told more than words would have. Mrs. Locke tapped her pen against the edge of her desk whenever Tom's name was mentioned, each tap like a heartbeat she could not slow. Miss Kara folded her arms tighter than necessary, her eyes flicking toward the hallway every few minutes as if expecting him to appear unbidden. Fear of a boy becomes heavier when it's tethered to a man, and Tom's uncle hung like an invisible chain at his side.

Leo and Alex said little, though they knew the shape of violence better than most. Having once lived by fists and taunts, they recognized the echoes in Tom's posture, the sharpness in his eyes, the way his silence baited a challenge. They did not add to the rumours, but their watchfulness spoke volumes. Jeremy, small but perceptive, asked them softly at lunch, "Is it true? About his uncle?" Leo's lips pressed into a line. Alex shook his head, not to deny but to silence. "Truth doesn't matter," Alex muttered. "It's what he carries into the room that counts."

Ty listened differently. Where others heard only noise, he sorted whispers into patterns, as though each word was a stone on a map he built in silence. His father had taught him to trust not the story, but the root. And the root was clear: Tom's uncle was the storm behind the boy, teaching through fear, striking through rage. Ty did not flinch at the thought. He only grew stiller, like the air before rain. Beside him, Jeremy leaned close, trying to catch meaning from the stillness, but Ty gave no answer. He never did until the moment mattered.

Sophie, ever sensitive to the undercurrents, pressed her hands together when she heard two older boys muttering near the lockers. "They say his uncle's worse than Jarod. Bigger. Meaner." She repeated it to Mila, her voice quivering with the weight of comparison. Mila frowned, shaking her head. "Doesn't matter who's worse. It matters that Tom brings it with him." Their words were sharp, young though they were, and I noted them carefully. Children often understood cruelty quicker than adults admitted.

The staff, though careful, could not hide their own divisions. Some argued for removal, others for another chance, all of them aware of the weight each choice carried. Principal Arnett folded his arms at every suggestion, unwilling to let the decision be hurried. Mrs. Dunlop's voice wavered when she asked whether vigilance would be enough, whether watching was the same as protecting. Ms. Henley, calmer, argued that stripping Tom from the school without confronting the root would leave the wound festering. But even she admitted that every rumour felt like tinder, waiting for one spark.

And so the hallways remained charged, not with laughter or chatter, but with the sound of names — Tom's, and his uncle's, carried from lip to lip until they became larger than the boys themselves. Every child repeated it differently, every teacher held it with caution, but none could let it go. I listened, unseen, recording not just the words but the fear beneath them. The uncle was not here, not in the school, not within these walls. And yet, somehow, every child walked as though his shadow had been cast over their shoulders.

Tom did not walk the hall like the others. Where Nico and Jasmin strode with the half-careless rhythm of children who trusted their footing, Tom's steps were lighter, measured, and always edged by hesitation. His eyes told the story before his mouth ever dared. They never settled forward. They slipped sideways, glancing over shoulders, searching corners, measuring distance to doors. Even when the corridor was quiet, he moved as though someone might step out of shadow, as though one wrong turn could summon hands rougher than words. He could laugh if pressed, even smile when someone tugged him into play, but his eyes never followed the curve of his mouth. They darted, betraying him, as if signalling he did not belong even in his own skin.

Jeremy saw it first, sharp as only a nine-year-old could. While the teachers debated lesson plans and classmates thought only of the next recess, Jeremy leaned against the wall, watching Tom's glance flick back again and again. "Like a rabbit," Jeremy murmured once, but not cruelly — almost with pity. A rabbit cornered knows no comfort, no matter how safe the meadow looks. Leo, standing beside him, followed Jeremy's gaze and nodded slowly. He had worn that look himself once, back when fists had been his only answer to fear. "That's not the look of a fighter," Leo said under his breath. "That's the look of someone waiting for a fight he can't stop."

Ty said nothing at first, though he watched just as closely. His father had taught him that eyes revealed more than mouths ever dared, and Tom's eyes were a ledger filled with accounts unpaid. Even when the boy sat in class, shoulders drawn in tight, pretending to scribble like the rest, his gaze never left the edges of the room.

It was as though every wall held a threat, and he was learning to read it, decoding danger where others saw chalkboards and books. When Mrs. Locke asked him to read aloud, his voice was steady enough, but his eyes betrayed him, flicking to the window, to the door, back to the clock. Always checking. Always waiting.

Nico noticed it too, though his words came heavier. "He's scared of everything," he whispered to Jasmin after Tom passed their desk, head bent low. Jasmin shook her head, not quite agreeing. "Not scared of everything," she answered softly, "just scared of being caught. There's a difference." Ella leaned across from her seat and added, "That's how animals look in cages. Like they don't know where to rest." None of them mocked him; none of them laughed. They only saw it and carried the weight of what his eyes revealed. Children, untrained though they were, understood when someone bore fear so deep it could not be hidden.

The teachers spoke of it too, though never in Tom's presence. Mrs. Dunlop once confessed in the staff room, her tone careful, "It's not the grades that worry me. It's the way he scans the room. I've only seen that in children who've lived through more than they should." Mrs. Haller nodded, recalling her own cousin who had grown up with a violent uncle. "It's a survival trick," she said. "They keep looking for the next blow even when it doesn't come." Mr. Clarke added nothing, but his silence was an agreement, his brow furrowed as if every flicker of Tom's gaze carved a deeper line across his forehead.

Even laughter could not disguise it. One afternoon, when Sophie dropped her books and Nico made a joke about her "tripping over invisible friends," the classroom filled with the kind of laughter that carries children along like a tide. Tom laughed too, a sharp sound, quick and almost convincing. But Jeremy, sitting only a desk away, caught the truth. Even as Tom's mouth split into a grin, his eyes betrayed him. They darted toward the back of the class, the doorway, the ceiling vent. Searching for something, someone, or perhaps only waiting for silence to collapse into noise again. Jeremy whispered later to Leo, "He doesn't want to be seen, but he can't stop checking if he is."

Ty studied it longest, noting every flicker like a code. He could tell when Tom thought he was unobserved: his eyes darted faster then, sharper, his shoulders jerking with each glance. Ty spoke of it only once, in a quiet moment when Jeremy pressed him for an answer. "He's not looking out of habit," Ty murmured. "He's looking because he's learned danger always comes when you stop." Jeremy didn't fully understand, but he nodded anyway, trusting Ty's certainty. And I, unseen and voiceless, recorded the words in silence.

Mila tried to reach him once, offering half a smile when he brushed past her in the hallway. "Hey, Tom," she said, as though the sound of his name might anchor him. He flinched, his eyes shooting left then right before settling on her only for a breath. "Hi," he muttered, already stepping away, the word swallowed by his need to move on. Mila watched him go, unsettled, then turned to Sophie. "It's like he doesn't know how to stand still." Sophie answered softly, "Maybe standing still hurts."

In group lessons, when Miss Kara explained fractions or Mrs. Haller outlined maps on the board, Tom's head bowed like the rest, but his eyes betrayed him. They skimmed the edges of his notebook, then leapt to the sound of footsteps in the hallway, then back to the teacher's hand. Even the flicker of fluorescent lights made him glance toward the ceiling as though expecting it to break apart. Fear lived in him like a second heartbeat, one that pulsed louder than the first.

Alex, who had once been a bully himself, saw the signs and spoke of them to Leo. "He's not scared of us," Alex admitted, "he's scared of something bigger. I know that look. I've seen it in mirrors." Leo did not argue. He only placed a steady hand on Jeremy's shoulder, wordless, grounding himself in the boy's quiet affection. It was proof to him that even those who carried fear could find anchor in love. Tom, though, had no such anchor yet. Only eyes that betrayed him.

The adults weighed it carefully, whispering in offices and corners. Mrs. Locke argued that expulsion would only confirm the boy's fear of being thrown away. Mr. Arnett shook his head, worrying aloud about safety, about the ripple one violent uncle could send through an entire school. "We protect one," he said grimly, "but risk the many." Ms. Henley countered softly, "We protect the many by saving the one. The uncle's shadow isn't his fault." Back and forth it went, their voices drifting like storm winds, never reaching Tom's ears but shaping his fate nonetheless.

And still, through it all, Tom's eyes never rested. At recess, when others hurled balls across the yard and shrieked with laughter, Tom stood at the edge, eyes darting, scanning fences, trees, the far-off corner where the street bent out of sight. When lunch ended, he walked back into the building as though checking the doorframe for ambush. Even his moments of stillness betrayed him, his gaze refusing the horizon, refusing calm. It was vigilance too deep to be habit. It was survival.

I, unseen, followed the flicker of those eyes, watching how even silence could not tame them. They told the story he would never speak: that home was not safe, that laughter was a mask, that every second of quiet was simply the breath before another storm. The others saw pieces of it, the children in fragments, the teachers in whispers, Ty in precision. But together it was enough to reveal the truth. The eyes told everything. Even when Tom said nothing, they screamed the life he carried.

Ty had the kind of silence that unsettled more than any raised voice. Where Nico barked jokes and Jasmin whispered clever asides, Ty simply sat, eyes steady, hands folded in a calm that never frayed. It was a stillness that carried weight, as though every glance he made had been chosen, deliberate, and precise. When Tom shifted uneasily in his seat, his eyes darting as always to door and window, Ty did not scold or smirk. He only observed, quiet and patient, like someone watching a storm gather far off and knowing where it would break. His silence was not neglect but certainty, a steadying presence that made others sit straighter without knowing why.

Jeremy often filled the spaces with words, his nine-year-old energy spilling into questions, comforts, and quick reassurances. But Ty understood what Jeremy did not: words could only do so much. A boy like Tom was not searching for chatter. He was testing whether anyone would see him without trying to change him, whether someone could hold still without demanding he explain his fear. Ty offered that unspoken answer. His gaze was level, his breath measured, his stillness unbroken even when Tom fidgeted or snapped at him to stop staring. That calm presence was louder than Jeremy's warmth, because it refused to move.

Tom hated it at first. The eyes that darted so quickly across the room always landed back on Ty, as though drawn against his will. He shifted in his chair, hunched his shoulders, angled his notebook to shield himself, but Ty's quiet attention remained. It was not hostile, not mocking, simply there. And that was what cut deepest. It meant Ty saw him fully and refused to look away. To Tom, who lived in shadows of avoidance, that patience was unbearable. He snapped once, muttering, "What are you looking at?" Ty did not answer with insult or denial. He only said, "I see you." The words carried no judgement, yet they pinned Tom more firmly than a reprimand ever could.

The others noticed the difference too. Leo, who had once been a storm himself, recognised the strategy in Ty's restraint. "He's breaking him without a blow," Leo murmured to Alex after class. Alex smirked, not in cruelty but in admiration. "No," he corrected, "he's not breaking him. He's waiting for him to break himself." Jasmin watched as well, her curiosity sharpened. "It's strange," she said, "Tom flinches at every teacher's shout, but with Ty it's like he doesn't know where to run." Ella agreed, whispering, "That's because Ty doesn't chase him. He just waits."

In the staff room, Mrs. Locke remarked on it, noting how Ty's patience seemed to reach Tom in ways adults couldn't. "He doesn't push," she said, "and that makes Tom nervous. Children like him are used to pressure, to noise. But silence? That's harder to fight." Mrs. Dunlop nodded gravely. "Sometimes the quietest watchers are the ones who see most. Ty may not be older, but he understands something we don't." Mr. Clarke leaned back, considering, and added, "It's the mark of discipline. He carries it the way soldiers do." None of them knew the depth of Ty's training under his father, but all could see the difference it made.

At recess, while others scattered across the playground, Ty lingered closer to Tom. He didn't crowd him, never forced company, only stood within sight, a calm anchor against the chaos. Tom's eyes betrayed his discomfort, flicking toward Ty again and again. He muttered to himself, kicked at the dirt, tried to lose him in the swarm of students. Yet when he glanced up again, Ty was still there — hands in his pockets, shoulders straight, watching without accusation. Tom's breath grew quick, his laugh sharp and hollow when someone tried to joke with him. But beneath it all was the unease of being seen too clearly.

## THE SMILE THAT BROKE

Nico teased Ty once, saying, "You're like a hawk staring at a mouse." Ty didn't laugh. He only answered, "Not a mouse. A boy who doesn't want to be seen." Jeremy, overhearing, tugged on Ty's sleeve and asked what he meant. Ty crouched down to Jeremy's height, voice low. "When you stop running from shadows, you learn to watch them. Tom is waiting for danger. I'm waiting for the moment he realises I'm not it." Jeremy nodded, though he didn't fully grasp it, sensing that Ty's certainty held more than words could teach.

The counsellor, Ms. Henley, began to notice the effect too. She had spoken gently to Tom, offered kind words, and met only shrugs. But after days of Ty's silent companionship, she saw something shift. "He's still afraid," she told Mrs. Haller quietly, "but he's less alone in it. Ty doesn't soothe him, he doesn't need to. He just refuses to leave." Mrs. Haller, tracing maps on her desk with a fingertip, murmured, "Sometimes that's all children need. Proof that someone won't disappear when it's hardest."

At lunch, Tom tried to provoke Ty once, snapping that he was "creepy" for always staring. The class went quiet, waiting for Ty's response. He didn't flinch, didn't argue. He only answered, "I'll stop when you stop looking for what scares you." The words weren't cruel, but they hit with a precision Tom couldn't escape. He shoved his tray aside, muttering under his breath, but when he sat again, his eyes still darted toward Ty. Only now, there was something else in them — not just fear, but confusion. Why didn't this boy fight back? Why didn't he turn away?

Sophie remarked on it later, whispering to Mila, "Ty doesn't scare him like the others do. He scares him because he doesn't move." Mila thought for a long moment before answering, "Maybe it's not fear. Maybe it's the first time Tom's being held still, and he doesn't know what to do with it." Sophie nodded slowly, watching Ty's quiet figure in the corner of the classroom, still as stone, unyielding as truth.

Even Mr. Takashi, standing outside the school in his plain RCMP jacket, observed the silent vigil of his son with pride and concern. He said nothing to Ty, not yet, but when Jeremy mentioned it later, Mr. Takashi replied simply, "Patience is the hardest strength. It unsettles those who have only known power through fear." He knew his son was carrying a discipline many adults had yet to master.

I, unseen, followed the rhythm of it all. Ty's silence against Tom's restlessness, his certainty against Tom's fear. Day by day, the calm carved itself deeper, and though Tom resisted, something in his eyes shifted, if only for a moment. He still scanned, still searched, but now when his gaze landed on Ty, it lingered longer than before. Confusion grew where once there was only fear. And in that confusion, perhaps, lay the first crack in the armour of shadows he wore.

The staffroom air was thick with tension, coffee gone cold in half-empty mugs, papers scattered as though even the desks could not bear the weight of the conversation. Mrs. Dunlop folded her arms tightly, her voice clipped as she insisted Tom had exhausted every ounce of patience the school could offer.

"We've given him warnings. We've given him counselling. And still, he lashes out. At some point we must ask: whose safety matters most? His or theirs?" Her words struck like a hammer, and yet, in the stillness that followed, softer voices pushed back. Mrs. Locke, her tone careful, answered, "Expulsion isn't a solution. It's a sentence. Children like Tom don't vanish when they leave here — they spiral."

Ms. Henley shifted uneasily, her counsellor's notebook pressed to her chest. "He is a child," she reminded them gently, though her voice trembled. "Not a case file. Not a problem to be pushed out of sight. If we send him away now, where will he go? Back to the same shadows that created this fear? That would not save anyone." Mrs. Haller, tracing her pen across a faded map of continents pinned to the wall, muttered, "And yet every day we gamble with other children's safety. One wrong move, one snap, and what then? How do we explain that gamble to the parents of his next victim?" Their words collided like stones, clattering against one another without finding rest.

Mr. Clarke leaned forward, voice steady but lined with concern. "We can't argue around the edges forever. We need to see what lies beneath. Boys don't learn to flinch at shadows for no reason. Something — or someone — is shaping Tom into this creature of fear. Expel him and you only cut away the symptom. Leave the root to grow, and it will poison him beyond repair." Mr. Arnett, the principal, rubbed his temple as if the weight of every voice pressed on his skull. "The board will demand answers," he sighed. "They will want to know why we harbour a danger. They will want to know what makes us think he can change." His uncertainty bled into the room like a slow fog.

The murmurs grew louder, fragments colliding. "Too many chances." "Not fair to the others." "What of his uncle?" "We cannot know for certain." "The risk is ours if we keep him." I drifted unseen among them, catching half-sentences and broken thoughts, piecing together the map of their doubt. They spoke not only of Tom but of themselves — of their fear of failure, of responsibility, of being the ones who either saved or doomed a boy teetering on the edge. And all the while, the boy himself was absent, spoken of as if he were only a shadow drawn on the wall.

Then the quiet was broken by a voice not expected in that room — Ty, younger than all, standing just inside the doorway, his presence sharper than their arguments. He did not raise his voice, but it cut through like a blade nonetheless. "Stop talking about him like he's already gone." They turned, startled, some indignant that a child had intruded, others too struck to protest. Ty's calm did not falter. He looked to the principal, to the teachers, and then said, "You argue over chances and punishments as though they will heal him. They won't. He doesn't need hypotheticals. He needs help."

Mrs. Dunlop's brow furrowed, defensive. "And what do you propose, Ty? You're eleven years old. This is not your decision." Ty met her gaze without fear. "No, it isn't," he answered plainly, "but I see what you don't. You watch his behaviour. I watch his eyes. He is waiting. Not to fight, not to win. He is waiting for someone to prove they won't leave him to the shadows. Expel him, and you prove the shadows right." Silence followed, heavy, uncomfortable. The teachers looked away, some ashamed, some unsettled, but none able to dismiss the certainty in his words.

Mr. Clarke cleared his throat, breaking the silence. "I have seen boys like Ty before. The calm ones who see what escapes the rest of us. Perhaps we would do well to listen." Mr. Arnett leaned back, his fingers tapping the table, eyes narrowing at Ty. "You say you have a plan. Then say it. What help do you believe he needs?" Ty drew in a slow breath, his voice even, unwavering. "First, stop speaking of him like a lost cause. Second, find the truth of the home he lives in. Fear like his doesn't come from schoolyard scraps. It comes from nights where footsteps in the hall mean danger. If you want to save the others, then save him first."

Ms. Henley, her hand trembling, whispered, "He speaks truer than many adults." Mrs. Locke nodded slowly, her eyes softening as she added, "We cannot teach our students that abandonment is a lesson. If we cast him out, we teach them cruelty." Mrs. Haller pressed her lips thin, but she said nothing more, her doubts quieted for now. And so the staffroom air shifted, less sure, more fragile, the debate unsettled but transformed.

I remained, unseen, and recorded the change. The room had not decided Tom's fate, but a boy of eleven had shaken the ground beneath their feet. For the first time, the murmurs did not sound like verdicts but like questions. Ty's presence had placed a mirror in their hands, and what they saw was not Tom's failure, but their own hesitation.

The room shifted the instant the door opened. Mr. Takashi did not need to announce himself; the rhythm of his step carried authority enough to still the arguments before his voice was ever heard. He wore no uniform, no badge pinned to his chest, only the quiet weight of a man who had seen truth too many times to tolerate half-guesses. His eyes swept the staffroom, resting on each face with an evenness that made them lower their gazes in turn. He set his briefcase down without ceremony, adjusted his jacket sleeve, and then, in a voice softer than any of theirs, said, "You are looking in the wrong place."

The silence that followed was not awkward but electric, charged with the knowledge that their debates had been stripped bare. Mrs. Dunlop, always the first to fill a void, shifted in her chair and asked, "What do you mean?" But her voice, sharp moments ago, had lost its edge. Mr. Takashi didn't pace, didn't need theatrics. He stood at the head of the table as though it had been his all along, his tone calm but anchored. "You look at Tom as if he creates storms from nothing. He doesn't. Children don't live in fear by accident. Something — or someone — placed that fear there."

Mr. Arnett, the principal, leaned back, hands clasped together tightly. "We've suspected home issues. But the parents… their records are clean. There's no history." His attempt at certainty faltered beneath the inspector's steady gaze. "Exactly," Mr. Takashi replied. "You've searched for evidence of broken parents, but Tom's mother and father are not the source. You are right to sense a shadow at home, but it isn't theirs. It belongs to another." The weight of the words settled on the teachers like dust on untouched shelves, heavy and unavoidable.

Ms. Henley whispered, "Then who?" The question barely reached the air before Mr. Takashi continued. "The uncle. Eight years older than Tom's father. A man with a history not written on any school records, but one known to police. Intimidation, violence, disturbances kept quiet by family loyalty. He slips through because he doesn't live here every day. But when he does, the house changes. Doors that were once safe become doors to fear." He paused, not for effect, but to let them feel the truth dig into their chests.

Mr. Clarke rubbed his chin, muttering, "That explains his eyes. The way they never rest. Always watching for footsteps." He looked at the others as if confirming what he had long suspected but dared not say. Mrs. Locke sighed deeply, closing her notebook. "We've been teaching shadows, not children," she said. "Every lesson we planned, every punishment we considered — all of it wasted if he goes home only to fight a battle we cannot see." Her words landed heavily, not as argument but as confession.

Mrs. Haller still tried to resist, though her voice had lost its earlier steel. "And what of the safety here? If he lashes out, if he harms another—" But she trailed off, caught under the unwavering calm of the investigator's eyes. Mr. Takashi did not interrupt. He waited, and when her voice fell silent, he answered without cruelty. "Then you protect him the way you would protect any child. You do not discard him. Fear turns fists loose when it has nowhere else to run. If you give him safety, the fists will still, the eyes will stop scanning. But if you cast him out, you send him straight back into the arms of the one who made him this way."

The teachers shifted in their chairs, some ashamed, some uncertain, but none unmoved. Mr. Arnett pressed his palms flat on the table and exhaled slowly. "So the question is not whether Tom deserves another chance," he said. "The question is whether we are willing to do the work to give him one." His voice lacked the easy authority of a principal. It sounded instead like a man finally stripped of excuses.

Ty sat near the corner, silent as his father spoke, but his presence was sharp, deliberate. He had known. His father's words were not revelation but confirmation. Jeremy glanced toward him, wide-eyed, but Ty only folded his hands calmly, as though all of this was unfolding exactly as it had to. I drifted closer to him, unseen, and watched the faintest flicker of relief touch his face. Not joy, not triumph — only the quiet knowledge that truth had finally been spoken aloud.

Mrs. Dunlop broke the silence again, her voice thinner now. "What do we do next?" It was not defiance but surrender, the question of someone who realised they had argued for the wrong things. Mr. Takashi lifted his briefcase, unclasped it, and spread out a single file on the table. Its pages carried reports, not guesses, the kind of truth that did not bend under debate. "Next," he said, "we stop chasing rumours and start building protection. For Tom. For every student who carries bruises you cannot see. We face the root, not the branches."

The air shifted once more, no longer the stale weight of endless arguments, but the sharper gravity of decision. The staff leaned in, eyes drawn to the file, as though within its pages lay the map they had been stumbling for. Even those who still doubted could not deny the solidity of facts, the immovable weight of evidence. And in that moment, every person in the room understood: the boy was not the problem. The shadow behind him was.

The room grew colder when the name surfaced. It was spoken without anger, yet the effect was sharp as though a stone had been dropped onto a table. Mr. Takashi's voice carried no tremor, no hesitation; the clarity made it undeniable. Tom's parents were not the storm. It was the uncle — older, harsher, with a history of intimidation that spilled into every corner of the house. A man who entered rooms like a shadow no one invited, filling silence with threats unspoken yet felt. Teachers sat back, the air knocked from their lungs. For all their guesses, none had landed on this truth. The uncle lived under the same roof, his presence staining evenings and mornings alike, the quiet of a child's room shattered by a fear that never loosened its grip.

Jeremy lowered his gaze, fiddling with the sleeve of his jumper. He didn't need details; the picture was already painted clear enough. A boy who never met the eyes of his classmates, who twitched at the sound of footsteps, who laughed without light in his face. That wasn't bad behaviour, it was survival. Nico whispered to Jasmin, his voice barely carrying, "So it wasn't the parents." She nodded, the realisation sinking into her expression. Even the students, hearing through cracks in the walls of adult conversation, understood more than anyone gave them credit for. They didn't need lectures to see what kind of damage an unseen adult could carve into a child's bones.

Ty remained seated, posture steady, his hands folded on the table as though anchoring the weight of what had just been revealed. He didn't rush to speak, because words too quickly thrown would sound like pity. Instead, he waited, allowed the silence to do its work, then reached for a folded piece of paper in his bag. Jeremy watched him slide it across the table toward Mr. Clarke without announcement. It was not a report, nor a demand. It was a letter, written by Ty's own hand the night before, as though he had known this moment would arrive.

Later, when the letter reached Tom, its lines would carry no sharp edges. Ty's handwriting was steady, each word measured, not as if written for school but as if carved for a friend who had never known the meaning of the word. He told Tom that he was not alone, not broken, not beyond reach.

He said plainly who his father was, not as a warning but as a quiet assurance — an RCMP investigator, yes, but more importantly a father who taught his son to fight shadows without turning cold himself. He explained that every one of them — Jeremy, Leo, Alex, Jasmin, Ella, Sophie, Nico, Mila — wanted to stand beside him. Not because they feared him, not because they wanted him under their control, but because friendship was meant to be given in truth, never forced by fear.

Mrs. Locke pressed a hand to her lips when she read a copy of the letter, tears gathering in her eyes despite her long years of teaching. "Children writing like this," she murmured, "and here we are, arguing over punishments." Her words were not a rebuke but a confession, the sort of admission adults rarely dared to make before students. Mr. Arnett leaned back heavily, fingers tapping against the table, as though trying to calculate the distance between the policies he upheld and the reality of what they were facing. The uncle's name was now an immovable presence in the room, a truth they could no longer sweep into corners.

Mrs. Dunlop cleared her throat, her voice brittle. "So what do we tell Tom?" she asked. Ty finally lifted his head, his eyes steady but soft. "You tell him nothing," he said, calm as stone. "You show him. You show him that when he looks up, he doesn't only see shadows. He sees people who don't leave." The words fell into the room like a verdict, not harsh, but final. Even Mr. Clarke, who had spent years carrying the weight of other students' secrets, nodded in agreement.

I drifted in the corner, unseen as always, but I felt the shift in the air. This was not about reports filed away in drawers or staffroom debates that ended when the bell rang. It was about a boy whose smile had never been real, whose laughter always broke too quickly, and who might, for the first time, read words on a page that told him he was worth something. Ty's letter did not erase the uncle's shadow, but it planted a light inside Tom that might, someday, grow stronger than fear.

Tom held the letter as though it were glass, fragile and easily broken. His fingers lingered on the creases Ty's careful folding had made, as if the neatness alone was proof that the words inside were meant to steady him. He read slowly, eyes tracing each line with suspicion that softened into something quieter, almost reverent. When the final word met him, he did not crumple it, nor toss it away as he might have done in other moments of pride. Instead, he reached for a scrap of paper, the edges torn from a workbook, and wrote only two words: thank you. He handed it back without ceremony, no speeches, no explanations. That was enough. In that small act, every child in the room saw something shift — not much, but enough to prove that Ty's effort had not fallen to silence.

Mr. Takashi's steady voice carried next, revealing what the files said. The uncle was no myth, no whispered figure haunting only Tom's imagination. Records spoke of fights, charges pressed and then withdrawn, angry nights that spilled into police reports, only to be buried beneath leniency. Assaults that should have led to consequences often slid through cracks left by paperwork or lack of witnesses.

# THE SMILE THAT BROKE

The uncle's history was a map of damage — tempers flared in public, grudges carried into fists, scars left both visible and hidden. The teachers, so often firm in their lectures and punishments, paled as the reality sat before them. What Tom endured at home was not an exaggeration, but a weight he carried into every classroom.

Mr. Clarke pressed his knuckles against his lips, his jaw locked, his usual confidence dulled into quiet dread. Mrs. Locke's pen hovered uselessly above her notebook, lines unfinished, her eyes glassy as though trying to picture what Tom's days must look like when the school doors closed behind him. Even Miss Kara, who never hesitated to snap sharp warnings at unruly children, sat back in her chair, humbled into silence. The room of adults, for once, carried the hush of students caught learning something they had no answer for.

Ty waited until their gazes circled back toward him. He was not smug, nor triumphant. His calm carried the sort of patience only an old soul could manage, far older than eleven years should have allowed. "You won't reach him with speeches," he said evenly. "You won't reach him with warnings either. He hears warnings every day of his life. To him, words are threats." He let that hang a moment, then leaned forward, eyes glinting with a quiet mischief that felt out of place among such heavy truths. "If you want to reach Tom, you have to stop being adults. You have to become kids again. Tell him a joke so ridiculous it cracks his armour before you even try to hand him a lesson."

The staff blinked, caught between confusion and disbelief. "A joke?" Mrs. Dunlop asked, her voice clipped by habit. "You're saying—" But Ty cut in, not rudely, but with a firmness that settled the debate before it could rise. "Yes. A joke. A fart joke if you have to. The kind that makes him laugh even when he doesn't want to. Because if he laughs, then for one second, he's not waiting for a door to slam at home. He's just a kid. And once you give him that second, you can give him more." The suggestion, outrageous as it sounded to their polished ears, made Jeremy's face brighten with recognition. He had always known Ty had a way of making heavy truths sound strangely simple.

Jeremy piped up quickly, eager to prove Ty's point. "He's right," he said. "Sometimes you've got to go silly before you go serious. Like when I told Nico that joke about the teacher who sneezed so hard she erased the board. He laughed, even though he was mad at me. It worked." Nico smirked faintly, confirming it with a nod. The other students, clustered near the back, leaned in. They didn't need charts or plans — they understood instinctively what Ty was saying. The line between cruelty and kindness was sometimes crossed with a punch, but sometimes crossed with laughter that healed instead of hurt.

Mrs. Haller shifted in her chair, her sternness easing into the faintest of smiles. "A fart joke?" she repeated, as though testing the weight of the words in her mouth. The students giggled at the sound of it, their tension broken just enough. Even Mr. Arnett, rigid as always in his suit and tie, sighed and rubbed his forehead, muttering, "If it works, perhaps we've been too serious all along." For once, no one argued.

The invisible weight in Tom's eyes hadn't lifted completely, but when Jeremy leaned close and whispered a ridiculous quip about someone sitting on a whoopee cushion during math class, Tom's lips twitched. It wasn't much, but it was something. A flicker of light behind the fear, small yet stubborn, like a candle refusing to be snuffed out. Ty caught it, gave the barest nod, and the class understood: this was how battles were fought now. Not with fists, not with punishment, but with fragments of joy sharp enough to pierce through walls of silence.

The narrator — I — lingered at the edge of it all, unseen but recording every moment. The shift was delicate, almost invisible to those who wanted big gestures, but it mattered. In one letter, in one thank you scrawled across a scrap of paper, and in the faintest smile wrung from a boy who had forgotten how, history itself had bent. The uncle's shadow remained, but Tom had been given a tool sharper than fear — proof that he could laugh without permission, and that there were people ready to protect that laughter.

Tom sat rigid at the back of the room, his posture as sharp as the corners of the desk he gripped. Every sound became a weapon. The scrape of Mrs. Locke's chair against the tile made him wince as though expecting a blow. The sudden slam of a locker down the hall twisted his shoulders inward, his breath caught halfway to his lungs. He wasn't just hearing noise — he was hearing signals, warnings only he seemed able to read. Where others dismissed the chaos of school life as background noise, Tom's body braced, trained by years of bracing for fists and words. Fear had been drilled so deep into him that it lived not only in his mind but in his very muscles, ready to jolt at every snap, crack, and slam.

The teachers saw it, though most didn't understand. They mistook his stillness for defiance, his wide eyes for insolence. But Ty knew better. He'd been watching all along, waiting for the right moment to show them what none of their lectures or rules could teach. He leaned forward from his chair, posture calm, voice quiet. "You see?" Ty said, pointing toward Tom's tightened fists. "That's not anger. That's fear. You can't punish it away. You can only melt it." His words settled across the adults like a truth they hadn't wanted to face, and Jeremy, sitting a row behind Tom, caught it too, his small eyes wide with recognition.

Mr. Arnett, ever the stiff principal, tried first. His idea of humour was as rigid as his tie. "Well, Tom," he began, clearing his throat, "I suppose if you were a geography map, you'd be the capital of—fear city?" His forced chuckle died before it left his lips, and the students groaned. Tom blinked but didn't move, his walls holding. Mrs. Locke tried next, stumbling over a pun about books and lockers, her voice tripping as though humour were foreign to her tongue. Tom's expression didn't change, though Jeremy whispered that he saw the faintest twitch in his jaw, a crack too small for the teachers to notice.

Miss Kara, never one to back down, decided boldness was the answer. "I once had a student," she announced, "who was so bad at fractions that when I told him to reduce, he brought me a salad." The class laughed politely, but Tom's shoulders barely shifted. Fear still gripped him. He flinched again when the classroom door opened with a loud creak. The attempt at humour had loosened nothing. His second skin of fear stayed stitched to him tightly.

# THE SMILE THAT BROKE

It was Ty who changed everything. He waited until the laughter quieted, until the teachers gave up with shrugs and embarrassed smiles. Then, without moving closer, he raised his voice just enough. "Alright, Tom. I've got one for you. What's the most musical part of a fart?" The room went dead silent. Teachers exchanged horrified glances, Mrs. Dunlop coughed into her hand, but the students leaned forward in glee. Ty's face remained serious, patient, waiting until Tom looked at him, puzzled despite himself. And then Ty delivered the line: "The toot-al scale."

For a heartbeat, no one moved. The joke hung in the air like an uncertain note. Then Jeremy cracked first, his laugh bursting like a kettle whistling off its lid. Nico followed, Jasmin slapped her desk, Sophie doubled over. Even the stern faces of Mrs. Locke and Miss Kara couldn't hold — they tried to hide their smirks behind hands but failed. And then, against every expectation, Tom's lips twitched, curved, and broke into a laugh so raw it startled even him. It wasn't polite, it wasn't cautious — it was a full, unguarded laugh, sharp and loud, echoing through the classroom like a trumpet he didn't mean to play.

The laugh rolled over him, shaking free what fear had locked tight. For once, the darting of his eyes wasn't searching for danger, but scanning the room to see if anyone had caught him laughing — and everyone had. Jeremy's grin stretched ear to ear, Leo patted Tom's shoulder once, firm and proud, and Alex muttered under his breath, "That's the first real sound I've heard out of him." The tension that usually weighed on Tom's back seemed lighter, if only for the span of a joke.

The teachers shifted uncomfortably, uncertain if they had just witnessed brilliance or rebellion. Mrs. Dunlop muttered something about inappropriate humour, but even she couldn't stop the corners of her lips from curling upward. Mr. Clarke shook his head, smiling outright. "Sometimes," he said softly, "the right kind of ridiculous is more powerful than the sternest rule." The class nodded, recognising that Ty had proven his point in a way no lecture could.

Tom's laughter trailed into a quieter smile, but the crack it left in his armour was permanent. He exhaled deeply, shoulders dropping, hands unclenching from the desk. The scrape of a chair still made him twitch, the slam of a locker still set his jaw tight, but something new had been planted among those reflexes: the memory that laughter could be louder than fear. Ty caught his gaze one last time, nodded once, and looked away, letting Tom hold the moment for himself.

I lingered unseen, carrying the echo of Tom's laughter in the folds of silence that followed. Fear was still there — fear made flesh, etched deep into his body — but now there was something else woven through it, a thread that no fists or shadows could rip away. Tom had laughed. And that meant, at least for now, he had begun to live.

Jeremy leaned in close to Ty as the room settled again, his whisper barely carrying beyond the space between them. "Maybe Tom's not quite beyond help," he said, his words soft but edged with the unease of a child who had seen enough to know what cruelty could do. It wasn't meant as kindness — Jeremy wasn't offering hope with a smile. He was simply telling the truth as he saw it.

And truth, even spoken gently, carried a weight heavier than pity. Ty didn't answer right away. He kept his eyes fixed on Tom, watching the way the boy's shoulders hunched, the way his hands fidgeted against the desk like he was still bracing for something to come. When Ty finally nodded, it was slow, deliberate, carrying the air of someone who understood exactly what Jeremy meant.

The nod wasn't agreement so much as acknowledgement. Ty already knew Tom wasn't lost. He had seen it in the laugh that broke free just moments earlier, the laugh that no one expected, the laugh that proved the boy still had something inside worth protecting. Jeremy glanced up at Ty, waiting for a response, but Ty said nothing. His silence was more powerful than words. And yet, beneath that calm, something else stirred — the beginnings of a plan forming in the quiet recesses of his mind. He would not fight Tom with lectures, nor argue with teachers about second chances. He would show Tom the truth the way it needed to be seen: directly, without filters, without the false comfort of softened words.

When Ty returned home that night, the house was quiet save for the faint scratch of his mother's pencil across her sketchpad. His father sat at the kitchen table with a folder open, papers stacked neatly in his careful way. Ty knew those papers weren't schoolwork. He had seen that same folder pulled out when his father was investigating cases that touched too close to children. He sat down quietly, waiting until his father's eyes lifted. "You want to know about Tom's uncle," Mr. Takashi said, his voice low, steady, as if he had been expecting this conversation all along. Ty didn't flinch. He only nodded. His father turned the folder so Ty could see the first page: charges, dates, police records that painted a picture more damning than words ever could.

"Do you think he should see this?" his father asked, searching Ty's eyes for hesitation. Ty thought of Tom's flinches, the darting eyes, the laugh that had cracked open something hidden. "Yes," Ty answered simply. There was no waver in his voice. Mr. Takashi studied his son for a long moment, then reached for a fresh sheet of paper. He wrote a single line in his neat script: Just thought you'd like to see this for yourself. He folded the note once, clipped it to the photocopy of the record, and slid it across the table. Ty pressed his small hand against it, grounding himself in the weight of what he was holding. He didn't smile. He didn't need to.

The next morning, Ty carried the paper in his backpack, the folder tucked between a math book and his English notes. He didn't rush to give it to Tom. Timing mattered. He waited until the morning class broke for recess, until the noise of chatter and footsteps filled the hallways, until Tom was at his desk pretending to read while his eyes darted restlessly to every corner of the room. Ty walked past him once, silent, just to feel the space. Then he circled back, dropping the folded sheet onto Tom's desk without a word. The sound of it landing was almost nothing, but Tom's head snapped up as if someone had shouted his name.

Tom's fingers hesitated over the paper, reluctant to touch it, afraid it might carry the sting of another humiliation. But curiosity won out. He unfolded it, saw the words clipped to the front, and froze. His lips moved soundlessly, tracing the line: Just thought you'd like to see this for yourself. His eyes narrowed as he pulled the note aside, revealing the photocopied record beneath. For a long moment he didn't breathe. His gaze swept across the black lines, the official stamps, the charges that seemed to echo everything he had lived without needing to be told. His face drained of colour. He read on anyway, devouring every word as if the truth would finally confirm what his body had always known.

Jeremy, from his seat across the room, watched Tom's reaction with quiet intensity. He saw the way Tom's hands trembled as he turned the page, the way his chest rose and fell like someone trying not to drown. Jeremy nudged Ty, whispering again. "You sure this won't break him?" Ty didn't look away from Tom. His answer came in the smallest shake of his head. "It won't break him," he said. "It will show him he isn't imagining it. That's worse than anything." Jeremy leaned back, thoughtful, realising for the first time that sometimes truth wasn't meant to comfort. Sometimes it was meant to free.

Tom folded the paper back up after what felt like hours, though only minutes had passed. He tucked it into his own notebook, pressing it flat as though it were evidence of something no one else would believe unless he held onto it. His eyes lifted once, scanning the room, landing briefly on Ty, then on Jeremy. For the first time, he didn't dart away. He held the gaze a second too long, a silent acknowledgment that he knew where the paper had come from, and that he hadn't rejected it. He hadn't thrown it in the trash or shoved it back into Ty's hands. He kept it. That alone said more than words.

Ty turned back to his notes without fanfare, calm as ever. Jeremy sat quietly, chewing over what had just happened, his earlier words echoing in his own head. Maybe Tom really wasn't beyond help. Maybe the paper on his desk had cracked something even deeper than laughter. And if that was the case, then Jeremy's whisper had been more than an observation. It had been a beginning. The thought weighed heavy, but it also carried the faint spark of possibility, like the flicker of light that sneaks under a locked door. And Jeremy, watching Tom stare down at the desk where the paper had been, knew he had been right to whisper it aloud.

The classroom was louder than usual, the hum of voices and scrape of chairs carrying the kind of careless noise children make when their own lives feel untouched. But within that clutter of sound, Tom sat still as stone, the folded paper heavy in his pocket, his eyes fixed on nothing anyone else could see. Ty leaned across the desk slowly, not drawing attention, his voice low enough to be carried no further than the boy beside him. "If he's thrown away now, he will never come back." The words were not wrapped in kindness, not painted with the softness of hope. They rang more like the toll of a bell, a warning that once sounded could not be unheard. Tom's jaw tightened as if he'd been struck, though no hand had touched him.

The weight of those words lingered between them longer than the chatter around them, pressing Tom into silence. He glanced sideways at Ty, eyes narrowed but not defiant, more curious than angry. He wasn't used to someone speaking of him like he mattered, even as a caution. Ty didn't shift under the stare. He reached calmly into his notebook, pulling free a folded slip of paper already waiting there. No fanfare, no speech, just a quiet gesture as he slid it across the desk. Tom's hand hovered over it like it might burn him if touched. Still, he picked it up, careful, unfolding it with the same tension he had shown the day before.

The letter was short, written in Ty's deliberate, steady script. If you ever want to know more about that report or anything else about your uncle, you only need to ask. You can write it down, or tell me quietly. I will get the answers for you. No tricks. No one else needs to know. The choice is yours. Tom read it twice, eyes tracing the lines as if searching for hidden barbs, the cruelty that usually lived in promises from others. But he found none. There was no mockery here, no trap waiting to spring. The letter opened a door, but only wide enough for Tom to step through when he was ready.

Tom pressed the paper flat against his desk, not stuffing it away this time, not hiding it like contraband. His thumb traced the edges again and again, the nervous motion betraying the storm inside him. For a boy so used to walls, this small slip of paper was heavier than the books piled in front of him. He stole a glance at Ty, but Ty was already bent over his notes, pencil in hand, the very picture of calm. There was no push, no urgency, only patience written across his posture. The offer had been made. It would not be withdrawn.

Jeremy, watching from across the row, caught the look that flickered across Tom's face — suspicion giving way, just slightly, to something less guarded. He leaned closer, murmuring so only Ty could hear. "Do you think he'll actually ask?" Ty didn't look up from his page. His answer came steady, unshaken. "That's not the point. He just needs to know he can." Jeremy frowned, not fully satisfied but unable to argue with the certainty in Ty's tone. The truth was, Jeremy had never seen anyone hand Tom a choice before.

The teachers at the front droned on about fractions, voices blurred in the background, but none of it seemed to touch Tom. His focus stayed locked on that note, his fingers smoothing the crease lines again and again. Across the room, Nico was whispering to Jasmin about the upcoming game, Ella and Sophie giggled over some private joke, Leo tapped his pencil against his desk in restless rhythm, and Alex leaned back in his chair, pretending to sleep. Ordinary children, ordinary noise. But at Tom's desk, something fragile was shifting, quiet enough that no one else saw it.

For the first time, the silence around him wasn't just the silence of being left out. It was the silence of a moment given freely, the absence of pressure, a chance to decide for himself. That small difference carried more weight than a dozen lectures or punishments. Tom tilted the paper slightly, hiding the words from prying eyes even though no one else had noticed them. His chest rose in a slow, deliberate breath. He was not ready to speak, not ready to ask — but the seed had been planted.

Later that afternoon, when the bell rang and the class spilled into the hallway, Tom walked slower than usual, dragging his feet just enough to stay behind. Ty noticed, but he didn't push. He let the distance stretch until Tom was near enough to brush past him at the door. A single glance passed between them — sharp, questioning from Tom, steady and unflinching from Ty. It lasted less than a heartbeat, but it was enough. Tom slipped the note into his pocket, not with the desperation of someone hiding evidence, but with the care of someone protecting something fragile.

That evening, as homework spread across desks and the classrooms emptied, Mrs. Locke noticed the strange stillness in Tom's eyes when she asked if he understood his assignment. He nodded quickly, avoiding her gaze, and shuffled away before she could say more. She didn't press, though. There was a new tension in him, but also a new light, subtle and fleeting. She couldn't place it, but Ty had already seen it clearly. Tom had been given something no one else had thought to offer: control over his own truth.

By the time Tom lay awake in his bed that night, the note remained tucked under his pillow, smoothed flat so the words wouldn't fade in the folds. He had not decided if he would ever ask, if he could summon the courage to know more than he already carried. But knowing the choice was his alone was enough to soften the edges of fear for just a moment. And for a boy raised in shadows, that was no small gift.

Ty, at home across town, folded his hands over his notebook after finishing his own work. He did not wonder if Tom would ask. He only thought of the doorway he had opened and how he would be ready when the boy stepped through. His words to Jeremy earlier were not hope and not guesswork. They had been truth, spoken as plainly as any warning. If Tom were discarded now, he would not return. But if Tom were given the space to walk forward on his own, perhaps for the first time, he just might.

The staffroom air was sharp with coffee and tension, the kind that staled too quickly when voices rose above polite tones. Mr. Clarke leaned forward, palms flat on the table, his voice measured but heavy. "We cannot throw him away. That boy is more than what he carries. He's living with fear that most adults would not withstand. Compassion isn't indulgence — it's survival for him." His words carried weight, not just for their truth but for the grief behind them. Every teacher in the room knew Clarke had spent years watching children break under the cruelty of silence. But his plea was met by the hard slam of Mrs. Haller's hand on the table, her tone clipped and unyielding.

"Compassion does not shield the other students from harm," she snapped, her voice cutting the stillness. "We are responsible for all of them, not only Tom. If he lashes out again, if another child is hurt, the weight of that will be on us. Do you want to explain to a parent why their child came home with broken bones because we were too soft?" The question hung like a blade over the table, sharp and unforgiving. Mr. Arnett, seated at the head, rubbed at his temple, eyes closed as though he were listening for reason among the noise. The divide had already split the room, the arguments carving fault lines no one seemed able to bridge.

Miss Kara, her voice quieter but no less fierce, added to the fracture. "We cannot gamble with lives, Clarke. Not when we already know the danger that lives under Tom's roof. Fear like that festers, and sooner or later it spills. I won't watch another Myles Neuts happen on our watch. Not here." Her words dragged silence into the room, a silence that pressed down on shoulders like stone. The mention of Myles's name was not careless; it was deliberate, and everyone felt its sting. Clarke's jaw tightened, but he did not retreat. He looked to the others, hoping one of them would remember the boy who had been lost because no one stepped quickly enough.

It was Ty who broke the silence, though he was not meant to sit among them as equal. The boy stood near the wall, too young for the weight in his eyes, his presence tolerated only because of his father. Yet when he spoke, the voices stopped, the quarrel stalled mid-breath. "If you give up on him now, you will not just lose him," Ty said plainly, his voice even but edged with steel. "You will make him into something you cannot control. Maybe you think you are keeping everyone safe by sending him away, but what you are really doing is planting the seed of someone you will fear in the future." His gaze swept the table, not flinching, not faltering.

Mrs. Dunlop, arms folded across her chest, shifted uneasily. "You speak boldly for someone not old enough to be in this room," she said, though the bite in her words softened at the edges. Ty didn't blink. "I've watched him," he replied. "More than you have. I've seen the fear under his skin, the way his eyes search corners. He isn't dangerous because he wants to be. He's dangerous because no one has given him another way to be. And if you throw him away now, if you choose fear over responsibility, then you will be the ones who made him what he becomes."

The words rattled, heavier than any of them expected from a boy of eleven. Nico, standing just outside the doorway with Leo and Jeremy, froze, catching the gravity that stretched in the air. They had heard Ty speak firmly before, but never like this, never with the weight of consequence dripping from every syllable. Mrs. Locke, who had said little until now, exhaled and leaned forward. "The child deserves the same protection we promise every other student. We cannot pretend we are guardians only for the ones who are easiest to guard. Clarke is right. If fear drives our decision, then we have already failed."

Mr. Arnett finally lifted his head, eyes heavy, his voice rough with the strain of leadership. "And if compassion costs us another student?" he asked. His words were not a rebuke, but a test, an attempt to find the line between mercy and duty. Ty stepped closer to the table, his small frame cutting through their larger shadows. "Then the answer isn't to abandon him," he said, unwavering. "The answer is to watch, to guide, to hold him accountable while still holding him close. If you drive him out, you will create the very monster you fear. But if you show him he is worth protecting, even when he doesn't believe it, then maybe — just maybe — he will learn to protect others instead of hurting them."

# THE SMILE THAT BROKE

The room quieted again, the divide not gone but weakened. Mr. Clarke's shoulders eased as he gave Ty a small nod, the rare gesture of a teacher yielding space to a student who had spoken wisdom greater than his years. Mrs. Haller still frowned, her hands clasped tight in front of her, but even she had no words left to counter the force of Ty's warning. For a moment, all that remained was the image of Tom's thin face, his watchful eyes, and the choice before them. The choice was not only about his fate, but about what kind of guardians they themselves wished to be.

Mr. Takashi, who had been silent all the while, finally added his voice, low and final. "You've all spoken of safety. But safety is not found in casting out the weak. It is found in making the weak stronger, in teaching them what strength really means. If you wish to keep the children safe, then begin here — with Tom. Because if you cannot save one boy under your roof, how do you expect to save the others?" His words sealed the room with finality, leaving no space for further protest. The teachers sat in uneasy silence, knowing the argument was far from finished, but also knowing the tide had shifted.

The motion to remove Tom no longer felt secure. It quivered under the weight of voices too strong to ignore. For the first time, the staffroom held not just debate, but a fragile sense of responsibility that no one could easily set aside. And though the divide still lingered, the crack of truth had been struck deep enough to demand attention. Ty stood back against the wall, his face calm, but his eyes never left theirs. He had not come to ask for mercy. He had come to demand that they see what they risked becoming if they let fear decide.

The silence that followed Ty's words felt too long, as though the staffroom itself had stopped to think. And then, unexpectedly, a smaller voice cut through, unsteady yet determined. Alex stepped forward from where he had been standing at the back, his hands curled into fists not from anger, but from nerves. "You all think Tom's dangerous," he said, his tone uneven but growing firmer with every word. "And maybe he is, maybe he's got more anger inside him than he can carry. But I know what that feels like. I know what it means to be the boy everyone whispers about, the one teachers watch twice as close, the one people expect to fail." His eyes darted briefly to Leo, then to Jeremy, then back to the floor.

Mr. Clarke's head turned sharply at the interruption, ready to caution him, but stopped when he saw the tremor in Alex's shoulders. It was not defiance this time, but courage breaking through the weight of shame. "If you had asked about me a year ago," Alex continued, "you'd have heard the same things you're saying about Tom. That I was cruel. That I hurt people. That I was the one you should be afraid of. And maybe I was. But if I had been thrown away back then, if you had decided I wasn't worth saving, I wouldn't be standing here right now. I'd be gone — and not just from this school." His words carried a raw edge, the kind that cracked open wounds not yet healed.

Mrs. Dunlop shifted in her chair, clearly unsettled. "Alex," she began, but he cut across gently, his voice firming as though it found strength in the very act of speaking. "No. You need to hear this. Because I was Tom. Not in the same way, not with the same uncle, not with the same fear.

But I was drowning in anger, and I used it to drown others. And you know what saved me? It wasn't rules, it wasn't threats. It was people like Leo, and Jeremy, and Ty. They didn't give up on me when they should have. They didn't throw me away. They kept reaching, even when I fought them off. And that's the only reason I'm standing here now, telling you this."

The teachers looked at one another uneasily, the weight of his confession bending their arguments. Mrs. Haller tried to hold her ground, her voice sharp. "You're saying we should risk the safety of dozens of children on one boy's redemption? That's too much to gamble." But Alex shook his head, eyes locked on hers. "I'm saying if you throw him away now, you've already made the choice for him. You've told him he doesn't matter. And when you tell a boy he doesn't matter, he will prove you right, no matter the cost. You call that safety? I call that cowardice." His voice cracked at the end, but it did not falter.

Leo moved subtly behind him, placing a steady hand on Alex's shoulder — not as reassurance, but as anchor. The tremble in Alex's voice steadied, and he pushed forward. "You think Tom doesn't hear the whispers? You think he doesn't know you're scared of him? He knows. He sees it in your eyes every time you look at him. And every time you show him that fear, it tells him he's already lost. If I had lived under that kind of shadow without anyone pulling me out, I would have gone down darker roads than you can imagine. Don't do that to him. Don't make him carry the blame for what was never his fault to begin with."

The room grew tighter, as though the walls themselves leaned closer to listen. Ms. Henley, the counselor, had tears pooling at the corners of her eyes, though she kept them hidden behind folded hands. Mr. Arnett sat straighter, but did not interrupt. For the first time, even Mrs. Haller had no words ready, her eyes fixed on Alex as though she were seeing him for the first time. The boy standing before them wasn't the shadow of the bully he once had been. He was the proof that change was possible, that a child could stumble in darkness and still be drawn into light.

"I'm not proud of what I was," Alex finished, his voice quieter now, but no less steady. "But if I hadn't been given another chance, if people hadn't believed I was worth saving, then I wouldn't be alive to tell you this. Tom deserves the same chance. Not because he's earned it, but because he hasn't had it yet." His last words hung in the air, fragile and heavy, as though daring anyone to cut them down.

The silence that followed was not the sharp silence of argument, but the aching stillness of truth. In that moment, the staff saw not only Tom's future at stake, but Alex's past stretched before them like a mirror. And mirrors, once revealed, are difficult things to turn away from.

The room held the echo of Alex's confession long after his words had finished. Chairs creaked faintly as teachers shifted, but no one seemed willing to break the silence first. It was as though a weight had dropped into the centre of the staffroom and pressed down on every voice.

Alex still stood near the centre of the room, pale but resolute, his chest rising and falling with the effort of what he had just forced himself to reveal. For a boy who once lived on lies and intimidation, truth came out of him like a raw wound. And then, beside him, Leo moved. He did not step forward with words or a speech. He only gave a single, deliberate nod.

The nod was firm, steady, and unmistakable. He was not adding noise to the argument, not layering another plea over Alex's. Instead, he stood there, his dark eyes locked on the staff, letting the silence carry his meaning. For Leo, silence had once been the cloak he wore when plotting how to hurt, how to gaslight, how to control. Now it was his armour in a different way — a stance, a refusal to let Alex stand alone. And though no words left his lips, the nod spoke of memory and survival. It said: Yes. He is right. I was there too. I was saved too. And I am living proof.

Mr. Clarke leaned forward slightly, his hands folding on the table. He had known both boys through their transformations, had watched Jeremy's affection and Ty's steadiness carve out a path for them. He needed no translator for Leo's silence. He saw the message as plainly as if it had been carved into the wooden floor. A teacher from the far side of the table muttered, "That's not enough," but her voice faltered almost immediately, because the nod kept hanging in the air like a stone that refused to fall.

Leo did not blink. He did not look down. He simply kept his gaze level, his jaw set, as though daring anyone to call him a liar about the life he had once lived. It was not the fiery courage of Alex's words but the grounded certainty of someone who had already walked through the worst of himself. The transformation in his posture was impossible to dismiss. He was not a child begging for belief; he was a witness testifying with nothing but his own presence. For some, that kind of testimony spoke louder than confessions ever could.

Mrs. Locke folded her arms, watching the boy closely. She had been the hardest to convince, unwilling to let empathy cloud her sense of order. Yet as she studied him, she could not deny the strength of that nod. He had not spoken to excuse himself or to paint a brighter version of his story. He had simply stood beside Alex, anchoring him, and in that act had anchored the truth as well. The resistance in her shoulders softened, though her mouth stayed firm. She would not admit it out loud, not yet, but she had been moved.

Ty, from his seat near the door, gave a faint exhale that might have been relief. He knew Leo's silence was not born of fear but of choice. Ty had seen enough to understand when stillness was strategy. He respected it, even admired it. His eyes met Leo's briefly, and for a second the two boys exchanged an unspoken recognition: one of them had chosen words, the other silence, but both carried the same weight.

Mrs. Dunlop rubbed her forehead, clearly torn. The memory of discipline met the challenge of redemption, and neither won easily. But even she seemed to pause when her gaze landed on Leo. Perhaps it was because she had watched him differently before — always the troublemaker, the sharp edge in the room. Now she was forced to witness him standing without defence, his silence transformed into defence of someone else. For her, it was an unsettling kind of growth, but it was growth nonetheless.

Jeremy, though not in the staffroom, would later hear about it from Mr. Clarke, and he would nod too when he heard. He would understand why Leo chose silence, because Jeremy knew better than anyone that Leo's words did not come easily when the heart was involved. His brother saved his words for moments when they mattered most, and sometimes that meant saying nothing at all. But Jeremy would also understand that the nod itself was Leo's way of protecting Alex, of lending him strength. It was his way of saying, I've got you, without having to form the words.

The staff looked back to Alex, then to Leo, as though weighing the two boys together. One spoke of a past that could have ended in ruin; the other confirmed it with nothing but presence. Together they formed an argument stronger than either could have managed alone. The air of the room thickened with the truth that stared every adult in the face: these were children who had been salvaged by compassion, and now they stood asking the same for another.

Even Mrs. Haller, whose sharp voice had dominated so much of the debate, found herself unable to speak. She glanced between the boys and then looked down at her papers, as if searching for something that would let her regain ground. But papers could not stand against lived proof, and she knew it. She might have pressed the point later, in calmer tones, but in that moment she could not muster a reply. The nod had silenced her more effectively than argument ever could.

In the back of the room, Ms. Henley's eyes glistened. She was not one to interrupt proceedings with her emotions, but her heart leaned naturally toward the children, especially those carrying burdens. Seeing Leo lend his strength to Alex without words reminded her why she had become a counselor in the first place. She pressed her lips together, saying nothing, but quietly resolved that she would not let Tom's story close before it had a chance to be rewritten.

The principal, Mr. Arnett, finally cleared his throat. His role was to balance safety and second chances, to weigh the good of the many against the salvation of the one. But he could not dismiss what stood before him. Two boys who might have been lost had proven themselves through transformation. And now they asked, not for excuses, but for the same chance to be offered to another. He felt the burden of leadership pressing tighter, heavier, but he also felt the truth of their plea taking root.

And so, without adding a single word, Leo had tipped the scale. His nod had become the hinge upon which the room shifted, not because it was loud or clever, but because it was undeniable. Silence had spoken, and for once, everyone listened.

# THE SMILE THAT BROKE

The letter sat neatly folded upon Tom's desk, Ty's careful hand sliding it there without a word. The paper carried more weight than its size suggested, the ink pressed deep as if to carve permanence into the truth it bore. At the top, a name — Myles Casey Benson Neuts, 1987–1998 — printed as clear as a gravestone. Beneath it, the lines unfolded like a memorial, a story told in plain sentences, without decoration, without evasion. Myles had been only ten, a boy no older than the ones sitting in this very classroom, when a bet that should have been forgotten turned into cruelty, and cruelty into death. Tom's eyes moved across the words slowly, though his body did not shift, and each sentence seemed to tighten his fists further.

The description did not soften the truth, nor did it spare him the harshness of the details. Myles was found in the washroom, his life ended not by choice but by the recklessness of others. The letter did not dress it up as tragedy alone; it named it what it was — a cruel prank that had stolen breath from a boy whose greatest crime was reminding another of a debt. Tom's breathing grew shallow as he read. He could almost see it, the lonely stall, the hook that should have held nothing more than coats, the silence that had filled those minutes until someone finally found him. The lines blurred in Tom's sight, but still he read on, absorbing each cruel fact as if it were etched into him.

When his eyes reached the note about Myles's parents — Mike and Brenda — having to make the decision to turn off the machines that kept their son's chest rising and falling though his mind was already gone, Tom's jaw trembled. He knew the word deceased. He knew what it meant for someone to be dead, but this letter showed him what it meant for parents to watch hope be extinguished in a room of machines and blinking lights. The weight of it pressed down until Tom's knuckles burned white. He tried to keep his face still, but a single tear escaped, betraying him before he could clench it back inside.

Here is what Tom Read:
Myles Casey Benson Neuts 1987 – 1998 • Burial Details Unknown Birth 14 Aug 1987 Ontario, Canada. Death 12 Feb 1998 (aged 10) London, Middlesex County, Ontario, Canada. Burial Details Unknown. Loving 10-year-old son to Mike and Brenda Neuts. Loving big brother to Dane Neuts. In the third grade, Myles Neuts made a $10 bet with a classmate to see who could colour a picture the fastest. Myles won the bet, but the student never paid up. When Myles reminded his classmate 2 years later, another student overheard and asked what Myles was talking about. Once he was told, that other student replied "We'll make him forget, on Friday."

On February 6th, 1998, Myles was found hanging on a coat hook in the washroom of his public school. He had been the victim of two bullies, aged just 11 and 12 themselves, who thought they were having a little fun with a simple prank. It was no joke. The 10-year-old boy died. In the span of ten to twenty minutes, while Myles was left to dangle by a shirt-collar and necklace, his breathing would stop, his brain would be denied oxygen, and for all intents and purposes, he was gone.

Six days later, after guarantees that their son would never regain consciousness, Myles's parents Mike and Brenda made the difficult decision to turn off his life-support machine. One of the boys never owned up and no one was ever found criminally responsible for his murder. The inquest into the manner of his death was deemed "undetermined." Myles' father has travelled coast to coast across Canada to raise awareness for bullying, as well as creating the Make Children Better Now Foundation in his honour.

Then his eyes fell upon the poem, written by Myles himself a year before he died. The words were simple, almost childlike, but they carried a wisdom that caught Tom off guard. "Peace is truth instead of lies, peace is love instead of hate…" He read them again and again, as if the repetition could force the lines deeper into his heart. The voice of a boy who would never reach eleven spoke to him across decades, telling him to be kind, to be truthful, to be better. The poem was no lecture. It was no sermon. It was just honesty, the sort of honesty Tom had never trusted anyone to give him before.

(Myles' Poem)
WHAT IS PEACE March 25, 1997 BY: Myles Neuts
"To me peace is love instead of hate, Peace is truth instead of lies, Peace is nature and a clean world, Peace is comments instead of complaints, So share instead of greed, Tell the truth instead of lies, Tell comments instead of complaints, Be kinder to others, Do what ever you can do to be more peaceful, If it means praying to God more, Or read more of the Bible, Don't swear or fight. Just be more peaceful, To yourself, and to others. I hope my poem has made you more peaceful, For our world."

Tom's throat burned as the last lines swam in his vision. "I hope my poem has made you more peaceful, for our world." He wanted to close the letter, to shove it away before the trembling in his chest could be seen, but his hands refused to move. Instead, his body locked tighter, fists clenched against the desk, shoulders squared as if bracing for impact. He did not speak. He did not need to. The tears that gathered in the corners of his eyes told more truth than words ever could. In the silence of that classroom, his grief was louder than a cry.

Harley stood near the back, arms folded but not in defiance. He watched the way Tom's silence filled the air and remembered his own, not long ago, when truth had finally cracked his mask. He glanced at Lisa, and she, too, understood. They did not speak, but their shared glance carried the same recognition: silence was no coward's refuge. Sometimes it was the only confession a child could give. Sometimes it was louder than shouting, sharper than anger. They, of all people, knew this.

Ty remained at Tom's side, unyielding in his calm. He did not push, did not explain the letter or demand a response. He simply stayed near, making sure Tom knew he was not alone at the desk, not abandoned to drown in a tide of words that had ended another boy's life. Ty's presence was its own anchor. He would stand there until Tom knew that silence was allowed, that silence did not mean weakness, that silence was not the end. Ty's steady eyes seemed to say, You do not have to speak yet. You are still safe here.

The teachers who had filled the room earlier with debate quieted one by one. Even the strongest voices among them could not break through the heaviness now hanging in the air. Mr. Clarke lowered his head slightly, recognising the lesson within Tom's clenched fists. Mrs. Locke stopped her restless pen-tapping. Even Mrs. Dunlop, who so often argued that safety came before sympathy, said nothing. The silence had caught them, too, showing them more about Tom's heart than any spoken explanation ever could.

Jeremy shifted in his seat, his young face etched with worry for his friend, but he respected the unspoken rule that had settled over them all. He didn't push a word into the space. He didn't say, It's okay, Tom, because he knew Tom wouldn't believe it yet. Instead, he let the silence hold, and for once, Jeremy allowed himself to be quiet, to watch and to learn.

Tom did not lift his head, did not unclench his fists, but his tears glistened in the light. His silence was not empty. It was full — of grief, of anger, of years of fear he could not yet speak aloud. The letter had cracked something within him, but it had not shattered him. Not yet. And perhaps that was enough.

In that room, among teachers and students who had argued, shouted, and whispered about what to do with him, Tom gave his answer in the only way he could: silence. And that silence, raw and undeniable, said everything.

The decision came slowly, as though the staff were dragging their feet across broken glass. Mr. Arnett pressed his palms flat against the desk, his face pale but set, and said the words no one wanted to voice: "We cannot expel him, not yet." The room held its breath. Mrs. Dunlop crossed her arms, her lips pursed as though swallowing bitter medicine, but she nodded in reluctant agreement. Safety still demanded caution, but there was a recognition—faint, strained—that cutting Tom off completely might sever him forever. They chose instead to hold him in suspension, neither embraced nor abandoned, left to stand on that narrow line between rejection and another chance.

Mr. Clarke exhaled, a quiet relief in his shoulders, though his eyes betrayed sorrow that they had not chosen trust outright. He knew what it meant to put a child in limbo, to tell him he could stay yet never assure him of belonging. He looked at Tom, whose face was drawn tight and unreadable, fists still knotted as though the verdict meant nothing at all. But everyone could see the tension in his shoulders, the subtle flinch of a boy who had grown too accustomed to being on trial, never sure if the gavel would fall in his favour or against him.

Ty did not flinch. He did not shift in his chair or bow to the hesitations that clouded the air. His gaze stayed fixed on Tom with a steadiness that felt older than his years. It wasn't defiance; it was certainty. To Ty, this half-measure was no victory, only a fragile foothold. But he would take it, and he would guard it with his own two hands if he had to. His silence was its own promise, one that Tom felt even if he didn't yet understand it.

Tom, for his part, sat suspended not just by the staff's verdict but by his own confusion. He knew enough to recognise pity when it was offered, and this felt heavier than that. Why would Ty, a boy not bound by blood or by obligation, choose to stand beside him? Why would he risk himself when everyone else pulled away? The questions churned inside him without answer, leaving him unsettled, almost angry at the weight of loyalty he hadn't earned. His fists trembled, not with rage but with bewilderment.

Mrs. Locke broke the silence with a softer tone than usual. "Trust isn't given freely," she said, almost as if to herself. "But neither should it be taken away forever." Her words didn't erase the tension, but they gave the staff something to cling to, a justification for the choice to postpone judgment. Still, her eyes flicked toward Tom with worry, as though she too could see the blade's edge he now balanced upon. One slip, and he would fall either into darkness or into the arms of those who refused to let go.

In the back of the room, Mr. Takashi straightened. He did not raise his voice, yet when he spoke, the weight of authority carried across every corner of the room. "He is not alone," he said. "As long as I draw breath, he will not be abandoned to the shadow of that man." He did not need to name the uncle again. Every adult in the room knew who he meant, and every student who overheard felt the steel in his words. It was not a promise made lightly.

Beside him, Mrs. Takashi rested a hand gently on her husband's arm before adding her own voice. "Children know when they are unwanted," she said. "They feel it sharper than most adults realise. If you hold Tom halfway between acceptance and exile, he will know it. And if he knows it, it will break him." Her words lingered longer than she expected, because they came not as argument but as truth delivered by a mother who understood how fragile a child's heart could be.

The staff faltered under their words. Some exchanged glances, uneasy with how close the Takashis had come to striking at their conscience. Yet the choice had already been made, and none dared to overturn it. Suspended. Balanced on the edge. Watched but not trusted. A fragile peace, as fragile as Tom himself.

Ty leaned ever so slightly closer to Tom, his voice quiet enough that only Tom could hear it. "They won't see it, but I will. I'm not leaving you." The words were steady, not pleading, not demanding, but certain. Tom blinked, confused more than comforted, yet he did not pull away. The very act of someone choosing to stay—when they had every reason to turn—was something new to him. He did not know how to hold it, so he held it the only way he could: with silence.

Jeremy, though younger, felt the tension settling in the room like a heavy fog. He scribbled in his notebook, not words of judgment but notes to remind himself later: Blade's edge. Second chances. Ty doesn't bend. He knew this moment would matter later, perhaps more than any of them yet realised. Even a nine-year-old could see the stakes.

The students who had gathered outside the door whispered about the verdict when they heard it. Some were disappointed, some relieved, some simply confused. But even they felt the fracture in the decision. It was not resolution. It was only delay. And delay carried its own dangers.

In the silence that followed, Tom's fists slowly uncurled. Not in surrender, not in peace, but in exhaustion. He did not raise his eyes. He did not thank anyone. But he did not resist Ty's quiet promise either. That was enough. For now.

And so the verdict hung in the air, postponed but not erased. A boy's future suspended, a school divided, and a single truth lingering beneath it all: Ty would not give up on Tom. Not today, not tomorrow. Not ever.

The hallways after the meeting felt longer than usual, as though the school itself had shifted beneath their feet. Tom walked slowly, not because he wanted to but because his body carried the weight of something unseen. His head was low, his steps heavy, and yet it wasn't the pace of guilt—it was the drag of chains invisible to everyone except those who had listened closely. Ty's eyes followed him, watching the way the late spring sunlight caught through the windows, drawing out Tom's shadow across the linoleum floor. It stretched ahead of him, tall and dark, as if mocking the boy who carried it.

Jeremy noticed too, scribbling another thought into his notebook, his young brows pressed together. "That's not just his shadow," he whispered to himself. "That's someone else's shadow he's carrying." The words made no sound beyond his lips, yet they settled into his chest with an ache he could not shake. For in Tom's silence and in his silence alone, they all had seen the truth: he bore the mark of his uncle's violence, a stain that lived in posture, in glances, in the way his fists refused to unclench even when no one threatened him.

Ty, standing at the far end of the hallway, kept his gaze steady. He understood what others missed. This was not simply fear of punishment or embarrassment from the verdict. No, Tom walked as if the very shape of his uncle followed him everywhere he went, burned into his skin and carved into his movements. A boy of thirteen should not walk like that. A boy of thirteen should not wear the burden of grown men's sins. Yet here he was, stretched out before the sunlight like the silhouette of a life he had not chosen.

The students who crossed paths with him parted without thinking, some whispering, others holding their silence. Sophie looked at Ella and shook her head, her face pale with pity. Nico's usual grin faltered, for even he felt the chill in that elongated shadow. Jasmin nudged Leo lightly, but Leo did not answer. He only stared, jaw tight, knowing better than most what it meant to live under the weight of someone else's cruelty. His nod earlier in the staffroom had not been empty—it had been recognition.

Teachers, too, noticed the strange heaviness clinging to the air. Mrs. Locke, who normally dismissed shadows as mere tricks of light, folded her arms and leaned against the doorway, unable to step aside from what she saw. Mrs. Dunlop spoke softly to Mr. Clarke, "It's like he carries more than just himself." Mr. Clarke, with sorrow in his eyes, only replied, "Because he does." The others said nothing, but each one knew that silence had its own language, and Tom's was screaming louder than words ever could.

Ty stepped closer as Tom reached the far corner of the hall. He did not touch him, did not call his name, did not demand his attention. Instead, he let the silence hold, as though to say: I see it. I see you. For Ty understood that Tom's shadow was not only his uncle's—it was also Myles Neuts'. The story told in the library, the story written into letters, now pressed against Tom like a mirror. Myles had been left alone once. Ty would not let Tom walk that same path, no matter how long his shadow stretched.

Tom's memory of Myles lingered, though he had never met the boy. He had read the words, seen the name on paper, and felt the tear between fear and shame rip open inside him. Myles had been ten, and Tom was barely older now. He knew enough to see himself reflected in that tragic story, knew enough to understand the danger of silence and the cruelty of those who pretend that pain is only a game. His fists clenched harder, but his eyes burned. He would not speak of it, not yet, but the shadow knew.

Jeremy, who had been watching quietly, nudged Alex. "Did you see?" he asked. Alex, still thoughtful from his admission earlier, sighed. "It's not just him. It's all of us. That shadow touches everyone if we don't do something." His words carried more weight than he intended, but they were true. For in schools, shadows do not belong to one child alone—they ripple outward, staining classrooms, playgrounds, and homes alike.

Harley, who had once stood in Tom's shoes but had chosen another path, leaned against the lockers, his arms folded. He glanced at Lisa, who was at his side, and for once neither of them spoke. They saw themselves in that shadow and did not need words to name it. Harley had been caught before he fell too far. Lisa had been pulled back before she struck one blow too many. Both knew the silence Tom carried. Both wondered if it would break him—or if, perhaps, it would finally lead him to the truth.

The sunlight shifted as clouds passed outside, but the shadow did not fade. If anything, it grew sharper, darker, a reminder that even in springtime light, the past has a way of etching itself onto the present. Ty's eyes narrowed slightly. He wasn't afraid of the shadow. He knew how to step into it without flinching, how to walk beside it until it lost its grip. Still, the sight hardened something in him: a resolve that Tom would not be left dangling between verdicts and whispers, between expulsion and forgiveness.

In the staffroom, Mr. Takashi's words echoed: He is not alone. And Mrs. Takashi's soft caution: Children know when they are unwanted. Both truths now pressed against Tom's back like the weight of the entire school. He did not see it, not fully, but he felt it. The undeserved friendships that wrapped around him without his asking, the strange loyalty of Ty and even Jeremy, confused him deeply. Why would anyone want him? Why would anyone care?

But the fact remained—whether or not he understood it—that they did. Ty had already chosen to stand in his corner. Mr. Clarke had pleaded on his behalf. Jeremy had spoken with compassion beyond his years. Even Alex and Leo, once bullies themselves, had stood silently in solidarity. The bonds were there, invisible yet unbreakable, tightening around him like ropes not meant to bind but to hold.

As Tom reached the end of the hallway, the late spring light caught his face, half-shadowed, half-bright. His fists were still clenched, but his steps had slowed, as if unsure whether to keep walking forward or stop. Behind him, the voices of teachers and students swirled in the distance, but ahead stretched nothing but light and shadow. Both awaited him. Both belonged to him now.

The invisible narrator caught the moment with careful clarity: shadows, after all, are not owned solely by those who cast them. They fall across everyone, stretching until they touch even those who did not ask to share them. And in that long stretch of darkness and light, every student, every teacher, felt their own shape shift beneath the burden. Tom's shadow, his uncle's shadow, Myles' shadow—they all lingered together.

It was not just the shadow of a boy. It was not just the shadow of an uncle. It was a reminder that everything casts something larger than itself, and that in the halls of this school, shadows stretch long.

## CHAPTER 12: THE LIBRARY CONFRONTATION

The library was never meant for such gatherings, and that was the first clue that something was unusual. Assemblies were always conducted in the auditorium, where the polished floor echoed with footsteps and the ceiling lights made everything feel too exposed. Here, within the library, there was carpeting beyond the twenty-foot threshold of the entrance, the kind that muffled sound and absorbed tension. Rows of chairs scraped across the uncarpeted tile as they were dragged aside, their legs screeching before settling into silence. Teachers stood stiffly against the walls, their arms folded, their posture rigid, as though the presence of books demanded stricter formality. Students, by contrast, slipped onto the carpet, sitting cross-legged or leaning back on their hands, the ease of their bodies clashing with the unease in the air.

The carpeted floor softened the chaos of movement, yet nothing could soften the feeling pressing against everyone's shoulders. Students knew instinctively this was not routine. The voices of their teachers, usually confident, were lower now, like threads pulled taut. The shuffling of feet and whispered questions drifted across the room, carried not by curiosity but by caution. Even the books, those shelves that loomed like silent sentinels, seemed to press in closer, as though listening. The smell of paper and dust clung thick in the air, mingling with the faint tang of polish left from the janitor's recent efforts. It was not the space of joy, nor of study, but of reckoning.

Ty entered quietly, his footsteps deliberate, not hurried. He carried himself differently than the rest of the students, not more important, but more certain, as though he already knew what the room would demand of him. His eyes scanned the scene without judgment, simply marking the lines of tension. When his gaze found Tom, seated awkwardly near the edge of the carpet, there was no scowl nor pity, only recognition. Ty took his place on the floor like the others, yet his presence drew subtle notice. He did not relax, nor did he fold into anxiety—he simply waited, the kind of waiting that suggests patience is its own form of strength.

Tom, by contrast, looked restless. At thirteen, taller than most of the others, he was caught between boy and man, his limbs too long for ease. He sat with one knee drawn up, his elbow propped on it, his jaw set hard as though he were biting back words. His eyes darted often, never settling. When another student's gaze lingered on him for more than a second, his shoulders tightened, and he shifted, giving the impression of a cornered animal searching for escape. If anyone noticed, they said nothing, but silence did not spare him. Silence made it louder.

Jeremy was the smallest body among them, only nine years old, yet he blended into the group as though age could not diminish his presence. He sat near Leo and Nico, his back straight, his eyes steady on the front of the room. He did not fidget, nor whisper, nor show fear. His role here was not to lead, but to witness, and in that way he carried more weight than his size suggested. Leo sat beside him with a protective stillness, not glaring at Tom, not posturing— just being near Jeremy as though that single act was enough to keep balance. Nico glanced often between them, loyal in his quiet, yet alert.

# THE SMILE THAT BROKE

The teachers along the walls did not relax, even as the students settled. Mr. Clarke clasped his hands before him, the posture of a man who has too much to say and no certain way to say it. His eyes flicked toward Mr. Arnett, the principal, whose jaw was rigid as though carved from stone. Miss Kara leaned slightly against a shelf, her arms folded, her eyes sharp with unease. Mrs. Dunlop, the vice principal, tapped one finger against her arm, betraying her nerves in the rhythm of impatience. Mrs. Locke stood closer to the group, her expression measured, her eyes scanning each student as if seeking a thread of calm to grasp. Mrs. Haller and Ms. Henley stood side by side, one stiff and formal, the other softer, her concern visible even in the slight bend of her shoulders.

Then came the moment when Mr. Takashi stepped into the room. His presence altered the space as if the air had shifted. An RCMP investigator, he did not enter as an officer but as a father, his wife just behind him, her hands folded in front of her, her quiet gaze carrying more compassion than words ever could. The murmurs in the room dimmed without command. Even Tom, who had looked ready to bolt at the faintest provocation, stilled in his seat for a heartbeat. The man did not demand respect; he carried it. His steps were slow, deliberate, and without hesitation, as though no fear in the room was greater than the ones he had already faced outside these walls.

The hush that followed was not silence but suspense. It held the air in a grip, leaving every cough, every shuffle of clothing amplified. It was in that waiting that the divide revealed itself. Students leaned closer together, whispering lightly before stopping as though speech itself would fracture the moment. Teachers shifted their weight against the walls, and their eyes betrayed the argument already forming in their minds—whether this gathering would save a boy or condemn him. The carpet beneath the children muffled sound, but it could not muffle fear, nor expectation.

The students did not yet understand why they were here, not fully. They had heard rumours in the halls, whispers carried between lockers and over lunch tables, but rumours do not prepare for truth. Here, truth waited. And truth was rarely kind.

The library had always been a place of learning, of books read silently, of whispered questions about forgotten homework. Today it was a stage. The walls of books formed a witness stand, each spine a silent observer. The air pressed heavy on shoulders too young for burdens this great, and still, none of them moved to leave. Something was coming. Something none of them could avoid.

Sixteen paragraphs filled the room, yet it was not the count that mattered, but the weight of anticipation. A story was about to begin, one not written in fiction but in the raw truth of what bullying could do. And though none spoke it aloud, every student felt it: after today, something would be different.

Mr. Clarke stepped forward, his shoes making the faintest sound against the carpet as he moved to the centre of the room. He didn't raise his hand for silence, nor did he wait long for the restlessness to ebb away. His presence was enough. His gaze travelled slowly across the sea of young faces, pausing on no one for too long, yet not gliding past them either. Each student felt seen, as though the weight of his words would fall personally upon their shoulders. The air in the library, already tense, drew tighter. He cleared his throat, but it wasn't nerves—it was simply the gathering of a voice that had chosen to carry truth rather than comfort.

"Respect," he began, his tone low but steady, "isn't a word for posters or assemblies. It's a word that should live in your bones. And courage—" his eyes shifted toward the teachers along the walls, then back to the students—"courage is not fists, or threats, or proving you are stronger than the person next to you. Courage is telling the truth, even when it burns. Courage is admitting what you have done, and what has been done to you. That is why we are here today." His words moved without flourish, yet they pressed into the silence like weights laid upon a scale.

The students listened differently than they would in a normal lesson. They weren't half-distracted or whispering under their breath. Instead, they leaned forward in increments, as though leaning into the truth might soften it. Some shifted uncomfortably, others pulled their knees tighter to their chests. They understood, perhaps for the first time, that this was not another lecture that would fade with the bell. This was an assembly of wounds—old and new—and Mr. Clarke had made it clear there would be no disguises, no softened endings.

Tom sat rigid on the edge of the carpet, his shoulders tight beneath his shirt, his fists balled in silence. His eyes darted from teacher to teacher, but when they landed on Mr. Clarke, he didn't look away. There was defiance in his stare, yes, but there was also something else—something buried deeper, the kind of look one carries when they know the truth being spoken is already part of them. His jaw worked, clenching and unclenching, but he remained silent, his body a knot wound too tight to unravel just yet.

Ty, seated not far from him, folded his hands in his lap and didn't shift. He watched, not as a boy listening to an adult, but as someone weighing the moment. His calm was unnerving in its quietness, and more than one student glanced toward him for reassurance without knowing why. Jeremy, smaller among them all, looked fixedly at Mr. Clarke's face, his lips pressed together as though holding back his own words. Leo sat close, his eyes sharper, scanning Tom's posture the way one watches a storm gather. Nico and Mila whispered briefly, but the whisper carried no laughter. It carried nerves, plain and unpolished.

Mr. Clarke's voice did not rise, but it thickened with the weight of memory. "We are gathered in this library because truth belongs in places of learning. We cannot fight lies with silence. We cannot answer cruelty by looking away. Today is not about punishment. Today is about opening the doors we have kept locked too long, so no one leaves this building without knowing what is at stake." He let the words hang, and the silence stretched until the very air seemed to hum with it.

The teachers shifted against the walls. Mrs. Locke's lips pressed together in approval, while Mrs. Dunlop's arms folded tighter as if bracing for conflict. Miss Kara tilted her chin slightly, her eyes sharp with suspicion, but she said nothing. Mr. Arnett, standing near the back with arms crossed, studied both students and staff alike, his face a mixture of calculation and concern. Ms. Henley's brow creased, her hands clasped in front of her as though in silent prayer, though she would never speak of it as such. Mr. Takashi remained steady near the door, his wife just behind him, their presence a reminder that what unfolded here reached beyond walls and into homes.

Mr. Clarke's gaze found Tom again, just for a second longer this time, and the pause was felt by everyone in the room. "There are stories in this building that cannot remain hidden," he said, his tone unflinching. "Stories of harm, of cruelty, of pain. And there are also stories of change, of courage, of second chances. But none of them mean anything unless we are willing to look each other in the eye and name them. Today, you will hear truths that are not easy. I will not ask you to like them. I will only ask you to face them."

The weight of the words pressed heavily, like stone upon fragile glass. A cough somewhere in the back broke the silence, but it did not lighten it. Students shifted again, some glancing nervously toward Tom, others toward Ty, who remained unflinching. The tension in the library was no longer about the oddity of gathering here instead of the auditorium. It was about the knowledge that something was about to break—whether silence, or pride, or denial, none could yet tell.

For a heartbeat, it seemed as though Mr. Clarke might continue, pushing further into the truths that waited, but instead he let the silence stretch and settle. He knew the words had already been planted, like seeds in soil too dry to receive them, but seeds nonetheless. The air quivered with anticipation, the kind of silence that makes even the turning of a page sound like thunder. And when his gaze lifted again, sweeping across every child and adult alike, it was no longer simply a welcome. It was a challenge.

Tom's body betrayed him long before his voice could. His knees bounced against the carpet, his heels thudding softly, a rhythm no one wanted to hear but everyone noticed. His arms folded across his chest, though the gesture had little strength in it—it was not defiance, but a shield. His back bent forward, shoulders hunching down, as though gravity itself was pulling him toward the floor. Still, he held his chin up, eyes flicking quick as a sparrow, darting from teacher to teacher, then to the rows of students around him. It was the look of someone who had learned long ago that danger hides behind ordinary faces.

Mr. Clarke paused, not speaking further. He knew enough about silence to let it work. But the pause only deepened Tom's restless shifting. His fingers tapped against his arms, a muted drumbeat of nerves. His shoulders rose and fell in uneven breaths, and still his eyes would not stop moving. They lingered briefly on Mr. Takashi by the door, then cut away quickly as if burned. He looked at Ty next, only to find those calm dark eyes already on him. For an instant Tom looked away, then forced himself to look back, unsettled by Ty's steady patience.

Sophie whispered softly into Jasmin's ear, "He looks like he's gonna bolt." Jasmin didn't answer, but her hand tugged at her sleeve, her eyes narrowing in Tom's direction. Nico shifted on the floor, uncomfortable, though not afraid. "He's not sitting right," Nico muttered under his breath, and Leo, seated beside him, gave a short nod. Jeremy said nothing at all, but the way his hands gripped the folded newspaper in his lap told enough.

The teachers along the wall noticed too, though they tried to pretend they didn't. Mrs. Haller straightened her glasses with a nervous push. Miss Kara's jaw tightened, sharp lines across her face. Mrs. Locke's brow drew down low as though she was ready to interject at any second. Mrs. Dunlop leaned closer to Mr. Arnett, whispering quickly, though the words were too soft to carry. The principal's answer was only a small shake of the head, his eyes fixed on Tom with a weight that measured everything.

Tom's shifting grew worse. He pulled at the hem of his sleeve, fingers twisting fabric into tight knots. He glanced at the exit twice in less than a minute, and then down at the carpet as if the floor could open and swallow him whole. The silence of the room made every movement louder, every fidget echo like a crack against stone. He cleared his throat once, sharp and quick, the sound out of place in the heavy stillness.

Ty leaned forward slightly, his voice even, quiet enough to reach only Tom. "Breathe." One word, not a command, but an invitation. Tom froze at it. His eyes flicked to Ty again, but his lips pressed tight, no answer given. His knees kept bouncing, though slower now, as though the one word had caught him by the collar before he could break.

Ms. Henley, the counselor, looked between Ty and Tom, her hand half-lifted to step in, but she let it fall back at her side. She had seen enough to recognise the rare thread being tied in front of her, and knew better than to snap it. Her eyes softened, her silence deliberate.

Jeremy whispered to Leo, "He's scared." Leo glanced back at him, shaking his head slightly. "He's angry." Both were right, and both wrong. Tom's body carried both weights at once, his posture split between collapse and explosion. His fists clenched, his jaw locked, yet his chest trembled with uneven breath. Every line of him said he wanted to run, yet every flicker of his eyes said he had nowhere safe to go.

The library felt tighter by the second. Students pressed closer to one another without realising it, the way a herd does when it senses a predator nearby. But here the predator wasn't Tom. It was something in his memory, something that had built him into what they saw now: a boy on the edge of cracking, folding under pressure he hadn't asked for but carried every day.

Mr. Clarke let his eyes linger on Tom a moment longer before shifting them away, a mercy disguised as disinterest. He turned slightly toward the teachers, saying nothing, but the message was clear: they could see for themselves what sat in front of them. Tom's posture had become a confession without a word spoken.

Tom's knuckles whitened as his fists pressed harder together, and then he let go, flexing his fingers as though they were tied too tightly. He adjusted his seat, leaning forward, then back again, as though no position in the world could hold him steady. He looked once more at Ty, and this time didn't look away. It was not a challenge, but a question: why do you keep watching me? Ty's only answer was his calm, a quiet certainty that unsettled Tom more than fury ever could.

The other students noticed the exchange. Mila whispered, "Ty isn't even blinking." Ella frowned and added softly, "He doesn't need to." Their words carried no mockery. It was awe, tinged with relief. Where they saw danger, Ty saw a boy caught in his own storm, and refused to flinch.

The tension thickened, the air heavy with it. Tom's posture, uneasy and shifting, was no longer just his. It spread across the room, infecting students and staff alike with a restlessness they couldn't name. The silence pressed harder, stretching toward the breaking point. And everyone, from the youngest child on the carpet to the oldest teacher at the wall, knew something was about to give.

The room shifted when Mr. Zenji Takashi rose from his chair near the back wall. He did not need to clear his throat or demand silence; the air seemed to draw itself around him. His suit was plain, his posture steady, his expression calm, but every teacher in the library recognised authority when they saw it. Ty's father looked across the room, not at the students first, but at the staff who lined the walls, the ones who had been whispering arguments about what to do with Tom. His voice carried smoothly, not loud, but precise. "My name is Zenji Takashi. I serve as an investigator with the RCMP, and I am also an advisor to the provincial board of education. More importantly, I am a father, and I know the faces of children who are in trouble when I see them."

Mr. Arnett shifted uneasily but gave a short nod, granting him the floor. Mrs. Dunlop folded her arms, but her eyes softened as she leaned her weight against the shelves. Mr. Clarke gave nothing away, except a faint flicker of relief that someone else had stepped forward. Tom's shoulders stiffened as soon as the words "RCMP investigator" reached his ears. His eyes darted straight to the door, but Ty's calm gaze held him frozen in place.

"I will not frighten you with what the law can do," Mr. Takashi continued, his voice measured, his eyes moving across students and staff alike. "I will not recite sections of the code or list consequences, though I could. That is not what this meeting is about." His words pressed gently, but firmly, into the silence. "What I will tell you is this: when young people lash out, when anger spills into harm, it is rarely born here." He tapped his chest once, not dramatically, but as a reminder. "It is carried here, from somewhere else."

Miss Kara frowned, her voice sharper than she meant it to be. "But what if that somewhere else keeps making this school unsafe?" She glanced toward Tom without naming him. "How much more are we supposed to excuse before we think about the others?"

Mr. Takashi turned his gaze on her, not unkindly but unflinchingly. "I am not asking you to excuse. I am asking you to understand. Those are not the same thing." He let the distinction hang in the air until even the students understood. Jasmin whispered to Ella, "He talks like Ty," and Ella nodded, leaning close. "It's the same eyes," she whispered back, "like he sees past everything."

Tom clenched his fists harder. His knuckles whitened as he muttered, "I don't need understanding. I don't need any of this." His words were low but carried in the tense silence. Leo leaned slightly forward, his hand pressed against the carpet, but said nothing. He had been in that same space once, and he knew silence could sting sharper than any lecture.

Mr. Clarke stepped in gently. "Zenji, the children—"

"I know," Mr. Takashi replied softly, never raising his tone. "And because they are children, we speak plainly. Fear is already their companion. They do not need more of it from us." He shifted his weight slightly, now looking directly at Tom. "You are thirteen, yes? Old enough to know the weight of your choices, but still young enough that every day ahead of you can be different from the last. Do you believe that?"

Tom's jaw locked. He stared at the floor, refusing to answer. Ty broke the silence for him, his voice low but steady. "He doesn't believe it yet." The students stirred at the sound of Ty's certainty. Mr. Takashi only gave the faintest nod in his son's direction, as if acknowledging an ally already standing with him.

Mrs. Locke's voice broke from the line of teachers. "So what are you suggesting? That we keep waiting until something worse happens? Until a child ends up in the hospital?" Her tone carried frustration, but beneath it was fear.

Mr. Takashi's answer came measured. "No. I am suggesting you stop treating this boy as a problem to be removed and start seeing him as a life that must be protected. Safety and protection are not enemies. They must walk together." His gaze swept the room again, making sure the students heard it as much as the staff. "Law is not only about punishment. It is about responsibility—for each of us, not just the one who stumbles."

Nico whispered to Jeremy, "He sounds like Ty when he's serious." Jeremy nodded, clutching the folded newspaper against his chest. "That's where Ty learned it," he whispered back. Alex, sitting cross-legged, kept his eyes on Tom, recognising the clenched fists, the darting eyes, the posture of a boy who wanted to break free but didn't know how.

Mr. Arnett stepped forward a little. His voice wavered but held its ground. "Zenji, you know the pressure we're under. Parents want answers. They want guarantees."

"There are no guarantees," Mr. Takashi said quietly. "Not in law, not in life, and not in this room. But there are choices. And the choice before you is whether you cast him out and make certain he is lost, or you keep him here and risk helping him find a different path."

Tom finally snapped his eyes up, his voice sharp, cutting through the stillness. "And what if I don't want your path? What if I don't want your help?" His voice cracked, betraying more than he meant it to.

Mr. Takashi didn't flinch. "Then you still have to hear it. Because whether you want it or not, you are not alone in this school. You do not carry only your anger. You carry what you leave behind on every face you touch. That is responsibility. And it will not leave you, no matter how much you deny it."

The room was silent. Not a student shifted. Even the teachers who had been ready to argue found no words. The warning was spoken, not in threat, but in truth. It was not fear he had laid in the library, but weight—the kind no one could ignore. And Tom, for the first time, had no place to hide from it.

The silence broke with a sound no one expected: the thud of palms slamming into a chest. Tom had risen so fast that his chair clattered backward, its wooden legs scraping the carpet before toppling onto its side. His arms shoved forward, his fists tight against Mr. Zenji Takashi's jacket, and the man staggered back two full steps. The library gasped as one, a collective intake of fear. For a moment even the air seemed to recoil. Books trembled in their shelves from the force of Tom's sudden violence, as though the walls themselves had felt the jolt of his fury. Students froze where they sat cross-legged on the carpet, the ripple of alarm running through them like a wave caught in a storm.

"Tom!" Mr. Clarke's voice cracked the air, sharp and urgent, but it could not erase what had already happened. Tom's chest rose and fell, his breathing wild, his eyes wide with a fury that was half anger, half terror. His fists clenched again, as though ready to strike, yet his whole body trembled as though even he wasn't sure if he wanted to finish what he started. Ty stood up slowly from the carpeted floor, not rushing forward, but the movement alone shifted the current of the room. His dark eyes never left Tom's, and though he said nothing, the steadiness of his posture began to pull the storm away from panic and toward focus.

Zenji Takashi had not raised a hand. He straightened his jacket calmly, though the mark of Tom's shove was still written in the creases. His silence, his refusal to react with anger, unsettled Tom more than any threat could have. "Don't just stand there!" Tom barked, his voice cracking under the weight of what he'd done. "Say something! Do something!" His words carried not triumph but desperation, as though begging for punishment to justify the chaos boiling inside him.

Mrs. Dunlop gasped audibly and reached toward the phone mounted on the wall. "He just assaulted—" she began, but Mr. Arnett caught her wrist before she could dial. His voice was low, firm. "Not yet." The students glanced at each other, eyes wide, breaths quick. Jasmin pressed her hands together so tightly that her knuckles whitened. Ella clutched Sophie's arm, whispering, "He's going to be arrested. They're going to take him away." Sophie shook her head, her lips pressed tight.

Ty took one step forward, his voice still calm. "He doesn't want to fight you," he said, not to his father but to Tom directly. "He never did. You just want to see if anyone will finally fight back." Tom's head whipped toward him, his eyes narrowing, his mouth pulling tight as though holding back a scream. "You think you know me?" he spat, his voice sharp and bitter. "You don't know what I live with. None of you do!" His fists remained balled at his sides, but his shoulders trembled under the weight of words that cracked wider than his shove ever had.

Nico half-rose to his knees, but Leo held him back with a hand pressed firmly on his shoulder. "Wait," Leo whispered, his voice steady. "This isn't over yet." Alex leaned forward, eyes trained on Tom, recognising too well the signs of a boy lashing out because he could not find another way to be heard. "I know that look," he murmured to himself, almost too low for anyone to hear. "It's the same one I wore."

Mr. Clarke stepped forward, his face pale, but Zenji Takashi lifted one hand slightly, stopping him without a word. Then, quietly, he spoke. "Tom, you just put your hands on me. Do you know what that means?" The words were not harsh, not shouted, but they carried the weight of authority that pressed against every heart in the room. Tom swallowed hard, his eyes flashing from fear to defiance. "I don't care!" he shouted, though the tremor in his voice betrayed the truth. "I don't care what happens!"

Ty's voice cut through again, softer this time. "Then why are you shaking?" The question pierced deeper than any punishment. Tom faltered, glancing down at his trembling hands as if they had betrayed him. His breath hitched, sharp and shallow, but still he refused to answer.

Jeremy whispered to Mila, who sat wide-eyed at his side, "He's not just mad. He's scared." Mila nodded faintly, her hand clutching the sleeve of her sweater. Sophie leaned closer to Ella and murmured, "Ty's going to stop him. Just watch." But even her voice held a trace of doubt.

The teachers along the walls remained frozen in place, unsure if they were witnesses to the beginning of disaster or the breaking of a cycle. Mrs. Locke folded her arms tightly, muttering to herself, "This is a police matter." Yet Mr. Takashi never once raised his voice or stepped closer. He let the weight of Tom's action hang heavy, like a shadow stretched long across the floor.

"Arrest me then!" Tom cried suddenly, his voice raw, his eyes glistening with unshed tears. "Go ahead, that's what everyone wants, right? Get rid of me, throw me out like I'm nothing!" His words cracked louder than the shove, tearing through the stillness like glass splintering underfoot.

"No," Zenji Takashi answered, his tone even. "That is not what I want. And it is not what you deserve." The words fell with a gravity that silenced even the whispers. Tom blinked hard, his mouth opening as if to argue, but nothing came out. His fists unclenched slowly, trembling as his arms hung useless at his sides. For the first time, the boy who had lashed out looked smaller, diminished not by punishment but by truth that stripped away the armour of rage he had worn so long.

The library was still. Every face, student and teacher alike, carried the weight of what had just happened. A boy had struck at the law itself and had not been crushed in return. Instead, the moment revealed the jagged edges of fear, guilt, and longing that no expulsion notice could erase. And as Ty stepped closer, his quiet certainty steady as a hand extended in the dark, it became clear that the shove was not the end of something. It was the beginning of a reckoning Tom could no longer avoid.

The library turned to stone. No one breathed, no one shifted; even the clock on the wall seemed to hesitate between its ticks. Ty's dark eyes flicked toward his father, searching, not for instruction, but for permission. Zenji Takashi gave him the smallest of nods, a gesture of trust, a silent understanding that the boy knew what must be done. In that heartbeat, the air was frozen in suspense, the future of a single thirteen-year-old boy balanced on the trembling edge of silence. Students sat rigid on the carpet, their faces pale, their eyes unblinking, afraid that the slightest sound would ignite the room into chaos.

Mrs. Locke's voice shattered the stillness. "Arrest him!" she demanded, her words sharp, cutting through the frozen air like broken glass. Her arms crossed tightly against her chest, her eyes narrowed, and she looked not at Tom but at Zenji Takashi, as though daring him to uphold the very laws he had sworn to serve. "He assaulted a police officer, an investigator, a father. There is no excuse for this behaviour." Gasps broke from the students, not because of Tom's shove, but because of the venom in her voice.

Zenji Takashi turned his head slowly toward her. His voice, when it came, was low and edged with steel. "Shut up." The words struck the room harder than Tom's shove had. Silence deepened, heavier than before, every pair of eyes widening in disbelief that such authority could speak with such bluntness. Mrs. Locke stiffened, her mouth opening to object, but Zenji raised one hand, silencing her before she could draw another breath. "You cause too many problems already," he continued, his gaze steady, unflinching. "You speak only from hate, and hate blinds you to the truth standing in front of you. You are wrong about this boy."

Tom's face twitched, the tension in his jaw faltering. For the first time, someone in authority had not condemned him outright, but had defended him—against another adult, no less. He shifted his weight uneasily, his fists loosening and tightening again as though uncertain what to do with them now that they weren't being used to push. A flicker passed through his eyes, one that neither rage nor triumph could explain. Confusion, perhaps even the shadow of gratitude.

Mr. Clarke stepped forward, his voice softer than usual, as though afraid to crack the delicate balance in the room. "We are not here to destroy him," he said, glancing from teacher to student, then resting his gaze on Mrs. Locke. "We are here to understand him. If all we do is punish, then we have failed him and ourselves." His words landed gently, but their weight was undeniable.

Mrs. Dunlop folded her arms, still uneasy, her lips pressed tight. "But we cannot excuse violence, not in this school. We cannot let this be forgotten." Her voice trembled, less out of anger than out of fear. "What if it happens again?"

"It will," Zenji Takashi replied evenly, his hands folded calmly in front of him. "If you turn him into an enemy, it will happen again. If you give him a chance to see a different path, he might yet take it. And I would rather risk teaching him than guarantee losing him." His eyes shifted back to Tom, the boy who stood rigid, trembling, unable to lift his head. "He is not your threat. He is your responsibility."

The students on the floor leaned into each other, whispering nervously. Ella covered her mouth with her hand. "Did he just tell a teacher to shut up?" she breathed. Sophie nodded, whispering back, "He did. And he was right." Their words carried among the younger ones, a ripple of astonishment that even authority could be challenged when it was clouded by anger.

Ty took another step closer, his voice quiet but clear. "Tom," he said, "you pushed my father. But he didn't push back. Doesn't that tell you something?" Tom's breath hitched, his eyes darting from Ty to Zenji, then back again. He opened his mouth to speak, but no words came. Instead, he dropped his gaze to the floor, as though the truth itself weighed too much to look at directly.

Nico whispered to Leo, "If it were anyone else, he'd be gone by now." Leo only nodded, his arms folded, his expression hard, but his eyes softening toward Tom. Alex leaned forward, his elbows on his knees, muttering, "I've been there. I know that look. That's the face of someone waiting to be discarded."

Mrs. Haller, who had said nothing until now, finally spoke, her voice low and hesitant. "Maybe Mr. Takashi is right. Maybe Tom isn't the danger we think he is. Maybe what we're seeing is the shadow of the danger he lives with every day." The words hung there, unchallenged, as though the weight of them could not be denied.

Mrs. Locke, pale and stiff, said nothing more. She turned her face away, her lips pressed into a thin, angry line. Her silence, this time, was not power but defeat. The authority she wielded had been stripped from her by truth sharper than any reprimand. And in that moment, the library remained frozen not with fear, but with the fragile possibility of change, a pause in time where one boy's fate balanced on the courage of those willing to stand for him instead of against him.

The silence was unbearable, a heavy cloth pressed over every breath, every thought. The adults seemed paralyzed, each waiting for the other to make the first move, while Tom's fists remained locked, his chest rising and falling in sharp jerks. Then, before anyone could speak, Ty rose from the floor. The motion was slow, deliberate, the kind that made everyone's eyes shift to him without command. He did not rush, nor did he falter. Each step was measured, soft against the carpet, and in those steps was a calmness that unsettled more than anger ever could. He walked not as a child out of place, but as though the ground itself had given him permission to stand where no one else dared.

Nico hissed a whisper, tugging at Jasmin's sleeve. "What's he doing?" Jasmin shook her head, unable to answer, her wide eyes fixed on Ty as though he carried some secret no one else could hold. Leo leaned forward, elbows resting on his knees, watching with a wary respect, while Alex muttered under his breath, "He's not going to fight him. He doesn't need to." Even Mr. Clarke, the one who usually shielded the children from moments too raw, stayed quiet. Something in Ty's stillness kept them all rooted.

Tom's eyes narrowed as Ty stopped a few feet in front of him. His fists flexed, his weight shifted, his body preparing for another shove, another defense. "Stay back," Tom growled, his voice hoarse, jagged with something that was not hatred but the sound of a cornered boy. His chest heaved, sweat glistening at his temples. He expected fists, he expected resistance, but Ty's arms remained at his sides, empty, open, as though he had walked into a storm without armour.

"No," Ty said simply, his voice clear, cutting through the tension like a blade of glass. He took another slow step forward, placing himself fully between Tom and the sea of adults and students watching. His eyes didn't waver. They held no accusation, no disgust, only a steady certainty that seemed older than his years. "I'm not here to stop you," Ty continued, his tone level, steady, "I'm here to ask you one thing." The room tilted toward him, every ear straining.

Tom swallowed, his jaw tight. "What?" he spat, though the word shook as it left his mouth. His fists rose higher, but they trembled now, less with rage than with fear. The library seemed to shrink, pulling every shelf, every wall, into this circle between the two boys. No one dared breathe loud enough to break it.

"Who are you really angry at?" Ty asked. His words were not shouted, not pressed with force. They were spoken like a stone dropped into water, rippling outward, finding every ear, every heart.

It was not a challenge; it was an invitation. And in that single question, the fight in Tom's shoulders wavered. His eyes flicked wildly, first toward Mr. Takashi, then Mrs. Locke, then to the floor. His chest rose high, a gasp catching in his throat, and for a moment, he looked less like a boy about to lash out and more like one standing on the edge of breaking down.

Mrs. Dunlop shifted uncomfortably, whispering to Mr. Arnett, "That's not safe—he shouldn't be this close." But Mr. Arnett raised a hand, his eyes fixed on Tom's trembling face. "Let him finish," the principal said softly. His words carried not just authority, but a recognition that what was happening now could not be undone by interruption.

Tom's knuckles whitened as his fists clenched tighter, but his lips quivered, betraying him. His eyes darted to the shelves, to the carpet, to anywhere but Ty's unwavering stare. "You don't know me," he muttered, though his voice cracked at the edges. Ty didn't flinch.

"I don't need to know everything," Ty replied. His voice lowered, almost intimate, though the whole room heard him. "I just need to know the truth of this moment. Because I don't think you're angry at me. Or at my dad. Or even at them." His head tilted slightly toward the wall of teachers, but his eyes never left Tom. "So who is it? Who are you really angry at?"

The words echoed in the silence, filling the space with more weight than shouting ever could. Tom's breath stuttered, his eyes glassy, his body caught between two worlds: the armour of rage and the collapse of confession. A muscle in his cheek twitched, betraying the battle inside. Jasmin clutched Ella's hand, whispering, "He's not yelling at him. He's… helping him." Ella nodded, her eyes wet, though she said nothing. Even Sophie, always the first to comment, pressed her lips together, watching with tears she refused to wipe.

Mr. Clarke leaned into Mr. Arnett's ear. "Do you see it? This is what we couldn't reach in him. Ty just did." Mr. Arnett only nodded, his throat too tight for words. Tom finally lowered his fists, not fully, but enough to betray the weight of Ty's question. His chest shook with uneven breaths, and though no words came yet, the silence that followed was no longer the silence of rage. It was the silence of a boy trying not to break.

The silence in the library pressed against every ribcage, an invisible weight no one could shrug off. Ty's question lingered in the air, heavier than any scolding or punishment ever could have been. Tom's lips twitched, his jaw set so hard it looked like his teeth might crack. His fists trembled against his sides, knuckles whitening with the force he poured into them. His eyes betrayed him, shimmering wet, but he refused to let a single tear fall. Instead, he twisted his face into something jagged, a mask of rage that shielded the pain beneath. The students shifted uneasily, their own eyes darting between Ty's calm frame and Tom's shaking body. It was not anger they were seeing—it was the visible strain of someone trying to contain years of hurt.

Nico leaned toward Leo, whispering low, "He looks like he's about to explode." Leo didn't answer, only narrowed his eyes, recognising something familiar in Tom's trembling stance. Alex muttered under his breath, "That's not fury. That's fear with teeth." Jasmin's hand clung to Ella's, both girls frozen, not daring to breathe too loudly. Mr. Clarke watched with a teacher's heart torn open, knowing this was a lesson no curriculum had words for. Mr. Arnett gripped the edge of his chair, torn between stepping in and knowing he'd only shatter the fragile thread Ty had spun.

Tom's breath rasped through clenched teeth. "You don't know anything about me," he spat, the words shaking. His voice cracked mid-sentence, betraying the war between holding back tears and releasing them. His chest rose high, desperate for breath, and his shoulders hunched as though trying to keep the world from seeing what lived beneath. He glanced at the adults, their stern stares burning into him, then back to Ty—who stood steady, unmoved, with his hands still resting calmly at his sides.

"I don't have to know everything," Ty said gently, his tone cutting through Tom's words like a clear chime in the storm. His eyes never left Tom's face, not mocking, not challenging—just present. "But I know this: you're not mad at me. You're not mad at my dad. You're not mad at them either." He flicked his eyes toward the row of teachers against the wall, then back again, steady as stone. "So who is it? Who are you really mad at?" His voice dropped softer still, so quiet that the silence had to lean in to hear it.

Tom's fists twitched as though to swing, but no blow came. Instead his arms trembled more violently, the tremors running through his shoulders like cracks in a wall about to give way. His lips parted, but no words spilled out—only a strangled breath that rattled as though pulled through glass. He blinked hard, lashes wet, and twisted his head to the side, refusing to look Ty in the eyes. "Shut up," he whispered, the words breaking in half, sounding less like a command and more like a plea.

Ty did not move closer, but he shifted one small step forward, not enough to invade Tom's space, only enough to be ready should Tom collapse. "I won't shut up," he said quietly, firm but kind. "Not until you stop fighting the wrong people. Not until you say it out loud, even just once." His calmness was not rehearsed; it was lived, the patience of someone who understood silence and carried it as an ally. His eyes softened, but his stance never wavered. "You don't have to tell them," he added, tilting his head slightly toward the rows of adults. "You only have to tell yourself. Who are you really angry at?"

Mrs. Locke opened her mouth, but Mr. Takashi raised a hand sharply, silencing her before a word escaped. His face was stone, unreadable, but his eyes carried quiet respect for the boy standing before his son. Mrs. Haller dabbed her eyes with a handkerchief, whispering something inaudible into Ms. Henley's ear. The counsellor nodded slowly, her gaze locked on Tom. Even she had never seen him this close to breaking.

The students on the carpet leaned forward, breaths caught in their throats. Sophie muttered into her sleeve, "Why does this feel worse than yelling?" Her eyes glistened. "Because yelling is easy," Mila whispered back. "But this… this is tearing him apart."

Tom finally raised his eyes again, locking them with Ty's. And there it was: the shimmer of tears not yet fallen, the fury struggling against grief. His voice broke into the air, jagged and raw. "I said shut up!" he barked louder this time, but his tone had lost its venom. It wasn't the bite of hate. It was the cry of someone begging not to be exposed. His fists rose again, not to strike, but to shield his face from the truth rising inside him.

Jeremy sat silently at the back, his hands clenched in his lap. He leaned toward Leo and whispered so quietly it was barely a breath, "He's not angry at us. He's angry at home." Leo nodded once, grave and slow, his eyes fixed on Tom.

Ty did not flinch. "Then say it," he said softly, steady as ever. "Say who it is. You don't have to fight me. You just have to tell yourself the truth. Because the truth is louder than this." He gestured slightly toward Tom's trembling fists.

The air in the library thickened, the weight of unspoken words pressing down. Tom's breath cracked, his lips twitching, the question digging into him deeper than fists ever could. And though no confession left his mouth yet, the crack in his armour was wide enough for everyone to see.

The stillness of the library shattered with Tom's voice, raw and jagged. "You don't understand!" he shouted, the words clawing their way from somewhere buried deep. His fists shook as though the anger itself had weight, dragging his body forward. "This isn't about school! It's not about him!" His eyes darted at Ty, then at Mr. Takashi, wild and untethered. "It's not about any of you!" His voice cracked on the last word, snapping the room's silence into fragments that could not be gathered back again. Students flinched at the volume, but it wasn't the sound that frightened them—it was the desperation beneath it.

Leo straightened, his jaw tightening, recognising the breaking point he once knew in himself. Alex whispered, "Here it comes," more to himself than anyone else, as though bracing for impact. Jeremy pressed his hand flat against his knee, his face pale. He knew Ty's question had landed its blow, but the wound it opened was bleeding more than anyone expected. Tom's breaths tore through the air, sharp and uneven, his chest heaving as though he had been running for miles.

"Then who?" Ty asked, his voice calm, steady. He did not step closer, did not push, only left the question hanging like a bridge. His eyes softened as he added, "Say it, Tom. We're here. We'll hear you." His arms lowered slightly, palms turned outward, not to catch, not to restrain, but to show they were empty. The invitation was there without demand: open arms, waiting if Tom needed them.

Tom's lips trembled before the word burst out like a stone thrown through glass. "My uncle!" His throat tore on the sound, his entire frame shaking as though naming it made it real. "He's the one! He's the one I hate! He's the one who—" His words broke apart into jagged sobs, each one louder than the last, fury and grief indistinguishable in their sound. Students stared in shock, teachers frozen where they stood, the truth finally pulled into the open air.

Mrs. Dunlop covered her mouth with her hand, her eyes wide. Mr. Clarke closed his eyes briefly, nodding as though he had expected this moment, though it wounded him to hear it out loud. Ms. Henley, the counsellor, leaned forward in her chair, her lips pressed together in silent recognition of the weight Tom carried. But it was Mrs. Locke who stiffened visibly, folding her arms in disgust. "We've all heard enough," she muttered, but Mr. Arnett shot her a warning glance, silencing her before she could poison the air further.

Tom's voice surged again, hoarse and furious. "And you! All of you teachers who wanted me gone!" His arm lashed out, pointing, his finger shaking with rage. "You wanted to throw me away like garbage! Like I didn't matter! Like I was just another problem you could get rid of!" His face twisted, wet with tears now, the mask of rage crumbling even as he shouted. "Do you know what that feels like? To already be trash at home—and then to come here and hear that maybe you're trash here too?" His voice cracked so hard on the last word it came out nearly broken, a cry more than a shout.

The room bristled with the tension of truth too sharp to ignore. Jasmin clutched Sophie's hand tightly, her eyes glistening with tears she didn't bother to hide. Mila's chin trembled, her voice whispering to no one in particular, "No one should feel that way." Nico looked down at the carpet, his fists clenched, unable to meet Tom's eyes but unwilling to turn away from the sound of his pain.

Ty finally moved—not toward Tom, but only enough to lower himself to the boy's level, so their eyes aligned. His voice was steady, anchored. "You are not trash," he said firmly. "Not here. Not to us. Not to me." He kept his arms open, still offering, still patient. "If you want them, my arms are here. But you don't have to take them yet. Just know they're here, and they'll stay here." His words were not a command but a promise, one boy's vow to another.

Tom's breathing rattled, his tears now falling freely, streaking his face as he glared at the ground. His fists loosened, only slightly, but enough for everyone to see the shift. He did not move into Ty's embrace, but he did not pull away either. His body, rigid for so long, trembled with the weight of confession and the fear of what would follow. For the first time, the wall around him cracked, and through that fracture, the truth had found its way out.

Mr. Takashi remained standing, silent, his eyes steady on Tom. He did not raise his voice, nor did he step in. He only nodded once at his son, the barest sign of approval, and then turned his gaze toward the row of stiff teachers. "This," he said quietly, though his tone carried more than any shout, "is what you nearly threw away." His words cut deep, leaving no room for reply.

The room was still, thick with the sound of Tom's uneven breaths. Students shifted closer together, some resting shoulders against one another as if bracing from the impact of what they had just witnessed. The library had become a courtroom, not of law but of truth, and the verdict was written on Tom's tear-streaked face. The first crack in the wall had come, and it could not be undone.

Tom's fury did not soften after naming his uncle; if anything, it swelled, filling the library like a storm no wall could contain. His chest heaved as words clawed out of him. "Do you think I don't see it in your eyes? The way some of you look at me—like I'm already lost, like I'm just one step from being locked up?" His voice shook but carried, every student listening as if their own futures were caught in his outburst. Tears tracked down his cheeks, but his fists swung upward as though fighting invisible chains. For the first time, he was not just raging at shadows—he was daring everyone to hear him.

And Ty, still in front of him, didn't move. His eyes locked on Tom's, steady as stone, a presence that said: I can hold this. His small shoulders, squared and calm, looked out of place before such fury, but no one doubted his strength. He did not offer words immediately. He let the air shake with Tom's voice. He let the library hear every note of rage. He let Tom's storm crash against something that would not crumble. The boy who had once said little now spoke louder by silence than any of the adults scattered along the walls.

Tom's shouting cracked further. "He's ruined me! Since I was five! He's made me hate myself, made me hate everyone else! And you people—" his arm shot out toward the teachers— "you were about to finish what he started! Throw me away, and then what? Maybe I really would have become the monster you thought I was!" His chest convulsed, half-sob, half-scream, and the words dissolved into shaking gasps. His body trembled from the force of holding back what his heart wanted to break into.

Still, Ty did not rush. He did not smother Tom with comfort or strip him of dignity by forcing calm. He only shifted his stance slightly, lowering himself to Tom's level again, his arms still open—not insistence, not demand, just there. His nod was small, but it carried power: You're right to be angry. I see it. I will not run from it. Keep going if you need to.

A hush fell heavier across the library, thicker than before. Students sat in rapt silence, breaths held, while teachers glanced at one another uncertainly. Even Mr. Clarke's throat worked as though words had formed and died there. Mrs. Dunlop's hand trembled against her cheek. Ms. Henley's eyes glistened, though she stayed composed. It was the quiet acknowledgement that Tom's anger, no matter how violent it sounded, had been earned. And only Ty had managed to stand inside that fire without flinching.

Leo muttered under his breath, "He's doing what I never could." Alex, beside him, nodded faintly. "No… he's doing what we never even tried." Their voices were nearly lost under Tom's uneven gasps, but the admission rang true. They had once broken others to make themselves feel whole. Ty was showing another way: to hold someone together long enough for them to see they weren't already broken beyond repair.

Jeremy, small in the back, clutched his notebook against his chest. His lips barely moved, but his eyes never left Ty. He had never seen anyone so young hold another boy's life so carefully without words, only presence. He thought of Myles, of the article folded neatly at home. If someone had stood like that for him… maybe. The thought hollowed him out, but it also carved something solid inside him: a vow to remember this moment, because it mattered.

Tom's arms sagged, his fists still tight but lowered to his sides. His throat worked around words that wouldn't come. For all his anger, all his noise, silence took him again—this time not as armour, but as exhaustion. He looked at Ty as though the weight of years pressed down through his eyes. His voice broke into a hoarse whisper, barely audible, "Why do you care?" The words were not accusation but bewilderment. He had never been asked to believe in kindness directed at him.

Ty finally spoke, steady and quiet: "Because you're not what he made you. And I'm not letting him win." His arms stayed where they were, his posture unchanged. He had said enough. The rest, he left for Tom to choose. That restraint, more than anything, broke through to the room watching. Strength was not in conquering. It was in waiting, in standing unbroken in front of someone else's breaking.

The air shifted. Students felt it before the teachers did, as though the floor itself leaned differently. A boy's scream had filled the library, but now another boy's silence ruled it. Not the silence of fear or rejection, but the silence of a space being held. The tension had not gone, but its edge had dulled, wrapped in something steadier. Ty, still only eleven, had shown a truth even the adults had missed: that sometimes the bravest act was not striking, not lecturing, not even comforting—but simply standing firm, letting another's pain exist without being erased.

The library did not breathe after Tom's words fell silent. Every teacher in the room carried a different shadow across their face, some rigid with anger, others pale with dawning recognition. Mrs. Locke was the first to break the stillness, her lips tightening as she hissed toward Mr. Arnett, "This is too far. Violence against staff is never excusable. He should be arrested." Her voice, sharp as glass, cut the hush in two. Several students flinched, not from Tom this time, but from the cold certainty of her words. Whispers began to ripple down the rows of teachers, hushed but heavy: "Police… suspension… safety first." The words sounded like verdicts, not solutions.

Mr. Clarke stepped forward, voice level but firm, "We are not in a courtroom, Margaret. This boy has carried pain none of us fully understood until now. You heard him. We cannot answer pain with punishment alone." His hands trembled at his sides, but his words did not. A few teachers shifted uncomfortably, caught between fear for safety and the conviction that compassion had just spoken through Tom's tears.

It was Ty, though, who moved before anyone else. The eleven-year-old walked a slow half-circle until he stood in clear view of the staff row. His dark eyes fixed on each teacher in turn, but when they settled on Mrs. Locke, the weight in the room changed. Students instinctively leaned closer. Even Tom lifted his head to watch. Ty's voice, though soft, carved into the silence with an authority far older than his years. "Mrs. Locke," he said, pausing just long enough for the air to strain, "you are a disgrace to me. You dishonour me by deciding this young man's worth is nothing before you've even asked yourself if he deserves saving."

The words landed like iron. Mrs. Locke's jaw tightened, her arms folding across her chest as though to shield herself. Colour rose hot in her cheeks, but no reply escaped her lips. Teachers glanced at each other in disbelief, some stunned by the audacity of a child, others struck by the clarity of his truth. A single cough from the back of the room broke the tension, but even that faded quickly as all eyes returned to the boy who dared speak so plainly.

Ty did not stop. He drew in a steady breath, his shoulders square. "I will not apologize for what I just said," he declared, his voice ringing across the library, "because the day we stop fighting for someone like Tom is the day we fail every student here. And I will not fail him." His words were not a plea; they were a challenge, sharp and unbending.

Silence pressed heavier than before. It was Mr. Zenji Takashi who rose next, calm as still water. His suit jacket shifted slightly as he straightened, but his eyes remained steady, not on his son, but on the teachers. "I agree with my son," he said simply. His voice carried no threat, only unshakable certainty. That alone sent another ripple through the staff. No one expected agreement, let alone such quiet conviction, from the man many viewed as authority incarnate.

Students watched with wide eyes, some gripping their knees, others whispering, "He said it… Ty actually said it." Nico's head tilted toward Jeremy, whose small fists pressed tight against his lap, pride flashing across his face. Jeremy whispered back, "That's what real courage looks like." Leo, sitting further back, lowered his gaze, a faint smile tugging at his mouth. "That boy fights harder for others than I ever did," he muttered, Alex nodding beside him.

Mrs. Dunlop, the vice principal, lifted a cautious hand as though to ease the storm. "Ty," she began, carefully measured, "this is highly irregular. You're not—" but she faltered, seeing the boy's steady stance, the unwavering calm beside Tom's still-shaking figure. For all her years in administration, she had never seen students hold a room this way.

Mr. Arnett finally cleared his throat, his voice rough but not unkind. "We will… discuss this further," he said, though his gaze lingered on Tom. The principal's words carried the weight of hesitation, a man trying to balance fear and duty. He did not silence Ty, nor did he reprimand him. He only allowed the moment to remain unbroken, and that, in itself, was a concession.

Mrs. Haller whispered to Ms. Henley, "He speaks with more authority than half this room." The counsellor nodded, her hand resting against her notebook, her eyes glistening as she watched Tom for signs of collapse. She knew what Ty had just done: given him cover, shielded him from the final blow of rejection.

Tom, for his part, had not spoken since his rage had cracked open into confession. But his eyes lifted now, wet and red, to look at Ty. Confusion and disbelief swirled there, but beneath it, the faintest flicker of something else: a question he was too proud to ask aloud. Why would you fight for me?

Ty answered without words, only holding his ground, his chest rising and falling steadily, his presence declaring silently: Because you're worth it, whether you believe it or not.

The sound of Tom's chair scraping against the library floor was louder than any words spoken that morning. He shoved himself to his feet, his body taut with fury, but there was no triumph in his face. His chest heaved as though the air itself was choking him, and his fists clenched until his knuckles blanched white. The students sitting cross-legged on the carpet drew back instinctively, watching him stumble toward the doorway. His shoes struck hard against the tile, each step a declaration that he could no longer bear the walls around him. This was not rebellion, nor was it victory—it was the only way he knew to keep from crumbling in front of them all.

The hush that fell in his wake was thick enough to smother. Teachers, lined against the walls, exchanged glances that carried both relief and dread. Mrs. Locke muttered something sharp beneath her breath, but Mr. Clarke silenced her with a glare. Mr. Arnett, standing near the entrance, did not move to stop Tom. Instead, his eyes swept the room, resting briefly on Ty, who was already upright, his dark gaze tracking Tom's retreating back. The principal gave the faintest of nods, a signal not of surrender but of trust. He knew better than to send another adult into Tom's storm. Ty had earned that chance.

Tom's footsteps echoed into the corridor, fading but not vanishing. Even the slam of the library doors behind him carried no finality—it was a sound of desperation, not rejection. The air inside remained charged, every student and teacher caught in the quiet aftermath. Sophie's eyes were wet, her hand pressed to her lips as if to hold back a cry. Nico leaned close to Leo and whispered, "He's not running from us—he's running from himself." Leo gave no answer, only a slow nod, his face shadowed by memories of his own broken exits years before.

Ty's father shifted his weight but did not pursue immediately. Mr. Zenji Takashi's hand rested briefly on the back of a chair as he addressed the room in a low, steady tone: "He needs space—but not abandonment." His words, simple as they were, left the teachers still and uncertain. No one argued. They knew what he meant. There was a line between discipline and desertion, and Tom had been balancing on that blade far too long.

Ty moved first, his steps silent but purposeful, his small frame cutting through the aisle of seated children. His face betrayed no anger, no pity—only an unshaken resolve. Jeremy shifted on the carpet, clutching his knees and whispering to himself, "He won't let him go too far." Jasmin, sitting beside Ella, reached for her friend's hand, their fingers knotting together as though to anchor themselves in the unease. None of them doubted Ty, though every one of them feared for Tom.

Mrs. Dunlop's voice broke the silence. "Shouldn't we—" she began, but Mr. Arnett cut her off with a quiet, "No. He's not in handcuffs, and I'll not put him there today." The principal's voice was weary but firm, and for once, no one challenged him. Even Mrs. Locke, arms folded tight across her chest, kept her silence. The library, usually a place of hushed whispers and turning pages, had become the stage for something rawer than any lesson taught from a book.

Ty's figure slipped through the doorway, the sunlight of the corridor spilling briefly across the carpet before the doors swung shut again. In that moment, the weight of trust shifted. Students who once looked to their teachers for answers now turned instinctively toward Ty, believing in his calm where the adults had faltered. It was not authority that gave him that power, but presence, and the certainty that he would not abandon Tom to his shadows.

Mr. Takashi's eyes lingered on the closed doors before he spoke again. "I will follow him shortly," he said, his voice measured, "but not to intervene. Only to stand where he can see that he is not alone." His words carried the quiet assurance of a man who had stood with too many broken souls before. He knew that rushing after Tom would drive him further into panic, but distance would tell a different story—that trust was still waiting when he chose to look back.

Ella leaned against Jasmin's shoulder and murmured, "Why does Ty care so much?" Her friend whispered back, "Because someone has to." Across the carpet, Mila wiped her cheeks and stared at the doorway as if she could will Tom to reappear. Alex exhaled sharply, his arms folded, muttering, "I used to walk out like that. Thought it made me strong. All it made me was alone." His words hung heavy, not just for the students, but for the teachers who had failed to see it then.

Mr. Clarke moved to the centre of the room, his hands clasped tightly. "We are not finished," he said quietly, but firmly. "What you saw was not defiance—it was a boy trying to survive. If you cannot tell the difference, then you have no business speaking of justice." His voice cracked, but his eyes remained fierce. The students straightened, sensing that they had witnessed a truth too often ignored.

The library's silence grew deeper, not empty but waiting. Ty's absence left behind not fear, but a thread of hope, thin but unbroken. Every ear strained for the echo of returning footsteps, but none came yet. Still, they believed he would succeed. Because Ty always did what no one else dared: he listened. And sometimes, listening was enough to keep another boy from vanishing altogether.

When Tom's footsteps thundered away from the library, every adult seemed to freeze. Mr. Clarke stepped forward as though to pursue, his hand half-raised, but Zenji Takashi intercepted him with a steady motion. His palm lifted, calm and commanding, and his voice cut through the hush: "Let me go." It was not a request but a certainty, the kind spoken by a man who had walked into storms far darker than this one. Mr. Clarke faltered, then stepped back, the tension in his jaw showing he wanted to object but knew better. He had seen the weight Mr. Takashi carried—not of force, but of presence—and it was a weight no teacher could match.

The RCMP investigator slipped out through the same doors Ty had gone moments earlier. His movements were neither rushed nor heavy; they carried the patience of a man who knew haste only fed panic. The faint slam of the doors settling closed behind him left the library bound again in silence, but outside, the corridors stretched with light. His shoes made no echo on the floor as he followed the invisible thread his son had already pulled toward Tom's pain. He walked not as a policeman but as a father, measured, deliberate, the embodiment of calm pursuit.

Tom had already reached the edge of the schoolyard, his body hunched against a fear that no one else could see. The spring sun poured down, gilding the grass with warmth, but he sat in its glow like a shadow refusing to dissolve. Ty was there, a few feet away, his knees bent, hands loose on his lap. He said nothing, only waited, his dark eyes fixed gently on the older boy. There was no judgment in him, no demand—just space held open until Tom was ready. For a long moment the scene was fragile, like glass, and it seemed one wrong movement could shatter it.

Zenji Takashi approached with the same softness his son had shown, each step slow, deliberate, unthreatening. He did not announce himself, did not call out Tom's name or clear his throat with authority. Instead, he let the sun carry him forward, his presence folding into theirs like a tide easing onto the shore. When he reached them, he did not stand above, towering over their bent shoulders. He lowered himself to the ground, settling beside them with the ease of a man unbothered by formality. The grass bent beneath his weight, and still he said nothing. He was simply there.

Ty shifted only slightly, glancing at his father, but offered no words. The boy knew this silence well; it was a silence that spoke louder than reprimands. Tom's breathing came fast, shoulders heaving, fists tight on his knees, but he glanced sideways when he sensed the added presence. For the first time since the shove, his eyes softened, only for a heartbeat, at the realisation that the man he had pushed away had come back—not to punish, not to drag him inside, but to sit with him beneath the sun.

# THE SMILE THAT BROKE

The warmth of the spring afternoon wrapped around them, distant shouts of children on the playground threading faintly through the air. It might have been an ordinary scene—three figures on the grass, pausing in the middle of a school day—but the quiet gravity of it turned the world still. Zenji Takashi's breathing was steady, a rhythm both boys could hear without trying. It matched the weight of Ty's calm, creating a circle in which Tom's anger, his fear, his shame, could settle without spilling over.

Slowly, Tom's hands loosened, though his fists did not open entirely. His voice remained buried, but his breathing eased, catching less in his throat. The sharp edges of his rage dulled, though they did not vanish. He stole another glance, first at Ty, then at the man who had sat beside them as though it were the most natural thing in the world. Neither pressed him, neither demanded, and it was that restraint—the absence of expectation—that softened something inside him he had not realised was clenched.

It was then, in the hush of the library lawn, that the three of them formed an unspoken pact. Not by words, not by rules, but by presence alone. Tom's fury had been chased by dozens of voices before, shouted down, condemned, or ignored. But now, for the first time, it was simply witnessed—watched with eyes that did not flinch, absorbed by shoulders that did not collapse. The sun warmed their backs, and the silence they shared became its own kind of language, one Tom understood better than any speech.

The grass bent beneath Tom as though it had been waiting for him all day. He dropped hard, his knees folding under him, and for a moment he pressed his palms against the soil as though to ground himself, to make sure the earth did not tilt away. Ty lowered himself without hesitation, legs crossed, hands open, his stillness deliberate. Zenji Takashi followed with quiet grace, settling beside them as though the act of sitting in the sun was as important as any speech he might make. The leaves above them swayed, scattering patches of gold across their shoulders and faces, a softer light than the flat glare of fluorescent tubes.

The silence held first, thick but not suffocating. Ty tilted his head back toward the branches, watching them stir. "The sun feels good," he said after a long pause, his voice even. "Much nicer than those buzzing lights inside." His words carried no lesson, no hidden point, only truth spoken plainly. The corners of Zenji Takashi's mouth lifted into a faint smile, the kind that came more from his eyes than his lips. "I agree," he murmured, his deep voice gentler than it had been in the library. Tom's head moved in a small nod, almost imperceptible, but it was there. A start, thin as paper but strong enough to hold weight.

The sound of the school carried faintly on the breeze—doors closing, a whistle from the far field, a ripple of laughter that came and went. Yet beneath the tree, time slowed, the outside world held at bay. Tom drew his knees closer, his arms folding across them, his chin dropping to rest against his sleeves. He did not speak, but his body betrayed him. The tension in his shoulders lessened by inches, his back curved not in defiance but in exhaustion. He was listening, even if his mouth refused to confirm it.

Zenji rested one hand on the grass, fingers brushing the blades in absent motion. His eyes studied the boy without pressure, the way a father studies weather: watching for signs, for patterns, for shifts that reveal what is coming. He said nothing more, for nothing more was needed yet. Tom felt that gaze, not sharp, not piercing, but steady, and he let his head sink further into the nest of his arms. His breath slowed. He was not yet ready to break, but he was no longer bracing himself to run.

Ty leaned back on his hands, tilting his face to the sun. "I like it out here," he said simply. "It's easier to breathe." His voice floated as light as the branches above, directed at no one, yet meant for both of them. Zenji's smile deepened at his son's instinctive wisdom. Tom gave another nod, more certain this time. His shoulders shifted, the motion of agreement unspoken but visible. Even without words, his body confessed that he understood.

The sunlight became their language, quiet and shared. Tom's fists, once hard as stone, now loosened until his palms rested against the grass. He traced the dirt with his thumb, not consciously, but in the small way a person does when they no longer need to hold themselves in a shield. His chest rose and fell in a more natural rhythm, less forced, less jagged. Ty saw it and let it pass without comment, giving Tom the dignity of discovery. Zenji did the same, waiting, allowing the boy to feel his own slow unraveling.

For a while they said nothing more. The birdsong returned, hesitant at first, then stronger, as though the silence had made room for its music. Tom listened, though he did not look up. His eyes blinked against the light, and his breathing evened with the soft rhythm of the leaves. Ty let his words rest where they were, not pushing further, not filling the space with questions. His father mirrored the stillness, a pillar of patience beside them both. The three of them sat as if carved into the afternoon—boy, boy, and man—different lives, different ages, bound for the moment by nothing but the sun.

The silence was not empty. It was layered, filled with the unsaid: the weight of a boy's fear, the steadiness of a father's presence, and the quiet assurance of a friend who would not abandon him. Tom's nods, small and fleeting though they were, meant more than entire speeches. He was not rejecting them. He was not pushing them away. He was hearing them—hearing the warmth, the patience, the choice to sit beside him rather than stand over him. That was enough for now.

Tom's voice was low, almost a whisper, the words dragged from some chamber inside him that had never known daylight. "It started when I was five," he muttered, his eyes still fixed on the grass. "The fists… the words… it never stopped. Not once." His shoulders hunched as if expecting the confession to bring punishment, but none came. Ty said nothing, only shifted slightly so that his hand rested lightly in the grass near Tom's, close enough to remind him he was not alone, but far enough to respect the space that boy still clung to.

# THE SMILE THAT BROKE

Zenji Takashi exhaled through his nose, quiet and steady, then rose to his feet. Tom flinched at the movement, but Ty's calm stillness held him in place. Zenji's voice was soft, steady, almost casual. "I'll get something to drink. Three root beers. I think we've earned that." He disappeared into the school without another word, leaving the boys in the sunlight, the sound of distant laughter and a lawnmower filling the gap. Tom blinked after him, confused by the simplicity of the gesture. For once, no adult was storming away in anger or dragging him back inside. He was being trusted to stay.

The silence stretched again, but it was softer now. Tom dug at the dirt with his thumb, carving invisible lines. "Five years old," he repeated, his voice thick. "Every day. No one ever believed me. Said I was lying, said I wanted attention. But it was real." He looked at Ty then, expecting disbelief, expecting the flinch that always came when truth became too heavy. But Ty only gave a slow nod, the weight of it grounding the air. "I hear you," he said quietly. "And I believe you."

When Zenji returned, he carried three glass bottles, cold enough to sweat in his hands. He offered one to each boy before lowering himself to the grass again, his movement unhurried. "Root beer fixes nothing," he said with a small smile, twisting off his cap. "But it makes the waiting easier." Tom hesitated, then opened his bottle, the hiss of carbonation sounding louder than it should. He drank, the sweetness grounding him in something strangely ordinary. For the first time in years, the knot in his chest loosened enough for him to keep talking.

What spilled from him over the next hour was jagged, uneven, but real. He spoke of nights where he learned to sleep with one eye open. Of fists that landed without warning. Of words that stripped the marrow from his bones long before the bruises faded. He told them about the silence in the house, how his parents pretended the uncle was just strict, how no one dared to acknowledge the shadows he dragged into every room. He told them about hating himself, about thinking maybe he deserved it. Each word fell heavy, but none of them broke the patience of the two beside him.

Ty didn't interrupt. He didn't rush in with comfort, either. He sat still, sipping his root beer slowly, nodding when it mattered, letting the boy speak until the words burned themselves out. Zenji added nothing more than the occasional murmur—"I hear you," or "That should never have happened." Nothing polished, nothing prepared, only truth layered gently against the boy's raw confessions. Tom noticed that neither of them looked away, not once.

By the time the sun began to shift lower, Tom's shoulders had dropped, his fists unclenched, and his voice had steadied. He leaned back in the grass, staring at the thin clouds crawling across the sky. "I never told anyone," he admitted softly, his throat tight. "Not one person." He blinked hard, the tears fighting to remain hidden. "I thought if I did, it would just make things worse."

# THE SMILE THAT BROKE

Ty tilted his head, studying him with the kind of patience only a boy who had seen shadows himself could hold. "You told us," he said. "And we're still here. We're not leaving." His words landed without force, without ceremony, but they carried weight. Zenji took a final drink from his bottle and set it in the grass, his gaze steady. "Tonight," he said, "you'll eat a full meal. You'll sleep without fear. And tomorrow—tomorrow we'll start making sure you never have to face this alone again."

Tom closed his eyes, the root beer bottle cooling in his hands. For the first time, the thought of a night's sleep didn't feel like a punishment. The fear was not gone, but it was no longer the only voice in the room. Between Ty's quiet strength and Zenji's steady presence, something new had entered his world. It wasn't safety yet, not fully. But it was the start of it, and that was more than he had ever allowed himself to hope for.

## CHAPTER 13: A NEW HOME, A NEW START

The Takashi house stood at the end of a quiet street, framed by tall maples whose branches filtered the afternoon light into scattered gold. Tom lingered at the gate with his small bag gripped tight in one hand, as if the straps themselves might anchor him to the world he had left behind. He had never been invited into a home like this before, not as a guest, not as someone expected, and certainly not as someone wanted. His chest tightened with the thought that any moment he might be told he did not belong here, that this threshold too was another trap. He cast a wary glance at the front windows, where curtains swayed softly, giving nothing away.

Ty walked a few steps ahead, glancing back at him with that same calm assurance he had carried since the library. "It's just a house," he said simply, though the weight in his voice suggested more. Tom wanted to believe him but felt the familiar churn in his stomach, the one that always came before entering a place where danger might hide. He kept his eyes on the steps, each one a reminder of how easy it would be to turn back. But the memory of Ty's steady voice and his father's quiet promise in the grass nudged him forward.

Mrs. Takashi opened the door before he reached it. She did not rush him, nor did she force a smile that might feel false. She stood with her hands folded in front of her apron, her voice soft and even. "Welcome, Tom," she said, as if the words had been waiting for him for longer than this single day. He shifted on his feet, the bag biting into his fingers. He had expected sharp tones or rules barked out like commands. Instead, her calm unsettled him more than warnings ever could. It left him without defence.

Zenji appeared behind her, his broad frame filling the doorway, though his presence was far from threatening. He inclined his head in greeting, a gesture that carried both respect and assurance. "Come inside," he said, as if it were the most ordinary thing in the world. Tom hesitated, his shoes still planted firmly on the edge of the step. He half expected that once he crossed the line, some punishment would fall, some accusation would strike him down. Yet Ty was already holding the door wide, his hand light on the frame, waiting without demand.

The house smelled faintly of cedar and something warm from the kitchen, perhaps bread or soup, though Tom could not tell. The scent tugged at him, stirring memories that hurt as much as they soothed. He stepped over the threshold at last, the wooden floor cool beneath his shoes. The bag in his grip felt heavier, as if it carried not just the scraps of clothing inside but every memory of fists and shadows he had ever known. His breath came shallow, but he kept moving, unwilling to falter now that he had crossed the invisible line.

Inside, the hallway opened into a living room where bookshelves lined the walls and paintings filled the spaces between. None of it was lavish, but it was alive with colour and care. Tom's eyes darted to the corners first, scanning instinctively for dark places where danger might crouch. Ty noticed but said nothing, only guiding him to the rug in the centre of the room. "You can sit if you want," he offered. Tom shook his head stiffly, unwilling to let go of his bag just yet. He felt like an intruder in a museum, afraid that touching anything might shatter it.

Mrs. Takashi stepped quietly past them and returned a moment later with three glasses of water set on a tray. She placed them gently on the table without comment, her movements graceful, unhurried. Tom's eyes flicked to her, waiting for the snap of disapproval that never came. She only nodded once, the faintest of smiles softening her face. Zenji lowered himself into a chair, his posture straight but not rigid. He spoke with the measured calm that had steadied Tom outside the school. "This is your place now," he said. "No tests, no traps. Just a roof and a meal. The rest comes later."

Tom clutched the strap of his bag tighter, his throat burning with the effort of holding back words he did not trust himself to say. He wanted to scoff, to push back, to insist that nothing was ever that simple. But the room did not allow for such defences. Its quiet was not the silence of fear but the silence of safety, an emptiness that asked nothing of him. Ty settled cross-legged on the rug, looking up at him as though the day were no different from any other. "You'll get used to it," he said softly. "It feels strange at first, but it's real."

Tom set his bag down at last, the sound of it hitting the floor louder than he intended. His hand lingered on the strap, unwilling to fully release it, yet the weight lifting from his shoulder was undeniable. He lowered himself onto the edge of the rug, knees drawn up, his back still wary and stiff. The others did not crowd him, did not press him for answers. They let him sit in that fragile balance, half in and half out, like a boy who had stepped across a threshold but was still deciding if he belonged on the other side.

And for the first time in years, he was given the space to decide for himself. The welcome had not come with speeches or commands, only the quiet certainty that he had a place here. It was a beginning, awkward and unsteady, but a beginning all the same. The door remained open behind him, the sunlight spilling through, and Tom could not tell if the ache in his chest was fear leaving or hope daring to enter.

The dining room of the Takashi home glowed softly under the hanging lamp, its light falling across a polished wooden table set with simple but careful precision. Tom stood awkwardly at the edge, his bag still clutched in one hand though he knew it was unnecessary here. The air was heavy with the smell of garlic, soy, and roasted meat, a warmth that filled the room without smothering it. Ty motioned him forward, his voice quiet. "Sit here," he said, pulling out a chair. Tom obeyed stiffly, lowering himself onto the seat as though it might collapse beneath him at any second. His shoulders hunched, and his hands gripped the edge of the table as though bracing for impact.

Mrs. Takashi entered with a tray, her movements steady and elegant. She placed dishes on the table one by one, not rushing, not fussing, as though she were painting each detail into place. A plate of steak cut thin, resting beside bowls of steamed broccoli, cauliflower, and bright baby carrots; a dish of glossy noodles that shimmered in the light. She glanced at Tom without pressure and spoke gently. "You can take as much or as little as you want," she said. "Nothing here will surprise you." Tom nodded, though his throat felt tight. He was used to surprises—ones that struck, ones that shouted, ones that never let him finish a meal.

Ty noticed the stiffness in Tom's shoulders and leaned close, his voice low enough that only Tom could hear. "You're too tense," he said, his eyes sharp but kind. "I can help." Tom frowned, unsure of what he meant, until Ty reached out and pressed two fingers gently against the muscle between his shoulder and neck. The touch was firm, not invasive, and a strange warmth spread through the knot. Tom jerked slightly, but the tension began to ease, almost against his will. "Acupressure," Ty explained, a small grin tugging at his lips. "It works." Tom blinked at him, bewildered. He had not known relief could come from something so simple, and for a moment he let his body rest against the chair rather than cling to it like armour.

Zenji sat down at the head of the table, his posture as straight as ever, though his tone was lighter than Tom had expected. "Let's eat," he said. "Conversation tastes better with food." He began with the vegetables, passing them around with deliberate care, allowing Tom to choose what he trusted. The boy reached hesitantly for carrots first, the bright orange safe and familiar. Mrs. Takashi passed him a plate with steak already sliced thin. "It's easier this way," she said quietly. "You don't have to fight with it." Tom nodded once more, awkwardly, but took a piece.

As the plates filled, the conversation began—not with interrogation, not with demands, but with small talk, light and gentle. Mrs. Takashi asked about his favourite subjects in school, though she did not press when he shrugged. Zenji spoke about a story from his work, though softened and chosen carefully for young ears, and Ty chimed in with a teasing comment that made even his father chuckle. Slowly, the words began to circle toward Tom, giving him space to step in if he wished. At first, he only listened, chewing slowly as though waiting for the trap. But the trap never came.

Ty picked up a piece of broccoli with his chopsticks, holding it steady between the thin sticks with the precision of someone who had practiced since he was small. Tom's eyes followed, fascinated in spite of himself. Ty noticed and grinned. "You don't have to use these," he said, wagging the chopsticks with ease. "But if you want, I'll teach you." Tom shook his head quickly. "I'd drop everything," he muttered. Ty laughed, not at him but with him, letting the moment lighten. "That's how you learn," he said, popping the broccoli into his mouth with exaggerated care.

Bit by bit, Tom found himself answering questions without meaning to. He admitted he liked reading when nobody was around, though he never told anyone at school. He admitted noodles were his favourite, though he had never eaten them this way before. Mrs. Takashi smiled gently. "Then eat what you like," she said, pushing the bowl closer. Tom hesitated, then helped himself, the steam warming his face. He realised, somewhere between bites, that no one was watching how much he ate, no one counting his portions or judging his pace. It was his choice, entirely his.

The hour slipped past unnoticed. The food became easier, the silence less heavy. Ty kept the conversation steady with small nudges, Zenji added humour in his dry, understated way, and Mrs. Takashi listened with a patience that felt more powerful than any lecture.

Tom spoke more than he expected—about classes, about the park near his house, about a stray dog he once fed scraps to. Each story left him surprised at himself, surprised that he wanted to share at all. He caught himself smiling once, faint but real, and quickly masked it with another bite of noodles.

When the plates were finally set aside, the room still hummed with the warmth of food and words shared without judgement. Tom leaned back in his chair, not fully at ease, but no longer clutching the table's edge as if for dear life. He realised, with a quiet jolt, that for the first time in longer than he could remember, he had eaten until he was full, and no one had taken that from him. The thought sat heavy in his chest, not with pain, but with something new, something close to peace. It unsettled him, but he did not push it away.

The Takashi family had not asked for gratitude, had not demanded trust, but in their careful silence and simple kindness, they had begun building something stronger than walls: the faint possibility of home.

The dining room of the Takashi home glowed softly under the hanging lamp, its light falling across a polished wooden table set with simple but careful precision. Tom stood awkwardly at the edge, his bag still clutched in one hand though he knew it was unnecessary here. The air was heavy with the smell of garlic, soy, and roasted meat, a warmth that filled the room without smothering it. Ty motioned him forward, his voice quiet. "Sit here," he said, pulling out a chair. Tom obeyed stiffly, lowering himself onto the seat as though it might collapse beneath him at any second. His shoulders hunched, and his hands gripped the edge of the table as though bracing for impact.

Mrs. Takashi entered with a tray, her movements steady and elegant. She placed dishes on the table one by one, not rushing, not fussing, as though she were painting each detail into place. A plate of steak cut thin, resting beside bowls of steamed broccoli, cauliflower, and bright baby carrots; a dish of glossy noodles that shimmered in the light. She glanced at Tom without pressure and spoke gently. "You can take as much or as little as you want," she said. "Nothing here will surprise you." Tom nodded, though his throat felt tight. He was used to surprises—ones that struck, ones that shouted, ones that never let him finish a meal.

Ty noticed the stiffness in Tom's shoulders and leaned close, his voice low enough that only Tom could hear. "You're too tense," he said, his eyes sharp but kind. "I can help." Tom frowned, unsure of what he meant, until Ty reached out and pressed two fingers gently against the muscle between his shoulder and neck. The touch was firm, not invasive, and a strange warmth spread through the knot. Tom jerked slightly, but the tension began to ease, almost against his will. "Acupressure," Ty explained, a small grin tugging at his lips. "It works." Tom blinked at him, bewildered. He had not known relief could come from something so simple, and for a moment he let his body rest against the chair rather than cling to it like armour.

Zenji sat down at the head of the table, his posture as straight as ever, though his tone was lighter than Tom had expected. "Let's eat," he said. "Conversation tastes better with food." He began with the vegetables, passing them around with deliberate care, allowing Tom to choose what he trusted. The boy reached hesitantly for carrots first, the bright orange safe and familiar. Mrs. Takashi passed him a plate with steak already sliced thin. "It's easier this way," she said quietly. "You don't have to fight with it." Tom nodded once more, awkwardly, but took a piece.

As the plates filled, the conversation began—not with interrogation, not with demands, but with small talk, light and gentle. Mrs. Takashi asked about his favourite subjects in school, though she did not press when he shrugged. Zenji spoke about a story from his work, though softened and chosen carefully for young ears, and Ty chimed in with a teasing comment that made even his father chuckle. Slowly, the words began to circle toward Tom, giving him space to step in if he wished. At first, he only listened, chewing slowly as though waiting for the trap. But the trap never came.

Ty picked up a piece of broccoli with his chopsticks, holding it steady between the thin sticks with the precision of someone who had practiced since he was small. Tom's eyes followed, fascinated in spite of himself. Ty noticed and grinned. "You don't have to use these," he said, wagging the chopsticks with ease. "But if you want, I'll teach you." Tom shook his head quickly. "I'd drop everything," he muttered. Ty laughed, not at him but with him, letting the moment lighten. "That's how you learn," he said, popping the broccoli into his mouth with exaggerated care.

Bit by bit, Tom found himself answering questions without meaning to. He admitted he liked reading when nobody was around, though he never told anyone at school. He admitted noodles were his favourite, though he had never eaten them this way before. Mrs. Takashi smiled gently. "Then eat what you like," she said, pushing the bowl closer. Tom hesitated, then helped himself, the steam warming his face. He realised, somewhere between bites, that no one was watching how much he ate, no one counting his portions or judging his pace. It was his choice, entirely his.

The hour slipped past unnoticed. The food became easier, the silence less heavy. Ty kept the conversation steady with small nudges, Zenji added humour in his dry, understated way, and Mrs. Takashi listened with a patience that felt more powerful than any lecture. Tom spoke more than he expected—about classes, about the park near his house, about a stray dog he once fed scraps to. Each story left him surprised at himself, surprised that he wanted to share at all. He caught himself smiling once, faint but real, and quickly masked it with another bite of noodles.

When the plates were finally set aside, the room still hummed with the warmth of food and words shared without judgement. Tom leaned back in his chair, not fully at ease, but no longer clutching the table's edge as if for dear life. He realised, with a quiet jolt, that for the first time in longer than he could remember, he had eaten until he was full, and no one had taken that from him. The thought sat heavy in his chest, not with pain, but with something new, something close to peace. It unsettled him, but he did not push it away.

The Takashi family had not asked for gratitude, had not demanded trust, but in their careful silence and simple kindness, they had begun building something stronger than walls: the faint possibility of home.

The room had been carefully prepared, the sheets drawn smooth, the curtains pulled halfway to soften the moonlight. To anyone else it might have seemed peaceful, even inviting, but for Tom the silence was too large, too open, too foreign. He lay on the king-sized bed, stiff beneath the covers, staring at the ceiling as if waiting for a noise that never came. The walls did not creak, the doors did not slam, and no voice barked his name from the hall. That very absence pressed against him like a weight. His hands twitched against the blanket, caught between relief and fear, because peace itself felt unnatural.

Down the hall, Ty lay awake on his own bed, eyes fixed on the shadows stretching across the ceiling. He had listened to the rhythm of footsteps earlier, the pacing back and forth, the restless shifting of a body unwilling to rest. Tom's silence was louder than words, and Ty had already decided he would not leave him to wrestle it alone. His father sensed it too. Zenji Takashi rose from his own room almost at the same moment, pulling on a robe with the calm precision of a man who had seen too many nights broken by ghosts. Their eyes met in the hallway, no words needed. Together they turned toward Tom's door.

Inside, Tom's breathing came fast and uneven, his eyes unfocused as old memories pulled him backward. He saw the cracked door, the heavy steps that always followed, the shadow that swallowed the light before fists did. His chest rose and fell quickly, his muscles braced for a strike that never came. He squeezed his eyes shut and whispered, "Not again… not again." It was the cry of a boy trapped between worlds, one foot in safety, the other still chained to fear. He didn't notice the door open, or the soft pad of Ty's feet crossing the carpet.

Ty reached the bed first, climbing onto the other side without hesitation. He leaned close, speaking low but steady. "You're not there," he said. "You're here. And I'm here too." Tom turned sharply, startled by the voice, but found only Ty's dark eyes fixed on him, steady as stone. The boy's arms wrapped around him with certainty, no hesitation, no pity—just the full-bodied hug of someone declaring *I love you enough to stay*. Tom stiffened at first, unused to touch that did not demand or harm, then felt the tension bleed out as he clung back, his hands gripping Ty's shirt like it might vanish if he let go.

Zenji stepped closer, watching the exchange quietly before resting a hand on Tom's shoulder. "No shadows here," he said softly. His voice carried the authority of a man who had spent his life chasing darkness, but also the gentleness of a father who knew how fragile trust could be. He leaned down, pulled Tom briefly into his own arms, and whispered, "You are safe in this house. Safe enough to sleep." Then he drew back, not lingering, respecting the boy's boundaries even as he offered what Tom had never known: unconditional protection.

Tom's breath slowed. His eyes were still wide, but the panic was fading, replaced by confusion at the unfamiliar warmth that surrounded him. Ty stayed pressed against his side, refusing to move, his presence heavy and reassuring. "I'll be here all night," Ty said, settling against the pillow. "You don't have to fight it anymore." Tom swallowed, his throat tight, and whispered back, "Why?" It was all he could manage, a single word drenched in disbelief. Ty answered without pause. "Because you don't deserve to fight alone."

Zenji nodded once, stepping back toward the door. "Pleasant dreams, Tom," he said simply, and for the first time in years those words did not sound like a lie. He closed the door partway, leaving the hallway light just bright enough to soften the room's edges, erasing the dark corners where shadows might hide. Tom felt his eyes burn with un-spilled tears, his body sinking into the mattress at last. His grip on Ty loosened slowly, but the boy beside him did not move away.

Minutes stretched into hours, the silence no longer hostile but warm. Tom's breathing evened out, his chest rising and falling with the rhythm of sleep. His face, tight with fear when he first lay down, now rested soft against the pillow, the lines of worry eased by the simple truth of safety. Ty kept his promise, his own eyes closing only when he was certain Tom had surrendered to dreams. On the other side of the door, Zenji lingered for a time, listening to the quiet harmony inside before returning to his own room.

That night, Tom slept without shadows. He dreamed not of fists or threats, but of something quieter, something he had never known but had always longed for: the feeling of being guarded by love strong enough to chase the dark away. For the first time in his thirteen years, he slept like a child should—peaceful, untouched by fear, and unafraid of waking.

The morning broke soft and golden through the curtains, slipping over the Takashi household with the quiet discipline of a family already rooted in its rhythm. Tom woke to the faint sounds of pans against the stove and voices moving through the kitchen like music. For a moment, he lay still in the vast king-sized bed, trying to decide if the calm he felt was real or just another fragile dream. But then came the scent of something rich and unmistakable—bacon crisping in a pan, butter melting on hot iron—and it stirred something inside him he hadn't felt in years. He rose slowly, running his hand through his hair, his body still unsure if it was truly welcome outside the bedroom door.

When he stepped into the hall, Ty was already waiting, dressed neatly, eyes bright as if sleep had cost him nothing. "Come on," Ty said, not commanding but inviting, his voice carrying the easy warmth of someone who knew the path by heart. Tom followed him cautiously, his bare feet padding against the floor. At the kitchen threshold, he stopped short. The room was alive with movement but not chaos. Mrs. Takashi stood by the stove, her robe tied at the waist, flipping pancakes with a practiced hand. Zenji sat at the table already, reading over a file but closing it immediately when his eyes caught Tom's. There was no judgment in that look, only welcome.

"Good morning, Tom," Zenji said evenly, his voice deep but kind. "Did you sleep well?" Tom hesitated, words tangled in his throat, then gave a single nod. He wasn't ready to admit aloud that he'd slept better than he ever had. Ty slid into a chair beside his father, motioning for Tom to sit across from him. "You should tell them what you want," Ty whispered, grinning. "They'll actually make it." Tom frowned. "What do you mean?" Ty shrugged. "Anything. Just ask."

Mrs. Takashi turned then, her eyes soft and bright. "Tom, breakfast is yours today. Tell me what you'd like." The words hung in the air like something impossible. No one had ever asked him that before, not once in thirteen years. Meals had always been whatever was shoved in front of him, and complaints never ended well. He looked at her face carefully, searching for the trap, but found none. His voice came low, almost uncertain. "Real pancakes," he said, his tone half-question, half-dare. "With bacon. And… and maple syrup. The real kind. Not the fake one." His cheeks burned as though he had asked too much.

But Mrs. Takashi only smiled wider. "Real Canadian maple syrup. The only kind we keep." She opened the cupboard and brought down the amber bottle, setting it on the table with care. "And bacon is already on the stove. You'll have it fresh and hot." Tom blinked, watching her move with effortless kindness, as though this were the most natural thing in the world. His chest tightened at the thought that maybe, just maybe, it could be real.

The pancakes came first, stacked neatly on a warm plate, steam rising in soft clouds. Beside them, strips of bacon curled golden and crisp, their scent filling the room. A tall glass of milk followed, cold and beaded with droplets that slid down the glass. Tom stared at it all, overwhelmed. Zenji leaned back slightly, his eyes never leaving the boy. "Go on," he said simply. "It's yours." Tom picked up the fork with a trembling hand, cutting into the soft pancake. The taste of butter and syrup melted on his tongue, sweeter and richer than he could have imagined. For the first time, food didn't taste like survival—it tasted like belonging.

Ty grinned across the table, stuffing a bite of bacon into his mouth. "Told you," he said between chews. "Best pancakes anywhere." Tom allowed a small laugh to escape, quiet and awkward, but genuine. Mrs. Takashi reached out then, touching his wrist lightly. "No rush," she said. "Take your time." Tom nodded, swallowing hard, not just the food but the ache in his chest. He ate slowly, savouring each bite, listening to the rhythm of the family around him.

The kitchen filled with small sounds—Ty teasing his mother about burning bacon, Zenji chuckling under his breath, the clink of plates and glasses. None of it sharp, none of it cruel. It was ordinary, yet to Tom, it was extraordinary. He found himself watching the three of them, studying how they spoke to one another, how laughter was allowed to linger without fear of reprisal. Every second etched itself into his memory as proof that such mornings could exist.

At one point, Mrs. Takashi asked gently, "Do you like the pancakes, Tom?" He nodded quickly, swallowing his mouthful before answering. "They're… they're perfect." His voice cracked, betraying more than he wanted, but she only smiled as though she understood more than his words. Zenji sipped his tea and added quietly, "In this house, Tom, no one leaves the table hungry. Not for food, and not for kindness." Tom froze at that, the weight of the words striking him harder than any fist ever had.

By the time the plates were cleared, Tom sat back with a fullness in his stomach and a strange warmth in his chest. He had eaten pancakes and bacon before, but never like this. Never when each bite had been given freely, never when each laugh at the table had included him. It felt foreign, yes, but it was the kind of foreign he wanted to learn, the kind he hoped would never fade.

And as he glanced around the table—at Ty's easy grin, at Zenji's steady calm, at Mrs. Takashi's gentle eyes—he realised something he hadn't dared to believe before. This wasn't just breakfast. This was the first rhythm of a life he had never thought he could have.

The day unfolded slowly, almost deliberately, as if the house itself wanted to give Tom time to adjust. Ty moved through each moment with ease, his calm setting the rhythm. After breakfast, he showed Tom where homework was done—never shut away in a bedroom, but at the wide oak table in the living room, with books spread across its polished surface. The air wasn't heavy with tension or dread; it was casual, natural, filled with the quiet shuffle of pages and the occasional hum of Mrs. Takashi sketching in her art corner. Tom sat at the edge, stiff at first, waiting for the sting of correction or the bark of an order, but none came. Ty nudged his elbow lightly. "This is how we do it here. Side by side. No pressure." Tom exhaled slowly, the tiniest crack forming in the armour he always carried.

When homework was finished, Ty gathered the notebooks neatly, placing them on the shelf with almost ritual precision. "We always clear the table," he said. "It's not just about the table. It's about respect." Tom raised an eyebrow. "Respect for a table?" Ty grinned. "Respect for the space. Respect for each other. It matters." Tom said nothing, but the idea lingered in his head long after the books were put away. Respect was not a word often spoken in his world, not unless it was demanded with fists. Here, it seemed woven into every small act, every quiet moment, like air.

Next came the chores. Ty handed Tom a rag and pointed toward the windows, their glass already clear but lined faintly with the fingerprints of yesterday's sun. "We keep things clean," Ty explained. "Not perfect. Just clean enough that it feels good to walk through." Tom hesitated, rag limp in his hand, unsure if this was a test or punishment. But Ty started wiping without ceremony, humming to himself, his movements steady. Tom watched for a beat before mimicking the motions. To his surprise, no one checked his work, no one judged the streaks he left behind. When Mrs. Takashi passed through, she only smiled. "Thank you, Tom," she said gently. Two words. Two words he had almost forgotten how to hear.

The chores ended as quickly as they had begun, and Tom stood awkwardly by the sliding doors that led out into the yard. Ty slid them open with a flourish, stepping aside as though unveiling a secret. "Come see," he said simply. Tom stepped out into sunlight and stopped dead. The backyard was unlike anything he had ever imagined. A Japanese garden stretched across the space, not sprawling but crafted with care—smooth stones winding between raked sand, a small pond reflecting the sky, bonsai trees standing proud in their quiet discipline. It was beauty, but not loud beauty. It was calm, deliberate, the kind that stilled the heart even as it caught the eye.

Tom swallowed hard. "This is your yard?" Ty nodded. "Our yard. Yours too, if you want it to be." Tom didn't answer, his eyes darting across every detail, searching for the flaw, the crack, the inevitable sign that it was not real. But the garden offered nothing but stillness. He crouched by the pond, staring at his reflection rippling in the water. For once, he didn't hate the boy who stared back.

Then Ty motioned toward a wooden structure at the far end of the garden. "That's the dojo," he said. Tom blinked, straightening. "You mean… a real dojo?" Ty's grin widened. "Of course. My father built it. It's where he teaches me. And maybe one day, he could teach you too." Tom's chest tightened, half in awe, half in disbelief. He had only ever seen such places in films or in books; the idea that one could exist in a backyard seemed impossible. Yet here it stood, polished wood gleaming under the sun, the faint smell of cedar carried on the air.

They stepped inside, and Tom froze again. The floor was smooth and cool beneath his socks, the walls lined with practice weapons, scrolls, and quiet symbols of discipline. The space felt sacred, not in a religious sense but in its weight, its respect. Ty bowed lightly before stepping onto the floor. "First rule," he said, "always respect the dojo." Tom awkwardly copied him, bowing shallow, unsure if he had done it right. Ty only smiled. "Good enough. The bow isn't about being perfect. It's about saying: I'm here. I'm ready."

For a while, Ty showed him the basics—not punches or kicks, nothing that would intimidate. Just how to stand, how to breathe, how to let his body find balance. Tom's muscles shook with tension, but Ty corrected him gently, his hands guiding without force. "You don't need to be strong all at once," Ty murmured. "Strength is the last thing that comes. First comes balance." Tom tried again, planting his feet, feeling the strange steadiness that came when he let the floor hold him instead of fighting it.

When they stepped back into the sunlight, Tom felt something new, something fragile but undeniable. The house, the table, the chores, the garden, the dojo—none of it had asked him to prove himself. It had only asked him to be present. Ty walked beside him, hands tucked into his pockets, his voice casual. "See? It's not so scary. It's just life. And life's a lot better when you let someone else carry part of it with you." Tom said nothing, but for the first time in years, he believed it might be true.

The afternoon had grown long, sunlight stretching across the garden until the stones glowed faintly gold. Tom sat on the back step, shoulders still tense despite the calm around him. Ty dropped beside him, tossing a pebble toward the pond. "You know," Ty began with a mischievous grin, "if you throw a pebble in just right, the fish will laugh." Tom blinked, suspicious. "Fish don't laugh." Ty smirked. "Not out loud, maybe. But in their heads, they're roasting us for staring at them all the time." Tom gave the smallest twitch of a smile, though he tried to hide it. Just then Nico and Jasmin slipped into the yard, their presence noisier than the wind. Nico immediately crouched at the pond's edge and said, "See? Look at this one. He's laughing at Tom already." Jasmin doubled over in mock horror, pointing. "Oh no, Nico, that one's laughing at your hair." The laughter bubbled sharp and sudden from Ty, spilling out into the air before anyone else could stop themselves.

For Tom, the laughter rose against his will, at first nothing more than a sharp exhale. But when Jasmin leaned dramatically toward him and whispered, "Don't worry, fish are picky. They only laugh at ugly people," the dam broke. Tom let out a short, startled laugh, quickly muffled with his hand. His face flushed red, as though laughter itself were forbidden, but Ty leaned closer. "There it is," Ty said warmly. "See? You've got it." Nico seized the moment with a grin. "Careful, Tom. If you laugh too hard, your face might crack. I heard it hasn't moved in years." That line made Tom choke out a snort he hadn't meant, and suddenly the silence of his world fractured into something far brighter.

Then Zenji arrived, carrying a tray of drinks, and Nico's eyes glimmered with mischief. "Uh-oh. Here comes the big boss." He straightened, adopting a deep voice: "Yes, Sensei, I'll never laugh again." Jasmin added quickly, "No, no, look serious! He'll know if you've been smiling." Tom watched the two of them put on over-the-top poker faces, but when Zenji raised an eyebrow, Nico cracked. "We were just teaching Tom how to frown, sir!" Zenji set the tray down with deliberate calm. "Oh? And do you succeed at this yourself?" Nico burst into laughter, pointing to Zenji's ever-stern expression. "See? See? He's a professional!"

Even Mrs. Takashi, who had come to call them in, shook her head with an amused sigh. "Professional is not the word, Nico. He was born that way." She turned to her husband and said dryly, "Your face has two settings: 'serious' and 'seriously worse.'" The children exploded in laughter, Ty doubling over while Jasmin clutched her side. Even Zenji himself cracked the faintest grin, which only fueled them further. Nico gasped through the laughter, clutching his chest. "She roasted you, sir. She roasted you in front of the fish!"

Tom's laugh began in a stifled burst but rolled out louder than he expected, so much that he startled himself. He bent forward, shaking, not with fear but with genuine laughter that reached his stomach for the first time in years. Jasmin leaned against him for support, giggling uncontrollably, while Ty thumped the grass with his fist, half from mirth, half from pride. Zenji sat down heavily on the step, shaking his head with mock resignation. "I see my honour is gone. My wife, my son, the neighbours' children—everyone has betrayed me."

Mrs. Takashi patted his shoulder with deliberate sympathy. "It's about time, Zenji. You take yourself too seriously. Even Tom knows it." She winked at Tom, who hiccupped mid-laugh but nodded anyway. Zenji placed a hand dramatically over his heart. "Tom, too? My last ally." Tom coughed between chuckles. "Sorry, sir. They're right." And then he burst into another fit of laughter, this time unrestrained, so loud it startled a bird from the nearby tree.

The laughter went on longer than any of them expected, swelling and falling in waves. Even Zenji allowed himself to join, though his laughter was deeper, slower, like gravel moving beneath the earth. When the noise finally subsided, Tom wiped his eyes with the back of his sleeve, breathless. "I can't remember the last time I laughed like that," he admitted softly. Ty nudged his arm. "Good. We'll make sure it's not the last." Tom lowered his head, still smiling in disbelief, as if unsure whether the joy would hold. But in that moment, surrounded by voices that wanted him, laughter that carried no cruelty, he felt for the first time that maybe he belonged.

The boardroom smelled faintly of polish and paper, the long table already stacked with files and reports that carried too many assumptions inside their pages. Mr. Arnett sat at the head, shoulders drawn back, while the other members of the board shifted in their seats, some eager to speak, others wary of the confrontation that was sure to follow. "We can't ignore this," Mrs. Locke began coldly, her voice sharp enough to cut the silence. "Tom poses a danger, not just to himself but to everyone here. The incident in the library proves it. He should be removed." A murmur of agreement rippled around the table, though not everyone was quick to nod.

Mrs. Dunlop, the Vice Principal, leaned forward, her eyes steady. "But we've all seen the reports. The issue isn't Tom's behaviour in isolation—it's what he's endured. You want to punish a child for surviving abuse? That isn't justice, it's cowardice." Mr. Clarke raised a hand gently, his voice softer. "We owe him more than abandonment. I teach him. I've seen the way he looks for escape, not violence. He needs help, not exile." Mrs. Locke pressed back against her chair with a scoff. "Help is fine in theory, but what happens when another student ends up in hospital? Do you plan to write their parents an apology?"

Before the argument could spiral further, Zenji Takashi cleared his throat. His calm presence alone hushed the room, though his words were measured. "You are treating this as if you are deciding the fate of a criminal. He is not a criminal. He is a boy. What you choose here will define him more than you realize. If you brand him as dangerous, you will create the very danger you fear." His words settled like heavy stones, but Mrs. Locke's eyes narrowed, ready to retort.

It was then that Ty, sitting beside his father, shifted in his seat. At eleven years old, his small hands folded over the polished wood, but his eyes burned with a certainty that silenced even the adults. "You're wrong," he said, his voice clear. Mrs. Locke blinked in disbelief. "Excuse me?" Ty leaned forward, unshaken. "You're talking about him like he's already gone, like he can't change. But I've been with him. I've sat beside him. I've heard his words when none of you would listen. He's not a threat—he's terrified. You can't punish someone for being scared. You can't throw him away because it's easier than helping him."

There was an uneasy shift among the members, some looking down at their notes as if suddenly ashamed. Mr. Clarke's lips parted slightly in admiration, but he stayed quiet, letting Ty hold the floor. Mrs. Dunlop glanced toward Zenji, who gave the smallest of nods, allowing his son to continue. Ty straightened, his small frame steady against the weight of so many older eyes. "You say you're protecting the school. But if you push Tom out, you're teaching everyone else here that the moment you're in pain, the moment you slip, you don't deserve a place anymore. You're teaching fear, not safety. And that will make every single student afraid to speak."

His words struck harder than any report could. The room went still, even Mrs. Locke faltering for the first time. Ty pressed on, voice unwavering. "You think removing him will keep everyone safe? No. It will just make him dangerous. If you make him believe the whole world wants him gone, then maybe one day he will act like you expect him to. And then it will be on you, not him, because you taught him that." He looked around the table, his eyes piercing each face, until even the most hardened officials shifted under the weight of his gaze.

Mrs. Haller, the geography teacher, broke the silence with a quiet breath. "He's right," she murmured. "If we close the door, he'll never have a chance to open it again." Ms. Henley, the counselor, folded her hands, her voice steady but heavy with meaning. "We've been given proof of what he endures at home. That alone explains much of his behaviour. We should not meet violence with rejection. We should meet it with support."

Mrs. Locke slammed her hand lightly against the table, though her voice lacked its usual venom. "So what then? We keep him here and hope he doesn't lash out again? That's your plan?" Ty's eyes sharpened, his words quick, precise, almost like an older man arguing in court. "No. The plan is to give him what he's never had before: consistency. A home where he feels safe. Teachers who don't quit on him. Friends who don't run. If you want safety, then give him no reason to fight."

For a long moment, no one spoke. The board members glanced between each other, some uncomfortable, some quietly moved. Zenji spoke last, his deep voice steady as stone. "I stand by my son's words. Expulsion is not an option. If you choose it, you will not only fail Tom, you will fail this school's purpose. Education is not meant only for the perfect child. It is meant for those who need it most."

Mr. Arnett finally folded his hands, his gaze sweeping the table. "We vote now," he said simply. Hands rose one by one, slower this time, until the count was clear. Tom would remain. The verdict was in, and for the first time, victory had been won not by authority, but by the voice of a boy who refused to let another be cast aside. Ty leaned back in his chair, breathing steady, though his eyes softened with relief. Zenji allowed himself the faintest smile. Mrs. Locke, though silent, sat stiffly with pursed lips, her defeat clear.

As the meeting adjourned, whispers followed Ty out of the room, half in disbelief, half in admiration. He had argued like a lawyer, stood like a soldier, and spoken like someone far older than his eleven years. Tom's fate had been sealed not by adults in power, but by the boy who had seen through his fear and fought for his place in the world.

Zenji Takashi rose from his chair with a slow, deliberate calm, placing a thick folder on the polished table before the board. He didn't need to raise his voice; the weight of his posture alone silenced the room. "This," he said evenly, resting a broad hand on the file, "is the record of a man you all have so far refused to see clearly." He opened the folder and spread several sheets across the surface—police reports, court documents, sworn statements. The stark black print underlined what had been whispered but never truly acknowledged: Tom's uncle was not a phantom excuse. He was real, violent, and unchecked.

The room shifted uncomfortably as eyes darted over the words. Assault. Disturbance. Threats. Each charge detailed with times, dates, and witnesses. Mrs. Haller leaned forward, her hand covering her mouth as she read aloud a line that chilled even the most skeptical: "Subject displayed extreme aggression toward minors in household, physical intimidation noted by neighbours." The silence thickened as Mrs. Dunlop whispered, "My God, this was under our noses all along."

But Mrs. Locke stiffened, her chin tilting upward in defiance. "Children exaggerate," she said sharply, though the tremor in her tone betrayed her faltering ground. "Families fight. We cannot condemn a man on the basis of heated words taken out of context." Zenji's eyes locked on hers, dark and unwavering. "This is not context, Mrs. Locke. This is evidence. Sworn, signed, and filed. You sit here and speak of safety, but your refusal to accept truth is what endangers children. You would rather discard a boy than admit you were wrong."

Ty sat straighter beside his father, his fists curled on the table, but Zenji's hand lifted subtly, calming him before he spoke again. "If you persist in denying irrefutable proof," Zenji said, his voice firm as stone, "then I will have no choice but to file for your dismissal from this school. You are entrusted with the care of children. Your negligence, your blindness, dishonours that trust. And I will not let my son, or any student, be placed under the judgment of someone who values pride over protection."

Gasps and whispers stirred across the room. Mr. Clarke glanced between the documents and Mrs. Locke, his brow furrowed in visible disgust at her stubbornness. Ms. Henley, the counselor, leaned forward, her voice quiet but clear. "You've seen the bruises. You've seen the way Tom flinches at every sound. Are you so determined to defend your opinion that you'll ignore every sign of truth?" Mrs. Locke's lips pressed thin, but she had no words to counter.

Mr. Arnett, the principal, cleared his throat heavily. "The evidence is plain," he said. "There is no more debate about where Tom's anger comes from. The question now is whether we help him heal, or whether we choose the coward's path and turn him out." His eyes lingered on Mrs. Locke, a silent warning that her stance was no longer tolerable.

Zenji gathered the papers back into the folder, his gaze never leaving her face. "This is no longer a matter of opinion," he said coldly. "It is a matter of duty. If you cannot accept this, if you cannot fulfil your duty, then step aside. This boy has suffered enough without educators adding to his punishment."

The silence that followed was suffocating. Even the tick of the clock on the wall seemed loud. Ty finally spoke, his voice steady and cutting through the tension like glass. "She won't answer, because she knows she's wrong." He glanced around the table, then back at Mrs. Locke. "Tom deserves better than excuses. And if you can't see that, then maybe you shouldn't be teaching at all." His words, young as they were, carried the sting of undeniable truth.

Mrs. Dunlop folded her arms, her voice tight but resolved. "Mr. Takashi is right. If Mrs. Locke refuses to acknowledge the truth, then she is unfit for this position. Children come first. Always." Several board members nodded in agreement, their earlier hesitation broken by the blunt evidence spread before them.

Zenji closed the folder with finality, the sound echoing like a gavel in the stillness. "This is the shadow Tom lives under," he said. "It will not vanish overnight. But it is our duty to show him that not every shadow holds power. That is how we break the cycle."

Mrs. Locke sat rigid, her eyes narrowed, but her silence condemned her louder than any words could. For the first time, the board was unified—not in fear, not in hesitation, but in the decision to stand with the boy they had once doubted. And at the centre of it all stood Zenji and Ty, father and son, resolute in the truth no one could deny.

Mr. Arnett had sat quietly through the heated exchanges, his spectacles balanced low on his nose, his fingers pressed together like a man trying to weigh the fate of a life in his palms. He had always been measured, never rash, and certainly never the sort to raise his voice in front of a board split down the middle. Yet as Zenji's evidence lay across the table and Ty's cutting words lingered in the silence, the principal slowly leaned forward, his tone heavier than anyone had ever heard from him before. "I have listened," he began, his voice deliberate, "to teachers, to investigators, and to a child who has shown more courage than some of us seated here. The conclusion is unavoidable. Tom does not need to be cast out. He needs stability. He needs safety. And he needs us to finally stop treating him as a threat when he is, in truth, the one under siege."

The room stilled. Mrs. Locke's lips parted in protest, but before she could speak, Mr. Arnett raised his hand to silence her. "You, Mrs. Locke, have had your chance to prove you could place the needs of students above your own bitterness. You have failed." His words were not shouted, but they struck with a force greater than rage. "You argue for expulsion as though it were discipline. It is not. It is abandonment. Worse, it is cowardice, and I will not allow cowardice to guide this school's future."

Mrs. Dunlop nodded slowly, relief flickering across her face as if someone had finally said aloud what she had been holding back. Ms. Henley placed a hand over her heart, whispering, "Thank you," though her words barely carried across the table. Mr. Clarke's eyes softened, pride evident in the principal's uncharacteristic steel.

Arnett removed his glasses and folded them on the table with care, his gaze sweeping the board. "It is my recommendation that Tom remain in this school under direct supervision, that his progress be nurtured, not stifled. He has endured enough punishment at the hands of those who should have protected him. We will not add our names to that list. And furthermore"—his eyes turned sharply to Mrs. Locke—"I will formally request your removal from this staff. You have lost the trust of your colleagues, and worse, the trust of your students. A teacher without trust cannot lead."

Mrs. Locke paled, her bravado cracking as she gripped the edge of the table. "You cannot—" she began, but Mr. Arnett's voice cut across hers, calm but immovable. "I can. And I will." His authority, long restrained by years of balance and caution, now came forward like a blade drawn from its sheath. The teachers around him sat taller, emboldened by his stance. Even Zenji, a man accustomed to command, inclined his head in recognition of the principal's resolve.

The shift in the room was tangible. Where moments before there had been division, now there was clarity. Leo glanced sideways at Alex, who smirked faintly as if to say the tide had finally turned. Nico whispered something to Jasmin, who nodded, her eyes wide as she absorbed every word. The students in the adjoining waiting area, though not privy to the documents, could sense the victory in the tones drifting out from behind the door.

Ty's gaze lingered on his father for only a moment before fixing on Mr. Arnett. For the first time since this began, he saw the principal not as a bureaucrat trapped between policy and conscience, but as a man willing to risk his position to defend a boy everyone else had nearly abandoned. Ty offered a short, respectful nod, one warrior to another, and Mr. Arnett returned it with quiet gratitude.

Mrs. Dunlop finally spoke, her voice steadier now. "Then let the record show," she said, "that the principal stands with the boy, and the board will follow his lead. Tom stays." Her statement was not a question but a declaration. The murmurs of dissent that might have followed died quickly under Zenji's watchful stare and Arnett's unyielding calm.

Mrs. Locke pushed back from the table, her chair scraping against the floor. She muttered under her breath about injustice, but her words carried no weight now. The tide had turned against her, and even she seemed to know it. Her silence, broken only by shallow breaths, hung like defeat.

Mr. Arnett folded his hands once more, this time with finality. "We are not here to debate Tom's worth. That has been settled. We are here to decide whether we as educators will do what we claim—to protect, to guide, to teach. Today, I choose to uphold that oath. And if that means one of us must leave this room in disgrace, then so be it." His gaze never wavered from Mrs. Locke, whose cheeks burned crimson beneath the weight of his stare.

The decision was made, not by vote, not by consensus, but by conviction. And in that conviction, Tom had been given something he had never known before: an institution willing to fight for him, not against him. The shadow of his uncle loomed still, but for the first time, a light had been lit in defiance of it.

The sun had barely shifted past noon when the group of students drifted together near the edge of the playground. They weren't loud, not this time. Jeremy's small frame stood a step behind Leo and Alex, who both crossed their arms like sentinels. Sophie, Ella, and Jasmin stood close enough to show they belonged to this moment too. Their voices dropped lower than the wind, but their intent was clear: they would not let Tom be cast out. Jeremy, his voice more steady than his years, looked up at the others and whispered, "We've seen too much to let them toss him away. If we give up on him, then we're no better than the people he's running from." None of the others argued. Instead, they nodded one by one, their silence becoming stronger than a shouted pledge.

Inside the school, Mr. Arnett lingered near his office window, watching the playground without really seeing it. The meeting had left him heavy, though resolute, and he knew the true work would begin now, when paper and promises would not be enough. His eyes caught a smaller figure approaching, and beside him, a taller shadow—Ty with his father, Zenji, and Tom trailing behind. Mr. Arnett did not summon them; they came of their own accord. He could see in their faces that this was not going to be a routine exchange. It was something more. Something binding.

Ty's steps were deliberate, neither hurried nor hesitant. He stopped directly before the principal, bowed his head briefly in respect, and then raised his eyes with a seriousness rarely found in children his age. Zenji placed a hand on his son's shoulder but said nothing; he, too, recognised when a voice needed to stand on its own. Tom lingered slightly behind, his body tense, but his gaze fixed on Ty as though waiting for proof that someone would truly take his side without condition.

Mr. Arnett cleared his throat, ready to speak, but Ty stepped forward before he could. "Mr. Arnett," Ty began, his voice calm yet unshakable, "you already know what I've done with Tom so far. You've seen that he listens to me, even when he doesn't want to. That's because he knows I'm not afraid of him, and I never will be." He glanced back at Tom, who stiffened but didn't look away. Ty continued, "But more than that, he knows I don't hate him. I want him to grow, even if it's hard. And I will stay with him through the good and the bad. I will not let him fall."

# THE SMILE THAT BROKE

The principal felt the weight of the boy's words settle in the room. Zenji folded his arms across his chest, silent but firm, allowing his son to take command of the moment. Tom shifted, a nervous sound escaping his throat, but Ty's hand motioned gently for him to hold steady. Then Ty spoke louder, clear and certain, so that no misunderstanding could cloud what he was about to say. "I promise." He drew in a breath, his posture straightening with solemnity. "I, Ty Shiro Takashi, swear an oath to guide Tom through his anger, his fears, and his pain. I will not let him waver or falter. I will not let him be lost. I will stand with him through the good and the bad until he can stand alone as the person he was meant to be. I will not break this promise."

The silence that followed was not empty. It was sacred. Zenji's hand tightened slightly on his son's shoulder, not in restraint, but in pride. Mr. Arnett felt something stir within him, a recognition that this boy had just pledged more loyalty and responsibility than many adults dared to shoulder. He had seen oaths written in ink and stamped with seals that carried less weight than the conviction in Ty's young voice.

Tom's eyes flicked to the ground, then back up to Ty. His jaw clenched, his breath caught, and for a moment it looked as though he might scoff or push the words away. Instead, his shoulders sagged under the enormity of what he had just been given. No one had ever vowed to stand by him before—not family, not teachers, not anyone. His throat worked soundlessly, but his eyes told the truth. He felt it. He believed it. For the first time, he allowed himself to believe that someone cared deeply enough not to walk away.

Mr. Arnett inhaled slowly, as though steadying himself before a verdict. "Ty," he said at last, his voice thick but steady, "your oath is heard. And I believe you. More than that—I trust you." He glanced at Tom, whose guarded stance had softened, if only slightly. "Tom, you need to understand something. This boy has just put his name, his honour, and his future on the line for you. You owe him your effort. Not your perfection, but your effort. Can you give him that?"

Tom hesitated, looking at the floor, then at Ty again. For once, he didn't try to find an excuse. He nodded slowly, one hand curling into a fist before loosening. "I… I'll try," he muttered, and though the words were small, they were honest. Ty gave a single, approving nod, as though the promise was already enough to begin.

Zenji finally spoke, his voice deep and measured. "A child's oath should never be taken lightly. But Ty does not speak as a child. He speaks as one who understands duty. I will hold him to his promise, as he will hold Tom to his effort. Together, they will not fail."

Mr. Arnett exhaled and leaned back in his chair, his decision already made. "Then so be it. Tom remains here, under this oath, and under Ty's watch. If there was ever a guardian fit for the task, it is him." He extended his hand first to Ty, then to Tom. Ty shook firmly, the promise sealed not only by words but by action. Tom, after a long pause, did the same. His grip was weak, but present.

Jeremy, peeking in from the hallway, caught Leo and Alex's eyes. They all understood without speaking: the pact was real, and it had grown far beyond whispered promises among students. It had become law in its own way, written not on paper but in the spirit of those willing to stand against shadows.

The words of Ty's oath still hung thick in the air when a shuffle of footsteps broke the silence. Lisa stepped forward, her arms folded across her chest, her chin lifted in that way that dared anyone to challenge her. She didn't wait for permission, didn't glance at the teachers or even at Zenji. She fixed her sharp eyes on Tom, who still lingered in the shadow of Ty's promise, and spoke without a trace of hesitation. "He's one of us now," she declared. Her voice didn't rise, but it carried with a certainty that filled the room. "And if you think I'm going to let him fall apart, you don't know me at all." The teachers blinked at her bluntness, but the students knew Lisa rarely wasted words.

Tom froze at her statement. He wasn't used to anyone claiming him, much less someone with Lisa's kind of force. His first instinct was to scoff, to push it away before it could cut him later. But there was no sarcasm in her face, no cruel twist in her tone. She said it the way one might announce the sky was blue or the floor was solid—it was fact, not sentiment. Lisa took a step closer, her stance protective, as if daring anyone in the room to contradict her. "I know what kind of storm you carry," she continued, softer now but no less fierce. "It doesn't just vanish. It takes time. And when it feels like it's too heavy to hold, I'll be there. Because I've carried it too."

Leo exchanged a glance with Alex, both recognising the weight of Lisa's words. Once, she had stood on the other side of the line—hard, sharp, and dangerous. Now she turned that edge into armour, not for herself, but for Tom. Jeremy's eyes flicked from Ty to Lisa and back again, seeing the bond forming not from pity, but from understanding. The adults shifted uncomfortably, unused to children speaking with such conviction, but no one interrupted. Zenji's gaze narrowed, thoughtful, as though evaluating Lisa the way he might assess an ally in the field.

Tom opened his mouth, but no words came. He looked at Lisa as though trying to measure whether she was mocking him, whether this was another trap dressed as kindness. Her stare didn't waver. "You don't have to believe me yet," she said firmly, her voice cutting through his doubt. "But you'll see it. I'm not going anywhere. You're not going to face this alone, not anymore." She turned slightly, addressing Ty without looking away from Tom. "You swore your oath. Now hear mine. I'll stand with him too. Even in his darkest moments, I'll be there."

Ty's lips curved into the faintest smile, the kind that acknowledged strength when he saw it. "Then it's done," he said quietly. "He's not just mine to watch over. He's ours." Tom flinched at the word, but again, something in him softened. The cracks in his defences widened, not through force, but through the strange persistence of people refusing to let him be alone. He clenched his fists once, then slowly released them, the gesture small but telling.

Mr. Arnett leaned back in his chair, exhaling. "I don't know what kind of group I'm looking at anymore," he admitted, glancing between Ty, Lisa, and the rest. "But it seems stronger than anything we could design ourselves." His eyes softened as they rested on Tom. "Maybe this is exactly what he needs." Mrs. Dunlop nodded faintly, her face drawn but contemplative, while Mr. Clarke allowed himself a rare smile, faint but proud. Only Mrs. Locke looked away, lips pressed thin, refusing to acknowledge the turn.

Lisa turned back to Tom, crouching so her eyes were level with his. Her tone gentled, but it carried the same unwavering steel. "I know you don't trust this yet. You probably think we'll get tired and walk away like everyone else. But we won't. I won't. You're one of us now, whether you like it or not." She extended her hand, not forcing, just offering. Tom stared at it for a long time, his jaw tightening as though weighing the risk. At last, he placed his hand in hers, a hesitant grip, but real.

The room seemed to release a breath all at once. Ty stepped beside them, his presence steady, and Leo and Alex moved closer too, forming a loose circle around Tom. For the first time, Tom was not standing alone in the spotlight of suspicion. He was surrounded, shielded by peers who had decided, without waiting for adult approval, that he belonged. And Lisa, with her sharp edges and blunt words, had carved the truth into stone: he would not walk this path without them.

For a long while, Harley stood at the edge of the gathering, his arms folded, his eyes fixed on the carpet rather than the people in the room. He had heard Lisa speak, had felt the echo of her vow in the silence that followed. He had watched Tom shift under her gaze, uncertain whether to believe her. And though Harley had always carried his words like weapons, now he chose them with care. When the silence threatened to stretch too long, his voice came low but firm, steady in its weight. "She's right," he said, no bravado in his tone, only truth. The room stilled again, because everyone knew Harley did not give his voice easily. When he spoke, it meant something.

Tom's head jerked slightly, eyes narrowing at Harley. Of all people, Harley was not the one he expected to hear support from. But Harley didn't leave space for doubt. He stepped forward, shoulders squared, his gaze unwavering. "I lived in shadows once," Harley said, louder now so even the teachers at the back could hear. "I know what it's like to be buried under anger, to think no one can understand. Ty pulled me out. Lisa showed me what it means to be stronger by standing still. And now, I make the same vow." He turned, looking directly at Ty and Lisa before facing Tom again. "I'll follow the same oath. You're not going to fall without me standing there to catch you."

Lisa's expression softened, her fierce mask slipping just enough to reveal a hint of pride. Ty gave a slight nod, his quiet approval more valuable than a hundred speeches. Jeremy exhaled, as if some invisible knot in the room had loosened.

The other students whispered, shifting on the carpet, feeling the weight of unity forming before their eyes. Harley, the one who had once been feared, had cast his lot not with authority, not with indifference, but with Tom. And with that, the group's voice became one.

Mr. Arnett cleared his throat, his voice steady but carrying a charge. "Then let it be known," he said, holding a slim folder in his hand. "The Board has made its decision." The staff tensed, eyes darting toward Tom, expecting news of exile, suspension, or worse. But Arnett's eyes swept past Tom and landed squarely on Mrs. Locke. "Effective immediately, Mrs. Locke has been given her two weeks' notice. The documents are official." He set the folder on the table with finality. "Her services are no longer required at this school. A replacement will be appointed."

Gasps rippled through the students, and even some of the teachers shifted in shock. Mrs. Locke's face flushed crimson, her lips pressed into a hard line. She opened her mouth, but no sound emerged. Instead, she gripped her papers tightly, the fury in her eyes saying what her tongue could not. Mr. Clarke, standing a little way off, adjusted his glasses and bowed his head, more in relief than triumph. Ty, however, stepped forward before Arnett could close the subject.

"If I may," Ty said, his voice calm but sharp enough to cut through the murmurs. "You don't need to search far for the right replacement." Arnett raised a brow, clearly unaccustomed to a child interrupting Board matters, but Ty pressed on. "Mr. Clarke is the one you want. No one else. He knows the language better than anyone. He's read more books in one year than most people will read in a lifetime." Ty's gaze didn't waver, his tone carrying the same gravity that had silenced teachers before.

Arnett frowned slightly. "And what makes you so sure, young man?"

Ty answered without missing a beat. "Because within this school year alone, he has read no less than three hundred and twenty-five books. Not skimming, not flipping pages. Reading. Absorbing. Every novel, every poem, every play—he's lived them. And more importantly, he knows how to share them." His voice did not shake, though he was eleven years old standing in front of principals and teachers. "You want someone who can teach English, literature, and creative writing with passion? Someone who can make us believe words matter? That's Mr. Clarke."

The library fell quiet. Teachers exchanged glances, some skeptical, others thoughtful. Mr. Clarke himself looked startled, as though unsure whether to step forward or remain invisible. His hands fidgeted with the edge of his sleeve, but his eyes shone with quiet gratitude. Arnett leaned back in his chair, considering, the weight of Ty's words pressing into him as surely as if another adult had spoken. He finally nodded once, slowly.

"Perhaps," Arnett said, his tone neutral but his eyes betraying respect, "we've underestimated the talents we already have in our building."

Zenji Takashi's deep voice followed, steady as stone. "I have read with your librarian," he said, his eyes on Clarke. "And the boy is right. There is wisdom here, not just knowledge. Do not waste it."

Harley folded his arms again, but this time it was not defensiveness—it was pride. He had added his voice, and now the momentum was irreversible. Tom, silent through the exchange, looked from Ty to Lisa to Harley, then to Mr. Clarke. For the first time, he seemed to recognise that this was no fragile promise spoken in haste. This was a wall being built around him, one brick at a time, and each vow added to its strength. He said nothing, but his silence now was not rejection. It was the beginning of belief.

The evening settled over the Takashi home like a warm blanket, soft shadows stretching across the polished wood floors and the faint sound of Mrs. Takashi humming in the kitchen as she washed the last of the dinner dishes. Tom sat stiffly on the edge of the couch, his small bag still resting by the door, as though he were afraid to unpack it, afraid to believe this wasn't temporary. His hands fidgeted restlessly, pulling at the loose threads of his worn sweater. Ty sat opposite him on the floor, legs folded comfortably, watching him in silence with that steady patience that always seemed to unnerve Tom more than any words could. For a long moment, the only sounds were the clinking of dishes in the kitchen and the faint hum of a ceiling fan. Then Tom's voice came, quiet and awkward, almost like he regretted speaking the moment it left his lips.

"Thanks," he muttered, staring at the floor rather than Ty. His voice cracked halfway, caught between boyhood and all the years of burden he'd been forced to carry. "For… for not laughing at me. For not…" He stopped, his jaw tightening, unwilling to finish the sentence. Ty tilted his head slightly, eyes soft but sharp with understanding.

Ty didn't tease him. He didn't make a joke or deflect with words. He simply pushed himself to his knees, crossed the short space between them, and extended his arms. It wasn't a small gesture, not a polite squeeze of the shoulder or a fleeting tap on the back. It was full and unreserved, an embrace that asked for nothing but gave everything. Tom froze, uncertain at first, but Ty's hold was insistent without being forceful, wrapping around him with a certainty that could not be questioned.

"You don't have to explain," Ty said softly, his cheek brushing against Tom's hair as he spoke. "I care about you. I see you. I'm here for you. You belong here. And most importantly…" He drew a breath, his voice lowering to a near whisper. "I love you." The words landed like stones on still water, sending ripples through the silence of the room.

Tom's shoulders shook, not from sobs but from the effort of holding back the wave of emotion that threatened to break free. No one had said those words to him without cruelty hidden behind them.

No one had embraced him without demand. He pressed his forehead into Ty's shoulder, his fists trembling as they slowly, reluctantly, unclenched. For the first time in years, his hands curled not into weapons but into anchors, gripping the fabric of Ty's shirt as though afraid to let go.

Zenji Takashi stood quietly in the hallway, unseen by either boy. His broad frame leaned against the doorframe, arms folded, his expression unreadable but his eyes glistening with quiet approval. He did not interrupt, did not break the fragile moment with authority or words of wisdom. Instead, he turned away, leaving the boys to their truth, trusting that some lessons could only be spoken in the language of love.

Mrs. Takashi, drying her hands on a towel, caught her husband's eye as he passed the kitchen. He gave her a single nod, and she smiled faintly, her heart warmed by the soundless exchange. In her mind, she whispered a prayer of thanks—not to any god, but to the strength of simple human kindness, to the chance that even the most broken child could be rebuilt when arms opened wide enough to hold them.

Back in the living room, the hug did not end quickly. It stretched on, past the awkwardness, past the hesitation, until it became something steady and real. Tom finally exhaled, a shuddering breath that carried years of fear and shame, and in that release came a quiet peace. He didn't say the words back—not yet—but the way his body leaned into Ty's, the way his grip refused to loosen, was its own answer. And Ty, wise beyond his years, understood.

The small bag by the door no longer looked like luggage waiting for escape. It looked instead like the first step in unpacking a life, piece by piece, in a place where belonging was no longer borrowed, but freely given.

The night in the Takashi household was a gentle one, carrying no echoes of raised voices or the thud of fists against walls. Instead, it hummed with the quiet rhythm of dishes drying in the rack, the faint notes of Mrs. Takashi's voice trailing off after a song, and the measured creak of the staircase beneath her careful steps. Tom lay in bed beneath clean sheets that smelled faintly of lavender, his eyes tracing the unfamiliar shapes of shadows on the ceiling. Every sound seemed strange to him—not threatening, only strange. He shifted beneath the blanket, expecting some reprimand for not sleeping yet, but none came. Only silence, soft and patient.

Mrs. Takashi entered with her quiet grace, a folded blanket draped over her arm. Without a word, she unfolded it and laid it gently over him, smoothing the edges across his shoulders with the tender precision of someone who knew what it meant to soothe without asking permission. Tom stiffened at first, unused to such kindness, but her touch was steady, neither hurried nor forced. She leaned down, brushing a strand of hair from his forehead, and kissed his cheek lightly. The gesture startled him more than any shout could have, yet he did not pull away. Something in the softness of it disarmed him completely.

His breath hitched, shallow, as he waited for the unease to come, for the panic that usually followed any closeness. But it did not arrive. Instead, warmth seeped into him, the warmth of a mother's quiet care—a warmth he had not known since he was too young to remember it clearly. His chest loosened, and his fists, usually curled tight beneath the blankets, slackened into the mattress. The room held no menace, only calm. For once, he let it hold him.

Across the hall, Ty lingered at the doorway, his silhouette framed in the faint glow of the hallway light. He didn't speak at first, only watched, his sharp eyes softer than usual. When Mrs. Takashi slipped past him, she gave his shoulder a gentle squeeze, a silent handover of trust, before retreating downstairs. Ty padded quietly into the room, barefoot and deliberate, and stood at the side of the bed.

Tom turned his head slightly, catching sight of him in the dim light. He didn't ask him to stay, didn't tell him to go. The silence between them stretched, but it wasn't empty. Ty lowered himself to sit at the edge of the bed, his presence more reassuring than any lock on the door could ever be. He leaned forward slightly, his voice low and steady, almost like a promise whispered against the night.

"I love you, Tom," he said. The words weren't forced or dramatic, but simple, direct, and unshakable.

Tom's chest rose with a long breath, and for once it wasn't sharp with tension. The words carried weight, but not the kind that crushed him. They pressed down gently, like the blanket Mrs. Takashi had tucked around him, grounding him in a way he had never known before. He didn't answer—not with words—but his eyes fluttered shut, his lashes damp with the tears he refused to shed. His body eased into the mattress, surrendering, at last, to rest.

Ty remained at his side, silent and unmoving, as the night grew stiller. Tom drifted, the sound of his own breath softening, his body curling slightly but not in fear—only in the fragile comfort of knowing he was safe. The world outside might still carry shadows, but within this room, there was only calm. And for the first time he could remember, Tom didn't brace himself for what would come when he closed his eyes. He simply let them fall shut, and the darkness welcomed him kindly.

The morning entered gently, the curtains stirring faintly as the first light of day pressed through the glass. For Tom, it was unlike any morning he had ever known. He hadn't woken with a start, heart racing, ears straining for shouts or footsteps in the hall. He had slept deeply, soundly, with dreams that carried no menace, only warmth. As he sat up on the edge of the large bed, the sheets still tangled around him, he blinked in disbelief that the night had passed without fear. He rubbed his eyes, stretched his arms, and for a moment simply listened to the quiet house. His body felt heavy, not from dread, but from true rest.

He shuffled off the mattress and padded into the washroom, where he tended to his first morning need, the ordinary routine every boy takes for granted. When he splashed cold water across his face, he caught sight of himself in the mirror. His reflection seemed different. His eyes weren't darting, his shoulders weren't tense. He lingered on his own gaze longer than usual, as if surprised that the boy staring back looked less like a cornered animal. He dried his face slowly, letting the towel rest against his skin longer than necessary, unwilling to let go of the strange calm that clung to him.

Downstairs, the house was alive with the sounds of breakfast—pans shifting against the stove, the soft clatter of plates being set out, the smell of something frying in butter. Tom hesitated at the foot of the stairs, his heart thumping not with fear but with something he couldn't yet name. He stepped forward anyway, letting the warmth of the kitchen draw him in. The moment he crossed the threshold, Ty's head turned toward him, eyes bright with the quiet knowing only he carried. Tom froze for a heartbeat, then without understanding why, he moved straight to Ty and pulled him into a hug.

The embrace was sudden, fierce, and uncalculated. Tom buried his face into Ty's shoulder as though he had carried a lifetime of words locked away, and they had finally broken free without speech. Ty stiffened only for a second, then wrapped his arms around Tom with a steadiness that anchored them both. Zenji rose from his chair, surprised, but before he could speak, Tom turned and seized him in the same way, clinging tightly. The man who had stood firm against boardrooms and teachers alike felt his throat tighten as the boy's arms gripped him with desperate sincerity.

Then Mrs. Takashi came into view, wiping her hands on a dishcloth, her expression softening as Tom's eyes found hers. He moved toward her, no hesitation in his steps, and folded himself into her arms. She held him as though he were her own, steady and sure, her cheek pressed against his hair. And then, as they all stood together, Tom drew back just enough to look at each of them, his chest heaving, tears shimmering in his eyes. His lips parted, trembling, and the words fell out unguarded, fragile yet undeniable.

"I love you," he said.

The room stilled. For Zenji, for Mrs. Takashi, for Ty, it was as though time itself halted around that confession. They had not expected it—not from this boy who had known only fear, anger, and silence. But the truth in his voice left no space for doubt. His tears streaked his cheeks, his chin trembled, and yet the words were steady, filled with a weight none of them could carry lightly. It was the first time Tom had ever given those words to another human being, and they landed with all the force of a breaking dam.

Zenji's eyes welled instantly, his stern face undone by the flood he could no longer hold back. Mrs. Takashi pressed her fingers to her lips, overcome by the tenderness of the moment. Ty, eyes shining, stepped forward again and pulled Tom back into his arms, this time with no hesitation at all. Together they whispered the words in return, each of them repeating them not as an echo but as a vow.

"We love you, Tom."

The embrace grew tighter, not crushing but complete, the kind of hug that promised permanence. It was a circle of arms and hearts, binding him not by obligation but by choice. Tom could feel the difference; this was not pity, nor duty, nor fragile charity. It was love in its truest form—accepting him in both his scars and his strength, claiming him as theirs without condition. He trembled inside it, letting the truth of belonging finally root itself where fear had lived too long.

The kitchen air was thick with the sound of muffled sobs and quiet laughter, tears mixing with the smell of maple syrup and bacon still warm on the stove. For the first time in his life, Tom understood what it felt like not to be a burden, not to be tolerated, but to be wanted. His words had set it free, and their response had sealed it. In that moment, standing in the sunlight streaming through the window, he was not a boy broken by an uncle's cruelty—he was a son, a brother, and a boy finally home.

The days passed more quickly than Tom ever imagined they could. He had counted time before by bruises and silences, but here, in the Takashi home, a week slipped by without a single moment of dread. At first, his body had twitched with old instincts, waiting for the sharp crack of a door slammed in anger, the heavy boots of his uncle echoing down the hall, but by the third day, something shifted. He caught himself laughing at the breakfast table without hesitation, leaning back into a chair without bracing for a blow, even leaving his bedroom door ajar at night. For Tom, that was the kind of freedom he had never tasted. It was as though his ribs had been wrapped in iron bands all his life, and now those bands had been cut loose.

Each morning began the same—pancakes or eggs or whatever Mrs. Takashi insisted he try, and coffee poured for Zenji that filled the kitchen with its warm, bitter scent. Ty chattered, sometimes with Nico and Jasmin when they visited, and the talk was never forced. They spoke of school, soccer, the little arguments that children make sound like wars but resolve in a minute's time. Tom listened, stunned at the ease with which this family spoke to each other, and by the end of the week he was speaking too. His words came hesitantly, but each one was accepted, no matter how clumsy, and the smiles around the table never mocked him.

The relief in his body was almost unnerving. He had lived so long with tension that he hardly knew how to carry himself without it. His shoulders, usually hunched high, now rested low. His fists, once tight without thought, now opened easily. Even sleep no longer came with ghosts tugging him awake; he lay down in that wide bed, the blanket tucked by Mrs. Takashi, and closed his eyes knowing no shadow would reach for him in the night. It was like being handed a life he didn't know he had been allowed to want.

But the sweetness of it carried a bitter undercurrent, one that began to gnaw at him by the seventh day. He knew this couldn't last forever. The school board would have its say. His parents would want him back, and the world beyond this house would demand an answer. The thought of returning to that old life sent a chill through him sharper than anything he had faced before. He had been given a glimpse of something better, something whole, and to lose it now would feel like a punishment worse than any strike from his uncle's hand.

That evening, after dinner, Tom lingered at the table long after the plates had been cleared. Zenji sat across from him, polishing his glasses, his face calm in that way that unsettled Tom because it was never false. Tom stared at his hands, the words rising like a storm he could no longer hold back. "I can't go back," he said finally, his voice raw, trembling but steady enough to carry truth. "They didn't stop him. They didn't protect me. They left me there, and I can't— I won't trust them again." His eyes locked on Zenji's, desperate for an anchor.

Zenji folded his glasses and set them aside, his gaze unwavering. "You want me to intervene?" he asked quietly. Tom nodded so fiercely his hair fell into his eyes. "Please," he whispered. "Help me make a case against them. If I can't stay here as your son, then I'll file for emancipation. I'd rather live by your rules, under your discipline, than go back to a house where every step ruins me." His plea wasn't a child's tantrum—it was the voice of a boy who knew the difference between life and survival.

Mrs. Takashi, standing in the doorway with a dish towel still in her hands, felt her heart fracture and strengthen all at once. She crossed the room and placed her palm gently on Tom's back, not pushing, not pulling, simply grounding him. Ty, silent at first, then spoke with a conviction rare for his eleven years. "He belongs here," Ty said firmly. "You see it, don't you, Dad? He doesn't just need us—he's already one of us." His words hung heavy in the room, a child's truth stated with more weight than any adult could muster.

Zenji leaned back in his chair, steepling his fingers beneath his chin. He studied Tom, not with suspicion, but with the kind of grave attention reserved for matters of justice. "Emancipation is not a simple thing," he said at last. "It requires proof, commitment, and courage. You'll be called to stand in front of people who will question everything you say. They will press you hard, Tom. They will ask why you would turn away from your parents. Can you face that?"

Tom's eyes filled, but his jaw hardened. "I already have," he replied. "I faced worse every day. I'd rather stand in a courtroom than live one more night in that house." His words struck the table like a stone, and silence followed. Mrs. Takashi brushed his hair back, her lips tightening against the tears threatening her composure. Ty moved his chair closer and simply rested his hand over Tom's, the silent promise clear: you will not stand alone.

Zenji nodded slowly, the decision settling in his bones. "Then we begin carefully. We build your case on truth. No exaggerations, no anger, only what has happened. Truth will do the work if you let it." His voice carried the weight of both law and love, the authority of a man who had seen too much, but also the steadiness of a father offering shelter. Tom sagged forward, half in relief, half in exhaustion, and allowed himself to believe, for the first time, that he might truly have a way forward.

The room seemed to breathe again. Ty gave his hand a squeeze, Mrs. Takashi kissed the top of his head, and Zenji leaned back with the faintest smile breaking through his sternness. Tom felt the corners of his mouth twitch, just barely, but enough to mark the beginning of something new. A week without fear had changed him already. Another week, and perhaps he could learn what it meant not just to survive, but to live.

## CHAPTER 14: THE COURT OF TRUTH

The room had gone still when Zenji set the folder on the table. He spoke in the calm, deliberate tone that left no gap for doubt, no room for denial. "These are the records," he said, sliding the files toward the attending officers. "Police reports, sworn witness accounts, and signed statements that show a pattern stretching back years. You will see the charges, the dropped cases, the violence that slipped through cracks in the system. No more cracks remain today." His words were not loud, but they carried a gravity that pressed against everyone present. Even the uncle shifted uncomfortably, his arrogance faltering as the officers leaned forward.

One officer flipped open the file, his eyes scanning quickly. "Multiple accounts of assault," he murmured, his brow furrowing. "Several dismissed, one stayed, two unresolved." He looked at Zenji, then at the man sitting across the room, arms crossed, face set in forced disdain. "You've kept busy." The tone was dry, but there was no mistaking the sharp edge beneath it. The uncle barked a laugh, but it cracked in the middle, the sound too thin to carry the confidence he tried to project.

Mrs. Dunlop, who had stood stiff against the wall, drew a sharp breath and whispered, "All this time, it was him." Her words were soft but cut into the silence like glass. Tom's shoulders tightened, his face pale, but he didn't look at her. His eyes were fixed on the officers, waiting for them to act, waiting for the weight of years to be lifted from his small frame. The uncle sneered, shifting again as if he could intimidate the air itself, but Zenji's steady gaze held him in place.

"Stand up," one officer commanded. The words were sharp, trained, impossible to ignore. For a moment, the man didn't move, his jaw tight, as though defiance might earn him some measure of dignity. But when the second officer's hand brushed the holster at his hip—not threatening, merely resting there—the uncle rose abruptly, his chair scraping loudly against the floor. Tom flinched at the sound, his body remembering too many slammed doors and overturned furniture.

The click of metal was louder still. The handcuffs closed around his uncle's wrists with a snap, final and unrelenting. The man twisted slightly, testing the strength of steel, but it was no use. He muttered something low and bitter, but the words were swallowed in the shuffle as the officers turned him toward the door. The once-proud bully, the shadow that had haunted Tom's every breath, was now reduced to nothing more than a criminal being escorted away.

Tom finally found his voice. It wasn't trembling, nor was it broken. It was sharp, quick, and cutting in its simplicity. "Later, loser." The words hung in the air, small in length but heavy in meaning, years of swallowed silence spat out in two syllables. One of the officers couldn't help himself—he chuckled, shaking his head as he opened the cruiser's back door. "Kid's got a point," he muttered under his breath, though loud enough for Tom to hear.

The uncle's face twisted, but there was no power left in his glare. He stumbled slightly as they guided him outside, his protests drowned by the sound of the car door slamming shut. Metal and glass closed around him like a cage. For the first time, Tom saw him not as the giant in the shadows, but as a man contained, small and ordinary, sitting powerless behind bars. The cruiser rolled away, its red and blue lights flashing against the afternoon air.

Inside the room, silence followed in its wake. Teachers looked at one another with expressions that ranged from shock to relief. Mr. Clarke rubbed his temples, his voice low as he said, "It should never have taken this long." Ms. Henley, the counsellor, nodded faintly but said nothing more, her eyes resting only on Tom. She understood the victory, but she also understood the cost.

Ty stepped closer to his friend, his presence quiet but steady. He didn't clap him on the shoulder or tell him "good job." He simply stood beside him, as if his silence was an anchor, holding Tom in place while the storm within tried to settle. Tom exhaled slowly, but his fists remained clenched, knuckles white as bone. Victory didn't always feel like triumph—it felt strange, jagged, unfinished.

"Come on, son," Zenji said softly, his voice breaking the silence. "We need to prepare for what comes next. This was one battle. The larger one begins in court." He spoke to Tom directly, not to the room, reminding the boy that the fight wasn't over, but it was no longer his alone to bear. Tom nodded faintly, his eyes fixed on the floor as if trying to make sense of the ground beneath him.

Mrs. Takashi moved quietly to Tom's side, her hand light against his back. "You did well," she whispered, her tone warm but firm. "You faced him without fear." Tom swallowed hard, unsure whether he believed it, but the words slid into the cracks of his doubt and gave him something to hold. She guided him gently toward the hall, her pace slow, allowing him to walk at his own measure.

As they moved, other students—Nico, Jasmin, Ella, Sophie—watched from the edges, unsure whether to speak or stay silent. Leo and Alex exchanged glances, memories of their own confessions still raw. None of them dared to interrupt the moment, but in their eyes there was recognition, even admiration, that Tom had found the strength to speak. Jeremy, standing small among them, whispered quietly to himself, "He said it. He really said it."

Outside, the air felt different. The cruiser was already gone, but the sound of its siren still echoed faintly in Tom's ears. He inhaled sharply, as though the world were larger now, the sky higher, the air clearer. Yet the knot in his stomach remained, twisting tighter with each step. He had told his uncle goodbye, but now he would have to tell a courtroom why.

## THE SMILE THAT BROKE

Zenji placed a hand on Tom's shoulder—not pressing, not pushing, only steadying. "You are not alone," he said. The words were few, but they were enough to remind Tom that the long shadow cast by his uncle was fading. What remained now was the truth, and the courage to speak it aloud.

Ty, walking just a step behind, leaned close enough for Tom to hear. "You ended it," he whispered. "Now we start again." Tom didn't answer, but the corner of his mouth shifted—just slightly—as if the weight of those words gave him something he had never dared believe in: the beginning of freedom.

The letter arrived not with ceremony but with the firm stamp of government across its face. The envelope, plain and heavy, was slid beneath the Takashi's door early in the morning, the ink of the seal still sharp. Zenji bent to pick it up, his movements deliberate, his expression unreadable as he set it upon the kitchen table. Tom's eyes followed it like prey follows a hunter, wary and expectant. Ty reached across the table, resting his fingers on Tom's arm, grounding him before the words inside were even opened. The silence was louder than the birdsong that drifted in from the garden.

When Zenji unfolded the papers, his voice carried the weight of finality. "A formal hearing has been scheduled," he read, scanning the lines. "You, Tom, are summoned, as are your parents. The court will convene in two weeks' time." His tone was steady, but beneath it lingered a heaviness that no father should have to read aloud to a boy not his own. Tom shifted in his chair, pressing his palms flat against his thighs, his breaths short and uneven. He did not ask questions—he already understood what this meant.

Mrs. Takashi set a hand on Tom's back, rubbing a small circle as she always did when words might do more harm than good. "This is not punishment," she reminded him softly. "This is the truth being called into the open." Her voice was warmth against the cold edges of the summons, a reminder that the papers themselves held no power compared to the hands around him. Yet Tom's eyes still flickered with unease, for paper had always meant warnings, suspensions, apologies demanded under threat. This was no longer school discipline. This was law.

Ty leaned closer, his tone quiet but unwavering. "It doesn't matter what they say. We'll speak the truth, and the truth will hold." He glanced at his father as if to borrow strength, then looked back at Tom. "And when you can't say it, we will." The promise was simple, but in Ty's voice it carried the solidity of stone. Tom nodded faintly, his throat tight, but he didn't look away. For the first time, he let himself believe that someone else might truly speak on his behalf without bending the story.

The day carried on, though the air in the house shifted. The summons sat folded neatly on the counter, as though watching them. Tom ate little, poking at his food, his appetite gone. Zenji let him be, knowing force would only add another layer of resistance. Instead, he kept the conversation light, asking Ty about homework, listening as Mrs. Takashi spoke about her latest canvas, coaxing laughter into the air so Tom could breathe it in without realizing he had. It was a gentle tactic, but one that pulled the boy back from retreating into himself.

At school, whispers had already begun. Students spoke of the arrest, of the uncle led away in handcuffs. Some said Tom would be taken away, others that he would never return. Jeremy overheard them in the corridor and squared his shoulders, saying only, "He's not gone. He's with us." The others—Leo, Sophie, even Harley—echoed it in their own way, ensuring the rumours did not become Tom's reality. In their eyes, the summons was not a death sentence but a chance at rewriting everything.

Teachers, too, held their debates. In the staffroom, Mrs. Dunlop urged caution, while Mr. Clarke argued with quiet intensity for compassion. "If you take away the only steady ground a boy has," he said, "do not be surprised when he falls." Mrs. Locke, stripped of her authority but still bitter, muttered about discipline and danger, earning nothing but silence from her peers. It was Ms. Henley who finally said, "It isn't for us to decide anymore. The court will weigh the evidence. What we can do is stand ready to tell the truth."

At the Takashi home that evening, Zenji gathered Ty and Tom at the low table, laying the papers flat. "We will prepare," he said. "We will not leave a gap for doubt, not a single question unanswered." His eyes moved between the two boys, resting longer on Tom. "But you must remember: this is not only about proof of what was done to you. It is about showing who you are now, and what you deserve going forward." Tom swallowed hard, the weight of those words pressing into his chest.

Ty reached across and tapped the edge of the papers. "Then we'll show them," he said firmly. "Not just with documents or words—but with how we live. With how we stand together." His conviction was unshakable, his youth no barrier to the strength behind it. Zenji inclined his head, a small smile tugging at his mouth. "Exactly," he said. "The court will see more than records. They will see family."

That night, Tom sat on the edge of his bed, staring at the moonlight falling across the floor. He held the copy of the summons in his hand, the letters heavy against his skin. Ty appeared quietly at the doorway, slipping inside without a word. He sat beside him, shoulder to shoulder, letting the silence stretch. Finally, Tom whispered, "What if they don't believe me?" His voice was thin, almost breaking. Ty didn't hesitate. "Then they'll have to believe me. And Dad. And everyone else who knows. The truth is too heavy to be ignored."

Mrs. Takashi passed by the doorway, pausing to see the two boys sitting together in the pale glow. She said nothing, only smiled faintly and continued on, her heart steady. She knew the next days would test all of them, but she also knew the foundation they had built could weather it. For the first time in Tom's life, he was not entering battle alone.

In the days that followed, the Takashis moved with quiet determination. Zenji spent hours organizing files, calling witnesses, ensuring no gap could be exploited. Mrs. Takashi prepared meals and created calm spaces, her art softening the sharp edges of tension. Ty shadowed Tom, not suffocating but steady, anchoring him with routines that reminded him he was more than a victim waiting to be questioned. They spoke little of fear, choosing instead to focus on truth, repeating it like a rhythm until even Tom began to breathe it in.

The summons, once a source of dread, became a symbol of the next step. It was no longer a threat—it was a door. And though Tom trembled at the thought of crossing it, he knew whose hands would steady him as he walked through. The Takashis had already set aside their fear, replacing it with resolve. They would face the courtroom not as three voices but as one.

The papers had been read aloud, the hearing date fixed, and the weight of it lingered in the Takashi home like a storm yet to break. Supper had finished, the plates cleared away, but Tom remained at the table. His hands rested flat against the smooth wood, his posture stiff, his eyes fixed on nothing but the shadows cast by the overhead lamp. Zenji sat opposite him, calm but alert, waiting for the words he sensed were pressing at the boy's lips. Ty perched at his side, his chin resting in his palms, watching Tom with the quiet patience that had become his strongest gift.

Finally, Tom exhaled, the sound sharp in the stillness. "I will not go back," he said, his voice firm though his throat trembled. "Not to them. Not to a house where I was nothing but a target." His eyes lifted, meeting Zenji's with raw intensity. "If they stood by once, they will stand by again. I will not live in a place where silence is permission." The words came in a rush, not of anger but of truth pressed so long against his ribs it could no longer be contained.

Zenji folded his hands, leaning forward slightly. His gaze carried no judgment, only a quiet respect for the boy's courage. "This choice," he said, measured and steady, "is not made lightly. You understand that the court will ask if this is anger speaking, or something deeper?" Tom's jaw tightened. "This isn't anger," he said, his voice almost breaking. "This is survival." The statement landed with the force of stone upon water, rippling through the room in silence.

Ty shifted closer, brushing his arm lightly against Tom's, a silent reassurance. "You don't have to prove that to me," he murmured. "I already know. And I'll say it as many times as I have to so they know too." He lifted his chin, his boyish face stern with conviction. "No matter what happens in that courtroom, I won't let you falter. You can lean on me." Tom looked at him then, startled by the certainty in a voice younger than his own, and for a flicker of a moment, belief cracked through the doubt.

# THE SMILE THAT BROKE

Mrs. Takashi entered quietly with a pot of tea, her movements graceful as she set the cups down before them. She said nothing, only laid a gentle hand on Tom's shoulder before returning to her chair. The warmth of her touch lingered even after she sat, a reminder that not all gestures needed explanation. Tom glanced at her, the words caught in his throat, but she gave him only a small nod, as if to say: it is enough that you spoke.

Zenji sipped his tea, then placed the cup down carefully. "The judge will ask why you cannot return," he said. "They will press, they will measure your words. Are you prepared for that?" Tom's hand curled into a fist, then slowly released. "I am," he said. "Because it's not about shame anymore. It's about truth. I would rather face questions in a courtroom than go back to a place where I was never safe." His voice steadied as he spoke, gathering strength from the very act of saying it aloud.

Ty grinned faintly, tilting his head. "You're stronger than you think," he said. "Most people would have crumbled by now. But you're still here, still fighting. That's not weakness, Tom. That's proof." Tom shook his head, uncertain. "Proof of what?" Ty's answer came without hesitation. "Proof that you're worth saving. Worth standing beside." The words hung heavy, not as comfort but as fact, and Tom let them settle, his chest rising in a long, unsteady breath.

The house around them seemed to lean into the moment. The hum of the refrigerator, the faint ticking of the wall clock, even the shifting of branches against the windows—all of it softened into a backdrop for the vow that had just been made. Mrs. Takashi smiled faintly into her tea, her heart swelling at the sight of two boys forging a bond through truth. Zenji's eyes, sharp and discerning, softened as well, recognizing in Tom not only the wounds of the past but the steel of someone determined to claim his own future.

Later, when the dishes were washed and the house quiet, Tom lingered by the doorway before heading to bed. He looked back at Zenji, his voice low but clear. "This isn't just your fight," he said. "It's mine. But I can't win it alone." Zenji inclined his head. "Nor will you. You have my word." Behind him, Ty piped up, "And mine." The room fell silent again, but it was not the silence of fear. It was the silence of an oath sealed in trust.

Upstairs, Ty followed Tom to his room, sitting with him a while before the lights dimmed. "You know," Ty said, lying back against the bed, "I've never seen you look so sure. It suits you." Tom rolled his eyes but smiled faintly, the expression awkward and unfamiliar on his face. "Don't get used to it," he muttered. Ty chuckled. "Too late." And though neither admitted it aloud, they both felt the shift—resolve had been spoken, and it could not be taken back.

When the house finally fell into full quiet, Tom lay awake, staring at the ceiling. The fear was still there, coiled tight within him, but it no longer dictated his every breath. He thought of the courtroom ahead, the questions, the scrutiny. Yet for the first time, he imagined standing there with people at his side who would not waver. Survival was not just clawing against the dark anymore—it was stepping into light with others who refused to let him fall.

By morning, the decision was set within him. He moved through the day with a quiet certainty, still cautious, still scarred, but no longer willing to be silenced. He had spoken the truth to the only family that mattered, and they had answered with loyalty. The summons may have forced his hand, but his resolve was his own. And as long as Ty's promise held, he knew he would not stand alone before the judge.

The house had gone quiet after supper, but the weight of tomorrow pressed against the walls like a gathering storm. Tom lingered in the kitchen, restless, pacing from the cupboard to the window before sitting back at the table. His shoulders were tight, his hands fidgeting with the edge of the tablecloth, pulling at a loose thread as though it held his thoughts together. Mrs. Takashi entered softly, her steps barely stirring the wooden floor, and she set down a small tray with two cups of steaming tea. "You shouldn't carry that much inside before you sleep," she said gently, sliding one of the cups toward him.

Tom muttered a quiet thanks, his voice low, not trusting himself to say more. He wrapped both hands around the warm cup, though he didn't drink. Mrs. Takashi sat across from him, her posture calm, her presence steady, as if she had all the time in the world to wait. "You're not alone in this, Tom," she said after a long silence. "Not tonight, not tomorrow, not ever again." Her hand reached across the table, resting lightly on his. The touch startled him at first, but then the weight of it sank in—not heavy, not demanding, simply there.

He stared at her hand for a moment before lifting his eyes. "What if they don't believe me?" he asked. His words cracked in the middle, the fear spilling through despite his best efforts. "What if the judge says I have to go back?" The tremor in his voice betrayed the boy beneath the scars, the child who had waited too long for someone to protect him. Mrs. Takashi's thumb brushed against his knuckles, grounding him. "The truth has a way of standing on its own," she said. "And even if others try to turn away from it, I will not. You are already my son in my heart. No court can erase that."

Tom's throat tightened, and he looked down quickly, blinking hard. "Why would you even say that?" he asked hoarsely. "Why would you claim me like that? I'm not even yours." His words carried no anger, only disbelief, as though the concept itself was foreign. Mrs. Takashi leaned forward, her voice soft but firm. "Because family isn't just who you are born to, Tom. It's who chooses you, and who you choose in return. And I choose you." The words slipped into the cracks of his doubt, filling them with something he could barely recognize: belonging.

The kettle clicked behind them, forgotten, but the tea on the table still sent up gentle curls of steam. Tom lifted the cup, sipping carefully. The warmth slid down his throat, steadying him more than he expected. "Nobody ever said that before," he whispered. "Not even my parents." His lips tightened around the rim of the cup. Mrs. Takashi's gaze softened, but she did not let go of his hand. "Then let me be the first. I see you, Tom. I believe you. And I will not let you be cast aside."

The words sat heavy in his chest, but they didn't crush him; they steadied him. He drew a shaky breath, daring to meet her eyes. "What if I'm not enough?" he asked. "What if all I've been is a mistake?" Mrs. Takashi's expression sharpened, her tone clear as glass. "You are not a mistake. You are a boy who has been asked to carry more pain than any child should. That doesn't make you broken—it makes you stronger than most grown men I've ever met. Don't let anyone tell you otherwise."

Tom pressed his lips together, fighting the sting in his eyes, but one tear slipped free anyway. He brushed it away quickly, embarrassed, but Mrs. Takashi only smiled softly. "There is no shame in tears," she said. "They don't make you weak. They show you're still alive, still feeling, still fighting. I would worry more if you had none left." She gave his hand a firmer squeeze, her steady warmth wrapping around him like a shield.

The kitchen clock ticked in the background, each second pulling them closer to the hearing. Tom took another sip of tea, slower this time, letting the quiet linger between them. At last he set the cup down, his voice unsteady but resolute. "I don't want to lose this," he said. "I don't want to go back." Mrs. Takashi's hand slid from his to rest over his forearm, her touch gentle but unwavering. "You won't lose this. Not if I have any breath left in me."

Outside, the wind rattled softly against the windows, but the kitchen remained warm, a cocoon against the world's chill. Tom leaned back in his chair, finally letting his shoulders drop a fraction. Mrs. Takashi watched him carefully, noting the subtle shift, the first loosening of fear in his posture. "Try to rest tonight," she said. "Tomorrow will be heavy enough without you carrying it in advance." He gave a small, uncertain nod, though his fingers still lingered against hers as if afraid to let go too soon.

When at last he rose from the table, he hesitated. "Do you really mean it?" he asked, his voice barely audible. "That I'm… already your son?" Mrs. Takashi stood with him, brushing a hand lightly against his cheek. "I meant every word. And I will keep saying it until you believe it yourself." She kissed his temple gently, then turned him toward the hallway. "Now go. Ty is probably still awake, waiting for you."

Tom paused at the doorway, one hand gripping the frame. He looked back once more, his face shadowed but his eyes clearer than before. "Thank you," he said simply. The words were rough, but the weight behind them was real. Mrs. Takashi only smiled, watching him disappear down the hall, her heart full but steady. Tomorrow would be a battle, but tonight, she had given him something no court could take away: a place where he belonged.

The hallway was dim, the only light coming from the soft glow of the lamp near the stairwell. Tom stood outside the bedroom door, his shoulders still stiff from the kitchen conversation, though something in his eyes had softened.

# THE SMILE THAT BROKE

Ty sat cross-legged on his own bed, waiting as though he had known Tom would stop by. He didn't rise, didn't rush, but when Tom stepped inside, Ty shifted slightly to the edge of the bed and patted the spot beside him. Tom hesitated, then sat, the mattress dipping under his weight. For a moment neither spoke, the silence hanging heavy, until Ty broke it with a steady voice.

"When they speak to you tomorrow," Ty said, his tone calm but unyielding, "they speak to me too." The words were not grand, not rehearsed, but the weight behind them was undeniable. Tom turned, studying him in the half-light. "What does that mean?" he asked, his voice rough. Ty held his gaze, refusing to let it falter. "It means you're not walking into that courtroom alone. Every word they throw at you, every question they fire, I'll be standing right there. If they want to challenge you, they'll have to go through me."

Tom let out a shaky breath, the sound almost like a laugh but too fragile to carry. "You're just a kid," he muttered, half in disbelief. "They won't care what you say." Ty's eyes narrowed, not in anger but in certainty. "They'll care," he replied. "Because truth doesn't need age to stand. It only needs someone who refuses to move. And I won't move, Tom. Not for them. Not for anyone." The firmness in his tone made Tom look down quickly, his fingers twisting in the blanket at the foot of the bed.

For a long moment, Tom said nothing, only staring at the floor. Ty let the silence stretch, patient in a way most children never could be. Finally Tom whispered, "What if I can't do it? What if I freeze? What if I mess it all up?" Ty leaned slightly closer, his hands resting on his knees. "Then I'll be your voice," he said. "If your words stumble, mine will stand. If you shake, I'll steady you. If you fall, I'll pick you up. That's my promise." The simplicity of it cut through Tom's spiraling thoughts, leaving him with nothing to argue against.

Tom lifted his head slowly, eyes searching Ty's face. "Why?" he asked. The single word carried the weight of all his disbelief, all the cracks left by years of neglect. "Why would you even care that much?" Ty's answer came without hesitation. "Because I see you," he said firmly. "Not just the anger, not just the fights—you. The boy who's been carrying more than he should. The boy who deserves better. You're not alone anymore, Tom, and I'll keep saying it until you believe me."

The words struck harder than Tom expected. His throat tightened, and he looked away, trying to hide it. Ty didn't push, didn't mock, didn't tease. Instead, he sat back slightly, giving Tom space while still holding the ground between them. "Tomorrow won't be easy," Ty added quietly, "but nothing worth fighting for ever is. What matters is that you don't have to fight it alone. I'll be right there, beside you, the whole way through."

Tom's hands clenched and unclenched, the tension running out in small bursts as though his body didn't know whether to collapse or hold on. At last, he muttered, "You don't even know what it feels like."

# THE SMILE THAT BROKE

Ty's voice softened, but his eyes never lost their steady light. "Maybe not all of it. But I know what it feels like to be pushed, to be doubted, to be told you don't belong. And I know what it feels like to prove them wrong." The conviction in his tone made Tom glance back, his expression caught between skepticism and longing.

The bedroom clock ticked steadily, filling the silence that followed. Tom finally leaned back, not into Ty directly but enough to close the distance between them. The shift was small, but it spoke louder than words. Ty didn't move away, didn't draw attention to it—he simply let the moment stand. "When they look at you," Ty said again, quieter this time, "they'll see me too. And they'll know you're not standing alone."

A silence settled that wasn't heavy this time but grounding, like the calm before dawn. Tom closed his eyes briefly, breathing out as if some of the weight had finally slipped free. "Alright," he whispered. "Alright." Ty gave the smallest of nods, his face calm, his posture relaxed but unbreakable. "Good," he said. "Because tomorrow, we show them who you are. Not who they think you are. Who you really are."

Tom's chest ached with the truth of it, the steady anchor Ty offered without demand. He leaned a little more, letting his shoulder rest against Ty's for the briefest of moments. Ty didn't shift, didn't flinch. He simply held the space, silent but firm, until Tom found enough breath to steady himself again. "Thank you," Tom murmured, so soft it barely carried. Ty gave no reply, only a quiet nod, but the promise between them was clear. Tomorrow, no matter what came, Tom would not face it alone.

The morning broke sharp and clear, with the kind of sunlight that felt almost cruel, too bright for a day so heavy. The courthouse loomed over them, a structure of marble and glass that seemed to press the air thinner with its weight. Tom's steps faltered as they reached the broad stone stairs, his eyes tracing the columns and the polished brass handles on the doors that looked as though they had never been touched by children like him. He shifted his small bag from one shoulder to the other, though it held nothing he needed, only the habit of carrying something when the rest of the world wanted him bare. Ty walked at his side, his posture calm, his gaze steady, his hand brushing Tom's shoulder every so often as though to remind him, wordlessly, you are not here alone. Zenji and Mrs. Takashi walked a step behind, their presence quiet but unyielding, the solid line that framed the boy between them.

Inside, the courthouse smelled faintly of polish and dust, the echo of their footsteps swallowed by high ceilings that stretched like a cathedral. Tom glanced left and right, his eyes catching on the armed guards stationed by the entrance, on the clerks carrying stacks of files tied neatly with string, on the faces of strangers who looked up with idle curiosity. Each stare made his chest tighten, but Ty's shoulder nudged against his once, light but certain. "Straight ahead," Ty murmured, his voice barely more than breath. Tom nodded stiffly, pushing the air back into his lungs, and let his feet follow Ty's rhythm rather than his own faltering steps.

The courtroom doors were carved oak, tall and heavy, the handles cool brass that shone under the morning light. As they approached, Tom's parents stood already near the opposite side of the hall. His father's face was drawn, unreadable, while his mother clutched her purse with both hands as though it were a shield. They didn't look at Tom directly, not at first. When they did, the glance was fleeting, and Tom felt the familiar hollow stir within him. It might have broken him then, that small dismissal, but Ty's hand rose again, fingers brushing just above his elbow, grounding him before the silence could echo too loudly.

The bailiff called for order, and the two groups were guided toward their sides. Tom's parents moved toward one table, their lawyer waiting with a thick file already open. Tom and the Takashis were led to the opposite table, where Zenji calmly laid down his briefcase, his expression unreadable yet resolute. Mrs. Takashi pulled Tom gently into the chair between herself and Ty, the small gesture saying without words, we sit together, always. Tom swallowed hard, his throat dry, but when he looked at Ty beside him, he found the boy's face calm, almost defiant, as though daring the very walls of the courthouse to test their strength.

The judge's bench towered above, empty for the moment, the seat raised high to cast every eye upward. Tom stared at it, his stomach tightening, imagining the questions that would rain down, the decisions made with a voice that carried the weight of law. For a fleeting second he thought he might run, might push back from the table and bolt toward the doors behind them. Ty leaned closer, his voice low but sharp as steel. "Stay with me," he whispered. The words weren't desperate, weren't pleading—they were command and promise in one. Tom nodded faintly, his body settling though his heart still raced.

Across the room, his parents shifted uneasily, the father leaning to whisper something to their lawyer while his mother sat stiff, her lips pressed in a thin line. Tom's eyes lingered on them longer than he meant, and a shadow crossed his face. They didn't look like villains in that moment, only small and afraid in their own way, yet the hurt remained, carved too deep to fade in one morning. Ty followed his gaze, then turned back sharply. "Don't," Ty said under his breath. "Don't carry their weight today. You've got enough of your own. Let them carry theirs." Tom blinked, the firmness catching him off guard, but he turned back to face the front, his shoulders squaring a little more.

When the judge finally entered, the courtroom rose together, the scrape of chairs echoing like thunder against the marble. Tom rose too, his knees weak, but Ty rose beside him, their movements aligned, a silent declaration. As they sat again, Tom's hand twitched against the table, fingers curling tight against the wood, until Ty slid his own hand over Tom's for a brief moment, not to hold but to steady. The warmth lingered even when Ty pulled back, and Tom knew then that whatever words were demanded of him, he would not be left to drown alone.

The doors closed behind the last stragglers, shutting the noise of the city away, leaving only the hum of the courtroom. For the first time, Tom did not feel like the smallest body in the largest room. He felt the weight of the Takashis at his side, the promise of Ty's unbroken gaze, and the certainty that when the truth was called upon, it would not stand alone.

# THE SMILE THAT BROKE

The room stilled the instant the judge entered, the shuffle of papers and muted whispers fading into silence. He was a man of late years, his hair more grey than black, his shoulders upright though worn by decades of decisions that weighed heavier than stone. The black robe flowed behind him as he climbed the steps to his bench, and when he turned to face the room, there was nothing hurried in his movements. His eyes swept across the chamber, cool and deliberate, as though each person there carried a measure of truth or falsehood that must be weighed. No one spoke, no one shifted. Even the guards at the doors stood a fraction taller, waiting.

Tom sat rigid at the table, his shoulders hunched but his eyes forward. The judge's gaze lingered on him longer than any file or folder, and Tom felt the weight of it press against his skin. His hands trembled where they rested on the polished surface of the table, the movement small but undeniable, and yet he didn't look away. The judge's eyes were not cruel, not piercing like blades—they were steady, probing, seeking the marrow of the boy before him. It was as if he meant to learn more from Tom's silence than from any word yet spoken. Ty noticed the tremor, and without shifting much, let his knee nudge gently against Tom's, steadying him.

The parents sat across the room, stiff in their seats, but the judge did not glance their way at once. Instead, he studied Tom's posture, his thin frame caught between fear and defiance, a boy forced into a role far too heavy. The lawyers shuffled their files, eager to begin arguments, yet the judge raised a hand and kept the silence in place. His eyes had not finished their work. He looked to Zenji briefly, acknowledging the RCMP investigator with a subtle nod, but his gaze always returned to Tom. The boy's fists clenched tighter against the wood, his knuckles paling, until the judge leaned forward ever so slightly and rested his chin on his hand.

The weight of that look wasn't condemnation; it was recognition. Tom wasn't being dismissed as a child unworthy of the court's time. He was being examined as though his truth mattered as much as any evidence the adults carried in their files. The boy felt the tremor in his chest ease just a fraction, the tight coil in his throat loosening under the quiet dignity of the judge's attention. Ty saw it too, the small shift, and allowed himself the faintest nod. He whispered so low only Tom could hear, "He sees you." Tom blinked hard, his jaw tightening, and he forced his shoulders to straighten though his hands still shook.

Mrs. Takashi's hand reached gently across the table, not to smother his trembling fingers but to lay her palm beside them, close enough that if Tom wished, he could touch it. He didn't, not yet, but the presence of it steadied him further. Zenji sat as still as a carved figure, though his eyes flicked once toward his wife and son with quiet approval. The judge watched it all, every tremor, every shift of posture, every breath Tom fought to keep steady. He was reading the boy like others might read a ledger, and the more he saw, the heavier the air in the courtroom became.

When the judge finally spoke, his voice cut the silence without force, low but firm. "This court acknowledges the presence of all parties," he said. The formality was expected, but then his gaze returned to Tom again. "We will hear the truth today—not just in documents, not just in statements, but in the lives affected." His words struck deeper than law; they landed like a recognition that Tom himself would be heard, not just spoken for. Tom's throat worked as though to answer, but Ty leaned in, murmuring, "Not yet. Just breathe." Tom nodded faintly, clutching the air in slow gulps, his eyes locked on the judge's.

The parents shifted uneasily under the prolonged focus, their lawyer attempting to interject, but the judge raised one hand and silenced the room again. "I have read what has been placed before me," he said evenly, "but the paper does not yet tell the story of the boy who sits here. That story will be told today." His eyes fixed on Tom once more, steady and unwavering. For a boy who had long lived beneath the shadow of violence, those words lit a small flame inside his chest. It frightened him, but it was the kind of fear that came with hope.

Tom swallowed, his lips parting as though to speak, then pressing shut again. Ty's hand hovered close, a silent shield waiting for the moment the boy might collapse under the pressure. The judge leaned back at last, shifting his gaze briefly to the lawyers, then the parents, then to Zenji and Mrs. Takashi—but each time his eyes returned to Tom, the gravity of it all resting on a single boy's trembling shoulders. The silence deepened again, but it was no longer empty; it was expectant, like the pause before a storm breaks.

For the first time since stepping into the marble halls, Tom felt he wasn't invisible. The judge had seen him—his fear, his resolve, his frailty, and his strength. And though the trial had yet to truly begin, Tom sat a little taller, his fists loosening just enough for his fingers to press lightly against the wood, steadying himself. Ty caught the movement and smiled faintly, his voice a whisper of iron. "You're stronger than you think."

Zenji rose when the judge gave the nod, his tall frame steady as if carved from the same stone as the courthouse itself. There was no flourish in his movements, no theatrics, only the precision of a man who had carried both badge and burden for many years. He set a thick folder on the table before him, the sound of it landing sharp against the hush of the courtroom. When he opened it, page after page of police reports, signed statements, and official seals glinted under the lights. His voice, low but commanding, filled the space without need for volume. "Your Honour, the boy seated here has lived under the shadow of a man whose record is neither brief nor misunderstood. The uncle is no rumour. He is violence documented."

He lifted the first document, a police file dated years back, and handed it to the clerk to be passed to the judge. "Assault charges," Zenji stated flatly. "Dismissed on a technicality, but the evidence was clear. A man hospitalised after an argument turned to fists and broken glass." The judge skimmed, his expression unreadable, but the weight in the room thickened.

Parents shifted in their seats, their lawyer frowning but silent for now. Zenji set down another paper, this one accompanied by photographs that made several teachers in the gallery glance away. "Property damage. Threats made to neighbours. Repeated complaints that never made it far enough to see trial." Each word came like stone placed on stone, building an unshakable wall.

Tom sat rigid, his eyes locked on the evidence as if each page were proof of the nightmare he had lived. Ty's hand rested lightly on the boy's shoulder, reminding him he was not alone in this moment. Zenji's voice pressed on, unwavering. "Statements from those who lived under his roof. One, a neighbour who saw bruises on Tom's arms when he was only six years old. Another, a teacher who noted repeated absences, and when asked, the boy claimed he was too sore to lift his arm for writing." Zenji did not raise his voice, but every syllable struck with the clarity of truth sharpened by years of discipline.

The judge leaned forward, his chin in his hand again, studying the papers with a slow, methodical eye. Zenji continued, this time holding up photographs sealed in evidence sleeves. "Here," he said, "is proof of the uncle's temper documented by police call-outs—walls broken by fists, shattered doors, blood spattered where furniture had been overturned. And here—" he held up another page, "—a sworn statement from a cousin who left the house after one violent encounter too many. She describes the uncle's rages, his fists, his drunken threats." A ripple of discomfort passed through the courtroom, a wave of unease settling heavy across the seats.

Mrs. Takashi sat with her hands folded in her lap, her eyes trained firmly on Zenji. She didn't flinch at the evidence, though her knuckles whitened as she held them together. Ty leaned closer to Tom, whispering softly, "This is not your shame. This is his." Tom's jaw clenched hard, a single tear slipping down his cheek though his gaze never wavered from the folder in Zenji's hands. The boy, who had lived so long believing his silence would bury him, now watched his suffering laid out for all to see, undeniable, unignorable.

The parents' lawyer shifted at last, rising as though to object, but the judge silenced him with a sharp glance. "He will finish," the judge said, his tone edged with finality. Zenji bowed his head in acknowledgement, then turned the page once more. "Hospital reports. A broken wrist on a young boy. Tom." His voice did not tremble, though the weight of the word struck deep. "The record says accident. The statement, however, says otherwise. The neighbour who took him to the emergency ward that night swore the boy whispered the name of the uncle before anyone else entered the room." Gasps slipped through the gallery, muffled quickly, but the echo remained.

Zenji did not falter. "This court deserves to see the truth stripped bare of excuses. This is no boy with wild temper alone. This is a boy who has endured, and who, if returned to that household, will endure again until endurance is no longer possible." His eyes fixed on the judge, unblinking. "The uncle is not simply a danger in past tense. He is a present danger, if the law does not sever his reach." With deliberate motion, he laid the final set of files before the judge, each marked with the seal of the RCMP, undeniable, official, permanent.

The silence after his words was the heaviest yet. No one moved. No one dared to breathe too loud. Tom stared at the polished wood table, his small shoulders shuddering, yet for the first time he did not shrink from the weight of his story. Ty leaned in again, whispering with steady certainty, "It's the truth, Tom. It's finally the truth." Zenji looked back at his son, then at the boy beside him, and for a moment the stern investigator softened just enough that his pride showed in his eyes.

The judge finally broke the silence, his voice steady but edged with gravity. "This evidence will be entered into the record," he said. "The court acknowledges its weight." His gaze swept across the room, pausing on the parents before returning to Zenji. "You have done this court a service by bringing it forward." Zenji bowed once, sharply, and then sat, the folder now empty before him. The wall had been built brick by brick, and it would not fall.

Tom's parents rose slowly when the judge gestured, their lawyer standing with them, papers already shuffled and set in order. The mother's hands trembled as she clasped them together, her gaze darting everywhere but toward her son. The father kept his shoulders stiff, his jaw locked, as though posture alone could lend weight to words that rang hollow before they were even spoken. Their lawyer began, voice smooth with practice, "Your Honour, my clients wish to make clear that they had no knowledge of the uncle's conduct within the home. They were as blindsided by this evidence as anyone here today."

The words echoed through the courtroom, too polished, too sharp-edged, and yet strangely fragile. The mother added in a wavering voice, "We—we never saw. If we had known, we would have stopped it." She glanced briefly at Tom, as if hoping for some sign of mercy, but his face remained stone. Ty sat forward slightly, his hand on Tom's arm, steadying him when the boy's chest heaved once with restrained rage. Zenji's eyes narrowed, his hand pressing against the table as though to keep his composure from breaking under the weight of such deflection.

The father finally spoke, his words clipped, defensive. "We worked long hours. We trusted family. If things happened under our roof, it was hidden from us. We cannot be blamed for what was concealed." The lawyer nodded at the statement, folding it neatly into his larger argument. "Your Honour, to punish these parents by stripping them of custody would be to wound a family already fractured. They did not wield fists. They did not strike. Ignorance may be unfortunate, but it is not malice." The lawyer leaned back slightly, satisfied, as if the carefully arranged syllables would outweigh years of pain carved into a boy's skin.

But the silence that followed was not one of agreement. It was heavy, strained, and filled with the unspoken truth every teacher, every student, every observer knew: silence was never neutral. Mrs. Takashi's eyes brimmed with restrained fury, though she said nothing, her gaze cutting into the parents with the force of a mother who understood the duty they had abandoned. The judge's brow furrowed, his pen tapping once against the bench as he studied their faces. Even the clerks shifted uneasily, glancing between the boy and the people who claimed to love him but had allowed his torment to fester.

Tom's hands clenched against his knees, his knuckles bone-white as his body trembled with rage he refused to loose. His voice did not rise, but his eyes spoke louder than words—burning, wounded, alive with the betrayal of years. Ty whispered close, low enough for Tom's ears alone: "You don't have to shout. They already know." Tom's head tilted, just enough for a tear to streak down his cheek, but he never let his gaze fall. His stare pierced his parents as if to carve into their very bones the knowledge they could not erase with excuses.

The father's words continued, brittle and defensive. "We cannot be expected to control what another grown man does when we are not present." But even as he spoke, the memories painted themselves across Tom's face—nights of yelling loud enough to rattle dishes, mornings of bruises hidden under long sleeves, the suffocating knowledge that his parents' silence had not been ignorance but a willful refusal to look too closely. The teachers in the gallery exchanged glances, many recalling how often they had seen Tom shrink from touch, how often excuses had been offered, how often the parents had smiled too quickly in meetings.

Mrs. Dunlop, seated in the row of staff, muttered under her breath, "They knew." Her voice did not carry far, but Ty caught it, his jaw tightening as he straightened his back. Zenji, seated beside him, laid one hand briefly on his son's arm, steadying not because Ty would erupt, but because he might speak out of turn. The judge held up a hand, halting the parents' lawyer before he could drone further. "Your son is thirteen," the judge said flatly. "Your home has been the stage of violence for nearly his entire life. Are you telling this court you noticed nothing?" The question cut through the room, a blade of truth pressed against the hollow shield of their claims.

The mother's lips parted, then closed again. No answer came that did not sound like surrender. The father shifted, his silence betraying him more than any false word could. Tom's body shook with silent fury, and for a moment his lips parted, but Ty's grip on his arm reminded him that his truth would come in its time. Tom's fury remained etched in his eyes, a fury that no lawyer's polish, no parent's plea, no claim of ignorance could erase.

For the first time in that courtroom, the parents did not look at the judge, or at the lawyer who shielded them with rhetoric. They looked at their son, and saw in his silence a verdict far harsher than any gavel could strike. Silence was not innocence. Silence was a confession of its own, laid bare for all to see. And Tom, thirteen years old, sat with the fury of a boy who understood too well what betrayal looked like when it wore the mask of ignorance.

The judge adjusted his glasses, his expression unreadable as he looked down at the boy seated among the Takashis. "Tom," he said quietly, "will you come forward, please?" The room shifted as the bailiff guided Tom toward the witness stand, but instead of keeping him at the usual distance, the judge gestured for him to stand closer—just to the side of the bench, within reach of calm authority but out of reach of intimidation. "I want you to feel safe," the judge said, voice steady, not softened into pity but weighted with respect. "Do you understand?" Tom nodded once, his chin high though his hands trembled. Ty caught his eye from across the courtroom, his small nod saying *you're not alone*.

When the judge asked, "What your parents just told this court—was it true?" the room fell into a silence so complete that even the scratching of pens ceased. Tom lifted his chin again, his eyes locked firmly on the judge's. "Your Honour," he began, his voice unsteady at first but growing stronger, "they lie as clear as I am looking at you right now." Gasps rippled across the room, teachers and clerks shifting in their seats, but Tom's voice only sharpened. "If their statements are false, I have the bruises to prove it. I'm not the only one who saw. Others have seen it with their own eyes. They stood there. They let it happen. They are just as guilty as my uncle."

The judge leaned back slightly, watching the boy's words cut through every layer of defence raised before. The mother lowered her head, tears sliding silently, but the father's jaw tightened, fists clenching at the table. Tom ignored them both, his gaze never leaving the judge. "I slept in fear most nights," Tom continued, his voice breaking once before hardening again. "I slept with my fists tight so I could be ready. I learned to listen for every floorboard creak, every door slam. I learned what it feels like when fists bruise not just skin, but something deeper that never heals."

The room was silent but for the boy's breathing. Even Mrs. Locke, who had once sneered at the thought of saving him, looked pale, her lips pressed together in a line she could not defend. Tom's eyes glistened but no tear fell as he continued. "Words cut too. They said I was nothing. They said I deserved it. And my parents—" he finally broke his gaze from the judge, glaring at the two seated at their table, "—stood by. They didn't swing fists, but they didn't stop them either. They left me there." His voice dropped low, a whisper heavy enough to crush the silence. "I will not go back."

The courtroom stiffened as though the air had frozen solid. The weight of his refusal filled the marble chamber, stronger than any testimony given before. Ty leaned forward, gripping the wooden edge of the bench, his small face fierce with pride. Zenji folded his hands over one another, steady as stone, while Mrs. Takashi wiped at her eyes. Even the judge's pen stilled, resting against the paper as he studied the boy before him—not as a victim alone, but as a young man claiming his truth.

"Tom," the judge said after a long pause, "you are under oath here. Do you fully understand the gravity of your words?" Tom's chin lifted higher, his voice clear and unwavering now. "Yes, Your Honour. I understand. That's why I'm telling you the truth. Because I want it to stop. Because I won't live that life again." The boy's fists unclenched at last, his open hands trembling at his sides as though freeing themselves of chains that had bound him for years.

Across the gallery, whispers rose among the teachers who had known him—Miss Kara pressing a hand to her chest, Mrs. Haller shaking her head with wide eyes, Mr. Clarke bowing his head as if in prayerful respect though no words were spoken. Mr. Arnett leaned forward, his jaw tight, as though regretting every moment he had once considered expelling the boy who now stood braver than most grown men.

The judge sat back, his eyes narrowing in thought, but no gavel struck, no immediate verdict came. Instead, he nodded once, a small gesture of recognition. "Thank you, Tom," he said simply. "Your truth has been heard." The words hung in the air, not final but heavy, their echo lingering in every corner of the room.

And for the first time in a courtroom lined with stone and shadow, it was not the authority of adults or the power of evidence that stilled the room. It was the voice of a thirteen-year-old boy, standing tall in defiance, declaring before all that he would not be sent back into silence, and that he would never again live in the shadow of fists and neglect.

The judge leaned forward, folding his hands as his eyes swept the courtroom. He had already seen the strength in Tom's words, and now his gaze turned to Ty, the boy who had stepped between violence and peace more than once. "Young man," the judge said, "I am told you wish to speak." Ty rose from his seat beside Zenji and Mrs. Takashi. He walked with steady, deliberate steps, his posture upright, his small shoulders squared as if he carried the weight of something far greater than his age. The bailiff looked uncertain, glancing at the judge, but the nod that followed gave permission. Ty climbed onto the witness stand, adjusted the chair without hesitation, and faced the court.

"Your Honour," Ty began, his voice clear, carrying further than anyone expected, "do not let my age fool you. I have an IQ over two hundred and twenty. I was born with high-functioning autism. I may be only eleven, but I understand more than most believe." A murmur rose from the gallery, but the judge lifted his hand for silence. Ty never flinched, never broke his rhythm. "I am here to answer anything you wish to ask me. I have taken care of Tom since the first day he crossed paths with me, though he did not know it at the time. I saw the bruises. I saw the anger. I saw the way he pushed people away. Adults feared him. Children avoided him. But I stood beside him."

He paused, his hands folded together atop the rail, his gaze locked on the judge. "I stood in the way when his fists rose. I blocked him, not with force, but with calm. I did it out of love, because I cared enough to know that he needed help, not punishment. Nothing more, nothing less. And then, when I discovered the truth of what he faced at home, it only made sense why he carried so much weight." Ty glanced sideways at Tom, who sat motionless, his throat tight, his eyes on the floor.

"Your Honour," Ty continued, "I heard his parents with my own ears. I was in the office with Principal Arnett. I heard them say he was dangerous, that he would tear someone apart if given the chance. They painted him as a monster. But it was a lie. I knew it was a lie because I stood right next to him, inches from his fists, and he never struck me. He didn't even try. He just knew I was calm. He felt that, and he chose to lower his hands. That is not what monsters do. That is what broken boys do when someone finally sees them."

# THE SMILE THAT BROKE

The judge's brows lowered slightly as he studied the boy on the stand. Ty raised a finger and pointed—not accusing wildly, but deliberate, calm, controlled. "And there was one teacher," he said, "who never cared. Who judged him. Who judged us. She sits here still, though she has already been given her notice to leave. She no longer represents this school. She no longer holds authority. She no longer holds truth." His finger dropped. Mrs. Locke stiffened, her jaw tightening, but no one in the courtroom challenged his words.

The judge asked, "Ty, what is it you believe this court must understand about Tom?" The boy straightened in his seat. "That he is worth saving," Ty replied firmly. "That he has already changed. I have seen him laugh, Your Honour, real laughter, the kind that breaks walls. I have seen him sleep without fear for the first time in years. I have seen him eat without suspicion, speak without rage. Progress does not come easy, but it comes. And if you send him back, you will destroy it all. I swear before this court, on my life and my honour, that I will not let anyone harm him again. Not here, not at school, not in any place where I stand."

The judge pressed, "You are only eleven. Do you truly believe you can carry such a promise?" Ty's answer came swift and certain. "I already have." He leaned forward, his small hands gripping the wood rail. "Every day, I stood between him and chaos. Every day, I saw a little more light come back into him. That is why I say this: Tom belongs with us. He is my brother now. And no law, no paper, no words of those who failed him, can erase that truth."

The words rang in the chamber, not shouted but steady, carrying the unmistakable fire of conviction. Ty's eyes never wavered, his back never bent, his tone never cracked. Around the courtroom, grown men and women shifted, their expressions altered by the knowledge that an eleven-year-old had spoken more truth in five minutes than many of them had in a lifetime. Zenji's lips curved into the smallest trace of a proud smile, Mrs. Takashi's eyes glistened, and even Tom—who had promised himself never to cry again—felt his throat tighten against the flood of tears waiting to break.

The judge leaned back in his chair, studying the boy as if measuring him against every expectation of childhood he had ever carried. "Mr. Takashi," he said carefully, "you have spoken boldly for one so young. But the court requires clarity. Why do you stand for Tom when others fear him?" The room held its breath. Ty shifted forward, resting his elbows on the rail, his small hands folded but his eyes unyielding. "Because I saw the truth before anyone else wanted to. I knew his anger was not born from cruelty. It was born from pain. I know the difference. I chose to care, Your Honour, even when it would have been easier to turn away."

Tom's head lifted slightly, his eyes red, his lips pressed tight. The judge caught the glance, noting how the boy sat differently now—no longer a shadow waiting to vanish, but a boy who felt the weight of another's courage standing in front of him. Ty's voice steadied as he continued.

"I have been at his side in every hallway fight, every classroom outburst, every moment when fear twisted into rage. I was there, calm, when he wanted to strike. I was there, quiet, when he wanted to scream. And he chose restraint, Your Honour, not because he feared punishment, but because he trusted me. If he can trust me, he can trust more. If he can trust more, he can heal."

The judge leaned forward. "You speak of trust and healing. But are you not too young to carry such responsibility?" Ty shook his head, his black hair shifting across his brow. "I am young, but I am not too young. I was born different, Your Honour. I see patterns in people. I hear truth even when others bury it. My age doesn't make me blind. It just makes me underestimated. And that is why I am here. To tell you that Tom is not dangerous—he is wounded. And wounds don't heal by sending someone back into the fire."

There was a pause before the judge spoke again, his tone softer now. "And what would you do, Ty, if this court grants Tom the chance to remain with your family? What is your role?" Ty drew a deep breath, his words precise, deliberate. "I will guide him, through the good and the bad. I will be his anchor when he trembles, his balance when he rages. I promise before this court and before you, Your Honour, I will not let him falter. I will not let him be forgotten. I will not let him be thrown away." He straightened in his seat, his small frame taut with purpose.

The silence stretched, broken only by the faint scratching of the clerk's pen. Ty lifted his chin, his next words heavier than anything expected from an eleven-year-old. "I, Ty Shiro Takashi, swear an oath before this court. I swear to help train Tom into the man he deserves to become. I swear to stand between him and harm. I swear to guard his progress, to nurture his strength, and to believe in him when others do not. I swear, Your Honour, to stand as his brother, not by blood but by choice. And I will not break this oath."

Gasps rippled through the courtroom, soft but undeniable. Mrs. Takashi pressed a hand to her lips, tears pricking her eyes, while Zenji sat tall, pride written in every line of his face. Tom stared at Ty, his chest rising and falling unevenly, his fists clenched not in anger but in the desperate attempt to hold himself together. He had never heard words like that spoken for him—not from parents, not from teachers, not from anyone. The judge sat in measured silence, his gavel untouched, his expression unreadable.

"Ty Shiro Takashi," the judge finally said, his voice steady but low, "your words will be entered into record as sworn testimony. This court has rarely heard such conviction from a man twice your age, let alone a boy of eleven. I will weigh your oath with the seriousness it demands." He paused, letting the statement settle across the room. "You may step down."

Ty nodded once, rising from the stand with calm precision. He stepped carefully down the stairs and returned to his place beside Tom, who could no longer contain the wetness in his eyes. Ty did not gloat, did not smile.

He simply placed a hand on Tom's shoulder, squeezing once, a silent assurance that his oath was not just words. The courtroom had witnessed something extraordinary, and though the gavel had not yet fallen, everyone present knew that the course of this trial had shifted on the strength of one boy's vow.

When Mrs. Takashi rose from her seat, the entire atmosphere shifted. Her presence was calm, yet commanding, as though she carried the weight of every truth unspoken. The judge watched her approach, noting how she moved without fear or hesitation, her steps steady as her gaze. She did not look at Tom's parents, nor did she allow her eyes to linger on the hushed crowd. She went directly to the stand, placed her hand where instructed, and swore the oath without faltering. Then she looked at the judge with quiet conviction, her voice warm but firm. "I am not here to speak of law, Your Honour. I am here to speak of love, and of truth."

Her words drifted across the courtroom, soft yet undeniable, as though every syllable carried an anchor. "This boy, Tom, has eaten at our table. He has slept beneath our roof. He has sat in silence at our side when words were too heavy for him to carry. He is not a stranger. He is not a burden. He is not a danger to us. He is already our son, whether this court recognizes it or not." She paused, letting the weight of her claim settle. "When he first came into our home, he could not laugh, he could not sleep, he could barely breathe without fear. And now—" she gestured faintly toward Tom, who sat rigid yet listening—"now he breathes easier. He laughs, even if only a little. He has begun to dream again."

The judge leaned forward slightly, studying her closely. "Mrs. Takashi," he said, "you speak with care. But what of the weight this boy carries? What of the danger that others fear?" She did not flinch. "Danger does not vanish by casting a child aside, Your Honour. Danger fades when love takes its place. Tom has lived in shadows for most of his life. In our home, he has slept without fear. He has eaten without shame. He has smiled without guilt. These things are not dangerous. These things are healing." She folded her hands together, her voice tightening with emotion. "And I tell you now: we will not let him go back to what broke him."

The parents shifted uncomfortably in their seats, their faces tight, but she did not spare them a glance. Instead, she pressed forward. "I have watched him sit at my table, staring at the plate as though food was a test he might fail. I have seen him wake in the night, trembling, until my husband and my son reassured him that he was safe. I have tucked a blanket over him when he fought to stay awake, fearing what dreams might come. And I have seen, slowly, the boy begin to trust. Not because we demanded it, not because we forced it, but because love does what rules cannot—it waits, it listens, it holds without judgment."

The room had fallen silent again, but it was not the silence of fear. It was the silence of listening. Even Mrs. Locke, bitter and unwilling, kept her tongue pressed behind her teeth as if words might betray her. The judge raised one brow. "And what do you ask of this court?" Mrs. Takashi's voice sharpened, though it did not rise.

"I ask nothing more than recognition of the truth already standing before you. This boy is ours, Your Honour. We are his family. His blood betrayed him. We will not. His name may not match ours, but his place does. To deny him would not protect him. It would destroy him."

She turned her head finally, not to the parents but to Tom. He sat frozen, his eyes glistening, his lips trembling. "Tom," she said softly, though her words reached every corner of the room, "you are mine. You are ours. And nothing they can say or do will change that." Tom's shoulders shook once, but he did not break. Instead, his fists unclenched for the first time that day, his palms open, resting against his knees. His breath came uneven, but it came freely, and that was enough.

The judge steepled his fingers, his face unreadable, yet the pause between his words carried weight. "Mrs. Takashi, your testimony will be recorded as spoken. This court recognizes your statement of intent." She inclined her head with calm respect, then stepped down, her back unbent, her presence leaving behind a quiet warmth that no paper, no file, no law could ever replicate.

When she returned to her seat beside Zenji, his hand brushed hers briefly, a quiet exchange of strength between husband and wife. Ty sat straighter too, his eyes alight, knowing that his mother had spoken with the same fire that burned in him. And Tom, though he said nothing, turned toward her ever so slightly, as though acknowledging, at last, that love might not be a trick, nor a fleeting dream, but something real enough to hold.

The hush that settled over the courtroom was not ordinary silence but something weighted, as though every breath hung suspended on a fragile thread. The clerk shuffled a stack of papers at the front bench, her hands precise but her eyes darting nervously between the judge and the assembled families. The officials at the side table leaned toward one another, whispering in quick bursts, their words muffled under the pressure of the moment. Even the officers stationed by the doors seemed less statuesque, their attention pulled toward the boy sitting in the centre of it all. Tom's chin remained level, but his hands trembled slightly against his knees. He had spoken his truth; now the judgment was no longer his to carry.

The judge removed his spectacles, setting them down with deliberate care, his gaze sweeping across the courtroom. It was not the glance of a man overwhelmed, but the stare of one who knew the gravity of what he held in his hands. His eyes lingered first on Zenji, who sat solid, shoulders squared, then on Mrs. Takashi, whose calm defiance glowed still from her testimony. Finally, the judge studied Ty, who leaned forward in his seat, unblinking, as if he were ready to shield Tom even here, in a chamber of law. The weight of all those words, all those truths, pressed into the judge's silence until the entire room seemed to lean with him.

The parents shifted uneasily at their table. Tom's father kept glancing toward the exit, his jaw tight, while his mother fumbled with a folded tissue she hadn't once lifted to her eyes. Their lawyer bent close to them, murmuring, but their responses were stiff, half-hearted, like actors who had forgotten their lines halfway through the play.

The murmurs around the room grew louder—teachers, board members, and spectators whispering their judgments long before the gavel had spoken. Mrs. Locke, seated behind the parents, sat with arms crossed, her expression caught somewhere between resentment and fear, unwilling to meet the eyes of those who had condemned her.

For Tom, each sound felt like thunder. The shuffle of shoes, the creak of wood, the faint scratching of pens across paper—every detail magnified under the strain of waiting. He glanced sideways, catching Ty's gaze for the briefest moment. Ty gave no smile, no dramatic signal, just a calm nod, the same gesture he had offered him countless times in school halls and during sleepless nights. That quiet assurance steadied him now, even as his stomach knotted at the uncertainty ahead. He knew one thing only: he would not go back, and that truth was written in his bones.

The judge finally leaned back, tapping his pen lightly against the desk. "This matter," he said, his voice carrying evenly, "is not a question of guilt alone, but of future. The evidence presented has been strong. The testimonies—" He paused, his eyes flicking briefly toward the Takashis. "—have been compelling. But this court does not make decisions lightly. The welfare of the child must remain the sole consideration." He turned his attention back to the officials, who murmured their acknowledgments, and then toward the parents, whose faces tightened at his words. "The truth has been spoken in ways that cannot be ignored. It is now the duty of this court to weigh it."

The officials leaned back, exchanging glances that carried no comfort. One scribbled furiously in his notebook, another whispered again, but the nods they gave to the judge were enough to show that something irreversible had already begun. The parents tried to mask their dread, but Tom caught it in their eyes—fear not of losing him, but of losing control. His mother's hand trembled as she set her tissue aside, and his father clenched his jaw so tightly it looked as though it might crack. Tom almost smiled at that, not out of cruelty but because for once, the fear was not his to bear.

Zenji leaned slightly forward, his hands folded neatly on the table, his expression one of patience carved from stone. Mrs. Takashi placed a hand lightly on his arm, not to soothe but to share the weight of the moment together. Ty, however, remained upright, his gaze never leaving Tom. In that gaze was not just loyalty but something fiercer, a promise that no matter what came next, Tom would not face it alone. Tom felt it, the warmth of that silent bond, and for the first time in a courtroom that smelled of old wood and cold stone, he allowed his breath to settle evenly in his chest.

The judge looked out again over the rows of teachers and school officials seated in the gallery. Mr. Clarke sat forward, his hands clasped together tightly, while Mr. Arnett's jaw was firm, his stance already clear even before the ruling. Ms. Henley kept her gaze fixed on Tom, her expression softened with quiet hope, while Mrs. Haller clutched her notebook to her chest as though bracing herself for the verdict. All of them knew that this was no longer just about procedure—it was about a boy standing at the edge of two lives, one that would break him, and one that might finally allow him to heal.

And in that hush, Tom understood the weight of the crossroads. This was not only about the uncle in prison, nor about the parents who looked at him now with thin masks of regret. This was about whether love could be recognized as truth inside a courtroom, whether the bond of chosen family could carry the same strength as blood. He clenched his fists once, then let them fall open again, palms resting steady. For the first time in years, he chose not to brace for impact but to stand ready for whatever judgment came.

The gavel had not yet fallen, but in that silence, every soul in the room knew that the decision was already being carved into stone. The whispers, the shuttling papers, the shifting bodies—all were nothing compared to the unspoken truth that wrapped itself around them all. The crossroads had been reached. Now came the path forward.

The judge leaned forward, his hands clasped tightly before him, his eyes fixed on the boy who stood straighter than anyone expected. "Tom," he said, his voice low but resonant in the chamber, "do you understand what emancipation means? To sever the ties of law and name, to declare that your parents no longer hold authority over you?" The weight of the words seemed to echo off the paneled walls. The court shifted, pens paused over paper, and every breath seemed to hold in wait for the boy's answer.

Tom did not look at his parents, nor at the officers in the room. His gaze locked only on the judge, unflinching despite the tremor of his small hands. "I understand," he said, his voice steady in the hush. "And I choose it. I choose them." His hand moved, gesturing faintly toward Ty, Zenji, and Mrs. Takashi. "They are my family now. They kept me safe. They listened. They believed me. My parents didn't. They let me suffer and did nothing. That is not love. That is not family." His words fell clean and final, sharper than any accusation an adult could craft.

A ripple coursed through the courtroom. Mrs. Dunlop shifted uncomfortably in her seat, her brows tight with sympathy, while Mr. Clarke leaned forward, his eyes glistening. Ms. Henley held her breath, visibly moved, while Mr. Arnett nodded slowly, as if Tom's words had sealed his conviction. Even the officers near the door looked away for a moment, hiding the sting of emotion that crept behind their eyes. The parents at their table froze; his father's face turned pale, his mother's lips pressed thin, her tissue clutched so tightly it tore in her fist.

Tom's voice softened but carried with a clarity that did not falter. "Your Honour," he continued, "I don't want to end up like Myles Neuts. I don't want to be another boy they read about in newspapers, another life broken by silence and cruelty. I don't want anyone else to ever go through what I did." His hand reached into the folded papers Zenji had given him, and he stepped forward, holding out a letter. The bailiff took it and placed it in the judge's hand. "That's about Myles," Tom explained, his voice trembling only once. "He wrote a poem about peace before he died. He should still be here. He shouldn't have been lost. I don't want to end up like him, and I don't want anyone else to either. I want it to stop—with me. With us."

The judge opened the letter with deliberate care, scanning the lines with a gravity that filled the chamber. The poem's simple truth, written in the hand of a boy lost too soon, seemed to hang in the air like a plea from the grave. "Peace is love instead of hate… peace is truth instead of lies…" The judge read quietly to himself, his eyes slowing over each line, his face tightening as though the child's words had carved directly into him. When he set the paper down, his gaze lifted to Tom, and for a moment his stern expression faltered into something deeply human.

"You carry a heavy weight for your years," the judge said finally, his voice quieter now. "A weight no child should have to bear. And yet, you stand here, asking not only for your own freedom, but for the hope of others." His eyes flicked briefly toward the parents, who sat silent and motionless, then back to Tom. "Tell me this, then. Do you believe, truly, that this home you've found—the Takashis—will give you what was denied you until now?"

Tom turned, his gaze sweeping to the family seated behind him. Ty leaned forward slightly, his eyes unwavering, his small but certain nod already the answer before Tom spoke. Zenji sat calm, his broad frame grounded as if no force could shake his resolve. Mrs. Takashi's eyes shone with quiet strength, her hands folded on the table, waiting not to claim him but to receive him. Tom swallowed, then turned back to the bench. "Yes, Your Honour. With them, I am safe. With them, I am loved. They're not perfect, but they don't need to be. They are mine, and I am theirs. That's all I need."

The room shifted again, a murmur passing through the gallery. Some officials scribbled furiously, others sat back in silence, and still others looked at Tom with a newfound respect that went beyond pity. Mr. Clarke's hand went to his mouth, overcome by the dignity in the boy's words. Mrs. Haller blinked quickly, fighting to compose herself. Even those who had doubted—those who had whispered about risk and danger—felt their arguments thin beneath the simple strength of his declaration.

The judge studied him for a long moment, then nodded, as if answering something beyond the courtroom. "Then I have no further questions." He tapped the letter once against the desk, his expression unreadable, but his eyes spoke a truth clear enough: the decision was being written already, not in law alone but in conscience. Tom's words had carved themselves into the record of the court.

In that silence, Tom's chest rose and fell with a calm he had not felt in years. He had spoken everything that mattered. He had chosen. And for the first time, he believed someone truly listened.

The judge's gavel struck the block with a force that startled even those who had expected its fall. The sharp crack carried through the chamber, reverberating off the paneled walls until it seemed to linger in the bones of every listener. Tom flinched, not from fear of punishment, but from the sheer finality of that sound. It was the sound of decisions, of authority, of power that reached further than his own hands could ever stretch. For a heartbeat, he believed it might mean his world was about to collapse.

But the judge's voice followed, calm and deliberate. "The matter of custody and emancipation is not to be taken lightly. I have heard the testimonies. I have seen the evidence. I will retire to conduct a final review of all materials before rendering my judgment." His eyes swept over the room once more, pausing briefly on Tom, before returning to the papers spread before him. "Until then, the boy remains in the care of the Takashi household under protective supervision." With that, he gave a single nod, and the gavel fell again, echoing like thunder striking stone.

Tom exhaled sharply, his breath catching as though he had been holding it since he first stepped into the courtroom. His fists uncurled at last, his knuckles pale from the grip he had held on his own knees. He glanced at his parents across the aisle; they sat stiff and silent, their faces unreadable masks, yet he felt no draw toward them, no ache for their comfort. Instead, he turned toward the only ones who had stood for him: Ty, Zenji, and Mrs. Takashi. The fear remained, but it was tempered by the knowledge that they had not left his side.

Ty leaned close, his small shoulder pressing gently against Tom's. He tilted his head just enough so his whisper carried, quiet but certain. "We're still here." The words were not dramatic, not a promise of impossible futures, but a reminder that at this very moment Tom was not alone. His lungs eased, the tightness in his chest loosening as if the air itself had chosen to return at Ty's command.

Around them, the courtroom stirred back to life. Papers shuffled, pens scratched notes across legal pads, and murmurs rose among the officials. Ms. Henley dabbed at her eyes discreetly, composing herself with the professionalism expected of her station. Mr. Clarke let out a long breath, his relief so obvious it made Mr. Arnett glance toward him with a knowing half-smile. Mrs. Dunlop leaned close to whisper to Miss Kara, but both stopped when Zenji turned his gaze briefly in their direction, firm and watchful.

Tom lowered his head, trying to hide the tears that burned in his eyes, but Ty's hand shifted, resting against his arm in a steady gesture. Zenji reached forward from the bench behind, placing a broad hand on the boy's back, and Mrs. Takashi's eyes met his with warmth that did not falter. None of them spoke, but the strength of their presence spoke louder than any argument his parents had tried to muster.

The parents themselves sat frozen, caught in the sharp light of exposure. His mother's jaw tightened as if she longed to speak, but the weight of the judge's declaration silenced her. His father's eyes shifted downward, his posture collapsing into something that looked almost like defeat. Neither reached for Tom, neither whispered his name. In their silence, they surrendered what little remained of their authority.

Tom looked back once, just enough to see their faces, then turned away. His shoulders squared slightly, not in defiance but in recognition that he no longer needed to seek anything from them. Whatever decision the judge made, the truth of who stood with him was already plain. He felt the edges of the fear ease again, leaving something new in its place—something he had not trusted himself to believe in until this very moment.

As the courtroom emptied, footsteps echoing against the marble floor, Ty tugged lightly on his sleeve, steering him toward the doors. "Come on," Ty said softly, his voice even. "The sun's still out. Let's walk in it." Zenji and Mrs. Takashi rose beside them, guiding without force, their pace set not by procedure but by patience.

For Tom, the gavel's thunder still echoed in his chest, but beneath it, Ty's whisper lingered stronger. *We're still here.* It was enough to steady him against the weight of uncertainty. He did not know what the verdict would be, not yet. But he knew one thing that mattered more than law or judgment: he was no longer alone in waiting for it.

The heavy doors of the courthouse groaned shut behind them, leaving the echoes of the gavel and voices sealed inside. The marble steps stretched downward, cool beneath their shoes, but the air outside was bathed in late afternoon light. The sun hung just above the rooftops, golden and steady, wrapping the four of them in warmth as though the day itself refused to yield to the darkness still unsettled in their hearts. Tom hesitated on the first step, his eyes narrowing as though he feared the weight of the building would reach out and drag him back inside. Ty, without words, placed his hand against Tom's elbow and guided him forward until they reached the middle of the broad staircase. There they sat, the courthouse at their back, the open world before them.

Tom lowered himself slowly, as if unsure whether he deserved the rest, but once seated, he leaned into Ty almost at once. The boy's shoulder pressed against his cheek, steady and unyielding, and Tom felt the tremors running through his own body ease with the simple contact. For so long he had only known shoulders that shoved or fists that struck; the unfamiliarity of resting against someone who held still and strong was nearly overwhelming. He exhaled shakily, the sound half a sigh, half a release, and let his weight settle.

Zenji stood a step above them, his arms folded loosely as he scanned the street. He was vigilant still, his eyes sharp as though expecting shadows to emerge from the edges of the sunlight, but his stance held no tension.

Mrs. Takashi lowered herself onto the stone beside the boys, her skirt pooling around her, her hand resting lightly on Tom's knee in quiet reassurance. Nothing was spoken yet, for all three of them knew words would only tangle what was already perfectly clear in gesture. The silence was heavy, but it was a silence chosen, not enforced, and in that difference lay a vast freedom.

Tom turned his head slightly, the warmth of Ty's shirt beneath his cheek, and whispered a breath too soft for anyone but Ty to hear. "I don't want to go back. Not ever." Ty's response was not verbal, not at first. Instead, he tilted slightly, giving Tom more of his shoulder, the motion subtle yet full of meaning. Then, quietly, as if speaking to the sun itself, he said, "You're not going back. Not while I'm here." Tom's chest tightened, not in fear, but in something unrecognizable at first—until he realized it was relief.

The moments passed, marked only by the distant hum of traffic and the occasional murmur of others leaving the courthouse. No one disturbed them, for it was obvious they were bound in something deeper than procedure. Tom lifted his head suddenly, his eyes bright with unshed tears, and before Ty could react he threw his arms around him. The embrace was fierce, desperate, yet filled with a tenderness that surprised even Tom. His voice cracked as he breathed into Ty's ear, "I love you." The words, raw and unpolished, carried more weight than any oath sworn within the courtroom.

Ty did not hesitate. He wrapped his arms around Tom fully, pressing his chest to his brother's as if sealing the vow. "I love you too," he said without falter. It was not the quiet encouragement he had offered before, but a declaration, firm and full, that could never be mistaken for anything less. Zenji and Mrs. Takashi exchanged a glance above them, their eyes shimmering with tears they did not attempt to hide. What had been forged through hardship had now been spoken aloud, and it could never be undone.

Tom pulled back only enough to look at Ty's face. His eyes searched, desperate for any trace of doubt, but there was none. Ty's gaze was steady, calm as stone, yet alive with the fire of loyalty. Tom felt his breath catch again, not because of fear this time, but because he realized he believed it. For the first time in his life, he believed that someone's love was not conditional, not fragile, not waiting to vanish at his next mistake. His lips trembled, but he managed a smile— awkward, crooked, and small, but real.

Zenji descended the final step and crouched beside them. He placed one hand gently on Tom's back, his voice low but firm. "What you feel now—hold it close. It will remind you in the days ahead, when doubt tries to return." Mrs. Takashi leaned forward, brushing a loose strand of hair from Tom's forehead, her touch motherly in every sense of the word. "You are not waiting alone anymore, Tom," she said softly. "Whatever happens next, we face it together." Tom's chest swelled at the word together, and his arms instinctively tightened again around Ty.

The courthouse behind them still seemed immense, its shadow stretching long across the street, but the sunlight on the steps cut through its darkness. Tom closed his eyes briefly, breathing in the scent of the warm stone and the faint trace of Ty's shirt against his cheek. For once, the waiting was not filled with dread, but with a fragile hope that felt almost strong enough to last. He had feared the future for so long, but here, with their arms around him and their words anchored in truth, he believed it might finally belong to him.

The world around them moved on—judges returning to chambers, clerks filing papers, strangers passing without notice—but on those steps, time seemed to slow. Tom's waiting had begun, but the weight of it no longer bent him to the ground. He sat straighter, his hand still clutching Ty's arm, his other hand brushing against Zenji's where it rested against his back. In the stillness, he understood the depth of what he had been given: love that would not falter, a brother's promise that could not be shaken, and a family that was no longer borrowed but his own.

For the first time in years, Tom felt certain of one truth—he was loved, and he loved them in return. And that was enough to carry him through the waiting hour, no matter how long it stretched, until the future finally spoke his name.

# CHAPTER 15: A FAMILY DECLARED

The bailiff's voice rang clear across the courtroom, commanding all to rise as the judge stepped back into chambers. The shuffle of chairs and the soft scuff of shoes on the polished floor echoed with reverence, every person in attendance knowing the next hour would decide the fate of a boy caught between ruin and redemption. Tom rose as instructed, his hands pressed tightly against his thighs, his back stiff with nerves, yet his eyes forward. Ty, only eleven years old, stood beside him, his small frame steady, his hand brushing against Tom's arm like an anchor reminding him not to drift away into fear.

The judge, robed in black, carried himself with calm authority as he settled back into his seat. His gaze was steady, his features stern but not cruel, as if he had long ago learned that truth rarely lived only on paper. "You may be seated," he declared, and the room lowered into silence, the shuffle of clothing and faint creak of benches settling like an exhale after a long held breath. The sound of the gavel striking the block cut through the quiet, a sharp reminder that this was no school assembly, no gathering in a library—this was a court of law.

Tom lowered himself into his seat, his shoulders trembling faintly, though he tried to disguise it with folded hands pressed against the table. He had endured many confrontations in school hallways, countless nights of fists and voices in the dark, but this space held a different weight. He knew that here, words would be written into record, and decisions could never be undone. Across from him, his parents sat in stiff silence, their faces carved into lines of false resolve. Their eyes barely glanced at him, as though the boy they had raised was now a stranger they wished erased.

Ty kept his presence quiet but firm. His hand rested lightly against Tom's forearm, a touch subtle enough to avoid drawing attention but strong enough to steady him. His eyes flicked upward only once toward the judge before settling back on Tom, silently reminding him he was not alone. Zenji Takashi sat just behind them, his presence immovable, like a stone wall built against storms. Mrs. Takashi, graceful and calm, folded her hands over her lap, her eyes never leaving Tom, as though her love could reach him even without words.

The judge glanced at the files stacked neatly on his bench, tapping them once before lifting his gaze to the room. "Court is now back in session," he announced, his voice even, carrying authority without the need for volume. The words struck the air with finality, sealing every person into the moment. Tom inhaled deeply, trying to draw courage from the presence at his side. The boy who once thought himself unwanted now found himself shielded by more than family—he was defended by those who believed in him without condition.

The teachers who had come to bear witness shifted uneasily in their seats. Miss Kara's hands fidgeted in her lap, her eyes fixed on the floor. Mrs. Dunlop pursed her lips, trying to mask her concern beneath professionalism.

Mr. Clarke, always calm, adjusted his glasses and studied the judge with careful attention, knowing the next words would set the tone for what was to come. Even the students allowed to attend—Nico, Jasmin, Ella, Sophie, Leo, Jeremy, Mila, and Alex—sat stiff and wide-eyed, understanding that this was no performance, no rehearsal. This was real, and Tom's life balanced on the edge of the judge's decision.

Tom shifted uneasily in his chair. His fingers twitched against the table as though he wanted to grip something but dared not show weakness. Ty leaned slightly closer, whispering just enough for Tom to hear, "We're here." The words were soft, but they sank deep into Tom's chest, a reminder that even if the room felt like a prison, he was not facing it alone. His breath steadied, though his heartbeat remained quick and sharp, hammering like a drum against his ribs.

The parents exchanged a fleeting glance across the table, their expressions stiff and unreadable. They had been summoned not by love but by duty, and the coldness in their gaze confirmed to Tom what he had already known: they did not return to claim him, but to preserve themselves. He swallowed hard, the bitter taste of betrayal heavy on his tongue. Yet beside him, Ty's stillness reminded him that betrayal could be met with loyalty, and lies could be answered by truth.

Zenji's presence in the second row loomed with unspoken power. He did not need to shift in his seat or make a sound to command attention. His file of evidence lay beside him, thick with the records of abuse and the shadows of a man now locked behind bars. He waited, not as a policeman prepared to enforce law, but as a father determined to defend his son—whether by blood or by choice made in love. The silence of the courtroom pressed down, but Zenji's silence carried more authority than the parents' words ever could.

The gavel tapped once more, not in anger but in order, as the judge cleared his throat. "The court resumes deliberations in the matter of custody and emancipation of Thomas McGill." The words struck Tom's ears with weight, his name carrying through the courtroom as though it belonged to a stranger. He clenched his jaw, forcing his eyes forward, refusing to let the sound undo him. Ty's hand remained steady against him, a reminder that even if his name was spoken like a file number, his life was not a case—it was a beating heart, defended by those who refused to abandon him.

Jeremy, sitting with the other students, shifted in his seat, his young face pale with worry. At nine years old, he did not fully understand the mechanics of law, but he understood enough to know that Tom's fate rested in this room. Beside him, Leo's silent nod served as reassurance, even if it was more for Jeremy's sake than for Tom's. The others leaned together, their quiet solidarity weaving into the tension like threads of hope that would not snap, no matter the weight placed upon them.

Mrs. Haller whispered softly to Ms. Henley, the counselor, her voice low but her concern sharp. Both had seen children falter under the weight of silence, but this boy had been dragged into a courtroom to prove his right to safety, a burden no child should ever carry. Yet they too knew the truth: Tom was not alone. He had an advocate in Ty, and through Ty, a family determined to shield him.

As the judge began to outline the order of proceedings, his voice even and precise, Tom sat straighter. Fear still clawed at his chest, but beneath it lay something steadier—resolve. The night before, Mrs. Takashi had called him her son, her voice unshaken, and he carried that truth into the room like armour. He would not fold, not now. He would speak when asked, and he would hold his ground, because love had finally claimed him, and he would not let it be taken away.

The courtroom doors closed with a faint echo, sealing them all within the chamber of truth. For Tom, it felt like both prison and sanctuary. The walls were high, the lights bright, but between Ty's hand on his arm and Zenji's watchful presence just behind him, he felt a strength he had never known. His parents might sit across the aisle, but they were shadows now. The light of family, true and chosen, sat with him.

The gavel struck once more, finalizing the opening of the session. "Let us proceed," the judge declared, his gaze falling on the boy before him. The moment had begun, and for Tom, there would be no turning back. He lifted his chin, swallowed his fear, and braced himself for the questions that would decide his life.

For the first time in years, he did not tremble alone.

The judge gave a small nod toward the parents' table, his expression unreadable as he invited them to speak once more. Tom's father shifted uneasily in his chair, adjusting his tie though it was already perfectly straight, while his mother folded her hands together as though rehearsed for a performance. Rising in tandem, they turned toward the bench, their faces composed, their eyes carefully trained to appear earnest. Yet to those who had lived beside Tom, their act was as transparent as glass.

"Your Honour," his mother began, her voice trembling just enough to appear rehearsed grief, "we are simply parents caught in unfortunate circumstance. We never wished for our son to be hurt. We never saw the signs. We believed he was safe." Her words floated across the courtroom like a frail veil, but every ear that had heard Tom's testimony recognized them for what they were: lies draped in false sympathy.

His father followed quickly, his tone heavier, attempting to add weight where his wife's words had faltered. "Thomas is our son," he declared firmly. "We did not abandon him. We did not fail him. The troubles he speaks of—these are exaggerations of a boy influenced by others. We are his rightful guardians, and he belongs under our care." His words struck the air with the finality of ownership, as though Tom were property to be reclaimed rather than a child pleading for his life.

Across the courtroom, Tom's fists clenched against his knees. He had already spoken, already looked the judge in the eye and declared the truth. He had offered bruises as proof, scars as testimony. To hear his parents repeat the same twisted story now, as though his words were nothing, sparked an anger in him that trembled at the edges of control. Yet he stayed seated, his breath sharp, knowing his time to speak again would come. Beside him, Ty's steady hand kept him from rising too soon, grounding him before fury betrayed him.

Zenji Takashi leaned forward slightly, his eyes narrowing but his body still. He had lived too long in rooms filled with lies to be shaken now. He knew this game: deny, deflect, discredit. Yet the weight of evidence on his lap and the quiet certainty in his son's poise assured him that the truth would prevail. He did not rise or interrupt, though every fibre of his being wished to shout the word "enough." Instead, he let their words hang hollow, waiting for the silence that would reveal them as empty.

Mrs. Takashi watched with quiet dismay, her hands folded calmly in her lap, her gaze locked on Tom. The boy's jaw trembled with effort, his chest rising and falling too fast. She could see the war inside him, the pull between the hurt of betrayal and the strength of love. She willed him silently to hold on, to trust that lies cannot stand when truth already has roots in the ground.

Mr. Arnett, seated near the front, shifted in his chair, his brow furrowed. He had heard these same statements before in his own office, the parents painting their son as dangerous, unstable, beyond saving. Now here in court, their script remained unchanged, a desperate play repeated before an audience that no longer believed it. He caught the judge's eye only briefly, but the look was clear: their words were not enough. Not anymore.

Among the students, whispers rippled like uneasy wind. Nico leaned closer to Jasmin, muttering that Tom's parents were only digging themselves deeper. Ella bit her lip, Sophie shook her head, and Leo's eyes burned with a quiet fury. Jeremy, wide-eyed, whispered to Mila that parents should love their kids first, not last. Their quiet voices never rose above a murmur, but their disbelief filled the silence between the parents' words, as though the children themselves served as jury.

The judge rested his chin against his folded hands, letting their plea run its course. His gaze never wavered from them, his eyes sharp, dissecting each phrase, each attempt to twist truth into pity. When their words slowed, the silence that followed was heavier than any gavel. The courtroom felt the hollowness, a performance played too many times before an audience too wise to applaud.

Tom's father pressed once more, his voice sharper, a hint of frustration leaking through. "Your Honour, our son has been manipulated. These… people"—his eyes flicked toward the Takashis—"have filled his head with stories, convinced him to turn against us. We ask only to restore him to his rightful home, where he belongs." The word "belongs" hung in the air like a chain, and Tom's shoulders stiffened as though those links were being fastened once more around his neck.

Ty turned his head slowly, his eyes piercing, his expression unflinching. He said nothing, but his gaze alone was enough to silence Tom's trembling. His presence was a shield, a reminder that chains can be broken when someone dares to stand unafraid beside you. For all the words being thrown across the courtroom, Ty's silence carried more conviction than their speech.

Mrs. Dunlop sat rigid, her lips pursed. Though she rarely revealed emotion, today her eyes betrayed her, flashing briefly with anger. She had seen too many children made to feel small by adults who ought to have protected them. To watch these parents cloak negligence as innocence stirred something fierce inside her, though her role demanded she remain silent. The same storm brewed quietly in Miss Kara and Ms. Henley, whose eyes spoke volumes that their mouths could not utter.

The judge finally leaned back, setting his pen against the desk with a soft tap. He allowed a moment of silence to stretch, the kind that demands reflection. Every person in the courtroom could feel that pause was not idle; it was the weight of a man who had heard lies before and was measuring them carefully against truth already spoken. The parents stood still, their faces drawn tight, but their words no longer carried power.

Tom's breath steadied at last. His voice had already cut through their performance in the session before, and he knew it had landed. Their repetition was only a shadow now, a desperate attempt to reclaim what they had lost. He did not need to rise, did not need to shout. The truth was already out, standing taller than their excuses. He looked at Ty, who gave him the faintest nod, and for the first time Tom realized he didn't need to fight alone.

The gavel tapped lightly, calling the room back to order. "The court has heard the plea," the judge said, his tone level but weighted. "It has also heard the testimony." No more words were needed to expose the difference between the two. Lies had been spoken, but truth had already been declared. The balance was shifting, and everyone in the room knew which side carried weight.

The parents returned to their seats, their eyes downcast, their act exhausted. Across the room, Tom sat straighter, his hand steady against the table, the shadow of fear lifting just enough to reveal the glint of hope beneath. For the first time in a long while, he felt that lies had not silenced him. Truth had. And truth was stronger.

The judge leaned forward, his spectacles catching the light as he surveyed the room. His gavel rested idle, yet his authority pressed down heavier than its wooden weight could ever manage. "We have heard the pleas of the parents," he said, his voice measured. "We have heard the testimony of those who have taken this boy into their home. But justice demands more than the testimony of guardians. I want to hear from those who have stood alongside him in the world beyond his front door." His gaze moved deliberately, sifting the crowd with the precision of a man who had lived his life weighing truth against deception. The silence thickened until his eyes landed squarely on Mr. Arnett. "Principal Arnett, you will rise."

The man shifted in his chair, adjusting his jacket before standing. His tall frame cast a sharp line across the courtroom floor, and though his expression carried respect for the setting, there was steel beneath it. "Your Honour," he began, his voice steady, "I have been the principal of this boy's school for years. I have seen children stumble, and I have seen them rise. But Tom's case has been one of the heaviest burdens to cross my desk." His words carried the weight of one who had chosen not to look away when others had, and it settled across the benches like dust long ignored.

Tom's eyes flicked toward him, searching for betrayal or doubt. Instead, he found a gaze that was earnest, steady, even protective. It unsettled him in the way kindness always did, but he did not turn away. Ty noticed and gave the smallest nod, silently encouraging Tom to listen, to trust.

Mr. Arnett folded his hands behind his back, continuing. "I will not pretend this boy came to me as an easy case. He was angry, volatile, and, at first glance, a danger to others. I had reports of fights, threats, behaviours that would have frightened most staff into throwing him out. I was close to believing it myself." His eyes cut briefly toward the parents, then back to the judge. "But what I saw was not a boy bent on destruction. What I saw was a boy carrying more than any child should ever be forced to bear."

Mrs. Dunlop shifted in her seat, nodding almost imperceptibly. Miss Kara folded her arms, her sharp eyes fixed on the parents as though daring them to contradict what was being spoken aloud. The students sat forward, breath caught in their chests. For once, the adults were saying the things they had all known but were powerless to prove.

"Your Honour," Arnett pressed, his voice gaining strength, "I have seen this before. I once took in another boy—Jarod. He was just as angry, just as broken. But he was not beyond saving. And the one who reached him was not me, nor any officer, nor even his teachers. It was Ty Takashi, eleven years old, who stood against his rage and refused to let him drown in it."

The judge raised a brow, his gaze slipping toward the boy seated calmly beside Tom. Ty did not flinch, his face calm, his hands still, as if waiting for his turn to confirm the story. Tom's breath hitched, glancing from Ty to the principal, beginning to understand that his story was not just his own—he was standing in the shadow of others who had walked the same path before him.

Mr. Clarke leaned forward now, whispering to Ms. Henley, "He's telling the Jarod story." She only nodded, her expression softening as memory flashed across her face. It was not just a story—it was a truth the staff had witnessed, proof that transformation was possible when someone dared to believe in the broken.

The parents shuffled uncomfortably, their act unraveling as the narrative shifted out of their control. Tom's mother pursed her lips, her father's jaw tightened, but they could not interrupt. The judge's eyes held them silent. The weight of testimony was now building against them, brick by brick, until their denials looked thin against the fortress of truth being constructed in that very room.

Arnett's voice dropped lower, quieter, though no less firm. "I tell you plainly, Your Honour: I see the same in Tom. A boy wounded, yes. A boy who has lashed out, yes. But a boy capable of healing, of growth, and of becoming something remarkable—if only he is given the chance. To send him back would not be justice. It would be sentencing him to despair."

Zenji's hand brushed against Mrs. Takashi's beneath the table, a silent acknowledgement of solidarity. She blinked once, steady, her chin held high, knowing that the fight was not theirs alone anymore. They had allies now—powerful voices that carried weight.

The judge tapped his pen lightly against the bench, the sound sharp in the stillness. His eyes never left Mr. Arnett. "And you are prepared," he said slowly, "to stand behind your words, should this boy falter?" The question hung heavy, testing resolve.

Without hesitation, Mr. Arnett straightened. "Yes, Your Honour. I stood behind Jarod, and I will stand behind Tom. Not as a rescuer, but as a man who refuses to abandon a child to darkness when light is within reach." His declaration rang through the chamber with a finality no parent's plea could imitate.

Tom's breath shook, his throat tightening as though the words had caught there too. He blinked furiously, but the wetness gathered anyway. To hear a man stand before a judge and claim him as worth the fight—it was more than he had expected. Ty pressed his hand briefly against Tom's arm, an anchor in the storm, and for once Tom did not pull away.

The judge leaned back, folding his hands together. His eyes swept the room again, no longer searching for actors but for truth. "Very well," he said quietly. "This court will hear new voices. We will hear those who have walked with him." His gavel tapped once, not to silence the room, but to open the door to further testimony.

And in that instant, Tom realized the tide was turning. This was no longer just a battle between him and his parents. It had become a gathering of witnesses—people who had chosen him, who would not abandon him. The court had called for voices, and they were rising.

Mr. Arnett adjusted his tie as he rose, his shoulders squared, his posture commanding more than respect. He had spoken before, but this time he spoke not as an educator or principal, but as a man carrying the weight of fatherhood. "Your Honour," he began, voice resonant across the chamber, "my name is Robert Arnett.

I stand here not only as principal of the school this boy attends, but as the legal guardian of a boy named Jarod—my adopted son." The declaration sharpened the silence at once. Heads turned, murmurs hushed, and Tom himself leaned forward, his eyes widening at the revelation. For years he had seen Mr. Arnett as the quiet authority behind a desk. Now, in this courtroom, he saw a man laying down truth like iron.

The judge's pen halted mid-note, his brows raised ever so slightly. "Adopted son," he repeated, his tone neither sceptical nor approving—simply drawing the thread. Arnett did not waver. "Yes, Your Honour. A boy once consumed by rage. A boy feared by his peers and distrusted by adults. A boy most would have written off as dangerous." His voice tightened, memories pressing through every word. "But he was not lost. He was not beyond saving. And I stand here to tell you, he is now my son, not by blood, but by choice—and choice is stronger than blood." The words struck the chamber like a bell, and for a moment even Tom forgot to breathe.

Arnett's eyes swept the court, his gaze a blade cutting through pretence. "I have seen what redemption looks like. I have seen what it takes to turn fury into discipline, chaos into peace. And I will not let anyone dismiss Tom as unsalvageable. I will not allow the same cycle of abandonment to claim him. Not while I stand here." His hand pressed firmly against the table before him, and his voice dipped low, steady as stone. "If anyone doubts me, let them stand and say so."

The challenge hung heavy, daring contradiction. The parents shifted uncomfortably in their seats, their faces stiff with indignation but their mouths frozen. None of the teachers spoke, though Mrs. Dunlop leaned subtly forward, nodding as if silently affirming his truth. The room was still, all except for the faint scratching of the judge's pen against paper, noting every word.

Arnett's tone hardened. "Your Honour, Jarod was the fiercest storm I had ever seen in a child. He tested every boundary, fought every rule, lashed out with fists that could break bone. Yet I refused to yield. And it was not me who broke through to him—it was Ty Takashi." His voice pointed toward the boy who sat straight, calm, as though waiting for that mention. "At a martial arts tournament, Jarod challenged Ty with every ounce of his fury. Ty stood his ground. He barely moved. And when the storm exhausted itself, Jarod found himself in Ty's arms, broken not by violence, but by strength tempered with mercy."

A ripple passed through the benches as the story settled, too vivid to dismiss as fable. The judge regarded Ty for a long moment, his eyes narrowing not in distrust but in assessment, as though weighing whether such a boy could truly carry the burden described. Ty did not flinch, his gaze steady, his hands folded neatly in his lap. Tom stared at him too, the story stitching itself into his understanding—proof that Ty's strength had been tested long before he arrived in his life.

"Your Honour," Arnett pressed on, "Jarod is now a young man who sits at my table, who calls me father, who no longer fears his own reflection. That transformation was no accident. It came from love, from persistence, from the refusal of those around him to abandon him. And that same chance must be given to Tom." His voice lifted, carrying across every row. "If not, then this court will be guilty not of justice, but of surrender."

The judge shifted in his chair, his lips pressed into a thin line. He tapped his gavel once, not in anger, but in pause, letting the words settle in the air. His eyes scanned the courtroom, searching not for evidence but for resonance. "Mr. Arnett," he said at last, "your testimony is compelling. But I would like corroboration. You spoke of Jarod, of change witnessed, of truths hard to face. This court must know if others can attest to what you describe." His gaze swept the rows, lingering on the benches where students sat nervously beneath adult scrutiny. His eyes landed on a boy—smaller than the rest, yet watching with intent. "Jeremy," the judge said, his tone direct, "stand."

The youngest of the group blinked, startled that the stern voice had chosen him of all people. Nine years old, with his hands folded tightly in his lap, Jeremy hesitated, then rose slowly, his knees shaking. The air shifted as whispers broke out, some disbelieving that a child could be called in such a solemn room. The judge silenced them with a sharp glance. "This court values truth, no matter whose lips carry it," he said firmly. "And sometimes, the youngest eyes see most clearly."

Jeremy swallowed hard, his face pale, his hands fidgeting as he stood in the shadow of adults. Yet when his eyes flicked toward Ty, then to Tom, he found something steadier. He remembered the times he had seen fists almost fly, the way Ty had stepped between, the way Tom had trembled afterward when he thought no one saw. He remembered the fear, yes—but also the quiet moments that proved it was not fury but hurt driving Tom's hands. And in that memory, courage rooted itself. He straightened, small but no longer shrinking.

The judge regarded him with a gentler gaze now. "Jeremy," he asked, his voice less a demand than an invitation, "you have been close to these boys. Tell this court—what have you seen?" The room hushed, every ear tilted toward the smallest voice in the chamber.

And in that fragile silence, Tom's heart thudded painfully in his chest. For the first time, it would not be an adult defending him. It would be a child, one who had no stake but truth.

Jeremy's voice came small at first, but every word carried a steadiness that belied his trembling hands. "Everything that Mr. Arnett stated," he said, his eyes fixed on the judge, "is one hundred percent truth and undeniable fact." The room, which had leaned forward expecting hesitancy, shifted back in surprise at the firmness of a nine-year-old's conviction. His words fell like stones into a still pond, rippling across rows of adults who had doubted whether a child's testimony could matter. Tom sat frozen, stunned that Jeremy had not only stood but had begun with certainty, not uncertainty.

The judge leaned back slightly in his chair, his expression narrowing to one of careful consideration. "Go on," he said, his tone not dismissive but encouraging. Jeremy nodded once, then folded his hands in front of him, his knuckles white, and spoke again. "I remember the boy Mr. Arnett spoke of. His name was Jarod. He came into school with nothing but rage in his chest and fists for his language. Every day felt like a storm walking down the hall. He wasn't safe, and everyone knew it. Kids moved out of his way. Teachers braced for fights. Nobody could stop him. Nobody—except Ty." The boy's voice cracked, but he pressed on.

The judge's gaze shifted toward Ty, who sat calm as stone, his face unreadable. Jeremy followed that gaze, then added, "It wasn't fists that stopped Jarod. It wasn't detention or punishment. It was Ty's eyes. His gaze. It was steady in a way I can't explain. When Jarod's storm came, Ty didn't fight him back. He didn't run either. He just stood there, looking at him. And somehow, that broke through when nothing else did." Murmurs stirred among the onlookers, but the judge lifted his hand, silencing them without effort.

Jeremy's words softened now, almost a plea. "Your Honour, if you don't believe me, then try it yourself. Stare into Ty's eyes. Look into his gaze the way Jarod did. Do it for just a few minutes, and then see how you feel. Because I promise you'll understand. You'll see what we've all seen—that it's not force, it's not fear. It's something else. Something that makes you stop running and start listening." His small hand lifted, pointing toward Ty—not accusing, but inviting, urging the most powerful man in the room to step into the quiet strength of an eleven-year-old.

The judge regarded Jeremy for a long breath, then turned deliberately toward Ty. "Very well," he said at last, his voice calm yet charged with curiosity. "I accept your invitation." A hush swept the room as though the air itself had frozen. Ty rose to his feet slowly, his posture neither proud nor timid, and stepped forward until he stood near the centre of the chamber. His eyes met the judge's with a steadiness so profound that even the shuffle of papers ceased. The marble walls seemed to amplify the silence, drawing every eye to the space between man and boy.

For a moment, no words passed. Ty simply looked at him, gaze unwavering, calm but not empty. The judge leaned slightly forward, his chin resting on one hand, studying the boy with the scrutiny he reserved for hardened witnesses. Yet the longer he stared, the more his stern features softened. The corners of his mouth twitched as if caught between disbelief and revelation. The boy's gaze was not defiance, not submission, but something rare—presence unbroken, a stillness that neither sought nor avoided power.

Minutes slipped by unmeasured. Murmurs tried to rise but were quickly stifled. The courtroom, so used to testimony of words, now found itself witnessing testimony without sound. Ty did not falter, not once. His breath rose and fell with rhythm, his hands resting lightly against his sides, his small frame carrying a gravity far beyond his years. The judge's pen, forgotten in his hand, slid quietly onto the desk. When at last he leaned back, exhaling, he did not hide the shift in his countenance. His eyes had lost their severity; they carried something closer to respect.

"Remarkable," the judge murmured under his breath, though the word carried far enough for the chamber to hear. He adjusted his robe, regaining his formal poise, then looked directly at Jeremy. "You are correct, young man. There is… something undeniable here." His gaze shifted back to Ty. "It is not often I encounter such steadiness—such clarity—in one so young. It cannot be taught. It simply is." The admission weighed heavier than any ruling he had yet given, and the silence that followed was no less binding than a verdict.

Jeremy sat down again, trembling with both relief and triumph. He glanced once at Tom, who stared back at him wide-eyed, disbelief flooding his features. For Tom, this was no longer just a trial—it was proof that even the smallest voices could shake the tallest pillars. And for the judge, though he said nothing more, his silence was louder than all the arguments put forth before.

"Your Honour," Mr. Arnett began, his voice steady but edged with feeling, "you have just witnessed what it is like to gaze into Ty's eyes. Now imagine that same gaze staring back at someone who is not calm, not curious, but filled with rage so fierce that fists become their only language. What do you suppose happens to a storm when it meets a wall that will not move?" He let the words hang for a moment, the weight of them pulling every eye toward Ty, who sat with his hands resting quietly on his knees. Then he turned back toward the judge. "I'll tell you what happens. It changes them. Because Ty isn't just looking at you—he's looking through you. And in Jarod's case, it was the first time anyone had ever truly seen him."

Mr. Arnett's voice deepened as he recalled the day of the martial arts tournament. "Jarod came into that ring a fireball. His fists moved like lightning, his kicks carried the anger of years. He wanted to break something, someone, anything that would remind him he was still in control. And yet, Ty barely moved. I was there. I saw it with my own eyes. He didn't meet force with force. He let Jarod throw the storm, and he deflected each strike as though it were nothing more than wind. Not mocking, not arrogant—just steady. It was the most patient resistance I have ever seen in my career as principal." The courtroom leaned forward as if the walls themselves wanted to hear.

"Blow after blow," he continued, "Jarod swung until his arms shook, but Ty never wavered. He turned each strike aside with the grace of someone far older than eleven. And when Jarod finally came at him with every ounce of fury left in him, Ty's body shifted just slightly. He used a single throw—one perfected not in violence but in discipline—and Jarod was sent flying through the air. He landed hard, not broken, but stunned. The crowd erupted. Some cheered, some gasped. But what silenced the room was what Ty did next."

Mr. Arnett's eyes found the boy again. "He didn't raise his arms in victory. He didn't gloat. He simply walked over to Jarod, crouched down beside him, and opened his arms. And in front of hundreds of people, Jarod—who had come in fists first, teeth bared—fell into them. He let the anger melt away, right there in Ty's embrace. That day, Your Honour, I learned something no law book had ever taught me. Sometimes justice is not in the strike. Sometimes it is in the stillness that follows."

The judge's gaze moved slowly from Mr. Arnett to Ty. His face betrayed nothing, yet there was a flicker in his eyes, as though he were weighing the meaning behind every word. Ty did not shift under the scrutiny. His stillness in that moment seemed almost to repeat the lesson Mr. Arnett described, as if the story and the boy's presence were one and the same. For the first time, the judge's gavel hand rested open on the desk instead of clenching the handle.

The silence in the chamber was interrupted by the sound of a door opening quietly at the back. A tall figure slipped in—Jarod himself. No announcement, no call from the bailiff, just the sound of his footsteps as he walked in and took a place along the side wall. His eyes scanned the courtroom, and for a moment, they met Ty's. The room collectively stiffened, expecting the old storm to rise again, but Jarod only inclined his head slightly, almost a bow, and remained silent.

Mr. Arnett turned toward the unexpected visitor, then looked back to the judge. "There is your evidence," he said, his voice almost breaking with conviction. "You do not need to take my word for it. Jarod is here, and his silence is proof enough. Ty did not conquer him with strength. He reached him with something stronger. And if he could change Jarod—if he could bring peace where fists once ruled—then I say to you, Your Honour, he can help Tom as well. He already has." The room was hushed, heavy with the kind of silence that comes when truth has no need for argument.

Jarod crossed his arms, leaning back against the wall. His jaw worked as if he wanted to say something, but instead, he only nodded again. It was the smallest gesture, yet in it lay more weight than any testimony. The storm that had once defined him was quiet now, held back not by force of law but by the quiet, unbreakable patience of a boy who refused to let anger win.

Jarod finally stepped forward, his presence tall, steady, and unlike the boy everyone remembered from the schoolyard. He did not rush or fumble with his words as he once had in the heat of temper. His voice, calm and even, cut through the courtroom with a gravity that surprised even those who knew him best. "What Mr. Arnett has told you," he began, his eyes fixed on the judge, "is one hundred percent true. I was there. I was the one who tried to break Ty down in that tournament. I came at him with everything I had—anger, fists, kicks, the need to crush anything that stood in my way. And he never once flinched. He didn't fight me with hate. He didn't try to hurt me. He just… stood. Every strike I threw, he turned aside. Every punch I aimed, he redirected. And when I had nothing left in me, he ended it with a single throw that left me on the floor, not broken, but humbled."

His hands moved subtly as he spoke, recalling the final technique. "He didn't slam me down like I deserved. He controlled it—he controlled me—so that when I landed, I had nothing left but the truth staring me in the face. I could see in his eyes that he could have done worse, much worse, but he chose not to. That was the first time in my life I realised strength wasn't in fists or fury. It was in knowing when not to use them. And Ty… he knew." Jarod's voice softened as though he were reliving the moment, and he looked toward Ty, who met his gaze without blinking.

The courtroom was silent. Even the shuffle of papers had stilled, as if the clerks and stenographers had forgotten their duties in the face of something greater. Jarod lifted his chin slightly. "There's an online video of that tournament," he continued, speaking with a strange mix of humility and pride. "Anyone can see it. It shows everything—my rage, his patience, the throw, and the way I fell into his arms afterwards. People cheered, but I knew it wasn't about winning. Ty didn't beat me. He saved me. And I'll never forget that."

He paused then, scanning the room as though challenging anyone to deny it. "Your Honour, I was the storm. I was the boy no one could reach, the one everyone thought was lost. But Ty reached me. Not by fighting back with hate, not by crushing me, but by showing me what real control looks like. What real love looks like." The word slipped from his lips without hesitation, and the judge's brow lifted faintly, as though surprised to hear it from a boy once defined by violence.

"I'm here now because I won't let Tom be lost the way I nearly was," Jarod declared, his tone tightening with resolve. "If Ty could change me—and believe me, I was worse than Tom ever was—then Ty and his family can help Tom too. I've seen it already. Tom has already started to change. I saw it in his eyes when Ty stood in front of him. I know that look. It's the same one I had when I realised I couldn't fight him anymore. That's not defeat. That's relief."

A ripple passed through the courtroom—teachers shifting in their seats, parents looking at one another uneasily, the judge leaning back as though absorbing a weight that grew heavier with every word. Jarod continued, his voice lowering but never faltering. "You can watch that video ten times or a hundred. It won't change the truth. Ty isn't just a boy. He's something else entirely. And if you give Tom a chance to stay with him and the Takashi family, I swear to you, you'll never regret it. Because if Ty can carry someone like me back from the edge, then Tom still has every chance in the world."

The last words lingered as Jarod stepped back, his head lowered slightly, as though the memory itself was both a wound and a gift. No one spoke, no one dared, because in that moment the courtroom had seen the proof not only in his testimony but in the boy he had become. He was no longer the storm. He was the calm after it—and Ty was the reason why.

The judge leaned forward in his seat, fingers steepled, his eyes not clouded with doubt but sharpened with interest. "Show me this video," he said at last, his voice carrying the weight of both curiosity and duty. There was no scepticism in his tone, no sneer that questioned Jarod's truth. Instead, it was the request of a man who wanted to see with his own eyes the moment that words could only hint at. The bailiff wheeled in a monitor, the kind usually reserved for cold exhibits—crime-scene photographs, autopsy reports, or signed affidavits—but today it carried something else entirely: proof of redemption. Jarod stood taller, though his hands betrayed the faintest tremor as he asked Ty and Tom to come forward with him. Together, the three boys faced the screen as the courtroom lights dimmed.

The video began in silence, showing the wide floor of the martial arts tournament, the polished wood reflecting harsh lights above. A younger Jarod, fierce-eyed and taut with fury, stormed into the ring. Gasps rose softly from the rows of benches as the audience saw what he had been: raw rage wrapped in a boy's body, fists clenched like hammers meant to break. The judge's gaze never wavered, fixed on the screen as Ty appeared opposite, calm even then, his stance still, his movements economical. Blow after blow came in the recording—Jarod's fury unleashed without mercy—yet Ty shifted, turned, and guided each strike harmlessly away.

Whispers spread in the courtroom as the video rolled. Teachers leaned forward, students in the gallery held their breath, and even hardened officials stared with the disbelief of those who had never seen patience wielded as a weapon. "Look at his feet," Mr. Clarke murmured softly, forgetting himself for a moment. "He doesn't move unless he has to." The recording reached the pivotal moment—Jarod lunging wild, desperate, his body a storm of fists—when Ty, with one precise motion, used his opponent's momentum to send him arcing through the air. For a frozen heartbeat, the room saw Jarod suspended, weightless, before gravity returned him gently to the floor.

The sound of impact echoed from the monitor, not the bone-breaking thud expected, but a controlled fall, guided by Ty's skill. The judge's lips pressed together, and his brow shifted, not with doubt but with an emotion few in the room could place. It was something close to respect. Yet the true climax was not the throw. The video showed Jarod, sprawled and shaking, broken not by pain but by the collapse of rage itself. He lifted his head, eyes wide and wet, and Ty—small, calm, impossibly steady—knelt beside him. There was no gloat, no sneer of victory. Only arms opening, wrapping around the fallen boy. It was that embrace, slow and unwavering, that silenced the tournament hall then, and now it silenced the courtroom.

When the screen froze on the image of Jarod weeping into Ty's chest, the judge lifted his gaze to the boy himself. Jarod stood rigid, his chest rising and falling with the weight of memory. "That was the moment," he said, his voice catching but not breaking. "The moment I stopped being a storm. Not because I lost. But because he wouldn't let me stay lost." His words echoed through the courtroom, sharper than the gavel, piercing through every defence, every doubt. He turned to Tom beside him, resting a hand lightly on his shoulder. "And I'm telling you now, he can do the same for you. Because he already has."

Tom shifted, his face pale yet softened by something unspoken. The judge leaned back in his chair, his eyes darting from Jarod to Ty to Tom, and then finally to Zenji Takashi seated nearby. The silence that followed was unlike any before. It was not heavy with dread or tension, but with awe. Even Mrs. Dunlop, whose usual caution had once been armour, wiped a tear discreetly from the corner of her eye. "It's not about fighting," Jarod added, his voice stronger now. "It's about surrender. That day I surrendered to someone who cared more about me than I cared about myself. And I'll never forget it."

The judge folded his hands once more, his voice measured, almost reverent. "The court has seen enough," he said, though his tone held more than procedure—it held the kind of gravity that comes when justice steps beyond law into truth. The screen was turned off, but the image lingered in every mind, carved deeper than ink or testimony. The boy who once had fists for a language had surrendered, not in shame, but in the arms of another child who refused to let him fall. It was not victory. It was salvation.

And as the lights rose again, no one moved, because the story had been told not in words alone, but in sight, in sound, in the undeniable proof of what love, patience, and unshaken courage could do when wielded by a boy named Ty.

Jarod stepped away from the monitor slowly, his breath shallow as though he had once again fought the battle of that day. His eyes, however, no longer carried the weight of anger—they held calm, the kind that only comes from knowing the storm has truly passed. He turned and faced Tom directly. For a long moment neither boy moved, the tension stretched like glass ready to shatter. Then Jarod crossed the short distance and pulled Tom into his arms. It was not a casual hug nor a staged gesture for the courtroom. It was firm, steady, and full-bodied, the kind of embrace that declared family even where no blood bound them. Tom stiffened at first, his instincts caught between fight and flight, but then his shoulders dropped. Slowly, hesitantly, his own arms rose and gripped Jarod in return. The courtroom exhaled together, a sigh of release that none had expected.

The judge leaned forward, his sharp eyes softening as he watched the two boys. For a man used to decades of testimony, deceit, and carefully scripted words, there was nothing performative about this moment. A faint look of peace crossed his face, the sort of expression that slips through when the heart is moved despite itself. He tapped one finger against the desk, a silent rhythm that betrayed thought, and then spoke with deliberate clarity. "This," he said, his voice quiet yet commanding, "is the evidence that cannot be placed into files or exhibits. This is the proof of what we are truly deciding." The courtroom stilled, even the faint scribbling of reporters' pens paused as though to mark the weight of his words.

Mr. Arnett, standing respectfully to one side, gave a single nod, his voice steady when he finally added, "Your Honour, I told you Ty could do what no adult could. But I must also tell you—Jarod stands here today not just because of Ty's discipline, but because Ty's compassion never wavered. Tom is walking the same path now. If Ty reached Jarod, then Tom too can be reached. No child is beyond repair if love holds fast." His eyes sought Tom's as he spoke, giving the boy not just words but belief, a hand offered across the gulf of doubt.

Tom's jaw slackened in disbelief. He had expected judgement, condemnation, perhaps even punishment—but not this. Not recognition from the very men who had the power to shape his fate. His chest rose and fell as though he had forgotten to breathe until that moment.

His eyes darted from Mr. Arnett to the judge, and then to Jarod still holding his shoulder firmly like an anchor. The weight of it all pressed against him, not as a chain but as a release. For the first time, he was not defined by fear or rage. He was seen, acknowledged, and—unthinkably—declared worthy of another chance.

The judge leaned back in his chair, his gavel untouched. "What I see here," he continued, his gaze sweeping the courtroom, "is the reason we do not close the door on children. If this boy beside Tom could be turned from wrath to respect, then it is our duty to see that Tom is not cast aside either. The law must protect, yes—but it must also recognise when protection means giving a child the chance to stand, not fall." His words struck like a bell, and their resonance filled every corner of the room.

Tom blinked rapidly, his throat tightening with the weight of feelings he had never allowed himself to show. His jaw trembled, and when he spoke his voice cracked, though the words were barely a whisper. "You… you really think I can change?" The question was not to Ty, not to Jarod, but to the world itself, as though daring it to finally answer him honestly. Ty, seated beside him, gave the smallest nod, his hand finding Tom's shoulder in quiet confirmation. He did not need to say the words; Tom already knew them.

Zenji Takashi sat straighter, his calm presence lending the moment its final weight. He did not interrupt nor embellish, for the scene itself was testimony enough. Mrs. Takashi wiped a tear from her eye, her hand tightening around her son's as though to remind him of the depth of their shared fight. Nico and Jasmin, from their seats behind, exchanged glances of quiet awe; even they, children though they were, understood the magnitude of what had just unfolded. Sophie leaned gently against Ella, whispering, "He's not alone anymore."

The gavel did not strike, but the decision seemed already to bloom in the air. The courtroom, once a stage for conflict, had become a space of undeniable truth. The hug between Jarod and Tom remained its centrepiece, a beacon no one could ignore. And though the verdict had yet to be declared, Tom felt for the first time in his life that the answer would not be abandonment.

The lesson had been made plain, not by law or argument, but by embrace. A child redeemed had extended his hand to another, and the world had borne witness. The judge's final glance at Tom carried no cruelty, only the simple recognition that the boy's life had just shifted. Tom sat in stunned silence, his jaw still slack, but behind his wide eyes burned something long forgotten—hope.

Mr. Arnett stood again, his shoulders square, his hands folded at his waist as though he carried not only authority but obligation. His voice, though not loud, commanded the silence with a firmness honed over years of guiding difficult children. "Your Honour," he said, his words deliberate, "I know this boy is not my student alone.

He is my responsibility, both as a principal and as a man who has seen far too many children slip through cracks that never should have existed. I will not allow Tom to become another name added to that list. Healing is not a straight path, but it is a path nonetheless. And if the boy chooses to walk it, then I swear before this court that I will walk it with him. I pledge myself as his ally. I will guide him, I will correct him when needed, and I will remind him of the strength he has already proven in choosing not to break." The stillness of the courtroom seemed to bend toward him, every figure listening, every breath drawn in anticipation of what would follow.

The judge leaned back slightly in his chair, his eyes narrowing, not in suspicion but in concentration. Mr. Arnett pressed on, his tone deepening with conviction. "If Tom falters, and he may, I will remind him of what he already is: more than what was done to him, more than the pain that has marked his childhood, more than the fear he has been forced to carry. He deserves the chance to prove himself, to rebuild, to discover the boy he was meant to be. I will not permit him to be discarded, not while I hold this position and not while I have breath left to speak." A faint tremor passed through Tom at those words, his jaw tightening, his eyes fixed on the man who, despite being bound by no blood, was vowing a loyalty stronger than kin.

Then Mr. Arnett shifted, not only in posture but in purpose, his words moving from pledge to proof. "Your Honour," he continued, "I stand not only on my word but on precedent. Some years ago, I took guardianship of a boy named Jarod. He was consumed by anger, violent in ways that frightened his peers and hardened the hearts of teachers around him. For many, he seemed irredeemable. But I saw in him a child worth saving. It was Ty who cracked through that wall first, Ty who disarmed him not only in combat but in spirit. But it was also an anger management program, run under supervision with school integrated, that finally steadied him. Jarod is there now, in that program, rebuilding himself day by day, and I stand as witness to his progress."

Jeremy, seated in the front row, nodded softly, his voice rising with permission from the judge. "It's true," he said. "Jarod's not gone. He's just away from school right now because of the program. He still learns, still grows. He's calmer, different. And he knows it's helping him." The boy's voice was quiet, but it struck through the room with the simplicity of truth. Tom's head turned sharply at the mention of Jarod, his eyes widening with a recognition of the name and the story already told of fists, defiance, and Ty's calm strength breaking through.

Mr. Arnett's words gathered strength again. "Jarod himself has declared this program the best thing that has ever happened to him. He is learning not only discipline but the art of controlling his fire instead of being consumed by it. He asked me to say this before the court, not for his sake but for Tom's: he believes Tom belongs there too. He believes Tom will not only benefit but flourish if given that chance. And if Tom does not wish to continue after trying it, that is his right. He may choose. But I will offer him that door, and I will walk through it with him." His hand pressed against the rail of the witness stand, his eyes locking with the judge's, clear and unwavering.

The judge leaned forward, his chin resting on one hand, and asked, "And you believe this will work for him? That he can face what is inside without collapsing beneath it?" His tone carried both skepticism and curiosity, the balance of law and compassion. Mr. Arnett inclined his head, unshaken. "I do not believe, Your Honour," he answered. "I know. Because I have already seen it once. Jarod was as far gone as any child I had ever met. If Ty and that program could bring him back, then Tom, who has already begun to show change, will not be lost."

Ty lifted his head at that, his voice steady and plain. "Your Honour, I'll go with him. If Tom goes into the program, then I will be there whenever he needs me. I won't let him face it alone." The words, unasked but freely given, slipped into the silence like iron dropped into water, pulling every heart deeper. Tom's eyes stung, and though he bit down on the inside of his cheek to stop the tremble, a single tear escaped. He wiped it away quickly, but the room had already seen.

Mrs. Takashi, seated at Zenji's side, touched her husband's arm, her voice gentle yet steady as she added, "We do not fear hard work, Your Honour. If it is discipline and love that Tom requires, he has both in our home. But what Mr. Arnett offers is another piece, one that reaches him in ways even family cannot. We accept it. And we will stand beside him while he tries." The words carried no embellishment, only truth.

The courtroom held its breath as Mr. Arnett finished. "Your Honour, I am principal by profession, but I am father by choice. And I choose to stand as ally for this boy, as I did for Jarod. Tom deserves no less." The silence afterward was not emptiness but respect, the kind that falls when a vow has been spoken that no one doubts will be kept. Tom sat rigid in his chair, but his wide eyes revealed the storm breaking into something else entirely: the fragile, new-born recognition that he was not fighting alone.

The gavel tapped once, not in anger but in precision, as the judge straightened in his seat. His eyes, sharp beneath heavy brows, fixed on Tom with the weight of a man who had decided to strip the room down to its bones. "This is no longer about sympathy," he said, each syllable carrying the ring of iron. "This is about emancipation. Tom, do you understand what that means? Independence is not merely freedom from pain—it is responsibility in every form. Housing. Guardianship. Finances. A name under the law. It is not simply choosing a new home; it is severing ties."

Tom did not flinch beneath the stare. His fists remained folded tight in his lap, but his voice cut clean into the silence. "Yes, Your Honour," he said. "I understand." His words, plain and unshaken, felt heavier than his thirteen years. Behind him, Ty sat straighter, his hand pressing once on Tom's arm in steady confirmation.

The judge leaned back, eyes narrowing further. "You say you understand. But tell me, what does it mean to you to be independent? What would you accept as consequence if this court grants your request?" Tom drew in a breath, the kind that rattled his chest before firming into resolve.

"It means I will not belong to people who allowed me to be hurt," he answered. "It means I will take the family that has already stood for me as my own. I'll learn what I must, do what I must, to stay safe and to grow. It means I won't be their son anymore—because they stopped being my parents long ago." His voice cracked once, not from weakness but from raw truth, and the court absorbed it like stone drinking rain.

Mrs. Dunlop stirred in her seat, her lips pursed in unease, but she did not interrupt. It was Zenji who shifted slightly forward, his calm presence filling the moment without words. Mrs. Takashi placed her hand softly atop her husband's, her eyes never leaving Tom's face, as though to steady him across the space that law still imposed between them.

The judge tapped his pen against the bench, the sound clicking like a clock in the charged silence. "You are aware," he continued, "that emancipation binds you to the choices you declare here. If granted, you will have no legal claim to support from your parents. Your protection, your guidance, your path, will fall entirely to those you name instead. Do you grasp the gravity of this?" Tom's shoulders squared, his voice dropping into something older than his years. "I do. And I want it."

Jeremy, perched anxiously at the edge of his chair, whispered low enough that only Leo beside him could hear. "He sounds older than all of us right now." Leo gave the smallest nod, his usual smirk erased, his eyes heavy with respect. Even Alex, leaning forward with elbows on his knees, seemed to carry the weight of what was unfolding.

The judge's gaze swept across the courtroom, lingering on Ty before returning to Tom. "And you would choose them?" he asked, his tone testing, pressing for hesitation. Tom lifted his chin. "I choose them," he said. His eyes flicked toward Ty, then Zenji, then Mrs. Takashi, and at last back to the bench. "I choose the people who stood when no one else did." His words carved into the stillness with finality.

Mr. Clarke, shifting awkwardly in his chair, muttered, "That boy knows exactly what he's saying." Miss Kara, arms folded tight, whispered back, "He knows more than half the adults in this room." Even the judge caught their murmurs, but he allowed them to pass, his focus never breaking from Tom's unflinching face.

Mr. Arnett, his voice softer now than before, added from his place at the stand, "Your Honour, I think the boy has already shown us that he comprehends every word. His resolve is not fantasy—it's survival. I stand by him."

The judge nodded once, the pen stilled in his hand. "Then let it be recorded," he said firmly, "that Thomas has spoken with clarity of understanding regarding the meaning of emancipation, and that his request will be weighed as more than the wish of a frightened child. It will be weighed as the declaration of one seeking rightful freedom." The gavel struck again, a single echo that trembled in the air, final yet not conclusive.

Ty leaned close enough that only Tom could hear. "You didn't just answer him," he murmured. "You told the truth, and truth holds." Tom's throat tightened, but for once he did not feel it as weakness. It felt like strength.

Zenji rose with the slow confidence of a man who had no need to embellish his words with theatrics. A thick folder rested in his hands, its weight a testament to months of preparation. The judge motioned for him to approach, and the shuffle of paper echoed in the room as he laid the file gently upon the bench. "Your Honour," Zenji began evenly, his voice steady, "we submit into record the documentation of our intent and ability to assume full guardianship of Thomas. What I speak now is not sentiment, but law."

The judge adjusted his glasses and leaned forward. His fingers brushed across the first stack of records, pausing as he skimmed the bold letters stamped in official seal. "Financial statements," Zenji continued, gesturing with measured hand, "detailing income stability, accounts in order, and a household that has been verified for readiness. Home inspections, conducted without warning, all passed and signed by independent assessors. And sworn affidavits from community leaders, teachers, and physicians, attesting to the environment my wife and I maintain." His voice did not waver; every syllable was clipped in its precision.

Mrs. Takashi sat composed at the table, her eyes not on the documents but on Tom, her gaze steady, motherly, immovable. She had already made her declaration in the quiet language of touch and tenderness. This was Zenji's realm: the hard lines of law, the armour of official records, the voice of accountability. Together they formed the balance Tom had never known— love on one side, law on the other, both unyielding.

The judge flipped a page and frowned lightly, though not with disapproval. "Mr. Takashi, I see here a statement of guardianship readiness signed by your own principal of employment." Zenji bowed his head slightly. "Yes, Your Honour. The RCMP has reviewed and approved this arrangement. They are aware of my son Ty's role in this matter as well, and the agency has no objections. Their statement affirms that I am in good standing to serve as both provider and protector under the law."

A stir rippled through the teachers seated along the wall. Miss Kara whispered to Mrs. Dunlop, "That's more preparation than most parents could ever dream of." Mrs. Dunlop pressed her lips together, unready to concede but unwilling to speak further against it. Mr. Clarke, his eyes wide behind his glasses, muttered just loudly enough for Nico to overhear, "It's airtight." Nico grinned faintly, tugging at Ty's sleeve, as if to say your family has this.

The judge lifted the affidavits next, glancing at the signatures lined at the bottom. "Testimonies from fellow educators," he read aloud, "and from community representatives who have interacted with Thomas in recent weeks." His gaze flicked briefly toward Tom, then back to the papers. "Each affirms the boy's improvement under your care, each attests that the environment is not only stable but nurturing." He set the papers aside carefully, almost reverently, as though they deserved more than a cursory glance.

Tom sat rigid in his chair, his hands balled into nervous fists on his knees. Ty leaned in and whispered without turning his head, "This is proof, not just promise. Watch." Tom's throat tightened, but he let his fists loosen, the words grounding him like stone beneath his feet.

Zenji spoke once more. "Your Honour, this is not merely about preventing harm. This is about giving Thomas a chance to thrive. My wife and I have sworn ourselves to raise him not as a case, nor as an obligation, but as our son. The paperwork before you is not a shield of emotion. It is the legal recognition of what is already true."

The judge tapped the file with his pen, his expression unreadable but focused. "The court acknowledges the submission of guardianship evidence. It will weigh heavily in the decision." His eyes lifted toward Zenji, lingering there as though testing his resolve. "You understand, Mr. Takashi, that this obligates you fully—financially, legally, and morally. Should emancipation be granted, the responsibility becomes yours without exception."

Zenji inclined his head, calm and absolute. "I accept it without hesitation." His words landed like stone upon the floor, leaving no room for doubt. Mrs. Takashi reached across and folded her hand gently over his, adding silently her agreement, her vow.

The courtroom held its breath, the weight of law and love fused at last upon the bench. And Tom, for the first time, let himself believe that this was not just a dream whispered in dark corners—it was becoming reality, carved into record.

The bailiff called the parents back to the stand. Their footsteps across the wooden floor echoed sharper than they likely intended, but their rigid posture betrayed the nerves they tried to disguise. They raised their right hands, swearing once more to speak nothing but truth, yet their eyes flickered nervously as they sat down. The judge fixed them with a level stare, folding his hands atop the bench. "Mr. and Mrs. Caldwell," he began, his voice even but edged with steel, "this is no longer about appearances. You are under oath. Explain to this court why you believe custody of your son should remain in your hands."

Mrs. Caldwell spoke first, her voice high and strained. "He is our child," she insisted. "Whatever mistakes were made in the past, they were never intentional. Families argue, Your Honour, families lose their tempers. But Thomas belongs with us. Blood should count for something." Her hand gripped the armrest of the chair as though anchoring herself, her knuckles paling under the pressure.

The judge listened without interruption, then shifted his gaze to the father. Mr. Caldwell cleared his throat, straightened his tie, and leaned forward. "Your Honour," he said, "it's easy to paint us as villains when every story told here has been against us. But Thomas has a home. He has a roof, meals, a bed. He is not neglected. We may not be perfect, but no parent is. Returning him to us is the rightful course of action."

Across the aisle, Tom's hands clenched at the words, his jaw tight. Ty reached over quietly, brushing his sleeve against Tom's, a silent reminder that he was not alone. Tom exhaled, his body trembling, but he stayed seated, letting the weight of the judge's questions carry instead of erupting in anger.

The judge leaned back, his eyes narrowing as he shuffled the papers Zenji had submitted earlier. "You claim to provide stability," he said, "yet medical records show repeated injuries without sufficient explanation. Police reports cite disturbances at your residence. Testimonies describe fear in your son's eyes, fear that no one has yet disproved." He set the papers down with deliberate care. "How do you reconcile these contradictions?"

Mrs. Caldwell shifted in her chair, her eyes darting toward her husband before returning to the judge. "Children fall, children bruise," she said quickly. "They fight with others, they get hurt at school. It doesn't always mean something sinister happened at home." Her tone sharpened as she spoke, but the tremor beneath it betrayed her.

Mr. Caldwell leaned in again, his voice louder now. "These so-called contradictions are misunderstandings. People misinterpret. They see discipline and call it abuse. We tried to correct Thomas when he lashed out, when he brought shame to the family. Isn't that what parents are supposed to do—guide their child?"

A murmur rippled through the courtroom at his words. Mr. Clarke adjusted his glasses, shaking his head slightly. Miss Kara pressed her lips tightly together, a frown carving lines into her brow. Nico whispered to Jasmin, "He just admitted it without even realising." Jasmin nodded grimly, her eyes fixed on Tom, who was staring at the floor.

The judge's voice cut through the murmurs. "Discipline is one thing," he said, his tone now heavy with authority. "But repeated physical marks, emotional terror, and neglect to protect a child from an abusive relative—those are not discipline. Those are failures of duty." He pointed his pen toward them, the gesture sharp as a blade. "And duty, above all, defines parenthood under the law."

Mrs. Takashi, seated beside Zenji, placed a gentle hand over her husband's. Her face was calm, but her eyes were unflinching as they remained fixed on the parents. Zenji himself said nothing, but his silence was weighted, an unspoken reminder that evidence already stood against them like immovable stone.

The father shifted uncomfortably. His tie suddenly seemed too tight, his collar suffocating. He tried again. "Your Honour, we did not know what Thomas went through with his uncle. We didn't see—"

But the judge interrupted, his voice striking the air like a hammer. "You lived under the same roof. You shared the same table. And yet you expect this court to believe you never saw what others clearly recognised? Ignorance is not innocence. A parent who turns away is as complicit as the one who strikes."

Tom's breath hitched, his head lifting for the first time since the questioning began. He stared at the judge with wide eyes, relief mingled with the ache of truth finally named aloud. His parents avoided his gaze, their eyes downcast, their arguments collapsing beneath the scrutiny.

Mr. Arnett stood briefly, asking permission to address the court. "Your Honour," he said with calm firmness, "I have seen this boy in my school for years. The contradictions you hear now are the same ones we've endured as staff. Excuses. Shifting blame. Never accountability." He gestured toward Tom, then toward Ty. "What he has found with the Takashis is not luxury—it is safety. That, above all, is what his parents failed to give him."

The judge nodded once, dismissing Arnett back to his seat. He turned again to the parents. "This court cannot rely on sentiment or claims of ownership. We rely on truth, evidence, and the welfare of the child. And in truth, your words falter."

Mrs. Caldwell's lips parted as though to protest, but no sound came. Mr. Caldwell pressed his palms together, whispering something inaudible under his breath, a plea perhaps, but not to anyone in that room. Their armour had cracked.

Ty squeezed Tom's hand briefly, leaning close enough for only him to hear. "The truth is stronger now," he whispered. Tom swallowed hard and nodded, his eyes wet but burning with newfound resolve.

The judge leaned forward, speaking slowly, each word measured. "This court will weigh all testimony and all evidence. But you, Mr. and Mrs. Caldwell, have given me nothing today that convinces me your home was safe, or that it could ever be safe again."

Silence followed, heavy as stone, every heart in the courtroom hearing what those words implied. For Tom, the balance had shifted. And for his parents, the ground beneath them had begun to crumble.

The gavel struck once more, and the judge announced a short recess. His tone carried no warmth, only the steady cadence of procedure, and yet the sound reverberated through Tom like a blow. The bailiff declared the court in recess, and the quiet shuffle of chairs filled the room as clerks gathered papers, voices low but constant, a hushed storm of whispers and movement. The machinery of the law had turned away from testimony, now grinding in its hidden gears, beyond reach of children or parents alike.

Tom sat down hard on the bench beside Ty, his hands clenched tight around his knees. He stared at the polished wooden floor, eyes fixed but unfocused, as though trying to read the future in its grain. Ty leaned close, brushing his arm lightly against Tom's, the same small gesture he had used in darker moments before. "Breathe," Ty murmured, not commanding but steadying. Tom tried, his chest shuddering as the air rattled against the knot in his throat.

Zenji placed a hand on his son's shoulder, his presence calm but immovable. "This is the hardest part," he said softly, his deep voice carrying like stone dropped into still water. "Now it leaves words and becomes judgment." Mrs. Takashi sat on Tom's other side, her fingers lightly resting over his wrist, not gripping but anchoring, a tether of quiet affection. Between them, the boy sat framed by strength and warmth, but still trembling.

At the back of the courtroom, Nico, Jasmin, Sophie, and Ella huddled together, their eyes following Tom without break. "He looks like he can't breathe," Ella whispered, her voice tight with sympathy. Nico shook his head. "He's not alone," he said firmly, though his hands fidgeted at his sides, betraying his own unease. Leo leaned against the rail, arms folded, his gaze locked steady on Tom as though willing him to remember that strength had already taken root within him.

Jeremy, smaller than the rest, stood a step away, watching with quiet eyes. He did not speak, for once, but the stillness of his presence pressed just as strongly as the words he had offered in court. He had seen too many children left behind by careless adults, and in Tom he saw the edge of that cliff again. But this time, the boy had hands holding him back from the drop. Jeremy's eyes shifted briefly to the judge's empty chair, then back to Ty, as though knowing instinctively that the outcome hinged less on the law than on the bond already displayed.

The parents sat across the aisle, hushed in conversation with their lawyer. Mrs. Caldwell gestured furiously with her hands, her lips tight with frustration, while Mr. Caldwell pressed his palms flat against the table, his jaw locked as though he were holding his own temper in place. They whispered, but the tension was visible even from across the room. The façade they had worn earlier had begun to fray, and even their lawyer's nods could not smooth the jagged edge of panic.

Clerks moved briskly between desks, delivering files to the judge's chambers. Each shuffle of paper, each soft click of a door carried the weight of the unknown. For Tom, the minutes stretched like hours, each tick of the clock another reminder that his future now rested in the hands of people he did not know, people who had never sat at his table, who had never seen his fists clench at the sound of a slammed door, who had never watched him shiver awake from nightmares.

# THE SMILE THAT BROKE

Ty leaned in again, his voice low enough only Tom could hear. "You already spoke the truth," he said. "You already stood tall. They can't take that from you." Tom swallowed hard, his throat dry, and whispered back, "What if they send me back?" His voice cracked on the final word, the fear uncoiled at last. Ty shook his head, unyielding. "Then I will stand with you there too. But they won't. They saw it. Everyone saw it."

Zenji added gently, "The truth is heavy, Tom, but it always finds balance. Judges know that. The weight is already tilting, not against you but for you." His eyes, dark and calm, met Tom's, and for a moment Tom allowed himself to breathe. Mrs. Takashi reached across and set her hand softly against Tom's cheek, a mother's gesture so natural it broke something inside him. He blinked rapidly, holding the tears at bay, but he did not pull away.

Across the bench, Mr. Clarke leaned closer to Mr. Arnett. "He's stronger than they know," Clarke said, gesturing toward Tom. Arnett nodded gravely. "He's stronger because he finally has a place to stand." The principal's eyes moved to Ty then, recognising again what he had told the judge: that this child beside Tom was not ordinary, but a bridge. And bridges do not crumble when the storm passes over them—they hold.

The bailiff announced that the court would reconvene shortly. The sound jolted Tom upright, his breath catching again. "It's almost time," he whispered, his voice small. Ty clasped his hand firmly, gripping once before letting go. "Good," Ty said. "Then they'll hear it one more time—that you belong."

As the minutes drained, the courtroom began to fill again with murmurs, every voice a ripple across a surface Tom could no longer control. He sat straighter, though his legs bounced slightly against the bench. Ty's calm presence steadied him again, as though the boy's stillness could be borrowed. The air grew thick, every shuffle of feet magnified, every cough slicing through the silence.

At last, the judge's door opened, and the clerks returned to their places. Papers were carried back to the desk, stacked neatly, waiting for his hand. The parents sat up straighter, their lawyer whispering urgent words they nodded at without hearing. Zenji exhaled once, as though steadying himself for the blow of the gavel. Ty squeezed Tom's hand again, harder this time, a reminder that whatever came next, it would not be endured alone.

The judge entered, his robe trailing slightly, his face unreadable as he reclaimed the bench. "Court will reconvene," the bailiff declared, and all rose to their feet. Tom stood too, his knees weak but his head held high, Ty at his side, Zenji and Mrs. Takashi flanking him. Whatever the machinery of law had ground toward in those hidden minutes, Tom knew one thing with certainty: he was not standing alone anymore.

The gavel struck once. The waiting was over.

The judge's return to the bench silenced the room before his gavel even struck. His robe flowed behind him as he sat, his eyes scanning the chamber with a weight that made every person stiffen. The sound of wood on wood rang out once, a sound sharp and final, commanding attention without need of repetition. "Be seated," he said, his voice measured, carrying both the burden and authority of the moment. The shuffle of bodies was subdued, everyone aware that the air now carried the scent of finality.

Tom sat rigid on the bench, Ty at his side, his hand resting lightly over Tom's arm. Zenji and Mrs. Takashi leaned in subtly, steadying presences on either side of the boy, their eyes locked forward as though bracing against a storm. Tom's parents sat across the aisle, their posture unnaturally upright, their lawyer whispering urgent counsel they barely seemed to hear. The students gathered at the back leaned forward in unison, every face taut with anticipation, as though they could will the words into existence.

The judge opened a file, turning a page slowly, his eyes scanning the lines though the decision had already been made. He cleared his throat once and began. "After careful review of the testimony, the evidence, and the recommendations presented, this court has reached its conclusion." His voice echoed through the courtroom, and Tom's breath caught, his knuckles white where he gripped the bench. Ty's fingers squeezed lightly, anchoring him.

"Thomas Caldwell," the judge continued, deliberately using the name recorded in the files, "is hereby granted emancipation from his parents." The words hung in the air, and though they were plain, their meaning struck like lightning. Tom's parents stiffened, their lawyer lowering his head. Tom blinked rapidly, his lips parting but no sound escaping. Ty smiled faintly, though his eyes never left the judge, as though refusing to release focus until every word was finished.

"This emancipation," the judge pressed on, "is not granted lightly, nor is it offered as reprieve from discipline or responsibility. It is granted on the grounds of failure of protection by the guardians assigned at birth. The evidence of abuse, neglect, and deliberate silence from the parents cannot be ignored." His tone hardened, and for a moment even the parents seemed to shrink under his gaze. "The law does not permit a child to be left in harm when alternatives exist."

Zenji straightened in his seat, his hand tightening briefly around Mrs. Takashi's. The judge glanced at them both before continuing. "Guardianship and custody are hereby transferred to Mr. Zenji Takashi and Mrs. Hanae Takashi, who have demonstrated not only willingness, but proven ability to provide the minor with care, stability, and safety. This custody shall be recognised under full authority of this court, effective immediately." A murmur swept the chamber, quickly hushed by the bailiff's sharp glance.

Mrs. Takashi's hand flew to her mouth, her eyes shining as she stifled a sob of relief. Zenji bowed his head slightly, a gesture of respect more than victory, his face calm though his shoulders eased visibly. Ty's chest swelled with quiet pride, though he kept his composure for Tom's sake. And Tom—he simply sat frozen, as though the words could not be real, his mind refusing to let them settle fully into place.

The judge paused, shuffling a page, and added, "A petition has also been filed for a legal name change, should the ward desire it." His eyes moved to Tom, steady and unblinking. "Do you, Thomas Caldwell, wish to legally change your name?" The room fell into such silence that even the faint hum of the lights above could be heard. Tom looked to Ty, then to Zenji and Mrs. Takashi, his lips trembling. Finally, he raised his head and answered clearly: "Yes, Your Honour. I want to be Tom Takashi."

The judge nodded once, as though expecting no other answer. "Then let it be entered into the record. Effective today, the minor shall bear the legal name Tom Shiro Takashi." He let the words linger, then struck the gavel firmly. "This court recognises the change of guardianship, name, and identity. So ordered." The strike of wood echoed once more, each beat finalising a chapter and opening another.

The parents sat stunned, their mouths parting as though to object, but no sound came. Their lawyer placed a restraining hand on their arms, shaking his head slowly. There was nothing left to argue, nothing left to fight. The law had spoken, and more than law, truth itself had found its home.

In the gallery, Nico whispered, "He's one of them now," and Jasmin clutched his hand tightly. Sophie wiped her eyes openly, not ashamed of her tears, while Ella leaned against Leo, who kept his jaw set, eyes still locked forward as though daring anyone to question what had just been secured. Jeremy exhaled softly, his lips forming a single word under his breath: "Finally."

Tom's shoulders sagged as though the weight of years had slid from him in a single instant. He turned to Ty, his mouth moving soundlessly before he managed to choke out, "Brother." Ty wrapped his arms around him immediately, holding him tight, his own composure cracking just enough for tears to slip down his cheeks. Zenji leaned forward, embracing them both with one broad arm, while Mrs. Takashi rested her hand on Tom's back, whispering, "Welcome home, my son."

The judge watched for a moment, his stern face softening almost imperceptibly before he returned to his papers. "This court is adjourned," he said, striking the gavel one last time. Chairs scraped softly, voices rose, and the world beyond the bench returned to motion. But for Tom, there was no sound, no sight beyond the arms around him, the voices of those who had claimed him not with law, but with love.

He stood at last, his legs trembling but his eyes brighter than they had ever been. The name still echoed in his mind—Tom Shiro Takashi. It was more than a name; it was belonging, it was promise, it was truth written into law. And for the first time in his life, the shadow of the past did not follow him out of the courtroom. He walked forward, not alone, but with family, declared and undeniable.

The moment the ruling was entered into the record, it was as if time itself paused. Tom sat frozen, his ears ringing with the sound of his new name. Tom Shiro Takashi. It did not feel foreign, nor did it feel like a mask placed upon him. It felt as though it had always been his, hidden in waiting until someone loved him enough to speak it aloud. His chest tightened, his breath unsteady, but when he looked beside him and saw Ty's calm certainty, Zenji's quiet strength, and Mrs. Takashi's unshaken love, the truth broke over him in waves too heavy to resist.

He leaned forward, his arms reaching first for Ty, clinging to him with a desperation that spilled into gratitude. Ty wrapped him tight, whispering nothing, only holding, as though every ounce of strength in his small frame was poured into keeping Tom steady. Zenji moved closer, pulling both boys against his broad chest with the practiced embrace of a man who had built his life around protection. Mrs. Takashi reached across, her hands warm against Tom's shoulders, her cheek brushing his hair as she whispered, "My son, my son."

Tears blurred Tom's vision until the courtroom itself vanished. For a moment, there was no judge, no gavel, no law. There was only the heartbeat of those pressed against him, the steady rhythm of people who had chosen him when all others had turned away. His fists unclenched, his shoulders sagged, and for the first time in years, he allowed his body to rest inside an embrace without fear of the blow that might follow. He let the tears fall freely, his voice cracking only to whisper, "Thank you."

Mr. Arnett stepped forward then, his hand resting firm on Tom's shoulder. His grip was not the hollow squeeze of acknowledgement, but the full weight of a man who meant his touch to last. "You've done well, Tom," he said softly, his voice low but carrying. "You stood when others would have buckled. You spoke truth when silence would have been easier. And now the world knows who you are." His eyes flicked briefly to Zenji and Mrs. Takashi, his expression saying more than words—that his loyalty would remain.

The children at the back—Nico, Jasmin, Ella, Sophie, Leo, Jeremy, and even Alex—rose quietly as if drawn by some unseen tether. They did not speak, but they did not need to. Their faces bore the evidence of what they had witnessed: a transformation not scripted by fairy tales but forged in the raw, unforgiving light of truth. Nico wiped his eyes quickly, pretending it was nothing. Jasmin leaned against Sophie, whispering, "He's safe now." Leo gave a solemn nod, his silence louder than any cheer.

Jeremy, younger and yet sharper than his years, caught Ty's eyes and then Tom's. His small chin lifted with pride. "You've earned it," he murmured, though it was quiet enough that only those closest could hear. Alex stood apart, arms folded, but his gaze lingered with respect that had been slow to grow and now refused to be hidden. In their own way, each child knew this victory was not just Tom's—it was proof that none of them needed to remain defined by the shadows behind them.

Tom pulled back slightly from the embrace, his breath still ragged, and looked at Zenji. "Is it real?" he asked, his voice cracked with disbelief. Zenji crouched so that their eyes met evenly. "It is real," he said firmly. "By law, by truth, by heart. You are ours, Tom. And we are yours." There was no hesitation, no condition. The words fell like anchor stones into Tom's chest, rooting him deeper than he had ever thought possible.

Mrs. Takashi brushed the damp strands of hair from his forehead, her touch as soft as when she had tucked him into bed the week before. "From the moment you walked into our home, you were ours," she said. "Today only gave the world the chance to catch up." Her lips pressed briefly against his temple, sealing the vow. Tom closed his eyes, letting the words soak through like rain into dry earth.

Ty shifted slightly, his arm still looped around Tom's back. "You're my brother now," he said quietly, but his words carried steel. "Not just here, not just today. Always. I will not let you down." His eyes did not blink, his tone did not waver. Tom, overwhelmed, pressed his forehead against Ty's shoulder and finally whispered, "I believe you." It was perhaps the bravest thing he had ever said, for belief required trust, and trust required letting go of the walls that had kept him alive.

The judge remained seated, observing without interruption, his pen resting still on the pad before him. Though his role was finished, he did not rise immediately. Something in his expression softened, his eyes lingering on the boy who had stood trembling and now sat surrounded by arms that refused to release him. For all the weight of law and evidence, the scene before him was what made the gavel's echo truly matter.

The parents shifted uncomfortably, their faces pale, their voices silenced by the inevitability of truth. Their son no longer bore their name, no longer their claim. The courtroom had stripped them of the illusion of guardianship, and in its place stood a boy reborn through choice and conviction. Their eyes darted toward the exit, but none looked back at Tom. And Tom, for once, did not care. He had no need of them any longer.

Mr. Clarke, standing quietly among the teachers, smiled faintly behind his spectacles. Miss Kara dabbed at her eyes, her usual stern composure faltering. Mrs. Dunlop stood with arms folded, nodding approval as though victory had been hard-won. Even Ms. Henley, who so often measured emotions with a counselor's calm, allowed herself the briefest exhale of relief. For once, the entire room seemed to agree on something undeniable: justice had landed where it belonged.

Tom inhaled deeply, his lungs filling as though with new air, cleaner than any he had known before. He straightened his back, not stiff with tension, but upright with dignity. When he opened his eyes, the fear that had haunted them for so long had retreated, replaced with something uncertain but strong—hope. He turned again to Ty, whispering, "Thank you, brother," and Ty only nodded, his silence steady, his eyes unyielding.

The family stood together at last, not bound by circumstance, but declared by court and by love alike. Zenji placed his arm around both boys, Mrs. Takashi completing the circle with her embrace. Mr. Arnett stepped aside, allowing the moment to breathe, though the pride in his gaze was unmistakable. The gavel's echo still lingered faintly in the mind, but it was no longer the sound of judgment—it was the sound of freedom, of beginning.

As the courtroom emptied, voices rose again, footsteps clattered against the tile, but in the center of it all stood Tom Takashi. His heart raced, but it no longer pounded with fear. It beat with the steady rhythm of belonging, of identity earned not by blood but by choice. He had walked in uncertain, trembling beneath the weight of chains he could not see. He walked out surrounded, claimed, and unbreakable.

And when the doors finally opened to let in the bright light beyond, Tom whispered the words he had once thought he would never say aloud: "I am home."

### CHAPTER 16: THE STORY OF MYLES

The library had been transformed once again, chairs drawn back in neat rows against the walls, leaving the centre carpeted floor bare for students to gather. The room was quieter than usual, but it was not silence born of fear. It was the kind of hush that comes when anticipation is shared, when every heartbeat seems to fall in rhythm with the person beside you. The sunlight streamed through the wide windows, catching on the dust motes that drifted lazily in the air, as though time itself had slowed for what was about to take place. The children sat cross-legged in lines, whispering here and there but never letting their voices rise above the thick blanket of expectation.

Tom walked in with Ty at his side, not at the back as he once might have done, but through the very centre of the room where every eye could see him. His shoulders were squared, not hiding but held with care, as though Ty's presence alone was the shield he had always longed for. Whispers ran along the floor, not the cruel kind that once trailed him through hallways, but soft murmurs of surprise, even awe. Some mouths hung open, others tilted in small smiles, but none dared mock him now. Tom was no longer the boy cloaked in the uncle's shadow. He stood as one who had been seen, believed, and lifted up by hands that would never drop him again.

Mr. Clarke stood at the front of the library, no longer merely the school's librarian but now wearing the role of English teacher, the very post he had earned after years of patience and quiet dignity. His presence set a tone of order, not the cold kind but the kind rooted in care. He adjusted the neat stack of papers before him, his eyes sweeping across the students as though measuring the gravity of the moment. He knew why they were here, and though his mouth carried the faintest smile, his eyes carried a weight that had not been lifted in decades. The story he would tell today was not one of fiction or gentle metaphor. It was the story of Myles, and the telling of it demanded nothing less than truth.

Ty sat down with Tom near the front, choosing a place where both could be seen, where neither could shrink into the crowd. Nico leaned slightly forward from his own seat, curiosity bright in his eyes, while Jasmin and Ella sat together, their hands brushing as though one needed the other's steady presence. Sophie glanced often toward Leo, her brow furrowed, sensing the heaviness in the air long before a word had been spoken. Alex stretched his long legs across the carpet with the casualness of someone older, yet even he, hardened by his own past, sat upright when the hush deepened.

At the side, Mr. Arnett, the principal, folded his arms but not in impatience; his posture was one of quiet guard, of someone making sure no interruption would disturb what had to be said. Mrs. Dunlop stood by him, her head slightly bowed as though she too felt the solemnity pressing in. Miss Kara tapped her fingers lightly against her notebook, the gesture small, but her eyes never left Tom, studying how the boy carried himself after weeks of turmoil. Mrs. Haller's usual sharp eyes were softened today, and Ms. Henley, the counselor, stood ready to anchor those who might need comfort when the weight of the tale became too much.

Zenji Takashi was there too, though he had positioned himself nearer the back with his wife, Keiko. They did not need to take the forefront; their son's steady presence had already proven itself stronger than most speeches could ever manage. Zenji's gaze swept the room, sharp enough to quell any unrest, yet it was Keiko's hands folded gently in her lap that set the tone of calm. Together they were watchful pillars, present not to overshadow the school's authority, but to make it clear that truth told in this place would be guarded well.

Mila slipped into the room last, her quiet steps unnoticed by most until she sat near Sophie and Ella, her soft smile adding warmth to the circle of friends who had long grown used to her gentle nature. She did not speak, but her eyes lingered on Tom, the unspoken message clear: he was no longer walking into spaces alone. With her presence, as with the others, the circle was complete.

Jeremy, younger than the rest, shifted in his seat with restless energy, but not with impatience. His wide eyes carried both dread and determination, for he knew what story was about to be told. He had held the article in his hands, traced the words with his small fingers, and memorised the name that was never to be forgotten. It was not his job to tell it today—Mr. Clarke would carry that burden—but Jeremy sat like a vessel, ready to hold each syllable as though he could guard it for the generations after him.

The library air thickened further when Mr. Clarke placed his hand on the top page of his notes and looked at the students. No one fidgeted now. Even the restless scuff of shoes against the carpet ceased, as though the floor itself had warned them to be still. There was no sound but the faint hum of the overhead lights and the distant ticking of the school clock, each second stretching like an hour. When he finally opened his mouth to speak, it was not the voice of a man reciting history. It was the voice of one who had lived through its echo, one who had carried the silence of a lost child across decades of halls and classrooms.

And so, the moment came. Tom leaned ever so slightly forward, not in defiance but in need, as if the story that was about to be told might finally untangle the threads of shadow still woven inside him. Ty's hand brushed his sleeve, steadying without drawing attention. Around them, every student braced in their own way: some with hands clasped, some with heads bent low, others with eyes fixed firmly on Mr. Clarke, afraid to blink lest they miss a word. What hung over them now was not fear of punishment or shame. It was the knowledge that they were about to hear truth, raw and unvarnished, truth that demanded to be remembered.

Jeremy broke from his place on the carpet with a burst of energy that no teacher tried to restrain. He darted across the library floor, his small shoes silent against the carpet, and without waiting for permission he wrapped his arms around Tom's middle. The gesture was not clumsy nor half-hearted—it was complete, chest to chest, Jeremy's face pressed into Tom's shirt as if to say what words would never catch. The room drew in a collective breath, as though witnessing something sacred, because in that moment the labels that had once weighed on Tom—troublemaker, threat, burden—were stripped away. What remained was a boy, claimed by another boy's arms, seen without hesitation.

Tom stiffened at first, his hands twitching at his sides as though unsure where they belonged. Years of bracing for a strike had taught him that sudden contact meant danger, not comfort. Yet Jeremy did not let go, not even when Tom's shoulders rose with tension. He simply held on with a persistence that only a nine-year-old could wield, pure and unflinching. Slowly, Tom's resistance melted, his arms lifting with effort until they folded around Jeremy. The hug, when it came, was not graceful, but it was real, and in that reality it carried more weight than applause or praise could ever offer.

Sophie followed next, her quiet steps carrying her into the circle Jeremy had opened. She knelt and placed her arms around Tom too, gentle yet firm, her cheek brushing his arm as though she were proving with her presence that Jeremy was not alone in his declaration. Ella came after her, then Jasmin, and then Mila, each one adding to the growing ring of warmth. They did not speak, for no speech was needed. Each hug became a sentence, and together they wove a story that Tom could not ignore: you belong here, you belong to us, and you are no longer alone.

Leo, taller and stronger, moved with hesitation, but when he stepped forward, the hesitation was not doubt—it was reverence. He remembered too well what it meant to be treated as an outcast, to stand in the corner of a room while others judged. When his arms wrapped around Tom, they were not the arms of someone offering pity, but of someone who knew the bitter taste of shame and the long road back from cruelty. Tom flinched less this time, almost leaning into Leo's grasp, as if the older boy's silent nod could pass to him the strength he had never thought to borrow.

Alex approached last among the students, his face serious, almost unreadable, and for a moment Tom braced himself for a different kind of contact. Yet Alex bent down and drew him into a hug all the same, whispering just loud enough for Tom alone to hear, "Don't think you're the only one who thought he was beyond saving. I was there once too." Tom's breath caught, and though he did not answer, his eyes softened, the sheen of tears threatening to spill but held back with effort. The library was utterly silent, not because it was demanded, but because every heart was caught in the sight of transformation unfolding right before them.

The adults exchanged glances across the room, each teacher struck by the fact that the children had done what lectures and policies had never managed. Mr. Clarke's face was unreadable, his hands tightening on the papers before him as though steadying himself for what was to come. Mrs. Dunlop pressed her fingertips together, blinking back unexpected tears, while Miss Kara brushed at her eyes with the corner of her sleeve, pretending it was only dust. Even Mr. Arnett, who had seen too many assemblies that ended in disappointment, felt his chest tighten at the sight. The authority of adults had not broken through Tom's armour—but the innocent insistence of his peers had.

Ty remained where he sat, his eyes steady, his expression calm, as though everything had unfolded exactly as he had expected. He had known Jeremy would be the first to move, just as he had known that once one child crossed the boundary, others would follow.

Ty's role was not to lead this moment, but to watch it unfold, to let Tom feel what it meant to be embraced without requirement. Zenji and Keiko, from their place near the back, understood this too. They exchanged a glance filled with quiet pride, not at their son's restraint, but at the circle of compassion the children themselves had built.

When at last the hugs ended and Tom sat back down, his shoulders no longer hunched but lifted just slightly, something had shifted in the room. The students did not cheer, did not clap, did not speak out in triumph. They simply resumed their places, the warmth still hanging like a veil over the gathering. Tom exhaled slowly, the sound barely audible, but it was enough. For the first time, he had been welcomed not with suspicion or conditions, but with the simple and undeniable truth of touch.

Mr. Clarke rose from his chair with the slow gravity of someone who knew the room was balanced on a fragile thread. He adjusted his glasses, the reflection of the library lights flickering across the lenses, and cleared his throat. The children turned toward him at once, sensing that what came next would matter. "Before we go further," he began, his voice low but steady, "I want to mark this moment. Tom, you returned today not as an outcast, not as a shadow, but as a student among students, and more importantly, as one of us." His words fell across the room like a benediction, not dressed in ceremony but carrying the weight of truth.

Tom shifted, uncomfortable with the sudden attention, his fingers knotting together, but Clarke did not allow him to retreat inward. The teacher stepped closer, setting his hand gently on Tom's shoulder, a rare gesture in a place where boundaries were strict and often cold. Yet the presence of Zenji Takashi, calm and watchful, gave the teachers a freedom they seldom dared to take. Clarke pulled Tom into a full-bodied embrace, one that stunned the students into silence. For the first time, an adult had spoken with actions what the children had already declared: Tom was loved, and he was no longer alone.

Mr. Arnett moved next, the principal who had too often been a man of measured distance. He crossed the space with deliberate steps and drew Tom into his own arms, a firm embrace that surprised even himself. "You belong here, Tom," he said, his voice breaking slightly. "Not because you earned it, not because you proved it, but because you are here, and that is enough." Mrs. Dunlop followed, tears in her eyes as she wrapped him in her arms, whispering that students like him needed to be held up, not thrown away. Even Mrs. Haller, known for her briskness, bowed her head and reached out her arms without hesitation.

The students watched wide-eyed, some with jaws slack, as the teachers—those pillars who so often kept themselves apart—embraced one of their own as though it were the most natural thing in the world. Zenji remained by the wall, his hands folded, but his approving nod was unmistakable. Keiko smiled softly, her artist's eyes catching the tableau as though it were a painting she would one day bring to canvas: a boy once lost in fear, now surrounded by a circle of arms, the lines of separation dissolving. For once, rules bent not to control, but to protect, and in that bending, something sacred was forged.

When Mr. Clarke finally pulled back, his hand still on Tom's shoulder, he turned to face the room. His voice carried new strength, firm and resonant, as though each word was carved into the wood of the shelves themselves. "Tom," he said, openly, so no one could mistake the depth of it, "you are truly loved here. You will never have to walk this journey alone, because we all stand with you. Not just today, not just when it is easy, but always." The words struck like hammers on the air, and though Tom lowered his head, his eyes burned with tears he could no longer hide.

Clarke let the silence settle before speaking again, his gaze sweeping across the faces of the gathered students. "But today is not only about Tom. Today is about truth—the kind that cannot be hidden, the kind that cannot be softened for comfort. There is a story that must be told, and Tom has asked to begin it." The room shifted uneasily, for stories told in this way were rare, and everyone sensed that the one they were about to hear was heavier than the ordinary tales of playground cruelty. Clarke's voice dropped a note lower. "The story is about Myles Neuts."

The name landed like a stone in the middle of a still pond. Whispers died instantly, and the weight of it hung over the gathering with solemn force. Jeremy's arms tightened around his knees, his face serious for once, while Leo's eyes flicked downward, recognising the sharp sting of shame that came with hearing the name of a boy broken by bullying. Sophie, Jasmin, and Ella exchanged uneasy glances, their hands brushing against one another as though to draw strength in quiet solidarity. Alex leaned forward, elbows on his knees, his usual smirk absent, replaced with the solemnity of memory.

Mr. Clarke did not let the silence grow stale. He raised his hand and gestured gently to Tom. "This story must be told not because it is easy," he said, "but because it is true. And Tom has chosen to stand before you, not to excuse his past, but to remind us all what silence can cost." He turned back toward Tom, nodding with encouragement that carried no demand. "Whenever you are ready, son." The word son slipped out naturally, and though Clarke did not notice it, Tom did. His lips parted slightly, his breath caught in his throat, and for a fleeting second, he felt the word rest on him like a cloak he had never dared to claim.

The library grew so quiet that the hum of the overhead lights seemed deafening. Every eye turned toward Tom, but not with judgment; rather, with expectation. Ty sat close enough to be felt, his calm presence anchoring him, while Zenji's steady gaze reminded him that there would be no punishment for speaking, no consequence except the freedom of truth. Mrs. Keiko Takashi folded her hands in her lap, waiting, her expression warm and open, as though telling him without words that art, even in speech, could heal wounds that seemed unending.

Tom swallowed, his throat tight, but he did not retreat. He stood slowly, his knees stiff, his shoulders trembling with the weight of the moment. Jeremy gave him a small nod, silent but powerful, as if to say that whatever words he found, they would be enough. The library held its breath as Tom looked around at faces young and old, waiting for him to carry the name of a boy whose life had been taken too soon into the centre of the room. At last, he inhaled and said quietly, "Then I will speak."

Tom's hands were already damp when he lifted them, his voice not loud, but clear enough to reach the teachers and the students gathered across the room. "Mr. Arnett," he said quietly, "could we… could we have some Kleenex boxes around here?" His request was not a demand but a plea, an understanding that the truth he was about to speak would not leave a single pair of eyes dry. The principal's face softened. He nodded without hesitation and signalled Mrs. Dunlop, who slipped out and returned within moments, her arms filled with tissue boxes. She placed them carefully along the walls, in the corners, and at the edge of the circle where the students would sit, as though preparing for a storm that could not be held back.

Mr. Arnett's voice, usually sharp in assemblies, dropped into something gentler. "Tom is right," he said, scanning the faces of his students. "What we are about to hear is not easy, and I won't pretend it will be. Take what you need. No one should feel ashamed of tears today." His words settled in the air, and even the teachers shifted uneasily, reminded that they were not immune to what was about to unfold. Ty's steady presence remained fixed beside Tom, his calm face holding no judgment, only assurance. It was enough to keep Tom from collapsing into the silence of old habits.

Chairs scraped against the carpet as students shuffled closer. Some were moved aside entirely, left stacked in rows against the library shelves, making way for a wide circle in the centre of the room. The carpet cushioned their steps, its deep fibres muffling the nervous movements as the children settled themselves cross-legged, knees brushing, forming a ring of quiet expectation. The teachers, for once, did not stand aloof. They too drew in nearer, folding themselves into the outer circle, uneasy but compelled by the weight of the moment. The hum of the overhead lights fell into rhythm with their breathing.

Tom stood at the centre, his shoulders pulled inward, his arms stiff at his sides. The circle pressed in around him, not with threat but with presence, a ring of eyes that waited, patient yet relentless. He shifted his weight from one foot to the other, resisting the urge to fold himself down into the carpet with the rest of them. He wanted to run, to vanish into the shelves, but Ty's gaze anchored him. Ty did not move, did not speak; his stillness was louder than any encouragement could have been.

Jeremy was the first among the students to break the tension, not with words but with action. He leaned forward and pulled his chair away, choosing instead to sit cross-legged on the carpet just a few feet from Tom's shoes. His small gesture spread like fire. Sophie, Jasmin, and Ella followed, lowering themselves onto the floor, their skirts and trousers folding neatly beneath them as they settled into the circle. Nico crossed his arms but joined in, his dark eyes watching Tom closely. One by one, the others followed, until there was no gap left, only a complete circle around a boy who had never been so exposed.

Zenji Takashi did not intrude on the centre, but his calm voice carried across the space. "A circle has no beginning and no end," he said softly. "It means that every person here carries equal weight. Tom, you stand in the middle, but you do not stand alone." His words steadied the atmosphere, lending the children something to cling to while keeping Tom from retreating into silence. Keiko, her hands resting gently in her lap, nodded in agreement, her eyes glistening already, her face open with the kind of love that made even silence feel like sanctuary.

Mr. Clarke lowered himself from the edge of the circle, no longer the teacher standing above but the participant seated among them. He set a box of Kleenex at his knee, then raised his eyes to Tom. "You do not have to hurry," he said, his tone stripped of every classroom authority. "The room is yours, for as long as you need." His words fell into the silence like stones dropped into a still pond, rippling outward, reaching both students and teachers alike. Even Mrs. Haller, whose sternness rarely wavered, bent her head and folded her hands, as if waiting in reverence.

The air shifted into something unspoken, the hush of expectation thick as fog. Tom's breathing grew shallow, his fists clenching and unclenching at his sides. He could hear the sound of his own pulse in his ears, the tremor in his breath fighting against the words lodged in his throat. Yet the circle remained steady, holding him upright with its silent demand and its silent promise.

At last, Ty moved—not forward, not to interfere, but just enough to tilt his head and meet Tom's eyes with the smallest nod. The kind of nod that did not push, but opened a door. Tom's lungs emptied, and for the first time, he inhaled as though the air itself was waiting to carry his voice. The circle, the tissues scattered around them, the adults who had bent their own pride to join the floor—it was all set for what could no longer be hidden.

When Tom finally spoke, his voice was rough, halting, but it carried through the circle clearly enough to reach every ear. "I don't know if I can do this," he confessed, his words trembling. "But I think… I think if I don't, I'll never be free of it." He looked down at his own hands, then slowly raised his head, catching sight of Jeremy's tear-bright eyes, Ty's calm resolve, and Zenji's unshaken stillness. The circle seemed to lean toward him, urging him on without words.

Mr. Arnett shifted from his chair, folding himself down cross-legged with the students, his knees cracking as he settled in, but his voice steady. "Then speak, Tom. Whatever you have, give it to the circle. It will hold." It was an invitation, not a command, and for the first time, Tom believed it might be true.

The library had changed. It was no longer shelves and books and carpet. It had become a vessel, a place where truth would be carried, no matter how heavy. Tom drew a breath, squared his shoulders, and prepared to bring forth the story of Myles Neuts, knowing the circle was ready to bear it with him.

# THE SMILE THAT BROKE

The library had already fallen silent, but when Tom's lips parted, the stillness seemed to deepen into something that pressed against every chest in the room. His voice caught, trembled, then steadied with an effort that could be felt more than seen. "Myles Neuts." The name did not echo, but it cut like glass through the hush, sharp and undeniable. Teachers drew in breaths they did not release. Students turned their heads as though caught by an invisible thread, every one of them bound now to the sound of that name. Even those too young to have ever heard it before recognised instinctively that it was not a name to be taken lightly.

The LED monitor at the front of the library flickered to life, a flat glow stretching across the circle of faces. On it appeared a single photograph, a young boy frozen forever at ten years old. His face, round with childhood, filled the screen, his eyes carrying a brightness that made the silence heavier still. No introduction was needed. Tom stepped slightly to the side, gesturing toward the image with a hand that trembled even as he forced it to remain extended. His voice cracked. "Look at this young boy here. I want you to remember his face." No one dared move. The moment carried a weight too sacred for shuffling feet or nervous coughs.

Sophie lifted her hand halfway, as though to cover her mouth, but let it fall again into her lap, her fingers curling tightly together. She stared at the screen as though trying to memorize every feature. Nico's usually restless body sat perfectly still, his chin tucked, his eyes darkened by a kind of respect he rarely showed. Even Jasmin, whose quick temper often flared at cruelty, pressed her lips into a thin line, fighting the sting of tears. Every child understood without words that this was no ordinary lesson, and that what was about to be spoken would never be forgotten.

Mr. Clarke, standing nearest the monitor, swallowed visibly before turning to the group. His hand, which usually carried books with casual steadiness, shook slightly as he adjusted the frame on the wall to remove a glare from the photo. He did not speak—he could not. Instead, he let Tom's words fill the air, knowing that nothing he might say could add or soften what already carried its own unstoppable force. Behind him, Mrs. Dunlop reached for a box of Kleenex and quietly set it in the centre of the circle, as though placing a shield against what was to come.

Tom's shoulders rose and fell as he drew in breath after breath, steadying himself against the swell of emotion threatening to consume him. He did not look at Ty, though Ty's presence at the edge of the circle was a constant weight, a steadying anchor. Instead, he kept his eyes fixed on the photo glowing above them. "I will tell you about him shortly," Tom said, his tone uneven yet strong enough to hold the room captive. The promise lingered in the air like a binding oath. No one doubted he would keep it, though the effort was carving its weight visibly into him.

From the corner of the circle, Ella whispered softly, almost involuntarily, "He looks so kind." Her words, though hushed, reached every ear in the silence. Tom's gaze flicked toward her, not in anger but in acknowledgement. "He was," Tom said simply, the words heavy with both truth and sorrow. He let them settle before returning his attention to the screen. The photo did not change, but somehow it seemed to grow larger, filling the library until it pressed against the hearts of everyone present.

# THE SMILE THAT BROKE

Mr. Arnett adjusted his glasses, clearing his throat, but he did not speak. His usual instinct to maintain order had deserted him. Instead, he found himself watching Tom with a kind of awe, the boy's posture stiff but unbroken, his voice carrying a weight far beyond his years. The principal leaned back in his chair, silent, letting the scene unfold without interference. Even Mrs. Haller, never one to hide her opinions, sat rigid and still, her sharp words dulled into silence by the sheer gravity of the moment.

Jeremy, who had been hugging his knees to his chest, leaned forward now, his voice uncharacteristically soft. "Tom... thank you for saying his name." The comment was not for recognition but for reverence. Tom blinked at him, his throat tightening, then gave a slight nod. He could not manage words in return, but Jeremy's statement had cut through his fear, reminding him that this was not a performance but an act of remembrance. That distinction steadied him, his feet grounding more firmly into the carpet beneath him.

The air grew heavier as the children's eyes moved from Tom to the screen and back again, as if weighing his words against the stillness of the photograph. They did not yet know the story, but the power of a name—spoken aloud, spoken true—had already begun its work. Kleenex rustled faintly as hands gripped them tightly, though no one yet allowed tears to fall. They were holding back, waiting for what was to come. The weight of expectation was almost unbearable, but none dared break it.

From the back of the room, Ms. Henley, the counsellor, folded her hands together, her expression more sorrowful than analytical. She had heard many stories in her time, sat through many confessions, but something about this—the way a boy no older than thirteen was shouldering the weight of another child's memory—struck her differently. She closed her eyes briefly, as if to steady herself, then reopened them, determined to be present in the moment no matter how hard it might prove.

Zenji Takashi's posture remained steady, his arms folded lightly, his gaze never leaving Tom. He did not interfere, nor did he attempt to soothe. He knew better. His presence was enough, and Tom knew it, even without looking at him. Keiko Takashi sat beside him, her face softened into an expression that carried both grief and pride. She held one hand over her heart, her breath measured, her eyes glistening but unyielding. Both parents understood the significance of this act, and both offered silent strength without a single word.

Tom's breathing steadied again, his chest rising with each deliberate inhale, his words carefully drawn out as though they weighed more than he could carry. "His name matters," Tom said, his voice clearer now. "It matters that you know it, that you speak it, and that you don't forget it." The students nodded, some slowly, others more urgently, their young faces solemn in a way that made them look far older than they were. Jeremy lowered his head, clutching a tissue, but refused to look away from the photo.

In the corner of the circle, Alex shifted uncomfortably, his voice gruff when he finally spoke. "People forget too easily," he muttered. "But not this time." His words earned quiet agreement from Leo, who glanced across the circle, his eyes damp but his jaw set. The boys, who had once carried their own shadows of cruelty, sat forward now as though lending their strength to Tom's act of remembrance. The transformation in their posture did not go unnoticed by the teachers.

As the LED monitor glowed, casting its faint blue light across the circle, the photo of Myles Neuts seemed to take on a presence beyond pixels and glass. It was no longer just an image—it had become a witness, a reminder, and a charge. Tom's voice cracked again, softer now. "You must remember his face," he said, each word deliberate, a command clothed in grief. "Because if we forget him, then everything we've learned here means nothing." The sentence landed like a stone, its truth undeniable.

Ty finally stirred, shifting just enough to let his voice break the stillness. "We hear you, Tom," he said, calm but unwavering. "We'll remember him." The affirmation, though brief, steadied Tom again. The circle, the photograph, the tissues waiting like sentries—it all seemed to bind together into a single moment, unbroken, unyielding. The library had become something more than a room. It had become a hall of memory, a sanctuary where the name of one boy, spoken aloud, could shake the silence of an entire school.

Tom stood a little taller, though his hands still trembled. The name had been spoken, the photo revealed, and the silence had been pierced. It was only the beginning, but already the circle knew that nothing would be the same again. Myles Neuts was no longer a shadowed story whispered in corners—his presence had been brought into the light, where it would remain.

Tom's voice was steadier now, but the weight in it could not be missed. "I learned everything I could about him," he said, his gaze never leaving the photograph of Myles on the screen. "I read reports, I read testimony, I pieced together what happened that February day in 1998." The words were not rehearsed; they came raw, shaped by long hours of quiet searching. The students shifted uneasily, sensing that the story would not shield them with soft edges. This would be truth, spoken without disguise, the way Tom had found it written in those old articles.

He paused only long enough to collect breath, then continued, "Myles was just ten years old, a boy like any one of us once was, or still is. He was in grade five, same as some of you sitting here now. That day, February 6th, 1998, he went into the washroom at school. What happened next was supposed to be a prank." The word landed bitterly, spat out as though it burned his tongue. "But it wasn't a prank. Not then, not ever. It was two boys, just eleven and twelve, putting him on a coat hook by his shirt collar. They thought it would make him forget some silly bet. But it didn't. It killed him."

A gasp shuddered through the room, not loud, but sharp, like wind through cracks in a door. Tom clenched his fists at his sides, his eyes flashing as he forced himself to continue. "He was left there, hanging.

For ten, maybe twenty minutes, his shirt and necklace cutting into him while he struggled to breathe. He stopped breathing. His brain stopped getting oxygen. By the time anyone found him, Myles was already gone in every way that mattered." He swallowed hard, his voice dropping lower. "Six days later, his parents made the choice no parent should ever face—they turned off his life support. Because Myles wasn't coming back."

Jeremy's small voice broke into the silence. "He was only ten." The words were half-statement, half-lament. Tom nodded stiffly. "Yes. Ten. Younger than Alex, younger than Leo, younger than most of you will ever want to think about. And no one was ever held criminally responsible. No one." His voice hardened, the injustice burning behind every syllable. "It was called undetermined. As if a boy's life can be something undecided, like a question left unanswered."

Mr. Clarke pressed his hand to his mouth, his eyes bright with tears he didn't hide. "I remember when it happened," he admitted softly, his voice quaking. "I was a new teacher then. I still remember the headline, the photo, the shock." Tom's eyes flicked toward him, acknowledging the words without breaking stride. "That's why it has to be remembered," Tom said firmly. "Because if we forget, then nothing changes. And it can happen again."

Sophie hugged her knees tightly, her lips trembling as she whispered, "They thought it was a joke?" Her question cracked under the weight of disbelief. Tom turned to her, his voice sharp but not unkind. "Yes. They thought it was fun. But it wasn't. A life ended because of their so-called fun. A boy died because they wanted to laugh." The bluntness stung, but no one in the room dared ask him to soften it. Even the teachers recognised the necessity of hearing it plain.

Ty's steady voice broke through the silence next, his words neither soft nor harsh, but absolute. "That's why we stand here now. Because one boy's story matters more than our comfort." His calm delivery reinforced Tom's truth, his presence acting as a pillar when Tom's own legs looked ready to give way. Tom drew a long breath, his shoulders dropping slightly, grateful for Ty's anchor without needing to say it.

Mr. Arnett cleared his throat, adjusting his glasses, but his usual authority faltered in the moment. "This is not an easy thing to hear," he admitted. "But it must be heard." He looked across the sea of young faces, his voice rough. "Every one of you has to understand: what seems like a game can end a life. We've seen it before. We cannot see it again." The words hung heavy, echoing Tom's determination.

Mila, her hands clenched around the tissue in her lap, finally asked, "Did his family… what did they do?" Her question was hesitant, fragile. Tom's eyes softened, just slightly, as he answered. "They mourned him. His father, Mike Neuts, travelled across Canada to tell Myles' story, to warn people about bullying, to keep his son's name alive. He even started the Make Children Better Now Foundation, because he didn't want anyone else to go through what Myles did." Tom's words cracked, but he pushed them out. "His family carried his memory forward because they refused to let him be forgotten."

The students sat straighter, some wiping tears, others staring hollow-eyed at the monitor. Alex leaned forward, his voice gruff. "If I'd been there…" He stopped, shaking his head, unable to finish. Leo put a hand on his arm, finishing the thought with a quiet, "So would I." The two former bullies sat united, their silence louder than most words. Tom caught their exchange and gave a slight nod, as though to say that even regret had a place in remembrance.

From the back, Ms. Henley's voice trembled as she added, "This is why we talk, why we listen, why we tell the truth. Children know when adults lie. They know when we try to soften it. And they deserve better." She looked at Tom with eyes that carried respect, not pity. "You're giving them better now."

Tom's breath shuddered, but he held his ground. "This isn't my story," he said firmly. "It's his. It's Myles's. And if we let it fade, then it could happen to anyone here." His eyes swept the circle, landing on each student, each teacher, each friend. "So remember him. Remember Myles Neuts. Because he matters."

The monitor glowed brighter in the dim library, casting its pale light across every face. In that circle, the students understood that this was more than a history lesson. It was a warning, a call, a truth that demanded to be carried forward. And for the first time, Tom did not look like a boy crushed beneath shadows. He looked like a voice chosen to carry another's name into the light.

Tom shifted his weight, his eyes locking on the glowing image of Myles, and when he spoke again his voice was softer, stripped of anger but edged with sorrow. "It all started with something so small, something you'd laugh at if you didn't know what came after. A colouring contest in the third grade. Myles and another student made a bet—ten dollars to whoever finished the fastest. Myles won. But the other boy never paid." He let the words settle, the absurdity of it hanging in the air, a childish game that should have ended in nothing more than sulking. The students leaned closer, as if the details themselves were heavy stones placed in their hands.

He drew a breath. "Two years later, Myles remembered. He reminded that student about the ten dollars. And that's when another boy overheard. He said: We'll make him forget on Friday." Tom's voice cracked on the word forget, his jaw tightening as he pressed on. "It was just words at first, but words can become weapons when someone believes them. And Myles never had a chance to prepare, because he didn't know how far they would take it." The circle sat hushed, the air tightening as the weight of those simple exchanges sharpened into something merciless.

Jeremy whispered, "Over ten dollars?" His voice was thick with disbelief. Tom turned his head, his eyes briefly meeting Jeremy's, and answered, "Yes. Ten dollars, and the need to laugh at someone else's expense. That's all it took. That's how cruelty works. It doesn't always roar in, it creeps in through small cracks, little betrayals that grow into something deadly." The truth stung more than if Tom had shouted. It forced every listener to think of moments they had brushed off as jokes, of promises broken, of dares tossed around without care.

# THE SMILE THAT BROKE

Mr. Clarke pressed a hand against his desk, his throat dry as he added, "It's always the little things that show us who people really are. And we miss them until it's too late." His words came gently, not to overshadow Tom but to underline what was already being revealed. Ty, sitting cross-legged across from Tom, watched him closely, his calm expression holding Tom steady without uttering a word.

Tom's gaze swept the circle. "That's what you need to understand," he said slowly. "The prank wasn't born in violence. It was born in arrogance, in a broken promise, in a laugh that never should have been made. Those boys thought they were clever, thought they were strong, but really they were just cowards looking for an excuse to humiliate someone." His words cut clean, sharper than anger could have. "And Myles paid the price. He kept his end of the bet. They broke theirs, and it cost him his life."

Mila's voice wavered as she asked, "Did anyone stop them?" Her hands clutched a tissue, her knuckles pale. Tom shook his head. "No. They were his classmates. They knew him. They laughed at him, and then they left him. No one stepped in. No one said stop. And that's what makes this story burn so deep—because it didn't have to happen." He exhaled shakily, his fists unclenching at last. "It was preventable. It should have been prevented."

Mrs. Dunlop dabbed at her eyes with the corner of her sleeve, whispering just loud enough for the room to hear, "Every child deserves better than that." Her words were half prayer, half confession, but no one contradicted them. They only deepened the ache that had already filled the library.

Ty leaned forward, his voice even, his eyes unwavering. "And that's why Tom tells it. Because one broken promise can turn into a broken life. And if we remember Myles, we remember to stop before it gets that far." His words carried like stone thrown into water, ripples spreading to every corner of the room. Tom gave a small nod, grateful for the hand Ty had placed invisibly on his shoulder through those words.

Leo clenched his jaw, then raised his hand slightly, speaking with a raw edge. "I've broken promises. I've used them to control people. To mock them." His eyes darted to the floor. "And I hate myself for it." Alex placed a hand firmly on his back, steadying him. "But you changed," Alex reminded him quietly. The exchange lit a spark of truth: healing was possible, even for those who had once chosen cruelty.

Tom's eyes softened briefly, his own anger shifting into something quieter. "That's the promise we need now," he said, his tone weighted but hopeful. "The promise that we won't laugh at someone's pain, that we won't break trust just to make ourselves feel powerful. That's how you honour Myles. Not by pitying him, but by learning from him." The words landed with finality, binding every student present to the reality of choice.

Mrs. Henley's voice trembled as she added, "That's the only kind of promise worth making—the kind that saves someone." She looked directly at Tom, her eyes brimming with a rare mixture of pride and grief. "And you've just made it."

The room fell into silence, not hollow but alive, filled with the weight of Myles's name, his story, and the lesson pulled from the smallest of beginnings. Tom straightened his shoulders, not out of pride but resolve. His voice carried one last time before the next chapter of truth unfolded. "The bet was never about money. It was about dignity. And when you strip someone of that, you take their life away piece by piece. Myles lost all of it in one moment. We can't let that happen again."

Tom's voice faltered as the photo of Myles remained lit on the monitor, its glow casting across every face in the circle. He rubbed his palms against his knees as though trying to steady himself, then finally spoke, his tone stripped of any shield. "It happened on a Friday. February sixth, nineteen ninety-eight. Myles went into the washroom at school, just like any other boy. He thought nothing of it. But the two who had made their plan—two kids, barely older than him—followed." His words cracked, but he forced them onward, steady enough to be heard.

"You need to understand," Tom pressed on, his chest tightening with every syllable, "this wasn't a fight. This wasn't an accident. This was a choice. They lifted him. They thought it was funny. They hoisted him by his shirt collar and necklace and left him hanging on a coat hook in one of the stalls." Tom swallowed hard, his eyes flashing to the floor. "He struggled. He couldn't breathe. And while they laughed, his body went still." The room seemed to shrink, the carpet beneath them a fragile island holding the weight of truth.

A sharp intake of breath broke from Ella, her hand flying to her mouth. Sophie leaned against her shoulder, eyes already swimming with tears. Mila pressed her forehead against her knees, shaking silently. The story was no longer distant; it was dragging them into the stall with Myles, forcing them to see what children were capable of when cruelty is left unchecked.

Tom's voice grew quieter, but each word landed heavier. "It only took ten… maybe twenty minutes. That's all. His brain was denied oxygen, and for all intents and purposes… Myles was gone." He clenched his fists until his knuckles whitened, trembling as he spat the next line. "And the worst part is—nobody came. He was left there. Alone." The silence that followed was punctured only by soft sobs and the faint hum of the projector fan.

Mr. Clarke lowered his glasses, dabbing at his eyes with a crumpled handkerchief. "Children are not meant to be left like that," he whispered, though his voice cracked too badly to continue. Jeremy's face burned red, his small fists digging into his lap. He didn't interrupt, but his whole body trembled with outrage, his breath coming shallow and quick.

Ty's eyes never left Tom. His stillness grounded the room, anchoring every floating emotion. He did not need to speak; his silence was its own vow of listening, of bearing witness. The weight in his expression alone told Tom to go on, not for himself, but for Myles.

Tom shook his head, his teeth clenched. "They thought it was a prank. A joke. But this was no joke. By the time anyone found him, it was too late. He was still there, on that hook, his life already gone." His voice dropped to a rasp, each word torn from him. "And the only reason we even know the details is because his parents had to hear them in court. His mom and dad had to sit there and be told what their son went through in his last minutes. No parent should ever… ever have to carry that." His eyes blurred, and he pressed his sleeve to his face, but the words would not stay buried.

Mrs. Dunlop quietly passed a box of tissues across the circle, but even she wiped at her cheeks as she did so. Nico, his voice hushed but fierce, muttered, "That could have been any of us." Jasmin nodded, holding his hand tight, as though bracing herself against the sharpness of the truth.

Mr. Arnett sat stiffly in his chair, his voice low but firm. "Every child in this school needs to hear this. Every child must know how quickly a life can be stolen, how fast laughter can turn to death." His words, though rough, carried a sincerity that was rare from him, one that landed squarely on the teachers along the wall who had once spoken of expulsion like it was a solution.

Tom glanced up again, his voice steadier now, though the pain lingered in every syllable. "This is why I tell you this story. Because Myles didn't get another chance. He didn't get to walk out of that washroom. He didn't get to grow up, or to sit here today. And it wasn't because of monsters, it wasn't because of men in dark alleys—it was because of classmates. Kids, just like us. And if you think it can't happen here, you're lying to yourselves." His eyes swept the circle, daring anyone to look away.

Sophie's sobs broke louder, and Lisa scooted closer to her, wrapping her arms around her shoulders without needing words. Leo leaned forward, gripping his knees, his face haunted with a memory he did not share aloud, but one that tied him to the story in a way he couldn't ignore. Alex kept his head bowed, as if ashamed, though his hand rested firmly on Leo's arm, grounding them both.

Ty finally shifted, his voice quiet but carrying. "Myles's story is not about the ending. It is about the choice that came before it. Every bully, every laugh, every shove… it adds up. And one day, there may not be a way back." His words rang clear, bridging the distance between past and present, Myles and Tom, the library and the washroom of St. Agnes School.

Tom closed his eyes briefly, the strain on his face softening just slightly. "That's why you remember him," he whispered. "That's why his name matters. Because if we let ourselves forget, then his death means nothing. And I refuse to let it mean nothing." His voice cracked on the last word, but he stood taller for saying it.

The library, once just a room of books and carpet, had become a courtroom of truth, every student and teacher both witness and jury. Myles Neuts, gone for more than two decades, stood among them through Tom's trembling voice, his presence undeniable. And in that moment, no one dared smile, no one dared speak—because they all knew they were standing at the edge of the same abyss, and now they had to decide if they would step forward, or finally turn away.

Tom steadied himself, the hush in the library drawing him deeper into the memory of a boy he never met but carried like a shadow. His voice dropped, raw against the silence. "Six days," he began. "For six days, Mike and Brenda Neuts sat by their son's hospital bed. Six days of machines breathing for him, doctors whispering updates that never changed. Six days of praying—not to saints or miracles—but just begging for his chest to rise on its own." He gripped the back of a chair for balance, his knuckles white. "And then the doctors told them what no parent should ever hear: their son would never wake up again. His brain had gone too long without air. He was alive in body only. Not in spirit, not in hope."

Jeremy's eyes glistened as he clenched his fists on his knees, his small voice trembling but unspoken. Ty's stillness anchored the moment, his calm gaze locked on Tom, lending him strength. Sophie pressed her face into her palms, her shoulders shaking, while Jasmin draped an arm around her without hesitation. The reality hung so heavy it pressed the room flat, as though even air had grown too dense to breathe.

Tom swallowed hard, fighting the knot in his throat. "Do you know what it means to sit by your child's bed for almost a week, watching them not move, not speak, not smile? Do you know what it means to keep hoping, even when the monitors tell you it's over? Mike and Brenda had to make a choice—a choice no one should ever face. On the sixth day, they gave the order. They told the doctors to turn off the machine. They watched their son's last breath, not because nature took him, but because cruelty had stolen him first." His voice cracked, and he pressed his sleeve against his face before forcing the words out again.

Mr. Clarke leaned forward, his face buried in his hands, glasses fogged. "No parent should ever—ever—be asked to do that," he muttered hoarsely, his voice breaking into pieces. Mr. Arnett sat rigid, his hand gripping the edge of his chair as though holding the entire school together by sheer will. Even Mrs. Dunlop, so steady in every crisis, lowered her eyes, a tear slipping silently down her cheek.

"Brenda held his hand as the machine went quiet," Tom said, his tone breaking under the image. "Mike stood by her, helpless, powerless, broken in two. Their little boy—ten years old—was gone. Not by sickness. Not by accident. But because children who should have been his friends chose cruelty, and no one stopped them. Six days later, his parents had to live with the sound of silence where their son's breath should have been."

Ella whispered to herself, "That could've been my brother," and buried her face in her lap. Mila, pale and tense, leaned against Leo, who pulled her close with his arm wrapped tightly around her shoulders. Alex stared at the floor, his lips pressed in a hard line, tears running down despite his clenched jaw. Their silence was no less than confession—they all knew too well what it meant for cruelty to steal a future.

Ty finally shifted, his voice calm but firm. "That is why we do not dismiss a bruise, or a laugh, or a prank," he said. "Because it builds. It builds until it ends a life. And then all that's left are parents forced to bury their child." His gaze turned across the circle, piercing, daring anyone to forget.

Tom nodded faintly, as though Ty's words had wrapped around his own. "Mike and Brenda didn't just lose a son that day. Dane lost his big brother. A family was torn apart. And it didn't end when the machines stopped. It never ends. They carry it every single day." His voice wavered but pushed forward, like a storm tearing itself open. "And when you laugh at someone's pain, when you think it's just a joke, remember that a joke killed a boy named Myles Neuts, and left his family broken forever."

The library felt smaller than ever, the carpet beneath them holding a grief that stretched far beyond the walls. Mr. Zenji Takashi lowered his head in respect, his hand resting gently on his son Ty's shoulder, a silent acknowledgment of both the truth spoken and the responsibility to guard against its repetition. Mrs. Keiko Takashi dabbed at her eyes, her artist's soul breaking beneath the weight of a child's life reduced to memory and mourning.

The students leaned closer to one another, as though needing proof of warmth, of presence, of life. Jeremy, unable to hold still any longer, whispered, "Never again." His words, though small, carried across the circle like a vow none of them could deny. Tom lifted his eyes then, his face streaked but his voice firm enough to stand. "That is why his name must be remembered. That is why you sit here today. Because Mike and Brenda chose to share their agony so no one else would face it. And now it is on us. We carry it too."

No one moved. No one breathed. The truth sat heavy on their hearts, carved into them by the image of two parents letting go of their boy after six long days of waiting. And in that silence, the legacy of Myles Neuts—ten years old, gone too soon—took root in them all.

Tom unfolded a sheet of paper with careful hands, as though even its creases carried weight too delicate to disturb. His voice lowered, steady but edged with tremor, and he said to the circle, "These are the words of Myles Casey Benson Neuts. He wrote them just one year before he died. Listen to them as though he were sitting here with us, asking you himself." The library fell utterly silent, the air so still that even the hum of the lights seemed to retreat. Tom began to read.

"To me peace is love instead of hate," he said, his voice softer now. The words hung in the space between children and teachers alike, bridging years and grief in their simplicity. A rustle came from the row of teachers as Mrs. Haller pressed a trembling hand to her mouth, already undone by the innocence that rang through every syllable.

Tom paused, his eyes scanning the next line as though steadying himself. "Peace is truth instead of lies." He looked around the circle, meeting the eyes of Sophie, of Nico, of Leo. None of them looked away. Each of them, in their own heart, knew how easy it was to choose lies, and how costly that choice could be.

He read further. "Peace is nature and a clean world, peace is comments instead of complaints." The gentle rhythm of the words, written by a boy not yet eleven, struck harder than any lecture ever could. Jeremy wiped his face on his sleeve without shame, his shoulders shaking as he whispered, "He was younger than me…" Ella reached over, sliding her hand into his without a word.

Tom's voice deepened, as though giving each line the reverence it deserved. "So share instead of greed, tell the truth instead of lies, tell comments instead of complaints." The words, so innocent yet so deliberate, pressed against the walls of the library like waves against rock. Even Mr. Clarke, who had spent years surrounded by books, bowed his head as though nothing he had ever read carried such weight as this.

By the time Tom reached the next lines, his own voice wavered. "Be kinder to others. Do whatever you can do to be more peaceful. If it means praying to God more, or read more of the Bible—" His throat tightened, but he forced himself onward, refusing to break. "Don't swear or fight. Just be more peaceful. To yourself, and to others." His eyes blurred, but he continued, determined to give every word back to the room as it had been given by Myles.

The library was drowning in silence and tears. Even the most hardened teachers could not contain themselves. Mrs. Dunlop's cheeks glistened as she reached instinctively for a tissue, while Ms. Henley let tears run freely down her face, her counselor's calm shattered by the boy's unguarded plea. Zenji Takashi sat still as stone, but his eyes, sharp and unyielding in every courtroom and investigation, now shone with sorrow he did not hide. Beside him, Keiko quietly reached for his hand, her artist's soul broken by the child's fragile truth.

Tom lowered his gaze to the last words. "I hope my poem has made you more peaceful, for our world." He folded the paper slowly, not to put it away, but as though tucking Myles himself back into a safe place. He looked around the circle, meeting every pair of eyes, and whispered, "He was ten. Ten years old, and he still had the wisdom to say what so many of us forget. He wanted peace, not for himself, but for everyone."

Jeremy's lip quivered as he spoke softly, "That's… that's all he asked for." Ty put his arm around him, steady, a silent reminder that grief was not his to carry alone. Mila pressed her head into Leo's shoulder, whispering that she could not bear it, while Leo simply wrapped both arms around her, grounding her in silence. Alex, always so hardened, bowed his head, tears dripping freely onto the carpet without care for who saw.

Mr. Clarke finally broke the silence. His voice was cracked, his chest heavy, but he said the words that every heart needed: "This is why we remember him. This is why we cannot fail each other." His glasses slipped down his nose, and he made no move to fix them. His eyes were locked on Tom, not as a teacher to a student, but as one mourner to another.

Tom held the folded paper against his chest and nodded once. "Myles asked for peace. We will not let his words vanish. Not while I'm here. Not while any of us are." His voice no longer trembled. It rang out clear, and in that moment, he seemed taller, older, as though the weight of Myles' plea had lifted him from boyhood into something greater.

No one moved. No one dared breathe too quickly. In that library, every student, every teacher, every soul present carried Myles' words etched into their hearts like scripture. And though the poem had ended, the silence it left behind was not emptiness—it was promise.

Tom's voice did not soften after the poem. If anything, it hardened, as though the weight of Myles' words demanded something more than sorrow. He looked around the circle of faces, his eyes red but unwavering, and he said, "Do you know what hurts the most about Myles' death? Not only that he died. Not only that two boys thought it was a game. It's that no one was ever held responsible. No one. The law looked at him—ten years old—and still called it 'undetermined.'" The words scraped through the silence like broken glass. Even Zenji Takashi, who had heard the worst of human cruelty in courtrooms, bowed his head.

Jeremy sniffled, his small hand clutched in Leo's, but his voice was steady when he asked, "No one? Not one person?" Tom shook his head sharply, anger tightening his jaw. "Not one. They let silence cover it. They let excuses cover it. And do you know what that silence does? It tells every bully that what they do doesn't matter. It tells every victim that their pain is invisible. That's worse than fists. That's worse than bruises. Silence eats at you, until you stop believing anyone will stand for you." His voice rose, not in rage, but in fierce truth.

Sophie's lips trembled as she whispered, "That's not fair…" Her words barely carried across the carpet, but Tom heard them. He crouched slightly, meeting her eyes. "It isn't. It was never fair. And Myles' parents had to bury their son knowing that the ones who did it walked away. No justice. Just grief." His voice cracked for the first time, but he forced the words out. "That's what silence does. It doesn't heal—it scars." The circle seemed to fold in tighter, as though every student wanted to shield themselves from the sharpness of that truth.

Mr. Clarke wiped his glasses with trembling hands, speaking low, "I remember the inquest. I remember how hollow it felt, how empty." He looked directly at Tom, as though finally confessing aloud. "You're right. Silence can be worse than violence." His voice faltered, but he did not look away. It was the first time any adult in the room had admitted the failure aloud.

Tom straightened again, his fists clenched, his chest rising and falling with effort. "I want all of you to hear me now. I will never, never let myself become that monster I was just a few days ago. I was angry, I was violent, I thought hurting people meant I was strong." His voice shook, but this time it was not weakness. It was the tremor of truth. "But the truth is, I was just broken. Broken like Myles, but in a different way. And if I had kept going, if I had stayed that person, then one day maybe someone would have been reading about me—about the lives I ruined." His breath caught, and his eyes brimmed with tears, but he did not falter.

Ty rose slightly from his seat, his steady gaze fixed on Tom. "You're not him anymore," he said quietly, his words more powerful for their calm. "You've already chosen different." Tom looked at Ty, eyes burning, and whispered, "Because you didn't let me fall. You didn't let them throw me away." The room stilled again, the students leaning forward as though trying to catch every word.

Tom turned back to the circle, his voice clear, each syllable landing like a promise. "I was put through things I can barely speak of since I was five years old. Things no child should ever endure. My uncle made sure I lived in fear, every single day. And I swore I'd never be weak, never be the one hurt again. That's how I became what I was." He took a step closer to the centre of the circle, his shadow crossing the carpet like a dark scar. "But today I make a different oath. I swear I will never let anyone else go through that, not if I can stop it. Not here. Not anywhere."

The students shifted, their eyes wide, their breaths unsteady, as though hearing the words of someone older than his years. Even Alex, who had once mocked Leo into cruelty, gave a slow, heavy nod. He understood the weight of promises made in the ashes of regret. Nico whispered under his breath, "That's how you change." Ella squeezed Jasmin's hand, both girls trembling, both girls nodding fiercely, as though Tom's vow had also become theirs.

Zenji Takashi finally spoke, his voice measured and resonant. "What you carry does not excuse what you've done. But today you've placed truth where silence once stood. And that is the first true act of justice." His words did not thunder—they were steady as stone. Keiko, beside him, lifted her eyes to Tom and said softly, "And it takes more courage than fists."

Tom breathed deeply, his body rigid but his voice steady. "I won't go back. Not ever. If I lose everything else, I will hold onto that." He opened his fists slowly, fingers trembling, and for the first time since he had entered the library that day, his hands hung free at his sides. It was as if the chains he had clutched so tightly had loosened, at least for the moment.

Jeremy stood and crossed the circle without hesitation, wrapping his arms tightly around Tom's waist. His small voice rose clear enough for everyone to hear: "Then you'll never be alone in it." Tom froze, his chest heaving, and then his arms lowered around Jeremy in return. The circle broke—not in fear, but in solidarity. Students moved closer, some laying hands on Tom's shoulders, some only sitting near, but all closing the gap that silence had once carved.

The library was filled with tears, but they were no longer only of grief. They were of defiance, of a vow shared. Tom had spoken the truth of injustice, and in return, the students gave him what he had never been given before: a place where silence would never again bury him.

Tom's voice steadied as he looked at the faces around him, his words slow but weighted. "Bullies are not born. They are made. Shaped. Allowed. Every cruel word, every silence, every time someone looked away instead of stopping it—that's how a bully grows." The words hit harder than any shout could have. The room was still, every student and teacher locked on him. "I wasn't born angry. I was taught anger by the fists of someone I should have been able to trust. And when no one stopped it, I believed it was the only way to survive. That's what bullies are. Broken kids taught to break others." His hands shook, but his eyes never lowered.

Leo shifted forward from where he sat, his voice rough but steady. "He's right." He looked across the students, his eyes filled with a pain they all recognised from his own confession weeks before. "I was one of them. I was given power, and no one stopped me. I thought cruelty meant respect. I thought fear meant strength. But it wasn't—it was emptiness." His words echoed Tom's truth, tying past and present together. He stood and moved to Tom's side, resting his hand firmly on Tom's shoulder.

Alex rose next, taller than Leo, his voice quieter but no less resolute. "I hurt him," he admitted, gesturing to Leo. "I drove him deeper into it, and in doing so, I turned into the very thing I hated most. I thought mocking him gave me control, but all it did was chain me to my own weakness." His shoulders squared as he stepped beside Leo, and then Tom, his presence forming a line of broken boys who had found new strength not in fists, but in truth.

Lisa, fierce as ever, broke the silence with her blunt tone. "I fought because I liked winning," she said simply, her eyes sweeping across the room. "I didn't care who I knocked down, as long as I felt taller. That was my truth." Her words were hard, but when she moved forward and took her place beside the others, her hands folded loosely in front of her, the room understood—admitting it was her way of tearing down the mask. "But I see now that winning like that makes everyone lose." She glanced at Tom, her eyes steady, and nodded.

Harley, taller than most, stepped forward with a hesitation that quickly turned to determination. "I was no better," he confessed. "I laughed while I tore people down. I thought it was survival, but it was nothing more than fear covered in noise. And it nearly destroyed me." His words cracked at the edges, but he stood straight and took his place in the growing line beside Tom. For a moment, the students simply stared, hardly believing how many of their once-feared classmates now stood united in truth.

Then, with a shuffling of feet and an awkward cough, Jarod came forward. His presence was heavier, his reputation still raw and frightening to many, but his eyes were lowered, not defiant. "I hurt more than I care to admit," he said, his voice carrying across the room. "And I know some of you will never forgive me. I don't blame you." He paused, drawing a deep breath. "But if Tom can stand here and say he won't go back, then I'll stand with him. Not because I'm clean. But because I refuse to let myself stay dirty." The silence that followed was thick, but Jarod didn't flinch. He took his place at Tom's side, completing the line of former tormentors turned defenders.

Tom looked across at them, his voice low but carrying. "Do you see this? This is what I mean. Bullies can become protectors if the cycle is broken. If someone says 'enough.' If someone steps in." He turned back to the circle, to the rows of students and teachers, his chest rising and falling with sharp breaths. "It doesn't erase the damage. It doesn't fix the past. But it stops the pattern from eating the future." His words settled like heavy stones, unmovable and undeniable.

Ty's voice rose then, calm but commanding. "What you're seeing is proof. Not excuses. Proof. Change happens when truth is spoken, when someone is willing to carry the weight instead of pretending it doesn't exist. These five are not perfect. None of us are. But standing here today, they've made a vow." His eyes locked with each one of them—Leo, Alex, Lisa, Harley, Jarod—and each nodded, their agreement silent but absolute.

The students shifted, the atmosphere taut with a mixture of disbelief and hope. Sophie whispered to Ella, "It's like the worst ones are the ones standing up now." Ella squeezed her hand, replying, "Maybe that's what makes it matter most." Their words, though soft, carried enough for others to hear, and heads began nodding around the circle. Even the adults exchanged glances, the reality of what they were witnessing slowly sinking in.

Tom raised his voice once more. "From this day forward, I refuse to be the person I was made into. I'll be the person I choose to become. And so will they. We stand together—not to hide what we did, but to make sure it never happens again." His eyes swept across the students, locking with those who had once feared him most. "That is my vow." The line of five behind him echoed the sentiment in their silence, their postures firm, their presence undeniable.

Mr. Clarke, who had listened with hands trembling slightly, spoke into the quiet. "Cycles are broken when someone chooses not to repeat them. Today, we all saw that choice." His voice wavered, but his eyes glistened with pride and grief. "And today, you've given this school something it has never had before—a chance to truly heal."

The silence that followed was different now. Not empty, not heavy. It was filled with possibility. The five who had once carried shadows now stood as beacons of what could change. And in that silence, the lesson of cycles had finally been spoken, heard, and believed.

# THE SMILE THAT BROKE

The words had been spoken, the lessons laid bare, yet what followed was heavier than any vow. Tom stood rigid at the circle's centre, his chest rising and falling as though the weight of Myles Neuts' story had pressed itself fully into his body. For a long moment, he stared at the image of Myles frozen on the monitor, the boy's young smile beaming across the library as though untouched by the cruelty of that day. Tom's throat worked, his jaw set, but no words came. Instead, a low, raw sound escaped him, almost foreign, almost startling—his first crack of grief breaking through. His fists unclenched, his body shook, and for the first time in front of his peers, Tom's defences dissolved.

His shoulders crumpled as he tried to hold himself upright, but his strength betrayed him. Tears blurred his vision until Myles' face on the screen became little more than a glowing blur. He shook his head, gasping through clenched teeth. "He was only ten," he muttered, not to anyone specific, but to the world itself. "Ten. And no one saved him." The words splintered as sobs tore free, the sound striking the room harder than any accusation. Students sat frozen, their own tears welling in response, teachers standing as though the air itself had turned heavier.

Ty was the first to move. Without a word, he crossed the small space between them and opened his arms. Tom did not hesitate. The boy who had fought, shouted, resisted, and denied every gesture of compassion now folded entirely, collapsing against Ty's chest with all the weight of his grief. His sobs muffled into Ty's shirt, his body trembling as though years of unspoken sorrow had been unleashed at once. Ty wrapped him fully, arms strong and steady, rocking him slightly, whispering nothing, offering only presence.

The library fell utterly silent save for Tom's sobbing. Each sound pierced the quiet like a blade, but no one flinched away. Nico wiped at his cheeks, his own tears falling unchecked. Jasmin leaned into Ella, her shoulders shaking as she clutched her friend's hand. Sophie buried her face in her palms. Even Leo and Alex, who had sworn to break their cycles, let their tears fall openly, their shame and their hope colliding at once. Every student, whether victim or former bully, felt the weight of what Tom carried—grieving for Myles, grieving for themselves, grieving for the pain that tied them all together.

Mr. Clarke, who had never let emotion unravel him in front of the students, turned his face away for a moment, his glasses catching the dim light as tears slipped down his cheeks. Mr. Arnett pressed a hand over his mouth, struggling with the composure expected of a principal but failing to mask the ache that seized him. Mrs. Dunlop's shoulders trembled as she pressed a tissue to her eyes, her quiet sobs betraying the vice principal's usually unshakable stance. Around the edges of the room, the teachers' silence was broken by sniffles and low murmurs of sorrow, the truth of Myles' death having found its way into their hearts through Tom's breaking.

Ty held Tom firmly, his small frame strong enough to carry the other's collapse. "You're safe," Ty murmured finally, low enough for only Tom to hear. "You don't have to hold it anymore." Tom shook his head against his shoulder, his sobs tearing out harder. "I never cried for me. I never cried for him. I don't know how." Ty's grip tightened, his cheek resting lightly on Tom's hair. "Then cry now. Cry for both of you." The words settled between them, quiet but true, and Tom's grief surged, pouring out like a storm breaking through walls that had held too long.

The other students began shifting closer, their circle pulling tighter as though the weight of Tom's grief drew them inward. Jeremy, usually eager with words, said nothing. Instead, he reached out and laid a hand gently on Tom's back, adding his quiet strength to Ty's. One by one, others mirrored him—Sophie, Mila, Leo, Alex—until a chain of hands rested lightly, not crowding but reminding him he was surrounded. No one mocked him. No one turned away. Every touch was steady, every gaze unflinching. For once, Tom was not the boy feared or avoided—he was the boy mourned with.

Zenji, standing tall but softened by the scene before him, exchanged a glance with his wife. Keiko clutched her tissue in one hand, but her other hand reached for Zenji's arm, squeezing tightly. Their son was holding a boy broken by years of cruelty, and in that moment they both knew Ty's vow was not empty—he had been born to carry this role. Zenji's voice was a whisper, reverent and heavy. "This is what healing begins with."

Minutes passed, though no one tracked the time. When Tom's sobs finally began to slow, his breathing ragged, he didn't pull away. He stayed pressed against Ty, his arms now clutching him in return, as though afraid letting go would mean returning to the shadows. Ty simply tightened his hold and whispered again, "You're not alone. Not anymore."

The image of Myles remained glowing above them, his poem and his story imprinted in every mind. Yet it was Tom's collapse, his open grief, that bound the lesson permanently in the room. In crying for Myles, Tom had opened the door for every student to grieve for themselves, for the scars they carried, for the silence they endured. And in Ty's arms, he had proven that grief could be carried, not hidden. That was the moment the room understood: cycles break not only with truth, but with tears.

When Tom finally pulled his head from Ty's shoulder, his face was streaked with tears but his eyes were clearer than they had ever been. He did not speak. He didn't need to. His grief had said everything. And the silence that followed was no longer heavy—it was sacred.

The dam had already broken, yet it seemed the flood was only beginning. Tom's sobs had cracked the silence wide open, but now the grief became something larger, something communal. Sophie clutched Ella so tightly their knuckles whitened, both girls pressing their foreheads together as tears streamed unchecked. Nico wiped at his cheeks with the sleeve of his shirt, but gave up when the tears kept coming faster than he could stop them. Jasmin's face glistened, her lip trembling as she leaned against Mila, who wrapped an arm around her without hesitation. It was no longer one boy's collapse they witnessed—it was everyone's. The room itself seemed to cry.

Leo, who once hid behind false bravado, did not bother to shield his face. His hands dropped into his lap, his tears falling freely onto his shirt. For years he had believed crying meant weakness, but in that moment, strength was no longer measured by silence. He wept openly, his sobs ragged, his eyes never leaving Tom who still clung to Ty. "I know," he whispered hoarsely, as though speaking to both Myles and Tom, as though confessing to everyone and to himself. It was not an excuse. It was truth spoken at last. His tears said more than his words ever could.

Jeremy, who had shifted closer with each passing moment, now wriggled himself firmly between Ty and Tom, his small arms wrapping tightly around Tom's trembling frame. He pressed his cheek against Tom's shoulder, eyes squeezed shut as his tears fell freely. "I love you," he whispered into Tom's ear, his voice breaking but steady enough to be heard. There was no hesitation in him, no shame. Jeremy's declaration pierced through the noise of crying, not as comfort but as truth. Tom shuddered at the words, his grip tightening on both boys, the shield around his heart splintering further.

The teachers, who once held the line between discipline and compassion, now found themselves undone. Mr. Clarke removed his glasses and set them on the nearest table, rubbing his eyes with shaking hands before the tears simply flowed unhindered. He was no longer the composed English teacher, nor the steady librarian who always had an answer—he was a man mourning the cruelty of the world, mourning a child he never met but whose story was now his own burden to bear. Beside him, Mrs. Dunlop lowered her tissue from her face, her chest heaving as she let herself cry as freely as the children. Even Mr. Arnett, the principal who had guarded his authority like armour, bowed his head into his hands, his shoulders quaking with sobs.

Ty remained the anchor, his arms still around Tom even as Jeremy pressed in and the others drew closer. His shirt was soaked, his shoulders aching, yet he did not move. He held them both, his strength unyielding. His eyes, though filled with tears of his own, never wavered. He looked across the circle, meeting each gaze, silently assuring them that this was not shameful, that this was healing. "Let it out," he murmured once, his voice quiet but carrying enough weight to ripple through the circle. And they did. No one resisted. The sound of grief filled the library, layered and raw, yet beautiful in its honesty.

Keiko Takashi clutched her husband's hand as tears streaked down her face, unable to stop herself from whispering, "They're learning what love truly means." Zenji nodded, his own jaw clenched tight as he tried and failed to stop his own tears from falling. He did not try to control them. For once, the RCMP investigator, the man so used to documenting facts and burying emotions, allowed himself to cry among children. He bowed his head slightly, a tear slipping from his cheek as he whispered to his wife, "This is the kind of justice no courtroom can give."

The circle of students seemed to pulse with shared sorrow. They reached for one another—hands linking, arms brushing, shoulders pressed together. Tom no longer wept alone. His grief had been absorbed, carried, and echoed back until it belonged to them all. Even those who had once inflicted pain—Leo, Alex, Lisa, Harley—sat within the circle crying as much for their past selves as for Tom and Myles. Each tear was confession, each sob a release, and for the first time the weight of silence did not crush them. Instead, it bound them together.

Tom could barely breathe from the force of it all, yet he did not pull away. His face pressed into Ty's chest, Jeremy clutched close at his side, and the warmth of others reaching in reminded him of something he had never known before: grief could be shared. For years he had believed sorrow must be swallowed, anger must be wielded, and pain must be endured alone. But here, in this library filled with weeping voices, he realised the truth. They were shouldering his grief with him. They were telling him, not with words but with tears, that he would never again carry it alone.

The sound rose and fell like waves crashing, until it finally softened into quiet sobs, the kind that left faces streaked, noses raw, and bodies drained. No one looked away in shame. No one wiped their eyes with embarrassment. They had all entered the grief together, and now, in this quiet, they emerged changed. Mr. Clarke's voice trembled as he finally spoke, "This is only the beginning." His words carried across the circle like a benediction, not of closure, but of commitment. They had wept, they had broken, and in that breaking they had begun to heal.

And in the centre of it all, Tom breathed deeply for the first time in years, surrounded by arms, by tears, and by love he never believed he would deserve.

Tom rose slowly from where he had been sitting, Jeremy still clinging to his sleeve, Ty's hand resting steady at his back. His face was swollen from tears, but there was no hesitation in his step. He turned toward the circle of classmates, teachers, and parents, the hush of the library pressing against him like a wall. The air smelled faintly of paper, carpet, and salt from tears. His voice cracked when he first tried to speak, but he did not retreat. He swallowed, looked once at the photograph of Myles glowing on the screen, and found his strength in the boy's eyes staring back. "I won't let this story fade," he said firmly. The room leaned in, every ear straining, every heart aching to hear more.

He lifted the article Jeremy had carried weeks before, the one with Myles' name typed in stark print. The paper trembled in his hands, not from weakness, but from the weight of carrying someone else's memory.

"Myles Casey Benson Neuts," Tom said clearly, "ten years old, born in Ontario, died in 1998. And the world moved on too fast." His voice shook, but not from fear—this time it was from fury carefully tamed into purpose. He let the words sink into the silence, not rushing, not filling the air with anything but truth. Jeremy's small hand tightened around his arm, and Leo's head bowed as if in reverence.

Tom's next words cut deeper. "He was not forgotten because he was weak. He was not forgotten because he made a mistake. He was forgotten because too many people stayed silent when he needed them to speak." His throat tightened as the tears threatened to rise again, but he steadied himself. Ty's presence anchored him, that quiet certainty pressing into his spine. Tom looked directly at his peers, eyes red and shining. "That silence nearly swallowed me too. And I will not—ever—let it swallow anyone else." The words landed like a strike, hitting not just ears but hearts.

There was a stillness in the room that carried weight. Even Mrs. Dunlop's tissue froze mid-air, her eyes widened as though she could not take another breath. Mr. Clarke adjusted his glasses, not to see clearer, but to hide his own tears as they fell onto his shirt. The children shuffled, some wiping their eyes, others clasping their hands in their laps as though they were praying without words. The photograph of Myles on the screen felt alive in the silence, watching them all, demanding this vow be made and kept.

Tom drew in a long breath and set the paper down carefully, as though returning a relic to its altar. "I used to believe anger made me strong," he admitted. His voice trembled, but he raised it higher, not hiding. "I used to think if I hit harder, yelled louder, or scared people enough, I'd never feel small again. But anger doesn't protect you—it eats you. It eats everything." He looked toward Alex, then Leo, who nodded faintly in shared understanding. "But compassion—compassion is the only thing that stops the eating. That's what I've learned. And that's what I'm choosing now."

Ty stepped forward then, not to take over but to stand shoulder-to-shoulder with him. He didn't speak at first, he only nodded to Tom, the way a brother would. Tom's voice grew steadier in that presence. "So I make this vow—here, in this room, with all of you as my witnesses." He turned slowly, making eye contact with Sophie, with Ella, with Nico and Jasmin, with every student who leaned in closer. His hands clenched and released as if the vow had to be wrestled free from his chest. "I will not let Myles Neuts' name fade. I will not let him vanish into silence again."

The sound of a chair scraped slightly as Mrs. Haller shifted, her eyes full and wet. The teachers looked among themselves, none daring to interrupt. Mr. Arnett, usually the voice of order, lowered his gaze as though humbled by a thirteen-year-old boy's truth. "From this day," Tom continued, "I will stand against the silence. I will protect those who feel they have no voice. I will not turn my back when cruelty hides in laughter, when lies are dressed as jokes, when fear stalks the hallways." His words came sharper now, like steel honed on stone. "Because silence is what killed Myles. And silence is what nearly killed me."

Jeremy leaned his cheek against Tom's arm, whispering again, "We won't let you do it alone." The words, though soft, rang clear enough for everyone to hear. Leo's hand rose, wiping tears furiously from his face, before he muttered, "Me neither." Alex followed, speaking more firmly: "All of us." Lisa crossed her arms, not to defend herself, but as if to seal her vow. Harley's voice was almost a growl when he added, "Count me in." And Jarod, who had hovered uncertainly near the edge, finally stepped forward, his head bowed. "I'll stand too," he said quietly. For once, no one doubted him.

Tom's voice faltered then, but Ty caught his shoulder, steadying him. He finished with words simple but powerful: "This is my vow. For Myles, for myself, and for every one of you. I choose compassion. I choose truth. And I will not let the silence win again." He lifted his head, tears running freely, but his eyes clear and unbroken. The vow hung in the library like a brand, something that could not be erased.

For a moment, no one moved. Then the sound rose—not of sobbing now, but of applause. Not the polite clapping of assemblies, but the fierce and raw pounding of hands that echoed off the bookshelves and ceiling. Teachers clapped, students clapped, even Zenji Takashi clapped once and then bowed his head low. The sound carried Myles' name through the library as if his spirit were being lifted back into memory. The vow was not just Tom's—it was theirs. And together, they knew it would hold.

Ty moved before anyone else could stir, his small frame walking with a certainty that made the entire circle of students shift back into silence. He stopped in front of Tom, who was still trembling from the weight of his vow, his face blotched from crying, his chest rising and falling as though he had carried the whole world in his words. Ty reached forward without hesitation, his arms sliding around Tom's shoulders, pulling him close. It was not a gentle pat, not a stiff squeeze of sympathy—it was a full embrace, tight and unyielding, the kind that said I love you, I see you, you are mine to protect. Tom's chest hitched, his own arms folding around Ty as if afraid to ever let go again. The circle drew tighter, and the vow that had once belonged to one boy now belonged to them both.

Tom's head dropped into the crook of Ty's shoulder, his tears falling freely, but for once there was no shame in them. Ty's voice carried low, steady, and strong, audible enough for every ear to catch. "Your vow is mine," he said. "I won't let Myles Neuts be forgotten. I won't let silence take another boy. We'll carry this together." The words were neither rehearsed nor theatrical, they were as simple as truth could be. The silence that followed was reverent, as if the library itself bowed down to what had just been declared.

Jeremy pushed forward then, his small body wedging between Ty and Tom, his arms wrapping clumsily around both of them. His face pressed into Tom's side, and his voice, muffled but steady, added, "I love you. Both of you. I'll never stop."

Leo and Alex exchanged a look across the circle, each seeing in the other the same memory of their own confessions weeks before. Without a word, they crossed the carpet, their steps heavy but purposeful, placing their hands on Tom's back, their presence a wall of strength. The circle began to shift, children pulling in closer, the carpet beneath them covered with knees, hands, and tears.

Lisa folded her arms for only a second before giving in, pushing forward to stand next to Ty. Her voice was blunt, unpolished, but truer for it. "Then count me too. If you fall, Tom, I'll fall with you. If you stand, I'll stand with you. But I'm not letting you go through this alone." Harley followed with his tall, awkward frame, his hand settling on Tom's shoulder, his jaw tight as though holding back his own emotions. His single nod, his firm grip, said more than words could. Even Jarod, who had lingered at the edge with uncertainty, stepped forward, shoulders slumped but eyes honest. "Me too," he muttered, almost ashamed. No one mocked him. No one doubted him.

Mr. Clarke was the first adult to move. He set his glasses aside, his eyes red, and walked into the circle of students. He bent slightly, his hand pressing gently against Tom's other shoulder. His voice cracked, but the words carried. "Myles deserved this—he deserves to be remembered by all of us. You've given him a brotherhood here, Tom. And you've given us courage too." Mr. Arnett stood just behind him, his usual formality broken, his face raw as he nodded his agreement. "You will not do this alone," he promised. Teachers who had been stiff and guarded softened, their arms folding across themselves, their eyes wet. Even Mrs. Haller clutched Sophie to her chest, nodding as if silently swearing her own vow.

Ty turned slightly, still holding Tom, and addressed the circle. "This isn't just his fight. It's ours now. Every one of us." His words didn't rise in volume, they didn't demand. They simply settled, firm as stone, undeniable. The circle bent closer, arms extending, shoulders touching, hands gripping. The bonds that had once been fractured by fear and cruelty were being rewoven with something stronger than any chain of silence. It was the brotherhood of memory—the choosing to carry another's pain so it would never be carried alone again.

Tom lifted his head, his eyes shining, though streaked with tears. He scanned the faces around him—Ty's unbreakable gaze, Jeremy's small determined arms, Leo and Alex's steady strength, Lisa's sharp promise, Harley's firm grip, Jarod's tentative step forward. He looked at the teachers who had softened, at the principal who no longer carried suspicion, and at Zenji Takashi, who stood tall at the back, his eyes filled with a father's pride. Tom drew a shaking breath and said only two words: "Thank you." His voice cracked, but the circle held firm, those words received as sacred.

The circle tightened once more, a collective embrace without arms, where every student, every teacher, every witness silently spoke their vow. The photograph of Myles still glowed on the screen behind them, his poem folded neatly on the table, his name alive in the air. And for the first time since 1998, in this small library, surrounded by children and teachers, Myles Neuts was not forgotten. His memory lived in the vow of a boy once lost and now found, carried in the embrace of a brotherhood that refused to let silence win.

Tom lifted his head once more and said one last vital, important statement to all, his voice steady even through the tears: "I want all of you to remember, that you are loved. Because I love each and every one of you. To me, you are my family."

The words fell into the room like a stone dropped into still water, sending rings of truth through every heart. Jeremy clung tighter to him, whispering back, "I love you too, Tom. Always." Ty rested a hand firmly on Tom's shoulder, pride radiating from his calm eyes. Sophie and Ella leaned into one another, tears running freely, their hands clasped together in silent agreement. Leo, once the bully, did not hide his face but let the tears streak down openly, proof that strength meant vulnerability. Alex bowed his head, humbled that someone could transform so much, so fast, and yet so true.

Mr. Clarke wiped his glasses with trembling hands, unable to disguise his weeping as anything less than love. Mr. Arnett, the principal, rose slowly, his voice breaking as he said, "You are not just students to me anymore. You are the reason we must never give up." Mrs. Dunlop and Miss Kara quietly passed boxes of tissues around, their hands shaking, while Mrs. Haller wept silently into her sleeve. Ms. Henley, the counsellor, whispered under her breath, "Finally," as though she had been waiting years for a moment like this.

Zenji Takashi bowed his head with reverence, his hand resting over his heart. Keiko Takashi dabbed at her eyes, pride and sorrow mixing in equal measure. And as the sunlight streamed through the tall library windows, no one moved to break the circle. For in that silence, in that love, they knew something greater than themselves had entered the room. It was not just Tom's voice. It was Myles's. It was every child who had ever suffered. And it was the vow of those still here, refusing to let another smile break unchallenged.

### CHAPTER 17: BUILDING NEW WAYS

The Takashi home was filled with a quiet solemnity, not the stillness of mourning but the breath-holding silence of something sacred. Zenji and Keiko stood on either side of Tom, one hand on his shoulder, the other guiding the pen that would change his life. The adoption papers rested on the polished table, each stroke of ink marking not the severance of an old life but the beginning of a new one. Tom's eyes watered as he wrote his name, now with the Takashi surname, and when the final flourish was done, he exhaled a breath he had not known he was holding. There was no audience beyond those who mattered. Yet the room carried the weight of generations, of honour, of family finally restored. The documents were not celebrated with balloons or a feast; they were folded carefully, tucked away as if to protect them from the wind itself. For Tom, they meant something greater than celebration — they meant belonging, and belonging meant life itself.

Keiko had prepared something beyond words, a gift that would hold the weight of tradition and the lightness of everyday comfort. From a wooden chest lined in soft silk she lifted four Deluxe Sashiko AtsuOri Samue outfits, the indigo stitching strong and elegant. Tom reached out as though afraid to touch, until Keiko placed them into his arms. The fabric was thick, handwoven with the same care one would show to a son. Zenji smiled, the rare kind of smile that softened the lines on his face, and nodded. "They are yours, Tom. Wear them in the dojo, wear them in the garden, wear them as you learn to carry yourself as one of us. These are not uniforms of discipline but clothing of respect. Respect for yourself, respect for this family." Tom clutched the garments close to his chest, his throat tight, his eyes refusing to release the tears that burned hot behind them.

The home itself seemed to shift around him, as though the garden and the wooden walls had known his name long before he arrived. The Japanese garden stretched outward like a painting in motion, with a pond that mirrored the clouds, koi gliding beneath lily pads as if they too welcomed him. A line of bonsai trees stood proud along the path, shaped by years of careful hands, their twisted branches echoing patience rather than force. The dojo sat at the far end, its sliding doors open to let in the spring air, tatami mats aligned in quiet readiness. Tom felt the weight of it all, the balance between order and beauty, and wondered if he would ever fit into such perfection. Yet for the first time, he dared to hope. He was not stepping into someone else's world anymore; this was his world now, and it was waiting to receive him.

Mr. Arnett had been present for the signing, a witness in the most personal sense, but his role that day grew far beyond the duties of a principal. Tom had chosen him, with all the seriousness of a vow, to be Uncle Ted. It was not asked lightly, and it was not received casually. Arnett bent slightly, as though lowering himself to Tom's level, though his broad shoulders still filled the doorway. His eyes, steady and kind, met Tom's with no hesitation. "If that is what you want, Tom, then that is who I will be. Uncle Ted." The boy's lips trembled, and then he nodded, and before the day had ended he was already calling the man "Uncle Ted" with the same conviction he had spoken "Mom" and "Dad." It was the weaving of a new net, one that would never let him fall again.

Evening came with the fragrance of Keiko's cooking, rice steamed in the pot, vegetables crisped in sesame oil, fish grilled to perfection. The dining table was not crowded with strangers but filled with friends who had become a circle of guardians around Tom. Ty sat tall beside his new brother, proud beyond measure, his smile brighter than the lanterns strung outside in the garden. Leo leaned across to tease Jeremy, whose grin betrayed a mixture of mischief and joy. Nico and Jasmin shared quiet words, Ella's laughter carried lightly over Sophie's quips, while Alex listened more than he spoke, his eyes softer now than they had ever been in his former life. Even Mila, who often hung back at such gatherings, leaned forward with bright eyes, as if drawn by the warmth of the family fire. Teachers were present too — Mr. Clarke, Mrs. Dunlop, Miss Kara, Mrs. Haller, and Ms. Henley — each finding their place as though the school itself had followed Tom home.

When Tom looked across the table, his gaze caught Ella's, and for a moment the rest of the world blurred. She sat with her dark hair falling loosely about her shoulders, her eyes glimmering with a knowing light that unsettled and fascinated him at once. For the first time in his life, Tom did not feel invisible to a girl. Ella saw him, truly saw him, and the realization sent a warmth through his chest that had nothing to do with food or family. He did not know what to call it yet, only that her smile lingered in his thoughts long after she looked away. Ella knew, too — her eyes returned, her lips curving as if to say she understood more than words could capture. Tom was startled by the power of it, by how quickly beauty could draw him forward, but he did not turn from it. He was part of this family now, and even love, unexpected and young as it was, belonged in it too.

The evening stretched with stories. Zenji spoke of honour, of what it meant to stand tall not by the strength of one's fists but by the steadiness of one's spirit. Keiko told of patience, how a bonsai grew not from force but from gentle shaping over years, a mirror of the way children grow when they are loved. Mr. Clarke recited lines of poetry, while Miss Kara and Mrs. Haller debated geography with a laughter that softened their authority. Even Mrs. Dunlop, whose reputation for severity was well known, leaned back with wine in her glass and a rare smile on her lips. Tom sat in the middle of it all, his eyes darting from face to face, storing away every gesture, every word, as though afraid they might vanish if he blinked. He did not speak much, but his silence was not the silence of fear; it was the silence of awe.

Later, when the lanterns burned low and the night air cooled, Jeremy slipped beside Leo, tugging gently at his sleeve. "He's home now, isn't he?" the boy whispered, his eyes fixed on Tom, who stood with Ty by the koi pond, laughter bubbling between them. Leo wrapped an arm around his little brother's shoulders, giving him a squeeze. "Yes," he said quietly, "he's home." It was a simple truth, yet it held the weight of every struggle, every broken piece, every hope that had finally come together. For Tom, the house, the family, the garden, the dojo, the laughter, even the quiet glance from Ella — all of it was proof that he was no longer wandering in search of love. He had found it, and it had claimed him fully.

The moment arrived with no announcement, no prepared speech, no call for attention. Tom simply stood in the doorway of the living room, where Keiko was arranging tea and Zenji was reading in silence, and spoke the words he had never before dared to speak aloud. His voice trembled at first, but then it steadied as though anchored by a truth older than himself. "Mom," he said, his eyes fixed on Keiko, and then he turned toward Zenji and breathed, "Dad." The air shifted at once, as though even the garden outside leaned in to hear. Keiko's hands froze mid-motion, her teacup nearly slipping from her grasp, and Zenji lowered his book with deliberate calm. There was no pause, no correction, no embarrassment in their faces. Only the quiet joy of two people who had been waiting, silently, for this day to come.

Keiko crossed the space between them, her bare feet whispering against the polished floor. She placed both hands on Tom's cheeks and pressed her forehead against his, her breath shaking but her smile unbroken. "Yes," she whispered, "I am your mother." Zenji rose, slow and purposeful, his presence commanding without force. He placed one hand on Tom's shoulder, the other on Ty's, and said, "And I am your father. You are my son. Nothing changes that now." Ty beamed so wide his cheeks hurt, nodding furiously as though to cement the words in stone. Tom's chest loosened with a relief so profound he nearly fell to his knees. For the first time in his life, he was not pretending, not borrowing the title of family from strangers. It was his now, and it could never be taken.

The news travelled swiftly through the school, not by whisper but by cheerful declaration. Ty could not contain his excitement, telling Nico, Jasmin, Sophie, and even Leo that Tom now had what they all knew he deserved. "He's got a real mom, a real dad, and a brother that's stuck with him for life," Ty announced with pride that spread like wildfire. The students, curious and bright-eyed, accepted it with the natural ease that only children have when truth carries no scandal. Even the teachers, those who had carried quiet worries about Tom's future, seemed lighter, as though a burden had been lifted from the halls. For once, the boy who had arrived carrying shadows now walked in the light of belonging, and it showed in every step he took.

That evening, when Tom returned to his room, he found something unexpected upon his bed. Folded neatly across his pillow lay a note written in careful, looping handwriting. He recognized Ella's style immediately, her flourishes and precise lines as deliberate as her laughter. She had slipped away quietly, saying she needed the washroom before her long walk home, but in truth she had left behind more than her absence. Tom sat heavily upon his king-size bed, smoothing the paper with nervous fingers before daring to unfold it. The words leapt at him with a clarity that left no room for doubt: "I am so happy for you, Tom. You've given us more than you'll ever know. What you did in the library about Myles Neuts, what you did for all of us, especially me, I will never forget. I am grateful, and I want you to know the truth. I love you. Not because of what you've done, but because you are yourself."

His breath caught, his eyes scanning the words again and again as though he might conjure them into permanence. He pressed the note against his chest, his heartbeat rattling beneath it like a drum too small to hold its rhythm. No one had ever written him something so raw, so fearless. Tom, who had known fists and cruel words more often than kindness, now held a confession that spoke of love. It unsettled him, not because he doubted it, but because he could not fathom what it meant to be loved without condition. He whispered her name into the stillness of the room, not loud enough for anyone else to hear, but strong enough for the word to steady him. Ella.

Meanwhile, Ella leaned against the bathroom sink, her hands gripping the porcelain as though it were the only thing keeping her grounded. Her cheeks burned with the courage it had taken to write that note, and though she told herself she had only gone to relieve herself before walking home, her heart betrayed her with every thrum. She knew Tom would find it, knew he would understand, and yet the vulnerability of it left her trembling. It was not a schoolyard crush she had written into words, not some fleeting infatuation born of convenience. It was the truth of a girl who had watched a boy stand in a library and speak boldly of a life lost, and in doing so reveal his own heart. She loved him not for heroics, but because he dared to be himself when others hid behind masks.

Dinner that night was lively, with voices overlapping, laughter spilling across the table, and plates being passed from hand to eager hand. Yet Tom hardly tasted the food, though he nodded at Zenji's stories and smiled at Ty's antics. The note in his pocket seemed to burn against his side, its presence a secret too enormous to contain. He looked at Ella across the table once, only once, and found her gaze waiting for his. Her lips curved ever so slightly, a smile that promised patience, a smile that told him she did not need an answer tonight. That single look steadied him more than the food could. It reminded him that even amidst the noise and the chaos of family, there could be quiet moments that belonged to only two.

After the dishes were cleared and lanterns lit in the garden, Tom wandered into the stillness of the pond-side path. The stars shimmered above, mirrored in the koi-filled waters, and he pulled Ella's note from his pocket once more. He read it under the soft glow of the lantern, each word deepening its hold. Behind him, Zenji's voice carried from the house, calm and sure, reminding Ty to prepare for morning practice, while Keiko's laughter followed in gentle waves. The world was no longer fractured for Tom; it was whole. And yet, within that wholeness, Ella's words carved a new space in his heart — a space both terrifying and beautiful. He folded the note carefully, not hiding it out of fear but treasuring it as one would treasure a seed. For seeds, he knew now, could grow into forests if tended with care.

Ty found Tom sitting just outside the garden after dinner, the lanterns flickering low and the voices of the adults carrying warmly through the sliding doors. He lowered himself beside him, his knees brushing the wooden step, and for a while they sat in silence, listening to the koi stir in the pond.

At last, Ty spoke with the frankness only a brother could muster. "You don't need to wonder anymore if you belong here. Blood doesn't make a brother, Tom. Living life together does. Sharing meals, training in the dojo, laughing in the same room—that's what counts." Tom glanced at him, uncertain whether to reply, but the conviction in Ty's tone left no doubt. He wasn't offering pity, he wasn't reciting something he'd been told. He was declaring what he believed. Tom's shoulders eased, as if a weight he'd been carrying for years had finally slipped to the ground.

The younger boy took a long breath before speaking, his voice low enough to nearly vanish with the wind. "I don't feel like an outsider anymore. I used to think I was always on the outside, watching everyone else have what I couldn't. Now it's different. I'm not looking in through a window anymore." Ty grinned, nudging his shoulder against Tom's. "That's because you're inside now. You've got a seat at the table and a mat in the dojo. You're not a guest. You're my brother, and nothing changes that." The words sank into Tom with the kind of depth no lesson at school could reach. He had heard people speak of family, but never had someone claimed him outright with such simplicity. He nodded, a small motion, but one filled with a courage he had never dared show before.

Later, back inside the house, Tom turned toward Zenji and Keiko with a look of hesitant curiosity. He fidgeted with his hands, as though ashamed to ask for something that might seem too grown up. "Mom, Dad," he began, his voice careful, "would it be all right if I tried coffee, just once? I've never tasted it before." Keiko looked toward Zenji, her expression a mixture of amusement and surprise. Zenji raised a brow, his face unreadable for a long moment, then gave a slight smile. "Coffee is no reward, Tom. It's bitter and strong. But if you wish to try it, you may. Only a little, with cream. Sugar is unnecessary. Sugar unsettles the stomach." Tom's eyes brightened with gratitude, as though they had just granted him entrance into another hidden chamber of adulthood. It wasn't about the coffee—it was about being trusted to ask, and trusted to receive.

Zenji prepared it himself, not with haste, but with the deliberate care he gave to every action. He poured a small measure of percolated coffee into a porcelain cup no bigger than his hand, and stirred in two measures of cream. The steam rose gently, carrying the sharp scent across the table. Zenji placed the cup before his son, not as a test but as a gift. Tom lifted it slowly, bringing it to his lips, the warmth surprising against his skin. The bitterness hit first, a strength he hadn't expected, but the cream softened it just enough to be bearable. He swallowed and set the cup down, his face caught between a grimace and a smile. Ty chuckled, leaning back in his chair. "See? Now you're practically an adult. Welcome to the club." Tom laughed too, shaking his head. "I'm not sure how you drink this every morning." Zenji simply answered, "Because it is not about liking it. It is about discipline."

The conversation shifted, but Tom's thoughts returned to the folded note still in his pocket. He had carried Ella's words with him since the moment he found them, but tonight he felt the need to share them, not hide them. After the dishes were cleared and the garden quieted, he stepped toward Zenji, holding the folded paper with trembling fingers.

"Dad, I want you to read this. And then give it to Mom, please." Zenji took it without question, unfolding the page with the same patience he had shown when guiding Tom through the adoption. His eyes moved steadily across the lines, his expression calm, though his breath caught once when he reached the final declaration. He read it again, slower this time, as if to weigh every word. When he finished, he folded it carefully and looked at Tom with a seriousness that did not frighten but steadied him.

Keiko received the note next, her hands delicate against the paper, her lips parting softly as she read the words. Her eyes glistened by the time she finished, though her smile carried a warmth that reassured Tom more than anything else. She laid the note flat upon the table and pressed her hand over it, as though sealing the promise inside. "Ella has given you a gift, Tom," she said gently. "Not the kind you can hold, but the kind you must honour. To be loved for who you are is the rarest gift of all." Tom lowered his head, overwhelmed, but Zenji spoke firmly. "Do not treat these words as a prize. They are not a trophy. They are a trust. If you return them with respect, you will have honoured her courage. That is what it means to be a man." Tom nodded, swallowing hard, his heart pounding with the weight of responsibility and the unexpected beauty of being seen.

Ty leaned against the doorframe, his grin tempered by respect for the moment, and called out with a chuckle, "See, Tom? Brothers tell each other everything. Even the scary things. Especially those." Tom smirked faintly, shaking his head, but there was no denial in his eyes. For the first time, he felt the binding of brotherhood not as chains but as a rope that pulled him closer, kept him steady, and gave him a place to belong.

The dojo held a silence of its own, a silence that hummed with discipline and patience rather than emptiness. Zenji stood at the head of the room, his presence filling the space without raising his voice. He motioned for Ty and Tom to kneel upon the tatami mats, the faint smell of straw rising around them as they pressed their knees into the woven floor. "Breathe," Zenji instructed, his tone both soft and commanding. "Do not force it. Breathe as the garden breathes, as the water moves, as the wind shifts in the trees." Tom closed his eyes, his shoulders tight at first, his chest fighting the rhythm. But gradually, guided by Zenji's steady cadence, his breath slowed. His fists unclenched, his heart steadied, and he began to feel strength where he once expected only tension. Zenji nodded. "Strength is not in your fists, Tom. It begins here," he tapped his chest gently, "with stillness."

Ty leaned back upon his heels, grinning as he opened his eyes and glanced at his new brother. "It feels strange at first, doesn't it? Like you're not doing anything. But that's the point. You don't always have to fight. Sometimes you just have to breathe." Tom exhaled sharply, the hint of a smile tugging at his lips. "I'm starting to see that," he admitted. The air in the dojo seemed to thrum with the rhythm of their breathing, the lantern light catching the sheen of sweat upon their brows, though they had barely moved. Zenji rose, satisfied, and left them with a nod. "Continue. Stillness must be learned together." His footsteps faded, leaving the brothers alone in the dim quiet of the dojo.

After a few more breaths, Ty stretched his legs and rolled his shoulders, turning toward Tom with a look that carried more weight than his years should have allowed. "There's something I want to tell you," he said quietly. "Jasmin and I… well, we're together. She's my girlfriend." Tom blinked, surprised by the frankness, but Ty pressed on, his words sincere. "It's not just about holding her hand or saying sweet things. It's about patience. About listening when she needs to talk, even if I don't have the answers. It's about being her sunlight, so she can grow." Tom tilted his head, curiosity plain on his face, and Ty continued, his voice steady. "If you give sunlight to a flower, it blossoms. But if you keep it in the dark, it withers. Ella… she'll need you to be her sunlight, Tom. And if you are, she'll give it back to you. That's how you both grow."

The words lingered between them, not heavy but deeply rooted, and Tom absorbed them as though they were part of the lesson Zenji had left them to discover. "I never thought of it like that," Tom said at last. "I thought you just… liked someone, and that was it." Ty chuckled softly. "It's not that simple. It's more like taking care of a bonsai tree." He gestured toward the one that stood upon the low wooden shelf by the far wall, its twisted trunk and delicate branches illuminated in the lantern's glow. "See that? It looks fragile, but it's strong because of its roots and its trunk. It can live longer than both of us if someone cares for it properly. That's what love is like. It's not about control, it's about shaping with patience, giving care, and never forcing it."

Tom rose to his feet and crossed toward the bonsai, his fingers hovering just above its leaves as though afraid to disturb it. "It doesn't look weak at all," he murmured. "It looks like it's survived everything thrown at it." Ty joined him, folding his arms with a smile. "Exactly. That's because someone gave it time. Someone gave it attention every day, clipping here, watering there, never too much, never too little. You'll understand that better with Ella as time goes on. If you rush, you'll break the branches. If you neglect it, it'll die. But if you stay steady, it'll thrive." Tom stared at the little tree with a reverence he had not expected. He saw in it a reflection of his own life—once neglected, nearly broken, but now being given care at last.

The brothers returned to the mats, their breathing steady once more, though the silence between them carried a new intimacy. Ty had not spoken as a child bragging of romance but as a young man passing wisdom to his brother. Tom felt honoured by the trust, the openness, and he stored the words away as carefully as he would guard a precious gift. He realized then that his place in the dojo, in the garden, at the table, was not given because of charity but because of love. A love that expected him to grow, to strengthen, and to give in return. And as the lanterns flickered against the polished wood, Tom vowed silently that he would not waste it.

The quiet of the Takashi home deepened after the evening meal, and Keiko retreated to her studio with its wide paper screens and faint scent of ink and cedarwood. Tom followed her hesitantly, his steps slow as though afraid he might disturb something sacred. She turned at the sound of his footsteps, her face lighting with welcome, and motioned him closer.

Upon the low table she set out a thick pad of drawing paper and a sharpened pencil, sliding them across the surface toward him with both hands, as though presenting a gift of great worth. "Here," she said softly, "you will find that patience does not need to be punishment. Patience can become art." Tom lowered himself to the cushion, his hands trembling slightly as he picked up the pencil, unused to such care being offered freely. The page waited in silence, an open space for him to discover himself.

Keiko sat beside him, folding her legs with the easy grace of someone long accustomed to stillness. She did not tell him what to draw, nor did she correct the way he gripped the pencil. She only watched, her presence steady, as Tom pressed the tip to the page. At first his lines wavered, hesitant and uncertain, the shapes unformed and restless. But as the minutes passed, he began to settle, the rhythm of sketching drawing him inward. His shoulders loosened, his breathing steadied, and soon shapes emerged that surprised even him: a curved line suggesting the flow of water, a sharp edge like the corner of a roof, a flower's outline bending toward unseen light. Keiko nodded approvingly, her voice calm. "Do you see? These are not mistakes. These are beginnings."

Tom paused, staring at the page as though it had revealed a secret. "I didn't think I could do this," he admitted, his voice low. Keiko's smile deepened. "Art does not begin with skill. It begins with courage. Every mark you make is a decision, and every decision is proof you dared to try." Her words carried no weight of criticism, only the freedom of discovery. For a boy who had once been punished for the slightest error, the absence of scorn felt almost impossible. And yet here he was, making lines that curved and bent, each one his own, and instead of fear he felt a strange warmth spread through his chest.

After a long silence filled only by the scratch of graphite, Tom lifted his head and asked shyly, "Mom, may I… may I make something for Ella?" Keiko's eyes softened, and she reached to place her hand gently upon his wrist. "Yes," she said simply. "Art is a gift when it carries truth, and truth is always worth giving." She rose briefly and returned with a brush, ink, and a sheet of finer paper. Setting them before him, she explained, "You may write her name in Japanese. I will show you." She dipped the brush into the ink and, with slow precision, began to form the characters, each stroke deliberate and fluid. "E-ra," she spoke gently as she painted, "this is how her name becomes part of our language."

Tom watched intently, his eyes fixed on the elegant movements of the brush. He took it from her carefully, his hand steady though his heart raced. His first strokes were uneven, the ink pooling too dark in places, too faint in others, but Keiko placed her hand over his, guiding him with patience rather than correction. Together they traced the name again, the brush moving in rhythm, until the characters took shape upon the page. When they finished, Tom leaned back, staring at the result with quiet pride. "It feels like more than just her name," he whispered. Keiko nodded. "It is. It is a piece of you, given to her."

The boy folded the paper carefully, his fingers brushing the ink as though afraid it might vanish. He tucked it against his chest, imagining Ella's smile when she would see it. For the first time, he realized that giving was not weakness, nor was it surrender. Giving was strength, a strength that built bridges instead of walls. And in that moment, with his mother at his side and the ink drying between them, Tom began to understand what it meant to create something not for survival, but for love.

The dining table glowed under the light of the hanging lanterns, the air heavy with the scent of rice, vegetables, and grilled fish. Conversation flowed easily among the children, bursts of laughter rising and falling, but at the head of the table Zenji spoke with the calm gravity that commanded attention without demanding it. He told a story from his boyhood, not polished, not exaggerated, but offered with the humility of a man who had lived long enough to see folly turn into wisdom. Tom leaned forward, elbows resting on the polished wood despite Keiko's gentle tap to remind him of manners, his eyes fixed on his father's face. There was no fear in him, no dread of ridicule, only eagerness. For the first time, Tom was learning without bracing for punishment. His mind, once a fortress against hurt, opened wide to receive the story.

Zenji's tale was of a time when impatience had nearly cost him dearly. As a teenager, eager to prove himself, he had ignored his teacher's instruction and rushed ahead in training. He described how he had tried to master techniques with force alone, believing speed and strength would make him invincible. Instead, he had struck poorly, fallen hard, and broken his wrist in the process. The room fell quiet as he recounted the memory, his voice even, his eyes betraying no shame. "Pain," he said simply, "is a teacher that cannot be bribed. It teaches with truth, not words." The children, even Nico and Jasmin who rarely stilled themselves, listened with unusual silence, their young minds catching the weight of the lesson hidden within the simple tale.

Tom shifted in his seat, his heart beating quickly. "Dad," he asked, the word still new and powerful on his tongue, "how did you decide to become an RCMP Investigator? Why that path?" Zenji paused, his chopsticks lowering to the edge of his plate, his gaze moving across the faces gathered at the table. Ty tilted his head, curious—he too had never heard the full story. Zenji folded his hands together, his voice quiet but firm. "Because I learned that protecting others matters more than proving myself. I had strength, but I wanted it to mean something. The uniform was not a badge of power, but of service. I wanted to use my hands not for fists, but for protection."

The children watched as Zenji leaned back, his eyes softening with memory. "I met your mother in the strangest of places. An art exhibit. I was in uniform, called to investigate a missing painting. She was standing in front of a blank canvas, sketching as though she could bring life back to what had been stolen. I spoke to her, thinking she was a witness. Instead, she became the only thing I could see in the room. I never found the thief that night, but I found your mother. And that," he concluded with a faint smile, "was the greater discovery." Keiko blushed slightly, lowering her gaze to her bowl, though her lips betrayed the smallest smile.

Tom sat transfixed, his fork forgotten, his food untouched. No one had ever told him a love story before, least of all from a father's mouth. His chest swelled with a mixture of awe and longing, as though the tale itself had wrapped around him. He rose from his chair impulsively, circling to where Zenji sat, and wrapped his arms around him tightly. His cheek pressed against his father's chest, his voice muffled but clear. "Thank you, Dad. Thank you for telling me." The embrace was not awkward, not unwelcome. Zenji placed his broad hand against the boy's back, steady and sure. He did not squeeze to dismiss, nor did he push away. He let the moment linger, giving Tom the space to feel it fully.

Around the table, the children exchanged glances that spoke volumes. Jeremy's eyes shone with quiet approval, Leo's jaw tightened as if holding back emotion, and Ella's gaze softened, her hand resting lightly upon her folded napkin. Even Alex, once hardened against sentiment, lowered his eyes with respect. In that moment, they all understood something greater than the story itself: Tom was no longer a visitor at the table. He was a son, and a brother, and nothing could take that from him now.

The morning sunlight poured through the tall windows of the English classroom, catching on the polished wood of the desks and the chalk dust that hung faintly in the air. Mr. Clarke was lecturing with his usual energy, weaving words into stories that made grammar and literature come alive. The students leaned forward in varying degrees of interest, some jotting down notes while others doodled quietly. Tom sat near Ty, his notebook open but his mind heavy with the weight of new beginnings. He had been welcomed into a family, claimed by parents, embraced by a brother, and surrounded by friends who treated him as one of their own. Yet the newness of it all sometimes felt fragile, like glass waiting for a careless hand to break it.

Mr. Arnett stepped into the room midway through the lesson, his tall frame and calm presence filling the space with the quiet authority of a man who did not need to raise his voice to command respect. He greeted Mr. Clarke with a nod before turning his eyes toward the students, scanning them with warmth rather than scrutiny. Tom, caught in the moment, lifted his head and without thinking spoke aloud, his voice carrying clearly across the room. "Good morning, Uncle Ted." The words slipped out as naturally as breathing, but the silence that followed fell like a heavy curtain. Every head in the room turned toward him, eyes wide, whispers rising like a quick wind. Tom's face went crimson, his heart hammering in his chest as realization crashed into him. He had revealed something private, sacred even, in front of everyone.

Without waiting for an explanation, Tom shoved his chair back and fled the classroom, his footsteps pounding down the corridor. His breath came sharp and ragged, shame burning hot in his throat. To him, it felt like betrayal—not of Mr. Arnett's trust, but of the intimacy of family itself. He imagined the students laughing, twisting his words, mocking the bond he had only just begun to treasure. He pressed his back against the cool wall of the hallway, sliding down until he sat on the floor, his arms crossed tightly over his knees. He could not bear to face anyone, least of all the man he had just called by a name so dear.

But Mr. Arnett followed, not with sternness or rebuke, but with the quiet patience that defined him. His footsteps echoed softly, unhurried, until he reached where Tom sat. He lowered himself without hesitation, his knees bending stiffly as he sat beside the boy against the wall. For a moment he said nothing, only offering his presence, letting the silence do its work. At last, he spoke with gentleness. "You did nothing wrong, Tom. You called me what I already am to you. That isn't betrayal. That's truth." Tom shook his head violently, his voice breaking. "They all heard me. Now they'll laugh. They'll think it's stupid. They'll say I made it up." His hands clenched against his temples, as though bracing for blows that never came.

Mr. Arnett reached out, pulling the boy into a firm embrace, his arm wrapping fully around him, his chest steady as Tom trembled. "Let them hear it," he said firmly. "Let them know. Because I am your Uncle Ted, whether whispered in private or shouted in the hall. You are not betraying me by speaking it. You are honouring me." Tom buried his face against the man's chest, the tears he had been holding back breaking loose, soaking into the fabric of the principal's shirt. The embrace did not loosen, did not shift with discomfort. It held fast, a shield against the shame Tom had built inside himself. Slowly, his breathing calmed, the panic melting into something steadier, something safe.

When at last they rose together, Mr. Arnett kept a hand upon Tom's shoulder, guiding him back into the classroom. The students fell silent as the door opened, their curiosity thick in the air. Mr. Clarke stepped aside, yielding the space to his colleague without question. Mr. Arnett moved to the front of the room, his voice steady, his eyes sweeping the faces of every child present. "You heard Tom call me Uncle Ted," he began plainly. "That is no mistake. That is who I am to him. I am his uncle, not by blood, but by choice. When someone chooses you as family, it is not a joke. It is the highest honour."

The room hushed, the weight of his words cutting through the usual chatter. Nico leaned forward, Sophie stopped her doodling, and even Leo sat straighter, his expression intent. Mr. Arnett continued, his voice carrying the warmth of truth. "Some of you have families who were given to you by birth. Some of you have families who found you later in life. Both are real. Both are strong. Tom chose me, and I accepted, gladly. That is something I hope every one of you finds someday—people who love you enough to claim you as their own, no matter where you began."

The students absorbed the words in silence, their eyes flicking toward Tom, but not with ridicule. There was curiosity, yes, but also respect, born of the authority in Mr. Arnett's tone and the sincerity in his eyes. Tom stood near the doorway, his chest still tight, but the shame was loosening, replaced with the strange warmth of being defended openly. Ty shot him a smile, small but certain, and Jeremy nodded quickly, his eyes bright with encouragement. Ella's gaze lingered longer, her expression soft and full of quiet pride. In that moment, Tom realized that what he feared as betrayal had become a bond, not just between him and Uncle Ted, but between himself and everyone who now knew the truth.

The first days of belonging carried with them both joy and unease. Tom walked through the house with lighter steps, yet at night he still lay awake, staring at the ceiling, waiting for the warmth to vanish. His heart remembered too well the times when kindness had been offered only to be snatched away, when affection had been a mask that hid cruelty beneath it. He had been conditioned to expect loss, not love. Every gentle word from Keiko, every steady nod from Zenji, every laugh from Ty was a gift he wanted to believe in, but fear told him it would collapse as everything else once had. That tension shadowed his face at odd hours, a cloud that appeared even on the brightest days.

Keiko was the first to notice. She saw it in the way Tom's smile faltered when she praised him, as though he feared the compliment might be a trap. She caught it in his hesitation when Zenji's hand reached for his shoulder, as though a touch of affection could turn to a blow at any second. She never scolded him for it, never demanded that he trust her. Instead, she moved closer with quiet grace, speaking to him in tones that invited rather than pressed. "Trust is not a seed that grows in one night," she told him one evening as she set down a bowl of soup before him. "It grows slowly, watered by patience, and sunlighted by truth. You don't need to rush. We will wait with you."

Zenji too sensed the unrest. His response was not to lecture, but to act in ways that could not be mistaken. He showed Tom how discipline was not cruelty, but care; how correction did not come with raised hands but with guidance. When Tom faltered in the dojo, Zenji's voice remained calm, his posture steady. "Strength is not perfection," he reminded him, "but persistence." The message was simple but profound: love did not retreat when mistakes were made. It remained. Tom, who had always braced for anger, began to exhale in relief each time Zenji proved again that his patience had no hidden blade. Slowly, the wall Tom had built around himself began to crack.

Ty's role was simpler, yet no less vital. He became Tom's mirror of constancy, never questioning his presence, never doubting his place. When Tom slipped into silence, Ty filled it with laughter. When Tom's eyes shadowed with fear, Ty nudged him with a brother's teasing until the tension eased. "You're stuck with us," he reminded him cheerfully one afternoon. "Doesn't matter how long it takes you to believe it. We'll still be here." Tom wanted to argue, to point out that nothing ever lasted, but he found the words dissolving on his tongue. Deep down, he wanted Ty to be right more than anything.

The turning point came quietly, without fanfare. Keiko sat beside Tom in the garden one late afternoon, the sun dipping low as the koi rippled the pond. She reached for his hand, not forcing but waiting. Tom hesitated, his fingers trembling, then placed his hand into hers. She squeezed gently, her eyes soft. "You are loved, Tom. Beyond what words can hold. Beyond what doubt can erase. You don't need to earn it. It is already yours." Tears blurred Tom's vision, spilling unashamed down his cheeks. He leaned into her shoulder, his breath breaking. For the first time, he believed. For the first time, he did not fear it would be taken back.

That evening, Ella arrived at the Takashi home, her presence carrying the nervous excitement of someone with a secret to share. She held a small package wrapped carefully in paper, her eyes searching for Tom as soon as she stepped inside. When she found him, she placed it in his hands with both of hers, her cheeks flushed. "For you," she whispered. He unwrapped it slowly, revealing a framed photograph of Ella herself, smiling with a warmth that needed no explanation. Alongside it lay another photograph: his own artwork, the Japanese characters of her name he had written under Keiko's guidance. She had captured it, preserved it, and given it back to him as though to say his gift had taken root.

Inside the frame was also a folded letter, longer than the first, written in her careful hand. Tom opened it with trembling fingers, his eyes scanning the words with growing wonder. Ella had written not just of her happiness for him, but of her gratitude for the strength he had shown in the library, for the truth he had spoken about Myles, for the way he had changed her own way of seeing the world. She confessed again her love, not as a fleeting crush but as a promise that she wanted to walk beside him, to share in his growth, to give and receive light as he had given to her. "You are my sunlight too," the letter ended simply, and Tom pressed it to his chest, unable to stop the tears that came again, this time not from fear but from joy.

Keiko and Zenji exchanged a glance as they watched him, their expressions calm but touched with pride. They saw the boy who once doubted every word of kindness now holding proof that he was loved, not only by family but by a girl who believed in him. Ty clapped him lightly on the shoulder, grinning. "See? Told you. You don't have to wait for love to vanish anymore. It's right here. And it's not going anywhere." Tom nodded, his voice too thick to speak, but in his heart he knew Ty was right. The walls were falling, and in their place, a life was being built—slowly, but strong.

Evenings in the Takashi household became a rhythm of gentle steadiness, the kind Tom had never known before. At the low table in the study, his books were spread neatly before him, not as instruments of torment but as invitations to explore. Keiko sat at his side, her hand resting lightly upon the corner of the page as she guided him patiently through each problem, never once raising her voice when he stumbled. Instead of dread, Tom felt curiosity rising in him, as if the very act of learning was an adventure waiting to be discovered. Each answer earned a smile, not scorn, and when the numbers tangled in his head, she showed him calmly how to untangle them again. This new way of study was foreign to him, but it was quickly becoming a place of safety.

Ty leaned over from the other side, his elbow nudging Tom with playful encouragement. "You've got this," he whispered whenever Tom hesitated, his grin breaking through the quiet focus of the room. Even the smallest successes—a line spelled correctly, a sum balanced neatly—were met with Ty's cheers. "That's my brother," he declared proudly, making Tom blush as though he had won a medal rather than completed a page of homework.

# THE SMILE THAT BROKE

Zenji would occasionally step in, standing at the doorway with arms folded, his voice steady as he reminded Tom that discipline was not cruelty but structure. "A mistake," he said, "is not a crime. It is a sign you are trying." Each phrase struck Tom deeper than the lessons themselves, reshaping the way he understood the meaning of learning.

One evening, as Tom leaned over his writing practice, Zenji sat with him and shared a story from his own childhood. His voice carried no bitterness, only truth. "Back home in Japan, when I was your age, education was not gentle. Straight A's were not a dream—they were a demand. Anything less, and punishment followed." Tom's eyes widened, his pencil stilling in his hand. Zenji continued, describing the strictness of the system: uniforms that dictated not only the cut of fabric but the very colour of socks, rules that extended even to hair and appearance, examinations that decided the course of one's future. "It was a place where failure was not allowed," Zenji explained, "and sometimes, children carried fear heavier than books."

The children at the table listened with fascination. Even Ty, who had grown up with Zenji, had never heard the stories laid out in such detail. Zenji spoke of the hours spent in after-school lessons, the culture of competition, and the expectation that every child must fit neatly into the mould. "There was little room for questions, only for answers," he said, shaking his head gently. "Some schools even had rules about hair length, or what colour underwear a student could wear. It was meant to shape conformity, but it often broke the spirit." He did not linger on cruelty, but neither did he soften the truth. His voice held both respect for discipline and sorrow for the rigidity that left little space for individuality.

Tom listened intently, his heart tightening at the thought of children punished for anything less than perfection. He lowered his gaze, whispering almost to himself, "I don't think I would have survived that." Zenji placed a hand upon his shoulder, firm but reassuring. "You would have survived, Tom. But you would have carried scars. That is why I choose differently for you. Here, mistakes are not a cause for shame, but stepping stones. You will learn with strength, not fear." The words pressed deeply into Tom's heart, undoing years of doubt. For the first time, he believed he could learn without waiting for punishment.

Encouraged by the warmth around him, Tom lifted his head and asked, "Dad, will you teach me Japanese? To read it, to write it, and to speak it?" His voice trembled with both eagerness and fear of asking too much. Zenji's eyes softened, and Keiko's lips curved into a smile. Ty grinned, thumping his brother lightly on the back. "Now you're talking." Zenji nodded slowly, his voice steady. "Yes, Tom. We will teach you. It will not be easy, but it will be worth it. Language is more than words—it is culture, it is history, it is a way of seeing the world. And if you learn it, you will carry more than knowledge. You will carry belonging."

From that night forward, Tom's notebooks filled not only with English lessons but with carefully drawn characters, each stroke a new act of trust. Keiko guided his hand with patience, showing him the flow of brush and ink, while Zenji explained the meaning behind the words. Ty, ever encouraging, tried to keep pace beside him, often making more mistakes than Tom but laughing freely at each one. The atmosphere of the house changed further, laughter mixing with study, the weight of fear replaced with the light of discovery.

Tom held Ella's framed photograph near his desk, her letter tucked safely within his books. Each time he practiced her name in Japanese, he imagined showing her, imagined her smile, and the effort felt worth every mistake. He no longer studied with the dread of failure but with the hope of giving, of sharing something meaningful. The boy who once braced for scorn now leaned into learning with eagerness, his fears slowly unraveling into something he had never known before: joy in discovery. And as Keiko often reminded him, discovery was the first step toward freedom.

The dojo smelled faintly of pine wood and tatami mats, the air cool with evening. Tom stood barefoot on the polished floor, his stance uneven, his body taut with determination and nerves. Zenji's voice carried through the space, calm but steady, instructing him to focus on his breathing before movement. Tom tried, but the eagerness in his limbs betrayed him. His foot slid where it should have grounded, his arms flailed where they should have held balance. With a sharp exhale, he stumbled forward and caught himself on his palms, his face hot with embarrassment. He braced for scolding, his body tensing instinctively, but none came. Instead, Zenji's voice was even, unmoved. "Stand again. Mistakes are part of learning. Breathe, Tom. Begin from stillness."

Tom rose slowly, his shoulders heavy with shame. Every failure echoed against the walls of his memory, dragging old fears back into the present. He wanted to shout at himself, to strike the mat in frustration, but Zenji's eyes held him steady. There was no anger there, no threat, only patience. "You do not fail when you fall," Zenji said softly. "You fail only when you refuse to rise again." The words settled in the silence, pressing into Tom's chest more deeply than any blow. He tried again, his hands trembling less this time, though the step that followed was clumsy once more.

Ty, watching from the side, laughed—not a cruel laugh, but a warm, knowing chuckle. "You should've seen me when I started," he said, his grin wide. "I lost my balance more times than I can count. Once, I even fell into the pond outside. Right in the middle of practice!" His laughter rang through the dojo, lightening the air, and even Zenji allowed himself a faint smile. Tom blinked, surprised, then let out a small laugh of his own, the knot in his chest loosening slightly. If Ty, who seemed so strong and steady, had faltered, then perhaps stumbling was not shameful after all.

Zenji called him to reset, reminding him once more to focus on breath before movement. "Patience is stronger than speed," he said. "Strength is useless without control. You must learn to master frustration before you master form." Tom inhaled slowly, his eyes closing briefly as he listened to the sound of his breath. He tried again, and though his stance wavered, his spirit steadied. Ty clapped from the side, cheering him as though he had won a medal. "That's it! You're already better than me on my first week." Tom's lips curved upward despite himself, the weight of fear giving way to determination.

For the next hour, the routine continued: fall, rise, reset, repeat. Each failure felt less final, each stumble less heavy. Tom learned to meet the mat with less shame and more resolve, his breath guiding him through the missteps. Zenji remained close, correcting with gentle adjustments rather than harsh words, guiding Tom's elbow here, his footing there. His presence was steady as a mountain, never once turning sharp or cruel. Slowly, Tom began to understand: patience was not a punishment for weakness, but the path toward strength.

By the end of practice, sweat lined Tom's brow, his chest rose and fell with exertion, but his eyes held a brightness not dulled by frustration. He bowed to Zenji, his form uneven but sincere. "Thank you, Dad," he whispered, his voice steadier than his stance. Zenji bowed in return, his eyes warm with pride. Ty bounded forward, throwing an arm around his brother's shoulders. "Told you the pond story would make you feel better," he teased. Tom laughed again, this time without hesitation, realizing that falling was not the end but the beginning of learning how to rise.

The dojo was quiet except for the measured breaths of the two boys. Tom stood in his stance, fists drawn close, eyes locked on Ty. His shoulders trembled, not from fear but from the desire to prove himself. He had always believed that strength meant striking harder, moving faster, never backing down. It was how he had survived before—by fists, by defiance, by never letting anyone see weakness. But Zenji's lessons echoed in the room, and Ty's calm expression challenged his old beliefs. Tom struck forward clumsily, but Ty stepped aside with ease, his motion swift but not aggressive. "See?" Ty said, smiling. "Strength isn't just about hitting. It's knowing when not to."

Tom frowned, his breath ragged as he reset his stance. "But if you don't fight back, they'll keep coming." The words came raw, pulled straight from memory. Ty tilted his head, his grin fading into something steadier. "Sometimes, yes. But sometimes, walking away makes them realize they don't control you. You don't have to give them what they want." He moved slowly, demonstrating a block without striking back, then lowering his hands altogether. "It's harder than fighting, believe me. But that's where the real strength is—choosing restraint when your body is screaming to swing." Tom exhaled slowly, his fists loosening, the weight of the idea pressing into him more than the training itself.

Zenji stepped closer, his voice measured. "A true warrior has nothing to prove. Violence is the last answer, never the first. Anyone can throw a fist, but not everyone can hold one back." Tom swallowed hard, staring at his knuckles. He wanted to believe, but the old anger inside him whispered otherwise. The anger told him fists solved problems quickly. Yet here, in the calm rhythm of training, his father's words carved a new truth into him. He lowered his arms, not in defeat but in thought. The silence that followed was heavier than any punch he could have thrown.

Later, Ty pulled him aside as they walked through the garden, the koi pond shimmering at their side. "You ever watch a praying mantis?" he asked suddenly, crouching to point at a small insect resting on a branch. Tom blinked, shaking his head. Ty grinned, leaning closer. "They wait. They don't waste their energy. They look so still, like they're doing nothing at all. But when the time comes, they move faster than you can see." Tom crouched beside him, his eyes following the creature's sharp posture. It wasn't swinging wildly, wasn't restless—it was patient, balanced, and ready. Ty's grin widened. "That's strength. Not force. Control."

The image stayed with Tom. He thought of the mantis waiting, silent but unyielding, and he felt something shift inside him. He realized how often his life had been the opposite—swinging, flailing, acting before thinking. But maybe there was power in stillness, in waiting for the right moment. Maybe there was even more power in choosing not to strike at all. The thought unsettled him, yet it sparked something new, something he couldn't ignore. For the first time, he wondered if his fists weren't weapons but tools, meant to be guided by patience instead of rage.

That night, as they sat together at the dinner table, Tom shared the lesson aloud. "Strength isn't fists," he said hesitantly, glancing toward Zenji for approval. "It's… it's walking away. Or waiting. Like the mantis." The words felt strange, as though he were speaking a language he had never known before, but Keiko's smile reassured him. "Yes," she said softly. "Strength is choosing what others cannot. It is harder than fighting, but truer." Tom's chest warmed, pride mixing with the unfamiliar calm of being understood. The boy who once thought only fists could save him now carried a different truth, one that promised a life beyond fear and retaliation.

The shift came quietly, like the slow turning of seasons, but everyone noticed it. Tom no longer moved through the halls with the guarded stiffness of a boy waiting for trouble. His steps were steadier, his gaze lifted rather than hidden. Where once whispers trailed him, sharp and curious about the scars of his past, now there was a calm in his presence that silenced speculation. He did not need to prove himself with words or fists. The calm itself became his answer. Students who had doubted him, or avoided him, found themselves watching the change with reluctant respect. Even the teachers, long cautious of how to handle him, began to see not a boy broken by anger but one slowly reshaped by love and discipline.

Mr. Clarke noticed first. He had seen boys bluff and posture, but Tom's silence carried no bluff. It was grounded. In English class, when debates turned loud, Tom no longer snapped at careless words. He listened, steady and thoughtful, and when he spoke, his voice carried more weight than the chatter of three others combined. Mr. Arnett—Uncle Ted to Tom—watched with quiet pride from the doorway during one such lesson, the corners of his mouth lifting as he recognized the fruit of patience. "That boy," he whispered to Clarke afterward, "is learning what most men never do." Clarke nodded, agreeing. Tom was not just fitting in—he was becoming an example.

Among the students, the change sparked its own conversations. Nico and Jasmin, once cautious around him, now laughed freely in his company. Sophie leaned closer when he spoke, her sharp tongue softened by the gentleness she saw taking root. Jeremy followed him everywhere, his admiration open, as if Tom's growth gave him a map for his own. Even Leo, who knew the shadows of bullying all too well, clapped Tom on the shoulder one afternoon and said simply, "You're not who you were. That's what matters." Alex, ever the skeptic, grunted but did not argue. The silence of his resistance was its own acknowledgment.

The rumours that had haunted Tom at first—the stories of his temper, the scars of his old fights—faded like mist in the face of his present self. A boy who once might have been feared was now sought out for his calm. He carried himself with a quietness that could not be ignored. And with each day, as he sat at the lunch table, walked the corridors, or stood in the courtyard, others felt the pull of that steadiness. He was no longer the boy on trial in the eyes of his peers. He was the boy building something new.

Ella noticed most of all. Her eyes followed him whenever he entered a room, her smile blooming whenever their paths crossed. When she found a folded letter in her hands—Tom's careful handwriting across the page—her heart raced before she even read the first word. She opened it with trembling fingers, scanning the lines slowly, as though afraid to miss even one syllable. Tom had written to her not with flowery phrases or borrowed words, but with the steady honesty of someone learning how to trust. He thanked her for her letters, for believing in him, for seeing what he barely saw in himself. And then, at the heart of it, the confession: he cared for her deeply, more than he knew how to explain.

Ella pressed the letter to her chest, tears welling in her eyes as the truth washed over her. For weeks she had given him her thoughts, her love written plainly on paper, never certain if he could return it. Now, here was his answer, simple and sure. Her tears fell freely, not from sorrow but from joy, as she whispered to herself, "All I want is to be with him." The photograph she had given him came back to mind—her smile captured in a frame—and she thought of how he must be looking at it now, knowing she was thinking of him just as fiercely. It was more than affection; it was a bond that grew with each shared truth.

At lunch the next day, Ella sat close beside Tom, her eyes brighter than usual. She said nothing about the letter at first, but when the noise of the cafeteria softened, she leaned in and whispered, "I read it. Every word. And I'll keep it forever." Tom's cheeks flushed crimson, but his eyes did not drop. Instead, he smiled back, shy but certain, and she knew then that no force could break what had begun between them. Around them, their friends laughed and talked, unaware that something far deeper had settled into place.

The schoolyard hummed with its usual chorus of voices, balls bouncing off pavement, and laughter spilling across the grass. Tom stood with Ty and Nico near the benches, the spring air sharp in his lungs, when a new boy pushed his way through the crowd. Daren had only been at the school a week, but his voice was already heavy with the edge of someone who needed to be noticed. He carried himself with that swagger Tom recognized too well—the careless tilt of the head, the smirk that dared someone to challenge it. Tom's chest tightened, his body remembering old patterns, but he stayed still, his breath slow. Daren's eyes narrowed on him like a hawk spotting prey. "So you're the one they all talk about," Daren said. "Doesn't look like much to me."

A ripple of silence spread across the group. Ty shifted beside Tom, his fists instinctively curling, but Tom lifted a hand, a small gesture of calm. His instinct screamed at him to respond, to swing, to prove himself, but Zenji's words, Ty's laughter, Keiko's patience—all of it rose within him like a wall against the tide. He inhaled deeply, his jaw tightening, then exhaled slowly as he stepped back. "Not interested," he said simply, his voice steady but not sharp. The words seemed to fall heavier than a blow. Students leaned in closer, expecting the snap of violence, but instead, they witnessed restraint.

Daren's smirk faltered for a moment, then sharpened as he tried again. "What's the matter? Scared?" The jab hung in the air like a baited hook. Tom's fists curled once, tight against his sides, but he forced them open. He looked Daren straight in the eye, and for the first time in his life, he let silence answer instead of fists. His step back was deliberate, a refusal without retreat. The crowd murmured, confused at first, then awed as they began to realize what had just happened. Strength had been shown not in blows, but in the choice to walk away.

Ella, standing at the edge of the group with Sophie, felt her heart thrum hard in her chest. She had feared the clash, braced for the worst, but what she saw instead left her breathless. Tom's restraint was not weakness—it was strength in its truest form. Her eyes followed him as he turned calmly from Daren, the curve of his shoulders firm and unyielding, his control unshaken. Her admiration swelled into something deeper, something that made her cheeks burn. She wanted, in that moment, to run forward and kiss him, to show him how proud she was, but she held herself still, her hands trembling with emotion.

Jeremy, who had been close enough to see Tom's fists clench and relax, beamed with pride. "He did it," he whispered fiercely to Leo, who nodded with a rare softness. "That's harder than any punch," Leo murmured, his voice carrying the weight of someone who knew the truth of violence. Even Alex, arms crossed as though unwilling to be impressed, couldn't hide the flicker of respect in his eyes. Around them, the whispers changed tone. Tom was no longer the boy they wondered about. He was the boy they admired.

Mr. Clarke, watching from the classroom window, felt the moment sink into him as deeply as it did into the children. He had taught about courage in words, in books and lessons, but here it was embodied in silence, in a single step away. He knew then this was a story he would tell future classes—not of violence, not of defiance, but of the day a boy proved that real strength lay in restraint. He turned from the window with quiet satisfaction, his heart lighter for having witnessed it.

As the crowd dispersed, Daren stood awkwardly in the middle of the yard, his smirk cracked, his bravado drained. He had expected a fight, a show of fists, and instead had been left with nothing. No victory, no power. Tom had given him nothing to feed on, and in that nothing lay defeat. Tom walked on, his pace steady, his friends falling into step beside him. Ty slapped his shoulder with a grin. "That," he said, "was the best move I've ever seen." Tom allowed himself a small smile, his breath loosening. For once, he felt not smaller for walking away, but larger, stronger.

Ella found him later, her steps quick as she caught up with him near the lockers. She hesitated only for a heartbeat before speaking, her voice hushed. "You don't know what that meant," she said, her eyes shimmering. Tom glanced at her, puzzled. "What?" She shook her head, a smile breaking through her tears. "Everything. It meant everything." She almost leaned closer, almost pressed her lips to his, but instead she reached for his hand, holding it tightly for a moment before walking away, her cheeks flushed crimson. Tom stood still, watching her go, his own chest thundering with something new and wonderful.

The Japanese garden lay bathed in the amber hues of late afternoon, the koi pond glimmering with ripples of fading light. Tom sat quietly on the edge of the wooden bridge, his legs dangling, listening to the steady hum of cicadas and the faint splash of water trickling from the bamboo fountain. For the first time in his life, silence was not a weight pressing upon him but a blanket covering him with comfort. Here, in this house, in this garden, with people who called him son and brother, he was learning what belonging truly meant. His heart swelled at the thought, both fragile and powerful, as though he held a secret treasure no one could steal.

Zenji and Keiko strolled the garden path, their presence calm and unhurried. Ty darted between stones and sand, laughing at his own attempts to balance like a tightrope walker across the stepping stones. Yet Tom was still, content simply to feel the earth beneath him, the house behind him, the family around him.

"This," he thought, "is home." It was not in the walls or the rooms, but in the way Zenji's steady voice reached him without judgment, in the way Keiko's smile never faltered when she said his name, in the way Ty's laughter folded him into brotherhood. He had stepped into their lives, and instead of being told he was an intruder, he had been given a place at their table, their dojo, their hearts.

Ella's footsteps approached quietly, hesitant yet purposeful, until she appeared at the edge of the bridge. She had never looked more alive to him, her eyes wide with warmth, her hair brushed by the evening breeze. For days, words had burned in her throat, letters written and folded had only carried fragments of what her heart carried whole. Now, standing in the garden, she found the courage that had waited patiently. She knelt beside Tom, her hand brushing lightly against his arm, and whispered, "I wanted to see you here, where you belong." The sincerity in her voice sent a shiver through him.

Tom turned toward her, the closeness startling but welcome. He searched her face for meaning, for the truth that her letters had hinted at but never said aloud. She leaned in, her breath soft upon his cheek, and before he could speak, her lips met his in a kiss so gentle it seemed to rise with the breeze rather than fall with force. His eyes widened, his heart raced, but instinctively he wrapped his arms around her, holding her close, not in desperation but in gratitude. The kiss lingered, tender and unhurried, and for Tom it was as though the garden itself had fallen silent to witness it.

When they parted, Ella's forehead rested against his, her cheeks flushed, her voice trembling as she breathed, "I love you, Tom." The words slipped into him with the force of truth, undeniable and real. His breath caught, his arms tightening just slightly as he whispered back into her ear, "I love you too." It was not rehearsed, not borrowed, but born from the moment itself, from every glance, every letter, every unspoken thought that had built toward this. She closed her eyes, a tear slipping free, though her smile shone brighter than the sun sinking behind the trees.

From the veranda, Zenji and Keiko stood side by side, watching with knowing smiles. Neither interrupted nor called out, for they understood the sacredness of first love. Instead, they exchanged a glance, a memory stirring quietly between them. Zenji's hand found Keiko's, their fingers intertwining as they remembered their own first kiss, the same nervousness, the same exhilaration, the same truth whispered between two young souls. Keiko leaned into him softly, murmuring, "Do you remember?" and Zenji chuckled low. "How could I forget? It felt just like this looks—pure, unshaken, true."

Nearby, Ty stumbled upon the scene as he bounded back across the stepping stones, his grin fading into wide-eyed surprise. Nico and Jasmin weren't far behind, pausing when they realized what they had walked into.

Sophie gasped, her hand flying to her mouth, while Jeremy tugged at Leo's sleeve, whispering, "What are they saying? What did they whisper?" Leo smirked knowingly, though his voice softened. "Something you'll understand when you're older, kid." Jeremy frowned but quieted, sensing the moment's weight. Even Alex, standing at the back with folded arms, let out a small sigh, his usual cynicism muted in the face of what was unfolding.

The friends didn't need to know the exact words, though they suspected. The way Ella clung to Tom, the way his arms cradled her gently, the way both of them glowed as though lit from within—none of it required translation. It was clear, even to the youngest among them, that something had changed forever. They had stepped across a threshold, not only in affection but in belonging. Tom was no longer the outsider proving himself; he was the boy loved, the boy chosen, the boy who finally believed he had a place where he mattered.

The evening settled softly upon the Takashi home, the lanterns in the garden glowing against the deepening sky. The circle of friends had long since scattered to their own houses, laughter and farewells trailing with them, yet Ella lingered still, her voice carrying gently as she spoke with Zenji and Keiko on the veranda. Tom and Ty sat cross-legged on the tatami mats in the living room, the sound of their laughter filling the space with warmth. For a boy who had once known only silence edged by fear, Tom felt as though the world had shifted into colour. Their voices bounced from wall to wall, stitched into the home as firmly as the beams themselves.

Keiko leaned in the doorway, her eyes softened with relief. She had worried that Tom's scars might take years to ease, that the rhythm of family might jar against old wounds. Yet here he was, laughing beside Ty as though they had been brothers since birth. Zenji joined her, sliding the door closed with a quiet motion. "Listen," he murmured, his voice rich with pride. "They're whole." Keiko's hand brushed his arm in agreement. To her, it was not simply that Tom had been adopted; it was that he had been sewn into the very fabric of their lives. Each laugh was a stitch, each shared glance between the boys a bond that could not easily unravel.

Ty leaned back on his elbows, a mischievous grin curling across his face. "So," he began, drawing the word out, "do you love Ella?" Tom's laughter stilled, though the smile did not leave his lips. He looked at his brother, the honesty already pressing to be spoken. "Yes," he admitted, his voice steady but tender. "I do. Very much." The confession came without shame, without hesitation, and Ty's grin only widened. He gave Tom's shoulder a playful shove. "Good," he said. "She deserves someone who means it." Tom laughed again, shaking his head, but inside he felt the truth settle deeply into his chest, undeniable.

The house itself seemed to cradle them. Four bedrooms stood within its walls, though only three bore the mark of family: Zenji and Keiko's room, Ty's, and now Tom's. Each boy had been given a king-sized bed, not for grandeur but for comfort, as though to say their worth could not be measured in half-steps. The fourth room, waiting always for guests, held the same warmth. Tom had not known spaces like this before—a home built with intention, each detail chosen not for show but for love. It was no palace, no estate, yet it carried a richness far greater than either could measure.

# THE SMILE THAT BROKE

Ella entered quietly, her cheeks faintly flushed from speaking with Keiko. She knelt beside the boys, her smile shy but unhidden, and for a moment it felt as though she too belonged in this circle, as natural as the sound of water over stone. Keiko followed her in, her voice calm. "Ella, your parents have agreed. If you'd like, you may stay with us tonight." Ella's eyes widened, her face lighting with joy as she nodded eagerly. "I would love that," she whispered, the gratitude in her voice ringing true. Tom's heart surged at the thought—she would be here, under the same roof, safe within the family's walls.

Zenji stepped back to the phone in the hall, finishing his call with Ella's parents. His voice, firm yet respectful, carried reassurance. He promised safety, care, and a home where Ella would be cherished like their own. When he returned, his expression was calm but his eyes gleamed with quiet satisfaction. "It's settled," he said simply. "Tonight she is ours to care for." Keiko reached to squeeze Ella's hand, her smile radiant. "Then welcome, dear," she said. "Tonight you are part of this house." Ella's lips trembled as though she might cry, but instead she bowed her head gratefully.

Ty grinned and stretched his arms behind his head. "Guess this house is never quiet anymore," he teased. Tom chuckled, though his gaze lingered on Ella, his chest tightening with a warmth that had no name before now. Keiko watched the exchange with the gentlest of smiles, her eyes glistening. To her, the picture was complete: two boys bound as brothers, a girl stepping bravely into love, and the walls of their home echoing with laughter instead of silence. It was not perfection, but it was wholeness—and wholeness was the truest gift she could ask for.

Morning light spilled into the Takashi home, warm and golden, slipping past shoji screens to rest upon polished wood floors. The air carried the faint scent of cedar from the garden and the crisp coolness of spring's last breath before summer. Ella stirred in the guest room, blinking against the brightness. She rose quietly, brushing her hair back with both hands, and when she stepped into the hallway, she found Tom waiting just outside, his posture hesitant but his smile certain. She moved without a word, wrapping her arms around him in a hug that was soft yet fierce. Her lips found his cheek in a quick kiss before pulling back with a shy grin. "Good morning," she whispered. For Tom, it was a beginning unlike any other.

Downstairs, Zenji had already prepared the percolator, its rich aroma weaving through the kitchen like a thread of comfort. He poured coffee into two small cups, adding only cream as he always did. Tom joined him at the table, his hands tentative on the porcelain, but his eyes shining with eagerness. Zenji raised his own cup in a quiet toast, and Tom mirrored him, sipping slowly. The taste was strong, almost bitter, but Tom held it proudly, swallowing as though proving something to himself. Zenji's gaze softened. "It's not about liking it yet," he said. "It's about sharing it." Tom nodded, his heart swelling at being trusted with such a simple, fatherly ritual.

Keiko set the breakfast table with quiet grace, Ty darting in and out of the kitchen with his usual boundless energy. Ella joined, carrying plates and helping without being asked, her laughter blending seamlessly with the household rhythm. To Tom, it felt like a picture he had once dreamed of but never believed he would live: family gathered, food steaming, the day beginning with peace instead of shouting. He caught Ella's smile across the table and felt that this house was no longer just a place of shelter—it was a home in every sense.

Later that morning, the students gathered in the classroom for one final assembly before summer break. The air buzzed with anticipation, desks scratched with names and doodles soon to be left behind for two months of freedom. Jeremy, perched at the front beside Mr. Clarke, cleared his throat. Though only nine, his voice carried the gravity of someone much older, a child unafraid to tell truths adults often avoided. He reminded the students that new ways are never built in leaps but in steps—small, deliberate, and steady. He spoke of Tom's courage, not in fighting but in walking away. He spoke of calling someone "Mom" for the first time, of trusting a home to be safe.

The classroom hushed as Jeremy continued, his tone firm yet warm. "New ways aren't easy," he said. "But they're better. They can last a lifetime if we keep walking them." His words settled into the room, not as lofty ideas but as simple truths each child could carry. Even the teachers, listening quietly at the back, felt the sting of recognition in their chests. It was not just the students who needed these lessons—it was everyone. Mr. Clarke's eyes glistened, and Mrs. Haller pressed a hand to her lips, humbled by the clarity of a child's voice.

Tom sat near the window, listening, his chest heavy with pride. He had been the example Jeremy pointed to, yet he knew it was not just his story. It was the story of every child who had been bruised, who had been told they could not change. His journey was proof that broken ways did not have to stay broken—that love, patience, and courage could remake even the most fragile of hearts. Ella squeezed his hand under the desk, and he turned to her with a smile that carried more than words ever could. Their bond, fragile yet certain, was its own step into a new way.

As Jeremy finished, the room broke into applause—not loud and raucous, but steady, a rhythm of agreement. Mr. Arnett stood, his presence quiet but commanding, and he spoke briefly of pride, of hope, and of his faith in each student seated before him. He did not give a lecture, nor did he promise that bullying or fear would vanish overnight. Instead, he echoed Jeremy's wisdom: "It starts with steps. Small ones. Steps that matter." The students nodded, some eagerly, others reluctantly, but all of them hearing the truth in his words.

The bell rang at last, releasing the tide of children into summer. Laughter and chatter filled the corridors, sneakers squeaking against polished floors, doors swinging wide to the freedom of two warm months ahead. Tom lingered near the lockers with Ella, Ty, and the others, each goodbye carrying more weight than it usually did. Ella leaned close, her eyes bright with tears not of sadness but of promise. "Stay safe," she whispered. Tom nodded, whispering back, "I will. We both will." Their fingers brushed, lingering, before she finally pulled away to join her family waiting outside.

Back at the Takashi home, the evening settled once more into the stillness of the garden. Zenji trimmed the bonsai with patient hands, Keiko hummed softly while preparing tea, and Ty sprawled on the veranda with a book. Tom leaned against the wooden railing, staring at the pond where koi flickered beneath the surface. He thought of Jeremy's words, of Ella's kiss, of the weight of coffee in his hand that morning, and he realized each moment was a step—small, deliberate, but unbreakable. His old ways had fallen like brittle branches. New ways had taken root, and they were growing.

Tom breathed deeply, closing his eyes. For the first time, he felt no fear of the morning to come. The path was not simple, nor was it guaranteed to be smooth, but it was his. And in that moment, surrounded by family and by love, he knew one truth that mattered above all: the ways he was building would last. And with Ella's hand in his, Ty's laughter beside him, and Zenji and Keiko's unwavering love, he would never again have to walk them alone.

## CHAPTER 18: A SMILE THAT BELONGS

The last bell had rung only yesterday, and already the air of freedom stretched itself over the town like a vast canopy. Children no longer carried the weight of assignments or the burden of bullies pressing against their shoulders; instead, they spilled out into the warmth of summer with laughter that reached into the streets and gardens. Tom felt it most keenly. The end of school was not simply the start of vacation—it was the opening of a door he had once thought forever closed. He stood at the threshold of something new, something wide and unbroken, with Ella's hand lingering near enough to remind him that he was no longer alone in it.

Ella, too, carried her own excitement in quiet ways. Though her parents had gone off with her aunt and uncle for a holiday camping trip, they had given her permission to remain with the Takashis, knowing she would be safe and deeply cared for. To her, this meant not merely the freedom of summer, but the opening chapter of something she had begun to long for all through the final days of school. Her relationship with Tom was still new, still tender, but she could already sense its roots pushing deeper into soil she trusted. Nights spent under the Takashi roof only deepened her feeling that she had stepped into a story that was meant to last.

The first morning of vacation broke without rush, without the clang of alarm clocks or the frantic shuffle of packed bags. Tom awoke slowly, as though his body already knew that the season itself demanded patience. He heard the faint hum of Keiko moving through the kitchen and the measured voice of Zenji greeting the day with calm. From the guest room Ella emerged, her hair slightly tangled from sleep but her smile as certain as sunlight. They met in the hallway, shy but eager, their words still few but their presence enough. For Tom, it was a kind of peace he had never known at this age—no shouts, no fists, no fear of what awaited at school.

They did not rush to fill the day with plans, nor did they measure time in hours. Instead, breakfast lingered into conversation, and conversation lingered into laughter. Ty leaned back against the doorway with his usual teasing grin, remarking that summer felt better when it was not running away from something. Tom chuckled, agreeing quietly, and Ella simply sat near him, brushing her fingers along the rim of her cup. Each gesture felt deliberate, each moment stretched to its full length. The day was not about reaching an end, but about staying present, as though the air itself held them in its open palm.

Later, they stepped out into the garden, the koi circling lazily in the pond while dragonflies skimmed the surface. Zenji joined them for a time, explaining how in Japan the first days of summer often carried the scent of festivals and family gatherings, of lanterns strung across streets and food shared beneath open skies. Ella listened with eyes wide, imagining each scene as though she stood among it. Tom listened too, though his attention often shifted to the quiet rhythm of Ella's breathing beside him. He was beginning to learn that peace was not only found in stories told, but in company kept.

Keiko spread a blanket across the grass, and they sat together beneath the budding branches of the bonsai trees. She explained how each one had been nurtured for years, shaped carefully but never forced. Ella traced the lines of the trunks with her eyes, nodding slowly. "It's like love," she said softly, and Tom felt his chest stir with something that reached beyond words. Keiko smiled at her, approving of the insight, but said nothing more. She did not need to. In the stillness of that moment, everything was already understood.

When evening drew close, lanterns were lit in the garden, casting a soft glow over the wooden beams of the house. The day had slipped past without urgency, each moment measured not by clocks but by heartbeats. Ella stayed close to Tom, sometimes brushing against him as though testing her courage, sometimes leaning nearer as though forgetting to hide her affection. Zenji and Keiko allowed it to unfold, watching quietly from the veranda. They remembered their own beginnings, when small gestures carried the weight of entire promises, and they knew better than to hurry what was already blooming.

That night, as crickets filled the air with steady rhythm, Ella chose her place once again in the guest room. Yet before retreating, she paused in the hall beside Tom's door. He had already turned down his bedding, ready for rest, but when she stepped close, he looked up at her with eyes that held no fear. "Good night, Tom," she whispered, her voice warm. He nodded, smiling faintly. "Good night, Ella." It was not grand, not dramatic, but in the simplicity of those words lingered a truth far larger than either of them could name.

The morning that followed was much the same—unhurried, deliberate, filled with quiet joy. Tom joined Zenji for coffee once more, the ritual already forming a rhythm in his days. Ella drifted into the kitchen, her presence a bright thread woven into the household. She hugged Tom lightly, pressing a kiss to his cheek before turning to Keiko with a question about the day's plans. It was not spoken in haste but in gentle curiosity, as though the possibilities stretched wide and endless before them. Tom felt his heart beat faster, not from fear but from the recognition that each step was part of something new.

And so the days of summer began—not in leaps, not in schedules marked upon calendars, but in steps so small they were easily missed if not noticed with care. Tom learned to see them, to hold them. Ella learned to treasure them, to carry them. Together they discovered that the beginning of summer was not about escape, nor about rushing toward an end. It was about breathing, waiting, and allowing what was real to take root. In this, Tom found his freedom, and Ella found her joy. Neither needed more than this—the slow unfurling of summer, day by patient day.

The morning sun fell across the polished floor of the dojo, its golden light reflecting off the wooden beams and spreading warmth into the cool space. Tom stood at the edge of the mat, his feet bare, his breathing steady, waiting as Zenji motioned for Ella to step forward. She hesitated only briefly, then slipped off her shoes and crossed to stand beside him.

Zenji spoke softly, his voice calm yet precise, introducing her to the slow, deliberate patterns of Taoist Tai Chi. "It is not about speed," he explained. "It is about rhythm, about finding stillness in the motion itself." Ella nodded, her eyes intent, determined not to miss a single word.

Tom smiled faintly as he demonstrated the first stance. His movements, though still learning themselves, carried a growing confidence, the kind only found through repetition and care. He lifted his arms slowly, bending his knees in a posture of rooted balance. Ella followed, her motions less certain, but Tom reached to adjust her hand gently, guiding her into the right form. "Like this," he whispered, his voice steady, his touch reassuring. Their eyes met briefly, and in that moment Ella realized that learning in the dojo was not just about discipline—it was about trust, about placing herself into rhythms that Tom already knew.

Zenji circled them quietly, watching with the keen eyes of both teacher and father. He corrected a posture here, adjusted an elbow there, never with criticism but always with patience. Ella found herself breathing more deeply, copying Tom's steady inhalations and exhalations until the rhythm became her own. "Balance," Zenji said softly. "Balance is not the absence of movement, but the harmony within it." The words sank into her mind, not merely as instruction but as something she carried into the way she stood, the way she breathed, even the way she looked at Tom as he mirrored her movements.

The practice continued, slow and deliberate, each motion flowing into the next like water sliding over stone. At first, Ella's arms trembled, her focus breaking when she lost her stance, but Tom was there each time, steadying her. His hand would rest against her shoulder or her wrist, a simple anchor that helped her return to the rhythm. She felt no shame in her stumbles, for Tom's quiet encouragement turned her missteps into lessons. "It takes time," he said gently. "But you'll feel it soon. It's like your body remembers even when your mind doesn't." His words eased her doubts, allowing her to trust the process.

When Zenji ended the session with a bow, Ella mirrored Tom, folding her hands and lowering her head with the same respect. The dojo seemed to hum with the weight of tradition, the polished wood carrying echoes of discipline and care that stretched beyond generations. As they stepped outside into the garden, the transition felt seamless, as though the lessons of balance had spilled naturally into the open air. The garden itself mirrored the dojo—quiet, deliberate, shaped with patience. The koi swam slowly in the pond, and the bridge arched gracefully across the water, inviting them to cross.

Ella walked beside Tom across that narrow bridge, her steps careful, her balance measured by what she had just learned. The water rippled beneath them, sunlight scattering across the surface like fragments of glass. Halfway across, she paused, turning toward him. He looked back, surprised by her sudden stillness, and in that pause something unspoken passed between them. Without waiting for permission, Ella leaned forward and pressed her lips softly to his. It was not hurried, not uncertain, but quiet and sure, like the forms they had just practised. Tom's breath caught, his heart leaping, yet his feet remained rooted firmly to the wooden planks beneath him.

For Tom, the kiss was not just affection—it was grounding. In that brief moment, he felt all the chaos of his past fall away, replaced by a calm that steadied him more deeply than any stance in the dojo. Ella's kiss reminded him that he did not need fists to be strong, nor walls to be safe. Her closeness anchored him, teaching him focus without fear. Each time she leaned into him, each time her hand brushed against his, he found himself more certain of the person he wanted to become. Not a boy trapped by anger, but one shaped by love and balance.

Ella pulled back slowly, her cheeks flushed but her eyes bright with certainty. She smiled at him, and Tom felt the tension in his shoulders ease as though she had brushed it away with her kiss. "See," she whispered softly, "you're steadier already." He laughed quietly, embarrassed yet warmed by her words, and took her hand as they crossed the rest of the bridge together. The koi swirled below, untroubled, and the garden seemed to welcome the quiet bond that had taken root between them. Zenji and Keiko, watching from the veranda, exchanged a glance, knowing the children had found something precious.

The day stretched onward, but neither Tom nor Ella felt the need to rush. They returned to the dojo later, their bodies tired but their spirits eager. This time, when Ella stumbled, Tom caught her and steadied her with a grin, as though the kiss on the bridge had given him a new strength of his own. He realized that balance was not just in stance or posture, but in the heart—learning to hold firm even when the world shifted beneath you. With Ella beside him, each motion felt easier, each breath deeper, each lesson more meaningful.

When the practice ended again, Tom bowed with gratitude, not just to Zenji, but to Ella, whose presence in the dojo had changed it from a place of discipline to a place of joy. She bowed back, her smile widening, and together they left the mats behind. As they stepped once more into the garden, Tom realized that every kiss, every glance, every shared rhythm was teaching him something far more valuable than he had expected. Balance was not about stillness. It was about love finding its footing in the spaces between breaths.

The dojo once again filled with quiet energy, the air alive with expectation as Ella stood on the polished floor, her feet shifting uneasily as she awaited Zenji's instructions. Unlike Tai Chi, Kung Fu carried a sharper rhythm, a more deliberate demand for precision. Ella tried to mirror Tom's stance, lowering herself into a form that felt unfamiliar, her weight uneven on her feet. Within moments she lost balance and stumbled, catching herself with a nervous laugh. Tom smiled gently, stepping forward, his hand brushing her elbow to steady her. "It's all right," he said softly, his voice carrying none of the harshness she feared. "Everyone falls at first. That's how we learn."

Zenji's gaze lingered on her for a moment before he nodded approvingly at Tom. "Yes. Teaching is not about striking down mistakes, but shaping them into steps forward." Ella straightened, cheeks flushed, but her eyes glimmered with determination. She tried again, focusing on her breath the way Tom had shown her.

Each attempt brought her closer to balance, though each misstep reminded her of how much patience it required. Tom stayed near, guiding her hands into alignment, showing her how to let her body move with intention instead of force. With every correction, his touch was light, never overbearing, and she felt steadier under his guidance.

Her love for Tom, though still young, became her anchor in those moments. Every time she faltered, she caught his gaze and found encouragement there, his eyes holding her steady where her legs could not. At one pause, he leaned forward, brushing a kiss against her cheek. It was brief, delicate, but its effect ran deep. Her breath steadied, her focus sharpened, and she held the stance without wavering. "See?" Tom whispered. "It's already in you. You just have to trust it." His words softened the edges of her frustration, turning the lesson into something beautiful rather than burdensome.

Ty, who had been watching quietly from the side, finally stepped forward, his grin wide as he prepared to add his own piece of wisdom. "Kung Fu is about balance," he said, his tone uncharacteristically serious for a boy his age. "But not the kind where you only think of your feet or your legs. It's all in here." He tapped his chest, directly over his heart. "And in here." He touched his forehead gently. "When the mind and the chest are steady, the body follows without question. It's like walking or crossing your legs—you don't think about it, your body already knows how." Ella and Tom listened intently, their eyes widening at the simplicity of his explanation.

Zenji smiled faintly, proud of his son for passing on the teaching with such clarity. "Exactly," he affirmed. "Balance begins in the heart and the mind. The body is the echo, not the source." Ella tried again, this time pressing her awareness into her chest and allowing her breath to guide her movements. She imagined her body flowing the way Ty described—like walking without thought, like breathing without command. Slowly, her stance held. The trembling in her legs eased, her arms steadied, and for the first time she felt the form align naturally. Tom's quiet nod of approval filled her with a surge of pride that no stumble could erase.

The practice continued, mistakes still present but now embraced as part of learning. Ella laughed when she fell, brushing off her knees with good humour, and Tom joined her in the laughter, showing her that even error carried its own rhythm. Each correction Zenji gave was delivered with gentleness, each reminder rooted in patience. Ty demonstrated the forms with boyish energy, exaggerating his movements just enough to make Ella giggle, easing her tension and reminding her that even discipline could hold joy. Together, the three of them shaped the lesson into something memorable—not a trial of endurance, but a celebration of persistence.

As the sun slanted through the high windows, Ella wiped sweat from her brow, her cheeks flushed with both effort and delight. She turned toward Tom, her eyes shining. "I never thought I'd be able to do it," she admitted, her voice breathless but triumphant. Tom stepped closer, pressing his forehead lightly to hers.

"You already could," he murmured. "You just needed to believe it." In that intimate closeness, Ella felt her earlier doubts dissolve, replaced by a steady confidence that reached deeper than she had known possible. She realized then that her strength was not only growing in her muscles, but in her heart.

When the lesson ended, Zenji bowed to them both, his eyes filled with quiet approval. Ella returned the bow, her movements more certain than before, and Tom bowed beside her, his pride unmistakable. As they stepped from the dojo into the cool air of the garden, Ella reached for Tom's hand without hesitation. The bridge arched before them once again, the koi swirling below, and as they crossed she leaned into him for another kiss. This one was longer, slower, filled with gratitude and certainty. Tom held her close, feeling her warmth and her strength, and he knew with unshakable clarity that her presence was what kept him grounded.

The garden, silent except for the trickle of water, seemed to hold its breath around them, as though witnessing the balance they had both discovered. Ty, watching from a distance, grinned mischievously, already teasing in his mind what he might say later, but he kept silent for now, respecting the moment. Zenji and Keiko exchanged another quiet glance, their hearts content. They saw not just children practising forms of discipline, but two young souls learning the truest lesson of all—that balance was found not in perfection, but in patience, humility, and love.

The garden breathed with summer warmth as the evening settled in, fireflies beginning their dance across the hedges and pond. Zenji had prepared a simple camp for the children in the far corner where the grass grew soft and the shadows of the bonsai trees stretched long beneath the lantern light. A canvas tent rose beside the koi pond, its edges anchored with care, though Tom and Ty argued playfully over which stake was straightest. Ella laughed at them both, clutching her blanket as though already planning her nest beneath the stars. It was not the wild woods, but here, within the walls of the Takashi garden, the night promised wonder just the same.

As the three children settled, Zenji's voice cut gently into their chatter. He spoke not of rules but of stories, weaving memories of his own childhood in Japan. His tone carried the rhythm of someone who did not merely tell history but lived it, describing festivals in Kyoto where lanterns floated down rivers like drifting constellations, and the discipline of his first dojo where patience was carved into every lesson. Ella listened wide-eyed, the scent of cedar and summer air wrapping around her like an invisible cloak, and she clung closer to Tom, eager not to miss a word.

When the stories eased, Ty leaned back against his blanket, looking at his father with a seriousness that belied his years. "You should tell them about chi," he said quietly. Zenji gave a faint nod, but Ty took the lead, his voice carrying the curiosity of a student turned teacher. "In Japan," he began, "we call it ki. It's not just one thing. It's your breath, your guts, your spirit, even the way your muscles and tendons work together. People think it's magic energy, but really, it's all the parts of you in harmony. That's what makes it real."

Ella tilted her head, curious. "So it's not like… some invisible power you can shoot out of your hands?" Her tone carried both teasing and sincerity, though her eyes shone with the earnestness of wanting to understand. Ty chuckled and shook his head. "No, nothing like that. It's not lightning or fireballs. It's when your breath matches your movement, when your body works with itself instead of against itself. That's ki. That's balance. And when you feel it, it's like you're stronger without even trying harder." Tom nodded quietly, recognizing the truth in his brother's words, though he still marveled at how easily Ty explained something so profound.

Zenji watched with pride, his gaze steady as his son spoke with conviction. "Ki," he added, "is cultivated. You grow it through discipline, through breathing, through stillness. It is not a gift someone gives you, but something you discover already within yourself." He drew in a slow breath and exhaled with such calm that the lantern flame between them barely flickered. "In the West, some call it superstition, or say it is not real because it cannot be measured. But the truth is simpler. It does not need measurement. It is lived. And those who live it know it." His words pressed into the silence like stones into water, rippling outward with meaning.

Ella pulled the blanket tighter, letting the warmth settle into her. "So it's like… believing in yourself, but deeper?" she asked. Ty leaned over, nudging her arm with a grin. "Exactly. It's believing so much that your body listens. When you trip, instead of falling, your body just knows how to catch itself. When you breathe right, your arms don't feel so heavy anymore. That's not magic. That's ki." Ella smiled faintly, resting her head against Tom's shoulder. His hand found hers beneath the blanket, and though he said nothing, the steadiness of his touch told her he understood what it meant to anchor someone else.

The night deepened, and the stars began to etch themselves across the sky, sharp and countless. Zenji pointed out constellations with the patience of a teacher, naming them in Japanese before offering their English names. Ella whispered each word after him, her accent clumsy but her effort sincere. Tom found himself quietly repeating them as well, his chest warm with the knowledge that he was learning pieces of a world larger than his own. The act of naming the stars in another tongue gave them new weight, as though they now belonged to him too.

After a pause, Zenji told them of how in Japan, children are expected to grow strong not only in study but in spirit. "We are taught discipline without question," he explained. "Uniforms, strict schedules, expectations so heavy they sometimes crush more than they build. But what I teach you here is different. Discipline does not mean punishment. It means patience. And patience, in turn, is freedom." Tom absorbed every word, his gaze shifting upward to the infinite sky, where patience and freedom stretched side by side. Ella nestled closer into him, her heart racing not from nerves but from a deep, unshakable peace.

Ty stretched his arms over his head, yawning, before sitting upright with sudden focus. "You know," he said with conviction, "people laugh at chi in the West, but that's only because they don't feel it.

You can't see breath, either, but you know it's real." He inhaled deeply, exhaled with force, then stood, performing a slow, deliberate stance on the grass. His movements were clumsy in the dark but carried the unmistakable rhythm of purpose. "It's real because it changes you," he added softly. "You just need to be patient enough to let it."

Zenji allowed the demonstration to stand without correction, his pride in his son's confidence clear. Ella clapped softly, her laughter light, though her admiration genuine. Tom gave a faint smile, knowing that Ty's words rang true. He himself had felt the difference—the quiet strength that had come not from fighting, but from walking away, from finding peace in restraint. The memory of Myles returned unbidden, the reason behind each new step, and his chest ached with the knowledge that the story he carried mattered most when told through the way he lived now.

As the fireflies continued their dance, the children finally lay back on their blankets, their eyes fixed on the star-splattered heavens. The garden was quiet except for the soft rustle of summer leaves and the distant sound of water spilling into the pond. Ella whispered, her voice drowsy but full of wonder, "Do you think the stars can feel us looking at them?" Tom squeezed her hand gently, whispering back, "Maybe. And maybe they smile too." In the stillness that followed, the night wrapped them in its calm embrace, and Tom felt for the first time that balance was not just in the dojo or in practice—it was in the quiet moments beneath the stars, when the world itself seemed to breathe with you.

The morning after the starlit camping in the garden, the world seemed fresher, as if the night itself had cleared away dust from the children's hearts. Ella lingered in the kitchen with Keiko while breakfast simmered on the stove, her hands folded in her lap, her cheeks glowing with a courage that looked fragile yet stubborn. She hesitated only a moment before her words poured out, steady and sincere. "Someday," she whispered, "I hope I can be Tom's wife." The admission hung in the air like incense, fragrant and impossible to ignore. Keiko set aside the teapot, her eyes softening as she turned to the girl.

Keiko did not laugh, nor did she brush the words aside with the easy dismissal of adults who hear childhood dreams. Instead, she listened deeply, her silence holding Ella's confession with the respect of a promise. "Your love is pure," she said after a pause, her voice steady. "It is not a small thing to say, Ella. Marriage is far away, yes, but the heart that wants it—that is already real." Ella's eyes brimmed with tears of relief, for she had feared being told she was childish, or naive. Yet here was Keiko, treating her words as truth, as something worth cradling.

Across the yard, Tom had drawn Ty aside beneath the shade of the small bridge in the garden. His voice carried the unease of someone uncertain whether he should even speak aloud what pressed at his chest. "Ty," he began, "I want to marry Ella too, when we're old enough. Maybe when the law says it's right, or maybe a little after, when we're ready." Ty blinked at him, then broke into a grin that softened into something more solemn. "That's not a small thing to say either. If you mean it, then you better treat her as though she's already your family." Tom nodded, the weight of his brother's words tightening his resolve.

Zenji, who had approached quietly, overheard just enough to draw the boys into conversation. He guided them to the shaded veranda, where a pot of green tea awaited, and sat them down with the patient gravity of a teacher about to unwrap something larger than their questions. "You speak of love and marriage," he said calmly, "but you also must speak of belief. Ty, you spoke of chi last night. Let me show you both sides of the river it flows." His tone was neither scolding nor indulgent, but carried the measured cadence of a man accustomed to balancing truth and doubt in equal measure.

He began with the arguments that gave chi its reality, the ones he himself had lived. "Many who practise feel it," Zenji explained, his gaze steady on Tom. "They speak of warmth, of currents, of a power that seems to move inside them. It becomes real because they experience it. It is not just imagination; it is breath in harmony with body. It is bones aligned with the earth. That is why Taoist arts, Tai Chi, and even acupuncture carry meaning. They have guided countless people to health, to calm, to strength without harm. You cannot dismiss what helps people live better, even if you cannot see it with your eyes."

Tom leaned forward, fascinated. Ella, who had rejoined them quietly, sat cross-legged beside Keiko, her eyes wide as though Zenji's every word might slip away if she blinked. Ty nodded knowingly, as if the ground beneath his father's words had always been firm. The air hummed with the sense that something vital was being passed down, not as myth, but as a lived truth that each child could carry.

Then Zenji shifted, his voice not colder, but sharper with clarity. "But not everyone believes. And they are not fools for doubting. Chi cannot be measured by science. No instrument can capture it. To many, that means it is not real. They call it pseudoscience, a belief dressed as proof. They say what we describe as chi is only biomechanics—how the body saves energy, how the nervous system fires, how heat moves. They see no force, only physics. And they are not wrong to point this out." The children sat straighter, realizing that his teaching was not meant to blind them, but to open their eyes wider.

"Some demonstrations of chi," Zenji continued, "are tricks. Sleight of hand. Deception. There are men who claim they can throw someone across a room with energy alone, but when tested, the illusion fades. These are reasons why many laugh at chi, why they dismiss it as a story for children. Science demands proof. Chi does not offer it." His words fell heavy, yet he spoke without bitterness, his voice steady as still water.

Ella frowned, glancing from Zenji to Tom. "But if it helps people," she murmured, "doesn't that make it real in some way?" Zenji's gaze softened as he inclined his head. "Yes. That is the heart of it. Whether chi is real energy, or only the harmony of your body and mind, it helps people heal. It makes them stronger. It gives them peace. And in that, it is real. For belief does not always need to be proven in a lab. It only needs to be lived."

Keiko reached across to place her hand over Ella's, her touch steady, grounding. "It is the same with love," she added softly. "No one can measure it. No one can weigh it. Yet when you feel it, you know it is there. Whether the world believes you or not, it is yours. It is real." Ella's breath caught, her heart swelling as though Keiko had taken her secret hope and painted it into words too perfect to forget.

Tom turned to Ty, his eyes alight. "So it's like when we train—when I breathe right, when I let my body follow instead of fight—it's real, even if nobody else can prove it." Ty nodded firmly, his grin returning. "Exactly. That's chi. And that's love too." The brothers exchanged a glance that carried no laughter, only the shared weight of a truth too large for their young shoulders, yet somehow fitting there.

Zenji leaned back, his hands folded in his lap. "So whether chi is a force, or only a word for balance, remember this: what matters is how you live it. If it makes you stronger, kinder, more patient, then it is real in the way that counts." He let silence settle then, allowing the lesson to sink deeper than any lecture.

The children sat together for a long time, the tea cooling between them, the cicadas beginning their chorus outside the open screens. Ella leaned against Tom's arm, whispering softly, "So I guess love is chi too." Tom blushed but did not turn away. He pressed his forehead against hers, murmuring back, "Then I'll never let mine break."

That night, as lanterns flickered against the deepening dark, Tom's mind echoed with both dreams and lessons—the hope of Ella's words about marriage, the patience of Zenji's teaching, and the grounding certainty of Ty's brotherhood. The summer stretched before him, not in weeks or months, but in moments to be lived, each one as real as the breath in his chest.

Keiko sat across from Ella in the quiet of the garden, the scent of jasmine mingling with the dampness of the evening earth. The lantern light caught the curve of her face, softened by years of patience and an understanding carved from many seasons of life. Ella's words about marriage lingered in the air, fragile and unpolished, yet filled with a sincerity that made them glow. Keiko folded her hands neatly in her lap and smiled—not with amusement, nor with dismissal, but with a gravity that showed she had taken the girl's heart seriously. "You carry a dream, Ella," she said gently. "And dreams are not foolish. But love, like the bonsai tree, does not blossom in a season. It deepens with roots first."

Ella tilted her head, listening with every fibre of her being, her cheeks still warm from the courage of her earlier confession. She was afraid, if only slightly, that Keiko would remind her of her youth and say the words most adults had said to her in the past—that she was too young, too naïve, too fanciful to speak of marriage. Yet Keiko's tone had none of that condescension. Instead, she drew Ella closer with her calmness, with the kind of listening that nurtured rather than shut down. "The bonsai tree looks delicate," Keiko continued, "but its strength is not in what you see above the soil. Its strength is hidden. Its roots wind deeply, slowly, steadily. Love is much the same. You may not notice it growing, but with care, it becomes unshakable."

Tom, who had wandered into the garden after finishing a practice routine in the dojo, leaned against the wooden post of the veranda, quietly observing. He saw how intently Ella listened to his mother, her hands clasped together, her eyes shimmering with hope and a bit of fear. His heart swelled with a kind of pride—pride that Ella loved him so openly, and pride that his mother treated her with such dignity. Ella was not just a guest in their home; she was being drawn into the circle of family by a bond that was invisible but unbreakable.

Keiko reached across the low garden table, her fingertips brushing the rim of Ella's teacup. "Love cannot be hurried," she said with quiet conviction. "If you try to force it into blossom too quickly, it will break beneath its own weight. But if you let it grow slowly—step by step, day by day—it will last a lifetime. Even storms cannot uproot what has sunk itself deep into the earth." Her words were not grand proclamations, but steady truths, the kind that folded themselves into memory and stayed there.

Ella's throat tightened. She looked down at her knees, then lifted her eyes again with the determination of someone who needed to be understood. "But I do love him," she whispered. "I don't mean just the way kids say it. I mean it here." She placed her small hand over her chest, her voice steady though her eyes brimmed with tears. Keiko nodded, her expression softening further, and she reached out to press her palm gently over Ella's hand. "Then let it stay there," she said. "Hold it, nurture it, and let it guide you forward. But remember—love's truest form is patient. It is not in rushing to tomorrow, but in cherishing today."

The girl's tears fell, but they were not heavy with sorrow. They were the tears of a heart that had been heard, honoured, and guided without dismissal. Tom, unable to remain silent any longer, stepped closer and sat beside Ella, his presence quiet but steady. He wrapped his arm around her shoulders and whispered, "I love you too, Ella. I'll wait with you. However long it takes." The words made her lean into him, her tears staining the fabric of his sleeve. Keiko did not interrupt. She simply watched, a small smile tugging at her lips, knowing her son was learning to speak truth with both courage and tenderness.

Zenji entered the garden a few moments later, his footsteps silent against the wooden boards. He did not intrude with questions but instead lowered himself onto the veranda beside his wife, studying the scene with his steady gaze. Keiko leaned towards him slightly and murmured, "She wants to marry him one day." Zenji's brow lifted, but instead of amusement, he simply nodded, as though the weight of a young heart's hope was something worth honouring. "Then let them water their roots," he said softly, "and the tree will grow in its time." His words folded seamlessly into Keiko's earlier counsel, two voices weaving a single truth.

Ella wiped her eyes and laughed softly, embarrassed by her own tears, though no one mocked her for them. "I feel silly," she admitted. "Like I shouldn't have said anything." Keiko shook her head immediately, the firmness in her eyes leaving no room for doubt. "Never feel silly for speaking truth. Love is never foolish when it is real. What matters is how you care for it, how you protect it, how you let it grow. That is the difference between a flower that wilts in a week and a tree that shades generations."

The lanterns in the garden swayed with the night breeze, their soft light pooling around the three young faces and the two adults who had chosen to guide rather than correct. Ella leaned her head against Tom's shoulder, her hand still held over her chest where Keiko's hand had been moments earlier. In that gesture, a promise had been planted—not a promise of marriage tomorrow, but a promise of patience, of growth, of tending something that might one day become as enduring as the bonsai in the Takashi garden.

Zenji lifted one of the smaller bonsai pots from the shelf along the veranda and placed it gently in Ella's hands. The little tree, twisted and gnarled yet undeniably alive, seemed almost to speak without words. "This is yours for the summer," he said. "Water it every day, tend to it, and watch what happens. If you can care for this little life with patience, then you will know what love requires." Ella clutched it as though he had handed her something sacred, her eyes widening with awe.

Keiko added softly, "It will not change quickly. But day by day, it will show you its strength. That is how love works too. That is how families grow, how marriages last, how bonds endure." The garden felt hushed, reverent, as if even the cicadas had lowered their voices to listen. Tom pressed another kiss to Ella's temple, not out of impatience, but as a quiet vow to walk beside her through every day that stretched ahead.

In that moment, under the swaying lanterns and the whispering leaves, the lesson settled into their hearts. Love was not in the rushing. Love was in the staying. And for Tom and Ella, guided by Keiko's gentle counsel, the staying had already begun.

The evening carried the hush of cicadas and the faint lapping of water in the garden pond, as though nature itself had chosen to listen. Tom sat on the veranda steps, the bonsai still resting in Ella's lap, its fragile strength silently echoing what Keiko had just shared. He lifted his eyes toward Zenji, who sat a little apart, posture upright yet relaxed, his gaze cast toward the lantern light that flickered across the raked stones. Tom's question broke the silence, unadorned but heavy with curiosity. "Dad," he asked, voice steady but soft, "can love really last forever? Or does it change into something else after a while?" His words carried not only the innocence of a boy just learning what it meant to be loved, but the fear of someone who had once lived in a world where affection was fleeting and broken.

Zenji turned his head slowly, his dark eyes catching the glow of the garden lanterns. He studied Tom for a moment, not with scrutiny but with the stillness of a man who believed every word deserved time before an answer. Keiko looked toward her husband, her lips curving with quiet expectation, for she knew the story he would tell, a story that lived deep in the marrow of their marriage. Zenji leaned forward, resting his forearms on his knees, and spoke in the even tone of one who measured his words with care. "Love does last forever, Tom," he began, "but it is not because it is easy. It lasts because you choose it every day. It endures because you tend to it, even when storms bend its branches and time wears its roots."

Tom listened, wide-eyed, as though he were hearing a secret never told in classrooms or books. Zenji's voice wove a memory into the night air, steady and deliberate. "When I first met Keiko, I was younger than I understood myself to be. I thought strength was in holding firm, in never bending. But Keiko taught me that real strength is found in patience, in listening, in allowing another's heart to rest safely against your own. She did not demand perfection, but she asked for honesty. And I learned to give it, even when honesty felt like weakness." His eyes softened as he turned toward Keiko, who met his gaze with the smallest of nods.

Zenji shifted slightly, his hand tracing the grain of the wood beneath him as if the memory itself were carved into it. "There were days," he continued, "when work weighed heavy, when mistakes tempted me to shut everyone out. But I chose to let Keiko in. I told her truths I was ashamed of. And instead of turning away, she stayed. That is when I understood—love is not something that happens once. It is something you do, again and again, even when it is hard, even when you feel unworthy of it." The words did not rise with drama, but settled like stones in water, rippling out into the listening hearts around him.

Ella clutched the little bonsai tighter in her hands, her breath shallow as though she were trying to memorise every syllable. Tom leaned forward, his elbows resting on his knees, eyes fixed on his father with unwavering attention. The simplicity of Zenji's tone carried more weight than any grand tale of battles or victories. This was not a story of conquest—it was a story of endurance, of a bond forged not in the moments of laughter alone, but in the quiet struggles that tested whether love was real or not.

"Keiko and I have known loss," Zenji said quietly, his voice dipping with memory. "We have seen days where silence lingered longer than words, where distance threatened to hollow out the closeness we had built. But each morning, we began again. We chose to stand side by side, to turn toward one another instead of away. That choice, repeated day after day, is what makes love endure. Not grand gestures, not promises made once, but the daily decision to hold fast, even when holding fast feels like the hardest thing to do."

Keiko's eyes glistened, though she did not interrupt, allowing her husband's truth to fall gently upon their son. She knew the weight of every word, for she had lived them with him, in moments unspoken to anyone else. Tom glanced between them, understanding dawning not in quick bursts but in the slow, steady glow of recognition. Love was not a fairy tale that ended when vows were spoken. It was work, patience, honesty, and above all, choice.

Zenji reached across the low table, his strong hand resting on Keiko's, and for a moment silence said more than words. "You see, Tom," he said at last, turning his gaze back to his son, "forever is not a single moment. It is made of many small moments. Every day that I choose Keiko, and every day she chooses me, forever grows. That is how love lasts. That is why I tell you it can endure." His tone was neither romanticised nor softened, but grounded in the lived truth of years.

Tom's throat tightened, the weight of the answer more than he expected, yet exactly what he needed. He leaned back slightly, processing, his young mind holding the concept like a stone he would turn over in his hand again and again. Ella shifted closer, brushing her shoulder against his, as though silently affirming that she too had heard and understood. For the first time, Tom realised love was not just in feeling—it was in action, in persistence, in the resilience to keep showing up.

Zenji lifted his gaze to the stars peeking through the canopy of the garden trees. "Do not ask if love can last forever," he said, his voice barely above a whisper. "Ask instead if you are willing to choose it again tomorrow. If you are, then forever will come on its own." The lantern light flickered across his features, catching the faintest curve of a smile, not sentimental but certain. Keiko squeezed his hand in agreement, the silent testimony of a woman who had walked every step of that truth with him.

Tom swallowed hard and whispered, "I want to love like that." His voice cracked slightly, not from weakness, but from the depth of longing the story had stirred. Zenji nodded once, firmly, as though sealing an unspoken vow between father and son. "Then learn patience, honesty, and choice. Do not demand love be easy, Tom. Let it be real." His words carried into the night, etching themselves into memory.

Ella tilted her face toward Tom, whispering so softly only he could hear, "We can choose too. Every day." He nodded, gripping her hand with a steadiness he had never felt before. The bonsai tree between them seemed to glow in the lantern light, its twisted branches holding the same promise Zenji had spoken—a promise of endurance.

The night grew deeper, the cicadas sang louder, yet the garden felt settled, anchored by truths too steady to be undone. Zenji's story, spoken without flourish, had given them something far more lasting than tales of grandeur. It had given them a map of how love survives, how it takes root, and how it endures storms. Tom and Ella sat beneath its weight, not crushed, but steadied—knowing that the love they carried had just been given a way forward.

And so, with the stars above them and the bonsai between them, the lesson of forever did not feel unreachable anymore. It felt possible. It felt real.

The summer air was thick with warmth, cicadas singing their endless chorus outside the open windows of the small community hall. Rows of folding chairs were set up, filled not with adults, but with children of every age—some no older than six, others just beginning to step into adolescence. Their parents waited at the back, some curious, others uncertain, but it was the children who leaned forward, whispering to one another, until the room fell silent as Tom stepped to the front. He was nervous, that much was clear in the way he clutched his paper notes, though he never looked down at them. Instead, he raised his head, and with a deep breath, he spoke not as a boy burdened by fear, but as one carrying the weight of truth.

## THE SMILE THAT BROKE

"My name is Tom," he began, his voice steadier than he expected, "and I'm here to tell you about someone who should never be forgotten. His name was Myles Casey Benson Neuts. He was just ten years old. He was like us, just a kid who went to school one morning and never came home the same. Myles lost his life because of bullies. Because no one stood up in time. Because adults looked the other way, or waited too long, and when they did find him, it was too late." The words dropped into the air, heavy yet sharp, like stones cast into a still pond. The children shifted uneasily in their seats, some staring at the floor, others staring straight at him, wide-eyed.

Tom paused only briefly, then went on. "I don't tell you this to scare you. I tell you because it's true, and because someone needs to say it. Myles deserves to be remembered. His smile deserves to be remembered. He was a boy who should still be here, playing soccer, laughing with friends, dreaming about the future. Instead, he's gone. But if we tell his story, if we learn from it, then we can make sure what happened to him doesn't happen again." The silence deepened, the weight of his honesty pressing into every corner of the hall.

Ella sat in the front row, her hands folded tightly in her lap, her eyes fixed on him. She knew how much courage it took to speak this aloud, how much it cost him each time. Ty sat beside her, nodding subtly, his steady presence like a silent drumbeat encouraging Tom to keep going. Zenji stood near the back with Keiko, neither interfering nor correcting, allowing Tom the space to stand on his own. Mr. Arnett, who had insisted this gathering be allowed, leaned against the wall with quiet pride.

Tom continued, his voice firmer now. "I want you to understand something. A bully's words or fists are not stronger than the truth. They tell you lies like, 'If you tell, you'll get hurt worse,' or 'No one will believe you.' That's what they want you to think. But bullies feed on silence. Every time someone stays quiet, they win. The truth is the only way to take their power away. Always tell. Always report them. Don't keep their secrets. Don't protect them with your silence."

Several children glanced at each other, as though silently asking if this could really work, if speaking up wouldn't make things worse. Tom saw their doubt, and he did not ignore it. "I know you're afraid. I was afraid too. Fear tells you to stay quiet, to hide. But listen to me—fear doesn't protect you. It only gives the bully more time. When you stand up and speak the truth, yes, maybe you'll shake, maybe you'll cry, maybe your voice will break—but the truth will always be stronger than fear." His voice rose slightly, not shouting, but carrying conviction that filled the room.

A girl in the second row lifted her hand timidly. Tom nodded at her, and she whispered, "But what if the bully finds out you told?" Tom did not hesitate. "If they do, then you tell again. And again. And you keep telling until someone listens and steps in. You don't stop, and you don't let them make you feel ashamed. Because bullies want you to feel like you're alone, but you are not alone. There are teachers, parents, police, principals, friends—you must find the right people and make them see. Never stop telling the truth." The girl lowered her hand, and though fear still lingered on her face, a flicker of understanding shone through.

He leaned forward slightly, resting his palms on the table in front of him. "Don't ever believe that fighting makes you weak. Standing up, telling the truth, even when your knees are shaking—that's the real kind of strong. And if you see someone else being bullied, don't wait for someone older to step in. Be the first voice. Say something. Get help. Pull the person away. Stand next to them so they don't feel alone. Because silence is what allows bullying to grow." The words struck hard, and many of the children shifted again, their faces flushed with something deeper than fear: the awakening of responsibility.

Zenji's face remained impassive, but inside, he felt pride swell at the clarity in Tom's voice. This was no longer the boy who had once struck first in blind defense. This was someone who had turned pain into something purposeful. Tom's voice softened slightly, as though speaking to each child personally. "You have a choice every day. You can let a bully's smile break your own, or you can stand so that others' smiles don't break. You can choose not to be silent. Myles didn't get the chance to grow up and make that choice again. But we do. We can make it for him."

The room was so quiet that even the cicadas outside seemed to hush. A boy in the back wiped his eyes quickly with his sleeve, trying to hide his tears. Another whispered something to her friend, who nodded firmly. Tom stood still, letting the silence linger, allowing each of them to carry the weight of what he had said. He knew this wasn't about making them like him, or about being admired. It was about giving them the truth, unvarnished and steady.

Ella's heart swelled as she listened, her pride so fierce it nearly spilled from her in tears. She had loved Tom for the way he was learning to breathe, to smile, to love her without fear—but this, standing tall and speaking truth, was the proof of the man he would become. Ty gave a small, approving smile, seeing in his brother the quiet strength Zenji had always spoken of.

At last, Tom's voice settled into its final note. "Don't let Myles be forgotten. Tell his story. Stand up. And never let silence win." He straightened, no longer nervous, no longer clutching the notes he hadn't even looked at. His hands were steady at his sides, his gaze direct. And in that moment, he wasn't just a boy speaking to other children. He was a living promise that pain can be turned into strength, that truth can outlast cruelty, and that even one child's voice can make a difference.

The children began to clap, hesitant at first, then stronger, filling the hall with a sound that pushed back every shadow. Tom bowed his head slightly, not as a performer but as one who honoured the moment. And as he stepped down to join Ella and Ty, his heart carried the certainty that Myles's story had been heard, and that it would live on—not in fear, but in courage.

The evening air was thick with the quiet hum of summer as children left the community centre, their small hands curled tightly around the edges of chairs and bags as though reluctant to let go of what they had just heard. Tom's words lingered long after the clapping had faded, hanging in the space between them like threads pulling at their thoughts.

For once, the chatter of dismissal was subdued, the footsteps slow and thoughtful, as though each child feared the noise of their shoes might shatter the weight that clung to the room. Some whispered Myles's name, careful and soft, as if it were something fragile, like glass held in cupped palms. Others walked in silence, replaying every word in their heads, unsure how to share them once they reached their homes.

Parents who had been standing at the back of the hall stepped forward now, gathering their children, but even they did not speak right away. They had heard everything. Every word Tom had chosen, every truth he had pressed into the air without hesitation. And though many of them had come only to keep watch, perhaps expecting a child's talk, they found themselves unsettled by the piercing clarity of his honesty. They exchanged quiet glances, parents recognizing in one another the same thought: these were not things easily ignored. One mother pressed her lips together and smoothed her daughter's hair, but her eyes betrayed an unease that would not be soothed by gestures.

In one corner, a father knelt down to face his son. "Is that true?" the boy asked him, voice low and unsteady. "That if you don't tell, the bully wins?" The father opened his mouth, then closed it again, struck by the bluntness of the question. Finally, with a weight in his tone, he said, "Yes. It's true. And I should have said it before. But you heard it tonight, and you remember it. Don't stay silent." The boy nodded, the words sealing themselves into his chest. It was not just Tom's truth now—it was his as well.

Another child, clutching her backpack straps, whispered to her mother, "Would you believe me if I told you?" The mother's hand tightened, guilt flashing across her face, for she realized that there had been times she had dismissed small complaints as ordinary squabbles. She bent lower, her voice trembling. "I promise you now, I will always listen. Always." The girl's eyes filled with tears, though not from pain, but from the sudden discovery that belief could be given so freely. That promise, simple as it was, carried more weight than years of unspoken neglect.

Not every parent reacted with ease. One man muttered about children being too young to hear such stories, his frustration masking his discomfort. But his wife placed a firm hand on his arm, silencing him. "No," she said quietly but sharply, "they needed to hear it. We all did." Her eyes held a strength that unsettled him, for she was right, and the truth had already been laid bare. It could not be folded away like yesterday's news. It demanded reckoning, even within the walls of their own home.

As they walked into the fading light, conversations began to break open like seeds splitting in the soil. Brothers spoke to sisters about what they had seen, parents asked questions they had avoided, and children shared secrets they had been carrying alone. For the first time, words that had been silenced by fear found their way into the open. Some trembled, others cracked, but they emerged nonetheless. The story of Myles had become more than Tom's memory—it was now a living message, carried in many voices, reshaping the evening into something larger than itself.

At the Takashi home later, Zenji watched with quiet satisfaction as Tom returned with Ella and Ty, his steps unhurried yet steady. "Do you know what you've done?" Zenji asked softly, his tone one of reverence rather than instruction. Tom lowered his gaze, uncertain, but Zenji pressed on. "You've given them a mirror. Not the kind that shows a face, but the kind that shows courage. They will carry that with them, and it will change things." Tom said nothing, only nodded, the words sinking deep into him, deeper than praise ever could.

Across the town, in houses where the weight of the evening followed the families inside, silence held for a time before words dared to break it. A mother folded laundry slower than usual, her son sitting on the edge of the bed watching her. Finally, he whispered, "Mom, there's something I didn't tell you before." She set down the shirt in her hands, her heart already tightening, and said, "I'm listening." And so it began, the unburdening, sparked not by lectures or lessons, but by a boy who had dared to speak truth.

Even those who did not speak felt a shift. A girl sitting at her desk traced circles into her notebook, remembering Tom's words: don't let silence win. She wrote them down, letter by letter, as though carving them into her memory. Another child, alone in his room, clenched his fists and breathed deeply, imagining what it might feel like to finally stand up for himself. These were small actions, unnoticed by the world, yet profound in their quiet beginnings. Seeds had been planted, and no one could predict how far the roots would spread.

Ella, curled up later with Keiko in the quiet of the Takashi home, spoke softly, "Do you think they'll remember?" Keiko smiled faintly, brushing a strand of hair from the girl's face. "Yes," she answered, "because truth has a way of clinging to us. Once you hear it, you cannot unhear it. And Tom gave them something real. That kind of truth doesn't slip away." Ella nodded, comforted not only for Tom's sake but for the sake of the children who had listened. She knew something had shifted in the air, and she felt privileged to have witnessed it.

The next morning, parents spoke to one another in passing, remarking on the talk, unable to let it rest. Some praised Tom's courage outright, others questioned whether it had been too heavy for young ears. Yet beneath their differing words lay the same quiet recognition: the conversation had begun, and there would be no returning to silence. It was uncomfortable, yes, but necessary, and for many it was the first step toward facing truths they had long kept buried.

Tom, unaware of the full ripple his words had caused, sat with Ty beneath the shade of the garden trees, staring at the koi moving slowly in the pond. "Do you think it mattered?" he asked softly. Ty glanced at him, his grin small but sure. "Of course it mattered. Sometimes all it takes is one person willing to say it. And you did." Tom breathed out slowly, the knot in his chest easing just a little.

For the children who carried his words home, the night became one of restlessness, filled with thoughts that would not settle. Some cried quietly into their pillows, not from sadness alone but from the realization that they had power they had not recognized before. Others dreamed vividly, seeing themselves standing tall, speaking truth where once they had remained silent. And though they were still children, with fears and doubts that could not vanish overnight, they awoke the next day slightly changed.

Myles's story had been retold, not as a tragedy to haunt them, but as a reminder that silence was a choice—and so was courage. Parents awoke with questions echoing in their minds, teachers prepared for conversations they could no longer avoid, and children carried themselves with a cautious new awareness. The weight of listening had settled in, heavy but necessary, and with it came the possibility of change.

And in a small bedroom where Ella's framed photo now rested on Tom's nightstand, Tom lay awake, staring at the ceiling, his thoughts tangled but firm. He knew he had done what needed to be done. Myles would not be forgotten, not now, not ever. And if one child somewhere spoke up because of what he had said, then every trembling word had been worth it. With that thought, he finally let his eyes close, not with fear, but with the steady comfort of truth carried forward.

The warmth of the afternoon lingered in the Takashi garden, the air filled with the faint trickle of water from the pond and the rustling of leaves stirred by the softest wind. Tom sat on the wooden step of the dojo, his hands resting against his knees, his thoughts still tangled in the echoes of yesterday's words at the community centre. He had not expected the silence that followed his talk, nor the way so many children had looked at him with eyes that brimmed with something heavy, something searching. The weight of it pressed on him still, and though he did not regret a single word, he wondered if he had carried it well enough. His brow furrowed as he thought, but before doubt could climb higher, Ella's shadow fell across him, her figure outlined against the dipping sun. She carried no hesitation in her steps as she crossed the boards and sat down beside him, her presence steady as stone.

She did not speak at once, choosing instead to rest her hand lightly against his arm, letting him feel that she was there without pressing for words. Tom shifted, his chest tightening with the unspoken question that lingered between them: had he done enough, had he been strong in the way that mattered? Ella's gaze softened as she studied his face, the boy she loved beyond words, the one who carried burdens that children should never carry. "You know what I saw yesterday?" she finally asked, her voice quiet but firm. "I saw someone who stood up without swinging a fist, and that's harder than anything else. That's why I'm proud of you, Tom."

Her words landed with the weight of truth, and Tom felt his throat close as though he had been struck with a sudden force he could not defend against. "Proud?" he asked, the word escaping him in a whisper, as though he had never been able to believe it belonged to him.

"Yes," she answered without faltering. "Proud of you, not because you can fight, but because you chose not to. Proud because you told the truth about Myles, even though it hurt to say it. And proud because you showed everyone that strength is more than fists." Her eyes shone, unwavering, daring him to doubt her.

Tom turned his head away, blinking hard as the knot in his chest loosened, replaced by a sharp ache that was almost too much to hold. No one had ever spoken to him like that before, no one had ever told him that his truth alone could be enough. He clenched his hands, unsure of what to do with the surge of feeling, until Ella leaned closer and pressed her forehead gently against his temple. "You don't have to keep proving yourself to anyone," she whispered. "You already are enough."

The words cracked something inside him, and he drew in a shaky breath, his eyes stinging with tears he tried to hide. But Ella saw them, and instead of speaking, she simply wrapped her arms around him, steady and sure. He leaned into her embrace, not as someone broken, but as someone finally finding a place to rest. It was not the strength of fists that kept him steady, but the strength of love pressed against his heart, quiet and unshakable.

When he finally found his voice, it came halting but clear. "I didn't know if anyone would listen. I didn't know if telling the truth would matter." Ella pulled back just enough to meet his gaze. "It mattered to me," she said firmly. "It mattered to every kid in that room, even if they don't say it yet. And it mattered because Myles's name is still alive on our lips. You gave him that, Tom. Don't you see? You gave him back a place in the world." Her words settled into him like roots sinking deep into soil, unshakable, alive.

He thought of Myles then, the boy whose story had clung to him since the moment he had first heard it. He thought of the children who had left the hall with new truths in their hearts, of the parents who had paused to listen when they had not before. And as Ella's words echoed inside him, he realized that she was right. What he had done mattered, not because it erased the past, but because it planted something for the future. The heaviness in his chest shifted, replaced by something steadier, something close to peace.

Ella tilted her head, her smile soft but unwavering. "You're not just strong because you can fight. You're strong because you chose love instead. And that's the kind of strength that changes everything." Her voice trembled slightly, not from doubt, but from the force of what she felt. Tom stared at her, stunned by the clarity of her love, by the steadiness that poured from her even when he faltered. For the first time, he allowed himself to believe it, to believe that maybe he was more than the boy who had once fought to survive.

They sat in silence for a while, the garden around them alive with the gentle hum of life—the koi stirring in the pond, the leaves whispering in the wind, the faint scent of earth and pine drifting on the air. Tom felt the rhythm of it settling into him, the same rhythm Ella had given him with her words. He breathed deeply, letting it fill him, letting it anchor him in the present. And when Ella finally slipped her hand into his, he held it without hesitation, their fingers entwined like two threads weaving into one cloth.

Later, when the evening deepened and lanterns flickered against the night, Tom whispered the words he had held back for so long. "Thank you." Ella squeezed his hand, smiling. "You don't have to thank me for loving you," she said softly. "That's never something you have to earn. It's already yours." The simplicity of her words struck him harder than anything else, for they held no condition, no demand—only truth, steady and unshakable.

When Keiko stepped into the garden a little later, she paused in the shadows, watching the two of them with a quiet smile. She saw not just children learning about love, but two souls finding strength in each other. She said nothing, only allowed them that moment, knowing it was the kind of moment that stitched itself into the fabric of a life.

Tom leaned his head back, looking up at the stars just beginning to scatter across the sky. "Do you think Myles knows?" he asked softly, almost to himself. Ella followed his gaze, her voice quiet but sure. "I think he does. I think he's smiling because of you." Tom closed his eyes, and for the first time in a long while, his heart felt light.

The night stretched on gently, and though words grew fewer, their meaning only deepened. Tom understood that Ella's pride was not fleeting, not tied to what he did or did not do—it was tied to who he was becoming. And in her steadfast love, he found the courage to believe that his smile, too, could one day belong.

The first warmth of the morning sun had already stretched its arms across the sky when the children made their way down the winding path to the river. The Takashi garden had given them peace, but the river promised freedom, a different sort of release where the weight of classrooms and lessons was replaced with rushing water and laughter. Tom walked at Ella's side, their shoulders brushing now and again, his heart tugging at the thought that this was his first true summer with family, friends, and a love that did not vanish. Ty carried a small satchel with fruit and bread, Nico balanced a ball under his arm, and Jeremy trailed behind, humming to himself as though even the rhythm of the world had become music. By the time they reached the bank, the river sparkled like glass beneath the sun, and the children's shouts filled the air.

Without waiting for ceremony, Ty tossed the ball into the water and dove in after it, his splash catching Nico square in the chest. Nico's sharp laugh broke out, and within moments the rest followed, shoes and shirts flung aside, their bodies cutting through the cool river as though it had been waiting just for them.

Tom hesitated only briefly, watching Ella step gracefully into the shallows, her toes curling against the smooth stones before she leaned forward and dove beneath the surface. He felt something tug within him, something deeper than joy—something like belonging. When he plunged in after her, the cold seized his chest but released it just as quickly, leaving exhilaration in its wake.

Jeremy, too small to trust the deeper current, stayed close to the edge, splashing with Sophie, both of them shrieking each time Ty sent waves toward them. Their laughter carried like bells across the summer sky, filling the air with a sense of pure childhood that no bully could reach. Keiko sat on the riverbank with a sketchbook balanced on her knees, her hand moving steadily, capturing not perfection but motion, the fluidity of bodies that belonged to the moment. Zenji stood nearby, hands clasped behind his back, watching with a quiet smile that betrayed both relief and pride.

Ella emerged from the water, shaking droplets from her hair, her smile dazzling with the kind of brightness that needed no words. Tom waded toward her, reaching out to steady her arm, though she hardly needed it. "Best day yet," she laughed, her voice carrying above the rush of the river. Tom nodded, water sliding down his brow, and for the first time, he laughed too, a laugh that felt unshackled, as though no part of his old life had followed him here. The sound startled even him, and Ella, catching it, threw her arms around him in the water, both of them nearly tumbling backward with the weight of it.

Nico called for a race, his voice bold with challenge. Ty smirked and accepted instantly, already slicing through the current before anyone else had agreed. Tom, swept up in the energy, joined them, his strokes strong but not desperate. The race was less about victory and more about the joy of moving together, of testing strength not against fists but against water. When Ty reached the far bank first, triumphant, he raised his arms with a cheer, while Nico groaned dramatically, and Tom laughed again, this time without hesitation.

Back near the shore, Ella waded in the shallows, her eyes following Tom as though she could see more than muscle and motion. She saw the boy who had been broken, now held together by threads of love, truth, and resilience. When he returned, chest heaving and cheeks flushed, she met him with a grin that softened into something quieter. "You look alive," she whispered when no one else was close enough to hear. Tom met her gaze, something in him tightening with gratitude. "I feel alive," he admitted, and the words were no small thing.

The children played for hours, diving for stones, inventing games only they could understand, their laughter echoing across the water like a chorus. Jeremy tried to balance on a half-submerged log and fell off more times than anyone could count, each tumble earning cheers and applause as though it had been victory itself. Sophie twirled in the shallows, her skirt clinging to her legs, while Mila floated on her back, eyes closed, as though the river had stolen her worries. The freedom was contagious, spilling into every motion, every sound, every smile.

By midday, the sun beat fiercely overhead, and Keiko called them ashore for fruit and bread. They sprawled on blankets, wet hair clinging to their necks, the taste of simple food richer than any feast. Zenji sat among them, his posture still straight but softened by the ease of the moment. He listened as they retold the morning's laughter, each child embellishing their role in the games until truth blurred into story. Tom listened, too, but more than that, he watched, his eyes taking in what his heart had always craved: a place where love was ordinary, where joy did not have to be earned through struggle.

When Ella leaned her head against his shoulder, he felt something settle deep within him, heavier than the river and lighter than the sky all at once. "This is the best summer," she murmured, her voice muffled by his damp shirt. Tom turned his head slightly, letting his cheek rest against her crown, his lips brushing her hair as he whispered, "It's only just begun." The words carried no fear of what came next, only certainty that this was real, this was his, and nothing could take it away.

Later, as the sun dipped toward the horizon and the water glowed gold beneath its touch, the children returned for one last plunge. Their laughter rose again, loud and free, scattering across the riverbank like sparks. Tom caught Ella's hand as they leapt together, the world exploding in light and water around them. When they surfaced, gasping, their faces broke into grins that mirrored each other, unguarded and true. For the first time in his life, Tom did not worry about tomorrow. He only knew the river, the laughter, the kiss of sunlight on water, and the girl beside him who made every moment feel like forever.

The cicadas were loud that afternoon, their steady chorus rising and falling as though they had been waiting all day for the arrival of a guest. The Takashi garden shimmered in the summer light, the koi pond catching flecks of sun while the bonsai trees stood as careful witnesses to everything that passed. Zenji was setting a low table on the veranda with a small pot of percolated coffee and a tray of steaming green tea when the sound of measured footsteps approached along the path. Mr. Clarke appeared with his familiar calm stride, his jacket folded over his arm in the heat, and a smile that revealed not formality but genuine warmth. The teacher's visits were rare, but this one carried a weight that was felt even before he spoke a word.

Keiko came forward with her quiet grace, bowing lightly before guiding their guest toward the shaded place near the veranda where cushions were already waiting. She poured the tea with practiced hands, her movements steady, her smile unforced. Zenji poured the coffee with equal care, sliding a small cup across the table toward Mr. Clarke. The simple act of hospitality carried a dignity that needed no embellishment. Mr. Clarke accepted both with a nod, his eyes lingering on the garden that seemed to breathe serenity into anyone who stepped within its borders. "This home of yours," he began, his voice measured, "is not just a place of living. It is a place of healing. And I see that most clearly in Tom."

At that name, Zenji's brows lifted, and Keiko's hands paused, though only for a moment, before she resumed pouring. Tom, who had been sketching in the corner of the veranda, looked up with a mixture of curiosity and hesitation.

It was not often that his teacher sought him out outside of school walls. Mr. Clarke turned slightly toward him, his tone softening as he continued. "I saw you, Tom, at the community centre last week. I did not step forward then, but I watched. You stood before children younger than yourself and spoke with a truth that could not have been borrowed from anyone else. You told them about Myles Neuts—not with fear, not with shame, but with respect and courage. That takes more than words. That takes heart."

Tom lowered his eyes, not from shame but from the strange weight of being praised in such a way. He fiddled with his pencil, turning it between his fingers as though it could anchor him. Zenji placed a hand lightly on his son's shoulder, a gesture of acknowledgment that spoke without words: accept this truth. Mr. Clarke leaned back slightly, sipping the coffee with appreciation before speaking again. "The staff at the school have spoken of you as well. Word travels quickly when a student transforms. They have noticed the calm you now carry, the way you step away rather than strike, the way you listen before you speak. This is no small matter. Many adults cannot master what you have begun to live."

Keiko's eyes glistened, though her smile never wavered. She folded her hands gently in her lap, looking at Tom with a pride that seemed to wash away every shadow of the boy's past. "He has worked hard," she said softly, her Japanese accent carrying the words with an elegance that made them weightier. "But it is more than work. It is love that sustains him." Mr. Clarke inclined his head in agreement, his eyes narrowing with quiet conviction. "Yes, and it is love that sustains us all, though too often it is hidden beneath fear or pride. Tom, you have chosen to let love speak louder than anger. That is why the school is proud of you. That is why I am proud of you."

Tom finally raised his eyes, meeting the teacher's gaze. He did not know what words could fit into the space that had just opened inside him. He thought of Ella's letters, of Ty's laughter, of Zenji's steady voice and Keiko's gentle counsel, of Jeremy's endless affection, of Mr. Arnett's embrace. All of it gathered within him until it pressed against his throat. At last, with a voice steadier than he expected, he said, "Thank you, sir. I just… I just wanted Myles to be remembered." His voice cracked at the name, but no one flinched away from it. Instead, Zenji's grip on his shoulder tightened, Keiko's smile widened, and Mr. Clarke gave a small nod that carried more meaning than a dozen speeches.

The conversation drifted into quieter waters after that, as talk of books and summer days replaced the gravity of remembrance. Mr. Clarke spoke of his own youth, of teachers who had guided him with both kindness and firmness, and of the lessons that had shaped him into the man he was now. Zenji listened with interest, occasionally offering reflections of his own, while Keiko asked gentle questions that revealed more of their guest's story. Tom sat close, listening, absorbing, realizing that wisdom was not only found in books or dojos but also in the living stories of those who had walked before him.

As the afternoon stretched on, Keiko refilled the tea cups, Zenji poured a second round of coffee, and Mr. Clarke leaned back, his face softened by the ease of good company. "Tom," he said at last, "there will always be those who test your strength, just as there will always be those who try to dim your light. But I see now that you will not bend easily to such shadows. You have learned that strength is not fists, but truth. That is the greatest lesson any teacher could hope to see lived."

When Mr. Clarke rose to leave, the cicadas had grown louder, as if marking the close of something important. Tom stood with him, bowing his head slightly in the way Zenji had taught him. Mr. Clarke placed a hand on his shoulder, squeezing once before letting go. "Keep teaching, Tom," he said quietly. "For every child who hears you, a seed is planted. And seeds, when tended, grow into forests." With that, he stepped down the path, his figure soon swallowed by the brilliance of summer light.

Tom remained on the veranda long after, the echo of his teacher's words lingering like a song he could not yet put into notes. Zenji and Keiko returned to their tasks, but Tom sat still, holding close the truth that had been spoken over him. For the first time, he believed not only that he had been saved from the shadows of his past, but that he had been chosen for something greater. And when Ella came skipping into the garden that evening, her smile wide and unguarded, he rose to meet her, knowing with certainty that his life had been rewritten in ways he had only begun to understand.

The first letter was written late one evening, the soft lamplight falling over Tom's desk while the garden outside rested in the hum of crickets. He had not planned it. The paper had been meant for sketches, but when the pencil touched the page, the words formed before he could think of them. "Myles was only ten years old," he wrote, pausing at the name as though holding it gently in his hands. "He deserved better than fear. He deserved better than silence." Tom pressed harder on the pencil, his hand trembling slightly. For the first time, he realized that memory did not have to remain trapped inside him. It could be offered, carried outward, shared.

When he finished the first page, he read it aloud quietly. His voice was steady, though his throat tightened with every line. He had not written for teachers or classmates. He had written for himself, for Myles, for the boy whose story had become part of his own. Yet when Keiko entered quietly with a cup of tea, she stood behind him, listening. She placed the cup gently by his hand, leaned down, and kissed the top of his head. "Keep writing," she whispered. "Every word is a seed of truth." Tom folded the letter carefully, almost ceremonially, and set it aside.

The next day, he handed that first letter to Mr. Clarke at school. The teacher read it slowly during the lunch break, his eyes darkening, his lips tightening. When he finished, he looked at Tom with a mixture of pride and sorrow. "I will show this to the staff," he said firmly. "It is not only children who need to hear these truths. Adults must be reminded as well." Tom felt a warmth spread through him, a strange relief. He had not expected the letter to be taken so seriously. Now he knew he could not stop at one.

By the end of that week, there were five letters. Some were shorter, no more than a page, others filled several sheets with his small but determined handwriting. Each one carried a different part of Myles's story: the silence in the washroom, the failure of those who should have seen, the hope that children would one day stand up for one another. Tom did not embellish. He did not soften. He wrote as plainly as a boy could, his sentences raw but sharp. "If we do nothing," one letter said, "we become part of the problem. A bully is not stopped by silence. A bully is stopped by truth."

Mr. Clarke began sharing the letters with other teachers, slipping copies into their mailboxes, reading portions aloud during meetings. Some teachers wept quietly, others sat rigid with the recognition of their own past failures. The letters spread like whispers through the halls, until parents began hearing of them as well. At first, Tom was embarrassed. He had never intended for so many eyes to see his private words. But then he noticed something: the way teachers began watching more closely at recess, the way parents spoke with greater seriousness to their children after school. The letters were doing what he alone could not.

Ella read one of the letters one evening while sitting beside him under the shade of the veranda. Her eyes lingered over the lines, her lips moving silently as she read. When she finished, she pressed the paper against her chest and whispered, "Tom, this isn't just writing. This is you giving Myles a voice." Her words carried such tenderness that Tom had to turn away for a moment, afraid of the tears rising too quickly. Ella reached for his hand and held it firmly. "Don't ever stop," she added. "Not until every child knows they are not alone."

Encouraged, Tom began writing more deliberately. Some letters he gave directly to Keiko and Zenji, who read them with reverence before sharing them with friends in the community. Others he entrusted to Ty, who delivered them quietly to classmates who had once suffered in silence. Nico, Leo, and Alex each asked for copies, promising to hand them to children they knew needed them most. What began as a single letter at a desk became a movement, small but undeniable. The letters were never the same, yet each one carried the same root: remembrance and hope.

One letter reached Mr. Arnett, who called Tom into his office not to discipline, but to thank him. He placed the letter flat on his desk, pressing his hand over it as though it were something sacred. "This," he said gravely, "is more powerful than any assembly I could ever hold. Children will listen to children when they might turn away from us adults. You are giving them reason to believe change is possible." Tom shifted in his chair, unaccustomed to such weight being laid upon him, but deep inside he knew it was true.

By mid-summer, copies of Tom's letters had found their way into the hands of parents who had never once spoken to him. Some came to thank him directly, stopping him on sidewalks, calling to him in parks, offering their own memories of what bullying had cost them.

Others wrote back, letters filled with gratitude, with confessions of long-held silence, with promises that they would no longer ignore the shadows in their children's lives. Tom kept every reply, folding each carefully and storing them in a box beneath his bed. It was not fame he sought, but connection. Every letter that returned to him felt like a thread being tied into a larger net of safety.

Still, the act of writing was not always easy. Some nights he sat staring at the blank paper for hours, the weight of truth pressing so heavily that no words would come. Zenji would sit quietly beside him then, sipping tea, saying nothing. Only when Tom looked up would he murmur, "Even silence can be part of the truth. Do not force it. Wait until the words are ready." Keiko, too, reminded him that every letter did not need to be perfect, only honest. Slowly, patiently, Tom learned to accept that even his pauses had value.

The more he wrote, the more Tom began to notice changes in himself. The fear that had once coiled around his chest loosened. The anger that had once boiled in his fists cooled. He began to feel not like a boy trapped by his past, but like a messenger chosen for a purpose he had not expected. His letters were no longer only about Myles—they were also about healing, about the possibility of a world where children could walk freely without fear. Each letter became both remembrance and promise.

When Ella read his tenth letter, she kissed him lightly on the cheek and said, "Do you realize what you're doing? You're building a wall of words stronger than fists." Tom smiled shyly, but the words struck deep. He realized that perhaps this was his true strength—not in combat, not even in restraint, but in the ability to write truth plainly enough for anyone to understand.

At the end of that summer week, Tom sat once again at his desk, pen in hand, the evening light fading into dusk. He wrote slowly, deliberately: "To every child who has ever felt alone— you are not forgotten. Myles is remembered. You are remembered. Together we can break the silence." He folded the page and sealed it with care, setting it atop the growing stack of letters. For the first time, he allowed himself to believe that his words might outlive him, carrying forward into classrooms and homes he might never enter.

That night, as the crickets resumed their song, Tom lay awake under the weight of a strange peace. He had once believed his past defined him, but now he understood: it was his voice, steady and unafraid, that would shape his future. And somewhere in the darkness, he imagined Myles smiling, not broken, but whole, carried into memory through every letter of hope.

The lanterns had been lit one by one, each wick catching with a small flicker until the garden glowed in soft amber hues. The Takashi garden, with its pond, its curved bridge, and its carefully tended bonsai, felt like a place set apart from the rest of the world. The night carried a stillness that asked for reverence, yet within that stillness, Ella's laughter lingered as lightly as the fireflies that drifted over the water. Tom sat beside her on the bench beneath the cherry tree, his hand brushing against hers, both pretending not to notice at first, as though touch itself was something fragile that might shatter if acknowledged too soon.

Zenji had retreated into the house, Keiko following after gathering the tea cups, leaving the two young ones alone with the glow of lanterns and the chorus of night insects. Ty had yawned himself to bed long before, giving Ella and Tom the rare gift of quiet without interruption. They sat without speaking, yet everything that mattered was already present in the silence. Ella leaned her head back slightly, letting the soft light kiss her face, and Tom watched her as though he were seeing something he had never seen before. For all that he had endured, all the shadows he had walked through, it was here, in this moment, that he understood what it meant to be safe.

Ella shifted closer, her skirt brushing against his leg, and the air between them felt charged, yet unhurried. She spoke first, softly, her voice a whisper meant only for him. "Tom, when I look at you, I don't see the boy who was hurt. I see the boy who is still here, strong, kind, and brave." Her words lingered like incense, curling through the air, settling in places he did not know had been empty. Tom lowered his eyes for a moment, embarrassed, but she reached out, lifting his chin gently with her hand. Their eyes met, and in that meeting, nothing more needed to be explained.

The kiss came naturally, not rushed, not stolen, but offered. Ella leaned in, her lips pressing softly against his, no hesitation, no faltering. This was no accident, no shy experiment—it was certainty, a declaration that belonged to both of them. Tom responded instinctively, his hands finding her shoulders, pulling her close with a tenderness he had never known he possessed. The lantern light shimmered across the pond as though it, too, leaned in to witness what had just happened, the garden itself holding its breath in reverence for this small, sacred moment.

When they parted, Ella kept her forehead pressed against his, her breath mingling with his own. "I don't ever want to lose this," she whispered, her voice steady though her hands trembled slightly. Tom closed his eyes and whispered back, "You won't. I'll never let go of this. Not of you." They both stayed like that for what felt like forever, their words sinking into the roots of the bonsai, into the ripples of the pond, into the quiet hum of the summer night.

The lanterns swayed slightly in the evening breeze, casting patterns of gold across the stones at their feet. Ella leaned back finally, her smile radiant, her eyes shimmering with certainty. Tom's heart swelled, not with the nervous rush of youth, but with something steadier, deeper. For the first time, he felt what it meant to belong to someone not because of circumstance, not because of need, but because of choice. And Ella had chosen him as surely as he had chosen her.

The kiss was not their first, but it was the one that marked the difference between beginnings and belonging. No longer timid, no longer uncertain, it carried with it a promise unspoken yet undeniable. Tom realized, sitting there beneath the lanterns, that this was the kind of love people built lives around. He had once thought himself broken beyond repair, but Ella had proven otherwise. Her certainty became his certainty, her strength became his strength, and together, they forged a bond that felt immovable.

# THE SMILE THAT BROKE

Keiko, watching quietly from the veranda with Zenji beside her, exchanged a knowing glance with her husband. They had not planned to watch, but the glow of lanterns had drawn them out once more. Keiko's lips curved into a smile, remembering her own youth, her own first kiss, the way such moments carved themselves into memory forever. Zenji rested his hand gently on hers and murmured, "They will be alright." Keiko nodded, her heart warmed by the sight of two young souls finding each other beneath the lantern glow.

Tom and Ella spoke softly after, about nothing and everything—the stars, the warmth of the night air, the sound of frogs croaking at the pond's edge. Yet underneath their words lay the unspoken truth: the kiss had shifted something between them. No longer just children exploring affection, they had entered into the beginnings of love that sought permanence. Tom found himself telling Ella about his dreams, about how he wanted to be strong not in fists but in words, how he hoped to protect others not with anger but with truth. Ella listened, her hand never leaving his, her heart swelling with pride.

When the time came to return inside, Ella rose slowly, her fingers tightening around his as though reluctant to break the spell of the garden. Tom stood with her, walking her to the veranda where Keiko waited with a gentle smile. Before she left, Ella turned back, kissing him once more quickly, but no less certain. "Goodnight, Tom," she whispered, her voice a blend of shyness and certainty. "I love you." The words echoed in him like a song that would never fade. He whispered them back, his voice steady and sure, and watched her walk away, lantern light following her path like a blessing.

Tom lingered in the garden long after she had gone, the air still carrying the warmth of her presence. He looked up at the lanterns, their glow soft yet unyielding, and realized that he, too, now carried such a light inside him. It was not a light given by circumstance or luck, but by choice, by trust, by love. For the first time in his life, Tom smiled without fear, without armour, without hesitation. And that smile, under the lanterns, belonged entirely to him.

As the night deepened, Zenji placed a hand on his son's shoulder and guided him toward the house. No words were needed. They both knew something important had taken place. Keiko touched his cheek gently before sending him upstairs, her eyes filled with quiet pride. Tom carried the memory of the kiss with him into his room, the letter from Ella resting on his desk, the framed photo beside it, and for the first time, he felt the room was not just a place to sleep, but truly a place of home.

That night, as he lay in bed, Tom replayed the moment beneath the lanterns again and again, not as a fleeting dream but as a promise. Ella's certainty had settled inside him, steadying his spirit like the roots of a tree that refused to be moved. He closed his eyes with a smile that remained until morning, a smile that proved he was no longer the boy who had been broken, but the boy who had been chosen, who had found his place, and who had learned the truth of belonging.

The lanterns burned down slowly outside, their flames shrinking, their glow softening, but the memory they marked burned on within Tom, brighter than any light could dim. By morning, the garden would return to its quiet beauty, but for him, it would forever hold the echo of a kiss that had changed everything.

The sound of laughter rippled through the Takashi home like music woven into the very timbers of the walls. Zenji and Keiko stood side by side near the veranda, their tea cups untouched on the low table, watching as Tom and Ty darted through the garden in playful pursuit of one another. Ella trailed behind, her own laughter ringing clear as she tried to keep pace, the glow of the lanterns reflecting in her eyes. It was not the noise of chaos they heard, but the rhythm of joy, the cadence of a home filled with children who knew safety at last. Keiko leaned slightly against her husband, her smile gentle yet full of awe, as though she could not quite believe the completeness of the life unfolding before her.

Zenji's arms were crossed, his stance still as disciplined as the man who had served as an RCMP investigator for many years, but his eyes betrayed the softness within him. He had once thought strength lay only in restraint, in duty, in service to the law. Yet here, strength appeared in another form—in the easy way Ty accepted Tom as his brother, in Ella's tenderness toward Tom, and in the way Tom himself had learned to smile without fear. Zenji exhaled slowly, his breath deep as he whispered, "Keiko, do you see it? This is what we built. Not walls. Not a house. A sanctuary." His voice trembled, not from weakness, but from the immensity of gratitude pressing against his chest.

Keiko reached for his hand and squeezed it, her touch grounding him. "Yes, Zenji," she murmured, her eyes still upon the children. "And it is more beautiful than anything I have painted, more delicate than any bonsai I have shaped. Because it breathes, and it loves, and it grows without fear." She remembered Tom's first arrival, the hesitation in his steps, the way his eyes had darted as though expecting to be struck for simply existing. Now, he moved freely, chasing Ty with a grin that belonged wholly to him. Keiko felt her heart swell, for she knew that scars remained, yet love had built bridges across every fracture.

The children collapsed onto the grass near the pond, Ty sprawled out dramatically as though defeated, Ella nudging him with her foot, and Tom grinning triumphantly beside them. The scene was so ordinary, yet to Zenji and Keiko it was extraordinary. The ordinary had not always been possible for Tom. Now, it was his. Zenji remembered his own childhood in Japan, the strictness of his schooling, the weight of expectation. He had learned discipline there, but not joy. Watching Tom now, he whispered a silent promise that he would never allow fear or cruelty to have the final word in this boy's life again.

# THE SMILE THAT BROKE

Keiko lowered herself onto the veranda step, setting her tea aside as she folded her hands into her lap. "They are whole now," she said softly, more to herself than to Zenji. "Tom was a boy who carried cracks so deep, I feared he would never believe love was real. But look at him. Look at how Ty draws him into laughter, how Ella steadies him. They are healing each other, every day." She tilted her head toward her husband, a knowing light in her eyes. "Even your stern lessons have softened, Zenji. You are gentler with Tom than you were even with Ty." Zenji chuckled, conceding the truth.

"It is because Tom needed something different," he admitted. "Ty was raised with love from his first breath. Tom had to learn what love was. If I had met him with only rules and severity, I would have driven him further into his own darkness. No, he needed my patience, my silence, and sometimes my laughter too. He needed to know I was not only a protector but a father. And now, I think—" Zenji's voice broke, and he cleared his throat before continuing. "Now, I think he knows."

The night breeze stirred, carrying the faint scent of the cherry blossoms in the garden, their petals trembling in the lantern light. Ella shifted closer to Tom, her head resting lightly on his shoulder, and though their whispers could not be heard, the image was enough to quiet both Keiko and Zenji. Their children were not simply surviving—they were living, creating bonds that would last beyond classrooms, beyond summers, beyond even their watchful eyes. For parents, there was no greater gift. Keiko leaned against Zenji's shoulder, her sigh one of contentment. "This is the family I always dreamed of," she whispered.

Inside the house, the walls held echoes of many stories—some painful, some joyful, all true. Tonight, those walls absorbed the sounds of play, of love spoken without words, of children belonging without hesitation. Tom's voice rang out as he teased Ty for his theatrical defeat, and the others joined in with laughter that rose to the stars. Zenji closed his eyes for a moment, imprinting the sound into memory. He knew storms would come again, that life would bring challenges and sorrows. But tonight, this moment was untouchable. It was the heart of what they had all fought for: peace within a family whole.

Keiko rose finally, her knees stiff, and called gently for the children to come in. They groaned in unison, unwilling to let the night end, but obedience came naturally here because love was never wielded as a weapon. Tom was the last to rise, brushing grass from his shirt, his smile still radiant. Zenji watched him closely, the boy who once walked in shadows now moving with the lightness of one who believed he was wanted. "Come in, son," Zenji said, the word chosen deliberately, the word carrying weight that filled Tom's chest with warmth.

As the children filed into the house, Keiko glanced back at the garden, at the lanterns swaying gently over the pond. She whispered a quiet thank you to the universe—not to any god, but to the fragile yet fierce current of life that had brought them here. For Tom, for Ty, for Ella, for the family they had become. Zenji joined her at the doorway, his hand at her back, his voice low but sure. "Keiko, we have done well." She nodded, and together they stepped inside, the sound of children's laughter leading them into the fullness of home.

That night, long after the lanterns had burned low, the house remained alive with the echoes of joy. Tom lay in his room with Ella's picture beside him, Ty stretched comfortably in his own, and Zenji and Keiko found themselves smiling even as sleep overtook them. For the first time, perhaps ever, Tom slept without dreams of fear. And that, Zenji thought as he drifted into rest, was proof enough that the family was whole.

The morning air in the Takashi home was warm with the scents of rice, miso, and the faint bitterness of coffee that Zenji had brewed for himself and Tom. The garden beyond the shoji doors was alive with the movement of koi gliding in their pond, cherry blossoms scattered like pink confetti upon the stepping stones. Tom sat near the low table, his posture steady, his hands resting lightly on his knees. But it was not his stillness that drew notice this morning—it was his smile. Not the guarded curve that once served as armour, not the polite mask worn for the world, but a true, unbroken smile that radiated from his eyes as much as from his mouth. It seemed to fill the house like sunlight flooding through open windows, something so rare and so fragile that Keiko, upon seeing it, held her breath as though afraid to break its spell.

By midday the quiet home had filled with voices. His classmates, having arranged to visit, spilled across the threshold with laughter, curiosity, and a hum of anticipation. These were the children who had once whispered of Tom in cautious tones, wondering if the rumours about him were true, if his troubled past would follow him forever. But today, the rumours were nowhere to be found. They saw him as he was now, standing tall beside Ty and Ella, his eyes calm, his smile steady. When they entered the garden, it was as though they had stepped into another world—one built not by walls, but by trust, patience, and belonging. Tom greeted each one with the ease of a boy who no longer doubted whether he deserved their presence.

One by one, the children moved to him, hesitant at first, until Ella, bold as ever, wrapped her arms around Tom and held him close. Her embrace was not shy but firm, a declaration in front of everyone that her love for him was unwavering. That broke the hesitation for the others. Nico was next, his grin wide as he pulled Tom into a brotherly hug, followed quickly by Jasmin and Sophie. Even Alex, once a bully himself, stepped forward with deliberate sincerity, gripping Tom's shoulders before pulling him into an embrace that spoke volumes. Jeremy clung to him too, his nine-year-old arms squeezing tight with affection that was as pure as it was unashamed. One after another, the children followed, until Tom stood surrounded by warmth, every hug a testament that his place among them was secure.

For Tom, each embrace carried weight beyond what the others could comprehend. He had once known only fists, shouts, and cold dismissals; now he felt the strength of arms wrapped around him not to hold him down, but to lift him up. His throat tightened as his classmates whispered words of friendship, words of gratitude for his courage in teaching them about Myles and about truth. They were not hugging a boy they pitied, nor one they merely accepted—they hugged a friend they cherished. For a moment Tom's eyes glistened, but he did not turn away. He let the tears rise, let them blur his vision, for they were not tears of pain but of recognition: he belonged.

Zenji and Keiko watched from the veranda, hands joined, hearts full. They had dreamed of this moment when Tom's journey into their family began—of the day he would not only call them "Mom" and "Dad," but stand before the world as a boy who knew love, who received it without fear. Zenji's voice, low and roughened with emotion, whispered, "Keiko, look at him. That is not the face of a boy lost anymore. That is a son who has found himself." Keiko nodded, pressing her cheek against his shoulder, her own tears falling freely. She whispered back, "This is the family he was always meant to have."

In the midst of the celebration, Ella lingered by Tom's side, her hand slipping into his with a quiet confidence. "You don't even know what you look like right now," she whispered, her voice quivering with emotion. Tom turned to her, puzzled, and she smiled through her tears. "You look happy. Really, truly happy. And that makes all of us happy too." Her words struck him deeply, for he realized then that his smile was no longer just his own—it was shared, a gift that radiated outward, touching everyone around him. He held her hand tighter, his heart steady with the knowledge that he had become the boy he once feared he could never be.

As the afternoon waned, stories were told in the shade of the garden, laughter echoing beneath the lanterns that hung waiting to be lit. Mr. Clarke arrived, his eyes wide at the sight of his students gathered not in classrooms but in fellowship. He placed a hand on Zenji's shoulder, his voice quiet yet sure. "I have never seen such change in a child. What you have given him here, Zenji, Keiko—it is beyond teaching. It is transformation." Zenji bowed his head slightly, acknowledging the words, while Keiko's smile only deepened, her heart swelling with gratitude.

Later, as the children prepared to leave, each gave Tom one final embrace. Nico slapped his shoulder, Sophie promised to visit soon, and Jeremy clung so tightly that Tom had to laugh gently to ease his grip. Even Alex's hug lingered, the former bully's voice low with sincerity: "You taught me more than I ever thought I'd learn, Tom. Don't ever forget what you've done." Tom nodded, humbled, and returned the embrace with genuine warmth. By the time the last of them departed, Tom's heart felt both full and light, as though every shadow had been swept away by the power of belonging.

That evening, the family gathered around the low table once more. Ella remained, her parents content to leave her in trusted company. The lanterns glowed over the garden, their light soft against the night air. Tom looked around—at Ty laughing as he retold one of Zenji's stories, at Ella leaning against his shoulder with trust unshaken, at Keiko's warm gaze and Zenji's steady presence. And for the first time in his life, Tom did not wonder if the love he felt would vanish. He knew it was permanent, anchored like the roots of the bonsai in the soil, tended carefully by hands that understood its worth.

Jeremy, as ever, found the words to close the day. Standing before his friends and family, his small voice carried surprising weight. "New ways aren't built in leaps," he said softly. "They're built in steps. Like calling someone Mom. Like choosing not to fight. Like smiling because you know you're safe." His eyes fell on Tom, and he added, "That's what you've given us, Tom. A smile that belongs." Silence followed, but it was a silence heavy with meaning, as every child and adult present felt the truth settle into their hearts.

Tom's smile broadened, unshaken and unafraid. It was his, and it belonged to everyone who loved him. As the lanterns swayed in the summer breeze, Tom realized that life no longer felt like something to survive—it felt like something to live. Tomorrow would bring new days, new lessons, and yes, new bullies to face. But tonight, surrounded by love and friendship, he knew with certainty: he would be ready.

**COMING SOON**

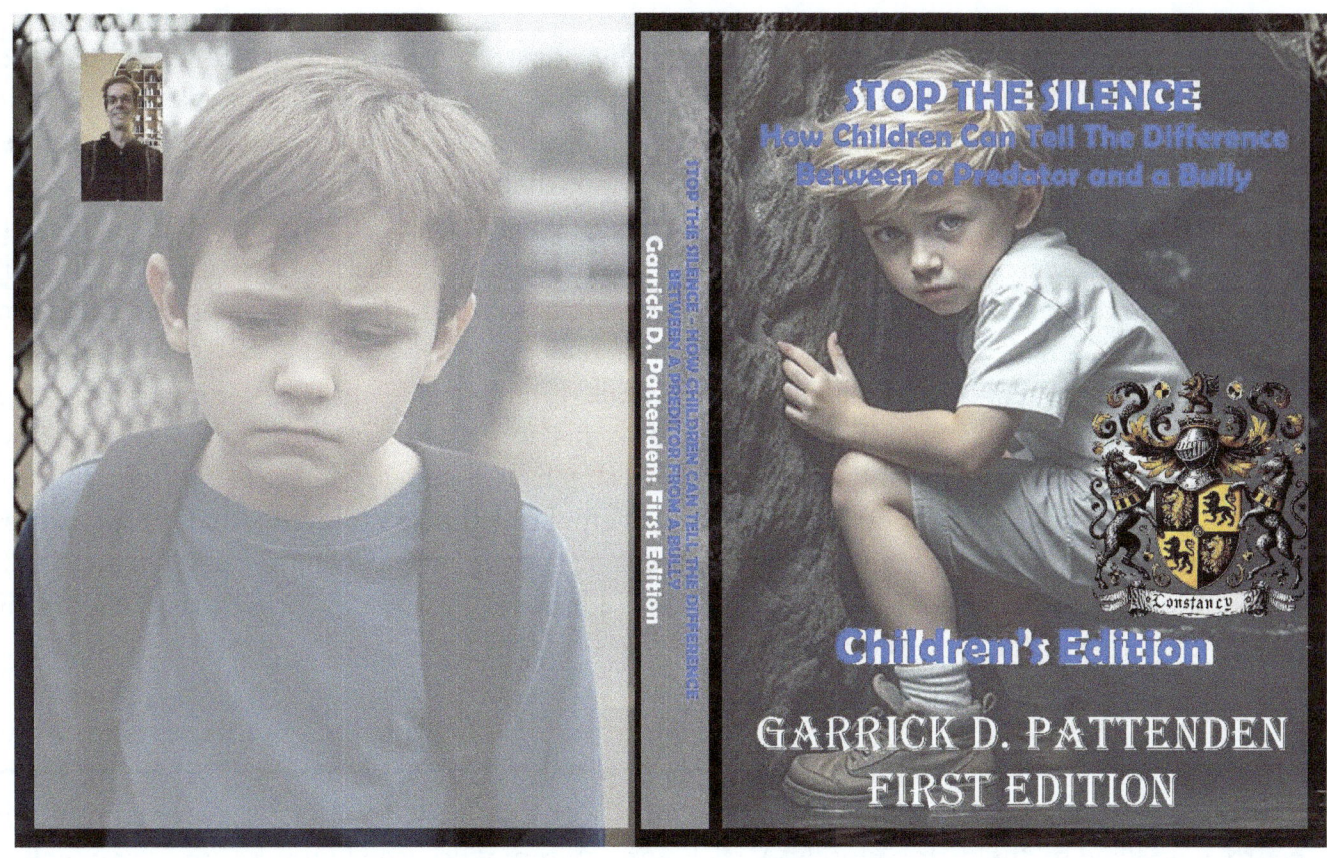

### EPILOGUE – A PREDATOR IN THE DAYLIGHT

The summer lingered in warm days that seemed endless, yet each child knew quietly that the season would eventually turn back toward classrooms and corridors. Tom no longer rose with dread, but with a sharper awareness of the world around him. Zenji's calm lessons, Keiko's gentle guidance, Ty's steady companionship, and Ella's unwavering love shaped his days with a strength he had never known. But alongside the laughter, the training, and the games, Tom held a truth: bullies had once been his battle, but predators were a different kind of enemy. They didn't shout in hallways or shove in the playground. They smiled, they flattered, they offered secrets dressed as kindness. Their power wasn't in fists or taunts—it was in silence.

Ty stood firmly at Tom's side, not just as a brother, but as his anchor. It was Ty who had once pulled him out of the storm of fists and anger, Ty who reminded him that brothers were not bound by blood but by courage. Now, as the Takashi family faced the harder truths of predators, Ty became Tom's mirror—never letting him forget that strength was measured not by how hard one struck back, but by how faithfully one stood guard. Their bond became the foundation of a circle that grew wider, a circle where no child would stand alone.

Ella's laughter filled the Takashi home, weaving her presence into every corner. She kissed Tom beneath the lanterns, leaned against him during summer walks, and became a steady voice of hope. Zenji and Keiko, watching quietly, gave their blessing, knowing young love could be a wellspring of courage. In that house, walls held more than safety—they held truth. They spoke openly of predators, naming the dangers others avoided: grooming, inappropriate touching, the manipulation of secrecy. The children heard the words, not softened, but explained with care, because Zenji believed children could only protect themselves if they were given the truth.

The circle of friends—Nico, Jasmin, Sophie, Mila, Jeremy, Leo, and Alex—grew tighter, their bonds now stronger than fear. They filled the Takashi home with laughter and cheer, balancing out the weight of lessons too important to ignore. Each of them carried scars, but together they carried them more lightly. They talked openly, even about things children usually kept hidden, agreeing that if someone older—or even a teenager—ever crossed a line, they would not be silent. "Predators don't care if you're afraid," Ty told them one night in the garden. "They count on it. But if you speak, they lose."

Predators had names now, not faceless shadows. Mr. Dwyer, the neighbour who always offered candy and asked children to keep visits secret. Cassie, a teenage girl at the park who lured younger kids with dares and promises. Mr. Lorne, a trusted volunteer at the community centre who liked to "help" too closely. Mrs. Trent, a parent who used kindness as cover, reaching where she had no right. Each name came with lessons: predators could be male or female, teen or adult, stranger or neighbour. They thrived on grooming—building trust, giving gifts, asking for silence, and slowly crossing boundaries. Zenji told the children plainly, "If anyone touches you in a way that makes you feel uncomfortable, or asks you to keep a secret that feels wrong, that is against the law. Speak. You are protected."

In late July, Tom stood before children at the community centre, his voice clear though his heart trembled. He spoke first of Myles Casey Benson Neuts, how silence had stolen his life, and then he warned of the silence predators demanded. "They'll tell you to trust them, to keep it between you, to never tell. That's how they win. But if you speak—even if your voice shakes—you break their power." Parents in the back shifted uneasily, but Tom refused to soften his words. He had sworn to honour Myles by telling the truth, and this was the truth every child deserved to hear.

Letters flowed in afterward—notes folded into his hands by nervous children, confessions shared by parents, acknowledgments from teachers who realized they had missed the signs. Tom kept them all in a wooden box by his bed, next to Ella's notes. To him, they were the same thing: proof of trust, acts of courage, sparks of change. At night, when he opened the box and read one or two, he felt Myles's presence close, his story alive in every truth spoken aloud.

Ella told Tom she was proud, pressing her forehead against his chest. "Not because you're strong with fists," she whispered, "but because you're strong with truth." Her kiss that followed was not timid, but a vow. Keiko, watching, reminded them that love was like bonsai—roots grew deep over time—but courage, she said, was sometimes as quiet as listening and as strong as standing close.

At the river, the circle of friends found freedom. Nico and Ty raced across the current, Jasmin laughed until she collapsed on the banks, Sophie sang against the wind, and Jeremy stretched his arms as if he could carry the whole world. Leo, steadier now, stood with Alex, both of them reshaping who they would become. Tom swam with Ella at his side, their hands linked beneath the surface, and he realized freedom was not about rule lessness. It was about living without fear, even when shadows lingered at the edge of the water.

Mr. Clarke visited before August ended. Over coffee and tea, he told Zenji and Keiko how proud the school was, how teachers had been struck by Tom's honesty at the community centre. Zenji listened with quiet gratitude, his hand on Tom's shoulder, steady and sure. For Tom, that weight meant belonging—the thing he had longed for all his life.

As the lanterns swayed one evening, Tom handed Ella a sketch, her name written carefully in Japanese strokes, blossoms drawn around it. She kissed him openly, her love clear. Zenji and Keiko exchanged a glance that spoke of memory, of endurance, of the same love they had built together. Tom trembled, not with fear, but with certainty that he was no longer alone.

Zenji's voice carried one night as the stars spread wide above them. "Love and truth are never about force," he told Tom. "They are about constancy." He spoke of resilience, of vigilance, of never turning away from what must be seen. Tom listened with tears in his eyes, daring to believe that truth, like love, could last forever. He whispered thanks, and Zenji's embrace answered louder than any words.

By the last weeks of summer, Tom no longer feared the love around him would vanish. Doubt had been replaced with trust, fear replaced with belonging. His smile no longer broke under weight, and when his friends gathered for one last evening before school, they saw it clearly. It was not the guarded smile of a boy hiding pain, nor the forced grin of one pretending to be liked. It was a true smile, whole and unbroken. They wept as they hugged him, one by one, knowing he had found his place, his family, and his strength.

Predators would still walk in daylight. Bullies would still stalk the hallways. But Tom was ready. With Ty as his anchor, with Ella at his side, with his family and friends surrounding him, and with the memory of Myles guiding him, he would face whatever came. His smile would not break again. It would belong—purely, fully, forever.

www.ingramcontent.com/pod-product-compliance
Lightning Source LLC
Chambersburg PA
CBHW080530300426
44111CB00017B/2662